SOUTHEND UNITED FOOTBALL CLUB

The Official History of:

The Blues

By: Peter Mason & David Goody

Published by:

YORE PUBLICATIONS

12 The Furrows,
Harefield, Middx.
UB9 6AT.

Printed by:
THE BATH PRESS

ISBN 1 874427 20 8

Acknowledgements

Thanks to: Joe Augur, David Axcell, Kathleen Branscombe, Sid Broomfield, Peter Cartwright, Dave Clark, Frank Dudley, Jack and Margaret French, Harry Glasper, Jim Goody, Karen Goody, Ted Hankey, Brian Horsnell, Harry and Jane Howe, David Jennings, Chris Jones, John Lester, Jimmy McAlinden, Judith McIntyre, Gerald Nevill, Ron Pountney, Doug Powell, Jack Rollin, Derrick and Beryl Sawyer, Ernie Shepherd, Alf Smirk, Henry Smith, Soccer Nostalgia, Ray Sorrell, Howard Southwood, Ray Spiller, Branch Warren, John Woodcock, West London Institute of Higher Education.

Special thanks to: Leigh Edwards and Brian Tabner
for additional statistical information.

And to the Evening Echo
for permission to reproduce many of the photographs.

Jacket design by Caroline Jefford

Dedicated to my dad, Tony, who took me to see my first Southend game, a 1-0 home victory against Barrow on 29 October 1971 (att: 12,410).

Peter Mason

Published by:
Yore Publications
12 The Furrows, Harefield,
Middx. UB9 6AT.

© Peter Mason 1993

....

British Library Cataloguing-in-Publication Data.
A catalogue record for this book
is available from the British Library.

ISBN 1 874427 20 8

CONTENTS

FOREWORD

HOUSE OF COMMONS
LONDON SW1A 0AA

Coming to Southend some twelve years ago from the City of Glasgow where football is very much a basic ingredient of the lifestyle of the people, I was fascinated to find that the Borough had a team which seemed to be somehow struggling along in the Fourth Division. Of course I came along to pay a visit and was depressed to see the state of the ground, the very small number of spectators, and then to hear about the Club's appalling financial position. However, it was encouraging to find that there was still a group of supporters and friends who had committed themselves to ensure that somehow this Club would survive. Since then Southend United have gone from strength to strength and have leapt up the various leagues. The ground has been improved quite dramatically and there is a great spirit of achievement.

The one thing which does still worry me is that the leading figures in the town are not aware of the huge benefit which can accrue to the Borough from having a team playing in the Senior Leagues. A good football team puts the Borough very much on the map and also provides a real focus for civic pride.

The other thing which I admire about the Club is the extent to which they maintain contact with the younger footballers in the Borough and do all in their power to make sure that adequate facilities for training and recreation are provided.

I join with many Southenders in congratulating Southend United Football Club on all it has achieved in recent years and to commit myself to doing all that I can to ensure that the Club will go from strength to strength.

Yours sincerely
Sir Teddy Taylor M.P.

By
Jimmy
Greaves

Southend's history has been more about the taking part than the winning, but dull it has never been! As you will learn in the following pages, the club has survived some turbulent times while walking a tightrope from which it would be easy to fall into oblivion. While the club has staggered from one financial crisis to another, the supporters have been remarkably faithful and the procession of teams wearing Southend's blue shirts have usually managed to serve up football of the entertaining, if unpredictable variety.

It was a deserved reward for the long-suffering supporters when the club at last made it out of the Third Division at the right end when promoted in 1990-91. This was a particularly proud moment for chairman Vic Jobson and his Board of Directors, who had hauled the club though a crisis that threatened its very existence. It's so easy to knock Vic and his colleagues, but they put action where their mouths are and thanks to them there is a solid foundation for the club to build on for the future.

This book gives a fascinating insight into the ups and downs of Southend United since the club was founded in 1906. Perhaps it was fitting that they once played at the Kursaal because the club has been riding a rollercoaster ever since.

There is only one disappointment for me about this official history of the Shrimpers. I find no mention of the fact that it was at Southend that I took some of my first as well as my final shots in football. I played on the Southend ground with the Chelsea youth team when I was sixteen and some thirty-four years later I played my last game at Roots Hall in my son Danny's testimonial match. I had no less a person than Frank Bruno as my powerhouse partner, so it was a knockout farewell for me.

The Kursaal has closed down, but Southend United lives on. This history of the club will give you all the facts and figures about the past. It's been more about taking part than winning, but it's also been about fun and entertainment. Long may it continue.

Jim Greaves

INTRODUCTION

Other teams dreamt of Wembley, some hankered for the first division championship or a place in Europe – but Southend only ever wanted second division status.

It was a modest ambition for a modest club, yet when it finally happened few could really believe it, least of all the seasoned supporters who'd seen Southend grind their way through countless years of third, and more recently, fourth division football. For the 'old uns' as much as the new core of young enthusiastic fans, the victory against Bury on 4 May 1991 which sealed Southend's promotion to division two was an emotional occasion. Football may be just a game, but genuine tears of joy were shed by many that day.

The 1990/91 season had certainly started with the normal talk of making the second division, but as usual it was more in hope than expectation. United had, after all, only just come up from the fourth division with a last ditch defeat of Peterborough the previous year, and most would have settled for a period of consolidation.

Manager David Webb had other ideas, however. In the summer he'd signed 21 year old scoring sensation Brett Angell from Stockport for £100,000, the man whose 15 League goals eventually did as much as anything to secure promotion. Webb had also completed a good piece of business with Crystal Palace when he snapped up the influential Chris Powell on a free transfer, slotting him into a young defence which improved by leaps and bounds throughout the campaign under the influence of swashbuckling skipper Paul Clark. Blond haired John Cornwell, too, made an early impact after being signed by Webb from Swindon for £45,000.

It was a dream start to a dream season; beating Huddersfield 2–1 in the opening game at the intimidating Leeds Road stadium and then putting together a run of five straight victories in the League. A mystifying 4–0 defeat at Stoke City deprived them of what would have been a record-breaking sixth win on the trot, then the bubble looked to have burst altogether when Crystal Palace demolished United 8–0 at Selhurst Park in the Rumbelows cup.

It was a temporary blip, however, and Southend were back on top of division three with a 1–0 away win against Mansfield, showing the fighting spirit which served them so well all year. By now the team was showing the shape it was to hold throughout the promotion challenge with Paul Sansome, Dean Austin, Chris Powell, Dave Martin, Spencer Prior or later Pat Scully, Steve Tilson, Paul Clark, Andy Ansah, Ian Benjamin and Brett Angell keeping a stranglehold on their places throughout.

A battling 1–1 draw with ten men against Birmingham City in October kept them in the hunt with main challengers Grimsby and Stoke. Crowds began to rise regularly above the 4,000 mark for the first time in years, Tilson began scoring too, and the terrier like Peter Butler won every ball going. They went back to the top with one of the most crucial wins of the season, a 1–0 victory at Griffin Park over Brentford, again with ten men, then boosted morale immeasurably by equalling the club record victory with 10–1 against Aldershot in the Leyland Daf cup.

Heading for the turn at Christmas, Southend began to open up something of a gap above the rest when they beat second placed Grimsby 2–0 in front of 8,126 at Roots Hall. Now seven points clear, they suddenly found themselves dealing with the unaccustomed attention of national newspapers, football reporters everywhere sensing that the seasiders were on the verge of something at last.

The Christmas period itself was something of a disappointment with two defeats and two draws, but Webb had enough confidence in his team to sign a new contract with the directors. He also made a key decision when he signed young Eire international defender Pat Scully on a month's loan from Arsenal. Scully's assured performances soon persuaded the manager to pay £100,000 to secure him on permanent terms.

Crewe boss Dario Gradi pronounced Southend *a formality for promotion'* after their 2–0 win at Gresty Road in January 1991, but Webb warned the exultant fans *'it's fatal to start looking too far ahead'.*

Rightly enough United's unbeaten home League record disappeared with a 1–0 Roots Hall defeat by Huddersfield, then they lost 2–1 on the plastic at Preston, relinquishing their third division lead to Grimsby in the process.

A crucial 1–0 win over Shrewsbury put them back on top in early February but after a freeze up they lost 2–1 at home to Reading, fuelling the doubters' worries that United were freezing up themselves. The steps towards promotion were indeed getting more nervous, and they looked anything but championship contenders in a 1–0 defeat at Grimsby in March. *'We seemed to show a lot of fear and gave them far too much respect'* said Webb afterwards, *'Some of our boys looked nervous and jittery, I want us to get back to playing with the freedom and flair which got us into this lofty position'.*

His players listened, returning to their more solid ways with consecutive 2–1 home defeats of Mansfield and Birmingham the same month, yet they'd dropped to second when an unfortunate 1–0 defeat at third placed Bolton in late March refuelled the nervous tension. By the beginning of April Southend were just three points above Bolton, five points ahead of the play off zone and nervously eyeing a late surge by Cambridge United, who had three games in hand.

By now, though, the fans were sensing glory – and they turned up in their thousands on 9 April for a Tuesday evening game at Brisbane Road against Leyton Orient. The vocal support was tremendous, the team performance magnificent, Andy Ansah crashing home after 17 minutes to leave Southend needing three more victories from the remaining seven games to go up.

'Southend are slowly convincing the south–east Essex public that second division football really is on the way' said the Daily Telegraph as a Roots Hall crowd of 8,622 saw them beat Tranmere 1–0 courtesy of a 42 minute Andy Ansah goal. The victory put them back into first place, but it also saw a penalty miss by David Martin, beginning a run of poor spot kicks which with hindsight probably lost United their chance of the championship outright.

Webb thereafter banned all talk of promotion in the dressing room but there wasn't much of it anyway after the next game, a miserable 2–0 home defeat against Wigan. That left five games to play; Southend still top and their destiny in their own hands.

On 27 April they took a giant step towards their goal by beating Exeter City 2–1 at St James's Park with a spectacular pitch length run and shot by Adam Locke, deflected in by Exeter defender Scott Hiley.

On 80 points and with two matches in hand over fourth placed Bolton (77 points), victory over fellow promotion seekers Cambridge in the next game would now assure Southend of division two status. Kick off was delayed by 25 minutes as the highest home crowd of the season – 10,665 – jammed in to see history made, but they witnessed Southend's only goalless draw of the season. The blues dominated the first half, but only a stunning save by Paul Sansome from Dion Dublin kept them level in the end and the result was satisfactory in the circumstances. Southend had maintained their slender one point lead at the top, now over Cambridge in second place and Grimsby in third. Once again they had only to win their next match to make sure.

Gigg Lane was the scene, a small, attractive ground on a beautiful sunny day. The team had flown up, the fans had followed in coaches and cars – and this was a make or break game. Bury had their own play off hopes, Southend were desperate for a win, but it began to look bad for United when Pat Scully was sent off for a hard tackle on 43 minutes. With the score at 0–0 the loss of such a key man – and with a whole half still to play – boded ill for the blues chances of even securing a draw, let alone snatching the win they needed.

Yet they came out fighting after the interval, determined to beat the odds and fired up by what they saw as Scully's unjust dismissal. Butler and Clark led the way with fierce combative tackling, Ansah made his usual darting runs, and Brett Angell charged all over the place.

For all that, neither goalkeeper had to make a save until Bury's Gary Kelly smothered a low 72nd minute shot from Ansah. At the other end United then survived a double scare when Liam Robinson's 30 yard drive forced Paul Sansome to fingertip over the bar and Valentine headed over from the resulting corner. It looked like the contest was going to burn itself out in midfield.

It looked like it, but it didn't. With just eight minutes to go Ian Benjamin, the man with the knack of scoring Southend's important goals, produced the most crucial yet.

It was a strike from an unpromising position, out of the blue really; Ansah's persistence winning him the space to get in a cross, Benjamin controlling, turning, and rifling into the corner with his left foot.

The explosion of emotion behind the goal and on the pitch was overwhelming. Fans tumbled over each other, the players jumped on one another's backs and just about everyone punched the air in celebration. But there were still eight minutes to go – longer, it seemed, than all the 85 years of Southend history that had gone before. Substitutes Chris Powell and John Cornwell held it steady at the back, the ball regularly went into touch and when Paul Sansome finally punted upfield with a minute or so of injury time gone, the referee's whistle sounded.

Scully was first on the pitch to congratulate his team mates and the celebrations lasted for at least half an hour after the match as the 1,500 travelling fans sang and danced on the terraces. Despite the supporters demands Webb didn't come onto the field; he was already in the dressing room bath with a glass of whisky in hand. But as the fans began their long happy journey home he paid tribute to the spirit of a club so long in the shadows.

'This was our little Everest' he said, *'I feel so pleased for the players and for everyone at Roots Hall, from the tea lady to the hardest fanatic on the north bank. Southend United has arrived at last, so let's all savour and enjoy it'.*

Having won the most elusive prize of promotion to the second division, Southend threw away the chance of the third division championship with a 1–1 draw against Orient and a 1–0 defeat versus Brentford, both at home. In the end they came second to Cambridge by one point when they should really have won, but it would be dishonest to say many of United's fans were upset.

Getting into the second division was all that mattered; Southend were now no longer a team of the lower echelons, they were in the top flight. For all the celebrations and the joy of the subsequent seafront procession, the magnitude of Southend's achievement didn't really sink in until kick off against Bristol City on 17 August 1991 – the first ever game in division two. What a privilege, what a magical moment to savour. If only the men and women who founded the club could have been there too...

GOLDEN MOMENT: Ian Benjamin turns to fire the goal which beat Bury

CHAPTER 1
EARLY DAYS

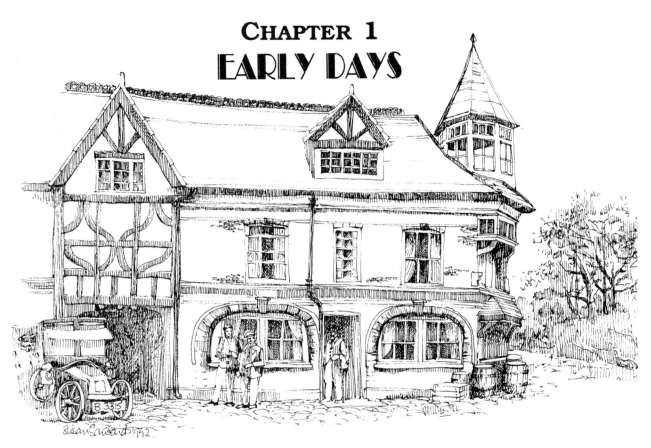

*Artists impression (Susan Saward) of the Blue Boar Inn in 1906
where it all began.*

Southend never did lack football teams – it just didn't have any good ones. By 1906, when it finally did get the side its 50,000 population merited, any number of senior clubs had already taken the town's name – most of them fairly nondescript outfits like Southend Victoria, Southend Corinthians, Southend Ramblers and even Southend Wesleyans. The top local amateur side, Southend Athletic, had been through some good times, but were hardly setting the world on fire either. They'd once played at Roots Hall Fields in Prittlewell, (the village whose 'south end' gave its name to the town) but now had a tenancy at Marine Park in the Kursaal, and played in red shirts and white shorts.

Athletic's poor showings during 1904/5 in the lowly South Essex League against the likes of Barking and Romford brought them only third place in a first division of just seven teams.

The Athletic reserves, who managed to field just five players in one embarrassing 1906 fixture, fared even worse in the division below, and the team as a whole showed such abysmal cup form that supporters were sarcastically promising to light celebratory bonfires if they beat local works side Arc in the final of the Chelmsford Charity competition. The fires in any case, were never lit; they lost 4–3. Even in 1906 fans liked a good moan, but the Athletic really were getting nowhere fast, and they were losing money into the bargain.

At the club's AGM on 16 May 1906 members heard that total gate receipts had almost halved from £427 to £240 and the President, Robert Jones, mooted the idea of attracting better players by turning semi-professional – an idea he had first brought up in 1903.

Little support was forthcoming, and although his plan (along with a possible move back to Roots Hall) was mulled over at great length, amateurism won through. In the face of what was nothing short of a crisis, the boldest move members could agree was a change of team shorts from white to blue.

With hindsight, that dithering AGM signalled the death of Athletic. The amateur game at the time was retreating into its own socially exclusive world, unable to cope with the rise of professionalism, and even though Athletic members knew moves had been afoot since April to create a strong professional club in the town, they chose to look the other way. It was a decision they were to regret, for within three days Southend United had been born.

The 19 May meeting at Prittlewell's Blue Boar Hotel which created Southend's new professional club was decisive and upbeat by contrast.

The foundations had already been laid a month earlier in the same hostelry – which was a stones throw from Roots Hall on the corner of West Street and what is now Victoria Avenue. Then, a band of local footballers and businessmen, driven on by Athletic's weak showing and local press complaints about the amateur side's 'dreary influence', had gathered on the evening of 19 April to talk about forming a new Southend club. Former Athletic player Andy Ducat, a Woolwich Arsenal and England star who'd been forced to leave the area in search of professional football, gave them his valuable support. By that time, led by Blue Boar landlord Oliver Trigg, the plotters had already managed to get a three year lease on the 6,000 capacity ground at Roots Hall, somebody had promised to buy shirts for the club, and they'd discussed semi-professionalism.

But in what might have been a holding operation, those present at the April meeting had voted unanimously to create a strong amateur team called Prittlewell United.

They aimed to enter as rivals to Athletic in the South Essex League and would play in royal blue, black collars and cuffs, and white shorts – blue, it seems, for no other reason than that Athletic played in red. Among the Blue Boar schemers was a Mr J Budd, former secretary of Southend Athletic, who told everyone there was room for two teams in the town. 'There are many who predict a short life for the new club', said the Southend Standard's football correspondent, 'but I believe it will be a team to be reckoned with before long'.

In the month after that April meeting, the plotters began to prove him right. If the Athletic members had taken the bull by the horns and responded with their own plan for a semi-professional team, 'Prittlewell United' may well have decided to throw their lot in with the Athletic rather than starting from scratch – and the club which now represents the town in the Football League could well have been playing in red.

As it was, the packed inaugural 19 May meeting, organised and inspired by Oliver Trigg, took the embryonic club's plans on by leaps and bounds. Horizons had widened, so the name Prittlewell was dropped – and the new team became Southend United. Prime mover and first club secretary Charlie Anderson, well known on the local cricket and football scene, said the Athletic had been 'fighting tooth and nail' to keep the new team out of the South Essex League – but in any case plans to play in such a lowly competition were dropped as unambitious. The newly elected directors were told to tout for professional players as well as amateurs, and an application was drawn up to play in the prestigious Southern League, frequented by emerging and powerful southern clubs like West Ham and Portsmouth.

It was more than the Athletic had bargained for, and shellshocked reds officials, already feeling the initiative being wrested away from them, made a hastily arranged trip to London four days later to apply for Southern League status too. Sadly – but typically – they were too late, and when news came through the following week that United had been elected to the League's second division, Athletic's obituary had virtually been written.

United's election caused great excitement in the town, and the Athletic were left behind amid all the Edwardian hat throwing and general commotion.

back George Molyneux, a rock steady defender who'd turned out for Southampton and Portsmouth, and Fred Watkins, a Welsh half back and Millwall player known as something of a joker. In goal Jack fixed up Charlie Cotton, once of Reading and Liverpool but poached from West Ham in the close season, and up front he had Arthur Holden from Portsmouth.

Just to rub salt into the wound, United had also been raiding Athletic of its best performers. The first player on United's books was William Thompson, a fearless, everpresent Athletic defender quickly joined by team

The new team had garnered 33 votes in favour of its application, beating Swindon Reserves (30) Royal Engineers (27) Wycombe Wanderers (18) and Tunbridge Wells Rangers (16). All of those teams received enough votes to get in anyway, but Hastings and Grays United were turned away.

Even as news of United's election was coming in, determined player hunting was in progress. By the third week of July, 30 year old former Plymouth Argyle manager Bob Jack, United's newly appointed player, manager and secretary, had been able to secure the signatures of 11 formidable professionals – among them two former internationals, one time England left

mates Jerry Thomson, 'Prince' Blott and Harry Owen, who all signed on professional terms, effectively forcing a depleted Athletic to amalgamate with Southend Victoria in June 1906. Other local sides also lost out to the promise of hard cash; Grays United were relieved of their skipper Ben Freeman and their forward Jimmy Axcell, whose grandson David Axcell is now a top Football League referee. Wanstead lost prolific scorer Harry Halse, who turned out to be United's best capture.

Fortuitously for Southend United, a Football League ruling meant that any players moving down to a Southern League club from the Football League outfits would have to go on a free transfer, but the non-leaguers cost money and the cash for those acquisitions (plus projected running costs of £40 a week) was to come from a share issue. At another packed and high spirited meeting on 5 July, this time in the local Masonic Hall, money raising plans were put on the table.

At the meeting, Southend United was formally declared a professional club, created a limited company, and 8,000 shares of five shillings each were put on the market. Trading in the shares, which aimed to raise £2,000, began on 3 August 1906 and closed two weeks later. Chairing the meeting was George Hogflesh, honorary secretary of the amateur running club Southend Harriers, who to cries of 'shame' revealed he had been much criticised by some harriers for taking part in the formation of a professional football club. There was a significant body of feeling against professionalism in the town, he said, but it was better to openly declare oneself in favour than to take part in 'sham amateurism'.

Secretary Charlie Anderson also said he'd suffered abuse for getting involved with professionalism, but was convinced he'd made the right move. There was a stirring supportive speech from Robert Campbell of Leyton FC, who'd helped Southend with their Southern League application – and the mood was so buoyant that plans to form a baseball team to play at Roots Hall on off-weeks even managed to find their way onto the share prospectus. Arsenal & Spurs had done likewise, but the plan never came to anything.

The list of directors of the company, registered at 15 West Street Prittlewell, read like a who's who of local self made men – formally named on the share prospectus were Charles Stein, a member of the Stock Exchange; Oliver Trigg, 'licensed victualler; George Hogsflesh, 'agent'; Frederick England, another licensed victualler, and Tom Tidy, a merchant and cigar importer.

Season tickets for Southend's 1908/9 campaign were available from Garon's Hairdressing Salon, price £2 2s for the stand or 12s 6d for the ground.

Many of them – particularly Oliver Trigg, who parted for good with a hefty £861 to get things going – quickly found themselves digging into their pockets as the share issue fell substantially short of its target.

By now, though, cash shortages could not halt the momentum and suddenly all newspaper sports coverage was of United. The players began roadwork under the supervision of trainer Arthur Norris, a former holder of the world 20 miles record, and a practice match was organised at Roots Hall for 25 August, the 'A' team versus the 'B' team, in aid of the Victoria Hospital. Punctually at six on a summer Saturday evening Oliver Trigg was given the honour of 'kicking off' amid loud cheers from a crowd of 850.

The 'B' Team, sporting most of the players who went on to form the first team, won 4–0 with 'considerable dash' and the Southend Standard predicted thousands of spectators to see some 'rattling good football' in the first proper match, two saturdays hence. Seven signings were made after the game but not everyone made such an impact. A mysterious figure called 'Dark' – allegedly a professional cricketer of some repute who once played for Norwich City – scored a goal for the B's at centre forward. But he was playing under an alias, and he never featured again.

Not everyone shared the majority enthusiasm for the new club, though. During the run up to the club's momentous first game – on 1 September 1906 at Roots Hall against Swindon Reserves in Southern League division II – a sarcastic *memorial card*' began circulating the town. Echoing the mock obituary which led to the creation of the Ashes for England v Australia test matches, it read:

'In memory of Southend Utd
Aged one
Interred in Root's Hall Field, Prittlewell
Another beastly body blow'

Exactly who had them printed remains shrouded in mystery, though fingers were quickly pointed at jealous Athletic officials. The Standard rather piously denounced the prank as *'childish and unsportsmanlike'*, worthy only of schoolboys.

The death of football at Roots Hall was severely exaggerated in any case. The game against Swindon Reserves, played in sweltering heat on a Saturday afternoon, was a huge success. The match was brimful of exciting incident from start to finish and professional football was judged a worthy addition to the town's activities, though United lost 1–0 after monopolising most of the play. As spectators swarmed onto the pitch after the final whistle guest of honour Nat Whittaker, secretary of the Southern League, pronounced everything 'first rate'. The United team that momentous day was:

*Cotton, Thomson, Molyneux, Johnson,
Owen, Freeman, Holden, Mitchell,
Halse, Watkins, and Jack.*

It was a good start to an even better season. Home gates, admission 6d, sometimes reached 3,000 – unheard of in an area brought up on the amateur game – and United could hardly have done better in their first campaign. Many of the teams they played were reserve sides of bigger clubs playing in Southern League division I, but United set about their job with relish and plenty of style. Most of the players were considered small in stature – six foot skipper 'Molly' Molyneux towered above his team mates – but they were big in heart and Southend quickly became known as a haven of direct, attacking, goalscoring football.

In the Southern League they averaged almost three a game throughout the season, even trouncing the once all–conquering Royal Engineers 12–0 in a home fixture on 15 September. And in the less important South Eastern League, which they won, much the same squad rattled in 90 over 19 games, chasing goals *'like a pack of hounds'*, beating Chesham Generals 13–0 and notching their 100th collective goal by Christmas.

Counting friendlies, United hit the back of the net a staggering 222 times in 65 games, conceding just 53 and losing only seven times. *'There is not another club in the country in any league or competition that has a goal record such as the United'* boasted the Standard. Their passing was *'pretty and effective'* but upfront Halse was ruthless. He bagged 91 goals in all competitions, catching the eye of several big clubs and eventually moving up North to Manchester United, where he won a cup winners medal and an England cap in 1909. Goalkeeper Cotton even managed to find his way onto the scoresheet twice – both penalties.

The result: Southend won the Southern League division II at the first attempt. The clincher, a Wednesday afternoon 2–2 draw against West Ham reserves on 3 April 1907, made the main news section of the local papers and pulled in a record Roots Hall crowd, probably 4,000. *'Such enthusiasm has never been seen like it in Southend before, even at the declaration of the poll at the general election'* screamed 'Ref' the Standard soccer reporter. Gate receipts from 47,000 paying customers during the season had reached £1,117.

Impoverished Athletic looked on forlornly. Even three months into that first 1906/7 season there were rumours of amalgamation, and in the summer of 1907, with United running 'smoking concerts' at the Blue Boar to raise funds for players' summer wages, Athletic decided to throw in the towel.

Officially there was a merger with United, but everyone knew it was no such thing, and most of the reds players were subsumed into the second eleven. The Athletic chairman, unable even to mention the name of his rivals, told members they were *'all aware of the reason why the club was not in such a satisfactory state as it was last year'*. *'The Athletic have passed away'* said the Standard, in a cruel reference to earlier controversies, *'but no mourning cards were issued'*.

All did not go swimmingly for United that summer, though. Promotion to the first division after their runaway victory was theoretically automatic, but during August 1907 fans were stunned by the news that an entirely new club, and a northern one at that, had been given Southend's place. Bradford Park Avenue, who had not yet kicked a ball but were loaded with money from the industrial north, effectively bought their way into the top flight, leapfrogging division II in their first season. Southenders were outraged, especially that *'the money bags of a northern club were accepted in preference to the rightful claims of a bone fide southern club'*. Southern League officials were accused of being 'capitalists' and 'bowing to commercialism'; it was one of several poor decisions by Southern League officials which eventually weakened its status.

The club had to swallow even harder when the by now hated Bradford Park Avenue used their money to lure away their tricky 21 year old forward Prince Blott before the start of the new campaign. But the cash from his transfer, plus money from Arthur Holden's simultaneous departure to Plymouth Argyle, came in handy – and there was nothing for it but to soldier on in division II. The 1907/8 season built on the success of the first year, starting with nine straight victories. Crowds rose steadily and United established themselves as a firm talking point. Some were shocked when betting slips started to appear at the ground, others complained of ill-mannered booing at some matches, and one local reporter accused fans of acting *'like men at some whippet races I've seen'.*

However uncouth, by April 1908 the fans had spurred United to league victory again. The players indulged in their own whippet fancier behaviour when an end of season draw between Hastings and Portsmouth reserves handed them the trophy. The cup, already in a cabinet at the Blue Boar headquarters (along with skipper

George Molyneux's four international caps), was brought down amid high revelry to be filled with ale. The team had lost only two League games all season, scoring 47 from 18 games against 16 conceded, but on the final day of the season against Wycombe Wanderers they came back down to earth with a bump. Held on cup final day in April, snow fell, Southend changed and warmed up in the cold for half an hour, but Wycombe refused to come out and the referee sent a telegram to say he couldn't make it to the ground. Postponed.

FOOTBALL !

AT ROOTS HALL, WEST STREET,
SATURDAY NEXT, 21. DECEMBER,
SOUTHEND UNITED RESERVES v

LIMEHOUSE TOWN.

Kick-off 2.30. Admission 4d (Ladies, Soldiers in uniform, and Boys, 2d.); Grand Stand, 4d. extra.

SOUTHEND UNITED'S ATTRACTIVE HOLIDAY MATCHES.
(All in South Eastern League, Division I.)
AT ROOTS HALL, WEST STREET.
WEDNESDAY (CHRISTMAS DAY), kick-off 11.20. a.m.,

v. HITCHIN TOWN.

THURSDAY (BOXING DAY), at 2.30 p.m.,

v. CHELSEA Res.

SATURDAY, 28th DECEMBER, at 2.30 p.m.,

v. WEST HAM UNITED Res.

WEDNESDAY, NEW YEAR'S DAY, at 2.30 p.m

v. FULHAM Res.

Admission To Ground, 6d. Ladies, Soldiers in uniform, and Boys, 3d.; to Enclosure and Grand Stand, 6l. extra.

19 December 1907

Despite a £50 a week wage bill for a fully professional first team and six paid men in the reserves, finances were stable enough for an emerging club. It wasn't unknown for Bob Jack to knock up the directors on the morning of an away game to borrow money for the train fares, but season ticket sales (10s 6d for the ground and £1 1s for the stand) brought in regular income with bigger matches – like a famous victory over Football League division two side Clapton Orient in the FA Cup that year – producing anything up to £80 a time.

With the help of a £700 transfer fee for Halse and Axcell to Manchester United the club had managed to accumulate more than £300 in the coffers since it had begun, and the Bradford debacle had taught directors the importance of having cash in the bank. More money was raised by issuing extra shares, and the application for election to Southern League division I went in.

THE REFEREE: "Yes, I know you've won, but how much money have you brought?"

Outraged: The Southern League's decision to give Bradford P.A. a division I place drew scathing comment in Southend.

As it was, United needn't have worried. Five vacancies had occurred, partly because some Southern League clubs, including Spurs, had been elected into the Football League second division, and in June 1908 Southend got their much sought after place with the big boys. Exeter, Leyton, New Brompton and Coventry joined them to play teams like Portsmouth, Millwall, Crystal Palace, Southampton and Bristol Rovers – the first teams, not the reserves this time.

JULY 2, 1908

Life in the Southern League proper was not easy, and even with their renowned fighting spirit Southend found it difficult to maintain their goalscoring exploits. Two train loads of Millwall fans helped swell a new record home crowd of 5,000 for the opening home game, a 3–0 win for United, but scores of freeloaders skipped their entrance fee by vaulting the enclosure railings. Opposing teams found Southend's defence only fractionally more secure during the 1908/9 season, although a final 12th position in a league of 21 was no disgrace for a club new to the scene.

United's very existence was threatened at the end of that season when plans for a third division of the Football League were drawn up without including Southend, Watford or New Brompton (later to become Gillingham), but spirited resistance led by Bob Jack and other United officials managed to kill the plan.

Close season improvements at Roots Hall meant crowds had remained relatively good, although when the Millwall gate was bettered early on against Southampton, and then for another new record of 7,200 versus eventual champions Northampton, there were complaints about congestion. The Northampton game brought in receipts of £191, and at nearby away games like Leyton or West Ham, up to 600 would follow the team. Money, however, was still tight, and a supporters committee formed by fans in March 1909 took on the job of raising money for the players' summer wages.

DEFENCE NOT DEFIANCE.

The defence of the Southend United was greatly admired at Plymouth.

THE BATTLE OF WOODEN SPOON
at Root's Hall, Jan. 30th, 1909.

(For the sequel see "Southend Standard" on Thursday next.)

The Wooden Spoon: "Now then, what am I going to have—Potted Shrimp or Boiled Bantam?"

In an enlightened move it also encouraged supporters to donate a shilling each to raise enough cash to buy shares, putting three of its members on the board and stumping up a £60 deposit towards the cost of erecting a stand on the West side of the ground. Blott, who had returned from Bradford, raised some cash by moving on again to join former team mate Harold Halse at Manchester United.

Money dominated the following 1909/10 season as the club languished near the bottom of the Southern League division I throughout the whole campaign. Even cup holders Manchester United failed to bring in more than 2,500 supporters when they visited the town on a sodden day for a pre-season friendly, Halse making a popular reappearance for the reds at his old ground. From the off financial problems stole most of the year's headlines.

By the end of the campaign, with the team narrowly escaping relegation in 20th position and still smarting from an 11-1 thrashing at Northampton (still the club's worst defeat in

any competition) United were £800 in debt. Directors were reduced to running money raising bazaars and paying for travelling expenses from their own pocket – which, in the case of one player, Walter Smith, was a not inconsiderable sum because he journeyed down from his home in Liverpool for every game. Ground admission was raised to a shilling over Easter (6d for boys, ladies and men in uniform) as gates dropped below 3,000 and receipts became increasingly meagre.

Most other Southern League clubs were facing similar difficulties, but manager Bob Jack, who found it difficult to run the team with so many off-field worries, unexpectedly decided to call it a day during the close season and went back to lead Plymouth Argyle, where he took up a lucrative offer.

It was a sad season in other ways – the town was shocked when jovial, much loved 30 year old keeper Charlie Cotton died in January 1910 from a kidney condition called Brights disease, leaving a wife and children.

C. COTTON (goalkeeper).

There were bizarre episodes too; centre half Harry Owen having to threaten legal action in November 1909 to stave off allegations from spectator Ebenezer Pepper that he'd been betting against his own side, and the club forced to pay a heavy £10 fine after revelations that the previous season it had deliberately fielded a suspended player, Leslie, under a false name.

But there were lighter moments. As a general election got underway in January 1910, while the team stayed at the Saracens Head in Lincoln before a game against Gainsborough Trinity, a crowd of 6,000 people swelled outside waiting for a balcony speech by the well known Conservative politician Sir Robert Filner. When Sir Robert failed to show, United's travelling reserve Maurice 'Dot' Cantor, who fancied himself as something of an orator, decided to come on as substitute. He addressed the crowd with vigour on the latest unionist thought but his political life proved even shorter than his footballing career. Most of his rhetoric was quickly drowned by cheering and hooting from the masses, although he did manage to keep going for 20 minutes. What little of his speech was audible was delivered, according to the local Lincoln paper *'at about*

250 words a minute'. With Cantor's help the Liberals held Lincoln.

The other bright spot was an end of season tour to Germany – an adventurous undertaking by a club so racked with money problems, but a great success nonetheless. A squad of 14 took the boat over in May, beat Berlin 4–0 and thrashed Oxford City 10–0 – almost certainly the first match on German soil between two English clubs. Out of six tour games they managed to win five, their only defeat against Berlina Hertna (3–1). Money still managed to rear its ugly head though – two players were marched off by German customs and held until they coughed up more than two shillings duty they'd been trying to avoid on some tobacco and a pack of cards.

United keeper Toone locks arms with his opposite number Eichelmann, in Berlin.

Germany aside, 1909/10 had been an unfulfilling season, so it was no surprise when United lost their way altogether in 1910/11, relinquishing the Southern League first division place they'd fought so hard for.

16

In the absence of Jack, the team was managed by Molyneux, whose actions were overseen for much of the season by a makeshift committee of directors – and it showed. Money matters got no better and standards began to slip. In an important FA cup qualifying game away at Enfield which kicked off at 2.45 on a Wednesday afternoon, Louis Parke, an occasional United player who'd come to watch a relative turn out for the home team, had to be drafted into the side after only ten blues players turned up. Officials managed to find him in the crowd and get him onto the pitch after ten minutes of play.

They won, but apart from a subsequent 5–1 defeat in a lucrative cup–tie against mighty Blackburn, played at Ewood Park despite a home draw – to raise more money – most was gloom during that 1910/11 season. The 'blues' even played in a ridiculous new strip of red and yellow hooped jerseys which home supporters found embarrassing, away fans found hilarious and the Southend Graphic dismissed as *'bilious'*. For a while Southend were called the *'beef and mustards'* but the new colours, like the team, dropped out of favour. By the time blue jerseys were reinstated in February 1911 United were heading for Southern League division II status.

New player/manager Joe Bradshaw took the team to within a whisker of going straight back up the following 1911/12 season, but again financial problems diverted attention from the pitch, and in February 1912 directors dropped a bombshell. The club owed £1015 and was seriously considering winding up voluntarily, a crisis precipitated rather ungraciously by one of the club's own directors, Thomas Buxton, who'd moved to Sidcup and now wanted to be paid back £90 he'd earlier loaned the club. When United said they couldn't pay straight away he issued a writ, and for two tense weeks the town stared at the possibility of what the Standard called *'the irretrievable calamity'* of losing its club. During that fortnight, though, a fund set up by mayor Chalton Hubbard managed to raise £600 in donations from townspeople.

The day was saved – cash collected for the team had even dwarfed donations to the Titanic disaster fund.

League joy may not have been forthcoming but United did at least win one trophy for the cabinet during 1911/12 – the handsome Southern Charity Cup, which was secured by Bradshaw's solitary goal against Coventry City in the final at White Hart Lane. Southend, still not finished with their sartorial adventures, played in a change strip of salmon and pink stripes.

Soccer life back in the Southern League division II was no great shakes – for players or fans – and it was imperative United got themselves out of what was threatening to become a football backwater. At a time of northern dominance, any team in the Southern League's first division could claim to be one of the 60 top clubs in the country, but division II was different.

Southend's 1912/13 season – the first to be played with goalkeepers restricted to handling in the penalty area – revolved around fierce clashes with gritty but obscure clubs like Aberdare, Custom House (in London's docklands), Luton, and Ton Pentre. Travelling, almost always by train, was fraught and gruelling, with the squad usually arriving on a Friday evening and staying at a local inn.

Crowds were small, and shares of receipts sometimes barely covered expenses. Pitches were often appalling, and a United league game at Newport was postponed that season because ground staff had attempted to dry out a badly drained pitch by sprinkling it with clinker and rubble from a builder's yard. United, who firmly declined to play, were given £15 towards their expenses after official league intervention, and managed to win the rearranged match later in the season, when improvised knee caps worn by the players still failed to prevent deep wounds and lacerations. In an earlier game at Ton Pentre the pitch was so muddy the referee actually lost his coin during the toss up and had to be brought a replacement.

Some of the grounds had a gritty atmosphere too. Custom House, for instance, where according to a local reporter *'even the most foul mouthed linguist could scarcely have visited the enclosure without adding some new words to his vocabulary'* was renowned for its hostile crowd.

There was light relief from division II earthiness when United landed a plum tie at Stamford Bridge against Football League first division team Chelsea, although they lost 5–2 and only 14,000 came to see the game on a filthy day.

But through it all Southend triumphed, the inspirational captaincy of Jerry Thomson and an unbeaten home record helping them to second place and promotion. Thanks to continued efforts from the mayor's fund and slightly better home gates, money worries (despite a loss of £703) were pushed to the background. The Standard rejoiced: *'In future we shall regard the horrible grounds of Glamorganshire and Carmarthenshire as awful nightmares of the past'* it said.

Southend, indeed, never darkened the second division's doorstep again, though the next two years back in division one against the likes of Crystal Palace, Portsmouth, Bristol Rovers and Cardiff City were hardly distinguished. Tram fares to Roots Hall were raised to a penny in anticipation of greater local interest during the 1913/14 season, though the move proved unpopular and the optimism was unfounded. Support did come from far and wide though – up to 200 fans regularly made the journey to home matches from Grays and Stanford, and crowds hovered around the 5,000 mark despite poor form.

The blues performed creditably in the cup, losing to Birmingham 2–1 in front of 19,000 at St Andrews, especially since Bradshaw rather foolishly decided to take his players up on the day of the game and they arrived only an hour before the kick–off after sitting in a cramped, delayed train for several hours. United's good recent run of cup performances was recognised the following year by exemption from the qualifying rounds, an honour not given to all Southern League clubs.

Leading Lights: founder Oliver Trigg (left), and former Athletic president Robert Jones.

18

Before a New Year slump Southend had played reasonably well with a young defence, and close season signing Lionel Louch further enhanced the club's reputation by becoming the first Southend player to win an international cap, albeit for England Amateurs, against Wales on 7 February. Keeper Thomas Clarke, unfortunately, undid all the good work when he was fined £5 by a local court for illegal street betting outside the Blue Boar. Clarke had been given previous warnings by the club, and he wasn't picked for a crucial end of season game against Plymouth the following week which pulled the club into a safe 16th spot from 20, just above the relegation zone. He disappeared from team sheets thereafter.

Boardroom turmoil surfaced during that 1913/14 campaign despite a balance sheet in credit for the first time. Bickering got so bad that club founder Oliver Trigg had to step in as chairman late in the season after previous incumbent and Roots Hall owner George Radford resigned because of *'personal insults'* directed at him during several acrimonious board meetings.

It was open warfare of a different and more serious kind – against the Kaiser – which dominated the following year. When Britain joined the fight against Germany in August 1914 Southend became the scene of the first air raid in the country. There were strong feelings in certain quarters that football should be abandoned, but others felt the game should continue as a necessary diversion, particularly for troops on leave or bored in their barracks.

Despite establishment disapproval of soccer's continuation, the terraces proved a useful recruiting ground. Southend mayor Joseph Francis addressed 1,000 fans who'd stayed on after a September 1914 match against Southampton, trying to recruit them to Lord Kitchener's Army. The sight of khaki uniforms on the terraces became familiar, and canaries fans at Norwich were surprised in October to find 1,000 soldiers from the Essex regiment and Southend H company *'cheering themselves hoarse'* in the crowd. They'd marched five miles eastwards from Costessey barracks to see United earn a 1-1 draw.

But the darker side of war quickly intruded on the club. Scotsman Billy Sutherland, who was signed as an inside forward for United in 1908 – then went with Bob Jack to Plymouth – was the first to be killed in action, serving with the Argyll and Sutherland Highlanders. A quiet, even tempered man, well mannered on and off the field, he was married to a Southend lady and was living in the town while playing for Chatham before he joined up. The diminutive Archie Wilson, one of the best right wingers United ever had, was also killed in France while serving with London Scottish, and so too was fearless Harry Owen, who'd played in United's first ever game and scored the only goal in that horrendous 11-1 defeat at Northampton.

As deaths in the trenches mounted and casualties began to rise in Southend itself, which was a prime and relatively close target for deadly German zeppelin raids, voices continued to be raised against football, even though upper and middle class pastimes like horse racing and theatre going escaped criticism. Many newspapers made their point by cutting match reports and publishing only results, and even the creation of a reservist Footballers Battalion, to which Southend's Woodward, Robson and Lonsdale enroled as privates, failed to help much in a public relations battle the game was losing quickly.

Southend, like other clubs, were pilloried for charging soldiers full price for admission, but gates were falling dramatically with so many fans away on duty, and less than 2,000 saw the home game against Norwich in February 1915. By the end of the season, with United again narrowly avoiding relegation in 17th place out of 20, courtesy of victories over Millwall and Plymouth, players were owed substantial sums in wages. United's £1,000 debts were by no means unique; all 60 first class English clubs managed to finish the 1914/15 season, but between them they had estimated debts of £¼m. The FA reduced maximum wages to £3 a week and abolished summer wages.

At the end of the season the football authorities bowed to intense pressure by suspending all soccer for the duration of the war.

Most of the United players joined up and manager Bradshaw went off to fight in France. For Southend a spell in hibernation was inevitable, but quickly a worse fate presented itself. At a meeting of shareholders in October 1915 the increasingly disgruntled former chairman George Radford, worried by threats of the club going into voluntary liquidation, said he would now only waive the £100 rent he was owed as owner of Roots Hall if the club surrendered the lease of Roots Hall immediately rather than in June 1916 when it was due to expire.

For reasons which remain unclear, the shareholders seem to have ignored that reasonable offer; instead granting use of Roots Hall to the armed forces without consulting Radford and therefore depriving him of potential rental income. Roots Hall was used for games in a new Southend & District military football tournament, which attracted 3,000 to the first game between the Lincolns & Leicesters v the Royal Field Artillery. But the standard of military football was poor, and by December a mere handful of spectators were watching.

Debts were still outstanding, and Radford's patience had snapped, but the shareholders were unwilling to go into voluntary liquidation because that would have meant relinquishing Southern League status, and the company continued in existence though the club remained only in name. In October 1915 the team's jerseys, footballs, corner flags and goalposts were auctioned.

Club founder Oliver Trigg died of a heart attack on 25 February 1919. Trigg, by then landlord of the Ivy House Hotel, had always dreaded the month of February – his father and two of his three brothers all preceded him to the grave during that month. Throughout his life, however, Trigg had been a cheery and genial character, popular with almost everyone and a well known supporter of local football, boxing, and billiards. A prominent freemason – like many of the Southend directors – he created his own Buffalo Lodge based at the Ivy House.

Little else happened for some time until a few days before the beginning of June 1916 when the lease on Roots Hall expired, and with lumps in the throats of many who attended, Messrs A Provost & Sons held an auction, at the ground, of what remained of the Roots Hall fixtures and fittings. As 100 potential buyers looked out over a pitch grown long enough to produce a crop of hay, everything went under the hammer. The grandstand, 122 ft long, went for £92 10s including dressing rooms and an office underneath – a paltry sum equivalent only to the recent cost of covering the small enclosure in front of the stand. The buyer, a lawyer called Flaxman, used the materials to repair his timber yard destroyed in Southend's first Zeppelin incendiary raid. More than 1,100 ft of fencing round the whole ground went for £15 10s after spirited bidding, and a timber refreshment bar fetched £2 10s. Total proceeds were just £137. From June 1916 Roots Hall ceased to be a football pitch and was converted into allotments to help the war effort.

An emotional 'Centre Half', the Southend Standard's loyal football correspondent, called it *'an inglorious and regrettable finale to the United's somewhat chequered career'*. After just ten years Southend United football club was dead – no players, no ground, no league to play in, not even a football kit to its name.

In September 1912, having arrived in south Wales at 9pm the previous night, blues players spent most of the Saturday morning prior to their match against Aberdare at the street funeral of a man who'd died in a local colliery accident.

CHAPTER 2
TWENTIES AND THIRTIES

No-one at home thought much about United during the horrendous events of the first world war, but many a homesick soldier remembered Saturday afternoons at Roots Hall with affection as he dodged death and boredom in the trenches.

In fact, when the Southend gasworks siren signalled the end of the war on 11 November 1918 it

Ted Grant: the new fairy godmother.

like turnstiles and goalposts which he'd bought in the Roots Hall auction just in case the club survived. West Ham, one of Southend's friends when the club was born, waived a £50 transfer fee they were owed, and offered to help with reconstruction. In December 1918 things were going so well there was even talk of Southend becoming a member of the newly

was the troops abroad as much as anyone who led calls for the resuscitation of the 'dear old blues'. Their letters from the front spoke of hopes that the team could be reassembled, so those at home began to act. Unlike other Southern League teams like Croydon Common, who wound up during the war and never recovered their old status, Southend at least still existed if only in name. And they had one remaining valuable asset – their Southern League membership.

Soon after armistice day, as renewed affection for United welled up throughout the town, two of the old directors put down £100 to refloat the club – providing 18 others would do the same. Previous benefactor Oliver Trigg was suffering ill health, so enterprising vice chairman Teddy Grant, United's new 'fairy godmother', donated back to the club essentials

touted third division, but the Football League temporarily abandoned those plans and Southend concentrated on getting ready for the Southern League again.

There was one problem, however. United needed to show they had a suitable ground before May 1919 if the Southern League was to let them play in the League, and with Roots Hall nothing more than a vegetable patch, United had nowhere to offer. After much dithering, and as the deadline fast approached, Southend Corporation, worried that the team would drop out of the League altogether, agreed in March to provide a pitch in Chalkwell Park (where Essex later played county cricket) for the first season back.

The first game at the Kursaal. August 1919, a practice match

Protests from local residents were ignored, but in any case the club came to a much better arrangement three weeks later when it finally secured a deal to play at Kursaal amusement park, the former haunt of Southend Athletic built only a few yards from the seafront.

As money rolled in from the townsfolk, work on the ground began and £3,000 of debts from before the war were virtually wiped out. More shares were issued, allowing United to pay £350 of the money they still owed players from before hostilities (a condition of them re-starting in the Southern League).

Poor Joe Bradshaw, owed £50 by the club since before the war, and perhaps expecting a land fit for heroes, returned from four years of hell serving in France to find his manager's job had been given to Ned Liddell, a former Clapton Orient defender who had stayed at home during the war and had been poached from a semi-managerial job at Arsenal. That incident left a sour taste in the mouths of many, but Liddell got to work in April 1919, desperately trying to find talent at a fair price. Players with any sort of reputation were now refusing wages of anything under £6 a week, and with the old Blue Boar HQ now defunct a 'towns meeting' was held at the Kursaal on 20 May 1919 to raise more cash.

Local Conservative MP Captain Rupert Guinness lent his weight to the efforts, 5,000 new five shilling shares were created, and the Daily and Sunday Express newspapers even donated a new kit, a set of parallel bars and some tug of war ropes for training.

Everyone got in on the act – the Kursaal owner David de Forest Morehouse threw in 50 guineas to a 100,000 shilling fund – and Liddell was able to sign Arsenal centre half Percy Sands during that summer. He also secured Billy Bridgeman from Chelsea and Lot Jones, a 16 cap Welsh international and former Manchester City player, who was brought in as an inside right. Seven pre war players signed up again including Wileman, Young and Burrill.

The first competitive game back – and the first ever at the Kursaal – was a 2–0 home defeat against Portsmouth on 30 August 1919 in the Southern League division II, but most were just glad to see the team back in action. Two days later United won for the first time at the new ground, 3–0 against Newport County, although the kick off at 6.10 pm was delayed because some players had arrived late on the ever unreliable Fenchurch Street line. Only by scrapping half time was the referee able to finish the contest with some light.

There were further train troubles in October, when a national railway strike prevented United getting to a League game at Norwich. The League committee initially fined them £50 for not chartering a charabanc instead – something which Brentford did for the next game at the Kursaal – but eventually backed down after an appeal.

That same month Lot Jones became the first player to win a full international cap while playing for Southend, receiving universal praise for his performance in the first Welsh victory over England since 1882. He won another cap for Wales during 1919/20, but stayed only one season at the club before becoming manager of Aberdare.

Famous double international Patsy Hendren, who played cricket and soccer for England, turned out for Brentford against Southend in October 1919 - and scored.

Football enthusiasm was greater than ever in the town but, perhaps because of the hard times and disruption imposed by the war, support didn't translate quickly into cash through the share issue – nor did it swell attendances dramatically. Home games were pulling in 5,000 top whack (generally double those before the war), but for Wednesday afternoon League games, kicking off while most people were at work, there were often less than 2,000 present.

Although the railway companies ran special football excursions to Southend from outlying towns like Pitsea, Tilbury and Laindon, and 60 fans regularly made the journey from Foulness Island, the big London clubs were a strong alternative draw, especially as so many Southenders worked in the capital. On Saturday mornings, when many of them had to work in the city, they would knock−off to the pub then catch a game at Highbury, White Hart Lane, or Upton Park rather than rush back to Southend for Southern League soccer.

With the wage bill high, money worries began to loom again and although the Christmas programme saw a Kursaal record of 6,877 against Swindon, the directors had little option but to switch a plum home cup tie against Sheffield United to Bramall Lane in the new year of 1920. Just to prove footballers were exponents of the cliche even in those early days Southend's new captain Henage Wileman assured everyone that the mighty Sheffield United *are only eleven men'* but his team still lost 3−0 in front of 39,700 − one of the biggest crowds ever to watch Southend.

Switching the tie was a good piece of business; Southend got an £841 cheque as their share of the takings. That allowed them to pay off every last halfpenny they owed from before the war, but two months later − in March − manager Liddell, tempted by greater financial security, defected to QPR after less than a year in the post. Managerless, the team sold centre half Maurice Woodward a few days later to Wolves for £700 and took a month to appoint Liddell's successor, Tom Mather, from Manchester City.

On the field it had been a reasonable season. The prolific pre war goalscoring had gone, but a very solid defence kept the side in the top half for most of the campaign and secured a final 11th position.

The referee of a December 1920 game at Fratton Park between Portsmouth and Southend was admonished by the FA after he ordered Pompey's Thompson off the field, then changed his mind and called him back.

The good foundations laid by Liddell, however, quickly disintegrated when he left. The ever present left back George Marshall, who'd joined just before the war, and principal goalscorer Frank Burrill both followed Woodward to Wolves for £800 each at the end of the season, forming an ex−Southend triumvirate who all played for Wolves in the cup final defeat against Spurs the following season. Outside left Jack Young also went, for £500 to West Ham.

The transfer deals helped the blues to a profit of several hundred pounds for 1919/20, but they weakened the side just as it was preparing to take on one of its most important steps. With one season completed since the war the Football League announced it would create a third division, using all the Southern League clubs to form its southern section with a northern section to be created a year later. Southend had become founder members of the third division south.

In real terms nothing much had changed − United would still be playing the same teams as before. But everyone knew they were now part of the Football League, a team to be reckoned with, just 14 years into their existence. The opening day of the third division crowned their new status, a bubbling crowd of 9,500 was present, easily beating the previous club record, to see a victory against Brighton.

As the crowds got bigger the atmosphere at the Kursaal became more charged. It was a tight ground, still being developed at considerable cost with extra banking, and sometimes difficult to police. Hundreds of spectators regularly got in without paying as attendances often pushed the 8,000 mark, and in the days when spectators were expected to be largely impartial, those within the enclosure were known widely for being uncompromisingly pro−Southend.

So marked was the extra support in that first third division year that when United drew second division Blackpool at home in the second round of the cup they refused lucrative offers to play away instead. Prices at the Kursaal were raised to 2 shillings (i.e. 10p) minimum for the game and 9,250 saw a momentous 1–0 win over supposedly superior opposition. With little traffic noise in those days, the roar when Joe Dorsett scored was heard by residents of Rochford three miles away; so excited were the players that, to general astonishment Dorsett *'was literally hugged by his colleagues!'*.

The cup proved a saving grace that season because although Southend avoided the re-election zone, the League position was never healthy. A dream third round home tie against Spurs in February 1921 (see games to remember) pulled in another record of 11,661, even though thousands of Spurs fans were frightened off by exaggerated reports of the Kursaal's limited capacity

They lost 4–1, but record receipts of £2,963 cushioned the blow and the club's following in the next three months belied their lowly position. More than 2,000 blues fans went to Gillingham on a flotilla of boats during March 1921 but a victory there was one of only 14 in the season. Crystal Palace became the first club to earn promotion to Division two by winning the third division south; despite a season of good crowds, keen local interest, an exciting cup run, and a healthy balance sheet Southend could only manage 17th out of 22.

The managerial and transfer upheavals at the beginning of the season had taken their toll – but there was worse to come. After an abysmal start to 1921/22 Tom Mather was effectively sacked halfway through the season and replaced by Ted Birnie, a former pre war Chelsea player. Birnie was to prove one of United's shrewdest managers during a valuable period of stability for the next 12 years, but he had little chance of reversing the decline when he took over, and Southend headed inexorably for re-election. So poor was the front line that Jimmy Evans,

United's left back, actually topped the scoring list that season, the only defender ever to finish a campaign as top scorer for a first class club. He was a fine player, becoming the second Southender to win international honours at the club and playing three games for Wales during 1922, but all around him there was chaos. United let in 74 goals while scoring only 34, finishing bottom and winning the reputation as *'the worst Southend team ever'*.

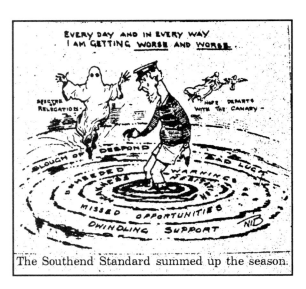

The Southend Standard summed up the season.

To make matters worse, the reserves – who might have been expected to produce a future more successful team – also managed to end up bottom in their competition, which had been formed out of the old Southern League.

Out of the depths of despair appeared optimism, though. When it came to re-election in May 1922, Southend finished top of the poll with only eight of the first and second division clubs failing to give their support. The club's re-election slogan had been *'Southend without its football would be as the sea without its salt'* and the results were widely seen as a vote of confidence in the team. Mayor John Francis promptly launched a £1,500 public appeal to rebuild the club, arguing that United had become 'an advertising medium for the town'. Southenders should emulate the *'shrewd northerners'* of Blackpool, he said, who had recently realised the value of their club and collected £3,000 to buy players.

By mid–July 1922 the fund had reached £600, allowing Birnie to sign ex–Manchester United player Billy Goodwin as centre forward. The new manager's clearout brought in many new faces to a squad of 19 professionals and several amateurs, returning to the clean attractive football Southend had always been known for. Goodwin proved a quick learner as well as a good buy, able to exploit the system used for the first five years after the war of playing teams home and away in consecutive weeks. By taking advantage of opposition weaknesses he'd spotted the week before, he inspired the blues with 21 League goals from 42 games during what was inevitably a transitional year.

A final 15th place was accepted by most in the circumstances as a fair effort, though Jimmy Evans – who'd chalked up another three Welsh appearances during the season – was not sorry to get a transfer to first division Burnley at the end of the campaign. Crowds which had dropped to an average 4,000 in the previous re–election year returned to the 8,000 mark, and a new home League highest of 11,000 was produced against Newport. Ted Birnie had created a good spirit in the side, so the following 1923/24 season was disappointing. Billy Goodwin broke his leg late–on, an injury more or less guaranteed to end a player's career in those days, yet even in his hour of despair Billy

(1923/24) Pre-season training at the Kursaal.

had heroically shouted *"Tell the boys to play up"* from his stretcher as he was led off. The boys unfortunately didn't play up, finishing 19th in the League and avoiding re-election by one point.

In a 1924 reserves game at home against Millwall the referee blew for full time after only 84 minutes. When his error was pointed out, he brought both teams back onto the pitch – but played just 2 minutes extra.

If the five seasons after the great war had been unfulfilling, the mid to late twenties proved to be much more fruitful.

Just as the country was going through something of a boom time United's playing fortunes picked up too. Trainer Bill Cartwright's new regime based around skipping, sprinting, and running down the seafront to Thorpe Bay pushed the club into a more efficient era, worthy of 'professionalism'. After the flux of their first 15 years, United had settled down. They could count on 5–6,000 loyal supporters, not great considering Southend's population was now 120,000, but Birnie cut his cloth accordingly and the club had some good times.

In 1924/25 the side was actually challenging for promotion to division two for much of the time, in second place by the end of January after beating Bournemouth 3–0, but eventually deprived by a bad patch in February and March when they dropped to a final but relatively pleasing 10th place – their best yet in the third division.

Despite the loss of 23 year old centre forward James McClelland to Middlesbrough for a record but undisclosed fee at the end of that season, Southend managed 10th spot again in 1925/6. Changes to the offside rule, which now only called for one player to be between the last defender and the keeper, penalised some teams but favoured United's quick accurate passing style.

With an improved Kursaal now theoretically capable of holding about 18,000, games on Christmas or Easter holidays were bringing in handsome sums of money, and on Boxing Day 1925 a new record of 13,500 was set against Bristol City.

That didn't stand for long though, because a month later came Southend's most momentous game yet, a spectacular 4–1 home demolition of second division Derby County in the fourth round of the FA Cup (see games to remember).

The victory brought Southend to national attention as never before and produced receipts of £1,226 from a crowd of 15,800. In the fifth round they drew Nottingham Forest, also at home; this time 18,153 turned out but saw United leave the competition after a 1–0 defeat. So it was that the season was remembered for its lucrative cup exploits, but it had been a successful one in the League too.

Fans on the Kursaal terraces were astounded in January 1925 when the referee gave Watford a direct free kick for a Southend foul inside the penalty area.

Billy Hick, who had come to Southend from Middlesbrough as part of the McLelland deal, turned out to be a good replacement for Billy Goodwin who never did properly recover from his breakage and ended up making Southend rock on the seafront after a spell with non-League Dartford. Hick scored 18 League and cup goals in *'rugged robust and resolute'* fashion, producing another 29 in all competitions during the 1926/7 season, when novelty big-game football commentaries began to appear on the radio. The 1926/7 campaign was the one blip in the late twenties, but a final 19th position was unflattering for a season which had seen the blues in 6th place approaching Christmas. Re-election was never a possibility, but a disastrous finish to the season put the team into freefall in the final weeks.

Surviving ledgers of local chemist shop Haughton & Sons show that opium, olive oil and smelling salts were the main items on the Southend trainer's monthly shopping list during the early 1920s. Bills usually came to around £15 a month.

United players in training with Indian Clubs before the cup clash with Forest, in February 1926.

The next year they ironed out the inconsistency and finished 7th, Hick again a key factor with 26 goals although he then went on to pastures new at Bristol City. United had been on the upgrade since Birnie arrived, achieving a blend of youth and experience best described by skipper Bert Rosier as *'a very happy family'*. Rosier, unfortunately, must have had one of those family rows – he ended up on the transfer list and was replaced as skipper by Dick Donoven.

A 12th position the following year, aided by 34 League goals from the erratic and often unfairly criticised ex–Sheffield United centre forward Jim Shankly – the highest seasonal total ever, either before or since – confirmed Southend's stability. But thoughts of the second division only realistically entered everyone's minds when United took top position in the League for the first time ever at the beginning of the 1929/30 season. Donoven's team created a third division record by winning their first five games on the trot, and the run of success began to pay dividends. On 16 November 1929 enthusiastic fans, inspired by the last few years of relative League prosperity, started a go ahead, sometimes radical supporters club which proved to be one of United's greatest assets in years to come. The old supporters club had faded out of existence years ago, but hundreds now took up membership of the new outfit, swearing to abide by its motto *'To help and not to hinder'* – also the philosophy of the National Federation of Football Supporters Clubs, which was formed early in 1927.

The supporters club soon began chaperoning visiting teams from the railway station to the ground and before long was organising its own version of the blues on tour – chartering charabancs to nearby away matches and even boats for games across the Thames at Gillingham. When cash stricken Merthyr Town arrived in March 1930 not having had enough money even to eat on the long journey to the Kursaal, the supporters club took them to Garon's Restaurant at their own expense before ferrying them in taxis to the ground. There could have been an ulterior motive though – extra portions of suet pud may have played a part in United's 6–0 win, Shankly scoring five.

(1931/32 season) Southend fans at the station ready to travel to the match at Crystal Palace. The 2–3 reverse was the first of the season – on 21 November!

Although Southend didn't stay top for long, promotion hopes continued until the Easter of 1930, when one point from three holiday games finally put the lid on things.

The blues finished 10th in the end with Bob Jack, their first manager, tasting success at last with Plymouth as he steered them to the second division after a decade of near misses.

The next two seasons were the high point of the Birnie era; two of the best Southend have ever produced. The bad cup form of recent years was to continue, but in the League even though only one club went up from each of the two division threes, United came tantalisingly close to promotion, finishing 5th in 1930/1 and an even better 3rd in 1931/2.

It was a period which also saw Southend's only game at Wembley stadium, though in bizarre circumstances.

The blues trotted onto the hallowed turf in a 6 December 1930 League match after Clapton Orient's new Lea Bridge Road ground had been declared temporarily unfit by the Football League.

Wembley was just about the only place available at short notice to stage two of the east London club's games – the other against Brentford – while pitch improvements were made. Mickey Jones thus became the only player ever to score a goal for Southend at Wembley, but United lost 3–1 in a game watched by what appeared to be only a handful of people. The crowd of around 2,500 was completely lost in the Empire Stadium, but it was an experience none of the side were ever likely to forget. On occasions during those successful two years United were undone by trying to play too much football, but such was their reputation that in April 1931 they were honoured by an invitation from the top Dutch side Ajax to play a friendly in Rotterdam.

They justified the fixture by beating what amounted to a Dutch B side 3–1.

Owen Williams, a former English international outside left signed from Middlesbrough in August 1930, should in theory have played an important part in that good spell but his 350 first class appearances had already begun to take their toll and an injury early on kept him out for long periods. Instead one of the keys to those good years was the healthy competition between the two centre forwards Fred Baron and Jim Shankly, neither of whom quite managed to assert himself over the other for a regular place, though Shankly usually had the edge when not injured.

Goalkeeper Billy Moore, who was honoured with an April 1931 benefit game at the Kursaal against Everton which United lost 6–2 in front of 8,164, was another key. Moore, Michey Jones, and Freddie Barnett were ever present during 1930/31, the latter two completing their 100th consecutive appearance as the team's right wing pair in November 1931. Barnett came from Spurs at the beginning of 1929/30 and Jones, full of tricks, from Everton at the same time.

Ironically gates for this rosy period were well below what had gone before – the depression had begun to hit hard, 1930/1 was a terrible winter for most spectators to endure without cover at the Kursaal, and home consistency always seemed to desert just as there was a big crowd in.

Supporters club membership had risen to 1,000, and in the summer of 1931, helping not hindering, it handed over £250 as the first of many valuable donations to the club.

At home maximum gates of 9 or 10,000 may not have been overly impressive but stories of Southend's stylish football went before them, and they were attracting huge crowds for away games when they sped off at the beginning of the 1931/2 season.

Still top after nine games (dropping a rare point to Thames, the new east London club which had stepped into Merthyr Town's division three south place) United drew a record crowd of 18,000 to Clapton Orient in October 1931. The following week their visit to Craven Cottage smashed Fulham's record by attracting an estimated 28,700, and at the end of November they finally lost their unbeaten run in virtually the last kick of the game in a 3–2 defeat to Crystal Palace at Selhurst Park in front of another contemporary record – 31,000.

In all Southend took a remarkable 24 points away from home that season, accredited by many to their lucky change strip of black and white stripes. But that Palace defeat triggered a mystifying deterioration which lost them the lead just before Christmas.

Then followed a disastrous set of results which was not stemmed until February. By that time United had dropped to 8th place, but began to pick up where they had left off before their aberration. Even so, the bad patch had been so debilitating that 24 points from the last possible 28 – including a 1–0 home win over Brentford in front of a new League record crowd of 17,025 – were still not enough to make up the difference. They went 14 matches without defeat to the end of the season and had been 15 games unbeaten at the beginning, but it was the in–between that had been their undoing.

Without the sag, promotion would have been a formality, everyone in the town knew it. As it was they had to be content with third place just four points behind the champions Fulham.

With Thames effectively bankrupt after only two years in the League, United became the first ever club to play their replacements, Aldershot, in division three south, winning 2–1 away from home in the opening game of the 1932/3 campaign.

> A reserves game at home to QPR in September 1932 drew a crowd of 6,138. Southend won 6–3.

But the winning streak which had begun the previous season couldn't go on for ever, and in September 1932 their 1–0 defeat at home to QPR became United's first loss since 13 February earlier the same year.

The League losing habit returned, but in the cup that year Southend beat Exeter, Scarborough, and Watford to reach the fourth round, setting themselves up with a repeat of the 1926 cup encounter with Derby, now a first division outfit with five internationals. It was a gallant fight at the Kursaal (attendance: 15,188), a 3–2 defeat after being 3–0 down which inspired them to better things in the League, where they'd reached 7th place in March 1933.

A final 13th position was down to inconsistency and, after the Shankly era, some weak finishing. Players were coming and going, and by now Ted Birnie was getting old enough to start thinking about retirement. Troubled by failing health, he would probably have gone early on during the 1933/34 season if a terrible start hadn't left United bottom of the table by December.

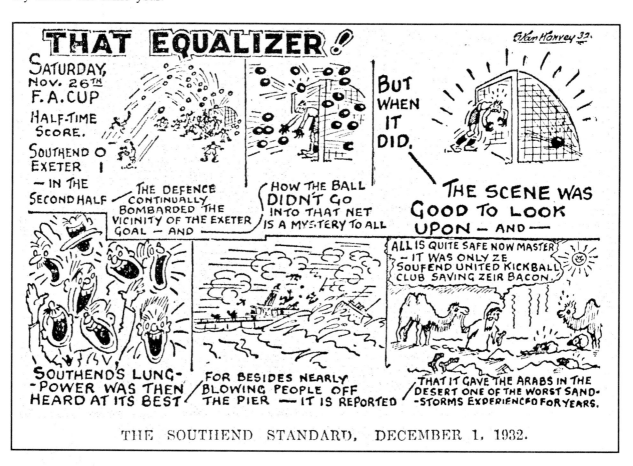

THE SOUTHEND STANDARD, DECEMBER 1, 1932.

Instead he decided to see the club clear of the re-election zone, which he managed by March, then handed in his resignation the following month.

Air travel was first used in soccer in September 1932, when Bristol Rovers arranged to fly one of their players, Vivian Gibbons, from Romford to Bristol so he could play in a midweek game against Southend.

Birnie's departure was one of several momentous upheavals in the period from March to August 1934. Shortly before his departure six of United's eight directors had resigned en masse, apparently over worries about whether money they'd loaned the club was safe, although everyone involved kept tight-lipped. Among those who left was the Kursaal managing director and one time club chairman David de Forest Morehouse, who died later that year aged 51; in his place came Captain Tom McEwan, secretary of the Greycing greyhound racing club based at an impressive new dog track at Southend Stadium in Grainger Road.

It wasn't long before most fans added two and two together and gossip about a move to the stadium began to spread. Sure enough, with Southend finishing a safe 16th as the 1933/4 season petered out, a seven year lease was signed with its owners in May.

A few days later, on 9 May 1934, the new directors found their new manager – David Jack, 35 year old son of the club's first boss Bob Jack. He was a tremendous capture, lured from the grasp of other clubs by a substantial offer and his local connections. He went to Hamlet Court Road School in Westcliff while his father was United manager, then began a magnificent playing career which took him to the very top. At Bolton he'd won two cup medals, playing in the famous white horse Wembley final, then at Arsenal under the great Herbert Chapman he'd captained England. Though still a player at Arsenal when he was approached for the Southend job, he brought a wealth of experience to United.

Making use of money handed over by the supporters club, Jack began some vigorous activity in the transfer market, building a much changed 24 player squad to serve the new management at a new ground. As seed was sewn in the centre of the dog track at Southend Stadium, the club unveiled its own flag, royal blue with the words *Southend Utd FC* across it in white letters, to be flown at the first match. Arrangements were made for bands to appear before games and a club signature tune called *'Play up the blues'* was composed for playing when the team ran out.

The townsfolk were buzzing with the possibilities, basking in the national attention Jack's arrival had given the side, buying season tickets like there was no tomorrow, and looking forward to second division football before too long.

Jack, of course, was more circumspect, and he was right to be. What had started as a season of great expectations soon became a flop of the highest magnitude; his debut outing as manager bringing Southend the ignominy of re-election for the second time. The boom interest of the summer had translated into good crowds (8,000 turned up for an early season reserves game at home to Spurs), and the season's average of 6,750 was better than many of the teams in the top half of the third division south. But for the loyal fans there was only one real highlight during that 1934/35 season – a huge 10–1 victory over non-League Golders Green in the first round of the FA Cup, which remains a record for the club, though it has been equalled since (see games to remember).

United eventually got to the third round, where they were knocked out 4–0 by Sheffield United at home in front of 13,712 during a 'pitiful' exhibition which typified much of the season's play. Between 5 May 1934 and 2 February 1935 they failed to keep a clean sheet for 26 consecutive games.

1934 – The playing staff during David Jack's first year at Southend. and.... a last look at the Kursaal ground.

End of an era: groundsman Bill Fitch locks the Kursaal gates for the last time, May 1934.

The move to the stadium – which with its dog track round the pitch lacked the atmosphere of the Kursaal – undoubtedly had a detrimental effect, and football is littered with teams who went through barren periods after making changes to their home surroundings.

But on the field under skipper Billy Carr, the team did not gel. United finished 21st out of 22 and were bottom or near the bottom for virtually the whole season. Jack's honeymoon period, if indeed he even had one, was short–lived in the extreme – there were even unfounded rumours that he would be leaving at the end of his first season. With only Bath City and Folkestone challenging Southend for their place in the League, re–election was never really in doubt, but it was a trauma the club could have done without. It was a costly year too – £2,460 on transfers and £2,700 to set up the stadium had contributed to a loss of just under £5,000.

Jack nevertheless continued his transfer dealing the next season, expanding the squad to 28 and capturing 31 year old Jimmy Nelson, a Scots international with two cup winners medals, from Newcastle United. Nelson became captain during 1935/6, guiding them to a marginally more respectable 18th position on the back of a strong defence held together by new Irish born keeper George Mackenzie, who replaced long serving Billy Moore.

Mackenzie, along with centre half Charles Turner, who'd come from Leeds, went on to win international honours with Eire while at Southend, but the biggest game for either of them came for the blues in the third round of the cup against second division championship challengers Spurs in January 1936.

More than 8,000 Southend fans in a White Hart Lane crowd of 48,839 saw what was one of United's best ever cup performances – an incredible 4–4 draw which earned them a home replay (see games to remember). They lost the return 2–1, in front of a new crowd record – 23,634 – at a stadium bursting its seams with more than 2,000 locked out. And this on a Wednesday afternoon.

March 1936 also saw Southend's first game under floodlights, an invitation match against a Dutch International XI played under the beams of fifty 1,000 watt electric lamps at the new Haarlem stadium in the Netherlands. The continental game didn't agree with United, though they stuck to their close passing style; five of the team had played abroad before, but under the bright lights and with a bewildering continental white ball rather than the British brown pudding they succumbed 4–0.

In what was otherwise a dull season for United, some of the more exciting moments were provided by farcical goings on at the FA. Upset by the sudden emergence of football pools, which appeared to be making money out of soccer without putting anything back, the old men of the FA sprang into action during February 1936. They decided to scrap the season's fixture list so that pools companies wouldn't know what games were going to take place on the coming Saturday. Unfortunately that meant the clubs didn't know either, and Southend were just as much in the dark as everyone else. In the first week after the FA's ruling United didn't officially find out they were playing Aldershot until the Saturday morning of the game, though they were supposed to be told in a cloak and dagger operation on the day before the match. Common sense eventually prevailed a couple of weeks later when the FA, tail between its legs, agreed to revert to the old fixture list and negotiate with the pools companies.

By now war clouds were gathering; Hitler had an iron grip on the German plain and a planned United tour to Germany in May was scrapped as the European mainland became an unpredictable place. Back home things began to look a bit better for Southend, who under the captaincy of Charles Turner during the 1936/7 campaign produced a spectacular 9–2 win over Newport, their record League victory, then moved into sixth, a position they kept close to all season. In April 1937, as British fascist Oswald Mosley visited Southend and former United manager Ned Liddell took Luton up to the second division as champions, United moved into their final resting place of 10th position.

Though groundsman Bill Fitch had tried his best to produce a decent playing surface at the stadium the directors experimented that close season with 23 sheep who were signed on amateur forms to graze the turf during the summer. The players, six of them also amateurs, concentrated on keeping up their training schedule; long runs along the seafront in the morning followed by ball practice in the afternoons, plus a few games of cricket against local sides at the weekend.

Harry Lane and Billy Dickinson had scored 16 League goals each in the 1936/7 season, which had seen the first experimental televised coverage of the national game, but manager Jack was still tempted to have a nibble at the great Dixie Dean when he became available on the transfer list. In playing terms the club had considerable assets – the whole United team was valued at £15,000 – and close links with up and coming Chelmsford City were beginning to bring forth some good players through an informal nursery system. But United still hadn't the attraction to draw really big time players, even on their way to retirement, and Dixie went to Notts County instead.

Secretary Manager:
DAVID B. N. JACK

Telephones { PRIVATE Leigh 76157
CLUB Marine 6463

Southend United Football Club, Ltd.

Members:—The Football League (Division III.) Essex County Football Association.
Football Association Cup Competition   London Combination

Telegrams:
JACK, STADIUM,
SOUTHEND-ON-SEA.

Registered Offices and Ground:
SOUTHEND STADIUM,
GRAINGER ROAD,
SOUTHEND-ON-SEA.

28th June 1937.

Gunner A.E.Hankey,
10th Field Brigade R.A.,
D E E P C U T, Hants.

Dear Albert,

Just a few lines to let you know that the Football Association have warned me as to my future reading of the rule concerning Service footballers. Naturally I am pleased to have got off so lightly.

Kindest regards,

Yours sincerely,

David B. N. Jack.

Letter from David Jack
to new keeper Ted Hankey.

In any case Bolan got off to a good scoring start in 37/38 and Southend again spent most of their time in the top half without seriously threatening promotion. In November Southenders crowded on to the head of the pier to see a demonstration of 'television', but mass production of sets had not yet begun to threaten attendances at games, and on Boxing Day 1937 a 2–1 home win against QPR drew a new record League gate of 17,000 – more than double the average.

In the cup they beat the famous but now declining Corinthians side whose right half, Caldwell, actually played in glasses, then defeated another of the famous amateur outfits, Walthamstow Avenue, before going out in a replay to 2nd division Barnsley in the third round. At last United seemed to be settling in at the stadium, improving their home record despite a long injury list, but the fans were not impressed when three of the blues' best players, Charles Turner (now captain of Eire), inside forward Harry Lane and left back Jack Everest, were transferred to West Ham, Plymouth, and Barnsley respectively for a combined £3,500.

Like previous managers, Jack was finding his team building efforts hampered by financial expediency, and when during a home game versus Crystal Palace in March 1938 there were no ball boys on one side of the ground sarcastic rumours began to circulate that they'd been transferred as well. 1938 also saw what would have been the first game against soon-to-be deadly rivals Colchester United, but the match had to be cancelled after Colchester officials forgot the date and failed to make the necessary arrangements at their end.

United finished 12th at the end of the 1937/8 season, a feat they repeated the following year with much the same squad. Five years at the stadium under Jack had produced little for the team, supporters had become jaded, and a borough now 150,000 strong was producing crowds of just 5–6,000. Among the fans was celebrity supporter Larry Gains, the popular black Canadian boxer who was commonwealth heavyweight champion from 1931 until 1934 and had settled in Southend to become a season ticket holder. His fame and Jack's name lent a certain sparkle to Southend during that time, but they were not particularly inspiring times for the club. The area needed a tonic, but it never came; instead life in Southend soon came to revolve around a series of air raid practices, listening to the wireless for news of Hitler's latest atrocities, and coming to terms with the idea of call-up.

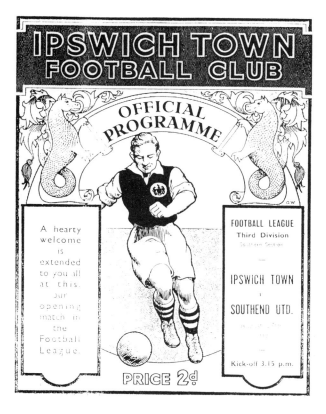

The 38/9 season began hopefully enough, United becoming the first ever team to play League Football against Ipswich, who'd replaced Gillingham when their re-election bid failed. They lost 4-2 away from home but were not defeated at the stadium until Swindon beat them 3-2 well into October 1938.

Preparations for war had begun to overshadow the 38/9 season by then; before a home game against Walsall in the same month teams and officials stood to attention in the centre of the field as the national anthem was played in *'a soccer tribute to peace'*. Later still in that same month French cup holders Olympic Marseilles, who were soon destined to fall under control of

Vichy France, visited the stadium for what was to be the last of United's growing list of international friendlies – at least until the war began.

Marseilles' goalkeeper Jaguare Vasconcellos, who had 13 Brazilian caps to his name, raised eyebrows during an exciting 2-2 draw by continually tapping his goal kicks just outside the penalty area to a defender, who then returned the ball so he could punt it upfield – a new innovation in England at the time.

The good FA Cup showing of late continued right up to the war, United beating Chesterfield 4-3 after extra time in a fiercely contested replay to set up a trip to Ewood Park against second division leaders Blackburn Rovers, where they lost 4-2. The Football League intervened after the Chesterfield game, fining three United players Bolan, Bell, and Smirk £3 each for bringing the game into disrepute.

But by now the threat of conscription was beginning to hang over most of the team. A planned continental tour was called off as Hitler went into Czechoslovakia and the nation began to prepare for the worst. The Football League tried to keep some semblance of normality going during the summer, issuing the fixtures as usual, deciding that players should at last begin wearing numbers on their backs, and allowing referees to wear black silk shirts rather than their customary blazers (a development first started in Essex).

But, anxious to avoid the kind of criticism which hit football in the opening months of the first world war, the FA acted quickly when war was declared on 3 September 1939. Southend had only managed to play three of their scheduled games before they heard the King make his radio announcement of hostilities while the players were having their customary Sunday morning drink and chat at the stadium. Within a week all football, except in the armed forces, was suspended. The United record for that truncated division three south campaign read: won 1, drawn 1, lost 1. Abandoned until further notice.

****

CHAPTER 3
WAR GAMES

As war broke out many of Southend's players began to move back to their original home areas to prepare for the call up, and others – like Len Bolan, who went to work at a munitions factory and Frank Walton, who moved to the car plant in Dagenham, took up war work.

But it didn't take long for the ban on soccer to be lifted; United were already playing a friendly against Norwich in front of 2,500 gas mask clutching fans at the stadium during the third week of September 1939. The next week they were playing Fulham.

The Home Office, soon aware that a phoney war was in the offing, and mindful of the morale boosting effects of the game, quickly gave the go ahead for the FA to launch a new war system based on regional leagues designed to keep travelling down to a minimum. At the beginning of October 1939 Southend had been allocated a place in what was known as South section 'A', joining Arsenal, Charlton, Millwall, Spurs, West Ham, Clapton Orient, Crystal Palace, Norwich and Watford.

There were restrictions on the size of crowds during wartime, but in any case the excitement of playing League football against the likes of Arsenal and Spurs wasn't quite what it might have been under normal circumstances.

Most of the teams had been decimated by the call up (Arsenal were eventually left with only two of their 42 professionals) and the majority of those who would normally have come to watch were in the forces too. The opening home game against Spurs, which Southend lost 2–1, attracted just 4,105 – and attendances got progressively worse as the weeks wore on.

The whole set up was scrappy in the extreme. Players in the forces were often refused leave to play weekend games, and promising new Southend keeper Ted Hankey, who sneaked away from the Royal Artillery to play under an assumed name for the reserves against Reading, lost his sergeant's stripes when his regimental sergeant major discovered the deception.

Teams were so short of players they were usually forced to use guests or inferior local amateurs to make up the numbers, and the standard of football began to show in some eccentric scorelines. United lost 8–1 against Charlton at the Valley in October 1939 in front of only 1,000, then beat Clapton Orient 7–0 at home a couple of weeks later before just 912.

Often out of their depth against the bigger teams and with money problems because of the poor crowds, United finished bottom of South 'A' with only four wins when their 18 match programme was completed in January 1940. David Jack started an appeal for £1,000 to keep the club afloat and supporters responded with £500, a marvellous effort considering the privations of war. The money allowed the club to take part in a revised set up which began in February 1940.

This time playing in South section 'D' with Watford, Crystal Palace, Clapton Orient, Aldershot, Norwich, Bournemouth, QPR, Brighton, and Reading they also had to fit in the hastily arranged war cup. This was played over two legs without non–League sides, but it created more interest than the new League set up.

In the second round of the war cup, which United reached after beating Watford 6–2, they drew a Nottingham Forest team which could only manage to field four of its own players in the first leg. Forest called on Aston Villa, Stoke and Bristol City to fill the gaps, but still managed to knock Southend out by winning 4–1. Jack was by now having serious problems putting out a side himself, even though lesser known players from Arsenal, Grimsby, Brentford, West Ham, and Spurs had all turned out in Southend colours.

Things gradually got more and more bizarre. The stadium grass grew long because it wasn't being cut regularly, games were becoming virtually meaningless, and almost all Southend's remaining players were working for the police war reserve, which often meant being on air raid duty at Shoebury Garrison the night before a game.

Southend entertained French side Stade Engheim-Ermont Club Athletique in a February 1938 joint benefit match for Billy Moore, Dicky Donoven, Jack Morfitt and Joe Wilson. But the longest name of any team to have played Southend is Utrechtse Sportvereniging Elinkwijk, a Dutch side who played the blues in a September 1965 friendly.

Wartime programme: note the air raid warning.

There were some understandably lethargic performances, yet the new South 'D' League ran well into the summer of 1940 despite the lack of interest, and teams were playing each other with monotonous regularity.

United's final South 'D' game against Watford, a 2–2 home draw in June which helped them finish fourth from nine, was their 7th encounter with the club since the beginning of the war league system. Familiarity was breeding contempt.

Southend itself began to feel the strains of war earlier than most in 1940. The town's strategic position at the head of the Thames, which German planes would follow on bombing raids into London, made it an important Luftwaffe target even during the 'phoney war'. With a convoy of warships almost permanently moored off the pier the town was declared a restricted zone, children were evacuated, and more than 700 high explosive bombs were dropped on the town during the war. It took its toll on the nerves too: George Winkfield, a Southend United director and motor engineer by trade committed suicide by carbon monoxide poisoning in his garage during May 1940. His business had suffered considerably during the war.

By August 1940 the government had decided soccer at the stadium was far too risky under the circumstances, and in any case the army needed the ground's facilities for training officers. United, now in some disarray but still keen to continue in the makeshift war competitions, had approached West Ham about ground sharing, with no luck. By the end of the month they'd instead fixed up a deal with Southern League Chelmsford City, who offered their New Writtle Street ground for hire.

Chelmsford had turned professional in the season before the war and despite being an unofficial nursery team for United were in better shape than Southend at that point. Relations between the two clubs had been close in recent years, so when David Jack was called up to work for Barclays Bank in the city, Chelmsford's manager Harry Warren began to look after United, filling any gaps with his own city players.

There were plenty of gaps too. Blues' first game at New Writtle Street was a practice match on 24 August, but army commitments meant only four United players could make it, so most of the ballast came from the Chelmsford squad. Fairly soon United teams turning out in League games were 60 per cent Chelmsford and 40 per cent Southend; later still virtually the whole team were Chelmsford players.

The new 1940/1 league, the third version to be tried since the war began, this time involved all the clubs in the south, but was based around a core of pre-arranged matches, with remaining fixtures left for clubs to fix up themselves. As this meant some teams would play more games than others, league positions were decided on goal average.

United, already wondering whether the whole idea was wise – and struggling for revenue because of pitiful crowds – kept going despite the early retirement of some bigger clubs like Aston Villa, Derby, and Sunderland. But the start to their new campaign could hardly have been worse. They lost the first game of the 1940/1 'season' 7–1 at home to an Arsenal side fielding the Compton brothers Denis and Leslie, Eddie Hapgood, and the great Cliff Bastin. Leslie Compton scored five.

As if that wasn't bad enough for the all important goal average, Southend then lost 7–0 to much the same team in the return game, played at White Hart Lane because Highbury had been bombed out of action. Further horrendous defeats at West Ham (11–0) and Norwich (8–4) – where United played with only eight men for half an hour because Sam Bell, Frank Walton, and Charlie Fuller arrived late after a car smash – began to emphasise just how ragged the Southend team had become. A scheduled match against Portsmouth was cancelled in September 1940 because United had problems raising 11 men, yet even when they did get something resembling a side together air raids would often scupper their chances.

Sirens continually interfered with a match at Clapton Orient in September 1940, forcing the players to go off after eight minutes. After a 75 minute wait they came back on the field to play, and attempted to finish the game by playing 40 minutes each way. But a quarter of an hour before the final whistle the planes came over again and the game had to be abandoned.

Other matches were similarly affected, and farce became commonplace. In a December 1940 game versus Spurs, Tottenham's guest right winger Tom Paton arrived ready for the kick off at Southend Stadium only to discover United had moved 20 miles away to Chelmsford; and in a game later during the year Harold Rickett, Southend's principal war keeper, walked off the field and refused to come back after ructions over an offside decision in a 7–0 defeat against Crystal Palace. Even a late league rally, which included good wins against Spurs (3–2), West Ham (3–1), and bottom placed Clapton Orient (9–3) failed to prevent Southend finishing 31st out of the 34 clubs competing in the south section, their average of 0.633 comparing with the 1.954 of champs Crystal Palace. The blues had managed to play 29 games, won 12, drawn 4, and lost 13, conceding 101 goals and scoring 64.

When the league had finished United fell out with the London clubs, who decided they no longer wanted the expense of travelling to some of the outlying teams like Southend, Southampton, Luton and Norwich. The league expelled the dissenting London clubs but with the system in chaos and the draw of the London clubs now gone, United needed a good run in the war cup to bring in some cash. They beat Millwall over two legs but were unlucky to draw in-form West Ham, the war cup holders, in the 2nd round.

The two legs attracted a total 9,000, a good tally for the war, but they were knocked out 4–2 on aggregate. At that point, and with Chelmsford owed rent money for the use of their ground, the Southend directors decided to call it a day. Their generous Chelmsford hosts, however, said they could wait for the money, and United struggled on for a while longer. An Easter crowd of 2,500 saw United win 3–1 against a Portsmouth side carrying seven of the team which had won the FA Cup in 1939 – perhaps their best wartime performance – but with travel from Southend virtually out of the question for the ordinary fan such feats were virtually irrelevant. Supporters could only read short reports in the local paper; reports which got shorter and shorter to save pulp.

In October 1941, with the current crop of meaningless games over and the authorities busy devising an even more labyrinthine league scheme, United wisely decided to call it a day.

They owed a sizeable £310 in rent to Chelmsford, they were travelling long distances to home and away matches despite the wartime conditions, and they were getting very little money through the turnstiles. Matches were being played away from United's home town, the team was fielding players whose army life now came before football, sometimes turning out sides with only one recognised United player – and losing most of their games into the bargain.

In their first war season United had used 45 different players, in the second another 26 new faces, making a squad of 71 with very little continuity. Only Stan Bell played with any regularity, by far the top scorer with 29 league and cup goals from 58 appearances over the two seasons. During that time 31 players filled-in for just one game and Southend used 34 guests.

While most other football clubs carried on, United became one of the 21 league outfits who went into hiding during 1942. The stadium echoed only to the sound of men doing army training, though later in the year the army did sanction its use for a rugby match, a one mile race, and a charity soccer game between the Royal Artillery and Southend Police (4–0). The following year they fitted in a boxing tournament, a softball game in aid of Merchant Navy Week, and an Army v Navy game graced by the great Arsenal & Scotland player Alex James (5–2), who was stationed at nearby Shoebury Garrison.

In the meantime, Southend United didn't stir at all until October 1944 when the prospects of an allied victory tempted the team to apply to play in the southern cup. The footballing authorities saw only a dormant club without players or a ground, so the application was unsuccessful. But talk of resuming the Football League began in earnest the following month, and as David Jack had drifted up north after his Barclays stint to become manager at Middlesbrough, United appointed Harry Warren as their new boss to represent them in early meetings of the two division three sections.

Unlike the 1914–18 conflict, there were merci-fully no war deaths at the club this time, but getting things going wasn't easy, and Warren spent most of his time trying to re-sign old players returning from all corners of the world. With peace near in May 1945 hopes were high that the stadium would soon be de-requisi-tioned by the government, and United directors filled in forms to enter the FA Cup. Rehabili-tation was on the way.

United's post war chairman Nevill Newitt was awarded the George medal during the second world war for his work with the bomb disposal section of the Royal Engineers.

Charity
Football Match
ORGANISED BY THE
Southend-on-Sea Constabulary
Recreation Club

ESSEX COMBINED SERVICES XI.
VERSUS
SOUTHEND COMBINED SERVICES XI.
AT SOUTHEND STADIUM
On Wednesday, 26th April, 1944
Kick Off 6.30 p.m.

PROGRAMME 2d.

PROCEEDS IN AID OF ESSEX COUNTY F.A.
PRISONERS OF WAR & REPATRIATED PRISONERS FUND

Football at last returns to Southend –
but it wasn't the blues.

CHAPTER 4
STARTING OVER

The players (Left to Right): Hankey, Harris, Sibley, Jones, Lane, Sheard, Hamilton, Smirk, Thompson, Jackson, Bell, Warren, Robinson and Bennett - report back to Grainger Road.

Preparations for peacetime weren't confined to the playing front. United now had money problems as their legacy of the war. Plans were hampered by the government's refusal to release the stadium as early as the club had hoped, but by July 1945 United had been accepted into the FA Cup and returfing had begun on their now bedraggled ground. The first post war game for United was a 2–1 defeat against QPR in the third division south (northern section), which pitched Southend into battle with ten other clubs north of the Thames – Port Vale, QPR, Watford, Notts County, Northampton, Ipswich, Walsall, Clapton Orient and Mansfield. Post war rules allowed each club a maximum of six guest players from other teams to make up the numbers.

With just 11 clubs in the division the 20 match programme was finished by the new year of

1946, United managing only 10th place with five wins. In the FA Cup, played for the first and only time on a two leg basis, United went out to Watford 4–1 on aggregate in the first round, but from a playing and financial point of view the northern section campaign was reasonably satisfactory considering all the obstacles United had to overcome. Club officials would often walk round the ground before a game with a board asking if anyone in the crowd had brought their boots and could play for the reserves. Troops had not yet returned in great numbers, but if they went to games in uniform they were charged the child rate of 9d admission, and on Christmas Day a win against Ipswich attracted a crowd of 9,000.

The balance sheet for the five years up to May 1945 had been less satisfying. The club had run up almost £2,000 in debts during the war, bringing its overall deficit to £7,657. Some of the directors who'd been against United continuing at Chelmsford claimed the chickens were now coming home to roost.

Once the third division south (northern section) had run its course, United took part in a third division south league cup competition designed to keep clubs occupied to the end of Spring 1946.

Like most of the competitions at the time it was a complex, rather strange affair, actually played on a league basis despite its cup status, with the top pair from each of two groups playing in the semi-finals. Long winded though it was it gave Southend the chance to build something of a team, with Leigh-on-Sea born former Southend schoolboy Cyril Thompson, who only turned professional at 27, making wonderful progress alongside centre forward Frank Dudley and speedy winger Alf Smirk. At one stage United had an excellent chance of making it to the semi-finals; in the end, they finished fourth in their group of 11 teams, losing only four of their 16 games.

Southend's squad still depended much on the whims of the armed forces, whose demands held sway over player availability. Big hearted centre half Bob Jackson – with Smirk and Thompson one of three ex-prisoners of war in the United squad – showed no ill effects of his stay courtesy of the nazis – and became the mainstay of a shifting team which used no fewer than 54 different players during 1945/6. Twenty of those were guests, most notably Stan Montgomery on loan from Hull City, and inside forward Ken Bennett from Spurs, but line ups were still necessarily makeshift, the demands on players significant and unpredictable. In April 1946 Alf Smirk played in the Army area final at Colchester in the afternoon then was rushed by car to Southend for an evening top-of-the-table clash for United against QPR.

Nonetheless United's first season after closing for the greater part of the war was far more satisfactory than most had expected. Support was showing first signs of the incredible post war boom and profits for 1945/6 reached £1,755. Familiar League and cup conditions

would return for the 1946/7 season, and United looked forward to normality.

In all, 24 players were offered terms for the first proper post war season, 12 full time, 12 part time, with some of the pre war men still in the services down to play either when they were demobbed or on leave. United were determined to run within their means so a small playing staff supervised by new trainer Wilf Copping, ex-Leeds, Arsenal and England international, kept expenses in check. The supporters club was back on its feet, ready to hand over cash. Former long serving coach Bill Cartwright joined the ground staff.

Post war wages were hardly attractive, even though agitation by the players union had managed to raise the maximum to £10 a week, and many opted to take 'proper' jobs which offered more security. But United had an additional problem – Southend's housing crisis. Manager Harry Warren travelled extensively trying to sign new staff, but had great difficulties finding homes – or even rented rooms – to offer players and their families.

Southend had for years been growing quicker than the housing market could accommodate, and landlord exploitation was commonplace. The club had half a dozen houses dotted around the neighbourhood, providing them as part of a signing-on deal in the hope that a player free from accommodation worries would be able to give his best. Even so, some of the more senior players were forced to take younger ones 'in digs'. Ted Hankey and his wife looked after Cyril Grant, Bobby Brown and Tommy Edwards for some time; it was a problem which was to dog the town and its football team for years to come.

The first game back in the third division south after the war could hardly have been more encouraging – a 3-1 home win over Walsall in front of 11,000. And the good news continued. Now playing meaningful soccer, free from the pressures of war, many of the opening games produced open exciting football, and Southend's team spirit was sky high. Cyril Thompson banged in three hat tricks before Christmas, Ken Bennett and Ted Hankey were often outstanding, and by November 1946, after a 5–1 away win at Norwich (attendance: 20,000) the blues were lying fourth. Special buses began running to games from Leigh, Shoebury, Rochford and Great Wakering. In the cup a 6–1 first round away win against what must have been United's most bizarre ever cup opponents – Brush Sports FC of the Notts & Derby League – was followed by a spectacular 9–2 victory in awful conditions against amateur cup holders Barnet. That set up a third round tie at Goodison Park against Everton, who had England keeper Ted Sagar and Scotland centre forward Jock Dodds in their team.

In those days a colour clash meant both teams had to change strip. United managed to loan Aston Villa's famous claret and blue kit, and Everton played in black and white stripes ('*white for surrender, black for mourning*' said Warren provocatively). Villa's cup achievements didn't rub off on the blues, but a 4–2 defeat in front of 50,124 was a good enough performance and after the game the club was inundated with transfer enquiries for several players. Even approaches from Hibernian, reputed to be the richest UK club at the time, were firmly rebuffed by Warren, who told all and sundry that Southend were buyers not sellers. True to his word, he signed centre forward Thomas Whalley from Arsenal before the season was out.

Though a bad spell towards the end of 1946/7 robbed United of a promotion place, they finished a successful eighth and for one of the few times in their history without a financial deficit of any kind. This without some of the players they were to rely on during the next few years, notably hard man Frank Sheard, who was still on Salisbury Plain, and Jack French (nephew of the pre war Jack French) who played most of his games for the army.

Hopes for the following season, then, were perhaps as high as they'd ever been; the side

was extremely fit, and there was quiet confidence all round. But they finished one place lower by the end of 1947/8, with a poor goal average and an uninspiring season behind them. Warren was favouring robust, high ball football at the time and the team, though a reasonable all round outfit, became workmanlike rather than skilful.

Southend's Grant challenges the Aldershot defenders in the 1947/48 home League match.

A wintry home match against Norwich City in March 1947.

Bournemouth lodged an official complaint in 1947 after the referee played only 85 minutes in a Christmas game against Southend at Dean Court. No action was taken.

In September 1947 Southend announced 'with regret' that cups and saucers used for refreshments at half time would be subject to a deposit of 6d 'owing to the great difficulty in getting replacements of crockery'.

Harold Shepherdson, No 2 to England manager Alf Ramsay, spent half a season as a player at Southend during 1948. He was signed from Middlesbrough, but picked up a serious injury soon afterwards and returned to Boro to begin his backroom career as their trainer.

Twenty members of the same Leigh-on-Sea family – 18 of them with the same name – each bought a season ticket for Southend's 1946/7 campaign – total cost £100.

Wilf Copping, who spent ten successful years as trainer at Southend after joining in 1946, died in July 1980 at Runwell Mental Hospital, aged 72. A much loved but rugged former coal miner from Yorkshire, he reputedly used meths as after shave, was capped 26 times for England, and played for Leeds and Arsenal between the wars.

SOUTHEND UNITED FOOTBALL CLUB LTD.

THE STADIUM,
GRAINGER ROAD,
SOUTHEND-ON-SEA
Phone 67819 & 67975 (private)

Player's Ticket

(Not Transferable)

11

Season 1948-49

Name ____________________

TRAINING RULES AND PLAYERS' INSTRUCTIONS

—o—

1.—All players must attend the ground at 10 a.m. daily (match days excepted), and shall be under the orders of the manager for the rest of the day.

2.—In case of illness or accident, players if unable to report at the ground must inform the manager as soon as possible. The Club's Hon. Medical Officer is Dr. A. G. Bewes, of 11, Wimbourne Road, Southend, and can be seen by appointment which must be made through the manager.

3.—Players must not invite friends into the grounds or dressing rooms at any time, nor must they invite friends into reserved compartments when travelling.

4.—Players will be provided with the necessary outfits, such outfits to be the property of the club.

5.—Gambling of any description is strictly prohibited.

6.—Smoking in the dressing rooms during training hours, or on any outward journey of an away match is strictly prohibited.

7.—All players must be on the ground 45 minutes before kick-off time for home matches, and at the station or place of leaving 15 minutes before the train or 'bus starts for away matches; when reserves are advised this also applies to them. Every player must inspect, and assure himself that he has his complete playing outfit before leaving the ground for away matches and be responsible for same on the journey.

8.—If players are injured whilst riding in or driving motor cars and as a consequence rendered unable to carry out their agreement it will be considered entirely their own responsibility.

9.—Players who wish to stay overnight or visit their homes during the season, must make their requests to the manager and must give him adequate time to make the necessary araangements.

10.—Any player absenting himself from training, or disregarding these instructions without leave from the manager, shall be held to have broken his agreement and be liable for suspension without pay, or be fined at the discretion of the directors.

11.—Any case of misconduct while on the field of play must be reported immediately after the match by the captain.

12.—Trainers must report to the manager all breaches of the above rules.

13.—Players must carry this card and produce it at the official entrance at all home matches. Players must under no circumstances allow it out of their possession, or allow any other person to use it.

14.—The foregoing Rules will be strictly adhered to, and players are requested to make themselves thoroughly conversant with same.

It is up to all the players of the Club to keep themselves as fit as possible, and to work harmoniously with one another. If any player has a complaint to make, do not breed discontent, but report same to the manager at once.

The Directors wish to point out the honourable position your club occupies in football, and to ask every player to assist them in uplifting the tone of professional football generally.

Everything possible will be done for your comfort and advancement, and you are asked to play the game in the true spirit.

Harry Warren.
Secretary Manager

Strict rules for the playing staff - 1948/49 season.

They certainly had no-one of the class of Notts County's Tommy Lawton, who played against United in the League twice that season, home and away. He scored both goals in a 2-1 win over Southend at Meadow Lane (attendance 35,000) but was fairly anonymous in the poor return match at the stadium.

Southend's Lawton of the late 40s and early 1950s turned out to be Irish International Jimmy McAlinden, signed from first division Stoke City for £6,500 by Warren early on during the following 48/49 season, just as Southend's steadiness was quickly turning into mediocrity. McAlinden proved to be arguably the greatest of all United players (see 'Players great and memorable') but for most of the 48/49 season the rest of the squad seemed to be on a different wavelength. The Irishman's vision caused a frisson of excitement at the stadium but too often those on the end of his perfect passes failed to do anything with them.

Poor form seemed to make no difference to the paying public, who packed the stadium almost to capacity against Millwall in September 1948 with an official gate of 20,000, and produced the most consistently high attendances in the club's history. Another 20,000 came in for a fogged off cup tie against Swansea, and even as Southend slipped to last-but-one in the League during March 1949 crowds rarely dipped below 10,000.

Attendances at away matches sometimes topped 30,000 and even reserves games packed them in – a combination game at Highbury against Arsenal drew a staggering 25,000. In November 1948, prompted by the growth of crowds, the stadium's general unpopularity with fans and the desire for a proper, non-rented club home, plans were unveiled for a return to Roots Hall – now a piece of wasteland – when the stadium lease expired in 1955.

A dog holds up the proceedings at Grainger Road.
Note the packed enclosure – for a reserve team match (versus Arsenal)

1949/50 team group with a difference, versus a local cricket team: (left to right) Copping, Gray, Warren (manager) Grant, Morris, Shead, Walton, Gawler, Pritchard, Jones, Hankey and (seated, centre) Nash.

Plotting the downfall of Leyton Orient in the FA Cup, 1949.
(Left to right): Wallbanks, McAlinden, French, Lindsay (back), Walton (back),
Wakefield, Sheard, Wilf Copping, Jones, Hankey and Clough.

The fans deserved better than the aimless stuff United were offering, but they did get some excitement towards the end of the season when their ever unpredictable side drew with League leaders Swansea at the beginning of April. Southend wrapped up the season with a 3–2 home victory over Notts County, their best performance of the whole campaign, to finish 5th from bottom.

From then on, despite the loss of Frank Dudley to Leeds for £10,000 (he'd scored 32 goals in his 88 Southend League appearances), and with the inspirational McAlinden at the helm as skipper, Southend began to get their act together. The new decade ushered in four of the club's best ever years.

The best of those four, in 1949/50, matched the third place secured in the 'if only' season of 1931/2, but this time in much steadier fashion. After six opening games Southend went to the top of the third south for the first time since that 1931 season, and were there or thereabouts for most of the campaign. In November 1949, they drew 2–2 with Swindon at the County Ground after an incredible six goals were disallowed, but they were at least consistent. The contrast between home and away form was startling; the first stadium defeat didn't come until February 1950 against newly relegated Nottingham Forest and the first away victory, against Millwall, had to wait until March. After the turn of the year the blues had drifted to 9th, but by April were second and had an outside chance of displacing Notts County at the top for the third south's only promotion place.

With four games left and needing a win against Northampton to keep their hopes up, they lost 2–1, then froze again in a 2–2 draw against Leyton Orient when a win on the last day would have given them the runners up spot and £220 in prize money. Instead, goal average got the blues a third place bonus of £165. Once again there was agonising about points dropped here and there, bits of bad luck and poor sequences, but few complained about a team which had equalled the club's best position.

A happy group of players – Wallbanks, Hankey, French, Davies and Wakefield –

Whatever the lost opportunities in the League, there were no grumbles about bad luck in the FA Cup, where United were beaten fair and square 4–0 in the third round that year away to Stanley Matthews's Blackpool. Southend's first and last encounter with the 'wizard of dribble' – and his team mate Stan Mortenson – quickly turned into a one sided contest. Poor Frank Walton, given the unenviable task of marking Matthews, gave away a penalty in the process, but it was an extra special game for United's keeper Ted Hankey, who went to Wellington Street school with Matthews in Hanley and used to knock him up on the way to Saturday morning schoolboy matches before the war. Matthews had by now become such an idol at Blackpool that his decision to take the club's tangerine colours for his racing silks was celebrated before the Southend game by a donkey parading around the ground in the club strip.

The unusual route from dressing rooms to pitch at Grainger Road,
where a plank was placed over the dog track.

The victory was never in doubt as far as Matthews' fans were concerned. A week before the game a lorry from a firm in Blackpool pulled into Southend gas works laden with materials for the stores, but when it was unloaded the workers also found three coffins warning Southend's travelling supporters of their team's fate in the cup. Inscriptions on the coffins said: *'Was it worth the bus and train fares? Southend United fell in the presence of duty. Send flowers and good wishes'.*

Chances of going one better in the League the next season were scuppered in the close season when McAlinden was suspended until 1 October 1950 after the FA found him guilty of receiving an illegal £750 payment as an inducement to join Portsmouth just after the war. Although the incident had only just surfaced, and had nothing to do with Southend, it was the blues who suffered (see bad times).

Architect Nevill Newitt, who resigned after 17 years as chairman later that season over arguments about the prospective move to Roots Hall, called McAlinden's suspension *'a staggering blow'.*

But the rest of the team – now boosted by the return of Joe Sibley from Newcastle United after three years away – rallied round.

McAlinden couldn't come straight back in October because he had flu, but he returned as skipper for the club's first ever League game against new third division south members Colchester United in October 1950. The Essex derby brought 21,000 to the stadium, and Southend won that first encounter 4–2 after young Reg Davies put them ahead after just 1½ minutes. The return match at Layer Road in March 1951 was equally satisfactory, a 3–1 win in front of 12,360.

Players in training at Grainger Road.

Later that month McAlinden also skippered the blues in another confrontation with their new rivals – a four a side sports quiz against Colchester United on Radio Luxembourg.

The Colchester result, plus an astonishing 8–2 home thrashing of Swindon after United found themselves losing 2–0 after 14 minutes, put Southend up to 5th and in contention. But Nottingham Forest, playing their only two seasons in the lower reaches, had been running away with the third division south that year and even though they met Southend on wonderful form at the stadium in April, losing 3–2, no-one could catch them.

United's scoring had been particularly pleasing in 1950/1; they finished with 64 goals at home, the highest total of home goals by any side in all divisions that season, and 92 in total – United's best ever. Sharing the League tally were Leslie Stubbs (19), the ever popular Albert Wakefield (15), Cyril Grant (12), Reg Davies (12) and Tommy Tippett (12), who moved to Bournemouth at the end of the season.

They took 7th place and finished the season off in some style by romping home 6–1 in a friendly against Racing Club from Belgium, a team boasting five internationals.

Much the same squad finished the following 1951/2 campaign in a fairly creditable ninth position, but created a bigger stir by making the last sixteen of the cup for the first time in their history. United reached the 5th round on the gallop, despatching Bournemouth 6–1, third division north Oldham 5–0, 2nd division Southampton 3–0, and previous round giantkillers Bristol Rovers 2–1 with a Jack French goal nine minutes from time. French's exploits helped him towards an England B trial at Highbury later on; Les Stubbs was also picked, but neither went on to full honours.

The reward was a home tie against second division Sheffield United on 23 February 1952, a 2–1 defeat in front of 21,887 for which the club raised the standard admission prices to 2s 6d. A seat in the west stand went up from 4s 6d to a very stiff 10s.

Typical scenes from the early 1950's
(Top): Players about to set off in the team coach for an away match.
(Bottom): The condition of the Grainger Road pitch often left a lot to be desired

(Above) Players on the boat to Germany during a 1952 tour.
(Below) Anderson scores from the spot on the tour

At the end of the season, players were given the news that the land needed to reconstruct Roots Hall had finally been bought for £11,000 from Southend Corporation. The money had been raised by the 6,000 members of the supporters club who'd set up a special Roots Hall trust fund – and now had their own supporters club band, the only one of its type in the country. Not long afterwards Reg Davies, now at Newcastle, activated a clause in his transfer deal by winning his first international cap, for Wales v Scotland. That brought Southend an extra £2,000 and Jack French's departure to Nottingham Forest further swelled the coffers. United were going to need all the money they could get for the Roots Hall move plus their yearly wage bill of £21,000, and with crowds consistently around the 8–12,000 mark they were in a healthy financial position compared to the troubled days before the war.

The fans, however, were none too pleased about the one sided transfer market activity, and in November 1952, when Great Wakering born Les Stubbs went to Chelsea for £10,000 they made their feelings known. A week later there were loud cries of 'I told you so' as United lost 3–1 to southern league minnows Bath City in the first round of the cup. It was the first time since gaining League status that Southend had been knocked out by a non–League side and the board moved quickly to announce it would not be selling any more players.

Nevertheless Major Alfred Hay, who'd taken over as chairman when Nevill Newitt resigned two years earlier, made things worse for himself when he tried to justify the Les Stubbs deal. He told the fans the transfer of their favourite had been *a wonderful piece of business for a one footed player'*, and within a matter of days he'd decided to make way for councillor Bert Smith, who linked his name firmly with the quest to move back to Roots Hall.

Other off field matters were to dominate the 1952/3 season too: in February 1953 floods devastated much of low lying south east Essex,

killing more than 100 people and doing particular damage to Canvey Island. Joe O'Neil, a young Aberdeen player on loan to Southend while on national service at Shoebury, had to pull out of the game against Bournemouth because the army needed him to fill sandbags after the flooding. United made plans to stage a game in aid of the flood relief fund.

Eighth place that year to add to 3rd, 7th, and 9th in the previous three left the club with a good sniff of division two and some creditable recent performances to look back on, but there'd been such a haemorrhaging of players that Harry Warren faced having to find ten signings to make up squad numbers for the next campaign. During the supporters club AGM a group of women members put down a motion that the manager should sign more handsome players to attract better female support, but good looks were the least of Warren's worries. He signed England amateur international Douglas Young during the summer but finding replacements for the likes of Stubbs, Davies and French – handsome or otherwise – wasn't going to be easy.

Predictably, Warren struggled – and so did the side, which spent most of the season in the nether regions of the table, even bottom at one stage. A final 16th place was no surprise to the fans, but the manager did make one excellent buy during the 1953/4 season, even if it was too late to halt the decline. In February 1954 he signed Roy Hollis, formerly of Spurs and Norwich, a lanky centre forward who was fast, direct, and had a goal scorer's instinct – even if he did miss as many as he put away. Bainbridge top scored that season with 12 but Hollis managed ten in just 13 games.

There were few bright moments for the supporters, save perhaps for the game against Brighton at the Goldstone ground, when United took the field in new away colours of red and green quarters. Eire surprised everyone in 1954 by picking goalkeeper Tommy Scannell to play against Luxembourg, even though he was playing in Southend's reserves, but the closest anyone else got to international football was a

Wembley team trip to see Hungary dish out their 6–3 footballing lesson to England. Southend were not good learners; they lost their next game 2–1 at home to Crystal Palace.

Crowds, in line with the post austerity middle 50s decline, shifted down to an average of 7,300, and the holes in the squad were widened at the end of 1953/4 when McAlinden, now in the twilight of his career, played his last game. After five years at Southend he decided to take up the player managership of Glenavon in his native Northern Ireland. Harry Warren led a spontaneous tribute of three cheers on the pitch after his swansong – a 4–1 home victory over QPR.

McAlinden's worthy inside right successor was stocky 29 year old Kevin Baron, 'the mighty atom' signed from Liverpool and one of six Scots in the squad for the following 1954/5 season. Essex cricketer Gordon Barker signed as a first team amateur, becoming the most successful of a trio of Essex players to turn out for the club. Trevor Bailey and Doug Insole, who between them played 70 test matches for England, had both helped the reserves after the war, though they made their footballing names with Walthamstow Avenue and Corinthian Casuals respectively.

Summer training began quietly while the town talked incessantly about two new phenomena – 'teddy boys' running rampage around the seafront, and the infamous, all pervading 'smell', now attracting the attention of government ministers and set to dog the Southend area for years to come, though it was eventually tracked down to oil refineries along the Thames estuary.

The team also caught the national limelight, going down 3–1 in a blaze of 3rd round cup glory in a return to first division Everton. The crowd of 53,043 was the largest ever to watch Southend but their previous 2nd round 3–2 win away against Bradford City on a gluey pitch was a more spectacular game – reckoned by those who saw it to have been one of the toughest, hardest matches in the club's history.

League–wise there were signs that the new side was beginning to gel in 1954/5, and a surge towards the end of the campaign put United into a final 10th place. The full 13 seasons at the stadium since 1934 had been steady but generally unfulfilling, yielding an average 11th spot in the third south table and a best position of third.

Players night 1950's style – a sing song around the piano.

They were marginally better times than at the Kursaal, where Southend averaged 13th place, also with a best of third. But everyone connected with the club hoped a new era could now be ushered in as the move to Roots Hall became reality. The last League game at the Grainger Road stadium was a 3–2 win against Brentford, tinged with sadness at leaving but shot through with anticipation as Southend prepared to begin a new season with their own ground and a push for the second division.

CHAPTER 5
A NEW HOME

A rare cup win, back in 1950 – The Essex Professional Cup – in the Upton Park dressing room after beating West Ham: (left to right) Clough, Wallbanks, Wakefield, Nash, Lindsay, Davies (front centre), Sheard (behind), Walton (with cup), Jones, Stubbs, French, Bert Smith and Harry Warren.

As the squad were beating Sliema Wanderers during a summer tour to Malta (although they also lost to Italian first division outfit Catania), last minute preparations at Roots Hall were being made. The entire cost of the project had been raised by the supporters club, which with the ground staff of no more than half a dozen had shaped a ground out of nothing – with a pitch now more than 30ft below the original Roots Hall level thanks to excavation of sand on the site since 1915.

The new ground had been two years in the making, and when work on constructing the west stand finished in 1955, it was finally in a fit state for play. The excitement of returning to the club's spiritual home – and one which the club finally owned – gripped nearly everyone in the town. For the first game at the new Roots Hall on 20 August 1955, gates opened just after midday for a 3.15pm kick off. Despite the rival attractions of carnival day, 17,700 came to see a fine 3–1 victory over Norwich on a gorgeous sunny afternoon.

Making his debut in that historic match was Sammy McCrory, a cool experienced inside forward who later went on to win his one and only Irish international cap with Southend. Joe Sibley, who'd made 200 appearances for the club since returning from Newcastle United, was on the team sheet but in the end not re-engaged for the club, and Warren had brought in a new trainer, Wilf Dixon from Aldershot.

Programme covers during the 1955/6 season proudly sported an aerial view of the 35,000 capacity ground, and the team took an immediate liking to their new, homely surroundings. In second position after 15 games, they played good football right through, despite a number of injuries, and although they were never really in with a shout for promotion, finished fourth as champions Orient romped into division two. Terrace supporters were more than happy to pay their 2s entrance fee to stand close to the pitch and relish an atmosphere far superior to the sometimes desolate stadium. The average attendance jumped to 11,379. Within five months a home fourth round cup tie against first division Manchester City had created a club and ground record of 29,500 with receipts of £5,572 (see games to remember). The match belonged to German keeper Bert Trautmann, who played the game of his life. A series of breathtaking saves drove the Southend crowd to distraction and kept City in the cup with a 1-0 win. *'We licked ten men but we couldn't beat the 11th'* said Kevin Baron afterwards. Manchester City went on to win the cup.

Though Roots Hall had no floodlights as yet, United played their first League game under lights at Coventry, a dull 0-0 rearranged match on a Monday night, 19 March 1956. The week before, McCrory had recorded another milestone by scoring a goal against Crystal Palace after ten seconds – almost certainly the fastest goal in the club's history. Jimmy Lawlor won himself a more dubious honour when he knocked out one armed referee Alf Bond with a fierce shot in the home game that season against Southampton.

The Coventry game had more significance than anyone realised, though, because it had given Harry Warren a chance to speak to the Highfield Road directors. In June, after 16 years of service with Southend, he announced he was going to become the Coventry manager. His new job made him the third south's most highly

paid manager and left a gaping hole at Roots Hall. Warren had always been larger than life, a huge bear of a man who had steered the club through its most successful period on limited resources.

Never again would the club see such an era of managerial stability, but his successor – Welshman Eddie Perry – was determined not to live in his shadow. Unlike Warren, who'd never been a top player, Perry came to United having won many of the game's honours with Fulham. He'd become assistant manager at Craven Cottage when he hung up his boots, and gained a reputation for spotting young talent. This was his first full managerial job and, lack of finances notwithstanding, he hoped to strengthen the club with judicious signings. Perry had an inauspicious start nonetheless, waiting ten games for a victory to come in the middle of September 1956, by which time his side had slumped to the bottom of the table. With the country going through its own crisis – in the Suez – he introduced a rather over elaborate passing style which sometimes confused his own players more than the opposition. It paid off handsomely in the cup, however, when after wins at Colchester United (4-1) and at Southern League Hereford (3-2), Southend drew second division Liverpool at home, continuing their fine cup record at home by winning 2-1. The directors made themselves popular for once by resisting the temptation to raise prices as they'd done against Manchester City – and were rewarded with an 18,253 crowd (see games to remember).

Better was to come, at least in attendance terms, when United drew another home tie against the previous year's beaten cup finalists Birmingham City. Kevin Baron, out for 11 months with a broken leg, failed to make the team despite scoring in his comeback the week before at Exeter. Instead acting skipper Jim Duthie – another Scot – led the team out in front of 28,964 fans. Birmingham, with England players Gilbert Merrick, Jeff Hall and Gordon Astall spoilt the party by meting out a 6-1 thrashing.

Things got better in the League after that, with Hollis (18 League goals) and McCrory (15) inspiring a great end of season rally and an eventual 7th position. Solid full back Sandy Anderson, already a veteran campaigner with a benefit game behind him though only 26, was the year's most improved player, eventually going on to the club record for League appearances – 452.

By now exotic summer tours were becoming par for the course, so once the 1956/7 season was over United set off for Austria and Czechoslovakia. Director Nelson Mitchell gave his Czech hosts an exhibition of 'rock n roll dancing' to break the ice, but the players were shocked by conditions behind the newly drawn iron curtain – so shocked perhaps that they didn't manage a win during the whole six match tour, though a 2–1 defeat against the Austrian B side in Vienna was no disgrace.

The tour also gave new centre forward 'Lou' Costello (real name Mortimer) a chance because Hollis had to stay back with business commitments. But there was a tragic note – new chairman Arthur Bewes had to return home when he became ill in Czechoslovakia and died a few weeks later, after only three months in office.

Eddie Perry's new team, now sporting Canadian right winger Errol Crossan, could count on good backing from the terraces. Petrol rationing during the Suez crisis had dropped average gates down to 9,565, but the following season they went back up to 11,000 and supporters club membership reached an all time high – a phenomenal 22,000. On the pitch, with new skipper McCrory (33 cup and League goals), Baron (5) and Hollis (21) there was much promise, but in 1957/8 the team again delivered solid League respectability rather than glory – another 7th place despite the club's equal highest points total to date (53).

Southend were one of only six clubs to have been ever present in the third division south, becoming a founder member in 1920 and staying there until its demise in 1958.

There was more excitement than mere statistics convey, though, because this was the last season of the old divisions south and north. The bottom 12 of the third south would – along with the bottom 12 of the third north – make up the fourth division next year. And Southend made sure they wouldn't drop with a 3–2 away win over Plymouth in April 1958. In the cup they drew Liverpool in the third round for the second season running, drawing 1–1 at Anfield in front of 43,454, and losing the replay at home 2–3 (16,655).

This was the year of the Munich air crash, when United players and fans stood in silence before the home game against Newport and the gulf between those first division teams playing in Europe and third division outfits like Southend seemed to have become even wider. United could content themselves with becoming founder members of the new third division, but Europe–wise had to make do with an off–season continental foray to the Netherlands and Austria, winning 2–1 against Sparta Rotterdam, playing seven games overall and losing just one – against Austria B.

It was unglamourous respectability next season too. A few new fashionable quiffs lent a touch of excitement to the team photo but it was 8th place by the finish of 1958/9. There was at least a consolatory feeling that United were now one step up from the League's fourth division basement, and there were new northern games to play in that first third division season. Gordon Banks became one of the greatest players to appear at a Southend ground when he turned out for Chesterfield in his side's 5–2 victory at Roots Hall, but there was the down side too, like losing 3–0 to Accrington Stanley and – horror of horrors – succumbing 1–0 away to Southern League Yeovil in the cup. This was also the first season that Southend hadn't played on Christmas Day, but more monumental than any changes in the League structure for the fans was a predictably unpopular switch in club colours for the following 1959/60 season, when United turned out in all white. Only one brave director voted against the change but on the terraces, where 'come on you blues' became redundant, there was a landslide against.

The directors argued that blue created too many colour clashes because it was used by more clubs than any other, and in any case the all white strip would be more striking under the club's new floodlights, which were switched on with minimal ceremony for a Monday evening League game against Mansfield on 7 September 1959. The game was watched by 11,416 novelty seekers, who continued to favour Monday night floodlit games above others but were more impressed by the lights than the strip, despite concessions to the past by way of blue neck ribbing and a blue stripe down the side of the shorts.

Full back Arthur Williamson made a record 219 consecutive league appearances for Southend between 14 January 1956 and 14 September 1960.

Another novelty that season was the sight of 16 year old local boy Bobby Kellard, the youngest player then to have played for United, trotting out on the left wing for his baptism at Valley Parade in a 3–1 defeat against Bradford City.

Three weeks later Kellard was selected to play for the England Youth XI, and he quickly established himself in the first team, making 19 more appearances that season even though he was too young to sign professional forms.

Despite local talent like Kellard and hours on the road looking for players, Perry had failed by the dawn of 1960 to build a squad capable of mounting a serious challenge for the second division. Criticism mounted as he spent more time away scouting, and after 3½ years at the helm he departed in February 1960, the shortest reigning manager since Tom Mather back in the early 1920s.

Former chairman Alf Hay, whose son–in–law Trevor Bailey had just joined the board, took over as acting manager in Perry's absence, steering the club through to the end of the 1959/60 season. He made himself unpopular by deciding to dispense with Sam McCrory at the end of the campaign but otherwise fared reasonably well, securing 12th place in the final table.

Unfortunately team spirit had been lacking, so former England international winger Frank

Broome was appointed manager in May 1960 to try to put things right.

Broome's stint lasted just six months as United's new white strip, modified for 1960/1 with blue shorts, began to look like something of a jinx. United were knocked out by Rochdale in the second round of the League Cup, were dumped from the FA Cup by Gillingham, and by November were lying below halfway. Broome went in the second week of the following month, with the club announcing it was £25,766 in the red – and things looking bleaker than they'd done for a long while.

The dismissal of Broome made little difference to the team's playing fortunes. Another former England international, Ted Fenton, was brought in as manager in March 1961 by Hay, who'd again acted as caretaker during the interim and was now entering his second spell as chairman following the resignation on health grounds of Bert Smith. But Fenton couldn't stop the rot and with one match remaining United needed a point at Grimsby to make themselves sure of staying in division three. They lost 1–0, but stayed up by the skin of their teeth in 20th position because Notts County beat Tranmere.

Top scorers that season were Peter Corthine and Jim Fryatt with only 16 goals each from 41 and 31 games respectively, so it was no surprise when Fenton released ten of his 25 professionals in the close season. Other desperate measures were needed – the directors decided *'after much discussion'* to revert back to the old blue shirts with white shorts, though this time with thin white stripes running through the shirts. Ground admission was now three shillings.

By November 1961 fans were so disappointed by the United drift they surged round the main entrance after a 3–1 home defeat against Northampton, calling on the directors to *'buy or resign'*. Chairman Hay claimed the protest had been organised by *'beatnik types – yobbos – call them what you will'*. But the fans, beatniks and all, were clearly upset.

A boycott began to take effect as only 4,754 turned up for the next home outing against Halifax – the smallest crowd at Roots Hall since it had opened – and a frustrated Bobby Kellard asked for a transfer.

Relegation was never really on the cards but pools entrants now regarded Southend fixtures as bankers for a draw; 16th position only confirmed to the fans that United were going nowhere fast. Fenton pronounced the season one of *'satisfactory consolidation'* but then executed the biggest clearout in the club's history, releasing almost half the squad.

Skipper Tony Bentley and winger Derek Woodley try out one of the cars that Ford loaned the club for a month during the 1963/64 season: Corsairs, a Zodiac and a Cortina.

Fenton's night of the long knives justified itself during the 1962/3 season when United pulled up to a final 8th place after setting off with five straight victories. The manager was now running a much happier ship, able to keep spirits high despite the huge winter freeze up. Nationally it went down as the season with the most postponed fixtures; in Southend the sea and Roots Hall both froze.

Snow deprived United of any home game between Boxing Day 1962 and 9 March 1963, creating a sticky fixture backlog later in the season. Weary players finished May 1963 with a tour to Ireland, where another cancellation robbed football programme collectors of a novelty; a match magazine of Southend United v Southend United. The scheduled game against the blues' namesakes, a team from Waterford, was called off at short notice.

September 1963 saw two firsts – the debut of the international Lambretta rally on Southend seafront, and United's first belated appearance in the third round of the League Cup. They were ousted 3–0 by Swindon, then suffered further humiliation at the hands of Yeovil,

going down 1–0 again in the FA Cup at the Huish. Crowds for visits to the Southend Odeon by the Beatles and the Rolling Stones threatened to eclipse anything United could muster that year, especially as relegation to the fourth was looming. Trouble between mods and rockers became a seaside pre-occupation and nothing the blues could do offered much of a distraction. Only Harry Threadgold's successor as keeper, Peter Goy, offered any consistently notable performances, yet he was not retained in May after the club eventually posted 14th place.

Fenton's reign was proving uninspiring. *'Ponderous, pathetic Southend'* was the verdict of former player Alf Smirk, now soccer reporter on the Southend Standard. As the Southend electorate returned Paul Channon and Stephen McAdden in the October 1964 general election, United fans were asked to cast their votes on a matter of equal local importance: could the declining support be attracted back by a switch from Saturday to Friday evening fixtures?

Newspaper ballot on Friday night football.

Talk of a switch had been running round the town for some time; other clubs faced with a national attendance decline had been experimenting with the idea, and United attracted a reasonable gate of 7,865 the previous season when they played a Friday evening game to avoid a Saturday afternoon clash with the televised Grand National. The first Friday night game had actually been played in May 1953 to avoid a clash with the cup final.

Supporters of Friday matches pointed to the much better attendances for United's occasional Monday night floodlit games, some argued that more than 2,000 amateur Saturday footballers would be able to see the blues on Friday, and others claimed gates would rise without the rival attraction of simultaneous big club fixtures in nearby London.

In an admirable display of democracy the club decided to put the arguments to the fans. Voting forms were handed out at the home match against Bournemouth on 28 December 1964, and 3,000 of the 6,219 who turned up made their mark. With added ballot sheets sent in via a tear-out coupon in local newspapers, a clear majority showed in favour of Friday evenings. Terrace merchants voted 3–1 in favour, stand supporters were evenly divided. The matter was put in hand.

Fenton had more immediate ideas about drumming up support, issuing an appeal for old rattles to be sent to the club so they could be issued to the crowd before games. Luck wasn't always with him, though a chance to generate more interest when United's big game against promotion-chasing Mansfield was chosen for Match of the Day went begging. The programme was cancelled to accommodate the funeral of Winston Churchill.

In the end a consistent mid table showing and an eventual 12th position left no-one at the club any nearer a solution to the problem of waning local interest. United were now well over £50,000 in debt, and in May 1965 cost-cutting measures forced Fenton to ditch eight year server Lou Costello, now a full back, and chief goalscorer Mike Beesley, who'd been signed for £8,000 from West Ham three years earlier. The manager chopped the squad by seven in all, then paid Charlton a new club record of £10,000 for South African born Eddie Firmani, a cultured former star of Inter Milan. It was to be Fenton's last act in charge; when his contract came up that same month it was not renewed 'by mutual consent'.

The directors had obviously been doing some prior managerial scouting because within a week aggressive Hartlepool manager Alvan Williams had been confirmed as Southend's new man in charge. His departure from Hartlepool opened the way for Brian Clough, whose similarly forceful personality sent the club on to better things. Williams was a strong character and disciplinarian too, but unlike Clough was able to turn a blind eye to the new trend of men growing their hair longer. *'I will not keep anybody out of the side because of the style of their haircut'* he announced magnanimously on his first day in charge.

Williams's fierce new regime of training, under the slogan *'speed, speed, and more speed'* produced some promising showings in pre season friendlies, and the first Friday night game of the season threw up a 2–0 home win against Swansea in August.

60

A mid-1960's training session on the beach.

A new FA ruling allowed Bobby Gilfillan to become Southend's first ever substitute in the third game of the season, replacing Bobby King. Friday crowds were good; 15,197 saw an October game against Millwall, but the early season form didn't hold up for long. The fans were pleased to see their team back in blue shirts and white shorts, but with their centre half idol Peter Watson forced to retire through injury, the previous season's leading scorer Gilfillan transferred to fourth division Doncaster, and only Eddie Firmani showing any real form, wins were few and far between.

In November 1965 United went through *'90 minutes of shame and humiliation'* during their worst ever Football League defeat, 9–1 at Brighton. That and several other defeats prompted former blues defender Frank Walton, now in the insurance business, to make an unsuccessful £50,000 offer to take over the club. Southend were now £60,000 in debt and spending more than £48,000 a year on wages, but the sticking point was Walton's insistence that the whole board should resign if he took over. In January, United launched a public appeal for £25,000 and announced staff cuts.

Having fun: Southend fans at Rotherham station, en route to the January 1966 match at Millmoor.

Secretary Harry Leaper and assistant trainer Jack French were the first victims, but the appeal was scuppered by on–field catastrophes which sapped public goodwill. The ever–critical Alf Smirk, who reported on Southend's 5–0 defeat at Swansea later that month, never showed any mercy to his playing successors. He described Southend as *'the biggest heap of footballing rubbish ever to enter the principality'*. Heap of rubbish or not, United were certainly not playing to their potential. By the end of May 1966 they needed a miracle to save them from the big drop to the fourth. As it was, even divine intervention couldn't have saved them from poor defeats at Scunthorpe and Grimsby which put the seal on things. After 46 years of trying, they'd finally flown the third division nest – but not in the direction everybody had been hoping for. A final 21st place had landed them fourth division status.

The comeback of cult figure Rodney Marsh produced a crowd of 3,092 for a Roots Hall reserve game against QPR during the 1967/8 season. Marsh, who'd been injured for some time, scored the only goal in QPR's 1–0 victory, prompting a celebratory pitch invasion.

The town took relegation hard. One newspaper correspondent suggested the club should solve its cash problems by ploughing up Roots Hall and growing potatoes; others sent in columns of anguished letters. In the last, meaningless home game of the season even a 2–1 win against Reading was greeted with a mixture of jeers and ironic cheers from 3,600 fun seekers.

Manager Williams, thankful for the diversion of England's 1966 World Cup victory that summer, responded with a limited reshuffle of his 15 full time professionals. United established themselves early on in the 1966/7 season as front runners in their new division, and as so often happens, better fortunes in a lower division boosted attendances. Crowd trouble began to be a regular occurrence around the country, but gates were usually above 8,000 and more than 12,000 came to see an October game against Port Vale.

Sixteen year old Bob Haddrick became the youngest player ever to turn out for Southend that month, beating Bobby Kellard's previous record, but he appeared only once more. Sixties cup non–achievement continued with a vengeance as the team lost 1–0 to Watford in the fourth FA Cup tie to be held between the clubs in six years, but in the League hopes looked good for a swift return to the third.

It wasn't particularly attractive football, but for Williams the ends justified the means. On the other hand, he may have seen the writing on the wall, because in April 1967, with United in 5th place and the promotion race hotting up, Williams announced that he'd decided to take the manager's job at Wrexham. The board, now under the influence of vice chairman Bill Rubin, a Chalkwell mail order footwear tycoon and ally of Frank Walton, accepted his decision.

Trainer Ernie Shepherd, who played for Fulham, Hull, QPR, and West Bromwich Albion after the war, took over as caretaker for the last few games as Rubin's money began to filter into the club. The new combative vice chairman paid for Southend's first ever flight to an away game, a crucial end of campaign clash with fellow promotion contenders Southport, though he may have wished he'd never parted with the cash when they went down 1–0. A similar scoreline against Stockport, who became champions, consigned United to 6th place and a second season in the fourth division.

Boardroom and dressing room discontent had been an unhappy feature of the 1966/7 season, but there were hopes of happier times under Shepherd, who was appointed manager with Geoff Hudson as assistant in the close season. The first club share issue for 60 years raised him £30,000 to buy players, and to all round embarrassment 'Shep' introduced the squad to regular ballet dancing sessions under the watchful eye of well known choreographer Gerry Atkins. Some thought they could detect extra poise in United's play that 1967/8 season, and under skipper Andy Smillie they certainly turned in some sparkling early form.

They were sitting pretty with ten games to go – 2nd behind Luton, well ahead of their closest rivals and with a recent 7–0 win over Workington behind them. Livewire centre forward Billy Best made an immediate goalscoring impression when he signed for £4,000 from Northampton in March; promotion looked a formality. Yet when it really mattered a seven match run in April brought only two points, landing United in 6th place for the second year running. Rubin declared himself 'choked', but it took another three seasons – and a couple of managerial casualties – before Southend got as close again.

What fans had hoped would be a brief stay in the basement was turning out to be an uncomfortably extended sojourn. United followers were used to chasing the elusive prize of second division status, not struggling to regain their place in the third, but they bore it well. In relative terms crowds in the late 60s were – considering the other attractions now on offer and the fortune of their team – probably the best in the history of the club.

So good in fact that Friday night games, which since the ballot had been played up to November and after February, were now extended to cover the whole year. Admission was a minimum of five shillings.

In 1968/9, wearing yet another changed strip – dark blue shirts and white shorts akin to Scotland colours – Southend managed 7th. Scottish International keeper Lawrie Leslie, who signed on a free transfer from Millwall, felt at home at least; he'd played behind similar colours five times for his country. Another Scot, John Kurila, signed from Northampton – and 18 year old Ian 'Chico' Hamilton came from Chelsea for an undisclosed but near record fee. Irish international Sammy McMillan captained the team to some respectable League results, but the blues made national headlines with two huge FA Cup successes against Southern League opposition, a 9–0 first round home win against Kings Lynn followed with a record 10–1 home victory against Brentwood in front of 13,107 (see games to remember).

Goalkeeper Lawrie Leslie in action during the 1968/69 season.

It was the best cup run for some time, brought to an end by Mansfield in the fourth round, and despite missing promotion United became the only League side to score more than 100 goals during the season.

The new strip was brought to a premature end in April 1969 when the Football League decided dark blue shirts clashed with the referees' tops. The club decided to borrow five different strips for the last five games of the season, then to ask the fans which they thought they should wear for 1969/70. There were plenty of voters – the season's 10,381 average was the fourth division's best, and higher than all but five of the clubs in the third. All five strips had blue as their main colour – but West Bromwich Albion's blue and white stripes with white shorts won the day.

The team were suffering from fatigue almost as soon as the 1969/70 had begun, battling for 330 minutes in the League Cup against Brentford before eventually winning through 3-2 in extra time of a second replay played on neutral territory at the Den. As usual the League Cup adventure was short lived, although this time they did manage to exit in the third round to Bradford City. Much more worrying was League form, which started badly and continued in the same vein, hampered slightly by a League decision to restrict the number of Friday games United could play.

By October 1969 the directors had seen fit to make Ernie Shepherd general manager with Geoff Hudson in charge of the team. Hudson's first move was to ban his players from the new Shrimpers Club, a successful set-up built at the back of the ground which was partly responsible for reducing the club's debt to £38,000 the previous year. Hudson gave no reasons for the ban, and though the players went to the press to complain, it stood. Skinheads now ruled on most terraces, and police paraded dogs at home games, but United fans won national approval for their behaviour. Only 2,887 of them saw the November game against Aldershot in snowy conditions – a new lowest ever gate at Roots Hall.

Injuries hit badly, and later in December, United postponed two games because their entire squad had flu. Hudson, only three months in the job, got the sack three weeks later as Southend reached 5th from bottom. Shepherd briefly resumed control for five weeks until Arthur Rowley, known throughout the country as the highest goalscorer of all time, was brought in to fill the gap. Rowley's instructions were to stop United's slide into the re-election zone, a feat he managed with minimum difficulty even though 17th place at the season's end was United's worst ever League position to date.

Given the board's increasing fickleness, Rowley did well to survive the 1970/1 season, when he took the team to an even lower 18th position. His side now played in all-blue with white socks after fans had written in saying they didn't like the blue and white stripes after all – and the League did an about face too, deciding to allow Southend to play freely on Friday nights again.

Not that either decisions made any difference to life on the pitch. Rowley's squad, by now sporting long hair and sideburns almost to a man, went through a hectic close season programme of friendlies, losing 1-0 at home to Italian League high fliers Fiorentina (8,769), beating Ghanaian side Accra Hearts of Oak 5-1 (3,193) and playing Clyde (4-2), St Mirren (1-0), and Dundee (0-5) in a Scottish tour. But when fourth division reality intruded, the familiar barren form of recent years continued.

One of the few bright spots of 70/71 was inflicting the first ever League home defeat on Cambridge United, who'd been elected to the fourth that season. But there were also smiles in the FA Cup, when new boy Bill Garner, signed from Bedford at the beginning of the season, hit a hat trick to help his team to a 7-0 first round defeat of Southern League Weymouth. For the third round – with the prize of a fourth round tie against Spurs beckoning – 16,668 flocked to Roots Hall, but United lost 3-0 to Carlisle.

Not long afterwards Terry Johnson, a new signing from Newcastle, promised better things by scoring in his debut against York. United, however, were in the nether regions of the fourth throughout the whole season; not

terrible, but frustratingly inconsistent. As Rowley and his players flew off for a ground–breaking post season tour across the iron curtain in the Soviet Union they knew they had plenty of work to do when they came back.

Southend in the Soviet Union:
Match programme Russian style
and.....
Pitch inspection
under the watchful eye of Lenin.

CHAPTER 6
THE YO-YO YEARS

Here we go: Arthur Rowley and team celebrate promotion
in April 1972.

With hindsight, season 1971/2 was the first year of what turned out to be two subsequent decades of to-ing and fro-ing between the fourth and the third division. These yo-yo years, broken only by United's promotion to the second division 20 years later, were certainly frustrating for the fans – and compared to the years of steady non-achievement in the third division not nearly so consistent. But they were far more exciting.

The sixth attempt to get out of the fourth division was successful. Apart from a nervous start, United spent most of 71/72 near the top, a happier team than for many years, given to having a laugh and bonded together by their Soviet tour, which was the first made by a British team for many years.

A first round FA Cup home win against Aston Villa, who were spending some time in the third division, brought record £5,500 receipts, 16,929 fans and a 1–0 victory squandered in the next round by losing to Ted MacDougall's Bournemouth. But attendances were soaring again as Southend bid for the title. A 2–1 Christmas win against Lincoln was watched by 15,434, the best Roots Hall League gate for years, but it was topped at Easter when 400 more saw the same scoreline against Doncaster, then the following month when 17,059 watched what they hoped would be the promotion clincher against Cambridge United. Southend lost that game 2–1 after keeper Derek Bellotti broke his collarbone and Peter Taylor, United's shortest player, replaced him between the sticks.

But they secured a third division place with their next game – a 1–1 draw at Scunthorpe. The key to promotion was Southend's refusal to admit defeat. Under skipper Joe Jacques they showed fine steam spirit and plenty of determination, exemplified by their back four and the hard work of front men Bill Garner and Gary Moore. Garner, who hit 26 goals, was the subject of an £80,000 offer from West Brom manager Don Howe, but the money was turned down.

Amid unprecedented scenes after the final game of the season versus Gillingham, thousands of the 15,854 fans crowded round the main stand to acknowledge their team's achievement. This was Southend's first promotion in any league since elevation to the first division of the Southern League in 1912/13. The players and the fans were ready to make the most of it.

Southend stalwart Tony Bentley, who'd once played 135 consecutive League games between 1964 and 1967, certainly shared in the euphoria when his benefit game against Stoke City a few days later attracted an impressive 11,500 fans to Roots Hall.

Promotion was good from the financial side too; gate receipts almost doubled to £80,395 for home games. Exhausted by their efforts, the players set off for a celebratory club holiday in Spain with wives and families in tow. Rowley stayed at home – he had some players to scout for.

In fact, except for the £15,000 capture of 21 year old Alan Moody from Middlesbrough, Rowley made few significant signings during the 1972/3 season. On the other hand he lost Bill Garner, his most valuable asset, to Chelsea. Garner made the right impression during a second round League Cup clash with Chelsea at the beginning of the 1972/3 season, a 1–0 defeat against a side boasting Harris, McCreadie, Hollins, Osgood, Houseman and future Southend manager Dave Webb. That game proved a financial jamboree for the club, with £10,000 takings from a 24,160 Roots Hall crowd; the deal which took Garner to Chelsea brought in £100,000. In the third division new local Rochford talent Peter 'Spud' Taylor found his way regularly into the first team, and United notched up their 1,000th home League game – against Bristol Rovers.

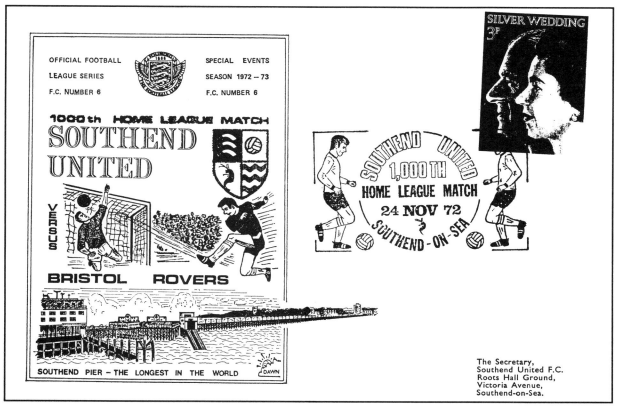

But on the whole, 14th place that season marked a return to steady third division mediocrity. The first away win didn't come until February 1973, six months into the campaign, when Gary Moore – a player often dogged by booing and jeering from the crowd – scored in a 1–0 defeat of Oldham. Apart from that, three of the more memorable games were friendlies – a 1–1 home draw against Zenith Leningrad, an 8–2 victory over Guernsey on the island's cycling ground, and a 3–0 home win against Dutch side Volendaam.

Peter Taylor's talents meant he didn't stay long at Roots Hall. Two months into the following 1973/4 season he was snapped up by Malcolm Allison, manager of second division Crystal Palace for £120,000, in real terms probably the biggest fee Southend have ever received for a player, though the figure was later exceeded.

It was money United couldn't refuse; for Palace money well spent. Taylor was not yet a class player, but Allison bought him hoping he would improve in a higher standard of soccer. That summer he and Bill Garner were picked as part of a massive 84 man squad brought together by England manager Don Revie for training in Manchester. Taylor eventually went on to win four caps for England.

Rowley immediately used the Taylor money to splash out £15,000 on Willie Coulson from Newcastle United, £7,000 on Stuart Brace from Grimsby and £12,000 on keeper Malcolm Webster from Fulham. Money from transfer deals was all the more important now because the once great supporters club was on its last legs, mainly due to a decision by Bill Rubin when he became chairman in 1969 to allow United to take over most of its more profitable activities. By December 1973 supporters club contributions had slumped to £2,000.

Things were tight nationally as well; the power crisis under prime minister Edward Heath had even been restricting United's electricity guzzling floodlit Friday night games, and on 24 February 1974 Southend consequently played their first ever League game on a Sunday

against Wrexham, drawing 10,054, the biggest crowd of the season thus far. When the floodlight ban was finally lifted on 20 March, United hadn't played under lights at home since 22 October 1973. National crisis or not, their mediocre form was unaffected, and they finished 12th at the end of the season.

Bill Rubin was still trying to cope with bubbling unrest in his boardroom when he warned fans they might see the erection of fences for the first time if trouble on the terraces didn't subside, but that didn't stop fighting in the north bank when 7,003 turned up for a post season testimonial game for groundsman Sid Broomfield against Chelsea.

There was valuable fresh blood in the shape of three new 19 year olds for 1974/5, Rochford born Tony Hadley, Alan Little from Aston Villa, and Ron Pountney from non-league Bilston. But middling form turned into much less than that after Christmas – and the third division was so close that season that in February 1975 talk of promotion hopes quickly turned into anxiety about relegation. A 1–0 end of season home win over Bury put paid to the worries, though only a freak set of results would have seen Southend go down. Highlight of the campaign had been a 2–2 home draw against Stan Bowles, Phil Parkes, and Gerry Francis of first division QPR in the third round of the Cup (attendance 18,100) before going out 2–0 in the replay. But all and sundry were exasperated by the post Garner/Best goal famine which was to continue into the next, far more frustrating season.

Long running talks had begun in April 1975 to lure Tottenham player Mike England to the club either as assistant manager or player/manager, but they eventually came to nothing when he opted for Cardiff City and Jackie Burkett, former West Ham full back who won an FA Cup winners medal with the Hammers in 1964, took over as United's trainer. Rowley, soldiering on in his quiet unassuming way, began to take the brunt of spectator criticism as his side sagged during 1975/6.

The season opened with a pitch invasion at Roots Hall as fans of newly relegated Sheffield Wednesday took exception to losing 2–1 in their first ever game in division three. Despite the big name opposition the crowd was only 6,775, the average dipped to 5,010, and in September a home game against Shrewsbury brought in just 2,992, at that time the second lowest United gate ever recorded. *'A big proportion of the United fans travel to Roots Hall from outside the borough'* explained the Southend Standard. *'A fan from Basildon for instance has to find a 61p train fare, 65p to get in the ground, another 10p for admission to the east stand and 5p for a programme that must be labelled among the worst in the Football League. With bus fares from Southend Central station and back again, a coffee, and perhaps a drink after the match, he has little change out of £2'.*

Coughing up such huge sums clearly wasn't the only factor, because United were also languishing at the bottom. *'I am sick'* declared Arthur Rowley after defeat at Brighton – and he wasn't the only one. In the FA Cup United were putting together one of their best ever runs, beating Swansea, Dover, Brighton and Cardiff to earn a fifth round dream tie at the Baseball Ground against Dave Mackay's Derby County (see games to remember). But in the League things were markedly different.

By March 1976 the fans were so disenchanted with the prospect of slipping down into the fourth again that they booed the Southend players even as they ran onto the field in a home match against Cardiff, then kept up the abuse throughout the game. East stand regulars threw cushions onto the pitch at the final whistle; those in other parts of the ground flung bricks and lumps of concrete.

Even so, a subsequent 2–2 draw with Wrexham did give United a last gasp chance of staying up – if they could win at Hillsborough. Their opponents, Sheffield Wednesday, also needed a win to avoid an unthinkable slide into the fourth and it was destined to be a blood curdling affair.

Southend gave their all, but in the end the nerves and the intimidating 25,802 crowd were too much to handle. The blues sealed their own fate by losing 2–1.

Vociferous support for a *'Rowley Out'* campaign towards the end of the season bore fruit when first the club sacked trainer Burkett then announced it was looking for a new manager. On the list of those linked with the job was the 32 year old boss of Lincoln City, a rising managerial star called Graham Taylor, former Fulham and England star Alan Mullery, and Dave Smith, recently sacked by Mansfield. During the second week of May 1976 Rowley was retained on a 'consultancy' basis after six years as manager, and Smith got the job.

Smith's extrovert qualities and enthusiasm for the game were in marked contrast to Rowley's quiet withdrawn approach. He quickly made himself popular with players and fans alike, but still the yo-yo bounced up and down. Within two seasons he had taken them back up to the third, but he also brought them back down again. He took over in the drought-hit summer of 1976, inheriting a squad whose reservoir of goals had also dried up. The defence, boosted by 18 year old schoolboy international Paul Clark, was sound enough, and during the 76/77 season conceded only 45 goals in 46 League games, a new club record.

But here, perhaps for the first time, was an era without a striker to catch the imagination. Croydon born 19 year old Paul Denny scored on his debut against Workington in September 1976, and centre forward Derrick Parker was brought in from Burnley to some effect, yet the season was characterised by low scoring draws – a record 19 of them in all. Selling Stuart Parker, the only consistent purveyor of goals over the past couple of years, helped matters none, though Smith did bring in some exciting chance creators like winger Colin Morris and midfielder Andy Polycarpou.

Tenth position in 1976/77 was purely down to lack of goalscoring, so when things began to gel a bit more up front the following 1977/8 season United shot to the top. Derrick Parker scored all four in an early 4–0 defeat of Torquay, League newcomers Wimbledon were dispatched 3–1 at Plough Lane, and fellow high fliers Watford (now under Graham Taylor) were beaten 1–0 at home in front of 10,990, the biggest League crowd for a long time.

Derby and Southend managed to find each other yet again in the FA Cup third round draw, the first division side (boasting Todd, Rioch, and Masson) coming out on top by the slimmest of margins, 3–2 at the Baseball Ground.

By April 1978, with much travelled Villa keeper John Burridge on loan, promotion in second place was virtually assured even though Watford had opened a commanding gap at the top. After the televised 1–1 Vicarage Road championship decider between Southend and Watford in front of 18,947, Graham Taylor's team paraded the trophy around the ground – and Dave Smith's eccentricities in the dug–out earned him a permanent slot on the Match of the Day's opening sequences.

Southend's own moment of glory came not long after as thousands swarmed on the Roots Hall pitch to celebrate a 3–1 victory over Rochdale which sealed second place. Once the joyful scenes had subsided backstage, Smith was discovered drying handfuls of soggy five pound notes on the radiator in his office. At the height of festivities he and assistant manager John Lattimer had been thrown fully clothed into the team bath.

There was plenty of room for self congratula-tion. Smith's boys had beaten their own previ-ous defensive heights by letting in only 39 goals from 46 League games and finished the season with ten away victories, beating the previous record of nine in the memorable 1931/2 season.

Amid all the joy there was one note of sadness though; 55 year old chairman Bill Rubin, who'd held his post for nine years, died of a stroke a few days after the last game of the season, only hours before he was due to take Smith for a celebratory dinner. His 40,000 club shares went to his two sons, and Frank Walton became the new chairman.

Smith took his players for a promotion wind–down in the seventies holiday mecca of Tenerife but the trip became more of a wind–up when it was partially marred by an all–in brawl during a 'friendly' against FC Cruse. Matters got out of hand when a Southend goal was disallowed, then Steve Yates took an elbow in the face; the United manager ran on to the field, called his players off and the game was abandoned.

Back home the 1978/9 third division campaign started with a defeat, then began to chug along nicely just below the promotion zone. New record signing Dave Cusack, £50,000 from Sheffield Wednesday made his debut as captain for the day in the centre of defence against his old side, and former Norwich City and Chicago Stings keeper Mervyn Cawston replaced the athletic Neil Freeman, who went to Birming-ham in the summer for £85,000.

Smith also speculated £2,000 of the club's money on the novelty of a video recorder that season; his office was regularly crowded with journalists and officials analysing previous games.

No tape was run through more times that season than the one which recorded a scoreless draw in a third round FA cup tie against Bob Paisley's European champions Liverpool. Un-doubtedly the strongest team United have ever played in any era, the Liverpool side they met on Wednesday 10 January 1979 had justified claims to being the best club side in the world; perhaps even one of the best club sides ever. Snowy conditions proved the leveller, and even though United were dealt with 3–0 in the replay, Southend's largest crowd ever went away proud of the achievement (see games to remember). Under the circumstances it was one of United's best ever results, and the 31,033 attendance that night is now unlikely ever to be beaten.

The packed South Bank for the record attendance match against Liverpool.

In the League, promotion hopes were kept on the back burner for most of the 1978/9 season, but in the end Southend needed a storming finish which they couldn't produce, and had to settle with 13th.

Any thoughts about consolidating on that respectable position the following year were immediately put in doubt when 13 United players were struck down with severe food poisoning after a buffet at a pre-season friendly against Dover. Only Colin Morris was fully fit as the season began, yet Southend still won their opening game and achieved their first measurable success in the League Cup, until now barren territory for the club. Having beaten Brentford and Bolton (their first ever win against a first division team) over the new two leg format, United held West Ham 1–1 in the sudden death third round at Upton Park, drew 0–0 at home in the replay, then returned to Upton Park via a toss of the coin for a second replay which they lost 5–1.

Not long afterwards Colin Morris joined Blackpool in exchange for Northern Ireland international Derek Spence, a hugely enthusiastic player who came close to beating George MacKenzie's club record of nine international caps while playing for Southend – and Keith Mercer was signed for £80,000 from Watford. Both of them, though, joined a team which had been trying to fight its way out of the relegation zone all season. Several good results just before Easter 1980 lifted hopes, but it was to no avail. United were back down to the fourth after just two seasons, relegated from the third in 22nd place and posting a loss on the year of £50,000.

> Southend midfielder Anton Otulakowski, who played in the late seventies and early eighties, also represented England at youth level as a gymnast.

Angry chairman Frank Walton rashly defied the yo-yo factor and promised the fans: *'This will never happen again as long as I live'*, publicly laying most of the blame at Dave Smith's door. *'He's had a totally free hand and must accept the responsibility'* explained Walton, *'He's spent around £200,000 on players who we expected to get us promotion, not relegation'.* Assistant John Lattimer became the fall guy, sacked just before the season's end, but Walton warned Smith he would be out too if the club was not doing well by Christmas of the new season.

Whether Walton's intervention had the desired effect, or whether Smith finally began to reap the rewards of his signings, Southend sped off at the beginning of 1980/1 – and never looked back. The team's 10th consecutive victory at home, 1–0 against Wimbledon in November, created a new club record of 19 consecutive home games without defeat. Roots Hall became a fortress, breached only during a 1–0 first round cup defeat against Hereford, who put the first home goal past Mervyn Cawston for 987 minutes. Defence, as always in the Smith era, was the strong point.

The football was entertaining and attractive, wholehearted Pountney the fans' favourite, Derek Spence named player of the year, and 17 year old Glenn Pennyfather bursting onto the scene. United won every home League game until January 1981 when they could only manage a scoreless draw with Northampton, and remained unbeaten at Roots Hall all season conceding only six goals at home, a fourth division record; milestones were broken left right and centre.

Yet the fans were staying away, now hard bitten and convinced that Southend wouldn't be able to stay in the third even if they did get promotion. Gates of 4–6,000 were condemned as *'a bad reflection on the town'*, especially as admission prices were among the lowest in the League, but many misjudged just how hard the disappointment of the previous year's relegation had hit morale.

So dominant were Southend that season that they actually clinched promotion as early as 29 March 1981, when a Sunday defeat of Aldershot by Torquay gave the blues the unassailable gap they required. Admission prices were reduced for the last home game of the season against Rochdale, when a 1–1 draw was

enough to make United champions of the fourth division – the first title they'd won since becoming champions of the Southern League division two in 1907/8 – 73 years previously. Southend's diamond jubilee season was certainly one to remember, because no fewer than 20 club records were shattered. Among them were the most successive home wins (18), the longest unbeaten home run (31), most wins in a season (30), fewest goals against (31), and the most clean sheets (25).

Chairman Frank Walton, buoyed by the championship, got into the club's first confrontation with the Southend council at the end of the season when local officials turned down plans to build a multi million pound supermarket on the car park behind Roots Hall's east stand. Setting the tone for a subsequent decade of mud slinging and controversy, Walton reacted by calling on the government to intervene. *'I'm fed up to the back teeth with listening to pipsqueak councillors airing their parochial little views'* he said diplomatically.

Smith, who was declared fourth division manager of the year, judged it *'a truly wonderful season for the club'*, then made sure he had no loose change in his suit before his ritual fully clothed bath. After a celebratory friendly match against Wolves, when skipper Micky Stead showed off the fourth division trophy and the players did a lap of honour, he also claimed his squad should never have gone down from the third in the first place, and that it was now *'good enough to go straight through the third division'*.

Not quite, but next season his team of winners did post the highest position since the third division south in 1957/8, finishing 7th at the end of 1981/2. The season of the Falklands war was the first year of three points for a win, a new system designed to produce more wins but which the blues, who commanded third place in the table as 1981 became 1982, ironically chose to christen with 15 draws. By April they were tenth but only eight points behind in a wide open division.

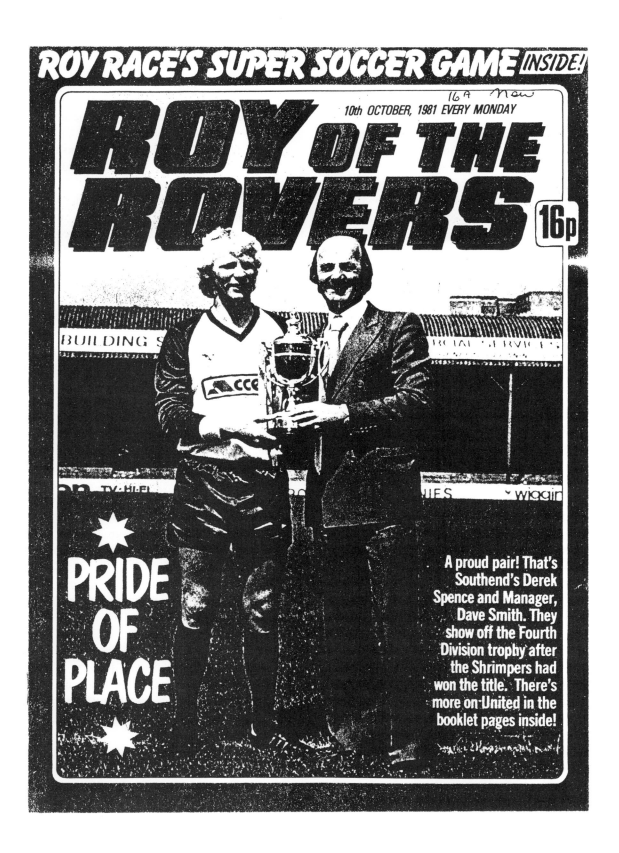

ROY RACE'S SUPER SOCCER GAME *INSIDE!*

ROY OF THE ROVERS

10th OCTOBER, 1981 EVERY MONDAY

16p

PRIDE OF PLACE

A proud pair! That's Southend's Derek Spence and Manager, Dave Smith. They show off the Fourth Division trophy after the Shrimpers had won the title. There's more on United in the booklet pages inside!

A sensational 5–3 away victory over Burnley that month kept slim promotion hopes alive until one too many of those draws made it mission impossible.

Supporters did celebrate promotion to the second division at Roots Hall that season, only they were from Burnley, who took themselves up by winning their return leg 4–1 in May. Home crowds were often below 4,000, despite the team's creditable performances; further indication during a time when crowds fell generally that United were heading for their most barren period on the terraces.

Efforts were made to win them back during 1982/3 – parachutists dropped onto the pitch for pre-match entertainment at the opening game against Lincoln – but displays on the field of play were hardly guaranteed to get them flocking in. In the FA Cup United finally laid the ghost of Yeovil, who'd beaten them twice in the same competition in 1958 and 1963, by thumping them 3–0 in the second round. That brought forward Jackie Charlton's second division Sheffield Wednesday, who were lucky not to lose a 0–0 draw at Roots Hall and were held 2–2 after extra time in the replay at Hillsborough thanks to a late Ron Pountney equaliser. United lost 2–1 in the second replay, a remarkable game involving an own goal, two penalties a sending off and the winners playing the whole of the second half with only ten men.

Once those dramas were over there was little left in the season. With Southend anchored midway in the table attendances plummeted to new lows, climaxing in an appalling 1,904 turnout against Walsall in April 1983. The only match in the latter half of the season to draw anything like respectable numbers was in the same month April against Bournemouth, purely because of one man. George Best, now 36, was having a brief revival as a player at Dean Court, and he put at least 2,000 on the gate at Roots Hall, tempting 4,275 into the ground. Woefully unfit but still with incredible gifts, he must have been just about the greatest player ever to step onto the turf at a Southend

ground, unless fans of Tommy Lawton, Gordon Banks and Bobby Charlton (who had appeared in 1974 as player manager for Preston) wish to argue otherwise. Best had a good game, turning his marker Micky Stead inside out and providing most of the footballing skills in a 0–0 draw even if he was operating at half pace.

Poor crowds Southend could do without. The club's overdraft now stood at £250,000 despite annual income from the Roots Hall market of £70,000, and Smith was forced to sell two of his best players, Dave Cusack and Anton Otulakowski, in a cash raising double transfer to Millwall. Others, including Paul Clark, who'd returned from a spell with Brighton, and Danny Greaves – son of Jimmy – were put on the market – and a final position of 15th didn't augur well for takings at the gates next season. After the last game of 1982/3 disappointed fans chanted for the resignation of Smith and booed his new chairman Mark Rubin, who'd taken over from Walton in March.

The club was vulnerable, and at least one man knew it. He was Anton Johnson, an Essex man and local butcher who was already chairman at Rotherham. Johnson sniffed blood at Southend, executing his takeover during one momentous June week. Smith, one of the club's most successful managers, was sacked without ceremony while he was on holiday, and the Rubin brothers Mark and Tony sold out to Johnson's 'consortium'. Whatever difficulties had gone before were about to pale into insignificance. Johnson was the worst thing that ever happened to the club.

To general astonishment the Crewe manager Peter Morris was moved quickly into Smith's position, though Smith conducted his own brief office sit-in until he got compensation. Then, as if to herald the start of a bizarre new era, United played Japan in a pre-season friendly, losing 1–0 to a goal by Masafumi Yokoyama, surely the most exotic name to have appeared on any scoresheet at Roots Hall.

Events ran too fast for most fans to keep up with, and by August soccer legend Bobby

Moore, who lived in nearby Chigwell, was moved in as chief executive: the last piece of Johnson's jigsaw. In a matter of two months Johnson had masterminded the biggest shake up of the club since David Jack had arrived in 1934. He changed personnel from top to bottom – a new board, a new chairman (Andrew MacHutcheon), a new first team coach (Colin Harper) and to go with them a radically different squad.

Not surprisingly in the midst of such chaos, 1983/4 was an unmitigated disaster. On the field a 4–1 September defeat at Preston equalled the club record of 12 consecutive League matches without a victory, despite the presence of on–loan Les Cartwright, a former Welsh international. Unfamiliar faces began to appear in the team as a desperate Morris opted for players who'd once been at the top level but were now on their way down; people like Billy Kellock from Wolves, Trevor Whymark and Kevin Steggles from Ipswich. Morris lasted only until February 1984, gates were now regularly under 2,000 and the town had turned its back on the new set–up.

Skipper Kellock in action against Northampton's Benjamin. The match in October 1984, 'attracted' 1,920 to Roots Hall.

Southend had been losing its faithful core over the last few years, now it had all but lost it altogether. Just 1,594 could bring themselves to turn up for a February game against Bolton.

Under the caretakership of Bobby Moore, the team bumped along the bottom of the third for the rest of the season, momentarily enlivened near the close when Malcolm Allison agreed to put in some part time coaching, but doomed to relegation even before they lost their last game against Wigan.

As they flew off for an ill–deserved tour of Sri Lanka, Bobby Moore was appointed manager on a four year contract and property developer Vic Jobson, the man who eventually got rid of Johnson, was elected a director.

Southend's failure on the pitch seemed of little concern to Johnson's new chairman Andrew MacHutcheon, who'd been telling anyone who'd listen that the 'winds of change' at the club would transform Roots Hall into a leisure centre as much as a football ground.

MacHutcheon had been exploring the idea of bringing greyhound racing to the ground, but the first step in the masterplan was an announcement in July 1984 that rugby league would be coming to town. In the wake of Fulham's semi–successful flirtation with the northern code, Maidstone–based Kent Invicta rugby league team were given permission to switch their operation to Roots Hall (see the grounds).

With the round ball Southend were even more pitiful, yet 20th place in the fourth division that 1984/5 season – unquestionably the lowest point in their history – was the least of anyone's worries. The club was on its last legs.

Boardroom battles had been raging as soon as the season got under way, with Jobson, MacHutcheon and Alan Gershlick all forced out in October.

Johnson brought in his London solicitor Michael Cranston as chairman and filled one of the vacant spaces with the former managing director of Rotherham, John Adams. Then, as a Football League investigation into Johnson's connections with other soccer clubs drew to a climax, rumours began to circulate that the club was dramatically in debt to the tune of £700,000.

By now confusion reigned. With the footballing authorities accusing Johnson of being 'evasive' and talk of a possible Board of Trade enquiry into United's affairs, police made a swoop on his Eastwood home during the early hours of 23 October 1984. Johnson was arrested, held, and questioned at Southend police station before being released later that day.

Investigations continued apace, but the bitterest blow was yet to come. Fans who'd saved up to £200 each in the club's Christmas loan fund discovered only a fortnight before the festive season that up to £70,000 of the money had gone missing. News of the scandal emerged shortly after an acrimonious five hour board meeting where exiles Jobson and MacHutcheon managed to secure the resignation of chairman Cranston and launch a struggle for control of shares once held by the Rubin family.

United admitted 'borrowing' cash from the fund which they later discovered they could not pay back – an angry crowd of savers at a subsequent loan fund meeting was only placated when Jobson, who'd managed to get back on the board, said he would make sure they had their money within seven days. The fraud squad began making its own enquiries while Robert Maxwell and Chelsea's Ken Bates came to the rescue, lending United the money to repay savers.

Humiliation then stacked upon humiliation when United striker Steve Phillips found the receivers taking over his club house in Leigh on Sea because of mortgage arrears, and the

Southend first introduced reduced admission prices for unemployed people in November 1984, when 15% of the town's working population were on the dole.

club was temporarily banned from the transfer market after missing a payment due to Portsmouth for winger Alan Rogers.

Jobson, now the majority shareholder, pledged to ensure shares would be spread over a wider base in future, and swiftly moved himself into the chairmanship as Johnson tried to extricate himself from the tangled web of his own making.

A few days before Christmas the Football League found Johnson guilty of breaching League regulations, banning him from ever becoming involved in football again. Southend, Rotherham, and Bournemouth were all found guilty of being controlled by a person involved with more than one club and were ordered to pay the costs of the League's inquiry, which had taken 16 months. An indignant MacHutcheon was banned too.

There was little to do but to pick up the pieces. The board fixed up an £800,000 remortgaging deal to reshuffle the debts, and Johnson's shares were blocked by the High Court. Jobson, more in hope than expectation, declared the nightmare over.

Needless to say, none of the calamitous happenings off the field did the team, or its manager, any good. Poor Bobby Moore, struggling to come to terms with his first Football League managerial job, had enough to contend with on the pitch without the club washing its dirty linen in public. Dressing room morale was rock bottom, there were problems even getting the players' wages, and the fans had more or less deserted what was undoubtedly a sinking ship. In February one of United's smallest ever home League crowds – 1,515 – watched a rare 2–1 win, over Halifax on a Friday night; sympathetic gatemen Mark Pearson and Mike Hillis gave the club back their £4 wages as a gesture of sympathy. As money got tighter Moore's squad got younger. 'Bobby's babes' were joined by Shane Westley, a tall volatile 19 year old from second division Charlton who did little to improve the blues already poor disciplinary record. As if the club didn't have enough problems, six sendings off and large numbers of bookings attracted disciplinary action against the club, frustration boiling over at the slightest opportunity. If it could have gone wrong it did that season, although everything was put into perspective when 52 were killed in the Bradford City fire disaster on the last day of the campaign. Southend players handed over ten per cent of their week's wages to the disaster fund in May and contented themselves with the one saving grace of their own season – that they'd managed to avoid the shame of having to apply for re-election, if only by the skin of their teeth on goal difference thanks to a victory at home to Torquay.

The ban on English clubs travelling abroad in the wake of the Heysel tragedy the following month had an immediate, bizarre effect on Southend during the close season when the club's planned summer tour to Scotland – deemed to be a foreign country by FIFA officials – had to be called off.

A 1985/6 Freight Rover Trophy first round tie against Northampton Town attracted just 683 hardy fans to Roots Hall.

Jobson, meanwhile, began his own close season controversy by unveiling plans for a new £14m 'super stadium' to replace Roots Hall. United would be playing there by the beginning of the 1986/7 season, he said – planning permission willing.

Moore signed 36 year old former West Ham and England full back Frank Lampard shortly afterwards, along with two of his best captures, Richard Cadette from Orient and Danny O'Shea from Exeter, both for £5,000. Amazingly, his side got off to a good start in 1985/6, Cadette playing brilliantly in a 5–1 thrashing of his old club, and the team fetching 14 points out of the first possible 18 to go top in September. Gates improved too, some now above the 4,000 mark, and there was a feeling that the worst was over.

By the turn of the year, however, the team had dropped to 7th, prompting a stony faced Moore to declare in January 1986 that thoughts of promotion were *'a sick joke'*. Jobson, too, had already written off the season, claiming that *'it would take a miracle for us to pull things round now'*.

Jim Stannard, who signed from Fulham in 1985, and returned to Craven Cottage in 1987.

Against such a background of despondency things could only get worse. Moore branded a 4–1 January home defeat against Colchester United in the Freight Rover Trophy *'without doubt the most pathetic, spineless and gutless performance I have ever witnessed from a bunch of professional footballers'*. What's more, he said, *'I have never felt so totally embarrassed by a display in all my life'*.

Frank Lampard was put in sole charge of coaching, but morale was on the slide. Moore played his dejected first team against Orient reserves to give them a confidence boosting victory but they lost 2–1, then midfielder Barry Silkman walked out saying *'I'm not bothered about kicking another ball for the club this season'*.

A freeze up in February didn't help, nor did some bad luck – in a 2–1 defeat against Stockport in March Clark hit the ball into the roof of the net but it bounced out sharply and the referee refused to believe it was a goal. In any case the fans now seemed to have little interest in United's fortunes. Just 1,006 watched a home game against Halifax in March 1986 – the lowest ever Football League gate at any Southend ground.

By early April a 3–2 defeat by bottom of the table Preston encouraged Lampard to quit his three month old coaching job, then after the full strength first team went out in the Thameside Trophy to Vauxhall Opel league team Walthamstow, Bobby Moore handed in his resignation on 25 April 1986. Though Moore hadn't had a good time at Roots Hall his departure still came as a shock, not least to the directors. The manager's decision capped what had already been a bitterly disappointing season, and they could not persuade him to change his mind. Moore did take the team up to the end of the campaign, however – ironically finishing his term with a 5–0 win over Rochdale and a 2–1 defeat of Port Vale.

Several well known names were connected with the empty Roots Hall managerial seat, among them Fulham and England player Alan Mullery,

John Pratt of Spurs and the betting favourite, former 1960s blues player Eddie May, who had recently been a coach at Charlton before resigning. In the end, though, it was a late applicant and dark horse who won the race.

Moore's replacement was another 1970s household name, former Chelsea folk hero David Webb, who'd had uneasy managerial spells at two other seaside clubs, Bournemouth and Torquay. Webb promised more grit and one of his trademarks – the creation of a settled side.

A 2–0 defeat away at Peterborough was hardly the ideal first match in charge, but a surprise 4–2 aggregate win against third division Brentford in the first round of what was now the Littlewoods Cup provided Webb with adequate consolation. The second round paired United with first division Manchester City, a Tuesday night all ticket affair at a Roots Hall now restricted to a farcical 12,000 because of safety restrictions.

As it was, the first clash between the two clubs since the famous 1956 'Trautmann game' drew only 6,182 – a reflection of just how much underlying support Southend had lost during the bad times.

A scoreless draw gave United an outside chance at Maine Road against a managerless Manchester City, but they went out after a brave 2–1 defeat and a fine display from Jim Stannard in goal. In the days between the two legs United chairman Vic Jobson had threatened to quit after councillors deferred plans for a new stadium, then there was more turmoil as Shane Westley and Paul Roberts were put on the transfer list following a backroom punch up. Both were back in the fold after a suitable cooling off period.

New £20,000 Swindon signing Martin Ling made an immediate impression, scoring on his debut against Crewe, and Cadette was attracting interest even though Webb had warned first division scouts: *'I'd sooner sell my wife'*. A whole week of training on an astro turf pitch in Basildon was to no avail when United visited that bane of the eighties, the plastic pitch at Preston, and lost 2–0.

Webb was suitably choked on the way back, when he was rushed to Chorley hospital after an altercation with a fishbone during the team's traditional fish and chips motorway meal.

By Christmas 1986 United were second in the fourth division and showing good form. Suspensions brought on by a poor disciplinary record didn't make things easy during the run in, but on 2 March 1987, with the team nicely poised for promotion, Webb shocked the town by quitting.

The manager of barely eight months stormed out of the club after a blazing row with Jobson over money for new players. Claiming to have been treated *'like a dirty rag'* he resigned with immediate effect, leaving Jobson to appoint 28 year old captain Paul Clark, a favourite with the fans, as caretaker player manager. *'If I'm honest I'd rather at this stage that David Webb was in charge'* admitted Clark.

The shock had a predictable effect on the pitch; three defeats out of the first four games under Paul Clark, then further gloom as England assistant manager Don Howe decided he couldn't take on a part time coaching job to help the club. With time running out, the promotion challenge was eventually resurrected by a 2–1 victory at Colchester, United's 1,000th League win. Webb's spectre was finally banished as third place United opened up a seven point gap above Wolves with a another 2–1 away victory, at Orient.

The real clincher – or so it seemed – was a home 1–0 win against Wolves in front of 10,369, United's biggest crowd for six years. But in the end it took a 2–0 victory in the last game of the season at Stockport to make sure. Richard Cadette's 31st goal and a strike by Glenn Pannyfather secured automatic promotion, one point ahead of 4th placed Wolves. About 500 blues fans on the Stockport terraces celebrated with the players afterwards; Wolves supporters who'd made the journey hoping for a Southend defeat went home dejected.

Richard Cadette celebrates with the fans at the Stockport promotion party.

The celebrations had hardly died down when Jim Stannard, one of the heroes of the season, signed for £50,000 to third division Fulham. A few weeks afterwards United's other star, Cadette, took a £120,000 move to second division Sheffield United and uncertainty began to hang over Clark too, bidding for the role of permanent manager after taking over the reins so successfully. In the end a disappointed Clark got the assistant manager's job, as Jobson lined up 41 year old Dick Bate for his first ever full time managership. Bate, assistant manager at Notts County, took over in June 1987.

His first significant signings were £14,000 Chris Ramsey, a Swindon full back who'd played for Brighton in the 1983 cup final and keeper Eric Steele, a £10,000 capture from Derby County. Responsibility for goalscoring after the departure of Cadette fell onto the young shoulders of 18 year old Richard Young, £25,000 worth of striker from Bates' old club Notts County, but it was a responsibility he could never live up to, especially with subsequent injuries.

Bate didn't have a happy time at Southend. During his short ten game spell with the club United conceded 32 goals and failed to win a League match. The early season nightmare included an 8–1 defeat at Gillingham, a result credited by Bate as *the most humiliating and embarrassing moment in my football life'* – and the worst Southend performance for 22 years. He had a 1½ hour clear–the–air meeting two days later, but the fog soon descended again and by the end of September 1987 his team had notched a further five defeats on the trot, including a 6–2 humiliation at Notts County.

With Southend sitting one place off the bottom, Jobson intervened. After a board vote of no confidence Bate was demoted to coach, an offer he rejected. Only ten weeks in charge and with the dubious honour of being Southend's shortest serving manager of all time he went back to Sheffield. Paul Clark was called back to take over, ironically only a few hours before a Littlewoods Cup second round tie against first division Derby County, set up by the only

victory of the Bate 'era', a 4–2 second leg defeat of Brentford.

So it was that Clark, and not Bate, presided over one of Southend United's greatest achievements – only their second ever defeat of a first division club. Derby County, fielding England players Peter Shilton and Mark Wright, succumbed 1–0 to a 28th minute Roy McDonough penalty, hit with such precision that one exuberant fan felt compelled to celebrate by racing onto the pitch and dropping his trousers in front of the main stand. That day – Tuesday 22 September 1987 – was simultaneously one of the most traumatic and joyful in the club's history (see games to remember). Life was nothing if not interesting.

Two League games later Clark was given the player/manager's job he'd been looking for, at 28 becoming the youngest manager in the Football League. The team celebrated with a 1–1 draw against League leaders Northampton, then produced another magnificent performance in the Littlewwoods cup return leg at Derby, drawing 0–0 to go through to the third round with an aggregate of 1–0. Only a cruelly deflected shot at Ipswich prevented United progressing further.

Southend had been transformed under Clark – or so it seemed. The players were brought back down to earth in November when third division leaders Sunderland shot seven past United, and Southend remained stubbornly in penultimate position. They had the worst defensive record in the entire country, but Clark showed some foresight by splashing out £45,000 on a striker – Cambridge United's David Crown – that same month.

More than enough money came in to balance that spending when midfield captain Glenn Pennyfather ended his nine year association with the club, second division Crystal Palace manager Steve Coppell paying £150,000 for him, then the biggest fee Southend had ever received.

After an unhappy time at Southend, Ramsey was transfer listed and fined a week's wages after an incident in which he was alleged to have deliberately elbowed a player in a reserves match against Billericay. By the end of January 1988, however, United had dragged themselves up to fourth from bottom, thanks mainly to goals from David Crown.

> *David Crown was top scorer for both Southend and Cambridge United at the end of the 1987/8 season, having moved to Roots Hall midway through the campaign.*

Progress was slow, but by the beginning of April Crown's goals and a new fighting spirit had pulled the blues two places clear of the relegation zone. Two crucial victories over Easter Bank Holiday weekend boosted United's survival chances, but they were still only out of the relegation area on goal difference. In the end it went right down to the wire.

Glenn Pennyfather

United moved into their last home match on 7 May 1988 against mid table Blackpool knowing victory would guarantee them third division soccer – and they thumped the tangerines 4–0. The game had been scheduled for a Friday night but the FA ordered it to be played on Saturday along with the rest of the crucial end of season fixtures. As it was, Southend took control of their own destiny, Peter Butler – signed from Cambridge United for £60,000 three months earlier – scoring after 28 minutes, Crown on 46, then Ling netting two in the last 12 minutes. Final position: 17th.

McDonough's poor disciplinary record (by March 1988 he was facing his third suspension of the season) threatened to upset United's chances during the following 1988/9 season. Now with new keeper Paul Sansome, a £40,000 signing from Millwall, the blues lost 3–1 on aggregate in the second round of the Littlewoods Cup against – again – Derby, now in division two, and took an early exit in the FA Cup, 3–1 away to Bristol City.

In the League continued poor showings had left the blues languishing at the bottom of the third again by November 1988, and newspaper stories began to link David Webb with a return to the club. Webb, who'd been out of football since leaving the blues, spent some time as a car salesman then admitted he'd been *'a damn idiot'* to leave the club. A week after the rumours began to circulate Paul Clark was given the fatal vote of confidence by the board and on 4 December 1988 Webb was brought in as general manager. That, he said, meant acting as *'a giant fly on the wall'* while Paul Clark remained in charge of team affairs – but it was less than a month before Webb, a strong personality who likes to have things his own way, had come off the wall to take sole charge.

Webb was soon to realise he'd inherited a struggling squad, and was quickly pledging to rebuild 'brick by brick'. After a turning point 4–0 defeat by Mansfield, teenagers Steve Tilson, Spencer Prior and Justin Edinburgh began to make first team appearances, but by May 1989 Southend had dropped into the relegation zone after hovering perilously one or two places above it for months.

The 1988 Club Christmas Card – but the 'New Stadium' never materialised.

United's loyal supporter Kathleen Branscombe of Westcliff
receives a life season ticket from Chairman Vic Jobson and Director John Adams
at a Blues Senior Citizens evening.

In the last game of the season, at home to Chester, Spencer Prior scored his first ever goal in a desperate 1–0 victory. That looked to have spared United the fourth division for the second season running until news came through that fellow strugglers Blackpool had got the win they needed – courtesy of an own goal – to stay up at the blues' expense. In the end United went down on goal difference, despite David Crown's 29 goals for the season.

Shane Westley went to Wolves in the close season for £150,000 and Southend started 1989/90 as 10–1 joint favourites for the fourth division championship. Within five games they'd justified favouritism by arriving at the top, but it was the Littlewoods Cup which again drew most of the attention early on, when defeat of Colchester in the first round set up a second round tie against Tottenham, the first time the two teams had met since 1936. Only a Fenwick goal separated the two sides in front of 15,734 at a White Hart Lane undergoing redevelopment.

The return leg was sensational; Southend won 3–2 and but for the away goals rule and the post which denied David Crown in the dying minutes, would have seen Southend through to the third round on aggregate (see games to remember). Still basking in the national publicity, it was back to reality the following week as the blues continued the good run with a fortunate 1–0 League win in their first ever game against Scarborough, newly promoted from the Vauxhall Conference.

And there was a further, more bitter, taste of reality soon afterwards when things went horribly wrong in the FA Cup against Vauxhall Conference side Aylesbury in November 1989.

Webb and his young squad should have seen the writing on the wall when a six day 'sun break' in Torremolinos prior to the game was drenched out by torrential rain, lashing the airport in Malaga and at one time casting doubts on whether the team would even be able to get back for the tie.

On the tight Aylesbury ground at Buckingham Road a week's worth of Spanish relaxation came to nothing when an 80th minute diving header from Glenville Donegal stunned everyone, including the 4,000 home fans. Shamefaced United players had tasted both sides of giantkilling within a few weeks – and it was back to the old cliche – concentrating on the League.

The League, mind you, was worth concentrating on. Under skipper Paul Roberts, United were still top after 17 games thanks to Crown's prolific scoring, and although a sag over Christmas took them off the lead, things continued to look good as the 1989/90 season came towards its end. Ian Benjamin came on loan from Exeter in March to replace the injured Crown, then signed permanently a few days later. Webb finally snapped up Andy Ansah on a free transfer from Brentford, a small tricky winger who'd been on his shopping list for a long time, and picked up defender Dean Austin from St Albans just before the deadline.

With five teenagers now in the side Webb was putting his faith in youth – and the youngsters repaid him. A 2–0 home win against Halifax in the penultimate game took the blues into third place. But enough for automatic promotion but they had to win their last match away at Peterborough – who were looking for a play off place – to stay there and ensure a trip to the third division.

In a tense finale, Crown gave United a two goal lead with strikes in the sunshine on 15 and 20 minutes, but Peterborough's Halsall set up a nail biting 40 minutes by scoring just after the break. A contingent of at least 1,500 United fans suffered further torture as referee Mike Reed played an incredible seven minutes of injury time, but superb performances from keeper Sansome and a defence marshalled by the ever determined Clark saw United through.

Drained of energy by the tension and the heat, but happy to celebrate with the fans behind the goal, United's exciting young squad had left it to the last minute, but they'd done it. And more than that – though they didn't know it at the time – they'd begun their historic journey towards the second division. The yo yo years were over.

****

Another celebration – this time in the Peterborough dressing room.

On the way up again.

(Top) Benjamin scores his spectacular first of the season, in the match at home to Crewe
(1st September 1990)

(Left) Martin salutes another Benjamin goal, the only one of the game at Mansfield, later in the same month.

Kick off in an October 1990 match against Lincoln City was delayed for two minutes while a 'canine calling card' was removed from the centre circle. 'Both sides by-passed the midfield in an end to end game' reported the Evening Echo.

PASTURES NEW

Life for Southend in division 2 – and subsequently the newly created division 1 – has opened up a whole new world for players and fans alike.

There are novel challenges, like remembering to look at the right league table in the Sunday newspapers, or getting used to the luxury of third round entry into the FA Cup.

And there are other bonuses too, like seeing Southend goals – and even live games – on TV. There are impressive new grounds to visit at famous big name teams like Newcastle, West Ham, Sunderland or Leicester. And there's more about the club in newspapers and maga–zines wherever you happen to live. What's more, Southend's spell with the top teams has given the club a big time feeling (despite the poor crowds) without the rat race mentality of the Premier League.

Whatever lies ahead, Southend United can pride themselves on achieving a lifelong ambition.

Whether they manage to stay in such exalted company or not, their first successful season in division 2 – and the fighting spirit since then – proves the club **is** capable of bigger and better things, whatever the sceptics have said over the years.

It would be an optimistic fan indeed who claimed Southend will never spend significant periods in the lower reaches again, for history has proved that United's natural home is in football's backwaters. But once an ambition has been achieved, it is surely easier to keep it in your sights – and it is easier to set new targets for future years.

The 1990/91 season was a natural breaking point in Southend's history, rather like a coming of age. The next part of the club's lifecycle looks set to be even more challenging – and just as fascinating.

Inspiring start to life in Division Two

SATURDAY should be the day when Blues reap due reward for their wonder start to life in Division Two.

Wolverhampton Wanderers will be in town and a combination of their traditional charisma and Southend's ... start points to a crowd of anything between

Angell stinger

By RAY CLARKIN

Sunderland 1 Southend 2

SOUTHEND put to shabby Sunderland to the sword. And their hotshot Brett Angell equalled a 64-year club record with his seventh League goal in successive ...

THURSDAY, JANUARY 2

Port Vale ......(0) 1	Ipswich ....(1) 2	
Hughes 56	Kiwomya 42 54	
	8,076	
Southend ......(2) 4	Newcastle ......(0) 0	
Angell 3 88,	9,468	
Jones 44,		
Ansah 56		
Sunderland ...(1) 2	Barnsley ....(0) 0	
Armstrong 23,	16,107	
Goodman 81		
Swindon ....(3) 3	Millwall ....(0) 1	
Shearer 21 43,	McGinley 63	
Ling 28	9,746	
Watford ....(0) 0	Tranmere ......(0) 0	
	9,892	

	HOME						AWAY						
	P	W	D	L	F	A	W	D	L	F	A	Pts
Blackburn	24	9	2	1	22	8	4	3	5	13	14	44
Ipswich	26	8	1	3	21	13	4	7	3	18	17	44
Southend	26	7	3	4	26	18	5	4	3	13	12	43
Middlesbro	25	9	4	0	22	6	3	2	7	11	19	42
Cambridge	24	5	5	2	17	9	6	3	3	20	18	41
Leicester	25	7	3	2	20	8	5	2	6	12	20	41
Swindon	24	7	3	2	23	14	3	6	3	21	15	39
Derby	24	5	2	5	16	12	6	4	2	18	14	39
Portsmouth	24	9	3	0	20	4	2	3	7	11	20	39
Charlton	24	5	3	4	14	13	5	4	4	13	13	36
Wolves	25	5	3	6	18	17	4	3	5	14	14	33
Millwall	25	4	1	6	15	19	5	5	4	23	20	33
Bristol C	25	7	4	2	17	11	1	6	6	13	23	33
Tranmere	22	6	5	1	16	12	2	6	3	9	12	32
Sunderland	26	6	4	2	19	11	3	1	10	16	26	32
Watford	25	4	2	7	13	16	5	2	5	16	13	31
Port Vale	27	4	7	2	16	14	3	3	6	12	20	31
Barnsley	27	6	2	6	18	17	2	4	7	11	20	30
Plymouth	24	8	1	3	15	13	0	3	9	10	23	28
Newcastle	27	5	7	2	24	19	1	3	9	12	29	28
Bristol R	26	3	6	3	22	22	3	3	8	11	21	27
Grimsby	24	4	3	4	16	16	3	3	7	12	23	27
Brighton	27	4	5	5	22	21	2	2	9	11	23	25
Oxford	24	5	2	7	20	19	1	1	8	12	22	21

Southend 3, Blackburn 0

KENNY DALGLISH and money-ladened Blackburn were shocked by 6ft 2in striker Brett Angell. He scored with two power–ful headers and in between laid on the other goal for Ian Benjamin.

Dalglish said it was Rovers' worst result since he took over.

Angell took his season's tally to nine goals and reached the 50-mark in the League.

He said: "We've been going through a sticky spell with just one point from our last four home matches. It was nice to bounce back."

Watford 1 Southend 2

Watford: James; Gibbs, Drysdale, Dublin, McLoughlin, Putney, Bazeley, Blissett, Butler (Morrow 81), Porter, Nicholas. Sub not used: Soloman. Goal: Porter (80 pen).
Southend: Sansome; Austin, Powell, Jones, Scully, Prior, Ansah, Cornwell, Tilson, Benja-min, Sussex (Angell 34). Sub not used: Hall. Goals: Sussex (3), Dublin (81 og). Booked: Scully
Att: 6,862. Referee: M Pearce (Hants).

86

CHAPTER 7
THE GROUNDS

Roots Hall – first time round

The Roots Hall

The real Roots Hall, the house which gave its name to United's football ground, was an ivy clad timber building dating back to the 18th century. It sat a mile away from the coast in four acres of ground stretching to the north of West Street in the pleasant, bustling village of Prittlewell, behind what is now the present ground's South Bank.

There had been a Roots Hall on the site for at least 400 years before Southend built their first ground there, although its name was originally Rowards Hall and it had been rebuilt since the very early days.

Occupied by a succession of well–to–do locals who sold parts of the grounds over the years, the house was eventually bought in 1876 by Daniel Gossett,

who later became mayor of Southend. Gossett lived there for 12 years before selling the house (and what was left of its land) in 1899. A few months later Roots Hall was demolished and the grounds became playing fields.

For the most part Roots Hall Fields, as they then became known, were used by Prittlewell Cricket Club. But they were also hired to anyone who could stump up the necessary cash, and Southend Athletic played there for a spell before moving to Marine Park near the seafront on the site soon to be known as the Kursaal.

For the founders of Southend United, who'd plotted their venture in 1906 no more than 200 yards away from Roots Hall at Oliver Trigg's Blue Boar Inn, the fields were a logical choice. They had little more than a certain rustic charm and the most limited of facilities, but they were close, available, and full of potential.

While Southend Athletic were displaying characteristic indecision about whether to make a move back to Roots Hall, United sprung into action by securing a three year lease on the ground. The pitch ran from north to south, as it does today, and although it had a pronounced slope from one end to the other, it was judged a satisfactory surface by the standards of the day. At 110 yards long and 73 yards wide it was of average size but had the smallest pitch area of any Southend ground.

Work began immediately on creating a muddy embankment which ran the complete length of the west side of the ground and could hold 2,000 'comfortably' – while on the east side Ducat's, a family firm run by the father of Southend born Woolwich Arsenal and England international Andrew Ducat, erected a 122 ft long, 200 capacity timber grandstand in time for the opening game. For the first month the players had to change in a small hut later converted to a tea bar, and in all other respects Roots Hall was nothing much more than an enclosed field surrounded by a white wooden fence just 7ft from the touchline.

> (Top) A civic watch inspection in front of the grandstand at Roots Hall in November 1914. (Bottom) Rural Prittlewell, and the entrance to the ground (on the left).

United's share prospectus claimed a 6,000 capacity, but that estimate wasn't tested in the early days, when crowds coming through the two turnstiles in West Street rarely amounted to anything more than 3,000 – respectable though that was for a new team. On the other hand the ground soon came in for praise from visiting teams and spectators. *'Upon entering the ground on Saturday I thought Southend were most fortunate to possess such a good enclosure'* wrote one visitor from the midlands, *'The playing space, although a trifle narrow, is a capital one, being well turfed and infinitely superior to many of the cinder heaps which do duty for football grounds in the vicinity of the midlands'*.

Others were complimentary too; only a month into the first season one correspondent felt moved to tell the Southend Standard how he was *'particularly struck by the ground, which I thought was an admirable one for a maiden team'*. He did however, have reservations about the danger to spectators standing next to the sharp projecting points on the fence surrounding the pitch. *'Needless to say the discomfort was exaggerated by the continuous crushing of excited persons in the rear'* he complained. *'Apart from this a player running at full speed near the boundary line and fully charged might possibly be the victim of a very serious accident'*. Another correspondent pointed out that *'spectators are too much on top of the wing men, who are often upset by disparaging remarks'*.

With United in a midweek league as well as Southern League division II – and Southend Corinthians using the ground on Saturdays when United were playing away – the Roots Hall pitch got plenty of use in its first season.

Gate money allowed some improvements in the following years, notably covering of the main east stand in 1909 and the erection of another more modest stand on the west side by the supporters committee. Regular appeals were made to builders for rubbish and earth to make embankments, but for the most part the rest of the ground remained uncomfortable and unsafe, with sections of the crowd slithering around in wet conditions.

Capacity had risen from the early days, but any crowd of more than 5,000 severely tested facilities. The ground record of 7,200 for a game against Northampton in 1909 produced predictable chaos, with myriad complaints about overcrowding and crushing. Journalists, too, regularly moaned about having to clamber up to a perilous, exposed perch on top of the grandstand, but they had to make do until a new secluded press box appeared amid general improvements in 1912.

The club's headquarters continued at the Blue Boar throughout, and essentially Roots Hall remained an uncomplicated, open ground.

So open in fact was the ground that the renowned aviator George Barnes chose Roots Hall as a runway to attempt the first ever flight in Southend. On 6 July 1910, under the auspices of the Southend United directors, Barnes attempted his flight in front of 2,000 people, but strong winds hampered his progress so much that after generating just enough height to avoid the dreaded fence, his Hunter monoplane came down fifty yards further on. Most spectators could afford a smirk because all but a few had slipped in without paying, but for the United directors their ingenuity was something of a financial setback. Barnes hardly enhanced his reputation a few weeks later by crashing at Folkestone and sustaining serious injuries.

Roots Hall was thereafter used for occasional non-footballing events – as when Southend rugby club opted to use its superior facilities for a big match against London Welsh in September 1912 – and by the summer of 1913 the ground had established itself as such an integral part of United's plans that the club began negotiations to buy it from its owner. Sadly the talks broke down at a crucial stage and when the first world war put a stop to the Southern League two years later a dispute developed over outstanding rent. Southend tried to generate money by sub-letting Roots Hall to the military, but by June 1916 when their lease ran out, there was no option other than for owner George Radford to hold an auction of Roots Hall assets to raise money.

The auction took place at the now disused Roots Hall – most of what was being auctioned, after all, now stood there in disrepair. Gales had brought down half of the roofing and the ground, according to one observer, made 'a desolate scene'. A week later work began on digging the pitch into allotments. After just ten years there, Southend's first, quaint little ground was no more.

The Kursaal

Southend's move to the Kursaal fairground was not one made of choice, but the club had 15 largely happy years within its grounds. It was an enclosure full of atmosphere, one of the most unusual settings for any ground, yet loved by those who saw the club flourish there in the 1920s and early thirties.

The Kursaal itself had opened to the west of the pier just behind the seafront in July 1901 as a place of leisure built around picturesque flower gardens and a trotting track which encompassed a football pitch used by Southend Athletic. In 1910 the trotting track was dug up, part of the grounds were let out as an amusement park and the whole complex changed its name to Luna Park.

Within two years, however, the area had been sold on to a Princeton educated American, Captain David de Forest Morehouse, who restored its original name and added extra attractions like a scenic railway and a ballroom. By 1919, when Southend were looking for a new post war home, Morehouse had the makings of what was to become one of the most popular amusement parks in the country – but for the time being he was glad of the extra income a football club would bring in.

Southend United Football Club,
LIMITED.

OPENING OF
NEW GROUND,
THE KURSAAL.

THE DIRECTORS EXTEND A CORDIAL IN-
VITATION TO ALL TO

A RECEPTION

To be held on the FOOTBALL GROUND from 3 p.m.
to 6 p.m. on

Saturday, 9th August, 1919,
FOR THE INSPECTION OF GROUND,
DRESSING ROOMS, ETC.

MUSIC AND REFRESHMENTS WILL BE
PROVIDED.

Admission   —   —   FREE.

Entrances: Woodgrange Drive (Beach Cars) and
Burdett Road, Marine Parade.

COME IN YOUR THOUSANDS AND SEE
WHAT A SPLENDID FOOTBALL GROUND
HAS BEEN PROVIDED FOR THE TOWN.

HIS WORSHIP THE MAYOR (Ald. F. W. Senier)
accompanied by the MAYORESS and Ald. JOHN
and Mrs. FRANCIS, have kindly promised to be
present.

Morehouse became intricately involved with efforts to revive United and a one year lease on their new ground was signed in April 1919 with an option for a further year and an eventual sale price of £9,500 if United were interested.

The new 115yd by 75yd pitch – by far Southend's biggest – was built on the east side of the Kursaal complex, partly over the original site of the trotting track, with a 'Beach End' to the south and the opposite goal backing onto Woodgrange Drive to the north. United had little time before the start of the first post war season to do anything more than lay the necessary 5,709 turfs and construct some rough banking – and even then had to postpone a preseason friendly against West Ham because the ground was unfit.

Fencing round the pitch was laid 9ft from the touch line, slightly further away than at Roots Hall but still close enough to allow the crowd to breath down players' necks. There was no stand of any description when the townspeople were invited to a public inspection on 9 August 1919 so most attention focused on the state-of-the-art dressing rooms in the south east corner, each boasting two large communal concrete baths, a hot geyser and a shower. In the same pavilion there was also a referee's room and a gym, plus living quarters for the trainer, a board room, and a clubhouse. Muddy entrances to the ground were built in Woodgrange Drive and Beresford Road but children found they could slip in unnoticed through the rickety fence backing onto Arnold Avenue on the east side.

The pitch was flat and far superior to Roots Hall, eventually winning a reputation as one of the best surfaces anywhere in the country. Portsmouth, Southend's first opposition at the Kursaal, liked the Cumberland turf so much they came away 2-0 winners on 30 August 1919 in front of 5,400, but two days later the first United goal at the ground – a penalty – set off a 3-0 demolition of Newport. Some believed United were spoiled by the perfect surface, which contrasted dramatically with some of the much rougher pitches around the country.

United claimed the Kursaal would eventually hold 35,000, but future attendances proved how inflated that estimate was. With just two small temporary stands in the first season, initially the club could only realistically cater for 3,000 fans in comfort, most of them still cruelly exposed to the winter wind and mists howling in from the sea. The Sheffield Daily Telegraph called it 'primitive' and one jaundiced football reporter claimed it would be difficult to find a bleaker ground in the country. *The wind cuts across with merciless incisiveness'* he complained.

Windy it might have been, but it was home, and Southend renewed their lease to 1924 at the end of the first season. Grandstand builders Humphries of London were called in during July 1920 to build an impressive £5,000 grandstand to hold 1,500 on the east side – and with additional terracing work supervised by trainer Jack Campbell, the stand and £3,000 worth of other improvements were finished in time for the beginning of the club's first season in the newly formed third division. Shortly afterwards the directors had to spend another £500 on 800 loads of earth to increase capacity to what they now claimed was 23,000. That was prior to the cup tie against Spurs in February 1921, but even so only 11,661 turned up after scaremonger reports in some London papers about the Kursaal's size.

League gates soon began matching that record during the following 1921/22 season, when the amusement park decided to erect a funseekers 'Waterchute' behind the Woodgrange Drive goal.

The chute became a well loved trademark to rank with Everton's church or Fulham's cottage and the ground began to gather something of a reputation.

By 1924 the Kursaal had been selected for the Essex Senior Challenge Cup final between Ilford and Grays Athletic – the first time the final had been played in Southend during its 40 year history – and Essex were playing county football there with regularity.

It was prestigious enough, too, for the Essex Provincial Grand Lodge of Freemasons to practice their handshakes there in July of 1924, but after Southend extended their lease still further and the Kursaal's record crowd of 18,153 attended a cup game against Nottingham Forest in 1926, the owners got ideas above their station. They decided to build a greyhound track round the pitch in May 1927.

The Kursaal track was only the second in the south of England, and news of its opening in June 1927 attracted punters from as far afield as Paris. It was a tight 500 yard course constructed in double quick time, running along the touchlines and cutting across the corners – to the dismay of long serving groundsman Bill Fitch. Unfortunately the hurried building programme created teething problems and thousands were disappointed when the inaugural meeting had to be cancelled an hour before the first race because no-one could get the hare to run.

The track eventually opened on 27 July 1927 in front of 5,000 people, by which time the FA had pronounced that greyhound racing and football were 'not compatible'. While the Kursaal owners digested the implications they met further trouble in August, having to call off a Sunday meeting after the Lords Day Observance Society ran a campaign with the rallying cry *'Greyhounds or God?'.*

The owners decided to carry on with the venture despite the FA's mutterings, and had even installed fifty 1,000 candlepower floodlights for the track by the end of October 1927, when another meeting had to be called off after the hare was three times caught and bitten to pieces. FA rules forbade use of the floodlights for soccer, but in murky conditions near the end of a November game against Bristol Rovers some bright spark illuminated the ground by turning on a whole section of the bulbs in the stand ten minutes before the final whistle. Flustered officials scampered backstage to turn them off before the FA got to hear about it.

Two different aerial views of The Kursaal. Note the Waterchute adjacent to the ground.

(Above) Match view from the Waterchute.
(Below) The Ordnance Survey map of 1921

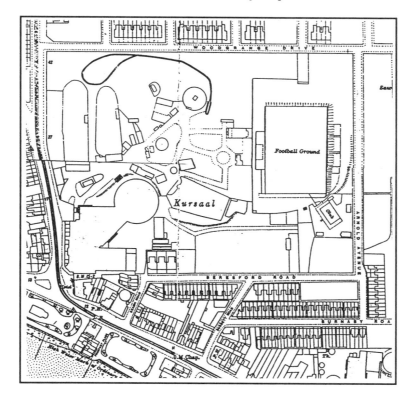

Lancaster Gate was actually more worried about the effect of the dog track on the pitch, which by the dawn of 1928 was showing distinct signs of wear and tear, especially in the corners. At a March 1928 meeting the FA warned it was considering action against clubs whose grounds were being interfered with by dogs.

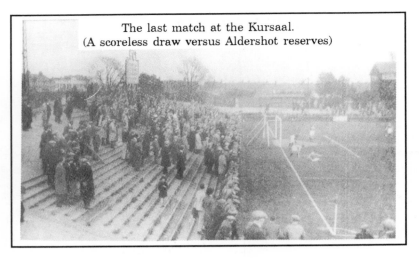
The last match at the Kursaal.
(A scoreless draw versus Aldershot reserves)

Four games were postponed because of the state of the pitch in that 1927/8 season, supporting the FA's view that what had been one of the third division's best surfaces was now being pawed apart. In the end it was the Football League who stepped in, ordering greyhound racing to cease at the Kursaal by 16 July 1928. Electric Hare Greyhound Racing Ltd took their equipment away; the experiment had lasted a year.

With the distraction of the dogs gone, Southend employed Messrs Flaxman to build a new west side stand, which was completed by December 1928. At 180ft long, 40ft deep and with a 25ft high roof it was almost identical to the opposite east side grandstand, although it had no seats and would hold 3,500 under cover.

Now the club had a much more respectable stadium – and one with great atmosphere at that. The few who still remember those days testify to the special feeling at the ground, a buzz generated by the close contact between players and fans, the compactness, even if it was rather open. If you had a big crowd at the Kursaal you knew you were at a football match – and the remaining years were good ones too, with Ted Birnie at the helm and the blues almost reaching the second division in 1931/2.

The sea fret still took its toll though; when Southend beat Chester 2–1 in 1933/4, 72 year old George Bunker had to be taken to hospital after sliding down the rain sodden mud banking, and in 1934 fans in the west stand sighed with relief when the supporters club finally fixed a glass screen to the exposed southern end of the west stand.

Ironically the screen served for only a few months, because in April 1934 a radically reshuffled board of directors decided to move to Southend Stadium, a new ground about three quarters of a mile further inland. United had to pay the Kursaal £250 compensation for breaking the lease, and the owners retained all the stands and fittings. It was an amicable agreement but a costly one for the club. After 15 years on the seafront, United were determined to start a new era under David Jack with a bigger, more solid ground. The final first team game at the Kursaal was a scoreless draw against Norwich on 28 April 1934, watched by 4,000. The gates were closed the following week after a reserves match against Aldershot, which also finished scoreless.

In November 1934 Captain de Forest Morehouse died, leaving the Kursaal under control of a trusteeship. The following month the west stand was taken down and the site was soon occupied by the famous 'Cyclone Roller Coaster', brought over from the Brussels Exhibition. Two years later the east stand, which had been sheltering untouched behind the roller coaster, disappeared too.

During the second world war the Kursaal and gardens remained open until Dunkirk in 1940, when the military requisitioned most of the site to set up a unit making uniforms for the forces. In 1948 it passed back into the hands of the Morehouse family and by the end of the 1960s was being acclaimed as *'one of the largest and best equipped leisure sites in Britain'*.

But the Kursaal's decline in the early 1970s was spectacular, and by 1979 even the famous wall of death had been pulled down. The domed entrance to the complex is now subject to a preservation order, but almost all the rest of the site has succumbed to a housing development. 'Prospect Close' now runs north to south right through what would have been the old centre circle. Not even the street names give a clue to the footballing dramas acted out there in the past.

Southend Stadium

Settling in: Fans get to know Southend Stadium
during one of the first games there – versus Exeter in September 1934.

Southend's third ground could hardly have been more of a contrast to its second. Its predecessor had been compact and cramped; the stadium was airy and spacious; the Kursaal was atmospheric and close to the action, the stadium was often subdued and crowds were set back. Even the pitches were poles apart – the Kursaal smooth and well grassed, the stadium bumpy and thinly sown. For many fans the move was a disappointing one, but for the club it was probably a wise decision. The new ground was an important factor in Southend's growing stability.

Built primarily as a venue for greyhound racing, Southend Stadium officially opened on 19 May 1933, five years after the failed dog track initiative at the Kursaal, with money raised by an oversubscribed share issue. It was an impressive new facility constructed on the site of former brick workings off Grainger Road, just a stone's throw from Southend's Victoria station – central and easy to get to.

United officials clearly had their eye on the space inside the oval dog track from day one, but the first public mention of a move there didn't surface until almost a year later when Captain Tom McEwan of the Stadium's 'Greycing Club' was appointed as a Southend United director in March 1934. McEwan's arrival had coincided with the departure from the board of the Kursaal's prime mover and now Southend chairman, David de Forest Morehouse, and it soon became clear that a ground move was under active consideration, even though United had two years of their Kursaal lease to go.

Negotiations with the Greycing Club began in May 1934 and within days the directors had fixed up a seven year lease at Grainger Road. The deal was rubber stamped on 4 June 1934 by the Football League, which had no objections to the grey-hound/football mix this time round, mainly because it would not affect the playing surface. A small army of workmen began to make preparations.

With a main stand and terracing already in place, their priority was the creation of a pitch, which was levelled and marked out in dimensions of 112 yards by 72 yards running north to south, then spread with 25 bushels of seed. Within two months the grass was established enough to host the first practice at the stadium, and a week later 7,000 came to see the debut League game there, a 2–1 win against Aldershot.

United fans were immediately impressed by the new facilities, though they were later to regret the distance thrown between them and the pitch by the dog track. Other more impartial observers were fulsome in their praise. *The stadium is an exceptionally spacious affair'* wrote one Exeter reporter, *'I have not seen a better ground in the course of travel to the headquarters of all the southern section clubs. The whole scene was in vivid contrast to the old and rather cramped Kursaal'.* The 1934 Football Encyclopedia judged it *'one of the best grounds in the south'.*

Those used to the privations of the Kursaal were certainly taken with the 2,000 tip up seats in the large west stand, and with the quickly constructed all standing popular enclosure on the eastern Sutton Road side, which brought total covered capacity to 9,000. The players, however, were less happy with the state of the clay–based pitch, which would become a quagmire with rain and bone hard during a dry spell. Four months into the first season groundsman Bill Fitch had to put in £1,000 worth of herring bone drainage, and in the summer of 1935 the bare pitch was completely relaid with 28,000 meadow turfs from a farm in Fambridge. Even so, the pitch never won a good reputation throughout the club's stay there and the ball would often bounce around like a pea on a drum in early season.

The best crowd in the stadium's first year was 13,373 against Sheffield United in the cup, but during the following season, in January 1936, another cup tie against Spurs set an all time record for the ground. Local contemporary reports put the crowd at 23,634, though a figure of 22,862 has often been quoted since. Whatever the true statistic, the game tested the stadium's capacity to the full, as 2,000 had to be locked out a quarter of an hour before kick off.

The stadium was a busy place, with dog racing on two weekdays and Saturday evenings after the game, occasional boxing matches and a number of local events. But by the late thirties it had still not won the hearts of United fans. *'The stadium is not a popular place from the spectator's point of view'* wrote one anonymous correspondent to the Southend Standard in 1937, *'Go to any ground you like and you will find the shilling supporter always stands behind the goalposts to see the goals scored. But if you do that at the stadium you are so far away you see very little of the play. The Kursaal had a better playing pitch and it was compact and homely. It wasn't necessary at the Kursaal either to have six little boys in the outfield to save 'boundaries''.*

Players of that era testify that the stadium was short on atmosphere unless there was a crowd of 10,000 or more, and there was speculation at the time that poor home showings were down to the lack of psychological backing from a crowd generally estranged from the action.

The footballing authorities indicated their approval of the ground in February 1938 by choosing it for a schoolboys' international trial, but the tide of terrace complaints could not be stemmed. *'To me the dog track is an insult'* raged one fan *'It's a kind of penance I am forced to undergo every time I enter the ground'.* *'One feels absolutely out of it'* said another.

By the close season of 1938 the directors had become so concerned by the grumblings and nostalgia for the Kursaal that they decided to allow shilling supporters into the 6,500 capacity covered standing area in the main eastern stand without paying extra to transfer. A few weeks later returns of a questionnaire sent to local residents confirmed that the stadium's impersonal surroundings were one of the biggest contributory factors to low crowds.

The outbreak of war a year later put paid to any further improvement plans – and forced the club to leave the ground. The army officer training corps requisitioned the stadium's facilities in August 1940, forcing United to switch to Chelmsford, although dog racing didn't finish until a month later in September 1940 when it was suspended *'owing to the present conditions'.*

The army officers destroyed all the club's pre war records and generally did the stadium no good at all, prompting a £271 compensation claim to the war department once hostilities ceased. Southend's victory celebrations got underway with a military tattoo at the stadium in June 1945, but returfing was needed before United could stage their first game back at the stadium against QPR in August 1945, a 2–1 defeat. Urgent repairs then had to be made when the public discovered that damage to one end of the ground made it as easy to see matches free of charge from the street as from the grandstand.

Dog racing didn't resume until nine months later in April 1946, when United found to their dismay that new Wednesday night meetings meant they had to play midweek games on Tuesdays or Thursdays. The late forties were a boom time for greyhound

The war hadn't changed the fans feelings about the ground, and their continued dislike of its 'wilderness' atmosphere – plus clashes with dog meetings – led the club to study the idea of buying its own purpose built stadium elsewhere in the town.

Early tentative enquiries to the council about land availability generated response, but the supporters club persisted, not least because the club's 21 year lease on the ground would be coming to an end in 1955. When fruitless negotiations started with the stadium owners about provision of floodlighting in

Coaching at the stadium during the 1947/48 season, under the guidance of Jimmy Hogan.

racing and meetings at the stadium began to attract in excess of 5,000. Protests from United fell on deaf ears because the dogs had primacy in the tenancy agreement.

By the time United found themselves playing their last game at the stadium, its official capacity had dropped to 20,000, and with the post war attendance boom over, average gates were now down to 9,000. The blues completed their 14th and final season inside the dog track with a 3–2 victory against Brentford on 30 April 1955, then moved on to their old home at Roots Hall half a mile to the north west.

1953, United officials were so set on moving that they asked for portable lights so they could take them to Roots Hall.

Football didn't disappear completely from the stadium when United left. The pitch was used by many local amateur sides, especially for finals, and in later years Ernie Shepherd and Arthur Rowley both hired the ground for United's reserve and youth team games. The dressing rooms were given a new coat of paint when amateur side Pegasus Athletic agreed to share the pitch with United's reserves in 1971, but greyhounds continued as the mainstay – despite a series of doping scandals which later led some London bookmakers to refuse bets on South-end races. In 1970 the stadium hosted the first round of the prestigious BBC TV Trophy, but the owners were already looking to diversify. In September that year an application went in for planning permission to build a second track on the nine acre site for speedway and stock car racing – but the council threw it out six months later. Ironically the ground had originally been built with planning permission for speedway as well as dog racing and football, but the Greycing club had never exercised the privilege; now it wanted to, the council stood in the way.

By the middle 1980s greyhound crowds had dwindled to less than 400 and profits had slumped dramatically. Although there were 127 meetings every year the stadium was being used only eight hours per week, generating barely enough income to support its 21 full time employees. With the council still deeply uninterested in any rescue packages, the hare made its final dash on Boxing Day 1985, shortly before the site was sold off to make way for a soulless Curry's superstore. Those who complained about lack of atmosphere at Grainger Road should see it now.

The Stadium in 1985.

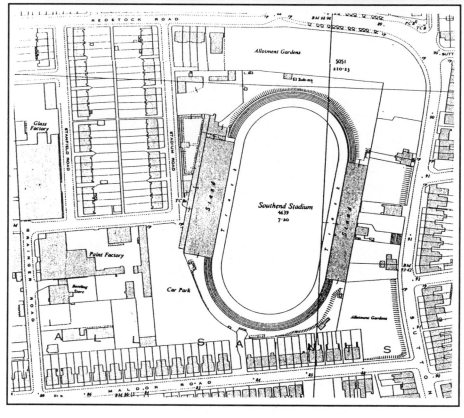

The stadium
c.1970

New Writtle Street

Ground sharing is usually fraught with difficulties, but Southend's time at New Writtle Street was relatively painless, thanks mainly to the generous hospitality of its owners, Chelmsford City.

United played their first proper game there in August 1940 against Arsenal and their last, before packing up, just over a year later in October 1941. Rent for each game was £10, but Chelmsford allowed the impoverished Southend board to run up a £310 slate. The hosts also picked up a huge kit and equipment bill thanks to the activities of 'souvenir hunters' from visiting teams during the war. Chelmsford had 50 towels when Southend first began using New Writtle Street, but by 1945 all but three had been pinched.

For a Southern League venue New Writtle Street was an impressive ground, its 18,000 capacity not far short of the stadium which Southend had temporarily vacated. Crowds in those war days barely topped 1,000 in any case, but Chelmsford City posted their record not long afterwards when 16,807 watched a southern league clash against Colchester United in October 1949. The ground had been opened in February 1923, with a 115 yard by 72 yard pitch running west to east.

Programme notes on 19 April 1941 prematurely predicted Southend's departure from New Writtle Street by claiming that the game on the following Saturday would be United's last of the war. *'We have some secret information that this will be the last war time match at home because the commencement of next season will see our empire forces victorious'* it revealed, optimistically. Once Southend eventually did call it a day in October 1941, Chelmsford played only intermittent friendlies until the Air Ministry requisitioned the ground in November 1942. The ministry set up a barrage balloon on the pitch and local firm Marconi used the main stand as storage space for components until the summer of 1945. With Southend back at their real home, Chelmsford kicked off their first post war Southern League match on 25 August 1945.

The ground is much changed these days, partly due to safety restrictions. The centre section of the main stand is the only significant feature remaining from the days when Southend lodged there, and the old 'barn' stand has been demolished. With a new capacity of only 2,800 New Writtle Street now takes second place in Chelmsford to the adjacent county cricket ground, scene of so many recent Essex triumphs.

New Writtle Street Stadium c.1957 – much the same as it looked during the war.

Roots Hall – second time around

Former player Dave Robinson surveys the rubbish tip that was to become the new Roots Hall

Roots Hall's temporary role as a first world war allotment came to an end when its new owners, the Southend Gas Company, discovered large deposits of sand on the site. The firm had originally intended to erect a gas holder on the land, but the inter war housing boom in Southend had created a huge demand for sand, so the opportunity at Roots Hall was too good to miss. Many a house in the area has foundations built with some of the material which lay beneath Southend's first football pitch.

When the sandpit was exhausted most of the area was taken over by the Gas Light & Coke Company, which used the huge hole created by quarrying as a dump for old cookers, piping and other gas related paraphernalia. Locals also took to throwing rubbish in the pit, and before too long it was littered with prams, oil drums and even old cars. Despite the dangers, children would sneak in to slide down the pit's overgrown sides on tea trays – or even to play football. A cycle speedway team called Prittlewell Pirates created their own ad hoc track there until they moved to a better venue at the Wakering sports ground in 1949.

By the time Southend United began looking at the site, few people in the area even knew it had once been the club's first home. The supporters club chose the quarry, after initial prodding from the council, because it was a natural bowl and was close to the centre of Southend; only later did some of its members discover they'd inadvertently planned a return to their old hunting ground.

Talks about a move began as early as the autumn of 1948, when press reports emerged of plans for *'a giant £500,000 stadium at Roots Hall which will be a centre for all sporting activities in the town'*. The scheme kicked off well when the council freed up the land by buying Roots Hall and tempting the Gas Light & Coke Company away by offering them a site on the new industrial estate in Eastwood. With the backing of mayor Johnson, a keen supporter who wanted to see work on the new ground started during his last year in office, United chairman Nevill Newitt began drawing up plans for an immense, completely covered complex with speed-way, dogs, cycle racing, swimming baths, squash, tennis courts and even a running track.

By June 1950 papers setting up a trust fund to raise money for the venture had been signed by the mayor, the United chairman and the chairman of the supporters club. But long sensitive negotiations were ahead, and Newitt's ambitious plans had already begun to make some members of his board uneasy. The cost of such a complex could ruin the club, they said, and wasn't one of the main reasons for moving to get away from the distraction of other sports? By February 1951 Newitt was sufficiently at odds with the rest of his colleagues to offer his resignation after 17 years, though he did still remain on the board.

With Roots Hall now in the hands of the council, events took a predictably ponderous turn. Only after protracted discussion did councillors approve a resolution in February 1951 to enter into talks with United about selling the land and then, to the relief of many, only on the basis that plans for speedway were scrapped.

The price was to be settled by the district valuer, but so many other snags arose that nine months later during the dark days of December 1951 United's new chairman Major Hay was sufficiently pessimistic to admit that a move *'may or may not happen in our lifetime'*.

Only in May 1952 did negotiations finally conclude with an agreed purchase price of £11,258 – money which had already been raised by the supporters club and could be paid in cash. Two months later the Salvation Army put hearts in mouths by lodging an objection to the new ground on the basis that it would create too much noise and disruption for their Millfield children's home, which was now perched along with the vicarage at the top of the south bank where the original Roots Hall had once been. The objections, fortunately, were overruled.

By now the expected cost had been chopped down to £100,000 with all of Newitt's more grandiose ideas rubbed out first by Major Hay and then by new chairman Bert Smith, the man responsible more than anyone for the success of Roots Hall. Capacity would be 35–40,000 with parking at the back of the main stand for more than 600 cars – and there were promises of a better deal for the lowly 'bob a nob' supporters behind the goals. The pitch would only be 15ft from the terraces – with no intervening dog track – and there would be covered terracing behind the north goal.

Work began in March 1953, just over two years before the lease at the stadium expired, when new groundsman Sid Broomfield, previously on Bert Smith's farm, pegged out a pitch 110 yards by 74 yards. The new field ran in the same direction as the original pitch at Roots Hall but was a yard wider – and more importantly, thanks to years of excavation, 36ft lower than it had once been.

First task for Broomfield and his bulldozer was to level out the pitch and to remove what large bits of rubbish he could. It was an unpleasant business, dominated by the all pervading smell of gas, but by August 1953 the pitch was in good enough shape for work to begin on creating terrace banks.

That was even harder work for Broomfield and a handful of men using just picks and shovels. Their excavations produced some interesting finds, including a roman coin discovered during digging of a foundation wall for the south west corner, and layers of buried shells laid out as if once washed up by an ancient tide. Evidence of early civilisation at Roots Hall had already come to light during the inter war years, when early iron age pots and stone age hand axes had been dug up in the sandpit. A number of graves were disturbed in 1926, fuelling theories that it was once the site of an ancient cemetery.

By May 1953 the visitors who regularly strolled down on Sunday mornings to look at progress could begin to see something resembling a ground. The workmen, helped by players and supporters, began to make the thousands of concrete blocks which would form the backbone of the main east stand and the perimeter walls. Support from local tradespeople, who gave materials freely and on credit, was exceptional. Shortly after seeding of the pitch began in May 1954 Nevill Newitt resigned from the board, complaining that no-one involved in the project knew anything about building – and that the Roots Hall project was turning into 'a retrograde step'. He was just about the only person who thought so.

The shell of the east stand went up in early 1955 and covers for the west and north stands were erected by Norwich agricultural builders Boulton & Paul just a few months before the scheduled opening. The north bank roof extended only the width of the penalty area and the west side was initially covered only on the back half of terracing; the 180ft east stand too, was much shorter than it is today and was only extended at both ends 13 years later.

Plans to build flats for players over the entrances in Fairfax Drive and Shakespeare Road were thrown out by the council and pressure from women supporters club members for a creche behind the main stand fell on predictably deaf ears.

The ground was eventually playable in June 1955, although another £6,000 was needed from the trust fund for finishing touches. Preparations began for the first game on 20 August 1955 against Norwich, a gloriously sunny day.

The supporters club band marched from Victoria Circus to the ground, then played a programme of music before community singing from a 17,700 crowd and at 2.30pm the ribbon cutting ceremony by Arthur Drewry, chairman and vice president of the FA. Mayor Connie Leyland received a £1,000 cheque from local newsagent and long standing benefactor Teddy Grant which paid for the erection of the north bank; the donation now remembered by a sign behind the goal. Before the players came onto the pitch to play a game worthy of the occasion, a 3–1 victory, the ground was dedicated by Archdeacon Gowing, Vicar of Prittlewell.

The opening match at Roots Hall, captured by a supporter's 'snaps'.

A supporters club meeting in October 1956 revealed that the total cost of buying and then developing Roots Hall had been £73,997, of which two thirds had already been paid off and £5,000 came in the form of an FA grant. So far the trust fund had raised £44,795 and the supporters club fully intended to raise the rest as well. *'Our castles in the air at Roots Hall have materialised'* declared supporters club secretary Jimmy Hummerston, *'We are well on the way to owning the finest football ground in either the second or third divisions. We have a ground of which we can be justly proud for eternity'*. The extent of the achievement was recognised throughout football; *'Southend United might almost be termed the bravest club in England, for while all of us are seriously troubled with declining attend- ances they have taken the bold step of moving'* said a piece in a Millwall programme of the time.

Southend's dream might have come true, but there was plenty of work still to be done. Much of the enormous south bank was still tufty grass and bushes, and other areas of terracing were not yet concreted. The entrances and car park were a muddy morass, there was no way in for disabled people and a second barrel on the west stand roof had to be erected to extend it up to the pitch during the first season. It took Broomfield and his helpers another five years to complete the terracing and various odd jobs kept him going for the next 30. *'We've never really finished'* he admitted when he retired in 1990.

Of more immediate concern was the pitch, which had been underlain with cockleshells, ash, and diagonal drains every eight feet but was lying on such hard compacted rubbish that water still lay on top. Stones, glass and other pieces of rubbish would habitually shift their way to the surface and when it was wet the place would stink.

For the first two seasons it was undoubtedly the worst pitch in England, infamous after the 1956 cup game against Manchester City for being a mudbath where even marking out the lines was sometimes impossible. Midway through a game against Cov- entry, Jim Duthie had the sole of his boot ripped off by the mud on the pitch, yet chairman Bert Smith allowed a showjumping event to be held on the turf at the end of that first season. Things got worse during 1956/7. Sacks often had to be used to soak up the water before games, and jokes began to circulate that Roots Hall was beginning to look like Southend foreshore at low tide.

'Skilful soccer is impossible on the Roots Hall swamp' reported the Southend Standard in February 1957, just before a grass expert spent two hours examining the pitch without being able to find a single worm.

During the summer of 1957, on the advice of the Sports Turf Research Institute, the pitch was dug up so that drains could be covered with nine inches of clinker and a further four inches of topsoil. One workman paid a price for his labours when the drainage drill he was drawing through the undersoil hit an old submerged cooker and turned the machin- ery over, breaking his leg. His sacrifice, and the £6,000 the club spent on the new pitch, was well worth it, because the surface settled down soon afterwards and is today highly thought of. Some measure of the improvement could be gauged the following year when Roots Hall was chosen to stage an amateur international between England and Iceland. The game was eventually called off *'due to the serious condition of British Icelandic relations'*, which had reached an all-time low over fishing limits. But there was recompense two years later when the English amateurs beat Scotland 2-1 there on 26 March 1960 (attendance 10,750).

Cost had taken floodlights off the shopping list for some time, but by August 1959 foundations for pylons were being built. An over-run meant the lights were not ready for the first game of the 1959/60 season as planned, but on 31 August they were switched on for a reserves game against Charlton. A week later, with new loudspeakers also on the go, they graced Southend's first League floodlit home match against Mansfield.

Six years into the new ground's life total spending on the venture had risen to £100,268, but Roots Hall now offered some of the most impressive facilities of any third division club. The Daily Mail called it the *'seaside Wembley'* and Kevin Keegan later dubbed it *'the Wembley of the lower divisions'*.

The ground hosted another England v Scotland amateur international in 1966 (3-3, attendance 4,946) and during the same year go-ahead was given for the creation of a 400 stall open air market in the car park, one of the most important money spinning ventures of subsequent years. The 'Shrimpers' social club opened in the summer of 1967, and the trust fund, which had been renting the ground to the club while it continued to raise money, finally handed over the premises in 1968.

A September 1970 report by the local chief constable put Roots Hall's capacity at 35,000, yet it was never seriously tested during the club's first 20 years there. Even the record attendance there – 31,033 against Liverpool in January 1979 – left spaces in certain areas of the ground. Six years previously, in August 1973, proposals for a new £1.1m canti-

SOCCER MARKET!

Roots Hall market – born in 1966.

lever stand were flourished in the fevered atmosphere created by plans for a third London airport at nearby Maplin sands. Maplin would increase the local population by 600,000 said chairman Bill Rubin, and Southend would have the base to support a first division ground. Flushed with money from Peter Taylor's transfer, Rubin said the plans were *'under active consideration'* but they came to nothing when the Maplin proposals were shelved.

Five years later an ambitious plan for a 10,000 sq ft supermarket and 20,000 sq ft retail store on the car park was submitted for council approval, only to be turned down after much revision and general to–ing and fro–ing in 1981. That turned out to be the first of many battles between the club and council which raged throughout the 1980s to the present day.

On the May bank holiday of 1976 Roots Hall played host to a music festival compered by Radio One DJ John Peel and headlined by Fairport Convention, making their UK debut. During the Anton Johnson era Roots Hall also briefly became a rugby league ground when the blue and white of Southend Invicta began appearing there in September 1984. The first match, on a Sunday against Bramley, drew just 358 spectators.

Within three months The Guardian's rugby league correspondent was reporting that *'not even Sid and Doris Bonkers can be seen in the dark dank streets around the Roots Hall stadium'*.

Southend certainly wasn't fertile territory for the rugby league code – even though Invicta took part in the second division and boasted one of the most famous of all New Zealand players, Mark Elia, as well as Australian international John Donnelly. By the end of the season crowds had dipped below 150 and the club had already reached a precarious position by the time only 85 turned up to see a home game against Huddersfield Barracudas. The league kicked Invicta out of the competition in August 1985, citing worries about *'the organisation and promotion of the club'*.

The ground was later used for a floodlit cricket match between Essex and Surrey on 23 September 1987, and during the post Anton Johnson era when cash was short, complicated wranglings developed over plans to move from Roots Hall to a site in Sutton Road three quarters of a mile away. But for the ground itself the most significant and damaging development came in 1988 when work began on the construction of more than 300 flats on the south bank. The subsequent development robbed the ground of its prize asset – the huge 72 step kop which could hold 13,500 and had accounted for almost half its capacity.

Six fans were later banned from the ground by chairman Jobson for agitating on behalf of the *'True Blue supporters club'*, which was opposing plans for a move. But when club calculations in the wake of the Justice Taylor report suggested it would cost £8m to bring the stadium into line with the recommendations, the search for a new ground intensified.

Brinkmanship has been the order of the day ever since; a move to Basildon the ultimate, unbearable spectre for many of the club's fans.

Work in progress, and,
the completed new look South Bank.

Roots Hall is not the ground it once was, but for most it remains Southend United's natural home – the place first chosen through sheer convenience, reinhabited many years later through sheer coincidence. The longest serving of all Southend's grounds, the only one they have owned and the only one to have seen division two football, Roots Hall is above all living proof of what can be done when fans, players and directors all pull in the same direction. *'If there is a monument to the British football supporter it is Roots Hall'* said Simon Inglis in The Football Grounds of England and Wales, *'here is a ground built almost entirely through the efforts of a small but dedicated group of people'*.

Fire has broken out at Southend grounds on three occasions. A discarded cigarette was blamed for a blaze in the grandstand at the Kursaal during a September 1923 match against Newport County, and smouldering floorboards burst into flames there against Brentford on Easter Monday 1932. Both fires were extinguished without injuries, although the second re-ignited three times before it was quelled. In September 1938 fire also broke out in the buffet at the south end of the Sutton Road grandstand on a Wednesday afternoon, destroying most of the club's food supplies.

CHAPTER 8
THE MANAGERS
BOB JACK
July 1906 to July 1910

Southend's first manager was a Scot, born in the Clackmannanshire town of Alloa where he began his soccer career playing for Alloa Athletic. He joined mighty Bolton Wanderers before his 17th birthday in 1895, establishing himself as a fixture on the left wing there for six years before spending a year at Preston North End and a further 12 months at Glossop. He then executed a bold move away from the northern smoke to newly formed Southern League outfit Plymouth Argyle, the club which captured his heart.

He spent two successful seasons at Plymouth as a player, then another as player/manager before quitting after a disagreement with his directors. Moving was a wrench, but he was welcomed with open arms at Southend where he signed an initial one season contract as player/manager/secretary on 30 July 1906. Jack's reputation and experience after 11 years as a player in the top flight was important to the fledgling club, but his most lasting contribution was his eye for promising young talent. With limited resources at his disposal, Jack decided to tap the local footballing scene – and he came up trumps. His sharp eye spotted Leigh on Sea player Jimmy Axcell and Wanstead striker Harry Halse, both signed in 1906 then swiftly sold on to Manchester United.

Jack was respected as a man of honour, but was not averse to bending the rules when it came to transfer fees. Manchester United were prepared to pay far more than the maximum allowed fee of £350 for Halse, so Jack threw in the useful Axcell as a 'passenger' for a further £350, effectively boosting Halse's price to £700. No one could touch him for it, and he followed up with further business the next year when artistic former Southend Athletic left half Prince Blott, whom Jack had nurtured into Ssouthern League football, also went for a substantial undis-closed fee to Manchester United.

On the field Jack only needed to play a limited part in Southend's first ultra successful season, but displayed his talents to much more effect in subsequent years, especially during the club's initial sojourn into the Southern League first division. His veteran status, dead ball skills and surprising pace helped steady the more inexperienced players in many of the bigger games. He also made a name as a bowls player, becoming Essex singles champion while with Westcliff Bowls Club and later representing the English Bowlers (despite his Scottish blood) against the Scottish Bowlers in 1922.

At 32 Jack was still playing by the end of the 1909/10 season when a lucrative offer from Plymouth tempted him back to Devon. He stayed there as manager for a phenomenal 28 years, taking with him his young son David, whom he'd long tipped to play soccer for England. Ever a good judge of promising talent, he was right, but even Bob Jack couldn't have foreseen that he would eventually return to Southend for a brief spell helping out his son with managerial duties. After Jack senior had retired from Plymouth at the end of the 1937/38 season, David brought his father to Southend stadium during the spring of 1939 as a scout and 'outside representative' – once again given the job of exploiting local talent – until the intervention of the second world war.

Bob Jack was a hugely influential figure in the early days whose financial acumen and scouting ability did more than anything to help United survive the early traumas. And he did what no other Southend manager has done by taking the club to two championships – albeit both in the Southern League Division II.

GEORGE MOLYNEUX
August 1910 to February 1911

'Molly' was appointed player manager at the beginning of the 1910/11 season as much for his past deeds and standing in the club as for any latent managerial skills. The departure of Bob Jack left a hole which no-one except Molyneux had the stature to fill, but his six months in charge proved a setback for the blues; setting off a chain of bad results which eventually dropped them back into the scrappy, second class football of the Southern League division II.

It was unfortunate that the season Molly took Southend to relegation should also have been his last in first class football, for he was the most inspirational player of the early days. Though he came to Southend with his international career well behind him it would be difficult to over-emphasise Molyneux's contribution on the field. In the frantic pace of Southern League football he was Southend's steadying influence, a calm, resourceful player who preached and practised safety above all. On the pitch and in the dressing room he was a player to be looked up to.

Molyneux started his career in 1897 as a left back at Everton, where he was born, but failed to make the first team and left for Wigan County the following season. There he played in the Lancashire league, which he later described as *'the roughest league in the world'*, but made good enough headway to transfer back to Everton and establish himself, this time in the first team. Two years later he joined Southern League Southampton where he spent five seasons in defence, played on the losing side in the 1902 FA cup final at Crystal Palace, and won all four of his England caps. His international debut was against Scotland in the May 1902 Ibrox disaster. Molyneux was chasing Scotland's Bobby Templeton on a run down the wing when the huge wooden stand behind the west goal collapsed, killing 26 people and injuring another 500. Although the game was completed to placate the 68,000 crowd, the tragedy had a deep effect on Molyneux who held vivid recollections of the events until his death forty years later. He won his three other England caps the following year against Scotland, Wales, and Ireland. In his halcyon days Molly was a friend and Southampton defensive partner with the legendary all round sportsman C.B. Fry, who asked him to

pose for illustrations in his series of articles called *'Illegalities of Football'* published in the Strand magazine. There could hardly have been a more ironic choice, for Molyneux was always a scrupulously fair defender who rarely gave away free kicks and harboured a loathing for anything unsportsmanlike.

He left Southampton in 1905 for Portsmouth, where he played one season before joining the debutant Southend side in 1906 as a 31 year old. From the moment he arrived at Roots Hall he was a favourite, known even to the youngest supporter because of his England caps and admired for his guts in joining such a new, unproved outfit. His wages as skipper in 1906 were £2 10s a week, and he remained at the helm on the pitch until his retirement as player/manager in 1911.

By then he was 'slow but sure', his six foot frame still towering above the rest of United's short squad, lapping up the crowd's frequent renditions of *'Molly I love you'* but increasingly inconsistent. Also a local cricketer of renown – he opened the batting for Leigh on Sea – his player/managership was extremely disappointing for everyone, but it failed to dim the average Southender's appreciation for the talents of a man who remained as popular when he retired with a benefit in October 1911 as the day he had joined. His six months as manager were dominated by the intervention of directors, who would often select the team and treated him as something of a puppet.

After Southend, Molly played more relaxing football with Colchester Town, then turned out for the army during the first world war, when he was a private. A lifelong bachelor, he spent the rest of his days in Southend as an engineer at the corporation sewage works, where he worked until his retirement in 1940. He lived for most of those years at 225 North Road, watching Southend games regularly and living quietly with his faithful landlady 'Mrs Young', who nursed him when cancer of the tongue struck in 1942. One of the most popular of all Southend players, an all time great defender – though not a success as a manager – the much loved Molly passed away in obscurity that year. The only mourners at his funeral were his three sisters.

JOE BRADSHAW
February 1911 to April 1919

Southend's treatment of Joe Bradshaw was, if truth be told, fairly shabby. Only a year after joining from QPR as new player/manager, contemporary accounts said the still youthful Bradshaw had *'his heart and soul in the club'*. A shrewd businessman off the field and versatility itself on it, his keenness knew no bounds and during the 1911/12 season he played in every position for Southend, including goalkeeper.

He was a clever player, though inclined in his enthusiasm to hold onto the ball too long, and despite declaring in 1912/13 that he'd henceforth be concentrating on his managerial duties, still took to the field in 27 League and cup games that year, helping his side to regain Southern League first division status.

Bradshaw went through difficult times as a manager, dogged by constant board bickering and in 1912 a horrendous financial crisis which prompted a town appeal to save the club from extinction (see 'bad times'). But he came through it all with enthusiasm undimmed and was still turning out, 'in emergencies only' during the 1914/15 season overshadowed by war.

In May 1915 he joined up and left for France, still owed the considerable sum of £50 in wages by a club which effectively folded during the war. After surviving four years in the fields of France he began to write to the local Southend papers from his posting in Theux, Belgium, urging *'a quick resuscitation'* of Southend United and offering any help he could when he was demobbed.

Yet when he returned on leave in April 1919 Bradshaw discovered his old job had been given to an Arsenal backroom boy, Ned Liddell, that very week. Many in the town were upset that the old manager hadn't at least been given first refusal of the job, but there was little the ever courteous Bradshaw could, or would, do.

In many ways though, Southend's ungraciousness was a blessing. When Bradshaw was officially demobilised in June 1919 he was free to accept an offer to take up a more attractive managerial job at Swansea, who under his guidance reached the second division and the semi-final of the cup. His success there lured him away in 1926 to Fulham, a team his father Harry, once the driving force behind the Southern League, had also managed. During his three years there Fulham dropped from the second division into the third south and he finished his managerial days with a four year stint at Bristol City. Ironically he was replaced at Craven Cottage by Ned Liddell.

EDWARD 'NED' LIDDELL
April 1919 to April 1920

Though 41 year old Ned Liddell was appointed as secretary/manager in the aftermath of the first world war, he finished his one year term at Southend as the club's first out and out manager because Harry Flowers, former secretary of the Birmingham Works Football Association, took over his clerical duties in January 1920.

Despite his relatively free hand, Liddell's one season in charge – when United came 11th in the Southern League division I – was decidedly non-inspirational. He was a straightforward, upright man who by virtue of his age had stayed at home during hostil- ities to help out Arsenal, representing Essex twice against the army (once as captain) during that time.

Born in Sunderland, he took his first step into the big time when he was transferred as a player from Seaham Harbour to Southern League Southampton, then took another move up by signing for Football League second division team Gainsborough Trinity. After an uneventful season in Lincolnshire he took up with Clapton Orient, serving 6½ years there as a half back and eventually winning his highest honour in a representative match for London against Birmingham.

Taking over Southend immediately after the great war was a particularly challenging job for someone in his first managerial post, but Liddell managed to sign on a number of pre war players and to capture Welsh international Lot Jones. His work impressed QPR enough for them to offer him their managership at the end of 1919/20 and he took it, though rather too hastily. When Southend came back with a better offer, Liddell found his interest in the blues rekindled but discovered he was already committed and had to leave. Liddell said at the time that he hoped to return to the Kursaal.

So when things broke down with QPR four years later few were surprised to see him back giving help to the then Southend manager Ted Birnie. He stayed for the duration of the 1924/5 season before becoming manager at Fulham in 1925, a job he held well into the 1930s. In 1936/7, after a spell as a West Ham scout and years on the fringes of managerial activity, he finally left his mark, joining Luton as manager and taking them to the championship of division three south in 1937, at the age of 59. He left Luton the following year, but was still in the game as chief scout for Brentford at retirement age.

TOM MATHER
May 1920 to January 1922

When Liddell went to QPR, the Southend directors were flooded with applications for the manager's post. Yet they chose instead to poach someone – Tom Mather from Manchester City, who had been one of the back room staff at city's old Hyde Road ground but was looking for the security Southend were prepared to offer.

A Lancashire man, the permanently bowler hatted Mather had become the Bolton manager in 1915, promoted from assistant. But after serving with distinction in the Navy during the first world war – narrowly escaping death at the hands of Atlantic U boats – he was torpedoed by his old club when he returned to Burnden Park. Like Southend's Joe Bradshaw, he too had to find another club when he discovered there was no job waiting for him. *'There are no half measures about Mather'* enthused the Southend Standard, *'He is a young man with plenty of vision and push and go'*. But Mather fared none too well at the Kursaal, guiding the blues to a shaky 17th in their first third division south season, then becoming the first United manager to be sacked when he left midway through the disastrous 1921/22 re-election season.

He clearly had talents, as his subsequent career showed, but at Southend they didn't blossom. United presented him with a gold wristlet watch at his last game in charge against Worksop in the FA Cup, but sitting quietly in the stand at that game was his successor Ted Birnie, ready to take up the seals of office two days later. Fortunately Mather's most successful days were still ahead of him – particularly at Stoke City, where he became manager in

October 1923. There, in a reign which lasted 12 years, he made his name as the man who signed Stanley Matthews. Mather approached Matthews – a Port Vale supporter – at age 14, but the youngster was forbidden to sign by his father. Undeterred, he spent the next year charming his way into the Matthews household, making frequent 'social' calls, and eventually signing the boy on amateur forms.

As Matthews approached his 17th birthday Mather went to even greater lengths to get him on professional terms, setting up a constant watch in case other clubs made a move, and instructing scouts to check registration plates of any suspicious cars.

'Tom was really desperate and confided that the signature meant so much that if Stoke lost me he would be in for the sack' said Matthews in his autobiography *'Feet First'*. *'He was always an active manager but on those few days he was like a man with St Vitus Dance – until the morning of 10 February 1932 when my father said to me 'If you want to sign, Stan, it's all right with me'. If St Peter had smiled and said 'step through the golden gates to heaven' Tom Mather could not have shown more relief'*.

Mather's courtship – and eventual friendship – with Matthews continued after he left Stoke to manage Newcastle from 1935 to 1939. When Stanley became restless in 1935 Mather journeyed overnight, to no avail, with a blank cheque in his pocket. After the war he finished management with a year at Leicester City from 1945–6.

TED BIRNIE
January 1922 to April 1934

Ted Birnie, if he was still alive, could even now lay good claim to being the most successful of all Southend managers. Ironically his first six months in charge coincided with the ignominy of finishing rock bottom of division three south. In reality though, the re-election course had been carefully mapped out by Tom Mather, his predecessor, who handed Birnie a demoralised team halfway through the 1921/22 season.

For the rest of his tenure Birnie guided United to third division respectability, his copybook occasionally blotted by the odd failure, as in 1923/4 and 1926/7 when Southend twice finished 19th, but otherwise a record to be reasonably proud of. The club was still only 16 years old when he took over, yet by the late 1920s and early 1930s he had made Southend one of the better third division sides. Without an inexplicable nightmare spell over Christmas 1931 he should have taken them up to the second.

Ted was a popular figure with the burgeoning crowds at the Kursaal, a loyal, painstaking servant who turned down offers from other clubs and presided over an era of financial improvement.

As a player he gave long service to the game as a top class half back, beginning at Newcastle United in 1897 and staying there until he joined Crystal Palace for a season in 1905. After four terms at Chelsea, where he teamed up with the man who was later to became his influential trainer at Southend, Bill Cartwright, Birnie broke his leg. He tried a season at Spurs but his first class career was over, and after non-league football in the North East, a spell as player/manager at Newcastle City and the intervention of the war, he became chief scout at Roker Park in Sunderland, only yards from where he was born and trained as an engineer.

It was from there that he joined Southend, initially saddled with rather too much intervention from the directors, but less so as the board realised they had employed a canny, assiduous man who was also a fine judge of a player. He was a quiet unassuming character who prided himself on being 'economical' and cutting expenses to a minimum; a good enough accumulator of money to retire from the job in his middle fifties, though he was by then suffering from ill health and died five months later in the autumn of 1934.

DAVID JACK
May 1934 to August 1940

Southend could hardly have got themselves a bigger name in football than David Bone Nightingale Jack. In many ways his partnership with the club was incongruous – one of the greatest of all English players teaming up with a modest third division outfit. But it was Jack's local connections more than anything which persuaded him to make the move. His father Bob Jack was the club's first manager, and he was educated in Southend at schools in Hamlet Court Road and Leigh Road. His memories of the town were happy.

At 35 Jack had no managerial experience to offer Southend, but he'd served for six years at Arsenal under the legendary Herbert Chapman, the first great manager in football.

A number of other clubs were confident enough of his leadership qualities to make a play for him too, but Southend clinched the deal with a huge offer of £750 a year – then the highest salary of any third division manager and a reflection of the man's status in the game.

Status he had aplenty. Born in 1899, Jack hit all the heights of the game during the inter war years as an inside right for Bolton and then Arsenal. He captained England four times and won nine international caps, took home three FA Cup winners medals, won three first division championships and became the first player to score at Wembley, for Bolton in the 1923 'white horse' final.

His mesmeric skills, cool brain and deadly finishing put him at the pinnacle of the game for a decade, the graceful 'master player' of his era. But Jack had initially flirted with a career as a civil servant before starting rather late in 1919 at Plymouth Argyle, where his father was manager. Brilliant close dribbling soon attracted first division Bolton, who snapped him up the following year. He won cup medals in 1923 and 1926 as the star at Burnden Park, scoring 143 goals during his stay.

Jack's sensational £11,000 transfer from Bolton to Arsenal in 1928, the first ever five figure deal, was the starting point for a transfer market spiral, but Herbert Chapman spent his money well. The subsequent forward line of Hulme, Jack, Lambert, James and Bastin was probably the best ever to turn out at Highbury, winning the cup in 1930 and three League championships in 1931, 1933, and 1934.

When Jack decided to go to Southend in 1934 he'd scored 258 goals and won every honour in the game. Despite being a chain smoker and lover of chocolates, he was still fit enough to play, and could have made a significant contribution on the pitch at Southend as well as in the managerial office.

Playing in the League, however, would have compelled him to sacrifice his big salary for the £8 a week maximum players wage, and though he did appear in occasional friendlies and once turned out in a blue shirt during a cup game against Crystal Palace in November 1936, United fans were never given a proper display of his playing talents.

Jack's appointment in 1934 coincided with a clear-out of the board and a switch to Southend stadium, encouraging the fans to speculate about a brand new era of achievement.

A strict disciplinarian, the new manager declared rather optimistically that he wanted Southend to play like Arsenal, but in his first season he took the team into the re-election zone.

It was undoubtedly a case of expecting too much too soon, but in the end Jack's years at the stadium produced only mid-table form, his best show a 10th position in 1936/7. He was a keen scout, travelling often to Glasgow, where he reckoned the best players were – and one day cast his eye over 132 different players. But he lacked his father's player-spotting instinct and though liked and respected by virtually everyone, he was perhaps rather too gentlemanly, sometimes too aloof, to establish a real rapport with the younger players.

Jack always had a keen head for business and figures (it was said he kept daily records of how many times he could head a tennis ball), so when the second world war broke out he took a job with Barclays Bank in the City of London. United's playing affairs were shambolic in any case, and with the temporary move to Chelmsford, Jack – who had voluntarily cut his wages to £5 a week – felt happier handing over control to Harry Warren.

After a rather bizarre wartime move up north to control a dog track in Sunderland he accepted a more fitting post in 1944 as manager of Middlesbrough, whom he kept in the first division for eight years. He resigned in April 1952, leaving the game to run a pub in Islington, north London, only to return a year later to finish his managerial career with the Irish club Shelbourne, where he took charge from August 1953 to April 1955. Thereafter he worked once again for the civil service – as an official in the Air Ministry – and renewed his connection with Southend United as their part time southern scout shortly before his death at 59 in London on 10 September 1958.

Jack's son, Ronny, didn't inherit the family soccer skills, but became a successful journalist with the Empire News, Daily Sketch, and News of the World, writing under the name David R Jack and ghosting books by Len Shackleton and Matt Busby.

He emigrated to Australia in the late 1960s and died shortly after retiring in 1990, aged 65.

HARRY WARREN
August 1940 to June 1956

Harry Warren's father, Ben, won 22 caps for England in the days when international games were thin on the ground, but Harry himself was never anything more than a journeyman professional.

Ben Warren died of a brain tumour at 37 when Harry was just 11, leaving the family in financial trouble. Harry went to work in the office of the local pit near the Derbyshire village of Newhall where he was born, acquiring the administration skills that made him such a successful manager in later life.

Everyone always knew him as 'Genial Harry' – six foot, 18 stone, a huge bear of a man since a knee injury had forced him to stop playing at Folkestone. He got so big in later years that before a close season cricket match between United and Newmarket Town he took two pairs of flannels to his tailor with instructions to *'make me one pair big enough'*. The tailor, according to contemporary reports, *'didn't have a scrap of material left, which is not surprising knowing his fine physique'*.

When he was old enough he signed as a centre half for Sheffield United, but after spells at Blackpool and Notts County eventually joined non-league Folkestone as player/manager in 1931.

As a manager at Folkestone he made his mark immediately, transferring no fewer than 25 players to League clubs and developing a reputation as a finder of fine footballers who could be sold on with handsome profit. Feted at Folkestone as the man who put the club on the map, Chelmsford City then poached him in April 1939 as part of their drive to gain full League status, and it was by this chance that he eventually acquired the Southend job.

Southend approached Warren about a wartime groundshare just as he was settling in at New Writtle Street, and with David Jack relinquishing his managerial job it fell on Warren to run what had effectively become a merged Chelmsford/Southend team.

A genuine football enthusiast with vast energy for organising, Warren refused to draw a soccer salary during the war, busying himself with all sorts of administrative wartime duties outside the game. He worked for the Ministry of Food distributing food parcels to badly bombed areas of London, became a sports officer with the home guard and chief volunteer fire officer for the Chelmsford area – carrying out all his jobs with renowned good humour.

When the war was drawing to a close in November 1944 Chelmsford graciously gave Southend permission to take Warren as their permanent manager, and he formally took up office in August the following year having never really had a chance to devote his time to Chelmsford.

City's loss, however, was Southend's gain, for Warren ranks with Ted Birnie and David Webb in the Southend success stakes, a dominant figure who could have remained manager until he retired if he'd not opted to go to Coventry in 1956. The move was a mistake, because he never achieved quite the same status or freedom at Highfield Road; Jimmy Hill, who fitted in far better, knocked him off his perch a year later.

At Southend Warren had been accustomed to having the run of the place. He'd brought the club into a strong financial position and built up several United teams held in high esteem by the rest of the football League, finishing 3rd in 1949/50 and 4th in his final year. He was a popular figure with the fans too, larger than life and a bigger local personality than most of his players. Always immaculately dressed in dark blue suits and homburg, he had a gift for saying the right thing at the right time, and was generous and charming in company.

In the dressing room, where he often exhibited his harder side, Warren seems to have been less popular. He deliberately left team building and morale to his trainer, the kindly but tough former Arsenal and

England left back Wilf 'Iron Man' Copping, who must be given much of the credit for the immediate post war successes. Unlike Copping, Warren never watched from the dugout during matches, only coming down from the stand to talk tactics or deliver broadsides at half time. But he could still get the best out of a player, and was keen on giving his squad a better deal than he'd had as a professional, fixing many of them up with club houses.

When he was sacked by Coventry in 1957, Warren left football altogether and came back to Southend. He employed his immaculate bookwork skills at Bates, Son & Braby, a local firm of solicitors, and was often seen in the directors' box at Roots Hall. Sadly, he died one year short of retirement in 1968, mourned by many at the club who'd appreciated his happy vigorous style.

EDDIE PERRY
July 1956 to February 1960

No Southend manager had a harder act to follow than Eddie Perry, the gentle Welshman who stepped into Harry Warren's shoes.

Perry came with a high reputation borne of a successful playing career and a post war coaching spell at Fulham, where he'd helped take the club to the first division. He'd played as a centre forward for Fulham either side of the second world war with a period at Doncaster Rovers in between, winning three caps for Wales in 1938.

Born in Rhymney, South Wales, Perry flashed to prominence with Merthyr Town in 1929/30 when he signed as an amateur one day, took professional forms a day later, and was transferred to Bournemouth within 48 hours. After a season with Bournemouth he transferred to ill-fated Thames (the third division south club which collapsed after only two seasons), and ended up at Fulham in 1931.

During hostilities he was picked for two wartime internationals and played as a guest for Brentford in the first wartime London Cup final at Wembley in May 1942. Post war, after finishing at Fulham, the FA sent him as a player coach to Norway for two summers, trying to revive the game there in the wake of the Nazi invasion.

As coach then assistant manager at Fulham, Perry developed himself a good reputation by discovering future England captain Johnny Haynes.

But in truth he was probably more suited to scouting and coaching than the cut and thrust of management, and when he got to Southend he was shocked by the tight budgets of lower grade football.

Within months he was having to deny rumours of a rift between himself and the players, fuelled perhaps by his constant trips to look for new signings. Regarded as the most travelled manager in the country, he missed eight first team games on the trot while off scouting in 1959 and spent much of his time nurturing *'Perry's puppies'*, the fruitful Southend United youth team he'd started up in 1957. His record as manager was respectable enough, but when things began to look ominous in the first half of the 1959/60 season Perry decided to quit, claiming he had no cash to strengthen the squad.

The board denied his allegations, but accepted the resignation nonetheless. Perry was never a good communicator and hadn't helped his own cause by splashing out on Les Stubbs and Alan Dicks, both of whom couldn't hold down a first team place after signing in a joint £12,000 deal from Chelsea. With more than a suggestion that his heart wasn't in the manager's role, he left saying he would quit football for a job with 'more security'.

In fact Perry was back in the game within two months as chief scout for Fulham, a role much more to his liking.

FRANK BROOME
May 1960 to December 1960

After years of relative managerial stability, Frank Broome's short six month presence at Roots Hall marked the beginning of a decade of chopping and changing at the top.

Like other clubs entering the modern era, Southend were now expecting their managers to come out of the office and onto the training ground. Sound administrative skills and an eye for a good player were no longer sufficient; managers now had to be tacticians, motivators, and coaches.

Whether 44 year old Broome had all those skills was difficult to judge from his short time at the club. A former England winger who began his playing days before the second world war with Aston Villa, he won his first international cap against Germany in the infamous 1938 Berlin 'friendly', when the FA ordered him and his colleagues to give the Nazi salute during the German national anthem. Six more caps followed before war deprived him of any more, and he built his subsequent managerial career on his international reputation.

Broome joined United on a week–to–week contract after being released from his manager's job at Exeter City, and signed five new players before the season. But he had to rely largely on Perry's old guard for the start of the 1960/1 campaign.

His squad began the season poorly and was soon criticised on the terraces for lack of fight. Though Broome was the first manager to establish real familiarity with his players, calling them by their first names and injecting a dry sense of humour into the proceedings, he seemed powerless to inject the spirit Major Hay, his demanding chairman, wanted.

Hay sacked Broome without ceremony just four months into the season, claiming his time as a top player had left him out of touch with the harsh realities of the game. *'Frank would make an excellent manager for a team of internationals, but we're in the danger zone and it doesn't look like his policy will pay dividends'* he declared. *'We've had three internationals as managers at Southend – David Jack, Eddie Perry and now Frank Broome – and none of them have been successful'*.

Dismissal left Broome bitter and bewildered. He'd moved with his family to Southend and refurbished his house despite the fragile nature of his contract – claiming he'd been promised at least a season to prove his worth. *'I wouldn't have taken the job if I hadn't been given that promise'* he said afterwards, *'I don't know what they expect after only four months, I'm not a magician and I can't make silk purses out of sows' ears'*.

Disillusioned by his treatment and saddened by the death of his father a month later, Broome decided to emigrate to Australia, where he coached the Bankstown club to their best ever season. He'd first been to Australia with an FA team in 1952 while he was with Notts County, the club he then joined as trainer and subsequently caretaker/manager before moving to Exeter.

Popular and highly respected throughout the game, he was perhaps the first victim of Southend's growing impatience at not being able to get that elusive place in the second division. In 1967 he returned to Exeter as manager, taking the helm for two years.

TED FENTON
March 1961 to May 1965

Despite his well known views on the managerial capabilities of ex-internationals, chairman Major Hay brought in another former England player, Ted Fenton, to replace the luckless Frank Broome.

Fenton had been manager at West Ham since 1950, celebrating a decade at Upton Park with a book called *'At home with the Hammers'*. But his long connection with the east end club was ended abruptly a year later in the spring of 1961 when a succession of defeats sent his team tumbling into the bottom half of the first division. Smarting from the sack, and with the South-end job newly vacated, Fenton's application joined more than 40 others on Major Hay's desk.

Hay thought he was up to the challenge – and challenge it certainly was. When 46 year old Fenton took over, Southend were drifting dangerously towards a first experience of the fourth division, and the new manager had some nervous end of season puffs on his ever present pipe as United's fate hinged on results of other matches. A final 20th position in that 1960/61 season was the worst display of his four year stay, and subsequent placings at 16th, 8th, 14th, and 12th left him with one of the least inspiring managerial records.

Fenton's youth policy ensured some useful players like Frank Banks, and he brought one of the club's most exciting players, Eddie Firmani, to Roots Hall. But the Fenton era was dogged by affairs at the bank, and he had to transfer more good players than he signed.

Well liked by the players, some felt he wasn't determined enough to be a manager, but his successful years at West Ham had disproved that. He'd been a top pre war player at Upton Park, appearing in an unofficial wartime international for England against Wales and returning to West Ham as assistant manager in 1949 after managing Southern Lleague Colchester United in their famous run to the sixth round of the FA cup – when the mayor said he'd done more for the town than anyone since Boadicea. His brother, Benny Fenton, later managed Colchester from 1955 to 1963.

In the end, despite his achievements at West Ham and Colchester, Ted Fenton probably didn't have enough talent to work with at Southend – and the results showed. When his contract at Roots Hall was allowed to expire 'by mutual consent' he left football, taking a pub in the Essex hinterland and spending his spare time riding horses. He died in a car accident aged 77 in 1992.

ALVAN WILLIAMS
June 1965 to April 1967

There was no forgetting Alvan Williams. Love him or loathe him – and most loathed him – he made an indelible mark on the club.

An aggressive, highly strung man with a huge frame reminiscent of Harry Warren, he joined Southend at 32, one of the youngest soccer managers in the country. In 1964/5 he'd covered himself in glory as boss of Hartlepool by preventing them from having to reapply for re-election for what would have been

the sixth year running, and he hoped to achieve miracles for Southend too.

As an undistinguished, aggressive player in the early sixties he'd given some clues about his future managerial character as a hard tackling centre half and blaster of penalties for Bury, Wrexham, Bradford Park Avenue and Exeter City. Born in Anglesey, he became assistant manager with Bangor City from 1961 to 1963, engineering a successful run in the European Cup Winners Cup which was ended only by a play-off at Highbury against Naples.

Once described rather flatteringly as *'a Welsh version of Tommy Docherty'* Williams immediately imposed his strict, disciplinarian regime on Roots Hall. He reorganised the club from top to bottom, virtually ending its carefully cultivated youth section and demanding *'100 per cent fitness and enthusiasm'* from the players. Training became a nightmare of long runs and weightlifting, the football direct and uncomplicated; anyone who didn't knuckle down was weeded out of what he called Southend's *'untidy garden'*.

Exuding confidence, Williams was appointed 'general manager' within four months, but results hardly justified his new status. Many of the players refused to respond to his tempestuous style, and by the end of his first season United had dropped out of the third division for the first time, having recorded their worst ever defeat – 9-1 at Brighton – into the bargain. Against expectations Williams then failed to bring his overly defensive team straight back from the fourth, and as his two year contract approached its end decided to pre-empt any move from the directors by becoming manager of Wrexham. At the racecourse ground Williams did several transfer deals with United, but lasted only a year before a drink driving charge led him to resign

and hand over to his assistant, former Southend player John Neal who went on to manage Chelsea. By now 46, Williams then drifted to north London, where he took a pub called the Robert Lee. As licensee of the pub in 1978 he was charged with murder after a fight with a 19 year old student he had thrown out for drunkenness. The student died of a brain haemorrhage, but the charges were later dropped at the Old Bailey because witnesses accounts were deemed unreliable. In the end he received a 12 month sentence suspended for two years after pleading guilty to causing an affray, then moved to Croydon.

Williams had become Southend's first genuine track suit manager, and he'd injected some badly needed competitiveness into the side, but he was manager during a period of great discord and discontent and his explosive temper upset more than a few people along the way. The son of a vicar, he was rather too fond of brandy and coke and would hardly speak a sentence without a swear word – yet could turn on the charm when he wanted. As a player at Bradford Park Avenue he'd lived in a caravan, and some said he had a bit of gypsy in him. Light hearted rumours persisted for years that when he left Southend he'd put a curse on the club, preventing it from ever reaching the second division. If he did, it eventually wore off 25 years later.

ERNIE SHEPHERD
April 1967 to October 1969

'Shep' as he was known to all and sundry, had been coach and then assistant manager to Alvan Williams during his stormy time at Southend. When Williams left, he was asked to become caretaker, then signed a two year contract halfway through United's second season in the fourth division.

A qualified FA coach, Shep had actually been at United since 1959, joining Eddie Perry from Bradford Park Avenue as trainer. A Yorkshireman, he'd joined Bradford City

as a 16 year old amateur but made his League debut for Fulham on the last day before the League was suspended in 1939. In a 20 year career in which he clocked up more than 500 first class appearances as a forward he went on to play for West Bromwich Albion, Hull City and QPR, and once played in front of 120,000 in Germany for London against Berlin. Now free to implement his own ideas, he began rebuilding a youth policy using local club Parkside as a nursery team and putting his respected tactical brain to good use with the seniors. Williams's formation was rejected as *a numbers racket'* and the football became more pleasurable to watch.

The directors limited their new manager to a squad of just 16 players, so it was fortunate that Shep had a knack for good value signings. He was most proud of capturing Billy Best from Northampton for £3,000, but also paid just £5,000 for Chico Hamilton from Chelsea, £10,000 to Bedford for Bill Garner, and a trifling £100 for local boy and future England international Peter Taylor.

He certainly made money for the club in the transfer market, though many of the players were only cashed-in later on under Arthur Rowley. What he didn't do, to the disappointment of the directors, was take Southend back into the third. His team should have done better than sixth place in 1967/8 when a late season collapse threw away promotion, and the following year despite a huge goals tally and a 10-1 destruction of Brentwood in the cup, they finished one place lower.

When the 1969/70 campaign started badly, Shep offered his resignation, but ten years at the club counted for much and chairman Bill Rubin asked him to stay on as general manager with Geoff Hudson looking after the team. When Hudson was sacked three months later Shep returned to team affairs for two months before the arrival of Rowley.

Rowley's appointment prompted Shep's departure and a brief time out of mainstream football during which he managed Southend's premier amateur club Pegasus Athletic, now playing at Southend stadium. Within a year though, he'd moved westwards to second division Orient, where as physiotherapist and youth team coach he spotted and nurtured a number of fine players, including Laurie Cunningham, John Chedozie and Glenn Roeder.

In 1976, after six years dividing his time between Orient and his part time job as England youth coach with Don Revie, he left to take up a six month management contract with the United Arab Emirates club Al Wasl in Dubai. No club appreciated his talents more, and six months turned into ten years. Revie asked him to be his assistant when he defected from England to manage the UAE national team but Shep was happy at Al Wasl, guiding them to the League title four times until his retirement in 1986.

GEOFF HUDSON
October 1969 to January 1970

Geoff Hudson's time in charge at Southend was nothing more than an interlude – three months and 12 matches in all. Of those dozen games United won only three and lost six, disappearing out of the FA Cup against Gillingham and reaching 5th from bottom before Ernie Shepherd was called back as team manager. Two months into the job, ironically, he'd promised to resign if Southend didn't get promotion to the third by 1971.

As a player with Gillingham in 1963/4, Hudson had known what it was to win the fourth division championship. He'd gone there after periods at both Bradford clubs, Halifax, Exeter, and Crewe – then left to join Lincoln and eventually Rotherham, where he ended his playing career. Hudson notched up 337 League appearances in all, scoring just once and joining Southend as a fully qualified coach at the age of 38, after a spell as trainer/coach with Southern League Cambridge United.

ARTHUR ROWLEY
March 1970 to May 1976

All football statisticians know Arthur Rowley: he is the man who scored more goals than anyone. Born in Wolverhampton, he began with the reserves at nearby West Bromwich Albion and went to Fulham in 1948 as part of a joint transfer deal with Ernie Shepherd, the man he succeeded at Southend.

In his first 22 games for Fulham Rowley scored 19 goals, but in his second season he broke a bone in his foot and was sold on to Leicester in 1950 for £12,000. He paid back every penny by scoring an incredible 200 goals at Filbert Street in just six years there. Rowley brought forth all the adjectives under the sun in Tony Pawson's book *'The Goalscorers'*, where he was described as *'Big, burly, bustling, courageous, hard hitting, powerful in the air and lethal on the ground'*. But he still had his detractors – those who said he was slow and ungainly, and others who claimed he was a poor worker.

After Leicester he continued the goal trail at Shrewsbury, where he took up as player/manager and eventually became the only person to score 20 or more goals in ten successive seasons, beating Dixie Dean's previous best of nine. When he hung up his boots Rowley had scored 434 goals from 619 games, but had never been picked for England – unlike his brother Jack, who scored over 200 goals for Manchester United and won six England caps.

Rowley left Shrewsbury in 1968 after ten years, having taken them from the fourth division to the brink of the second. He became manager of second division Sheffield United the same year, building most of the team which reached the first division after he left under a cloud in 1969. Seven months later, aged 43, he joined Southend on £7,000 a year.

A quiet, even introverted man who was modest about his past achievements, Rowley took United back to the third in his second full season at Roots Hall but after three moderate seasons brought them back down again – and lost his job as a consequence.

By the last few months of his tenure, as United were heading for 23rd place in the third division, he was sharing managerial duties with coach Jack Burkett. Fans began a *'Rowley out'* campaign and the writing was on the wall. Throughout it all Rowley remained his characteristic, unemotional self.

When Dave Smith was appointed in his place the directors kept him on in a 'consultative' role and gave him a testimonial against Leicester City, but he was soon off – and spent the rest of his managerial career in the non-league world as assistant manager at Telford and manager at Oswestry Town in the Northern Premier League.

DAVE SMITH
May 1976 to June 1983

Despite Arthur Rowley's short term retention as a consultant when 42 year old Dave Smith took over in May 1976, it was made quite clear from the start that Smith was 'number one'. Anyone who'd come across Smith's extrovert, forceful personality knew there was never any question of anything else.

Smith had a long and fairly distinguished career playing for Burnley, Brighton and Bristol City before taking up coaching appointments with Sheffield Wednesday and Newcastle. He had tasted success at Sheffield Wednesday in 1966 when the owls reached the FA cup final and at Newcastle three years later when the magpies won the Fairs Cup. After a spell as Arsenal's reserve team manager he went into a full managerial job at Mansfield in 1974, leading them out of the fourth division as champions in his first season and taking them to the quarter finals of the League Cup.

Smith's feats at Mansfield encouraged Southend to approach him without even advertising the manager's job, and he accepted despite having to drop back into the fourth division. A tough, competitive Scot from Dundee – the first Southend manager from north of the border since Bob Jack – he soon built on his hard man reputation, using what the Evening Echo called *'an iron fist in a velvet glove'*. A good public relations man who always had a ready quip, he was above all a good man manager – prepared to be tough with those he thought needed it, but gentle and persuasive with those who responded in other ways.

After seeing his new team lose 3–0 to Tilbury in the Essex Professional Cup he accused them of being 'non–tacklers' and soon beefed up the defence, creating the most impenetrable of all Southend back lines and smashing several long held defensive records during his stay. Smith was also a believer in wing play at a time when the notion had gone out of fashion, but to some extent his eventual downfall was a persistent lack of goalscoring up front.

A good motivator who soon discovered how to establish a rapport with his players, he tapped into local amateur sides, re–establishing a relationship with Southend teams which had lain dormant for years.

Tenth position in 1976/7 didn't reflect the extent of the turn around he'd achieved with much the same squad as Rowley, but Smith was unflappable and continued his policy with success the following season when United went up to the third in second place. In October 1978 he signed a four year contract after months of procrastination, but after taking the blues down to the fourth again two seasons later was warned by chairman Frank Walton that his future was at stake. He responded by winning the club its first proper championship, running away with the fourth.

That achievement – plus 7th place in the third division the following season – must make Smith one of the top five best managers the club has had, but his record was sullied by the team's inability to make the third division its long term home once again. By the end of a disappointing 1982/3 season fans were calling for his dismissal, yet no–one really expected him to get the boot when he did. Smith was on holiday with his wife in Tenerife when a message arrived to say the board had sacked him; after seven years a victim more than anything of Anton Johnson's determination to make a mark on the club he'd just gained control over.

A typically determined Smith returned from his holiday to stage a sit–in at his office, eventually suing the club for damages and getting a pay off. Relegation the next season was comment enough on the effect his departure had on the players, but Smith himself went on to better things at Plymouth in 1984, where his lively bubbling style brought Argyle to within a whisker of the first division, before he left Devon in 1987 to manage Dundee briefly during the 1987/8 season. He then left football.

PETER MORRIS
August 1983 to February 1984

By strange coincidence the man who followed Dave Smith into the South-end managerial chair had also followed him into the manager's job at Mansfield.

A one time midfielder with Ipswich and Norwich, Peter Morris had taken over at Field Mill in 1976 when Smith left for Southend, going one better than his predecessor by lifting Mansfield up to the second division in the 1976/77 season – as champions of the third. Since then he'd been at fourth division Peterborough, narrow-ly missing promotion in each of the three years he was there, and at Crewe Alexandra during 1982/3 where he'd declined a new contract in the hope of getting a better job. On paper bringing in Morris was a good move for Southend, but this was the chaotic Anton Johnson era, and his six months at Roots Hall were night-marish.

Amid bitter recriminations over the sacking of Smith he arrived at Roots Hall a few days before the beginning of the season to find a squad of only ten players, of which two were goal-keepers. There was no money for significant signings, and he relied too heavily on the dwindling skills of ex first division players. By February 1984 the board had decided he must go, announcing that *'despite our wholehearted support he has failed to bring the team to the required stan-dard'*.

Morris was a laid back, unassuming manager in the mould of Arthur Rowley, given to practising with his golf balls on the Roots Hall pitch. But he was trying to do his job at a time dominated by brash, overpowering personalities in the boardroom. Dozens of more forceful managers would have struggled too.

BOBBY MOORE
June 1984 to April 1986

Jack Charlton aside, members of England's 1966 World Cup winning squad have been peculiarly unsuc-cessful as soccer managers, and Bobby Moore was no exception.

Moore's exceptional playing record was always going to boost expecta-tions above reasonable levels, but during his stay he witnessed the two most unhappy years in the club's history. One of the most revered England players of all time, lifter of the Jules Rimet trophy, and a foot-balling legend, it must have been hard to take. Certainly former players talk of his frustration at having to work in a lesser standard of football, of the poor communi-cation skills which eventually opened up something of a gulf between himself and the squad.

With the continual distraction of the Anton Johnson saga behind his back Moore presided over relegation in his first year and 20th position in the fourth division during his second. As with his predecessor Peter Morris, it would be wrong to ignore the effect of behind the scenes confusion on Moore's record,

though his only other managerial stint, at non-league Oxford City, saw few high points either. When he left Southend, age 45, it still came as a surprise; he had the backing of the board, but could not be persuaded against resignation with three games of the 1985/6 season left. His con-tract had more than two years to run but Moore wanted to go *'for personal reasons'* – which later turned out partly to be connected with a drink driving ban. He did admit, however, that *'obviously the position of the team might have influenced my pos-ition'*.

Moore spent the summer of 1986 on a working holiday in Mexico for the World Cup, then made his move into public relations, eventually switching to a loose form of journalism as sports editor of the controversial Sunday Sport newspaper.

His connections with Roots Hall were not severed entirely though – a few days after his departure as manager he agreed to serve on the board, a job he still holds to this day.

DAVID WEBB
June 1986 to March 1987
December 1988 to May 1992

David Webb was the man who achieved what all his predecessors couldn't, and for that alone he must go down as the most successful manager in Southend's history.

But Webb has plenty of other claims to the title. During his first spell with the club he was responsible for taking Southend back up to the third in 1986/7 (although he left shortly before the celebrations). And in 1989/90, during his second stay, he again took the club out of the fourth before going on to the second division. In just four and a half seasons at Roots Hall he gained promotion to a higher division three times.

In his first period at the club 46 year old Webb took Bobby Moore's signings and galvanised them into a winning outfit. He'd grabbed eagerly at the chance to resurrect a management career which, after promising beginnings with Bournemouth from 1980 to 1982, had reached a dead end at Torquay in 1984/5. Within weeks Southend were in promotion contention.

Webb's downfall at Southend, however, was his love–hate relationship with chairman Vic Jobson, a pairing at once productive and self destructive. With promotion almost assured in March 1987 Webb got involved in an ugly row with Jobson over money for new signings – and stormed out. Strong personalities both, neither would budge an inch, and a parting was inevitable.

Webb had been a strong willed, enthusiastic full back for Chelsea when he scored the winning goal against Leeds in the 1970 Cup Final, a member of their victorious European Cup winners cup team the next year and after 299 appearances in a blue shirt a player at QPR, Leicester, Derby and Bournemouth before taking over as manager at Dean Court in 1980. With appearances before his Chelsea days at Orient and Southampton he managed 553 games in his League career.

Those who'd worked for or played with him over the years knew Webb as a likeable but forceful Eastender unlikely to give way in any confrontation. But a year and a half after he'd walked out on Southend, Jobson and Webb patched things up; Webb again eager to get back into management after a period away from the game as a car salesman, Jobson keen to see his former manager's motivational talents back in harness. It was a rematch worth the effort, for within 2½ years Southend were in the second division.

Ironically Webb first took Southend down from the third to the fourth, although he inherited a team in poor shape midway through the season. From then on his enthusiasm and knack for inspiring loyalty brought a squad of young, competent, players to heights nobody had really expected of them.

Even in Division Two he helped the players blossom, and only another debilitating clash with Jobson as the season neared its conclusion marred a successful campaign which could even have seen Southend promoted for the third time running. Webb left United this time with a managerial reputation strong enough for him to be linked with some of the top clubs: a far cry from his unhappy departure in 1987, when he disappeared into temporary obscurity.

DICK BATE
June 1987 to September 1987

There was no stranger tenure than Dick Bate's. He stepped into his first full time manager's job with chairman Jobson's full backing as *'the ideal man for the job'* and stepped out ten games later with an appalling record behind him. Bate hadn't been expected to get the job in the first place, mainly because caretaker manager Paul Clark had just completed David Webb's preparatory work by taking United to the third division. But Jobson had been persuaded to look at the Notts County assistant manager by Sheffield Wednesday boss Howard Wilkinson, and liked what he saw.

Bate began his professional soccer career in 1963 playing for Sheffield Wednesday's youth team, but after three fairly unsuccessful years at York City decided to give up the game in 1968, working for a decade as a teacher. In 1978, after a spell as manager of non–league Buxton, he was offered a job as youth coach with Sheffield United, switching in 1980 to a full time FA coaching post in the North West. Five years later he joined Jimmy Sirrel's fourth division Notts County as first team coach, leaving the club as assistant manager after an offer of the manager's job was suddenly withdrawn.

Shortly afterwards he was at Roots Hall, admitting his main strength was on the coaching side but promising to create an *'entertaining, disciplined and organised'* team, then adding: *'I'm sure I can also adapt into management'*.

After a run of six defeats on the trot, starting with an 8–1 battering at Gillingham, a vote of no confidence signalled that the directors had soon come to feel otherwise. Bate was offered demotion to coach, which he refused, and Paul Clark stepped in as player manager.

Short though his reign was, Bate kept his name uppermost in the club's thoughts for some time afterwards by suing for compensation. Despite his double quick dismissal he'd actually been on a two year contract and had turned down offers from Torquay and the Malaysian national team to join Roots Hall. Later, after a spell as Leeds United's youth development officer under his old friend Howard Wilkinson, the Malaysian offer was renewed – and taken.

PAUL CLARK
September 1987 to December 1988

It was a case of second time lucky for Paul Clark when Dick Bate's departure handed him the manager's job. As caretaker player/manager after Webb's walk–out at the end of the 1986/7 season, Clark had helped the club reach the third division, and he was hoping the directors would give them appropriate recognition. They didn't, but when Bate lost his job after three months Clark eventually got the chance he had wanted.

At 29 Clark became the youngest boss in all divisions and the first Southend player/manager since Joe Bradshaw in 1911. A terrace favourite for his crunching tackles and a fine leader by example on the field, he'd begun as an apprentice at Southend after a sparkling schools career in Basildon which brought him England schoolboy and youth caps.

He moved to Brighton in part exchange for winger Gerry Fell in 1978 and played 79 games in the second and first divisions before returning to Roots Hall in 1982. When he became player/manager he'd already notched up 185 first team games for United,

and his fighting spirit began to rub off on the team. Though the disastrous form of Bates' time was hard to shake off, he made an almost immediate impact, when on the very day he took over, Southend beat Derby in the Littlewoods Cup (see games to remember).

The burden of managing and playing at such a young age was a heavy one even for Clark to carry, however, and his first season in charge was far from satisfactory as United avoided relegation to the fourth by the skin of their teeth.

Three months into the 1988/9 campaign Webb arrived as general manager; it was only a matter of time before he asserted control over team matters.

Clark remained to give sterling service in the surge to division two, but was tempted by a better contract to move to Gillingham at the beginning of the 1990/91 season, thereby missing out on a return to football at the higher level he'd once known.

123

CHAPTER 9
PLAYERS GREAT AND MEMORABLE

On the statistics alone, **Sandy Anderson** would have claim to being one of Southend's best players; the defender who appears in all the soccer annuals as the man who made most League appearances for the club. In fact he joined the team he served for so long almost by accident. A 5ft 10in red haired Scot, he played for Scottish junior side Newburgh FC before moving as a PT expert to Shoebury Garrison on the outskirts of Southend, from where Harry Warren signed him as a 20 year old in April 1950. National service continued to play havoc with his availability until demobilisation, but from thereon he established himself as an indispensable, if rather one footed, member of the side.

By May 1957, when the club rewarded Anderson with a benefit, he was already spoken of as a 'veteran', even though he was just 27. He missed two penalties in one match against Port Vale in April 1951, but continued as an occasional spot kicker throughout his career, scoring eight goals. Never a full back with excessive flair or imagination, he was a defenders' defender, thin but admirably fit, committed to safety first and a staunch club loyalist who clocked up 452 appearances before his retirement from the game. He played his last game for Southend, aged 32, on 17 November 1962 at Swindon, never playing for any other first class club, though he later appeared in non-league soccer in Kent and is still a regular, white haired spectator at Roots Hall games today.

Statistics are not everything, however, and left back **Jimmy Evans** – who played for United in the early twenties – would almost certainly have the strongest claim to the title of 'best Southend defender'. Evans, like Anderson, was a popular favourite – *'a splendid and wholehearted servant'* of United with a sunny disposition which endeared him to the fans.

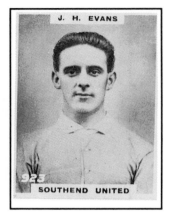

He played 3½ years for United after joining from his home club Rhyl in 1919, winning four international caps for Wales during his stay at the Kursaal and proving the mainstay of what was one of United's poorest ever squads.

As the star player Evans pulled in the princely sum of £4 a week in 1919/20, earning himself a ten shilling rise the following year when he became, of all things, Southend's top scorer. As a spot kicker he would signal to the referee from the back that he was about to take the kick, then would run straight in from his deep position without stopping, to crack the ball into the net. His 10 goals from the penalty spot in that 1921/22 re-election season put his goal scoring colleagues in the shade and his fearless approach made him a natural choice for Wales in the home championship games of early spring 1922. His debut against Scotland at Wrexham in February 1922 brought rave reviews, which were duplicated in his next game against England at Liverpool, even though he was played out of position on both occasions at right back.

On the field Evans was a hard tackling, ever willing player given to acrobatic clearances and 100 per cent effort, but away from the ground he was known throughout the town as an unassuming man with a penchant for clean living and abstemious habits; a stark contrast to some of his drinking, gambling colleagues. His £1,000 transfer to Burnley in April 1923 was a huge blow to manager Ted Birnie, who'd cleared out virtually everyone except Evans since the first world war and was now building his defence around him. Evans was not keen to go, but first division Burnley's reputation and the personal terms they offered him were good enough inducement. He played his last game for Southend away at Brighton, then appeared for one last time in blue at the Kursaal in a charity match.

Curiously, Evans failed to win any more international caps once he left Southend; after Burnley he moved on to Swansea in October 1926 before returning to Rhyl, where he finally retired in 1932. He remained in touch with the game well into the 1950s as steward of Rhyl supporters social club, where he worked for 30 years, and died in his beloved home town aged 81 in 1975.

DAVE ROBINSON TESTIMONIAL EVENING
TUESDAY, 21st APRIL, 1970

SOUTHEND UNITED F.

DAVE ROBINSON

No-one quite managed to step into Evans's defensive boots during the remainder of the inter war period but **Dave Robinson** matched him for effort. At ease either as a right or left back, Robinson had been a first division player with Leeds from 1922 to 1928 before moving to, and seeing out his playing days, at Southend, until a broken leg against Norwich forced him to quit in 1940. A tough little scot, he'd survived a breakage to his other leg at Leeds after playing on it for 40 minutes, and he played some of his best football at the Kursaal when he was an integral part of the 1931/2 side which came so close to the second division. Only 5ft 5ins, he was hard as nails, a first class exponent of the sliding tackle and nicknamed 'cannon ball Robinson' for his huge clearances. He began his football at junior south of Scotland clubs Lockerbie and

Eskdale, then played for Solway Star in the ill fated Scottish third division, which folded after just three seasons. He came down to England to join Workington, but played there just one season before being spotted by Leeds. A hard worker on and off the field, Robinson later became an institution at Southend, following his playing career after the war with 13 years as United's assistant trainer to the two Wilfs – Copping and Dixon – then the years up to his retirement as a member of the Roots Hall ground staff. In 1970 he was awarded a lucrative testimonial game against Aston Villa, and when he died aged 86 in August 1986 he was still doing odd jobs around Roots Hall after almost 60 years with the club. A minute's silence was observed in his honour before the game against Hartlepool immediately after his death.

The inter war years were also graced, if that is the appropriate word, with two of the most fearsome United defenders. Even in an era when most full backs were nothing more than 'stoppers' required to up-end anyone who got near them, **Dennis Thornhill** and **Harold 'Choppy' Wallbanks** instilled special fear among Southend's opponents.

Denis Thornhill

Thornhill, a left half, came from Wolves in 1948 and was known to the stadium faithful as 'the nutter'. A hard man who rather incongruously ran a neat little coffee shop in Sutton Road during the summer months, he was prone to aggressive behaviour even off the field. According to one popular story Thornhill provoked raised eyebrows and not a little embarrassment when, as an injured spectator during one home game against Plymouth, he bellowed from hushed terraces at his fellow players to 'take out' the Argyle goalkeeper, who'd been forced to become an outfield player after breaking his arm earlier in the match. 'The nutter' felt his defensive colleagues were allowing the shaken, virtually useless keeper too much leeway.

'Choppy' Wallbanks was widely believed to have acquired his nickname because of his frightening tackling, but it almost certainly came from his appropriately named birthplace, Chopwell in County Durham. Harold was one of five footballing brothers, known collectively as the 'choppy chappies', who played for various professional clubs from 1929 to 1948. He joined Southend from Fulham in 1949.

Frank Sheard was in much the same mould; a pugnacious, thick-necked centre half with a bull terrier build. A one time RAF police officer, Sheard became something of a cult figure in the post war years at Southend, known for his prodigious sliding tackles, loved for his uncompromising style, but not always given full credit for his tactical nous. His greatest achievement was bottling up the great Tommy Lawton in the 1947/8 season against Notts County, but the performance which most epitomised his character was against Bournemouth, when he took a kick in the mouth requiring ten stitches but refused to leave the field and reduce his side to ten men. Skipper McAlinden described him as *'the bravest centre half I had the pleasure of playing with'*.

Peter Watson

Sheard's eventual successor was **Peter Watson**, perhaps the best third division centre half of the early to middle sixties, and a United ever present until vision problems brought on by a fractured jaw put an end to his career at the beginning of the 1965/6 season. Watson transferred to Southend in 1959 from Nottingham Forest, where he'd been a player since coming through the youth XI. He played 45 League games in his first Southend season, clocking up 263 appearances in all competitions for United during six subsequent campaigns, and building a reputation as a true 'club man'.

At 6ft 1in Watson was commanding in the air, like his brother Dave, who went on to play for England in the same position. A thorough, sometimes dour defender who soon became an inspirational skipper and crowd idol, his limitations were occasionally exposed by classier players, but Southend were thankful on many occasions for his steady control of the back line. It was said of him that if he ever

stayed down he would be needing a stretcher, not a sponge, so it was ironic that his career came to a premature end after his injury during a short summer tour of the Netherlands. He was so fast and so naturally fit that everyone had expected him to continue for years to come, and without him United were relegated to the fourth division for the first time. Blighted by double vision, Watson tried a comeback in October 1966 but managed only three games before another knock spurred doctors to advise retirement. After a benefit game between Southend and an international managers XI he moved back to his native Nottingham.

The central defender of the 70s and 80s was undoubtedly **Alan Moody**, whose huge number of appearances for Southend came over 11 years at the club and gave him United's highest appearance total of 506 games, although he played six fewer League games than Sandy Anderson. Once a ball boy in the 1966 world cup game between England and Argentina, Moody was bought from Middlesbrough in 1972 and immediately settled in well, first under Arthur Rowley and then Dave Smith. Always a man who appeared to play within himself, many thought he could have progressed to a higher grade of football if he'd had more ambition, but no-one at Roots Hall had cause to bemoan his failure to move on. More than being a great defender, Moody was the best penalty taker Southend ever had. By 1978 he'd scored 24 goals from the spot in 27 attempts – almost always in the right hand corner just inside the post – and he went on to bag many more goals for the club by the time he retired in 1983. He even created a club record by scoring penalties in four consecutive League matches in April 1976. At his testimonial game against West Ham in May 1983 6,000 fans came to say goodbye.

In more recent years **Paul Clark** established himself as the crowd's favourite; a dogged, ever-safe defender much in the mould of that other eventual player/manager George Molyneux, who served United from 1906 to 1912, the best defender of the early days, and like Clark able to command his area of the pitch despite being short on pace (see managers).

Of United's goalkeepers none could have been more popular than the much loved eccentric **Billy Moore**, custodian in the late twenties and early thirties. Born in Sunderland, Moore joined Southend from Leeds in June 1925 and made himself the crowd's favourite with his asides and practical jokes for more than a decade. Something of a hearthrob as well as a character and comedian on the field, he always wore his trademark red jersey and cap between the sticks; a dashing and acrobatic keeper (if sometimes erratic), whose bravery eventually brought him one too many injuries. He was also keenly protective of his reputation, so protective in fact that when he was sent off for a goalmouth incident in 1932 he took off his jumper and tied it round his face to avoid the shame, much to the largely concealed amusement of the crowd. Also an excellent pianist, he carved a name for himself away from the game tinkling the ivories in local clubs, and was by all accounts the life and soul of any party.

Moore was first onto the team sheet throughout most of his time at Southend, earning a joint end of season benefit match with Jack French in April 1931 against Everton, during which the great Dixie Dean acted as linesman because he was not fit enough to play. The following 1931/2 season Moore began to show the first signs of mortality as he was dogged by injuries for most of the campaign. He was back as an ever present the next year and was the oldest servant of the club in 1935/6 when injuries began to hit again. New manager David Jack confined him to the reserves by bringing in the younger and more proficient Eire international keeper **George Mac-Kenzie**, who dominated the scene for many years to come. Moore left football, with 304 Southend games under his belt, to earn his living back in the north east as a shipyard worker.

Moore could have no complaints about being ousted by MacKenzie, who was almost certainly Southend's best ever keeper. MacKenzie was first spotted by David Jack in 1933 playing Scottish junior football, but with Southend then reliably served by Billy Moore, he tipped off his father Bob, who was managing Plymouth Argyle. MacKenzie signed for Plymouth on condition that Southend would have the option on him later.

His chance came with Moore's injury in 1936 and he seized it firmly in his first season. Incredibly small for a keeper at 5ft 7in and just under ten stone, he was nonetheless cool as ice and created such an impression that he was soon tipped for international honours.

Though he was brought up in Scotland, MacKenzie was born in Ireland and by the end of the season was picked for the Eire squad with team mate and Southend centre half Charles Turner. MacKenzie went on to become the player to win most international caps as a Southend player, nine in all, before his last game against Germany in 1939. His first caps came in two 1938 World Cup qualifiers against Norway, then against Poland and Czechoslovakia – followed by matches against Sweden, Poland, Hungary and Germany in 1939.

Charles Turner's Eire debut against Switzerland was followed in 1937 with matches as skipper against Germany, Hungary, Switzerland and France; five caps in all while he was at Southend. After leaving Southend in 1938 he played with MacKenzie in the World Cup qualifiers but made only one subsequent appearance for Eire, bringing his eventual caps total to ten against Hungary in 1939. A relentless stopper and quick mover who joined Southend from Leeds in the summer of 1935, Turner put in some masterly performances for Southend, notably against Spurs in the momentous FA cup 4–4 draw at White Hart Lane in 1936.

Ted Hankey

After the second world war **Ted Hankey** stole many headlines and became a crowd pleaser before six footer **Harry Threadgold** made the keeper's job his own, joining Southend from Sunderland in 1953 and retiring ten years later in 1963. Threadgold, who served with the marines during the war and was a useful boxer, turned professional with his local club Chester in 1947, and spent only a year at Sunderland before his surprise move to United.

Not the best, but perhaps the bravest keeper United ever had, he was as wholehearted as they come, suffering so many head injuries that some claimed he was a little punchdrunk by the time he packed up to become manager of the Ship Hotel on Southend's Eastern Esplanade. He was once left out of the team at his own request because he didn't like playing under floodlights.

Harry Threadgold

Of modern keepers, **Mervyn Cawston** has the best record. He completed 985 minutes at Roots Hall without conceding a goal during the opening months of the 1980/1 season – ten whole matches, plus 85 minutes, with a clean sheet. During that remarkable campaign he also conceded just six home goals and kept a Southend record of 25 clean sheets.

Jimmy McAlinden

Further up the field, **Jimmy McAlinden** must surely have been Southend's greatest ever player – inspirational skipper, midfield general, soccer artist, Southend loyalist and international footballer of repute.

Like so many of United's best players, McAlinden hailed from Ireland, where as a teenager he played for Belfast Celtic, won an Irish cup winner's medal, two international caps for Northern Ireland in 1938 and 1939, then moved across the water to play for Portsmouth .

One of the many players of his generation whose careers were robbed of their peak years by the second world war, McAlinden's finest moment came as a 21 year old when he played in the Portsmouth team which beat Wolves 4–1 in the 1939 cup final (the year Wolves players were given monkey gland injections to make them perform better). Cruelly deprived of a stage for his young talents over the next seven years, he returned from Ireland after the war to re–sign for Pompey as a 28 year old inside forward. Amid the turmoil of post war football he was picked twice by Eire in 1946, who played him against Portugal and Spain before he won his third cap for Northern Ireland against England in 1947.

He played at Fratton Park for the 1946/7 season, but then moved on to play for a year at Stoke City before signing with Southend in October 1948.

Though now 31, McAlinden's arrival at Southend caused great excitement in the town, for here was a man still capable of producing high class football. His transfer fee of £6,500 – then a Southend record – was fully and immediately justified as he showed skills seldom, if ever, demonstrated by a Southend player. Despite his wasted war years – or perhaps because of them – 'Jimmy Mac' was now in many ways at his peak, and the Southend crowds appreciated it. A top earner and star on the pitch, he was ordinariness itself in the town – a very quiet, church going man who shared club 'digs' with a number of United players during his stay by the sea.

An outstanding, cultured passer of the ball who always wore the number eight shirt, McAlinden no longer had the pace of his early days, but he still had a vision rarely seen in the third division. A strong, impish 5ft 8in, he was not a great goalscorer, except from the penalty spot, and preferred the role of provider, suffering throughout his stay at the stadium from having to work with players who only occasionally displayed his shrewd tactical awareness.

During McAlinden's first season, when he won his fourth and final Northern Ireland cap, also against England, far too many of the openings he created were wasted in front of goal, but it was no coincidence that the following season, under his guidance, United came within a whisker of reaching division two. In subsequent seasons as skipper he led them to 7th, 9th, and 8th in the third division south before a disappointing 16th in his last campaign – and when he missed 11 games in 1950 through suspension over illegal payments he'd allegedly received at Portsmouth, chairman Nevill Newitt described his loss as 'a staggering blow' (see bad times).

The fans knew Jimmy Mac was a 'proper footballer' and it was often said that he was too good for Southend, but he only wanted to move if it meant a better grade of football – offers from other third division clubs were regularly turned down. Only when the player/ managership of Northern Ireland's Glenavon came in April 1954 did he decide to leave. After his last game at the stadium (a 4–1 victory over QPR), manager Harry Warren led the crowd in three cheers as he walked off the pitch to thunderous applause. *'His displays will long be remembered by home supporters whose tribute to a great player now in the twilight of his career was spontaneous and from the heart'* said the Southend Standard.

The second of United's three great post war Northern Ireland players was **Sammy McCrory**. McCrory started at Windsor Park for Linfield in 1944, then moved two years later to Swansea where he scored 20 goals in their promotion year of 1948/9. Ipswich paid £18,000 for him in a double transfer deal with Jim Feeney and he later went to Plymouth for £6,000 before joining Southend in June 1955 for £1,000.

From then until his transfer to Southern League Cambridge United on 1 July 1960, McCrory made a huge impact on Roots Hall, like McAlinden an intelligent distributor of the ball but also a prodigious poacher of goals and a great header of the ball. Lightly built but assertive in front of goal, he made 222 appearances and hit the back of the net 99 times for United, scoring 11 goals in 39 games during his final 1959/60 season. In March 1956 he also scored what was almost certainly United's fastest ever goal, after ten seconds against Crystal Palace at Selhurst Park.

He will always be remembered, though, for his extraordinary international debut in November 1957, which he made at the age of 33. The rest of the United squad were there to watch him score a breathtaking long range goal at Wembley which gave Northern Ireland a sensational 3-2 victory against England – their first for 30 years and only their 5th since 1882. He'd given 12 years and three stone in weight to Duncan Edwards, one of the greatest footballers in the world at the time, but he outshone him.

The papers called it 'Sam McCrory's day' and for a short while he was the centre of unaccustomed press attention. Then the oldest player to win his first cap for Northern Ireland, the journalists labelled him *'the forgotten man of football'* which proved an appropriate tag, for despite being chaired off the Wembley field by his colleagues, McCrory never won another cap for his country – even though he was picked for the World Cup party for Sweden the following year. He eventually returned to Northern Ireland in 1962, where after a spell as player/manager at Crusaders he decided to retire from professional football and set up a pub in Belfast's Shankill Road.

United found a 16 year old local boy called **Bobby Kellard** they thought could replace McCrory as an inside forward. Kellard, a pupil at Fairfax High School, actually made his debut as a left winger while McCrory was still playing in October 1959, at the time becoming the youngest player ever to turn out for the blues. His progress was spectacular, immediately establishing himself as a regular and playing that same year – as an enforced amateur because of his age – in a trial for the Great Britain olympic games team.

A mercurial player, Kellard never quite matched the successful heights of his sparring partner Terry Venables, the Dagenham schoolboy he played with for Essex. But he was a third division star at Roots Hall, making 113 appearances and scoring 17 goals before leaving for Crystal Palace. He made a name for himself at a succession of clubs thereafter, including Portsmouth, Ipswich, Leicester City and Bristol City, where he was signed for a record £30,000 in 1968 by manager Alan Dicks, himself a former Southend player.

Ron Pountney had one of the biggest hearts of all Southend players, a 5'6" midfield action man who gave nothing less than maximum effort throughout the whole of his ten successful years at the club. Stylish with it, he was enthusiasm personified; as keen on the training ground as on the pitch itself.

On the other hand he was extremely unselfish, a generous creator for others who could have scored many more than 35 goals if he'd been prepared to have a go more often himself. It was his finishing instinct which first persuaded Arthur Rowley to sign Pountney from Bilston, the non-league midlands team he'd turned to after playing just one League game for Walsall. He arrived at Roots Hall in January 1975 determined to make full use of his second chance, and ran his way into the affections of all United fans after a season settling down.

Pountney's best football was played under Dave Smith, with whom he struck up a profitable father–son relationship.

Smith made Pountney his player of the year for six out of the seven seasons he was manager, and he won the supporters player of the year award a record three times. As a pivotal member of the 1980/1 team which won the fourth division championship he became one of the few Southend players ever to take home a championship medal.

Always a happy, chirpy player, Pountney was never the complaining type, even when he dropped out of favour under Bobby Moore. But he took the decision to give him a free transfer at the beginning of 1984/5 very hard, and was even more hurt when his scheduled testimonial against West Ham, which had been postponed because of a fixture clash, was never re-organised. After 349 League appearances he drifted into non-league soccer, playing for a number of Essex and Kent clubs, including Chelmsford and Basildon, and now works as a painter and decorator.

Of the out-and-out attackers, few at Southend could have been more devastating than **Harold Halse**, the small centre forward from Leytonstone who alas only served the club for two seasons before being snapped up by Manchester United in 1908. His phenomenal 91 goals in Southend's debut campaign came from a huge number of games, but he was prolific nonetheless.

When the fans learned of his transfer there was huge disappointment and crowds fell significantly in the following weeks.

Halse began his playing career at Wanstead before switching to Southend, and was moved to inside right at Old Trafford – a sign of his versatility. He scored two goals for England against Austria in 1909, his only international cap, and represented the Football League once in 1908 and twice in 1911.

Always an opportunist, he also scored six in Manchester United's 8-4 win against Swindon in the same year, only the third time the feat had been achieved up to that point.

After winning a cup medal with Manchester United against Bristol City in 1909 – the first former Southend player to do so – he won another for Aston Villa against Sunderland in 1913, then appeared on the losing Chelsea side in the 1915 final. After the war he ended his League career with Charlton, from 1921 to 1923.

Only **Jim Shankly** reached comparable goalscoring heights for Southend before the second world war, though he was never in Halse's class. The brother of Liverpool legend Bill Shankly, Jim set a club record in 1928/9 of 35 cup and League goals in a season, a record which held until Sammy McCrory matched it 29 years later. A former Sheffield United player, he was prone to scoring in bursts between injuries and was a collector of hat tricks. Yet for all that he was never a crowd pleaser and was towards the end of his career often the target of crowd barracking.

Roy Hollis

After the war **Roy Hollis** stood out above the others, in more ways than one. A tall gangling centre forward of the middle 1950s, he was top scorer three seasons in a row from 1954 to 1956 and remains the club's biggest collector of goals, with 135 during his seven years at Roots Hall.

A native of Great Yarmouth, where he began his soccer career playing for the town club, Hollis was signed by Harry Warren in 1954 from Spurs after a previous spell at Norwich, and was fortunate at Southend to be able to feed first off the service of McAlinden, then McCrory.

Although his talents were recognised by selection for a third division representative game in 1956/7, he was known rather harshly in some circles as 'gormless Hollis', a reflection perhaps of his awkward, stiff legged style which lulled many opposition defenders into a false sense of security. But he was nothing if not goal hungry, held the line together extremely well, and with inside right Kevin Baron formed one of the best frontline partnerships United ever had. Hollis could miss the easiest of chances – and he was certainly not pretty to watch – but he put away enough to land himself in the Southend hall of fame.

Sixties star **Eddie Firmani** was in a different class altogether, even though he was on the way down when he reached Southend. Born in Cape Town, South Africa he left his native country to start a football career at Charlton in 1950 and became the first British based footballer to leave for Italy.

At Sampdoria he became the idol of Genoa, receiving more than 100 fan letters a day at the peak of his popularity, when he also represented Italy as a centre forward. After success at Inter Milan, who signed him for a colossal £88,000, he wrote a 1959 autobiography called *'Football with the millionaires'* – and returned to Charlton four years later a much wealthier man.

Firmani signed for Southend after two years at Charlton in June 1965, smashing the club record with a £10,000 transfer fee and top scoring in the 1965/66 relegation season with 20 League and cup goals. Always an intelligent, charismatic player, he found lower division football rather too easy, even with reduced mobility well into his thirties, so was not impressed when he found himself unable to hold onto a first team place in the following fourth division campaign. He was never a good trainer, though, and a rift with the other players developed when they discovered just how much more he was earning than they were. In March 1967 he went back to second division football with Charlton as player/manager for a fee of £2,000.

Peter Taylor

Peter Taylor was perhaps the best locally produced Southend player since England star Andy Ducat came out of Southend Athletic shortly before United were born. Known during his Southend days by his schoolyard nickname 'Spud' Taylor hailed from Rochford where he was spotted at King Edmund Comprehensive School. He was initially signed on schoolboy forms by Crystal Palace, who let him go, then was rejected by Tottenham at White Hart Lane. Ironically both clubs were to pay huge fees for him later in life after he'd got the start he needed at Roots Hall.

Southend signed him as an apprentice just a few hours before his 17th birthday and he made his first team debut at the age of 18 against Barrow. During the 1972/3 season he finally began to make an appreciable impact as a mazy winger full of potential, if not yet producing consistently brilliant performances. When flamboyant Crystal Palace manager Malcolm Allison moved in for him in October 1973 he made an offer Arthur Rowley couldn't refuse – a club record £120,000.

At Palace, Taylor tasted second division football for a season, only to fall back with the side to the third at the end of 1973/4. Such was his impression on the game, however, that he became one of the few third division players ever to be capped by England – four times in all – during the 1975/6 season, two against Wales, plus one each against Northern Ireland and Scotland. After three seasons at Palace he joined Spurs for £200,000, but was never capped again.

In 1977 Taylor returned to Southend to open a sports shop in Hamlet Court Road, but when he finished with first class football turned out for Chelmsford City and then became manager of Dartford. He is currently assistant manager at Watford.

One man who played against Peter Taylor on the internatonal stage was **Derek Spence**, the third in the triumvirate of great Southend players from Northern Ireland. Spence, in fact, was probably the best forward to play for Southend, winner of 29 international caps, 16 of them as substitute, and scorer of three goals for his country. More than that, he was a hugely enthusiastic individual who spurred on the players round him to better things, willing to do almost anything for anyone off the field and a great supporter of local charities.

All bar five of his Northern Ireland caps had been collected by the time he joined United from Blackpool in a December 1979 swap for Colin Morris, but while at Roots Hall he went on to play Israel, Austria, Scotland, Sweden and France. His first cap came at Bury in 1974/5, winning another eight caps there before moving to Blackpool for the 1976/7 campaign. At Roots Hall he was named player of the year by the fans in the record breaking 1980/81 season and the next season played during the summer for See Bee in Hong Kong. Spence also turned out for Olympiakos in Greece and Crusaders in Northern Ireland, and eventually returned to Bury in 1983/4 after making 113 appearances and scoring 34 goals for Southend.

Lot Jones became the first Southend player to claim full international honours when he filled the inside left spot for Wales against England at Highbury in March 1920, helping his side to their first victory (2–1) over the English since 1882. He'd already won 18 Welsh caps while at Manchester City (the first in 1905), and took his tally to 20 at Southend before leaving at the end of 1920 for managerial jobs at Aberdare, Wrexham, and eventually Oswestry. Before the first world war **Lionel Louch** had won his 8th cap as an amateur international for England while at Southend in 1914.

In June 1953, United signed 24 year old **Douglas Young**, an English amateur international and Walthamstow Avenue full back who made 40 appearances for the club. **Tommy Scannell**, whose son Tony stars as DS Roach in the TV soap 'The Bill', made one appearance for Eire in 1954, against Luxembourg, while on Southend's books. Scannell's only other representative game was for an Eire XI against Celtic.

Like most lower division teams, United have signed several former internationals over the years, with varying impact. **Fred Watkins** of Wales and **George Molyneux** of England were the first two, brought in during the club's debut season, though the former was not a successful signing. Watkins' best days were with this three previous clubs – Leicester Fosse, where he made his Welsh debut in 1898, Aston Villa, where he won his 3rd and 4th caps in 1900, and Millwall, where he played his last (5th) game for Wales in 1904. Ex Clapton Orient outside left **Owen Williams**, one of the fastest players of his time, joined United in 1930 from Middlesbrough with two English caps during 1923 and 350 first class appearances to his name. He fared marginally better during his stay, but 5ft 8in full back **Jimmy Nelson** proved to be Southend's most useful former international during the inter war years.

Nelson joined United at David Jack's behest in June 1935 at the age of 34, by then the holder of two FA Cup winners medals with Cardiff City in 1927 and for Newcastle United in 1932. He'd also won four caps for Scotland – against Wales and Ireland in 1925, as captain of the Scottish 'Wembley Wizards' who thrashed England 5–1 in 1928, and against France in 1930.

Appointed Southend skipper from the off, he immediately struck up a solid defensive partnership with his compatriot David Robinson, a double act which stayed intact until the second world war. After hostilities, when he retired from soccer, Nelson managed the Spread Eagle pub next to Roots Hall (which was owned by Southend chairman Bert Smith) until taking his own pub, the Greyhound Inn at Cardiff.

T. MARTIN

In 1937 Jack also signed **Tudor Martin**, a former Swansea centre half who'd been capped once for Wales against Northern Ireland when playing for Newport County seven years earlier but made little impact for Southend. He'd previously turned out for West Brom, went from Newport to Wolves for a substantial but undisclosed fee in 1930 and joined Swansea in 1932.

Goalkeeper **Norman Uprichard** won 18 caps for Northern Ireland, but played just 12 games for Southend after signing in 1959 from Portsmouth. He won 13 of his international appearances at Pompey, the other five at his previous club, Swindon, and took part in the 1958 World Cup in Sweden. A broken arm sustained early on at Southend severely restricted his effectiveness, and he was released after making no impression in May 1960.

In September 1967 former Manchester United and Northern Ireland inside forward **Sammy McMillan** joined Southend from Wrexham, where he'd been for four years, in one of several lease-lend arrangements set up by the club with former Southend manager Alvan Williams. At Manchester United McMillan had won two caps for his country against England and Scotland in 1962/3.

The following year Scottish international keeper **Lawrie Leslie** came to Roots Hall on a free transfer from Millwall at the age of 33. Leslie started at Hibernian, but won his five Scottish caps at Airdrieonions during the 1960/1 season.

From there he moved south to West Ham, then to Stoke and finally Millwall, where he was brought in to replace Alex Stepney. Totally fearless, he reckoned to have broken nearly every bone in his body during his career.

Former Ipswich star **Trevor Whymark**, who'd won a single England cap against Luxembourg in the 1977/8 season, made his debut for Southend against Bristol Rovers in January 1984, and a year and a half later in July 1985 **Frank Lampard**, who played twice for England while at West Ham, joined for a brief spell at the end of his career. In September 1983 **Les Cartwright**, six times capped by Wales while at Coventry and Wrexham in the early 1970s, joined Southend on a loan spell from Cambridge United.

In 1991 assertive defender **Pat Scully**, who'd made one full appearance for Eire while at Arsenal as a substitute against Tunisia in 1987, signed on for United after a loan period, going on to become a key member of the team which made it to division two. Webb also brought in **Kevin O'Callaghan**, who was picked 20 times for Eire while at Ipswich and then Portsmouth.

Peter Taylor and Harold Halse weren't the only players who went on to win international honours after leaving Southend. **Reg Davies**, who was transferred from Southend to Newcastle for £10,000 in April 1951, left Harry Warren to rue what might have been when he went on to win six Welsh caps up to 1958/9.

Despite his young talent, Davies had spent most of his time at Southend in the reserves, partly because his favoured position was occupied by Jimmy McAlinden. **Phil O'Connor**, who made one full appearance for Southend in the 1969/70 season, later played for Australia in 1983.

Cultured left half **Dougie Wright**, who played for Southend in the 1936/7 season was transferred to Newcastle in May 1938 for £3,000 and played for England the following year against Norway, his only honour – despite being the idol of St James Park just before the war. He picked up serious wartime injuries to his leg at Dunkirk but returned to Newcastle in 1946 and the great Len Shackleton, in a moment of extreme generosity, later claimed he had been *'twice as good as Bobby Moore'*.

Dougie's father **John 'Jocky' Wright** was one of Southend's most loved early players, brought to the club at age 27 in 1908 by his friend Bob Jack, whom he'd played with at Bolton and Plymouth. Jocky, who played on the left wing at United, was actually picked for England when he played for one of his other previous clubs, Sheffield Wednesday, but was dropped at the last minute when officials discovered he was born in Scotland.

He retired after two years at Southend, working as a coach painter on Southend Corporation trams for many years until he died during 1946 at his house in Roots Hall Avenue, next to the site of the pitch he had once graced. His other son Billy Wright also played professional football for Bolton and Reading.

The other father and son pairing to have played for Southend was **Bob and David Jack**, though David's first team appearances were restricted by the wage limit on players.

After the second world war half back **Jack French**, nephew of the powerful Jack French who played before the war for Southend, followed in his footsteps by signing for United after being released by Middlesbrough – now managed, coincidentally, by David Jack.

Jack French junior was a much admired player, a little short of pace but skilful and more of a ball player than many half backs of his day.

In April 1948 he featured in a fateful Army Cup Final replay at Aldershot as captain of the Royal Armoured Corps against 121 Training Regiment, when two players were killed by lightning. French was taking a throw-in as the lightning struck, knocking all the players, officials and most of the 6,000 crowd to the ground. There was no rain or any sign of the impending flash before the fatal incident and as casualties – many of them temporarily blinded – were taken to hospital, the game was abandoned. Among the spectators was Southend manager Harry Warren.

In 1952 French signed for Nottingham Forest, where he had a successful time before a debilitating injury kept him out of the side. He returned to Southend for another season but was then forced to retire and became player manager of Basildon in 1957.

Two sons of famous footballers have also turned out for United – **Len Goulden**, offspring of 1940s Chelsea and England star Roy Goulden, who played as an inside forward – the same position as his dad – for Southend in 1961 and **Danny Greaves**, son of Jimmy Greaves, who was forced out of the game by a horrendous knee injury in 1989. Jimmy skippered an All Stars XI at Roots Hall in Danny's 1990 testimonial.

Some Southend players made bigger names for themselves in other fields, like England and Essex cricketer **Trevor Bailey**, who was born and bred in the Southend area, played for United reserves as an amateur, and eventually became a director of the club until 1966. Bailey, along with fellow Essex and England batsman **Doug Insole**, played for the reserves while at Cambridge University but with the added distraction of cricket eventually opted for senior amateur football at Walthamstow, with whom he won an amateur cup final winners medal at Wembley in front of 100,000.

Fellow Essex post war cricketers **Terry Kent** (one appearance) and **Gordon Barker** (61) also played for United, as did **Stan Montgomery** (100), who played for Glamorgan County Cricket Club.

Montgomery, who was the son-in-law of Jimmy Nelson, joined Southend after the second world war from Hull City, skippered the team on a number of occasions, and left for first division football at Cardiff in November 1948.

Of those who went on to make waves in football management **John Neal**, future boss of Wrexham (1968–77), Middlesbrough (1977–81) and Chelsea (1981–85), played 111 times for Southend between 1962 and 1965 and **Alan Dicks**, who managed Bristol City for 13 years up to 1980, played at Roots Hall before starting his managerial career as coach/manager to Jimmy Hill at Coventry in 1962. United keeper **Don Mackay**, who played 15 games

for the club from 1972–74 at the end of his career, went on to manage Dundee (1980–83), Coventry (1984–6), Blackburn Rovers (1987–91) and is now in charge at Fulham. **Chris Turner**, who appeared at Roots Hall during the 1980s, has managed Cambridge United and Peterborough, and **Kevin Fallon**, who made four League appearances for Southend, went on to manage the New Zealand national team just after the 1982 World Cup. In 1985 former blue **Dave Cusack** became Doncaster manager, lasting two years until a move to Rotherham. And in 1989 **Colin Morris**, the former winger who made 133 appearances for United, became boss of fourth division Scarborough.

Frank Walton

Frank Walton, on the other hand, became that rarity in football; a player who eventually took over as chairman of the club he once played for. A competent left back for Southend in the 1940s, he made money in insurance when he left the game and took control of the board in 1978.

Youngest ever United player was **Bobby Haddrick**, who made his debut on 14 October 1966 at 16 years and 177 days – weighing in at 13 stone despite being only 5'9½". First black player was Barbados-born **Micky Welch**, who made his debut in February 1985, and made a total of five appearances. Most gutsy were **George Falconbridge** who played occasionally in the 1920s despite having sight in only one eye, and **Cyril Thompson** who spent five years in a German prisoner of war camp before signing with Southend in 1946. Thompson didn't begin his career until the age of 27 but became popular at the stadium for his attacking play and was transferred to Derby in 1948.

Two years later he moved to Brighton, shifting to Watford in 1952 and finishing his career at Folkestone where he scored more than 100 goals. A Leigh-on-Sea man, he later worked as a British Rail electrician and died at the relatively young age of 53.

Southend goalkeeper **Trevor Roberts**, who succeeded Harry Threadgold between the posts in the sixties, died young too.

Trevor Roberts

A university man and Welsh amateur international who was eventually signed for Liverpool by Bill Shankly, Roberts was taken by a brain tumour as a 30 year old in 1972, echoing the tragic death at the same age of fellow United keeper **Charlie Cotton** in 1910 (see early days).

Kevin Baron

A year before Roberts' death, one time United skipper **Kevin Baron**, Southend's 'mighty atom' of the late fifties, died in Ipswich aged 45. A former Liverpool player, he'd made 138 League appearances for Southend between 1954 and 1958, scoring 45 League goals before signing for Northampton. His brother Gerard died in tragic circumstances too – at 67 he was the oldest victim of the Hillsborough disaster in April 1989.

H. WILEMAN

325 SOUTHEND UNITED

Another former Southend skipper, **Henage Wileman**, took his own life in 1926 by poisoning himself with disinfectant. Only 36 when his body was discovered on the banks of the River Trent in Nottingham, Wileman had separated from his wife, was out of work and depressed.

At Southend before and after the first world war he'd been a player of 'dauntless spirit'. Sturdily built, he scaled 12 stone despite his 5ft 6in frame and was signed by Joe Bradshaw in 1911, top scoring in his first two seasons with 17 and 27 goals. Wileman was rather taciturn and gruff, but to those who knew him intimately he was straightforward, loyal and kindly. In 1919 at Northampton when he failed to equalise with a last minute penalty he refused to speak all the way home, and if he had a weakness it was that he didn't take to misfortune well.

There was, alas, much misfortune in his life. Apart from marital problems he suffered the death during the first world war of his brother, who played for Luton, and his soul mate at Southend, Archie Wilson, both of whom were killed in France. After a December 1920 benefit game which drew 10,000, he made his last appearance for United on Boxing Day 1921 when he twisted his knee so badly he could never play again. Shortly afterwards, he drifted up to Nottingham after an unsuccessful spell as licensee of the Hare and Hounds in Stoke Newington, north London.

In August 1924, 22 year old new signing **Archibald Jackson** poisoned himself when he drank half a pint of his landlady's 'spirit of salts'.

Jackson, who hailed from Gourock near Glasgow, had only been in Southend a few hours when the incident happened and was reported dead in some London papers, though he survived after hospital treatment. The youngster claimed he'd drunk the poison by mistake, but unsympathetic Southend directors took a dimmer view – they slapped a permanent suspension on him for trying to commit suicide.

Other former United players remain in the fans' consciousness for no other reason than the pleasure they gave during their stays at the club. The goalscorers are, naturally, always remembered – like the quiet, reserved **Dicky Donoven** who started with Nottingham Forest and Mansfield Town, where he scored 118 goals in three seasons, before joining United for the 1925/6 campaign.

Brett Angell

Or **Billy Hick**, the hard, uncompromising forward who like 1990s hero **Brett Angell** scored in seven consecutive League games in 1927/8; **Ernie Edwards** of the same era who ran a stall at the Kursaal where he invited punters to knock down three skittles with a Southend United football; the handsome **Fred Baron**, who took up a tobacconists shop at the Kursaal in the late 1930s after his playing days at United and Liverpool; and winger **Harry Lane** who played before and after the second world war, known as the 'corner king' for his nasty inswinging corners which he sometimes even scored from.

After the second world war there was **Joe Sibley** who went to Newcastle and back, and nice guy **Frank Dudley**, who played from 1946–49, joined Leeds United and later headed Southend council's

cemeteries department after leaving the game. Later still there was the naturally talented individualist, **Ian 'Chico' Hamilton**, snapped up by Ernie Shepherd for a bargain £5,000 from Chelsea as an 18 year old. He'd been the youngest player ever to play for Chelsea as a 16 year old under Tommy Docherty, then was christened 'Chico' by Dave Sexton *'because he thought I was cheeky'*. He later went on to play for Aston Villa and Sheffield United.

John McKinven

Other favourite of the sixties was the exciting **John McKinven**, a long serving former 'Busby Babe' who joined Southend from Raith Rovers on a free transfer in 1960 and left for non-league Cambridge United in 1969, after 286 League appearances and 62 League goals for the blues, narrowly missing Irish international honours during his period at the club. One of the most wholehearted players of the same era, **Tony Bentley**, joined from Stoke City as a right winger in 1961 but finished up a full back and coached football at Thorpe Hall School.

In the early seventies there was livewire **Billy Best**, who hated training but top scored three seasons in a row up to 1972, and became only the second United player to have scored more than 100 goals for the club (123) before going back to Northampton, and **Bill Garner** an inconsistent, fiery tempered six footer bought from Bedford Town and sold onto Stamford Bridge for £80,000.

Billy Best

Micky Stead made 341 appearances altogether after signing from Spurs in 1978 for £50,000 and **Anton Otulakowski** became a player of tremendous vision who later packed up through a bad knee injury.

In the 1980s tiny **Richard Cadette**, originally from non-league Wembley and one of United's first black players, defied the tall lumbering defenders of the fourth division, setting games alight with his breath-taking goals. And **David Crown** made himself into a scoring machine before disappearing to Gillingham. All have served with distinction even if the fortunes of their team have not always shown it.

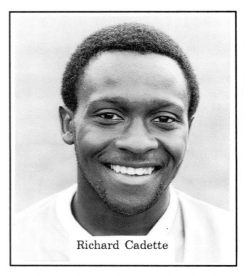

Richard Cadette

Mickey Stead

David Crown

CHAPTER 10
HELPING NOT HINDERING

Not many supporters clubs would merit more than a few lines in any team's history, but Southend's is different. Almost from its inception, the Southend United Supporters Club was one huge success story.

There had been a supporters committee in the early days, formed in 1909 to make contributions to players' summer wages, but by the 1920s, a victim of the first world war, poor organisation and indifference, it had fallen into abeyance. When a small band of enthusiastic fans tried to rekindle interest in the summer of 1929 they found little initial support but after putting a notice in the programme during the autumn were surprised when their inaugural meeting in the Clarence Hall on 16 November 1929 was packed out. The new supporters club adopted the motto *'To help – not hinder'*, affiliated itself to the Federation of Supporters Clubs and voted schoolmaster Charlie Benson – who was one of the linesmen in Southend's first match – as its first chairman, though he soon gave way to architect Nevill Newitt.

Early supporters club chairman, and later chairman of the football club itself: Nevil Newitt M.B.E. G.M.

Within two weeks the new club had swung into action, providing stewards and turnstile operators for a match at the Kursaal against Brentford on 30 November 1929 and laying on its first away excur-

sion to Clapton Orient on the 7th December. By Christmas it had organised buses to games from outlying districts like Rayleigh, Rochford, and Shoebury, and membership had shot up to 550 in just over a month. Later that season it took 360 fans across the Thames to the game against Gillingham on a hired boat called The Prince of Wales, and began entertaining players before home fixtures.

It was a dynamic start which the close knot of friends who ran the club wanted to build on. By the end of February 1930 the mainly female entertainment committee had laid on its first dance and staged its debut whist drive, the successful mainstay events of the club's money raising activities for the next 30 years. People began to join just for the social events and by the end of its first half season, when Benson was able to hand United a sizeable £125 cheque, membership stood at 800. In October 1930 the Federation of Supporters Clubs decided to hold its annual conference in Southend in recognition of the burgeoning interest in the town.

Progress from then on was swift. In its first full season the supporters club took charge of compiling, printing and selling the four page programme, adopted full control of catering arrangements at the Kursaal, and set up a *'Penny on the Ball'* competition in which the owner of the winning number got to keep the match ball. It bought and operated a new half time score board, built two new tea bars, and raised enough money to cover the Kursaal's west stand, all with an entirely voluntary staff. The appetite for work was enormous, the involvement in the club's affairs unprecedented, and the United directors couldn't believe their luck. They voted chairman Nevill Newitt to the board in 1933 and during the following years he became the fans advocate as chairman of the United board itself. *'The supporters club is the greatest asset the club ever had'* he said in 1934, the year he was instrumental in moving the club to the Stadium.

HOME from HOME
A CUP OF TEA LIKE MOTHER MAKES AT
The Supporters' Refreshment Buffets

INJURIES.

As usual we had a crop of injuries during the practice matches, the most serious being sustained by Russell, an amateur residing in the Borough. He had the misfortune to crack the left arm bone during the final practice match, We are glad to state that the arm is going on well and we hope he will soon be able to play again, and at the same time we extend to him our sympathy in his misfortune.

Hall is the only player on the books who has not been able to report fit for to-day, but it is expected he will make his initial appearance for the Club on Wednesday next v. Coventry Res..

LUCKY NUMBER PROGRAMME

The draw for the Football will take place at half-time as in past seasons.

Membership grew dramatically in the thirties as United went through some relatively successful years on the field. By the beginning of the 1935/6 season membership was up to 3,107; by October of the following year Southend was widely credited with having *'the largest and most powerful supporters club in Great Britain'*. Brimming with funds in 1937, the club became the first in the country to move into its own fully licensed social club and headquarters, at the old Southchurch unionist club in Sea View Road, Thorpe Bay, fully equipped with resident steward and four billiard tables.

Luxurious HQ apart, the club was never allowed to detach itself from the ordinary fans, and during the depression years it would regularly raise money to provide free tickets for local unemployed people. As late as March 1938, 120 unemployed men enjoyed a home game against Crystal Palace courtesy of the supporters club, but soon afterwards the footballing authorities put a stop to such hospitality on the grounds that giving away free tickets did not conform to the rules. The club continued to give much of its money to local charities, won two prizes in the Southend carnival, and gave valuable financial support to local amateur football teams.

When the King announced the declaration of war the following year, United's players listened to his speech in the dressing room on a wireless set donated by the supporters club. But even the hostilities failed to curb the club's activities – the members who remained behind channelled their fundraising efforts into sending parcels of cigarettes to British troops – 100,000 fags in all.

It was after the war, in fact, that the supporters club saw its greatest days. Under new chairman Charles Clenshaw, a local confectioner, the post war soccer boom increased membership to almost 6,000, and although Ipswich was now temporarily claiming the biggest membership of any supporters club, Southend was still firmly at the top when it came to financial contributions made to the host club. By 1949 United had already accepted more than £25,000 in cheques when a new challenge was thrown down – to build Roots Hall.

The supporters club set about its task with characteristic vigour. By 1952 it had £16,000 in the specially created Roots Hall fund, even though it had raided £2,000 from the kitty during the previous March to help United cover losses caused by a fall in attendances. Whist drives and dances continued apace, and the creation at the beginning of the 1952/3 season of a 40 strong Supporters Club Band – the only one of its kind – added further fundraising potential with appearances at the Cliffs Bandstand and other venues. The band also occasionally provided entertainment at away matches.

In the end, the supporters club almost singlehandedly raised the £74,000 to build and develop Roots Hall. To all intents and purposes it was their ground, and until the trust handed it over to United in 1968 was the only enclosure in the country actually owned and bought by the fans themselves. More than that, the intense community effort which the supporters club had spearheaded contributed to a genuine family feeling at Roots Hall which persisted for many years.

The unique Southend United Supporters Club band in action.

Those who stood on the terraces singing 'Abide with Me' at the opening Roots Hall game felt they had contributed, in however small a way to what they saw in front of them – and that must have been a significant factor in making Southend one of the best supported third division clubs for the next two decades.

As part of its commitment to the town as a whole, the supporters club also put up money to start football broadcasts to local hospitals, pioneered by commentators Bert Heigho and Wally Jones. The first broadcast, on 23 August 1956, took advantage of a new Roots Hall commentary box at the back of the east stand and a direct GPO line to Southend General Hospital. From there it was 'rediffused' through the wards onto the ordinary radios sets, then by private line to other hospi-

tals in the area. Match programmes were delivered to the bedside by the supporters club, who raised the initial £120 a year costs jointly with Toc H. Later broadcasts of Southend games were taken all over the country, notably in the 1957 third round tie against Liverpool when 29 Merseyside hospitals received the commentary.

By the time Roots Hall had been completed, the supporters club was claiming a phenomenal 18,000 members, thanks mainly to a weekly pools competition which had begun generating £10,000 a year for the trust fund. At its peak in 1957 there were 20,000 members, once again making the club the biggest in the country, and by the end of the 1961/2 season every last bit of the ground had been paid for.

Two years later the club declared it had raised £200,000 for United since its inception, but that figure seemed to become something of a watershed. With the breathless Roots Hall campaign over, the by now ageing leading lights of the supporters club were making ever more urgent appeals for younger fans to step forward. In 1966 a Southend Youth Supporters Club was formed, and two of its members, Peter and Alan Bushell, spent over 4 years filming the life and times of the club for a full length 'feature film' called *The team we call United'*, shown to fans at the Shrimpers Club.

The overall momentum, however, was difficult to maintain – and in March 1967, with membership sliding to 7,000, new United vice–chairman Bill Rubin dealt what was to be a fatal blow to the club's chances of reversing the decline by appointing a Southend United commercial manager, Harold Rumsey. To the supporters club's dismay, Rumsey's job was to take over the key functions which had always been the preserve of its members, like catering and programmes, – with a view to making money directly for the football club itself. To those of the older generation, like supporters club vice-chairman John Woodcock, who pronounced himself *'amazed'* that the club wanted to get rid of volunteer staff and replace them with paid workers, it was a baffling decision. But for Rubin, who saw the supporters club as an anachronism, it was a way of putting United on a more professional footing during a time when football was becoming big business.

For the supporters club, whose band had now also lost their pre-match musical slot, it was the beginning of the end. With its money raising activities hijacked and with a 1973 FA ruling which deprived the club of its right to run the pools competition, it was only a matter of time before it faded from view. Similar organisations throughout the country were in a compatible position, but by 1973 the Southend supporters club shop was rarely open, and members

---

Southend United Football Supporters' Club —— Nº 04742

MEMBERSHIP RECEIPT 1954-5
Expiry date—7th May, 1955

NAME (block letters) W. Frost

ADDRESS 185 Greenswood Lane Hockley

SUBSCRIPTION s. d. Received by

1:0

This receipt must be produced when claiming Competition Prizes

Peter (left) and Alan (right) Bushell film the 'Team we call United'.

could manage only a £2,000 donation to club funds – small money compared to the halcyon days. *'It hardly warrants our existence'* admitted gloomy financial secretary Cecil Henderson. *'Without a supporters club there would have been no United'* said Woodcock, but no-one was listening.

An injection of young blood came in 1974 when 24 year old Mike Bailey became the youngest ever supporters club chairman, but he effectively presided over its death. Three years later in 1977 it was announced that the supporters club was to be 'reactivated' yet the new version was largely a creation of the football club and it didn't inspire loyalty from the fans. There was no recreating the original, tightly knit body of people.

With hindsight the supporters club may have been guilty of over generosity. On top of the thousands it handed over, the hundreds of voluntary hours working turnstiles, pouring cups of tea and compiling programmes, the supporters gave away their biggest asset – Roots Hall. And they got nothing in return. In all its time the supporters club bought just over 800 shares in the club; nowhere near enough to exert any influence in the boardroom, despite the presence of several ex-supporters club members over the years.

Some still believe much more of the money should have gone into buying a controlling interest in the football club rather than propping up transfer deals and paying overdrafts. At least one director often advised them to do just that, but the advice was never taken. From any standpoint the supporters club was a glorious success but with a little more foresight it could have created a momentous precedent. The Southend fans, more than any others in the country, had a chance to run their own club, but they didn't take it.

CHAPTER 11
BAD TIMES

The bad times have been mercifully few at Southend, even though bigger clubs might sometimes have looked down with pity on a team so stubbornly confined to the lower regions of the League.

On the field of play there has been the odd woeful season or two, but unlike many teams Southend have never experienced a sustained period of failure lasting anything more than three seasons. For most of their footballing life United have given the fans a run for their money, even if they havn't always delivered what they have promised. They've been a steady, undramatic club, neither under-achieving nor playing above themselves, not sleeping giants, not perpetual minnows.

On the financial side, in a game where mere survival is often the priority, Southend have indeed, survived – most of the time with relative ease, but occasionally not without a fight. They have walked the tightrope on more than one occasion, but have only twice come close to folding altogether and their support has, until recent times, been reasonable considering the club's limited achievements.

Without the bad times, in any case, it is difficult to appreciate the good ones. Southend's misfortunes have nearly always ushered in a new era of relative success, which is reassuring in football because the next bad time is usually just around the corner.

****

Re-election

It's hardly to Southend's credit that they've been up for re-election twice, but they can take some comfort from the fact that other more illustrious teams, like Crystal Palace and Norwich City, have been in a similar position on a greater number of occasions – and that 60 other clubs have had to apply for re-election at least once in their lifetime. In any case, it is now 57 years since United last put themselves in danger of slipping out of the Football League.

In truth, both of United's re-election bids – either side of Ted Birnie's time as manager – were far less dramatic affairs than everyone had expected.

In 1922 there was certainly more anxiety. The club, after all, was only 16 years old and into just its second season with the new third division south. At one stage non-league Pontypridd were staging such a bullish campaign that the Southend directors began to feel more than a little nervous about the forthcoming result. Yet when the Football League announced the results at noon on 30 May 1922 United came top of the voting with 36 votes, four ahead of fellow third division strugglers Exeter City, who polled 32.

The vote of confidence in the club proved a turning point, encouraging locals to contribute to a mayor's fund for new acquisitions and allowing Ted Birnie to execute a beneficial clear out of players and training staff. The Southend Pictorial Telegraph reflected the general relief and sense of pride;
'This satisfactory culmination to weeks of anxiety was not brought about without much hard work and personal influence' it said.

The playing record for 1921/22 was: played 42, won 8, drawn 11, lost 23, goals for 34, goals against 74, points 27 – with the side finishing 22nd, an appreciably worse performance than during 1934/5 when David Jack's re-election squad produced the figures: P42 W11 D9 L22 F65 A78 P31, finishing 21st.

Nonetheless no-one was proud that Southend were up for re-election again. The 1934/5 season was an abysmal one; United moved into bottom position on 3 November 1934 and stayed there, with the exception of one week, for the rest of the season. Only on 13 April 1935 did they manage to sneak above Newport County on goal average. Injuries played their part, plus 'a strange apathy' among the forwards who wasted scores of clear cut chances, only coming to life in the last few games of the campaign. *'In match after match the United have proved to possess individual players as good as any in the division but they have failed to fit into the machinery of team work so essential to success'* said the Standard.

The re-election candidates facing Southend and Newport were not strong, however. New applicants Bath City could show a credit balance of only £52 and an average 3,000 crowd; their fellow hopefuls Folkestone had £100 in the bank but gates of just 2,100. With third division status Bath estimated their attendances would go up to 5,500, Folkestone said they would attract 8,000, but both were probably being optimistic. In any case Southend could boast an annual income of £15,156 plus an average gate already of 6,750, despite such a poor season. Newport were averaging 5,720 per match and pulling in £9,038 a year.

Not surprisingly then, voting at the 3 June 1935 meeting of the Football League came out strongly in favour of Southend. United directors heard at the Holborn Restaurant in London that they'd been re-elected with 48 votes, with Newport also retaining their third division south spot. For Bath, who received six votes and Folkestone, just one, the campaigning had been wasted. Chairman Nevill Newitt emerged to tell the press: *'I felt confident all along that we should secure re-election and was very pleased at the unanimous way the southern section representatives voted for us'.*

Not that re-election was always such a formality; Thames, Aberdare, Merthyr, New Brighton, Ashington, Durham, and Nelson all lost their places in either the third south or third north before the creation of the fourth division in 1958. Southend's relatively accessible geographical position, it's acceptable facilities, financial stability and its hitherto satisfactory playing record were collectively more than enough to convince most clubs to deliver their vote.

Whether United's standing in the game would have been high enough to avoid re-election 50 years later in 1984/5 is another matter, but in any case a last gasp win against Torquay on the final day of the season kept Southend out of the fourth division drop zone. With the club on its last legs and two of its senior officials banned from football, third time may well not have proved so lucky.

STANDARD JUNE 1. 1922.

SOUTHEND UNITED RESTORED TO LEAGUE.

PROCEEDINGS AT MONDAY'S MEETING.

ANXIOUS PERIOD AT AN END.

THE FUTURE OF THE CLUB.

INTERVIEW WITH THE CHAIRMAN.

After a period of grave anxiety in which the future of the Southend United has hung in the balance, the Football League, on Monday, granted it a new lease of life and restored it to membership of the Third Division. It is good news for the town as a whole, for it would be a bad blow to the Borough if, after the many years of strenuous labours, wholehearted service and money spent, Southend had been deprived of its first-class professional team. Supporters of the club who have enthusiastically and loyally followed its doings over many years will be gratified and pleased that its career has not been summarily cut short and hope that now a new start will be made which will bring honour and credit to the Blues and the Borough. Exactly how difficult and anxious has been the time preceding Monday's meeting probably only those intimately connected with the situation can realize. Not only during the past week-end, but for several weeks before the Southend United directors have been engaged in a fight for the life and future of the club. They had many difficulties to overcome. They were up against some past prejudices; they had to fight a tremendously strong, well financed opposition, and they received practically no assistance from their neighbours in distress, Exeter City. The popular personality of Mr. Peter O'Rourke, the ex-Bradford City manager, who has now taken charge of the Pontypridd Club, had worked wonders on behalf of the Taff Vale Club, his active canvass in the North, a significant backing from the *Athletic News*, which came out on the morning of the meeting with a photo of the Pontypridd ground, and a strong plea for the club, combined with a very considerable spending of money by that organization made their opposition to the retiring clubs a real danger.

◇ ◇ ◇

There were two other applicants in Llanelly and Bath City, but they were never serious opponents. When the representatives of the various clubs composing the Football League foregathered in London, on Saturday, for the business of the meeting early on Monday the

Financial troubles

There have been two significant financial crises at Southend – both at Roots Hall but 72 years apart.

The first, in 1912, was nowhere near as far reaching or debilitating as the second, but was in many ways the most serious, for it hit a club just six years old. The crisis came out of the blue on 22 February 1912 when directors were handed a circular informing them that Thomas Buxton, the man who'd taken over the Blue Boar inn from Oliver Trigg in 1907, was now calling in a £90 loan he'd given to the club several years before. Buxton's move took the club by surprise, not just because he was actually a United director, but also because most loans offered to the club by insiders were anything but, and were usually written off by the generous benefactor several years later. Buxton, however, was moving to take up another business in Kent and was obviously keen to clear the decks. When his fellow directors told him they couldn't produce the cash right away, he slapped a writ on them for the full £90.

Buxton: precipitated crisis.

Buxton's very public move set off a frightening chain of events for United, as other creditors suddenly realised they might also be unable to get their loans back or have their bills paid. Within a week the club was forced to call a shareholders' meeting *'with a view to voluntarily winding up the company'*. The local papers began writing United's obituary.

A meeting one week later heard that United had no assets of any value because – contrary to popular conception – its grandstand and fixtures were owned by the landlord of Roots Hall, not the club. It owed £456 to various local tradespeople and a further £559 to its directors, although all bar Buxton on the board were waiving their claims for the time being.

The irony of the crisis was that United were actually in their best financial shape since the club had begun in 1906; now able through rising gate money to keep the club running without recourse to further borrowing – and sufficiently flush over the preceding couple of years to have chipped away at the debt they did have. Plenty of other southern league clubs were having cash flow problems at the time; Buxton's impatience triggered a financial hiatus at Southend which could have been set off in any of the preceding years. Nonetheless, with no immediate source of money at hand and only two weeks to act, the only option United's shareholders had was to set up a last ditch appeal, which they launched immediately after their own meeting.

Backed by the supporters committee, Mayor Chalton Hubbard's dramatic plea for donations produced a heartwarming response – and not just from the Southend public. Among many contributions from outside the town, West Ham supporter George Webb presented Southend with £10 from a special collection made at Upton Park during a game against Millwall. Home gates rose by at least 1,000 during the two weeks of the appeal and there was a bumper crowd at Roots Hall on 11 March for the game against Cwm Albion of South Wales, when local MP Rupert Guinness and the vicar of Southend afterwards told 4,000 fans that the £26 collected at the ground that afternoon had raised the fund total to £390 by the end of the first week. It was a happy, celebratory meeting made all the better by a 7–0 victory. It left no-one in doubt that the £450 target would be reached in time.

By the end of the fortnight the townspeople had taken the Mayor's fund to a breathtaking £600, effectively freeing the club from all its remaining debt and cementing United's place in the town's affection once and for all. Buxton had his money, the players had their wages, the people had their team and within a year they were all rewarded when United won promotion to the Southern League division I.

The financial crisis of 1984 was hardly as inspirational, nor was it as clear cut. Many of its details still remain shrouded in mystery, but the problems appear to have begun in June 1983 when Essex butcher Anton Johnson, former owner of a nightclub in Rayleigh, took control of the club by agreeing to buy 44.9 per cent of the share stake from chairman Mark Rubin and his brother Tony, who'd been running Roots Hall since their father had died.

Johnson certainly inherited a debt problem – there was a £250,000 overdraft by the time he arrived – but under his controversial regime things began to slide even further. Just over a year later in October 1984, when he'd been ousted by Vic Jobson, the debt had climbed to a staggering £700,000 – and no–one really knew where the money had gone. For the first time since the dark days of the great war players began missing wage payments, and scandal surrounded the club as it emerged that the supporters loan fund had been raided. Two months later, after police investigations into Johnson's affairs, the Standard Chartered Bank effectively suspended his stake in the football club by announcing that no–one would be able to buy his shares without their authority.

Johnson was a flamboyant, charismatic man who could sometimes draw even the hardest sceptic into his web, and he certainly entangled many people at Roots Hall. Three years after he left, United were still chasing him for alleged debts of £25,000, and four other creditors wanted to talk to him about another £139,000. In June 1988 Johnson was declared bankrupt, tracked with little success by private detectives who'd been sent to look for him in the United States. The High Court heard he had effectively split his shares four ways in a company called *Splintcourt* and two of his three associates, former solicitors Geoffrey Myerson and John Hillman, were also now bankrupt.

The third associate, William Harris, was branded as a 'thoroughgoing liar' in a High Court case four months later, over a deal he'd signed in which £70,000 paid for the lease of the Roots Hall market went not to the club but to an Isle of Man company operated on behalf of Anton Johnson by his 'front man' Andrew MacHutcheon, who'd briefly been chairman of United. High Court judge Mr Justice Millet ordered Harris to pay back all the profits from the market since March 1984 and labelled the absent Johnson a 'confidence trickster'. Awarding costs of £250,000 to the club, he said United directors had fallen victim to 'concentrated fraud'.

For morale as much as cash flow the whole affair was disastrous. Money had haemorrhaged out of the club at a frightening rate, and it was going to be difficult to recover. Even worse, the Johnson affair had severely disillusioned many thousands of Southend supporters, especially those who had saved with the club's loan fund. It was no coincidence that playing fortunes reached their lowest point in 1984 and 1985, no coincidence either that the smallest ever home crowd came in the same week that United was forced to negotiate a huge £800,000 remortgaging deal with the Business & Mortgage Trust.

After that it could only have got better, but it took time. Some might liken the Johnson affair to a devastating bush fire, clearing all in its way ready for the renewal which promotion to the second division delivered six years later. Others might claim that unlike the financial crisis of 1912, which brought most elements of the club and town together, the mess of 1984/5 opened up wounds which have still not healed.

Detectives called in as ex-Blues boss vanishes

Anton Johnston

CREDITORS of Anton
hired an

Crowd disturbances

Violence and football, indeed violence and most mass spectator sports, have always been bedfellows – whether the authorities like it or not. A cursory glance at the history of any first class soccer club will reveal unsavoury crowd incidents, and the history of Southend is no exception.

On the other hand, Southend fans have acquired a deserved reputation for being some of the most peace-loving in the business. Arrests at Roots Hall even in modern times have been consistently below levels at other comparable clubs, and during the 1987/8 season United came second from bottom in the national arrests 'league table' with just three collarings during the whole campaign. Even in the late sixties, when crowd violence was more prevalent but went largely unnoticed by the politicians, United fans won a 1969 commendation in the rather bizarre 'John White crowd behaviour awards'.

Ironically, United's fans probably suffered from a worse reputation in the early days, when they were generally noted for being one sided and rather too vociferous for Edwardian tastes. The partisanship prompted a number of critical letters from visiting fans to local newspapers, but it didn't provoke anything more than spirited banter until October 1908, when United's FA Cup game at Leyton was stopped by the referee as rough play and tension on the field spilled over into fighting on the terraces.

With few fans able to afford long trips to away matches, the potential for trouble was greatest at derby games with London clubs or across the Thames at the Gillingham side New Brompton. In January 1909, just three months after the Leyton fracas, there were serious incidents at a Roots Hall fixture against New Brompton which was marred by fighting at the end of the match. As the final whistle blew one livid Brompton supporter rushed onto the pitch, kicking the linesman and aiming a punch at the referee. The offender was quickly escorted away for his own safety by policemen, but was met outside the ground by a hail of stones and potatoes from United supporters. He needed further protection on his tram journey to the railway station, but was met at the terminus opposite the Middleton Hotel by an angry crowd of 1,000, baying for his blood. Police drew their truncheons and locked him in a waiting room until his connection came.

Further small scale disturbances made the headlines before the first world war, but were rarely reported in the sensational tones accorded to modern day violence. They were often treated, in fact, as part of the general spectacle, as during a United trip to Millwall in 1914 when one reporter referred gleefully to 'two or three free fights amongst spectators which created a little diversion'.

Post war, a far more serious set of circumstances at a game involving Southend merited the attentions of a special FA commission investigation. Several hundred blues fans had travelled by charabanc to the match against Crystal Palace in November 1920, only to become embroiled in serious 'spectator misconduct' after the game. Most of the violence came from Palace fans who, incensed at United's 3-2 victory, crowded onto the pitch and kicked the referee 'so badly he was incapacitated'. Also mauled were United skipper Reid and a number of other blues players. An FA Commission subsequently ordered the Palace ground to be closed for a fortnight.

Referees, in fact, seemed to be a greater target of violence in those days than opposing fans. Protection of officials became a prime concern in the 1920s, so United directors were sorely embarrassed when in November 1925 a referee scheduled to take charge of a Southend reserve match at the Kursaal was sent an anonymous letter advising him that a bed had been booked in advance for him at Southend infirmary. Purporting to be from a committee member it signed off: 'I trust the crowd will not be too rough on you', but the game passed off without incident and the pre-booked bed remained empty.

The letter writer was never caught, but the following month the net was set wider in a search for another anonymous offender who threw a snowball at the band before kick off in a cup game against Dulwich Hamlet. The snowball hit one member of the Shoeburyness Railway Silver Prize Band with such force it knocked his front teeth out – an injury, according to match reports, 'which is a serious matter for him, as he is a solo cornet player'. In a public appeal for information, manager Ted Birnie pointed the finger at the Kursaal's west side enclosure, but collective silence ensued.

The Kursaal faithful had clearly not learned their lesson even by 1932, when the referee walked off the pitch to call for a police guard after being persistently pelted with snowballs from all sides in a home match against Clapton Orient.

Reserve games were not free from incident either, especially when they involved one of the big London sides. In January 1926 national newspapers were outraged by a 'riot' of Southend fans after a reserves fixture against Spurs. To the annoyance of a large crowd, fighting between players on the Kursaal pitch went largely unchecked by the referee, who ran off at the final whistle closely followed by terrified Spurs players and several hundred angry fans. Some reports claimed that anything up to 2,000 United supporters stayed behind breaking windows and besieging the locked Spurs dressing room. Only a police escort ensured a safe passage for the Tottenham squad, but surprisingly no official disciplinary action was ever forthcoming.

The FA took a much tougher line five years later when another Kursaal reserves match, against Southampton on Boxing Day 1930, sparked missile throwing and pitch demonstrations. The Essex County FA judged the crowd's reaction to the sending off of Fred Baron unacceptable, cautioning the club about future conduct and ordering it to place FA warning notices about behaviour in the programme and in prominent positions around the ground for the rest of the season.

In the end, a switch away from the charged atmosphere of the Kursaal to the barren lands of Southend stadium proved a far more effective dampener. Only one unsavoury incident of note occurred there, during a controversial knife edge cup game against Chesterfield in January 1939. With United winning 4–3 in extra time on a quagmire of a pitch, the referee awarded a dubious penalty to Chesterfield right on the final whistle and allowed added time for the kick to be taken. The ugly mood of the 12,000 strong crowd was made worse when United's Bolan was sent off for protesting.

'I could see what was going to happen, so I hurried round to the dressing room and gathered every police officer I could find' said Major Hay recalling the scene many years later. *'The penalty kick was saved by MacKenzie and then the crowd swarmed over the pitch. The police escorted the referee from the field with difficulty then the crowd formed up outside the dressing room and hurled stones through the windows'.*

At Roots Hall in September 1962 the referee again had to be smuggled out of the ground after a local derby clash against Colchester ended in a violent pitch invasion. Thereafter police dogs became a familiar site at every home match as sporadic but usually minor terrace fights continued throughout the sixties and seventies. Only in 1988 were security fences erected on the South Bank, described by vice chairman John Adams as *'a monstrous carbuncle on the face of an old and valued friend'*.

(Above) The fences go up, in December 1988.
(Right) Nicked: A fan is led away after terrace fighting between Southend and Watford fans (August 1976).

Disciplinaries

United's first clash with the footballing authorities took only three years to arrive when Bob Jack paid the penalty for sailing too close to the wind in 1909. The manager earned the club a not inconsiderable fine of £10 10s in November when the authorities discovered he'd been 'wilfully misleading' the authorities by registering a certain W. Leslie as a professional player for Southend during the previous 1908/9 season. Leslie, it turned out, was not Leslie at all – he was W. Askew, a 21 year old under suspension for various misdemeanours until the end of the 1910 season.

Askew had played for a number of clubs during his ban but United were unlucky enough to get caught red handed, and the investigating commission openly admitted the blues were being severely punished *as a warning to all clubs'*. In February 1921 however, United were fined £10 for wrongly approaching Arsenal player Henry Allen while he was still on the Highbury list, although he was allowed to sign for Southend shortly afterwards and made 24 first team appearances.

Jack's eventual successor Joe Bradshaw also fell foul of the rules in October 1912 when the FA penalised him for a technical 'oversight' when he was filling out exemption forms for the cup. The FA insisted Bradshaw's error meant United must now play in the preliminary rounds of the FA Cup rather than qualifying automatically for the first round proper. In the end it mattered little, for United beat Southend Amateurs 5–0, Walthamstow Grange 6–2 and Leytonstone 5–0 to get there.

Football League and FA attention had also been drawn in the early days to fevered betting activity around the Roots Hall ground before matches, though in the end they both preferred to let the police deal with gambling through the courts. As early as 1908 large numbers of illegal betting slips were circulating on the Roots Hall terraces – and the Spread Eagle pub just behind the ground became an acknowledged haven for unlawful gaming even into the 1920s.

When United later announced plans to build a greyhound track at their Kursaal ground FA worries about the intrusion of betting surfaced again, with officials issuing several subtle warnings on their concern about the link between dog racing and football. When Southend directors failed to take the hint the Football League eventually moved in to ban dogs altogether.

FA sanctions hit Southend again two years later when the game against Southampton reserves was disrupted by crowd trouble (see above), and nine years further on the game against Chesterfield, which also sparked off a pitch invasion, led to an FA inquiry. The investigating committee, however, was more interested in the behaviour of several Southend players who'd surrounded the referee to protest about a last minute penalty.

In an era when player dissent was a rarity, United's angry response had caused comment and considerable interest outside the environs of Southend, especially as Bolan had brought attention to himself by achieving an even rarer feat – being sent off. The men at the FA took a dim view of the proceedings, suspending Bolan for seven days and fining him £3 *'for using threatening language to an official'*. His colleagues Bell and Smirk (who threw mud at the ball as it was being prepared for the spot kick) were also fined £3 each for *'bringing the game into disrepute'* and the FA ordered costs of the inquiry to be borne by United.

After the second world war United were effectively penalised for alleged misdemeanours at another club when blues skipper Jimmy McAlinden was fined £50 and suspended for a staggering four months in May 1950. An FA investigation concluded that McAlinden had taken £750 as an illegal 'under the counter' signing on fee from Portsmouth manager Jack Tinn just before the war, but even though he was now playing for United, the club had to suffer his absence for 11 games. Southend's sole consolation was that McAlinden's lengthy ban was served for the most part in the close season.

That incident proved to be United's last significant clash with officialdom until its most serious run-in with the Football League during December 1984 when the club's one time owner Anton Johnson and former chairman Andrew MacHutcheon were banned for life from football. The team also attracted an FA warning a few months later for a huge tally of disciplinary points under manager Bobby Moore, but managed to stay out of real trouble until 1989 when United were *'strongly reprimanded'* by the Football League following a commission inquiry into allegations made by Maidstone United. The Kent club, whose admission to the fourth division had been opposed by Southend, complained about alleged lack of hospitality during a League match at Roots Hall early in the 1989/90 season. United were warned that any repeat *'will not be tolerated'*.

CHAPTER 12
GAMES TO REMEMBER

THE DERBY DOUBLE

Southend's two greatest victories came against Derby County, 61 years apart.

The first of them, in an FA Cup tie on 28 January 1926, infected the town with football fever. Derby were then a second division outfit, but unbeaten all season, perched at the top, and still with a formidable reputation as one of the elite founder members of the Football League. Southend, 8th in the Third South, only 20 years in existence and six years in the Football League, had made some waves in previous cup games, but this year had progressed to the fourth round by beating Dulwich Hamlet (5–1), Gillingham (1–0), and Southport (5–2).

A home draw promised great excitement, and the fans were not let down. Though there was still room for another two or three thousand at the Kursaal when the whistle blew for kick off, 15,800 had turned up, breaking the previous ground record by a clear 4,000 with receipts of £1,226. Never had a feverish atmosphere like it been seen at Southend; Derby were a team worth watching, graced by England internationals George Thornewell on the right wing and Harry Storer at inside right, yet they were beaten – and beaten resoundingly. Even the old hands in the crowd said it was the club's greatest performance to date – 4–1 against a side which went on to win promotion to the first division that season, the heaviest defeat inflicted on Derby all year. *'Southend were the best team I've seen all season and we haven't seen such a good team at Derby for a long time'* said one visiting Derby fan.

Hero of the day was Southend's Fred Graver, who came in as a last minute replacement when inside right Jim Bissett pulled out because his brother died. Graver filled the position admirably, and capped a fine performance by getting United's second goal. For the first 15 minutes exchanges had been even, but once Southend established the lead through Andrews they went on to dominate most of the game. Graver's opportunist 35th minute strike put them 2–0 up at half time and they went three goals ahead when Hick, playing on his own up front, rounded Derby keeper Olney in the 65th.

Hick followed up with another six minutes later, though there was a suspicion of offside, then Murphy got Derby's consolation with a cross-cum-shot which baffled Billy Moore. Each United goal was cheered ecstatically; with such force that one man living five miles away in Hadleigh reported hearing the roars.

There was similar excitement in the rest of the country, where football fans received the result with barely disguised amazement. *'Such a sweeping victory for the third division side was just about the last word in shocks'* said the Derby Daily Express, *'There is no mystery about County's defeat'* said the Derby Daily Telegraph, *'The Rams went into the contest with something approaching contempt for the opposition, persisted in playing the wrong type of game, and were taught a lesson that should do them good in the quest for other honours. Southend were supremely indifferent to the greatness of the opposition and fought with tremendous enthusiasm'.*

United's reward was a 5th round home tie against second division Nottingham Forest which they lost 1–0 at home in front of 18,153. But they also got a handsome payback for the pleasure they'd given the townsfolk when wealthy supporter Ernest Mogford took the first team and managerial staff to the National Supporters Club for a slap up meal and evening's entertainment, all expenses paid.

One other man was also congratulating himself over the Derby triumph – Herbert Upton of Westcliff, who'd dreamed of a 4–1 Southend victory the night before the game. Working in the city of London on the Saturday morning he'd told all his work pals of the premonition, then bent the ears of just about everyone standing on the terraces near him before kick off. *'If anyone questions my dream forecast I can give them the names and addresses of about 50 well known Westcliff residents whom I told this to on Saturday morning'* he later publicly told sceptics.

Teams:
Southend: Billy Moore, Jack French, Tommy Sayles, Fred Jewhurst, Frank O'Rawe, Jack Andrews, Hughie Morris, Fred Graver, Billy Hick, Bill Shaw, Steve Smith.
Derby County: Olney, Wightman, Ritchie, McIntyre, Thoms, Plackett, Thornewell, Keetley, Bedford, Storer, Murphy.

The first Derby cup match
Rolling on to victory:
United players in training.

The programme cover

Southend's second victory over Derby, on the evening of 22 September 1987, was, if anything, even more sensational. United were going through their worst spell in the third division, had the poorest defensive record in the country and a few hours previously had sacked their new manager Dick Bate. Yet under the hastily installed Paul Clark they produced their first ever home win against first division opposition. The only previous victory against a top flight team was away to Bolton in the 1979/80 League cup.

It was certainly a bad night for Derby, who had Bobby Davidson sent off in a passionate Littlewoods Cup encounter after 70 minutes for arguing with the referee. But Southend showed they had spirit which the fans had doubted existed during the first few weeks of the season. Like the 1926 encounter, Derby had England internationals in striker John Gregory, defender Mark Wright and goalkeeper Peter Shilton, but there was little any of them could do when Ross McLaren handled impetuously in the 28th minute to give Southend's Roy McDonough a penalty kick.

McDonough drove the kick hard and low past Shilton, who went the wrong way, setting off huge celebrations. Shilton had a number of important saves to make later on to deny United a bigger lead, and earlier, in the seventh minute 18 year old Lee Nogan (on loan from Oxford United) had beaten him only to see his shot rebound from the inside of the post. Eric Steele kept his first clean sheet of the season.

The Daily Telegraph called it *an epic performance* the Daily Express *a sensation*, but ironically it had almost never happened. To add to their early season scoring woes, their managerial instability and flagging morale, United suffered a burst water main at Roots Hall two hours before kick off. As plumbers battled to get it under control and with chaos all around, a postponement looked on the cards. But alternative arrangements were eventually made for the players to shower at the nearby Access Sports and Social Club; the greatest inconvenience fell on the disappointing crowd of 4,605, which had to go without tea and coffee at the refreshment bars.

Teams:

Southend: Eric Steele, David Martin, Peter Johnson, Adrian Burrows, Shane Westley, Derek Hall, Martin Robinson, Glenn Pennyfather, Lee Nogan, Roy McDonough, Martin Ling.

Derby County: Shilton, Blades, Forsyth, Williams, Wright, McLaren, Sage, Gee (Garner 75), Davison, Gregory, Callaghan.

Bangkok Post

Established in 1946

BANGKOK FRIDAY OCTOBER 9, 1987

● English League Cup

Derby, Chelsea, Portsmouth fall

London (AFP) — Struggling English Third Division side Southend pulled off a League Cup "giant-killing" act on Wednesday when they dumped First Division Derby out of the competition in the second-round.

And, after West Ham's ignominious exit at the hands of

The news reached far and wide!

What made that September 1987 victory so much sweeter was an equally memorable follow-up game with exactly the same line up in the second leg at a rain soaked Baseball Ground on 7 October 1987. Despite their 1-0 turnover at Roots Hall few in the Wednesday night Derby crowd of 12,118 expected their team to leave the competition at Southend's behest, but a 0-0 draw ensured just that.

United's defence showed no signs of being the most vulnerable in the League as ferocious tackling and tight marking kept Derby's attack largely out of the game. For the Blues it was another moment of joy to be savoured, for Derby the first omen in a season which eventually saw them relegated. *That's got to be one of the greatest nights of my career'* said United keeper Eric Steele, who'd been transferred from Derby to Southend in the summer.

United's record against Derby has always been good, in fact. On Valentines Day in the 1976 FA Cup they lost just 1-0 at the Baseball Ground against one of the greatest ever County sides. Derby were 3-1 favourites for the cup with Rioch, Leighton James, Gemmell, McFarland, Francis Lee and Charlie George – yet they found Southend a real handful. A 33rd minute goal by Rioch was enough, but United had a goal disallowed and the 5,000 blues fans in a crowd of 31,918 went away pleased with a gutsy performance. In January 1977 they lost 3-2 in a close fought FA cup third round match, Derrick Parker scoring both United goals.

In the other of Southend's four FA Cup meetings with Derby, United also came close to victory during a 3-2 defeat in 1933 at home. Claiming revenge for their 1926 defeat, Derby – now in the first division and sporting six internationals – deserved their victory, although Southend's decision to play goalscorer Jim Shankly in a depleted defence was a bad one. Derby went ahead 3-0 with three goals in 25 minutes, but strikes by United's 'Tot' Pike and Jimmy Morfitt gave County some anxious late moments.

TED HANKEY'S GAME

When popular goalkeeper Ted Hankey left for Bristol with the rest of the Southend team at 9.00am on 5 October 1946 he could scarcely have realised he would be contributing to one of the most remarkable United victories ever recorded – and without even taking the field.

Hankey travelled with the other ten players, plus one reserve, to Paddington, where they caught the 11.15 to Bristol for their Saturday League game against Bristol Rovers at Eastville.

The players settled into their reserved compartments only to hear minutes before the train left that the restaurant car – which was supposed to be serving them their pre-match lunches – hadn't been hooked to the train. After a mad scramble in the station's overcrowded refreshment room some of the players managed to salvage a few sandwiches before the off, but the prospect of playing on near empty stomachs pleased no-one.

Worse was to follow, however, when soon after passing Reading a group of players engrossed in a game of solo whist were disturbed by a crash of glass in the corridor. When they looked out of their compartment they saw a pool of blood on the floor and a pale Ted Hankey in a state of near collapse, wobbling around near a broken window. Hankey had tried to force open the jammed window with rather too much pressure, accidentally smashing it and cutting both hands, one severely.

As trainer Wilf Copping dealt with the bleeding wounds, Hankey insisted he could still play, but everyone knew he had only a slim chance. When the team arrived in Bristol there was no option but to take the keeper to the hospital, where the cuts had to be stitched as the rest of the team headed for the ground.

On the way to Eastville manager Warren extracted an agreement from the players that news of Hankey's misfortune would be kept quiet for as long as possible, mainly to reduce the psychological boost to the opposition of knowing United had no goalkeeper. Warren knew that before the kick off club officials would, as custom dictated, ask him for any team changes, and that he would be quizzed by the local press on his line up. To his great surprise however, not a single official or journalist made any enquiries about the team when he arrived at Eastville – and as kick off approached the Southend players in the dressing room heard an announcement that the United side was as per programme, with no changes. Warren had no inclination to let anyone know otherwise, for if Rovers had known that travelling reserve Bob Jackson was now donning Hankey's trademark American cap it would have been as good as a two goal start.

Jackson, who'd never kept goal in his life, certainly looked the part to the Bristol crowd, performing a 'tuning up' dance and rolling the ball out proficiently during the game, but the few in the know could hardly suppress their sniggers, despite the seriousness of the situation.

In the opening exchanges Southend steered clear of trouble but the misfortunes which had begun with the restaurant car in Paddington were to continue. Before half time Jackson himself had started to limp, Alf Smirk had gone off to get three stitches in a deep cut over the right eye, skilful defender Arthur Harris had pulled a muscle, and Cyril Thompson was dazed and shaken after a crunching tackle. To make matters worse Frank Walton was playing in splints after cutting off the end of his finger the previous week, and the second half turned into a tense affair for the few Southend fans who'd made the journey down. Play was consistently in the Southend half throughout, yet amazingly it was

down to Bob Jackson that Rovers only scored one goal in a 3–1 United victory – and that goal, he later claimed, only beat him because he lacked enough height to reach the swerving shot from Lewis on the left wing.

The win took Southend to 5th in the League but more than that it created a marvellous team spirit. As Ted Hankey, hands bandaged, bounded onto the pitch after the game to congratulate Jackson, the awful truth began to dawn on the Rovers players. Jackson had played so well that Rovers manager Brough Fletcher actually complimented Warren at the final whistle on his goalkeeper, but his face dropped when he was told Jackson was normally a centre half. The Bristol evening paper, still none the wiser, told its readers:
'Hankey did well in goal'.

There was elation back home as returning fans and players related the heroics. *'For their courage and strategy Southend have earned the admiration of the football world'* enthused the Southend Standard, *'Even though most of them were unaware of the difficulties, the 9,500 spectators cheered the team as they left the field and one went so far as to send a large box of cigarettes to their dressing room'.* After their exertions, mostly on an empty stomach, a few more sandwiches might have been better.

Teams:
Southend: Bob Jackson, Stan Montgomery, Tommy Linton, Arthur Harris, Frank Sheard, Frank Walton, Joe Sibley, Alf Smirk, Frank Dudley, Cyril Thompson, Harry Lane.
Bristol Rovers: Wear, Peacock, Watkin, Bamford, Warren, Whitfield, Petherbridge, Pitt, Lambden, Carr, Lewis.

The real **Ted Hankey** in action one month earlier, in the 1–1 home draw with Ipswich Town.

TRAUTMANN IN THE MUD

Glorious defeats – especially in the FA Cup – can bring any lower division club just as much national attention as efficient wins, and Southend's extraordinary 1–0 defeat against Manchester City in the fourth round of the FA Cup on 28 January 1956 was undoubtedly in that category. It was United's most memorable and exciting match for many reasons, but for one above all others – the breathtaking goalkeeping of Bert Trautmann.

Former German paratrooper Trautmann proved he was the best goalkeeper in the world that day, and many years afterwards described the game at Roots Hall as *'possibly the finest of my career'*. His side won 1–0, but everyone agreed it was only Trautmann who kept them in the match.

Both teams played in a changed strip, United in old gold shorts and shirts, City in claret and blue, and even the build up to the match was extraordinary.

Groundsman Sid Broomfield attempts to whitewash the touchlines.

Four days of almost continuous rain made the already muddy Roots Hall pitch, struggling in its first season to retain some sort of shape, nothing short of a swimming pool.

Yet when referee Ernie Crawford made a lengthy 45 minute inspection on the Saturday morning he delighted everyone by pronouncing it fit for play, his decision perhaps swayed by the tremendous work of 20 volunteer supporters who'd toiled dawn to dusk during the previous week mopping up and scooping away gallons of muddy water. They'd rolled lorry loads of sand and cockleshells into the pitch, yet conditions were still so bad by kick off it was difficult even for groundsman Sid Broomfield to mark out the lines.

Many said it was a game that should never have been played, but when rain began to arrive again an hour and a half before kick off Ernie Crawford knew a postponement was out of the question. Already thousands were ankle deep in mud on the terraces, eventually swelling the crowd to a new record of 29,500. The disappointment – and the ensuing chaos – would have been huge.

Considering the appalling conditions (it sometimes took four or five kicks to shift the ball from a puddle) the match was played with impeccable sportsmanship. Crawford, who later went on to officiate in the 1966 World Cup and take charge of games in 17 countries, said years afterwards that the game was *'the most wonderful I have ever refereed'*. He only had to blow for four fouls throughout the game and when the final whistle blew all 25 men on the field were given a rapturous ovation by the crowd. *'I have never been so satisfied in my life'* he said, *'Everybody on the field never thought it would last 90 minutes. I suffered so much cramp on the train to London that both my legs shot out straight in front of me'*.

The Sunday Pictorial's Frank McGhee reckoned the players had fought against *'the grimmest conditions I have ever seen'*, the People's Ralph Hadley christened it *'a ghastly Paschendale of a pitch'* but in the dressing room no-one wanted to talk about anything else except the phenomenal performance of Trautmann. Little Joe Hayes had scored City's winner against the run of play with a soft shot after 23 minutes which deflected away from keeper Harry Threadgold's reach and trickled agonizingly over the line.

Thereafter it was Trautmann who kept the Manchester men in the game, pulling off a succession of breathtaking saves which drove the Southend crowd to distraction.

Trautmann produced the first of his superhuman saves a minute from half time when he threw himself instinctively at a deflected cross from Lockhart and turned it beyond the corner of the goal, leaving Baron and Hollis with heads in their hands. In the second half Lockhart sent Hollis splashing through the water towards goal, controlling the ball wonderfully before picking his spot and firing a perfect low drive just inside the far post – only to see Trautmann leap across out of the mud and tip it round.

So it went on, with Trautmann defying anything the United forwards could throw at him. Hollis had a superb game, but no matter where he put it Trautmann was there. Even from a huge scything scrimmage in the goalmouth the city keeper emerged triumphantly with the ball, 'wriggling like an eel' from underneath a heap of players. It was his day and that was that.

Trautmann's most breathtaking save came, inevitably, from Hollis when initially diving the wrong way he twisted in mid air and managed to finger tip the ball away. *'I could see the ball going beautifully right into the corner of the net, then at the last split-second Trautmann's finger came from nowhere'*, said Hollis. *'He's the greatest goalkeeper I've ever seen'*.

Trautmann, ever modest, told one reporter as he staggered back to his team coach after the game: *'A goalkeeper can only look good against a good team'*. Coming from the man who had won the hearts of all Southend supporters, even though he'd stopped their team, it was the best compliment the United players could have hoped for. Just for good measure city skipper Roy Paul, one of four internationals in the Manchester side, declared he would never play a tougher game in his career. *'These Southend boys gave everything they had in the second half and then kept coming'* he said. It was a measure of Southend's achievement that Paul went on to raise the cup for Manchester City in the final that year. City played exceptionally well for the rest of the tournament, but Trautmann had won them the trophy at Roots Hall.

Southend United Football Club Ltd.

ROOTS HALL
Victoria Avenue, Southend-on-Sea

This portion to be retained

F.A. Cup (4th Round)

o. SOUTHEND UNITED v

1. MANCHESTER CITY

SATURDAY, 28th JANUARY, 1956.

Kick-off 2.45 p.m.

EAST STAND
VICTORIA AVENUE

RESERVED SEAT	BLOCK	B
10/-	ROW	R
(including Tax)	SEAT	37

Teams:

Southend: Harry Threadgold, Dennis Howe, Arthur Williamson, Jim Duthie, Jim Stirling, Jim Lawler, Crichton Lockhart, Sam McCrory, Roy Hollis, Kevin Baron, John McGuigan.

Manchester City: Trautmann, Leivers, Little, Barnes, Ewing, Paul, Spurdle, Hayes, Johnstone, Dyson, Clarke.

THE SPURS TRILOGY

There can have been few more spectacular Southend games than the incredible 4–4 draw in the third round of the FA cup against Tottenham Hotspur at White Hart Lane on 11 January 1936. Second division Spurs had prepared for the game by visiting the brine baths under Southend pier (a favourite haunt of the big London clubs), then dining at Garons on half a dozen oysters each and a bottle of stout. United followed them back to London on the Friday night, treating themselves for once to a night in a hotel.

More than 8,000 Southend folk followed them the following morning along the arterial road in a convoy of taxis, coaches and cars, crowding the pubs along the way and chartering special trains each carrying 500 people. On a pleasant sunny afternoon they mingled in a huge crowd of 48,839 at White Hart Lane, yet even those who believed Southend would put up a good fight weren't prepared for what was to happen.

It was an unforgettable end–to–end contest, with more incident and excitement packed into 90 minutes than many fans had seen in a whole month of matches. Played in a whirl of excitement but a clean encounter despite its great pace, the action began from the first minute. Twice Southend took the lead and twice they went behind, only to draw back level.

United opened their scoring after just four minutes when Bolan took advantage of a ball put out to him by Stevens, racing through to beat Spurs keeper Hooper with a fine high shot.

After an equaliser Southend's Nelson, trying to dispossess Welsh international winger Willie Evans, gave away a penalty which Howe missed. Yet further slack play by United gave Spurs the lead when Robinson (who had something of a nightmare) mishit a clearance for Sargent to pounce on.

Bolan sent the Southend followers wild with a perfect equalising header to make it 2–2 and for the next quarter of an hour up to half time the game was dominated by the blues. They forced corner after corner without adding to the score and Hooper made three exceptional saves. Shortly after half time Southend went 3–2 up when a cross from Oswald was dropped by Hooper and Bolan knocked the ball over the line for a hat trick against his old club. Things became easy for United for a period only for Robinson to back pass to the feet of Sargent, who beat MacKenzie to make it 3–3. Vigorous Southend appeals for a penalty were later turned down, then 25 minutes from time Howe crashed in a terrific drive from 30 yards which MacKenzie could only pat down for Morrison to touch over the goal line.

It looked like Southend's splendid resistance had come to nothing, but with 20 minutes to go Lane made it 4–4, setting up a nerve wracking final quarter of an hour. The sighs of relief when the final whistle went weren't confined to White Hart Lane: 150 people who'd gathered outside Standard House in Southend's Cliff Town Road cheered with delight when the telegraph announcing the score was put up in the window.

Mackenzie, the Southend goalkeeper, saves against Spurs.

SPURS SCORE FOUR GOALS

But Have To Fight Again

...TRICK

Teams:
Southend: George MacKenzie, Jimmy Nelson, Dave Robinson, Jimmy Deacon, Charles Turner, Billy Carr, Len Bolan, Fred Cheesmur, Leo Stevens, Harry Lane, Bert Oswald.
Spurs: Hooper, Channell, Buckingham, Howe, Rowe, Phypers, Sargent, Duncan, Morrison, Bell, Evans.

The replay on the following Wednesday afternoon caused enormous excitement, packing the stadium with its record crowd of 23,634. But the game could hardly have been a starker contrast, a ragged affair with little action, made even scrappier by a layer of frost on the bumpy pitch. People were sitting on the stand roof hoping to see an unchanged Southend team win the prize of a fourth round tie against first division Huddersfield, but goals in the 7th and 22nd minutes by Sargent and Evans shattered their dreams. Among the 2,000 who couldn't get in to see the 2-1 defeat were a train load of supporters who came down on the one o'clock from Fenchurch Street, which broke down on the way.

Those two cup games were Southend's first encounters with Spurs since a February 1921 clash at the Kursaal in the third round of the cup. On that occasion there was talk of switching the tie to White Hart Lane, but manager Tom Mather and the directors were bombarded with hundreds of letters asking for the fixture to be played at Southend – and apparently arguing for an increase in admission prices if necessary.

The board decided to raise the standard entrance fee from one shilling to three shillings with the stands one guinea and 10s 6d. In the two weeks before the game significant ground improvements were made, but the final crowd was a disappointing 11,661 mainly because only 1,500 Spurs fans made the trip. Alarmist reports in London papers like the Tottenham Weekly Herald had told them that Southend's ground was 'lilliputian'.

The gate receipts of £2,963 remained a record for a long time to come, however.

The match itself turned out to be controversial in the extreme. Spurs were outplayed in the first half but United had what everyone thought was a perfectly good goal disallowed, and saw three strong penalty appeals turned down. With the score at 1-1 just before the interval, Southend finally got a spot kick after inside right Tommy Nuttall was pushed off the ball by Smith. United skipper Arthur Whalley placed the ball on the spot ready to take the kick, but referee Noel Watson insisted on moving the ball to what he thought was a more precise position. Whalley moved it back again, the referee replaced it once more, and the skipper got a warning that any subsequent adjustments would lose his team the penalty opportunity. A seething Whalley, who was a highly strung character at the best of times, blasted the kick well wide, much to the anguish of the Kursaal crowd.

That incident proved the turning point of the match. In the second half Whalley charged around in an angry haze, his fellow players lost their composure, and Joe Walters had to leave the field with an injury. After what turned into a 4-1 defeat one of the linesman added to the post match controversy by publicly criticising the referee. The disallowed goal by Walters was at least a yard onside, he said, and if he'd have been the man in charge it would have stood. Spurs, riding their luck, went on to win the cup that year against Wolves.

Teams:
Southend: Tom Capper, Andrew Newton, Jimmy Evans, Henage Wileman, Arthur Whalley, Blakey Martin, George Nicholls, Tommy Nuttall, Albert Fairclough, Joe Walters, Joe Dorsett.

Spurs: Jacques, Clay, McDonald, Smith, Walters, Grimsdell, Banks, Seed, Cantrell, Bliss, Dimmack.

The other great encounter with Spurs came in 1989, when United, in their fourth division promotion season under David Webb, pulled off only their third ever defeat of a first division club by beating Tottenham 3-2 at Roots Hall in the second leg of the Littlewoods cup. The victory, in front of a restricted crowd of 10,400, was not quite good enough to knock Spurs out of the competition, because they'd already beaten Southend 1-0 at White Hart Lane in the first leg and went through

on the away goal rule. But it was certainly a shaker for manager Terry Venables and his star studded squad. The Spurs side which the blues defeated on the night of 4 October 1989 was packed full of internationals, including two of the very best – Gary Lineker and Paul Gascoigne. Home fans had paid up to £15 to touts for £5.50 tickets to see their team play one of the most glamorous sides in the country, yet Tottenham could hold out for only five minutes before Martin struck with a header from a corner.

Spurs struggled for another half hour until David Crown punished an error by England's Gary Mabbutt by putting the ball across for Gary Bennett to score United's second, amid frenzied scenes, in the 41st minute. Clive Allen got Spurs back on terms shortly afterwards, then a 55th minute equaliser by Nayim looked to have put the game beyond the home side. Instead, Southend almost achieved what would have been a momentous shock. In the 67th minute Bennett, who by now had a broken nose, managed to flick a Paul Brush free kick past Spurs keeper Eric Thorstvedt to make it 3-2 and give Venables's side a tense 23 minutes to the close.

With the overall aggregate score standing at 3-3 there were near misses at either end in extra time with David Crown and Gary Lineker both foiled by the post, before the final whistle gave Spurs their away goal victory.

It was a furiously paced, hectic game which saw sendings off for United's Roy McDonough in extra time and £1.7m Spurs striker Paul Stewart after 49 minutes. Stewart's dismissal led to angry after match exchanges between Venables and David Webb over whether United skipper Paul Roberts had feigned injury from Stewart's elbow in the incident which led to his dismissal. In an outburst which Venables was later to regret, he called Roberts a 'Con man'. Spurs ended up apologising for speaking out of turn and the Sun newspaper paid libel damages for making similar remarks, although the FA decided to take no action other than to issue a stern warning.

Teams:

Southend: Paul Sansome, Andy Dixon, Paul Roberts, David Martin, Spencer Prior, Paul Brush, Jason Cook (Mario Walsh 89), Peter Butler, David Crown, Roy McDonough, Gary Bennett.
Tottenham Hotspur: Thorstvedt, Thomas, van den Hauwe, Fenwick, Allen (P Walsh 90), Mabbutt, Nayim, Gascoigne, Stewart, Lineker, Sedgley.

SCOUSE ADVENTURES

Liverpool have proved exciting opponents on more than one occasion, though United have only played them five times. Their first ever encounter came on 5 January 1957 in the third round of the FA Cup, a year after the momentous game against Manchester City and refereed coincidentally by the same man, Ernie Crawford. Again the sticky Roots Hall pitch played its part in the drama, helping Southend to a shock victory over a Liverpool team which eventually finished third in the second division that year.

Not that everyone found the eventual 2-1 scoreline completely unbelievable. As the cloth sacking and mangles were brought out again at Roots Hall, some national newspapers had even predicted United could pull off a win, even though their intricate short passing game under new manager Eddie Perry didn't suit the quagmire conditions. *'It's the team with the hardest kick that wins'* predicted Perry.

In the end Perry credited the win to a Southend man who didn't play – injured skipper Kevin Baron, who played on the losing side for Liverpool in the 1950 cup final against Arsenal and dished up the inside information on his former colleagues before the game. Perry handed Baron the floor in the pre-match briefing and it turned out to be a good decision. Baron's biggest tip was to shut out Liverpool centre forward Billy Liddell, who later admitted in his autobiography: *'there was no disputing that Southend were the better team'*.

Liddell it was who forced a brilliant save from Southend keeper Harry Threadgold only ten minutes from the end with the score at 2-1.

Yet at the other end Liverpool's outstanding Scottish international keeper Tommy Younger – reckoned to have been one of the top four in the world – had to make many more important interventions. Liverpool fell into the trap of trying to play too much football while United, much fitter and familiar with the vagaries of their much maligned pitch, swung the ball about more, keeping it on the better patches out on the wings. Two of Southend's five Jimmys – Duthie and Thomson – got the all important goals, Duthie, the Scottish born skipper, after only three minutes with a spectacular drive after beating four men. Though the score at half time was 1-0, Southend could have been four up but for classic

160

keeping by Younger. As it was, Liverpool's Wheeler calmly put in a loose ball shortly after the restart to equalise.

Liverpool kept up the pressure for the next 15 minutes but lost the initiative for the remainder of the match, and Thomson's winner came eight minutes from time after he brushed off one tackle and slotted a low shot under Younger. With the 18,500 crowd roaring for the whistle, United ended the game as they'd started, in attacking mode, having just earned their 9th corner of the game.

'Liverpool's reputation foundered in the mud at Roots Hall, but they cannot blame the mire for this defeat' said the Sunday Express, 'From the outset they were faced by a resolute Southend who were superior throughout nearly all the 90 scintillating minutes'. 'Southend's forwards put a strong Liverpool defence completely out of their stride' said the Daily Mail, 'They always looked the more menacing side and only brilliant goalkeeping by Tommy Younger saved Liverpool from humiliation'.

Teams:
Southend: Harry Threadgold, Arthur Williamson, Sandy Anderson, Jim Duthie, Jimmy Stirling, Jimmy Lawler, Gordon Barker, Sam McCrory, Roy Hollis, Jimmy Thomson, John McGuigan.
Liverpool: Younger, Molyneux, Moran, Saunders, Hughes, Twentyman, Liddell, Wheeler, Arnell, Melia, A'Court.

The papers were predicting that Southend's 'suet pudding pitch' would help them in their subsequent fourth round game when they drew Birmingham City, previous years losing finalists, at home. They were wrong; despite the backing of a 28,964 crowd they went down 6–1 in one of their least distinguished cup performances. They should have listened to Jim Duthie, who said before the game *'I promise you the pitch is if anything to our disadvantage. We are a footballing team and we prefer hard grounds'*.

The following year United drew Liverpool again in the FA Cup, drawing 1–1 at Anfield in front of 43,454, then losing 2–3 in an exciting replay on a much improved Roots Hall surface (attendance: 16,650). But it wasn't for another 21 years that the two met again, also in the FA Cup, for the game which created Southend's all time attendance record – 31,033.

By then Liverpool had transformed themselves from the second division outfit of the middle fifties to one of the best club sides in the world, earning a place in Europe for 15 consecutive seasons up to the FA Cup third round game at Roots Hall on Wednesday 10 January 1979. More than 13,000 had turned up to a game against Brentford the previous week just to get vouchers for the cup match, but they were disappointed when snow caused postponement of the big event on the Saturday.

So it was that United's biggest ever crowd turned up on a Wednesday, an electric atmosphere never reproduced at Roots Hall before or since. Millions more saw highlights of Southend's achievement on TV that night, a spirited 0–0 draw against a side packed with world class players. A carpet of snow made things easier for United, but Liverpool manager Bob Paisley readily admitted the home side were worth the replay. If anything Southend had the slight advantage throughout the match, creating the better of the few chances there were. The best arrived in the first half when Gerry Fell sent Derrick Parker through the middle with only Clemence to beat, but his shot was easily smothered. In the final ten minutes there was further drama as supporters and players leapt in the air for a penalty when Parker went sprawling. TV replays, however, showed the referee was right to turn it down. Cawston saved a curling lob from Hughes and dived bravely at Fairclough's feet, but the key to United's defensive victory was two fine performances from Moody and Hadley, who shut Dalglish out of the game. *'They were truly magnificent'* said Dave Smith after the game, *'I've been getting a bit fed up with telling people we've got players of quality at the club – perhaps there's no need to after this performance'*.

Teams:

Southend: Mervyn Cawston, Micky Stead, Steve Yates, Micky Laverick, Tony Hadley, Alan Moody, Colin Morris, Ron Pountney, Derrick Parker, Phil Dudley, Gerry Fell (John Walker 68).
Liverpool: Clemence, Neal, Hughes, Thompson, Kennedy, Hansen, Dalglish, Case, Fairclough, McDermott, Heighway.

It took 39 minutes of the replay at Anfield for Liverpool to assert their superiority, a goal by Jimmy Case rewarding some cool, disciplined football. Parker had missed a golden opportunity for Southend when he headed over after 16 minutes, but it was the best chance of the match for Southend in a 3–0 defeat rounded off by a 73rd minute goal by Dalglish and a Kennedy shot just before the final whistle. United got a genuinely warm reception from an appreciative 37,000 crowd, of which about 4,000 had made the 550 mile round trip from Southend.

Roy Hollis celebrates during the 1958 FA Cup third round replay at home to Liverpool

TEN ONE!

To have beaten any team 10–1 once is fair going, but to do it three times is beyond the call of duty. Southend's highest score is actually 12–0 against the Royal Engineers during 1906, but that was in Southern League division two, which couldn't truthfully be counted as first class soccer. Since then 10–1 has become something of a favourite.

The first time United produced that scoreline was on 24 November 1934 against Golders Green in the FA Cup first round.

It was an inauspicious cup christening for the Athenian league side, who'd only been playing under their new name for a year, having previously been known as Hampstead FC. It could even have been 11–1 if Harry Lane hadn't missed a penalty in the first minute, but Golders Green began pluckily enough, their English amateur international Freddy Evans matching his opponents blow for blow during much of the first half until Southend scored after 24 minutes. The first goal was the best, an accurate pass from Billy Carr finding Fred Cheesmur who,

with his back to the goal, flicked the ball sideways through the defence to Harry Johnson who netted with a beautiful shot. Thereafter it was only a question of how many United were going to get, even though Golders Green keeper Godding pulled off some fine saves and would have had good claim to any man of the match award.

A healthy stadium crowd of 8,500 saw the amateur side crumble to 3–0 down by half time, then capitulate completely in the second phase as Johnson brought his tally to five and Cheesmur ran the defenders ragged. A mild foul by Richardson on Johnson gave Carr a penalty and Harry Lane added number five in bizarre fashion, inadvertently kneeing the ball in from short range. Cheesmur snapped up two and Jimmy Deacon got the other odd goal. For Southend, lying bottom of the third south, it was a tremendous boost for morale. For Golders Green, riding high in the Athenian league with five league victories out of nine, it was a graphic illustration of the gulf between amateurs and professionals.

Teams:

Southend: Billy Moore, Jack Morfitt, Lawrie Kelly, Norman Mackay, Joe Wilson, Billy Carr, Harry Lane, Harry Johnson, Fred Cheesmuir, Jimmy Deacon, Bert Oswald.
Golders Green: Godding, Boston, Richardson, White, Broadis, Bucci, Breagan, Edwards, F.Evans, T.Evans, Drinkwater.

Thirty four years later, on 7 December 1968, Essex part timers Brentwood received the same treatment – this time in the second round of the cup. Their manager Dave Bumpstead, a former Orient, Millwall and Bristol Rovers player, had conceded victory even before the match, but he hadn't expected complete humiliation.

The headlines called it 'the massacre of Roots Hall', all the more impressive because United had despatched Kings Lynn 9–0 in the previous round – dubbed 'the slaughter of the innocents'. But the first half gave little indication of the fireworks to come. Just over 13,000 home fans admittedly saw the match begin in spectacular fashion with a Gary Moore goal after just a minute, but Brentwood then equalised through Stratton on 17 minutes and created difficulties for the home side for another quarter of an hour.

At the interval United were winning 3–1 thanks to a 20th minute header from Moore and 35th minute strike by Sammy McMillan.

The southern leaguers contained the pressure after the break until Moore came up with two more brilliant headers in the 52nd and 63rd minutes, giving him four. Extraordinarily, though, he was to be outdone by fellow striker Billy Best, who'd been having an outstanding game even though he was not yet on the scoresheet. The first of Best's five arrived after 71 minutes, but the remaining four came in the final six minutes of the game. On 84 minutes he headed in a Hamilton cross, on 87 he nodded in a Birks centre, on 88 he hammered in the ball after a goalmouth scramble, and on 89 – to the biggest cheer of the day – he brought up number ten by dribbling the ball around keeper Dunbar. Of the 22 goals United had scored in that year's FA cup, Moore and Best had provided a staggering 17.

Teams:
Southend: Trevor Roberts, Tony Bentley, Graham Birks, Sammy McMillan, Micky Beesley, John Kurila, Eddie Clayton, Phil Chisnall, Gary Moore, Billy Best, Chico Hamilton.
Brentwood: Dunbar, Jones, Butterfield, Maynard, Loughton, Stevenson, Foster, Mansfield, Stratton, Dilsworth, Hyde.

Just to prove they could do it against League opposition as well, Southend cracked in ten versus Aldershot two decades later on 6 November 1990. A paltry 1,281 witnessed the spectacle, not just because it took place on a wet Tuesday night but also because the match was in the preliminary round of the unfashionable Leyland Daf Cup for third and fourth division clubs.

Those who bothered to make the trip were well rewarded by a merciless display from a blues team which a month earlier had been on the receiving end of its own humiliation – an 8–0 defeat against Crystal Palace in the Rumbelows cup. Financially hamstrung Aldershot were little more than punchbags for the United forwards, who began the evening with a fine goal at the north bank end from Steve Tilson after six minutes. Tilson followed up again with a looping back header into the left hand corner on 14 minutes, then Brett Angell produced a hat trick in the space of 16 minutes, volleying in on 25 minutes, rounding the uncertain 'shots keeper Jon Sheffield after 32, and climbing high to head in on 41. With a 5–0 lead at half time cynics were expecting the usual dull second period which often follows a goal glut, but Southend were in no mood to rest on their lead. Ten minutes into the second half Spencer Prior got his first goal of the season, a perfectly executed downward header from a corner

on 55 minutes, then on 68 – with Aldershot looking clumsier by the minute – Ansah powered a shot in from just inside the penalty area. By now playing with total confidence, the blues got their 8th on 74 minutes, a curling shot from Angell into the right hand corner, and their 9th smacked in from a couple of feet by Benjamin. Tilson got his hat trick with ten minutes to go, but it was Aldershot who had the last laugh, Dale Banton showing admirable fighting spirit to come back with the best goal of the game on 83 minutes.

The pity was that so few people saw the game, but the club laid on a special showing of the match video on a giant screen at the Shrimpers Club two days later. Shellshocked Aldershot manager Len Walker was not present for the re-run – he had no wish to relive what he readily described as the most embarrassing night of his football life. *'I don't think I ever got beaten by double figures even when I played in the cubs'* he said, *'We were second in every department, we were ripped apart by a superb team'*.

United manager David Webb said there were no superlatives to describe the result. *'I want them to celebrate tonight's win because results like this come only once in a lifetime, but I can assure you it will be business as usual when they report back for training on Thursday'*.

Teams:

Southend: Paul Sansome, Dean Austin, Chris Powell, John Cornwell, Spencer Prior, Steve Tilson, Peter Cawley, Peter Butler, Andy Ansah, Ian Benjamin, BrettAngell.
Aldershot: Sheffield, Brown, Cooper, Randell, Wignall (Banton 25), Flower, Whitlock, Puckett, Williams, Henry, Stewart.

APPENDIX
STATISTICAL SECTION
Key to statistical section

The majority of the information contained within this section is self explanatory,
however the following notes have been added, to avoid any confusion.

Section 1 – Who's Who.

Every player to have appeared for Southend United in the Football League, FA Cup, Football League Cup (and subsequent names), and Associate Members Cup (and earlier and subsequent names) have been included.

Separate columns give brief personal and career details of each player. The place of birth is given in the second column, followed by the date (or year) of birth. The player's previous club, where known, is given ('Fr:') in the next column, followed by the date of transfer (month/year). League and Cup appearances for Southend follows ('Apps.'); a plus (+) figure indicates additional substitute appearances (but not unused 'appearances'). The next line, 4th column, indicates the club, where known, that the player moved on to, plus the date (month/year where known); Goals scored for Southend United ('Goals') are shown in parenthesis. Where a player has returned to Southend United, additional lines of information are given, and the total number of appearances and goals scored for the club are given.

Section 2 – Match Statistics.

Football League match numbers (1 to 42 or 1 to 46) are given in the first column and repeated in the column prior to the team line-ups. Own goals (O.G.) and scorers are given, and included in each 'Appearances and Goals' table. Goals scored from a penalty are indicated (pen). Venue, (H) = home match, (A) = away match. Neutral venues are indicated. Official attendances (or newspaper reference approximations), where known have been given. The eleven players in the starting line-up (1 to 11) refer to the shirt numbers, and – in pre-1939 line-ups – the normal acceptable positions (e.g. '1' = goalkeeper, '2' = right back, ... '11' = left winger, etc.) 'Used' substitutes ('12' or '13') replaced the numbered player (shown in parenthesis). Unused substitutes ('appearances' have **not** been included in the table) have been included (where known) in the line-ups, and can be identified since no number in brackets follows their name. Abbreviated Cup rounds are self-explanatory, e.g. Q = qualifying, R1 = first round; R1L2 = first round second leg; R1r2 = first round second replay, etc. Players' seasonal summaries are given in the 'Appearances and Goals' table, a plus (+) figure indicates substitute appearances. League table summaries are given below the 'Appearances and Goals' table, including the final League position ('Ps.'), and points ('Pts.').

SECTION 1 – WHO'S WHO.

A

						League	Cup
ABBOTT, Peter	Rotherham	01/10/53	Fr: Crewe Alexandra	07/77	Apps.	26+1	2
					Goals	(4)	
ADAMS, Billy	Tynemouth	03/11/02	Fr: West Ham	01/37	Apps	13	
			Retired	05/37	Goals		
ALBESON, Brian	Oldham	14/12/46	Fr: Darlington	07/71	Apps.	109+1	10
			To: Stockport County	03/74	Goals	(9)	(1)
ALLEN, Edward	London		Fr: Local (Amateur)	07/20	Apps.	5	
					Goals		
ALLEN, Henry	Stratford	1896	Fr: Gnome Athletic	07/20	Apps.	23	1
			To: Gillingham	08/23	Goals		
ANDERSON, Bill	Lochore	06/11/26	Fr: Hibernian	05/54	Apps.	16	
			To: Weymouth	07/56	Goals	(1)	
ANDERSON, Sandy	Auchtermuchty	20/02/30	Fr: Newburgh Juniors	04/50	Apps.	452	31
			To: Folkestone Town	07/63	Goals	(8)	
ANDREWS, Jack	Darlington	1898	Fr: Shildon C.W.	05/25	Apps.	74	7
			To: Darlington	08/29	Goals	(1)	(1)
ANGELL, Brett	Marlborough	20/08/68	Fr: Stockport County	07/90	Apps.	79+6	13+1
			Still with club		Goals	(36)	(13)
ANGUS, Mike	Middlesbrough	28/10/60	Fr: Scunthorpe United	08/83	Apps.	1	
			To: Darlington	03/84	Goals		
ANSAH, Andy	Lewisham	19/03/69	Fr: Brentford	03/90	Apps.	83+4	10+3
			Still with club		Goals	(19)	(4)

Name	Place	DOB	Transfer	Date			
ARMITAGE, John	Chapeltown	21/08/97	Fr: Oldham Athletic	06/29	Apps.	9	
			To: Northampton Town	05/30	Goals	(2)	
ASHWORTH, Barry	Stockport	18/08/42	Fr: Bangor City	07/63	Apps.	31	5
			To: Hartlepool United	03/65	Goals	(5)	(1)
ASHWORTH, Joe	Huddersfield	06/01/43	Fr: Bournemouth	07/67	Apps.	36	3
			To: Rochdale	07/68	Goals	(2)	
AUSTIN, Dean	H. Hempstead	26/04/70	Fr: St. Albans City	03/90	Apps.	96	13
			To: Tottenham Hotspur	06/92	Goals	(2)	(1)

B

Name	Place	DOB	Transfer	Date			
BABER, John	Lambeth	10/10/47	Fr: Charlton Athletic	09/66	Apps.	72+10	9
			To: Margate	07/71	Goals	(18)	(1)
BAILEY, Jack	Grays	1901	Fr: Sittingbourne	08/26	Apps.	78	
			To: Thames	07/31	Goals	(22)	
BAINBRIDGE, Ken	Barking	15/01/21	Fr: Reading	02/53	Apps.	78	4
			To: Chelmsford City	06/55	Goals	(25)	
BALDWIN, Harry	Bolton		Fr: Bolton League	07/20	Apps.	14	
			To: Bolton Wanderers	08/23	Goals	(2)	
BANKS, Frankie	Hull	21/08/45	Fr: Juniors	10/62	Apps.	79	10
			To: Hull City	09/66	Goals		(1)
			Fr: Hull City	12/76			
			To: Coaching staff				
BARKER, Geoff	Hull	07/02/49	Fr: Hull City (loan)	12/70	Apps.	25	1
					Goals		
BARKER, Gordon	Leeds	06/07/31	Fr: Bishop Auckland	12/54	Apps.	57	4
			To: Chelmsford City	06/59	Goals	(9)	(1)
BARNARD, Chris	Cardiff	01/08/47	Fr: Apprentice	08/65	Apps.	4+4	3
			To: Ipswich Town	07/66	Goals		(3)
BARNES, Edward	Royston	21/07/98	Fr: Watford	07/20	Apps.	1	
			To: Charlton Athletic	12/20	Goals		
BARNES, Harold	Aldridge		Fr: Aston Villa	06/22	Apps.	5	1
					Goals		
BARNETT, Dave	Lambeth	24/09/51	Fr: Apprentice	09/69	Apps.	48+9	9
			To: Folkestone Town	07/73	Goals		
BARNETT, Fred	Dartford	04/04/98	Fr: Tottenham Hotspur	07/29	Apps.	174	13
			To: Watford	06/34	Goals	(35)	(3)
BARON, Fred	Prudhoe-o-Tyne	29/12/01	Fr: Liverpool	03/27	Apps.	62	2
			Retired through injury	05/32	Goals	(42)	
BARON, Kevin	Preston	19/07/26	Fr: Liverpool	05/54	Apps.	138	12
			To: Northampton Town	09/58	Goals	(45)	(1)
BARROW, Billy	Cardiff	1911	Fr: Margate	02/34	Apps.	34	2
			To: Bournemouth	06/35	Goals	(3)	
BATEMAN, Arthur	Cleethorpes	15/03/08	Fr: Grimsby Town	05/33	Apps.	19	3
			To: Brentford	01/34	Goals		
BAYLISS, Len	Alfreton	28/04/99	Fr: Mansfield Town	05/25	Apps.	8	
					Goals		
BEACH, Doug	Watford	02/02/20	Fr: Luton Town	07/47	Apps.	41	1
			To: Colchester Utd.	07/49	Goals		
BEANLAND, Tony	Bradford	11/01/44	Fr: Southport	03/66	Apps.	57	3
			To: Wrexham	07/67	Goals	(3)	
BEAUMONT, Percy	Mexborough	03/09/97	Fr: Barnsley	06/26	Apps.	30	2
					Goals		
BEESLEY, Micky	High Beech	10/06/42	Fr: West Ham United	08/62	Apps.	198+14	23+4
			To: Peterborough United	07/65	Goals	(45)	(4)
			Fr: Peterborough United	08/67			
			To: Dover	07/71			
BELL, Sid	Burnhope	06/02/09	Fr: Tottenham Hotspur	05/37	Apps.	84	10
			To: Millwall (guest)	09/41	Goals	(16)	(2)
			To: Chelmsford City	07/48			
BELL, Stan	West Ham	28/10/23	Fr: Local	07/48	Apps.	3	
			To: Monarchs F.C.	07/49	Goals		
BELL, Tommy	Heworth	11/04/01	Fr: Leeds United	06/25	Apps.	91	4
			To: Portsmouth	03/28	Goals	(2)	

Name	Birthplace	DOB	Transfer	Date		Apps	
BELLOTTI, Derek	West Ham	25/12/46	Fr: Charlton Athletic	12/71	Apps.	76	6
			To: Swansea City	05/74	Goals		
BENJAMIN, Ian	Nottingham	11/12/61	Fr: Exeter City	03/90	Apps.	106	15
			Still with club		Goals	(26)	(3)
BENNETT, Bobby	Harrow	29/12/51	Fr: Staines	06/72	Apps.	1	2
			To: Scunthorpe United (loan)	10/73	Goals		
			To: Wimbledon	05/74			
BENNETT, Gary	Kirkby	20/09/63	Fr: Chester City	11/88	Apps.	36+6	7+1
			To: Chester City	03/90	Goals	(6)	(4)
BENNETT, Ken	Wood Green	02/10/21	Fr: Tottenham Hotspur	06/46	Apps.	50	4
			To: Bournemouth	06/48	Goals	(10)	(6)
BENNETT, Walter	Sheffield		Fr: Chelsea	05/24	Apps.	7	
			To: Doncaster Rovers	08/25	Goals		
BENTLEY, Tony	Stoke	20/12/39	Fr: Stoke City	05/61	Apps.	379+2	38
			To: Folkestone Town	07/71	Goals	(14)	(3)
BEST, Billy	Glasgow	07/09/43	Fr: Northampton Town	01/68	Apps.	225+1	21
			To: Northampton Town	09/73	Goals	(106)	(17)
BINKS, Sid	Bishop Auck.	25/07/99	Fr: Portsmouth	06/28	Apps.	14	
			To: Fulham	02/29	Goals		
BIRD, Dickie	Llandrindod Wells	05/01/08	Fr: Sheffield United	10/36	Apps.	10	1
					Goals	(1)	
BIRKS, Graham	Sheffield	25/01/42	Fr: Peterborough United	01/66	Apps.	139+1	13
			To: Chester	10/69	Goals	(1)	
BISSETT, George	Cowdenbeath	25/01/??	Fr: Pontypridd	05/24	Apps.	58	7
			Retired	05/26	Goals	(14)	(4)
BISSETT, Jimmy	Dundee	19/06/98	Fr: Ebbw Vale	05/22	Apps.	33	4
			To: Rochdale	05/23	Goals		
BLEANCH, Norman	Heddon	19/08/40	Fr: West Ham United	07/61	Apps.	3	
			To: Bradford Park Avenue	11/61	Goals		
BOLAN, Len	Lowestoft	16/03/09	Fr: Tottenham Hotspur	07/35	Apps.	104	17
			Retired during war		Goals	(20)	(7)
BOLLINGTON, John	Belper	1892	Fr: Army	08/19	Apps.	1	
			To: Brighton	09/20	Goals		
BOOTH, Dennis	Ilkeston	09/04/49	Fr: Blackpool	03/72	Apps.	77+1	6
			To: Lincoln City	02/74	Goals	(1)	
BOOTH, Robert	Hartlepool	20/12/90	Fr: Birmingham	07/22	Apps.	27	4
			To: Swansea Town	06/23	Goals	(1)	
BORLAND, John	Rutherglen	09/11/03	Fr: Merthyr Town	05/29	Apps.	21	
			To: Barrow	06/30	Goals	(3)	
BOYCE, Tommy	Paisley		Fr: St. Mirren	07/27	Apps.	7	
			To: Clydebank	05/28	Goals		
BRACE, Stuart	Taunton	21/09/42	Fr: Grimsby Town	10/73	Apps.	106+6	16
			To: Falmouth Town	07/76	Goals	(39)	(4)
BRADBURY, Terry	Paddington	15/11/39	Fr: Chelsea	09/62	Apps.	160+1	15
			To: Leyton Orient	06/66	Goals	(19)	
BRADSHAW, John	Burnley	1892	Fr: Burnley	06/13	Apps.	1	
			To: Swansea Town	07/19	Goals		
			Training Staff (Emergency appear.)	07/22			
BRAND, Ray	Islington	02/10/34	Fr: Millwall	08/61	Apps.	22	2
			To: Hastings United	07/63	Goals	(9)	
BRAYSHAW, Walter	Denaby		Fr: Blackburn Rovers	05/26	Apps.	13	
			To: Denaby United	01/28	Goals	(5)	
BREWSTER, Bill	Kinglassie	04/08/33	Fr: Chelsea	08/55	Apps.	2	
					Goals		
BRIDGE, Jackie	Gt. Wakering	30/05/32	Fr: Juniors	08/50	Apps.	53	3
			To: Gravesend & Northfleet	07/56	Goals	(3)	
BRISLEY, Terry	Stepney	04/07/50	Fr: Orient (loan)	03/75	Apps.	8	
					Goals		
BROADHURST, Jack	Birkenhead	11/03/18	Fr: Tranmere Rovers	08/38	Apps.	1	
			To: New Brighton	03/39	Goals		
BROOK, Reg	Nottingham	1912	Fr: Coventry City	05/36	Apps.	3	2
			To: Bristol City	06/37	Goals		
BROOKS, Sammy	Brierley Hill	28/03/90	Fr: Tottenham Hotspur	12/23	Apps.	12	
			To: Kidderminster Harriers	06/25	Goals	(2)	

Name	Birthplace	Born	Transfer	Date		Apps	Goals
BROPHY, Tom	St. Helens	08/01/97	Fr: Aberdare Athletic	08/27	Apps.	42	1
			Retired	05/30	Goals		
BROWN, Ernie	South Shields	03/02/21	Fr: Newcastle United	02/47	Apps.	18	1
			To: Hartlepool United	01/51	Goals		
BRUSH, Paul	Plaistow	22/02/58	Fr: Crystal Palace	01/88	Apps.	69+4	13
			To: Enfield	07/90	Goals	(1)	
BRYAN, Billy	Doncaster	1912	Fr: Walsall	05/36	Apps.	7	
			To: Swindon Town	07/37	Goals		
BRYANT, John	Saltcoats		Fr: Merthyr Town	05/29	Apps.	2	
			To: Taunton United	06/30	Goals		
BUDDERY, Harry	Sheffield	1889	Fr: Portsmouth	11/21	Apps.	25	2
			Retired	05/22	Goals		(1)
BULLOCK, Peter	Stoke	17/11/41	Fr: Birmingham City	02/65	Apps.	12	
			To: Colchester United	10/65	Goals	(2)	
BUNGAY, Frank	Sheffield	1909	Fr: Huddersfield Town	05/33	Apps.	2	
			To: Boston United	08/34	Goals		
BURKE, John	London		Fr: Local	02/30	Apps.	1	
			To: West Ham United	03/30	Goals		
BURNS, Frank	Workington	11/11/24	Fr: Swansea Town	07/52	Apps.	89	4
			To: Crewe Alexandra	11/56	Goals	(14)	
BURRIDGE, John	Workington	03/12/51	Fr: Aston Villa (loan)	01/78	Apps.	6	
					Goals		
BURROWS, Adrian	Sutton In Ashfield	16/01/59	Fr: Plymouth Argyle (loan)	09/87	Apps.	6	3
					Goals		
BUSHBY, Billy	Shildon	21/08/14	Fr: Shildon C.W.	07/34	Apps.	40	6
			To: Southampton	06/39	Goals	(12)	
BUTLER, Ernie	Middlesbrough	28/08/24	Fr: Stockton	08/48	Apps.	36	2
			To: Darlington	06/53	Goals	(3)	
BUTLER, Peter	Halifax	27/08/66	Fr: Cambridge United	02/88	Apps.	135+7	25
			To: Huddersfield Town (loan)	04/92	Goals	(9)	(3)
			To: West Ham United (loan)	07/92			
			To: West Ham United	08/92			
BUTTERS, Guy	Hillingdon	30/10/69	Fr: Tottenham Hotspur(loan)	02/90	Apps.	16	2
					Goals	(3)	

C

Name	Birthplace	Born	Transfer	Date		Apps	Goals
CADETTE, Richard	Hammersmith	21/03/65	Fr: Orient	08/85	Apps.	90	14+1
			To: Sheffield United	07/87	Goals	(49)	(7)
CAGIGAO, Francisco			Fr:		Apps.	1	
			To:		Goals		
CAIRNS, Colin	Alloa	17/09/36	Fr: Camelon Juniors	02/58	Apps.	2	
					Goals		
CAMERON, Bobby	Greenock	23/11/32	Fr: Gravesend & Northfleet	10/63	Apps.	3	
			To: Adamstown (Australia)	06/64	Goals		
CAMPBELL, Joe	Walker-on-Tyne	31/10/03	Fr: Yeovil & Petters	05/29	Apps.	7	
			To: Dartford	07/30	Goals		
CAPPER. Tom	Newton-le-Willows		Fr: Southport	07/20	Apps.	78	6
			To: Wigan Borough	02/23	Goals		
CARR, Billy	Horden	07/03/05	Fr: Huddersfield Town	07/34	Apps.	95	9
			Retired during war		Goals	(1)	(1)
CARTWRIGHT, Les	Aberdare	04/03/52	Fr: Cambridge United (loan)	09/83	Apps.	2+2	1
					Goals		
CAWLEY, Peter	Walton-o-Thames	15/09/65	Fr: Bristol Rovers	07/90	Apps.	6+1	3
			To: Exeter City	11/90	Goals	(1)	
CAWSTON, Mervyn	Diss	04/02/52	Fr: Norwich City (loan)	08/74	Apps.	208	34
			Fr: Chicago Sting	08/78	Goals		
			To: Stoke City	03/84			
			Fr: Chelmsford City	11/84			
			To: Woodford Town	08/85			
CHAMBERS, David	Barnsley	06/06/47	Fr: Cambridge United	10/68	Apps.	52+10	3+1
			To: York City	03/71	Goals	(5)	
CHAMBERS, John	Birmingham	07/10/49	Fr: Aston Villa	07/69	Apps.	6+1	0+1
			To: Bromsgrove Rovers	07/70	Goals		
CHEESMUR, Fred	Wandsworth	1910	Fr: Sheffield United	07/34	Apps.	31	8
			To: Folkestone	08/36	Goals	(8)	(6)

Name	Birthplace	DOB	Transfer	Date			
CHISNALL, Phil	Manchester	27/10/42	Fr: Liverpool	08/67	Apps.	137+5	19
			To: Stockport County	09/71	Goals	(28)	(4)
CLARK, Jimmy	Kilwinning		Fr: Benburb Star	07/34	Apps.	23	1
			To: Derry Hibs	06/36	Goals	(6)	
CLARK, Paul	Benfleet	14/09/58	Fr: Apprentice	07/76	Apps.	300+11	44+4
			To: Brighton	11/77	Goals	(4)	(3)
			Fr: Brighton	08/82			
			To: Gillingham	07/91			
CLAYTON, Eddie	Bethnal Green	07/05/37	Fr: Tottenham Hotspur	03/68	Apps.	69+2	11+1
			To: Ashford Town	04/70	Goals	(16)	(2)
CLENSHAW, Les	Southend	1908	Fr: Westcliff (Amateur)	08/24	Apps.	131	9
			To: Chelmsford (Loan)	07/25	Goals	(28)	(2)
			To: Barrow	05/34			
CLOUGH, Jimmy	Newcastle	30/08/18	Fr: Crystal Palace	05/49	Apps.	34	3
			To: Barrow	07/50	Goals	(7)	(1)
COLLINS, Steve	Stamford	21/03/62	Fr: Peterborough United	08/83	Apps.	51	8
			To: Lincoln City	03/85	Goals		
CONWAY, Herman	Gainsborough		Fr: West Ham United	08/45	Apps.		2
			Retired	05/46	Goals		
CONWAY, Jimmy	Motherwell	27/08/40	Fr: Norwich City	10/63	Apps.	31	3
			To: Partick Thistle	07/65	Goals	(9)	(1)
COOK, Jason	Edmonton	29/12/69	Fr: Tottenham Hotspur	06/89	Apps.	29+1	8+1
			To: Colchester United	07/91	Goals	(1)	(1)
COOKE, George	Clowne	20/11/99	Fr: Portsmouth	05/25	Apps.	2	
			To: Wigan Borough	07/26	Goals		
COOMBS, Frank	East Ham	24/04/25	Fr: Bristol City	06/50	Apps.	20	
			To: Colchester United	07/51	Goals		
COOPER, Mark	Wakefield	18/12/68	Fr: Exeter City (loan)	03/90	Apps.	4	
					Goals		
CORBETT, Vic	Birmingham		Fr: Manchester City	05/35	Apps.	1	
			To: Brierley Hill Alliance	08/36	Goals		
CORNWELL, John	Bethnal Green	13/10/64	Fr: Swindon Town	07/90	Apps.	56+6	9
			Still with club		Goals	(2)	
CORTHINE, Peter	Highbury	19/07/37	Fr: Chelsea	03/60	Apps.	73	2
			To: Chelmsford City	06/62	Goals	(24)	(1)
COSTELLO, Lou	Dagenham	08/07/36	Fr: Aldershot	05/57	Apps.	251	15
			To: Chelmsford City	06/65	Goals	(15)	
COULSON, Willie	North Shields	14/01/50	Fr: Newcastle United	10/73	Apps.	51+1	7
			To: Aldershot (loan)	02/75	Goals	(4)	
			To: Huddersfield Town (loan)	11/75			
			To: Darlington (loan)	01/76			
			To: North Shields	06/76			
COWAN, Ian	Falkirk	27/11/44	Fr: Dunfermline Athletic	07/70	Apps.	3	1
			To: Australia	06/71	Goals		
COX, Arthur	Nottingham		Fr: Mexborough Town	06/22	Apps.	1	
					Goals		
COX, Charlie	West Ham	31/07/05	Fr: West Ham United	02/33	Apps.	2	
					Goals		
CREWE, Billy	Bolton	1898	Fr: Merthyr Town	05/29	Apps.	1	
			To: Wigan Borough	09/30	Goals		
CROMPTON, Arthur	Birmingham	14/05/03	Fr: Tottenham Hotspur	05/30	Apps.	56	2
			To: Brentford	02/32	Goals	(20)	
CROSSAN, Errol	Canada	06/10/30	Fr: Gillingham	08/57	Apps.	40	5
			To: Norwich City	09/58	Goals	(11)	
CROWN, David	Enfield	16/02/58	Fr: Cambridge United	11/87	Apps.	113	19
			To: Gillingham	07/90	Goals	(61)	(8)
CUNNINGHAM, Dave	Kirkaldy	10/08/53	Fr: Brechin City	04/73	Apps.	55+4	4+3
			To: Hartlepool (loan)	03/77	Goals	(4)	(1)
			To: Swindon Town	06/77			
CURRAN, Jimmy	Ryton-on-Tyne	1902	Fr: Barnsley	05/32	Apps.	2	
					Goals	(1)	
CUSACK, Dave	Thurcroft	06/06/56	Fr: Sheffield Wednesday	09/78	Apps.	186	26
			To: Millwall	03/83	Goals	(17)	(3)

D

Name	Birthplace	DOB	Club	Date			
DALEY, Peter	Liverpool	14/02/70	Fr: Liverpool	08/89	Apps.	0+5	
			To: Chelmsford City	07/91	Goals	(1)	
D'ARCY, Tommy	Edinburgh	22/06/32	Fr: Hibernian	05/56	Apps.	4	
					Goals		
DAVIES, Baden	Barry		Fr: Barry	08/28	Apps.		1
			To: Barry	03/29	Goals		
DAVIES, George	St. Georges, Salop		Fr: Wellington Town	06/22	Apps.	63	7
			To: Wellington Town	05/24	Goals	(11)	(2)
DAVIES, Hadyn	Troedyrhin		Fr: Troedyrhin	05/29	Apps.	7	2
			To: Lincoln City	08/30	Goals		
DAVIES, Len			Fr: Army	07/46	Apps.	3	
					Goals		
DAVIES, Reg	Cymmer	27/05/29	Fr: Southampton	07/49	Apps.	41	1
			To: Newcastle United	04/51	Goals	(18)	
DAVIS, Edward	Larne		Fr: Larne	08/38	Apps.	5	2
			Retired during war		Goals	(4)	(2)
DAYKIN, Harry	Somercotes	1909	Fr: Alfreton Town	05/27	Apps.	1	
			To: Fulham	08/28	Goals		
DEACON, Jimmy	Darlington		Fr: Wolverhampton Wanderers	10/34	Apps.	100	13
			To: Hartlepools United	06/39	Goals	(3)	(2)
DELF, Barrie	Southend	05/06/61	Fr: Southend Sunday League	03/83	Apps.	1	
			To: Dartford	08/86	Goals		
DELLOW, Stan	Willesden		Fr: Bradford City	06/21	Apps.	21	3
					Goals		
DEMELLWEEK, Johnny	Plymouth	10/01/07	Fr: Plymouth Argyle	05/35	Apps.	6	
					Goals		
DENNIS, Harold	Newark		Fr: Huddersfield Town	05/26	Apps.	11	
			To: Grantham Town	06/27	Goals	(2)	
DENNY, Paul	Croydon	05/09/57	Fr: Apprentice	09/75	Apps.	8+1	
			To: Wimbledon	08/77	Goals	(2)	
DICKER, Les	Stockwell	20/12/26	Fr: Tottenham Hotspur	07/53	Apps.	17	2
			To: Chelmsford City	06/55	Goals	(7)	(1)
DICKINSON, Harry	London		Fr: Local (Amateur)	03/20	Apps.	3	
					Goals		
DICKINSON, Billy	Tophock,Lancs	18/02/06	Fr: Rotherham United	05/36	Apps.	59	9
			To: Hull City	05/38	Goals	(26)	(5)
DICKS, Alan	Kennington	29/08/34	Fr: Chelsea	11/38	Apps.	85	3
			To: Coventry City	02/62	Goals	(2)	
DIXON, Andy	Louth	19/04/68	Fr: Grimsby Town	07/89	Apps.	24	6
			To: Gateshead	07/90	Goals		
DIXON, David	North Shields	1899	Fr: Birmingham	05/25	Apps.	4	
			To: Rhyl	06/26	Goals		
DIXON, Tom	Seaham Harbour	17/09/99	Fr: Clapton Orient	06/27	Apps.	249	16
			Retired	05/34	Goals	(7)	
DOBSON, Harry	Newcastle-on-Tyne		Fr: Newport County	02/22	Apps.	102	7
					Goals	(20)	
DONNELLY, Jim	Mayo	18/12/00	Fr: Accrington Stanley	05/24	Apps.	42	3
			To: Brentford	06/25	Goals		
DONOVEN, Dickie	Bulwell	20/06/00	Fr: Mansfield Town	07/25	Apps.	318	14
			Retired	05/35	Goals	(55)	(3)
DOREY, Charlie	London		Fr: Local	06/22	Apps.	51	4
			To: Guildford United	07/25	Goals		
DORSETT, Joe	Brownhills	11/04/88	Fr: Colne	07/20	Apps.	35	3
			To: Millwall	05/21	Goals	(3)	(2)
DOWNEY, ?			Fr:		Apps.	1	
			To:		Goals		
DOWSETT, Dickie	Chelmsford	03/07/31	Fr: Tottenham Hotspur	05/55	Apps.	20	
			To: Southampton	07/56	Goals	(4)	
DREYER, Henry	Sunderland	09/03/92	Fr: Crystal Palace	05/23	Apps.	22	3
			To: Boston Town	01/25	Goals		
DUCHART, Alex	Falkirk	03/05/33	Fr: Hibernian	05/56	Apps.	8	
					Goals	(2)	

Name	Birthplace	DOB	From/To	Date		Apps	
DUCK, George	Tottenham	22/05/52	Fr: Millwall	06/71	Apps.	3	
			To: Wealdstone	07/72	Goals		
DUDLEY, Frank	Southend	09/05/25	Fr: Local	08/46	Apps.	88	4
			To: Leeds United	08/49	Goals	(32)	(1)
DUDLEY, Phil	Basildon	17/02/59	Fr: Apprentice	02/77	Apps.	109+3	20+2
			To: Chelmsford City	06/83	Goals	(3)	
DUFFY, John	Dundee	24/08/29	Fr: Celtic	05/54	Apps.	114	4
			Retired	05/60	Goals	(4)	
DUGGINS, Eric	Tamworth	24/11/28	Fr: Portsmouth	07/52	Apps.	28	
					Goals		
DUNCAN, Bob	Kirkcaldy	02/11/43	Fr: Juniors	08/61	Apps.	7	1
			To: Ashford Town	08/62	Goals	(2)	
DUTHIE, Jim	Letham, Angus	23/09/23	Fr: Hull City	05/53	Apps.	160	10
			Retired	05/58	Goals	(8)	(1)
DYER, Steve	Chelmsford	21/03/54	Fr: Apprentice	03/72	Apps.	60+8	7
			To: Weymouth	03/77	Goals		

E

Name	Birthplace	DOB	From/To	Date		Apps	
EDINBURGH, Justin	Brentwood	18/12/69	Fr: YTS	08/87	Apps.	36+1	8+2
			To: Tottenham Hotspur (loan)	02/90	Goals		(1)
			To: Tottenham Hotspur	06/90			
EDWARDS, Andy	Epping	17/09/71	Fr: West Ham United	12/88	Apps.	17+3	4
			Still with club		Goals	(1)	(1)
EDWARDS, Ernie	Stourbridge	17/02/92	Fr: Newport County	06/23	Apps.	92	6
			To: Dudley Town	06/26	Goals	(4)	(1)
EDWARDS, Tommy	Llanelli	13/03/23	Fr: Fulham	03/48	Apps.	12	1
			To: Leicester City	12/48	Goals	(1)	
EGAN, Harry	Tibshelf	23/2/12	Fr: Brighton	06/36	Apps.	6	
			To: Aldershot	05/37	Goals		
ELLIOTT, Alex	Liverpool	1898	Fr: Wigan Borough	07/21	Apps.	8	
			To: Crewe Alexandra	08/23	Goals		
ELLIOTT, Dave	Tantobie	10/02/45	Fr: Newcastle United	02/71	Apps.	174+4	16
			To: Newport County	07/75	Goals	(9)	
ELLIS, Peter	Portsmouth	20/03/56	Fr: Portsmouth	09/84	Apps.	12	0+1
			To: Havant Town	11/84	Goals	(1)	
ENGWELL, Micky	Grays	27/09/66	Fr: Juniors	08/84	Apps.	7+2	1+1
			To: Crewe Alexandra	10/86	Goals	(3)	
EVANS, Billy	Llanigloes		Fr: Swansea Town	06/21	Apps.	62	4
			To: Queens Park Rangers	09/24	Goals		
EVANS, Jimmy	Rhyl	29/12/94	Fr: Ton Pentre	08/19	Apps.	99	7
			To: Burnley	04/23	Goals	(14)	(1)
EVANS, Tommy	Durham		Fr: Rotherham County	05/23	Apps.	27	
					Goals		
EVEREST, Jack	Currah	1907	Fr: Cardiff City	07/36	Apps.	49	6
			To: Barnsley	02/38	Goals	(2)	

F

Name	Birthplace	DOB	From/To	Date		Apps	
FAIRCLOUGH, Albert	St. Helens	04/10/91	Fr: Manchester City	05/20	Apps.	24	2
			To: Bristol City	03/21	Goals	(15)	
FALCONBRIDGE George	Ilkeston		Fr: Ilkeston United	05/27	Apps.	19	2
			To: Grantham Town	09/29	Goals	(2)	
FALLON, Kevin	Maltby	03/12/48	Fr: Sligo Rovers	07/70	Apps.	4	
			To: Ilkeston Town	06/71	Goals		
FELL, Gerry	Newark	01/03/51	Fr: Brighton	11/77	Apps.	43+2	9
			To: Torquay United	07/80	Goals	(10)	(2)
FELL, John	Quebec, Co.Durham	14/05/02	Fr: Leeds United	05/27	Apps.	30	2
			To: Hartlepools United	06/28	Goals	(3)	
FERGUSON, Brian	Irvine	14/12/60	Fr: Hull City	08/83	Apps.	31+10	7
			To: Chesterfield	10/84	Goals	(6)	
FERGUSON, Jackie	Maybole	29/08/39	Fr: Airdrie	06/67	Apps.	13+1	1
			To: Ayr United	07/68	Goals	(2)	
FIRMANI, Eddie	South Africa	07/08/33	Fr: Charlton Athletic	06/65	Apps.	55	7
			To: Charlton Athletic	03/67	Goals	(24)	(4)
FIRTH, Joe	Glasshoughton	27/03/09	Fr: Leeds United	06/35	Apps.	33	3
			To: York City	06/38	Goals	(12)	(1)

Name	Birthplace	DOB	Club	Date			
FIRTH, Robert	Shelton	20/02/87	Fr: Port Vale	07/22	Apps.	37	4
			Retired	05/23	Goals	(1)	(1)
FITTON, Fred	Bury		Fr: Rochdale	11/31	Apps.	3	
			To: Accrington Stanley	07/32	Goals	(1)	
FLATT, Colin	Blyth	30/01/40	Fr: Leyton Orient	06/66	Apps.	20+2	2
			To: Wisbech Town	06/67	Goals	(8)	
FLOWERS, Alf	Southend		Fr: Local (amateur)	08/21	Apps.	5	
					Goals		
FOGG, Ron	Tilbury	03/06/38	Fr: Grays Athletic	08/59	Apps.	2	
			To: Weymouth	06/60	Goals		
FOGGO, Ken	Perth	07/11/43	Fr: Portsmouth	09/75	Apps.	30	5
			To: Chelmsford City	06/67	Goals	(6)	
FOGGON, Alan	Chester-le-Street	23/02/50	Fr: Sunderland	06/77	Apps.	22	4
			To: Hartlepool (loan)	02/78	Goals		(1)
			To: Consett	07/78			
FORD, Andy	Minehead	04/05/54	Fr: Bournemouth	05/73	Apps.	135+3	17
			To: Swindon Town	08/77	Goals	(3)	
FORD, Arthur			Fr: Ancoats F.C.	12/20	Apps.	7	3
					Goals		
FORRESTER, Tony	Parkstone	14/01/40	Fr: West Bromwich Albion	04/59	Apps.	10	
					Goals	(1)	
FORSTER, Billy	Walker-on-Tyne	28/05/09	Fr: Newcastle United	08/38	Apps.	6	
			To: Bristol Rovers	07/39	Goals		
FRANKLIN, Graham	Bicester	25/01/57	Fr: Lowestoft	12/77	Apps.	1+5	
			To: Basildon United	08/82	Goals	(1)	
FREEMAN, Neil	Northampton	16/02/55	Fr: Grimsby Town	07/76	Apps.	69	7
			To: Birmingham City	07/78	Goals		
FRENCH, Jackie	Stockton		Fr: Middlesbrough	03/25	Apps.	174	10
			To: Brentford	08/32	Goals	(2)	
FRENCH, Jackie W.	Stockton	19/01/25	Fr: Middlesbrough	02/47	Apps.	187	11
			To: Nottingham Forest	11/52	Goals	(19)	(3)
			Fr: Nottingham Forest	07/56			
			To: Folkestone Town	06/57			
FREW, Jimmy	Kilmarnock		Fr: Chelsea	05/27	Apps.	56	3
			To: Carlisle United	05/29	Goals		
FRIEL, Benny	Glasgow	16/09/41	Fr: Dumbarton	06/63	Apps.	17	3
			To: Dumbarton	06/65	Goals	(8)	
FRYAR, Buck	Shoeburyness	25/07/11	Fr: Shoebury Town	08/31	Apps.	39	1
			Retired during war		Goals	(19)	(1)
FRYATT, Jim	Southampton	02/09/40	Fr: Charlton Athletic	06/60	Apps.	61	3
			To: Bradford Park Avenue	06/63	Goals	(24)	(1)
FUCCILLO, Lil	Bedford	02/05/56	Fr: Tulsa Roughnecks (USA)	12/83	Apps.	40+5	3+1
			To: Peterborough United	08/85	Goals	(4)	

G

Name	Birthplace	DOB	Club	Date			
GARDINER, John	Chester-le-Street	05/11/14	Fr: Holfords F.C. (amateur)	05/46	Apps.	1	2
					Goals		
GARNER, Bill	Leicester	14/12/47	Fr: Bedford Town	11/69	Apps.	101+1	9
			To: Chelsea	09/72	Goals	(41)	(6)
GATES, B			Fr: Local (amateur)	08/24	Apps.	1	
					Goals		
GAWLER, Ron	Canterbury	10/07/24	Fr: Canterbury City	06/49	Apps.	8	
			To: Tonbridge	06/51	Goals	(1)	
GIBBONS, A.S.	London		Fr: Dartford (amateur)	02/22	Apps.	5	
					Goals	(1)	
GIBSON, Billy	Manchester		Fr: Blackpool	05/30	Apps.	10	
			To: Macclesfield Town	08/31	Goals		
GIBSON, Bob	Washington	29/12/16	Fr: Army	08/46	Apps.	2	
					Goals		
GIBSON, Tommy	Maxwellston	23/10/88	Fr: Notts. County	06/23	Apps.	5	
			Retired	05/24	Goals		
GILFILLAN, Bobby	Cowdenbeath	29/06/38	Fr: Newcastle United	06/63	Apps.	65+1	4
			To: Doncaster Rovers	11/65	Goals	(33)	(2)
GLOVER, Alan	Windsor	21/10/50	Fr: West Bromwich Albion (loan)	01/76	Apps.	0+1	
					Goals		

Name	Birthplace	Born	Transfer	Date		Apps/Goals		
GODDARD, George	Guildford		Fr: Sunderland	07/35	Apps.	34	5
					Goals	(18)	(1)
GOODWIN, Billy	Staveley		Fr: Manchester United	07/22	Apps.	84	7
			To: Dartford	08/27	Goals	(32)	(3)
GOODWIN, Steve	Chadderton	23/02/54	Fr: Norwich City	06/75	Apps.	68+7	9
			To: Jovik (Norway)	05/79	Goals	(10)	(1)
GOODYEAR, George	Luton	05/07/16	Fr: Luton Town	07/47	Apps.	59	2
			To: Crystal Palace	06/49	Goals	(1)	
GOULDEN, Roy	Ilford	22/09/37	Fr: Arsenal	05/61	Apps.	9	1
			To: Ipswich Town	07/62	Goals	(2)	
GOY, Peter	Beverley	08/06/38	Fr: Arsenal	10/60	Apps.	118	6
			To: Watford	07/64	Goals		
GRAHAM, Jimmy	Corby	13/01/11	Fr: Hartlepools United	05/36	Apps.	4	
			To: Clapton Orient	05/37	Goals	(2)	
GRANT, Cyril	Wath	10/07/20	Fr: Fulham	03/48	Apps.	175	8
			To: Gravesend & Northfleet	07/55	Goals	(63)	(1)
GRAVER, Fred	Craghead	08/09/97	Fr: Leeds United	05/25	Apps.	10	1
			To: Wallsend	06/26	Goals	(1)	(1)
GRAY, Harry	Hemsworth	26/10/38	Fr: Bournemouth	06/48	Apps.	19	
			To: Ashford Town	06/50	Goals		
GRAY, Terry	Bradford	03/06/54	Fr: Huddersfield Town	07/79	Apps.	106+4	13
			To: Bradford City	08/82	Goals	(28)	(2)
GREAVES, Danny	Upminster	31/10/63	Fr: Tottenham Hotspur	01/81	Apps.	30+19	3+1
			To: Dagenham	03/84	Goals	(14)	
GRIEVESON, Harry	Easington	10/04/41	Fr: Sunderland	07/61	Apps.	24	1
			To: Sittingbourne	06/62	Goals	(1)	
GUTHRIE, Chris	Hexham	07/09/53	Fr: Newcastle United	11/72	Apps.	107+1	10
			To: Sheffield United	05/75	Goals	(35)	(5)
GYMER, John	Romford	11/11/66	Fr: Apprentice	08/84	Apps.	30+25	9+2
			To: Crewe Alexandra	07/87	Goals	(12)	(1)

H

Name	Birthplace	Born	Transfer	Date		Apps/Goals		
HADDRICK, Bobby	West Ham	01/05/50	Fr: Apprentice	08/65	Apps.	2	
			To: Hastings United	07/67	Goals		
HADLEY, Tony	Rochford	05/07/55	Fr: Basildon United	07/74	Apps.	272+22	41+2
			To: Colchester United	08/83	Goals	(19)	(2)
			Fr: Colchester United	08/84			
			To: Chelmsford City	07/85			
HAGUE, J. Keith	Duffield	1913	Fr: Derby County	05/36	Apps.	39	8
			Retired during war		Goals	(1)	
HALL, Almer	Hove	12/11/12	Fr: Tottenham Hotspur	07/37	Apps.	37	4
			To: Bradford City	06/39	Goals	(10)	
HALL, Billy	Consett		Fr: Blackpool	05/29	Apps.	1	
			To: Crook Town	06/32	Goals		
HALL, Derek	Ashton-u-Lyne	05/01/65	Fr: Swindon Town	08/86	Apps.	122+3	27
			To: Halifax Town	07/89	Goals	(15)	(4)
HALL, Joe	East Holywell		Fr: Backworth Percy	07/22	Apps.	57	7
					Goals		
HALL, John	Southend		Fr: Local (amateur)	07/32	Apps.	2	
					Goals		
HALL, Marcus			Fr: Tottenham Hotspur	08/90	Apps.	1+2	
			Still with club		Goals		
HALLEY, George	Kilmarnock		Fr: Burnley	11/22	Apps.	21	2
			To: Bacup Borough	07/24	Goals	(2)	(1)
HALSTEAD, Fred	Crawshawbeath		Fr: Blackpool	05/21	Apps.	24	1
			To: Hartlepools United	06/22	Goals	(3)	
HAMILTON, Chico	Streatham	31/10/50	Fr: Chelsea	09/68	Apps.	34+2	4
			To: Aston Villa	06/69	Goals	(11)	(1)
HAMILTON, David	Carlisle	08/02/19	Fr: Newcastle United	05/46	Apps.	4	
					Goals		
HANKEY, Ted	Stoke	24/05/14	Fr: Army	06/37	Apps.	125	9
			To: Tonbridge	06/50	Goals		
HARDING, Steve	Bristol	23/07/56	Fr: Bristol City (loan)	01/76	Apps.	2	
					Goals		

Name	Birthplace	Born	Transfer	Date		Apps	Goals
HARMSTON, Mick	Sheffield	07/04/50	Fr: Sheffield United (loan)	12/70	Apps.	1	
					Goals		
HARPER, Bobby	Glasgow	06/06/20	Fr: Newport County	07/50	Apps.	6	
			To: Linfield	06/52	Goals		
HARRIS, Arthur	Coventry	28/07/14	Fr: Nuneaton Town	07/36	Apps.	114	15
			To: Nuneaton Town	06/47	Goals	(1)	
HARRIS, Fred	Rothwell	1884	Fr: Swansea Town	07/21	Apps.	20	1
			To: Kettering Town	05/22	Goals	(2)	
HARRIS, George	Southend		Fr: Local (amateur)	09/21	Apps.	3	
					Goals		
HARRIS, ?			Fr:		Apps.		2
			To:		Goals		
HARRISON, Mike	Leicester	21/02/52	Fr: Birmingham City	07/72	Apps.	16	2
			To: Yeovil Town	06/73	Goals		
HARVEY, Albert	Southend		Fr: Southchurch (amateur)	05/23	Apps.	3	
					Goals		
HARVEY, J			Fr:		Apps.		2
			To:		Goals		
HATFIELD, Ernie	Mansfield	16/01/05	Fr: Wolverhampton Wanderers	05/31	Apps.	51	6
			To: Dartford	08/33	Goals	(3)	
HATTER, Steve	East Ham	21/10/58	Fr: Wimbledon	03/85	Apps.	61	7
			To: Maidstone United	07/86	Goals	(2)	
HAWARDEN, Andrew	Bolton		Fr: Bolton League	10/21	Apps.	10	
			To: Tranmere Rovers	07/22	Goals	(1)	
HAYDOCK, Frank	Eccles	29/11/40	Fr: Portsmouth	01/69	Apps.	28+3	6
			To: South Africa	06/70	Goals	(4)	
HAYES, Billy	Croston	08/11/96	Fr: Brighton	06/24	Apps.	51	3
			To: Accrington Stanley	06/26	Goals		
HAYNES, Robert	Desborough		Fr: Desborough (amateur)	10/20	Apps.	1	
					Goals		
HEATHCOTE, Peter	Leicester	13/11/32	Fr: Juniors	11/51	Apps.	2	
			To: Gravesend & Northfleet	08/53	Goals		
HENDERSON, Jim	Kelty		Fr: Manchester City	05/20	Apps.	23	2
					Goals		
HICK, Billy	West Pelton	13/02/03	Fr: Middlesbrough	03/25	Apps.	106	7
			To: Bristol City	05/28	Goals	(69)	(7)
HIGGS, Frank	Willington Quay	1907	Fr: Carlisle United	07/37	Apps.	2	
			To: Barrow	08/38	Goals		
HILLAM, Charlie	Burnley	06/10/10	Fr: Clapton Orient	06/38	Apps.	13	1
			Retired during war		Goals		
HIND, Billy	Gateshead		Fr: South Shields	05/25	Apps.	6	
					Goals	(2)	
HOCKEY, E			Fr:		Apps.	1	
			To:		Goals		
HODGE, Jimmy	Stenhousemuir	05/07/91	Fr: Norwich City	09/23	Apps.	18	3
			Retired	05/24	Goals		
HOGG, George	Kiveton Park		Fr: Lincoln City	06/26	Apps.	2	
			To: Mansfield Town	06/28	Goals		
HOLBORN, Harry	Gateshead	1915	Fr: Stanley United	07/34	Apps.	1	
					Goals		
HOLLIS, Roy	Yarmouth	24/12/25	Fr: Tottenham Hotspur	02/54	Apps.	240	20
			To: Chelmsford City	03/60	Goals	(120)	(15)
HOLTON, Pat	Hamilton	23/12/35	Fr: Chelsea	08/60	Apps.	11	2
					Goals		
HOPE, Phil	Birtley	1897	Fr: Blackburn Rovers	06/26	Apps.	9	
			To: Clapton Orient	06/27	Goals		
HORN, Graham	Westminster	23/08/54	Fr: Charlton Athletic	12/77	Apps.	9	2
			To: Aldershot	01/80	Goals		
HORNE, Alf	Birmingham		Fr: Hull City	05/27	Apps.	30	2
			To: Manchester City	03/28	Goals	(10)	
HORSFALL, George	Perth, Australia	19/09/24	Fr: Southampton	07/49	Apps.	1	
			To: Guildford City	08/50	Goals		
HORSFALL, Tommy	Hamilton	07/01/51	Fr: Dover	11/72	Apps.	11+5	
			To: Bury (loan)	11/73	Goals	(1)	
			To: Scunthorpe United (loan)	11/73			
			To: Cambridge United	12/74			

174

Name	Birthplace	DOB	Transfer	Date		Apps	Goals
HOUGHTON, Bud	India	01/09/36	Fr: Birmingham City	10/58	Apps.	68	5
			To: Oxford United	03/61	Goals	(32)	(1)
HOWARD, Stephen	Sunderland	1897	Fr: Blackpool	05/21	Apps.	15	
					Goals	(1)	
HOWE, Denis	West Ham	14/09/28	Fr: Darlington	08/54	Apps.	101	7
			To: Aldershot	07/58	Goals		
HOWE, Tony	Colchester	14/02/39	Fr: Colchester United	07/64	Apps.	2	1
			To: Clacton Town	07/65	Goals		
HOWLETT, Bobby	Basildon	12/12/48	Fr: Chelsea	09/67	Apps.	4+2	1
			To: Colchester United	07/69	Goals		
HULL, Jeff	Southend	25/08/60	Fr: Apprentice	08/78	Apps.	10+5	3+1
			To: Basildon United	07/81	Goals	(1)	
HUMPHREYS, Joe	Newhall		Fr: Aston Villa	07/22	Apps.	16	
			To: Burton Town	06/23	Goals		
HUMPHREYS, Ron	Tonypandy	04/04/25	Fr: Snowdown Colliery Welfare	12/45	Apps.	3	1
			To: Folkestone Town	07/47	Goals		
HUNT, Peter	Stepney	02/07/52	Fr: Apprentice	09/69	Apps.	50+6	4+2
			To: Charlton Athletic	12/72	Goals	(1)	
HUTTON, Alec	Edinburgh	10/10/41	Fr:	08/63	Apps.	1	1
					Goals		
HYSLOP, Christian	Watford	14/06/72	Fr: YTS	08/89	Apps.	12+1	1
			Still with club		Goals		

I,J

Name	Birthplace	DOB	Transfer	Date		Apps	Goals
INGLE, Steve	Bradford	22/10/46	Fr: Bradford City	01/67	Apps.	14+1	
			To: Wrexham	07/67	Goals	(3)	
JACK, David	Bolton	03/04/99	Fr: Arsenal	07/34	Apps.		1
			To: Middlesbrough (Manager)	1944	Goals		
JACKSON, Bob	Cornsay	12/05/15	Fr: Stanley United	07/34	Apps.	93	11
			To: Folkestone Town	07/48	Goals		
JACKSON, Wilbert	Halifax	04/08/04	Fr: Stoke City	07/34	Apps.	3	
					Goals		
JACQUES, Joe	Consett	12/09/44	Fr: Darlington	10/69	Apps.	85+2	8
			To: Gillingham	11/72	Goals		
JAMES, Charlie	London		Fr: Clapton (amateur)	08/29	Apps.	1	
					Goals		
JARVIE, John	Easterhouses	19/10/00	Fr: Portsmouth	03/28	Apps.	13	
			To: Watford	07/29	Goals		
JEFFERIES, Syd	London	1897	Fr: Green Weir (amateur)	07/21	Apps.	2	
					Goals		
JENNINGS, Walter	Grimsby	20/10/97	Fr: Swansea Town	05/22	Apps.	15	
			To: Boston Town	08/24	Goals		
JEWHURST, Fred	Hoxton	1897	Fr: Charlton Athletic	02/24	Apps.	117	9
			To: Clapton Orient	06/27	Goals		
JOHNSON, George	Sheffield	1903	Fr: Swansea Town	06/23	Apps.	62	5
			To: Newport County	06/26	Goals	(13)	(1)
JOHNSON, Harry	Radcliffe	04/12/10	Fr: Oldham Athletic	05/34	Apps.	26	5
			To: Exeter City	06/36	Goals	(15)	(7)
JOHNSON, Joe	Leigh-on-Sea		Fr: Leigh (amateur)	09/28	Apps.	45	
			To: West Ham United	06/32	Goals		
JOHNSON, Kevin	Doncaster	29/08/52	Fr: Sheffield Wednesday	09/72	Apps.	12+4	0+1
			To: Gillingham (loan)	02/74	Goals	(1)	
			To: Workington	07/74			
JOHNSON, Peter	Harrogate	05/10/58	Fr: Exeter City	08/86	Apps.	126	25
			To: Gillingham	07/89	Goals	(3)	
JOHNSON, Terry	Newcastle	30/08/49	Fr: Newcastle United	01/71	Apps.	156+2	12
			To: Brentford	11/74	Goals	(35)	(3)
JONES, Benny	Newtown	29/01/07	Fr: Nelson	08/34	Apps.	3	
					Goals		
JONES, Bertram	Merthyr		Fr: Ewyllrhsdyn	07/34	Apps.	1	
					Goals		
JONES, Charlie	Oakdale	20/11/11	Fr: Tottenham Hotspur	05/37	Apps.	22	4
			Retired during war		Goals	(2)	
JONES, Emlyn (Mickey)	Merthyr	29/11/07	Fr: Everton	07/29	Apps.	220	16
			To: Shirley Town	07/36	Goals	(30)	

Name	Birthplace	DOB	Transfer	Date		Apps./Goals		
JONES, Keith	Dulwich	14/10/65	Fr: Brentford	10/91	Apps.	33+1	2
			Still with club		Goals	(5)	(1)
JONES, Ken	Keighley	09/02/41	Fr: Army	10/60	Apps.	87	5
			To: Millwall	09/64	Goals	(34)	(2)
JONES, Len	Barnsley	09/06/13	Fr: Plymouth Argyle	08/49	Apps.	29	4
			To: Colchester United	07/50	Goals		
JONES, Matt	Chiswick	09/10/70	Fr: YTS	07/88	Apps.	2+3	0+1
			To: Chelmsford City	07/90	Goals		
JONES, Tommy	Cardiff		Fr: Bristol City	06/21	Apps.	3	
					Goals		

K

Name	Birthplace	DOB	Transfer	Date		Apps./Goals		
KANE, Stan	Workington	17/04/12	Fr: Liverpool (trial)	05/36	Apps.	2	
					Goals		
KAY, Harold	Barnsley	24/04/00	Fr: Barnsley	06/23	Apps.	11	
			To: Barrow	06/24	Goals	(1)	
KEEFE, David	Dagenham	23/06/57	Fr: Apprentice	07/75	Apps.	4+2	
			To: Torquay United	08/77	Goals	(1)	
KEELEY, John	Plaistow	27/07/61	Fr: Apprentice	07/79	Apps.	63	13
			To: Chelmsford City	07/80	Goals		
KELLARD, Bobby	Edmonton	01/03/43	Fr: Juniors	05/60	Apps.	106	7
			To: Crystal Palace	09/63	Goals	(15)	(2)
KELLOCK, Billy	Glasgow	07/02/54	Fr: Wolverhampton Wanderers	09/83	Apps.	53	9
			To: Port Vale	12/84	Goals	(8)	(4)
KELLY, Lawrie	Bellshill		Fr: St. Anthony's	06/34	Apps.	20	4
			To: Bristol City	06/36	Goals		
KENT, Terry	Battersea	21/10/39	Fr: Local	05/58	Apps.	1	
			To: Millwall	08/60	Goals		
KERRINS, Pat	Fulham	13/09/36	Fr: Crystal Palace	07/61	Apps.	11	1
			To: Romford	08/62	Goals		
KETTLE, Billy	South Shields	10/09/98	Fr: Ebbw Vale	07/21	Apps.	31	2
			To: Grimsby Town	07/22	Goals	(1)	(1)
KING, Bobby	Edinburgh	07/09/41	Fr: Glasgow Rangers	08/63	Apps.	77+2	7
			To: Romford	08/66	Goals	(2)	
KIRKALDIE, Jack	Coventry	02/08/17	Fr: Nuneaton Town	08/36	Apps.	1	
			To: West Ham United	03/37	Goals		
KURILA, John	Glasgow	10/04/41	Fr: Northampton Town	07/68	Apps.	87+1	14
			To: Colchester United	05/70	Goals	(1)	(1)
KYLE, Maurice	Darlington	08/11/37	Fr: Oxford United (loan)	03/70	Apps.	8	
					Goals		

L

Name	Birthplace	DOB	Transfer	Date		Apps./Goals		
LAMB, Steve	Southend	02/10/55	Fr: Apprentice	10/73	Apps.	6+1	1
			To: Chelmsford City	07/76	Goals		
LAMB, Walter	Tarleton		Fr: Swansea Town	05/25	Apps.	1	
					Goals		
LAMPARD, Frank	West Ham	20/09/48	Fr: West Ham United	08/85	Apps.	33	5
			To: Coaching staff	06/86	Goals	(1)	(1)
LANE, Harry	Hednesford	21/03/09	Fr: Birmingham	05/33	Apps.	220	25
			To: Plymouth Argyle	03/38	Goals	(64)	(11)
			Fr: Plymouth Argyle	05/46			
			Retired	05/49			
LAVERICK, Micky	Trimdon	13/03/54	Fr: Mansfield Town	10/76	Apps.	108+2	17
			To: Huddersfield Town	07/79	Goals	(18)	(1)
LAVERTY, Pat	Gorseinon	24/05/34	Fr: Sheffield United	07/60	Apps.	21	2
			To: Wellington Town	06/61	Goals	(6)	(1)
LAWLER, Jimmy	Dublin	20/11/23	Fr: Portsmouth	01/49	Apps.	269	19
			To: Chelmsford City	07/57	Goals	(17)	
LAWRENCE, George			Fr: Darlington	08/21	Apps.	18	1
			To: Abertillery	07/22	Goals		
LAWSON, Jim	Glasgow		Fr: Army	02/21	Apps.	19	
					Goals		
LEE, Norman	Trealaw	29/05/39	Fr: Bournemouth	02/62	Apps.	22	
			To: Romford	07/63	Goals	(1)	

176

Name	Birthplace	DOB	Transfer	Date		Apps	
LEIGHTON, Billy	Wallsea	08/12/14	Fr: Newcastle United	05/38	Apps.	16	2
			Retired during war	07/69	Goals		
LESLIE, Lawrie	Edinburgh	17/03/35	Fr: Millwall	07/68	Apps.	13	2
			To: Millwall (Trainer/Coach)	07/69	Goals		
LEWIS, Bernard	Aberfan	12/03/45	Fr: Watford	09/70	Apps.	55+3	5
			To: Chelmsford City	07/72	Goals	(6)	(1)
LEWIS, Harry	Merthyr		Fr: Arsenal	05/32	Apps.	18	3
			To: Notts. County	06/33	Goals	(6)	
LIEVESLEY, Wilf	Staveley	06/10/02	Fr: Manchester City	06/22	Apps.	7	
			To: Exeter City	06/23	Goals	(1)	
LIGGETT, Norman	Thornaby	21/07/41	Fr: Middlesbrough	07/62	Apps.	1	
			To: Kings Lynn	07/63	Goals		
LINDSAY, David	Cambuslang	29/06/26	Fr: Sunderland	05/48	Apps.	52	1
			To: Yeovil Town	07/51	Goals	(1)	
LINDSEY, Keith	Scunthorpe	25/11/46	Fr: Cambridge United	01/69	Apps.	89+2	11
			To: Port Vale	12/71	Goals	(4)	
LINFORD, John	Norwich	06/02/57	Fr: Ipswich Town (loan)	03/83	Apps.	6	
					Goals	(3)	
LING, Martin	West Ham	15/07/66	Fr: Swindon Town	10/86	Apps.	124+12	26+1
			To: Mansfield Town (loan)	01/91	Goals	(30)	(6)
			To: Swindon Town	05/91			
LINTON, Tommy	Falkirk	15/10/20	Fr: Army	08/46	Apps.	67	4
			To: Tonbridge	07/49	Goals		
LITTLE, Alan	Horden	05/02/55	Fr: Aston Villa	12/74	Apps.	102+1	15
			To: Barnsley	08/77	Goals	(12)	(1)
LLOYD, Brian	St. Asaph	18/03/48	Fr: Stockport County	09/69	Apps.	46	6
			To: Wrexham	08/71	Goals		
LLOYD, Charlie	North Shields	27/09/06	Fr: Hull City	05/28	Apps.	1	
			To: Loughborough Corinthians	08/29	Goals		
LLOYD, Jack	Bristol		Fr: Yeovil & Petters	07/29	Apps.	4	
			To: Crystal Palace	08/30	Goals		
LOCK, Kevin	Plaistow	27/12/53	Fr: Fulham	08/85	Apps.	10	1
			Joined coaching staff		Goals		
LOCKE, Adam	Croydon	20/08/70	Fr: Crystal Palace	08/90	Apps.	23+15	6+1
			Still with club		Goals	(4)	
LOCKHART, Crichton	Perth	06/03/30	Fr: Chertsey	08/50	Apps.	45	5
			To: Rochdale	06/57	Goals	(11)	(1)
LOGAN, James	Lochgelly		Fr: Plymouth Argyle	09/21	Apps.	3	
					Goals		
LOUGHRAN, Joe	Consett	12/08/15	Fr: Burnley	09/49	Apps.	147	11
			Retired	05/53	Goals	(1)	
LOUKES, Gordon	Sheffield	15/06/28	Fr: Sheffield United	07/51	Apps.	2	
			To: Gravesend & Northfleet	07/52	Goals		
LOVE, Alistair	Edinburgh	09/05/55	Fr: West Bromwich Albion	05/74	Apps.	6+5	2
			To: Newport County	07/75	Goals		
LOWDER, Tom	Worksop	17/10/24	Fr: Southampton	05/53	Apps.	21	1
			To: Boston United	06/54	Goals	(3)	
LUMSDEN, Alex	Fife	24/05/46	Fr: Camelon Juniors	02/66	Apps.	2	
					Goals		
LUMSDEN, Jimmy	Glasgow	07/11/47	Fr: Leeds United	09/70	Apps.	12	
			To: Leeds United (coach)	07/71	Goals		
LUNN, Fred	Marsden		Fr: Bristol Rovers	07/23	Apps.	7	
			To: Nuneaton Town	08/24	Goals	(2)	
LYMAN, Colin	Northampton	09/03/14	Fr: Northampton Town	07/33	Apps.	1	
			To: Northampton Town	07/34	Goals		

M

Name	Birthplace	DOB	Transfer	Date		Apps	
McADAM, Tom	London		Fr: Tufnell Park	07/37	Apps.	2	1
					Goals	(1)	
McALINDEN, Jimmy	Belfast	31/12/17	Fr: Stoke City	10/48	Apps.	217	14
			To: Glenavon	07/54	Goals	(12)	(1)
McCLELLAND, Jim	Dysart	11/05/02	Fr: Raith Rovers	07/23	Apps.	26	3
			To: Middlesbrough	03/25	Goals	(17)	(5)
McCRORY, Sammy	Belfast	11/10/24	Fr: Plymouth Argyle	06/55	Apps.	205	17
			To: Cambridge United	05/60	Goals	(91)	(8)

Name	Place	Date	Transfer	Date		Apps	Goals
MacDONALD, Elias	Prestwich	11/04/98	Fr: Southampton	06/24	Apps.	37	3
			To: Southport	06/25	Goals	(1)	
McDONALD, Jack	Maltby	27/08/21	Fr: Southampton	05/53	Apps.	28	
			To: Weymouth	07/55	Goals	(6)	
McDONOUGH, Roy	Solihull	16/10/58	Fr: Colchester United	08/83	Apps.	185+23	31+3
			To: Exeter City	01/84	Goals	(34)	(5)
			Fr: Cambridge United	08/85			
			To: Colchester United	10/90			
McGUIGAN, John	Motherwell	29/10/32	Fr: St. Mirren	05/55	Apps.	125	13
			To: Newcastle United	07/58	Goals	(34)	(3)
MACKAY, Don	Glasgow	19/03/40	Fr: Dundee United	07/72	Apps.	14	1
			To: Bristol City (Coach)	06/74	Goals		
MacKAY, Norman	Edinburgh	26/05/10	Fr: Plymouth Argyle	09/34	Apps.	32	2
					Goals		
McKECHNIE, Ian	Lenzie	04/10/41	Fr: Arsenal	05/64	Apps.	62	10
			To: Hull City	08/66	Goals		
McKENNA, Peter	Liverpool		Fr: Chelsea	11/31	Apps.	2	
			Contract cancelled	12/31	Goals		
McKENNA, Tom	Stewarton	27/09/07	Fr: Merthyr Town	06/29	Apps.	10	
			To: Portadown	06/30	Goals		
McKENZIE, George	Dublin		Fr: Plymouth Argyle	06/35	Apps.	120	22
			To: Hereford United	06/39	Goals		
MacKENZIE, Ian	Rotherham	27/09/50	Fr: Sheffield United (loan)	03/75	Apps.	5+1	
					Goals		
McKINVEN, John	Campbeltown	01/05/41	Fr: Raith Rovers	05/60	Apps.	284+2	19+1
			To: Cambridge United	12/69	Goals	(62)	(4)
McMAHON, Hugh	Mexborough		Fr: Mexborough Athletic	05/33	Apps.	10	1
			To: Reading	06/34	Goals	(3)	
McMAHON, John	Manchester	07/12/49	Fr: Preston North End (loan)	09/70	Apps.	4	
					Goals		
McMILLAN, Sammy	Belfast	29/09/41	Fr: Wrexham	09/67	Apps.	76+1	12
			To: Chester City	12/69	Goals	(5)	(6)
McNEIL, ?			Fr:		Apps.	0+1	
			To:		Goals		
McNEILL, Ian	Glasgow	24/02/32	Fr: Brighton	07/62	Apps.	41	2
			To: Dover	07/64	Goals	(3)	
MADDIX, Danny	Ashford	11/10/67	Fr: Tottenham Hotspur (loan)	10/86	Apps.	2	
					Goals		
MAIDMENT, Jimmy	Sunderland	28/09/01	Fr: Thomsons Welfare	06/23	Apps.	13	
			To: Newport County	07/24	Goals		
MANSFIELD, Ron	Romford	31/12/23	Fr: Millwall	11/52	Apps.	8	
			To: Sittingbourne	07/53	Goals	(3)	
MARSDEN, Eric	Bolsover	03/01/30	Fr: Crystal Palace	10/52	Apps.	14	1
			To: Shrewsbury Town	03/53	Goals		
MARTIN, Blakey	Bradford		Fr: Derby County	07/20	Apps.	75	5
			To: Llanelly	06/22	Goals	(1)	
MARTIN, David	East Ham	25/04/63	Fr: Wimbledon	08/86	Apps.	186+8	38+2
			To: Colchester United (loan)	04/92	Goals	(19)	(8)
			Still with club				
MARTIN, Jimmy	Stoke		Fr: Blackpool	02/29	Apps.	3	
					Goals	(1)	
MARTIN, Tudor	Caerall	20/04/04	Fr: West Ham United	02/37	Apps.	57	6
			Retired during war		Goals	(28)	(2)
MATHER, Edward	Westhoughton		Fr: Bolton League	07/20	Apps.	3	
			To: Leyland	07/21	Goals	(1)	
MATHER, Stan	Bolton	1905	Fr: Bolton League	07/20	Apps.	2	
					Goals		
MATHEWS, Frank	London	07/01/48	Fr: Apprentice	01/66	Apps.	20+6	3
			To: Torquay United	06/68	Goals		
MATTHEWS, David	Hackney	20/11/65	Fr: Walsall	03/88	Apps.	1+5	1
			To: Dagenham	12/88	Goals		
MATTHEWS, Paul	Leicester	30/09/46	Fr: Leicester City (loan)	09/72	Apps.	1	
					Goals		
MAY, Eddie	Epping	19/05/43	Fr: Dagenham	01/65	Apps.	106+4	7
			To: Wrexham	06/68	Goals	(3)	

Name	Birthplace	D.O.B.	Transfer	Date			
MAY, Harry	Glasgow	15/10/28	Fr: Barnsley	09/55	Apps.	19	2
			To: Gloucester City	07/56	Goals	(1)	
MAY, Warren	Southend	31/12/64	Fr: Apprentice	01/83	Apps.	77+12	10
			To: Maidstone United	07/86	Goals	(4)	
MAYCOCK, Harry	Rotherham		Fr: Scunthorpe	07/23	Apps.	3	
					Goals	(1)	
MAYES, Ken	Wickford		Fr: Barking (amateur)	06/31	Apps.	5	
					Goals	(1)	
MERCER, Keith	Lewisham	14/10/56	Fr: Watford	02/80	Apps.	131	19
			To: Blackpool	08/83	Goals	(35)	(1)
METCALF, Colin	Norwich	03/03/39	Fr: Norwich City	09/64	Apps.	3	
			To: Wisbech Town	07/65	Goals		
MIDDLETON, Billy	Boldon Colliery		Fr: Aberdeen	06/23	Apps.	30	1
			To: Brighton	06/24	Goals		
MIDDLETON, Ray	Retford	08/12/33	Fr: Bulford United	11/57	Apps.	5	
			To: Luton Town (trial)	07/58	Goals	(1)	
MILNE, Johnny	Aberdeen	27/04/11	Fr: Plymouth Argyle	06/37	Apps.	66	12
			To: Barrow	08/46	Goals	(1)	
MONTGOMERY, Stan	West Ham	07/07/20	Fr: Hull City	09/46	Apps.	96	4
			To: Cardiff City	12/48	Goals	(7)	
MOODY, Alan	Middlesbrough	18/01/51	Fr: Middlesbrough	10/72	Apps.	444+2	60
			To: Maldon Town	05/84	Goals	(41)	(3)
MOORE, Billy	Sunderland	1903	Fr: Leeds United	06/25	Apps.	285	19
			Retired	06/36	Goals		
MOORE, Gary	Sunderland	04/11/45	Fr: Grimsby Town	11/68	Apps.	156+8	16+1
			To: Colchester United (loan)	03/74	Goals	(46)	(9)
			To: Chester City	08/74			
MOORE, Howard	Canterbury	05/03/47	Fr: Gillingham	01/68	Apps.	6+1	
			To: Port Vale	07/69	Goals		
MORAN, Paul	Enfield	22/05/68	Fr: Tottenham Hotspur (loan)	03/91	Apps.	1	
					Goals		
MORFITT, Jack	Sheffield	28/09/08	Fr: Bradford Park Avenue	06/32	Apps.	66	15
			Retired through injury	06/36	Goals	(16)	(7)
MORRIS, Colin	Blyth	22/08/53	Fr: Burnley	01/77	Apps.	133	23
			To: Blackpool	12/79	Goals	(25)	(5)
MORRIS, Freddie	Sheffield	11/03/20	Fr: Barnsley	01/49	Apps.	34	2
			Retired	05/50	Goals	(16)	
MORRIS, Hugh	Hardgate		Fr: Nottingham Forest	09/25	Apps.	117	9
			To: Newport County	07/29	Goals	(14)	(1)
MORRISON, Willie	Edinburgh	31/03/34	Fr: Sunderland	01/58	Apps.	60	1
			To: Bedford Town	06/60	Goals	(4)	
MORTON, Geoff	Acton	27/07/24	Fr: Watford	02/52	Apps.	25	2
			To: Exeter City	09/54	Goals		
MUNCIE, Bill	Carluke	28/08/11	Fr: Leicester City	05/38	Apps.	14	5
			To: Crewe Alexandra	09/46	Goals	(2)	
MURPHY, John	Greenhead	03/11/01	Fr: Norwich City	05/26	Apps.	3	
			To: Scunthorpe	06/27	Goals		
MUSTARD, John	Boldon	1905	Fr: Burnley	12/33	Apps.	20	1
			To: Crewe Alexandra	07/34	Goals	(3)	
MYERS, Colin	Sheffield	1894	Fr: Bradford City	07/20	Apps.	23	1
			To: Aberdare Athletic	07/21	Goals	(2)	(2)
MYTON, Brian	Strensall	26/09/50	Fr: Middlesbrough (loan)	11/71	Apps.	0+1	
					Goals		

N

Name	Birthplace	D.O.B.	Transfer	Date			
NASH, Paddy	South Bank	30/06/19	Fr: Middlesbrough	12/47	Apps.	57	2
			Retired	05/51	Goals		
NEAL, Dean	Edmonton	05/01/61	Fr: Millwall	01/86	Apps.	35+5	8+3
			To: Cambridge United (loan)	12/87	Goals	(6)	(3)
			To: Queens Park Rangers (loan)	06/88			
			To: Fisher Athletic	08/88			
NEAL, John	Silksworth	03/04/32	Fr: Aston Villa	11/62	Apps.	100	11
			To: Wrexham (Trainer)	08/66	Goals	(1)	
NELSON, Garry	Braintree	16/01/61	Fr: Juniors	07/79	Apps.	106+23	12+3
			To: Swindon Town	08/83	Goals	(17)	(1)

Name	Birthplace	DOB	Club	Date		Apps/Goals	
NELSON, Jimmy	Greenock	07/01/01	Fr: Newcastle United	06/35	Apps.	73	8
			Retired	05/39	Goals		
NEWELL, Paul	Woolwich	23/02/69	Fr: YTS	06/87	Apps.	15	3
			To: Leyton Orient	08/90	Goals		
NEWTON, Andrew	Romiley		Fr: Manchester City	07/20	Apps.	29	4
			To: Accrington Stanley	07/21	Goals	(1)	
NICHOLL, Terry	Wilmslow	16/09/52	Fr: Sheffield United	05/75	Apps.	50	9
			To: Gillingham	10/76	Goals	(3)	
NICHOLLS, George	London		Fr: Chelsea	06/19	Apps.	20	1
			To: Ton Pentre	06/21	Goals	(1)	
NICOL, Jim	Middlesbrough		Fr: Middlesbrough	05/30	Apps.	15	
			To: St. Johnstone	07/31	Goals	(7)	
NOGAN, Lee	Cardiff	21/05/69	Fr: Oxford United (loan)	09/87	Apps.	6	3
					Goals	(1)	(1)
NORRIS, Graham	Hampton	08/02/54	Fr: Crystal Palace (loan)	03/73	Apps.	1	
					Goals		
NUTT, Gordon	Birmingham	08/11/32	Fr: Arsenal	10/60	Apps.	16	2
			To: Eindhoven (Holland)	06/61	Goals	(2)	
NUTTALL, Tommy	Bolton		Fr: Everton	07/20	Apps.	57	6
			To: St. Mirren	07/22	Goals	(10)	(2)

O

Name	Birthplace	DOB	Club	Date		Apps/Goals	
OAKES, Jack	Winsford	13/09/05	Fr: Crook Town	05/31	Apps.	2	
			To: Clapton Orient	04/32	Goals		
O'BRIEN, Jon	Southend	02/11/61	Fr: Maldon Town	01/85	Apps.	11	
			To: Chelmsford City	07/86	Goals		
O'CALLAGHAN, Kevin	Dagenham	19/10/61	Fr: Millwall	07/91	Apps.	2+6	1
			Still with club		Goals		
O'CONNELL, Iain	Rochford	09/10/70	Fr: Trainee	08/88	Apps.	0+4	1
			To: Dover Athletic	08/91	Goals		
O'CONNOR, Phil	Romford	10/10/53	Fr: Apprentice	06/68	Apps.	1	
					Goals		
O'NEIL, Joe	Glasgow	15/08/31	Fr: Aberdeen (loan)	11/52	Apps.	24	1
					Goals	(11)	(1)
O'RAWE, Frank	Uphall		Fr: Preston North End	08/24	Apps.	50	8
			To: Brighton	06/26	Goals	(2)	
O'SHEA, Danny	Kennington	26/03/63	Fr: Exeter City	08/85	Apps.	117+2	19+1
			To: Cambridge United	08/89	Goals	(12)	
OSMOND, Avery	Huddersfield	25/12/24	Fr: Peterborough United	05/48	Apps.	2	
			To: Betteshanger Colliery Welfare	07/49	Goals		
OSWALD, Bert	Bo'ness	20/12/10	Fr: Sheffield United	07/34	Apps.	123	14
			Retired during war		Goals	(21)	(3)
OTULAKOWSKI, Anton	Dewsbury	29/01/56	Fr: West Ham United	03/79	Apps.	161+2	26
			To: Millwall	03/83	Goals	(8)	
OWERS, Adrian	Chelmsford	26/02/65	Fr: Apprentice	02/83	Apps.	19+9	2
			To: Chelmsford City	06/85	Goals		
OXLEY, Cyril	Whitwell	02/05/04	Fr: Liverpool	09/28	Apps.	15	1
			To: Kettering Town	03/29	Goals	(6)	

P

Name	Birthplace	DOB	Club	Date		Apps/Goals	
PARKER, Derrick	Wallsend	07/02/57	Fr: Burnley	02/77	Apps.	129	20
			To: Barnsley	02/80	Goals	(43)	(8)
PARKER, Stuart	Preston	16/02/54	Fr: Blackpool	07/75	Apps.	62+2	12
			To: Chesterfield	02/77	Goals	(23)	(8)
PAVITT, Bill	West Ham	30/06/20	Fr: Fulham	05/53	Apps.	79	5
			Retired	05/55	Goals		
PENNYFATHER, Glenn	Billericay	11/02/63	Fr: Apprentice	02/81	Apps.	232+6	34+1
			To: Crystal Palace	11/87	Goals	(36)	(7)
PETERS, Tom	Droylsden	22/10/20	Fr: Doncaster Rovers (guest)	08/45	Apps.	1	
			To:		Goals		
PEYTON, Gerry	Birmingham	20/05/56	Fr: Fulham (loan)	09/83	Apps.	10	
					Goals		
PHILLIPS, Jack	Barry		Fr: Barry	08/24	Apps.	8	
			To: Merthyr Town	06/25	Goals	(1)	

Name	Birthplace	DOB	Transfer	Date		Apps	Goals
PHILLIPS, Steve	Edmonton	04/08/54	Fr: Northampton Town	03/82	Apps.	157+1	23+1
			To: Torquay United	01/86	Goals	(66)	(6)
PIDGEON, Henry	London		Fr: Queens Park Rangers	11/21	Apps.	17	2
			To: Yeovil & Petters	06/23	Goals	(4)	
PIEKALNIETIS, John	Penrith	23/09/51	Fr: Nottingham Forest	04/71	Apps.	1	
			To: Yeovil Town	06/72	Goals		
PIKE, Tot	Sunderland	25/03/07	Fr: Birmingham	06/30	Apps.	69	3
			To: Norwich City	06/33	Goals	(19)	(1)
PLUM, Seth	Tottenham	15/07/99	Fr: Chelsea	07/27	Apps.	10	
			Retired through injury	05/28	Apps.		
POLYCARPOU, Andy	Islington	15/08/58	Fr: Local	09/76	Apps.	41+20	6
			To: Cambridge United	08/81	Goals	(10)	(1)
POUNTNEY, Ron	Bilston	19/03/55	Fr: Port Vale	01/75	Apps.	327+22	51+3
			To: Chelmsford City	07/85	Goals	(26)	(9)
POWELL, Billy	Sutton-in-Ashfield	21/07/01	Fr: Grimsby Town	05/30	Apps.	1	
					Goals		
POWELL, Chris	Lambeth	08/09/69	Fr: Crystal Palace	07/90	Apps.	87+2	14
			Still with club		Goals	(1)	
PRICE, Arthur	Sheffield		Fr: The Wednesday	11/22	Apps.	1	2
			To: Scunthorpe	08/24	Goals		
PRICE, Duggie	Swansea	17/11/31	Fr: Swansea Town	01/58	Apps.	91	3
			To: Hull City	09/60	Goals	(41)	(1)
PRICE, Ken	Dudley	26/02/54	Fr: Dudley Town	05/76	Apps.	1	
			To: Gillingham	12/76	Goals		
PRIOR, Spencer	Rochford	22/04/71	Fr: YTS	07/87	Apps.	90	14
			Still with club		Goals	(3)	(1)
PRITCHARD, Harvey	Meriden	30/01/18	Fr: Manchester City	02/47	Apps.	71	3
			To: Folkestone Town	06/52	Goals	(8)	
PRITCHARD, Phil	Stourbridge	09/01/65	Fr: Stoke City (loan)	03/84	Apps.	9	
					Goals		
PROUDFOOT, James	Chester-le-Street	31/01/06	Fr: Notts. County	08/33	Apps.	10	1
			To: Yeovil & Petters	12/33	Goals	(1)	
PRYDE, Bill	Falkirk	20/05/19	Fr: Bo'ness	07/47	Apps.	17	
			Retired	05/49	Goals		
PRYER, Terry	London	04/12/67	Fr: YTS	10/85	Apps.	2	0+1
					Goals		
PUNTON, Bill	Glenkindrie	09/05/34	Fr: Newcastle United	07/58	Apps.	38	2
			To: Norwich City	07/59	Goals	(6)	
PURDY, Albert	Edmonton	15/03/99	Fr: Charlton Athletic	05/25	Apps.	43	3
			To: Brentford	05/28	Goals	(1)	
PURDY, Arthur	Evenwood	23/07/04	Fr: Luton Town	05/26	Apps.	2	
			To: Durham City	08/27	Goals		

R

Name	Birthplace	DOB	Transfer	Date		Apps	Goals
RAFTER, Sean	Rochford	20/05/57	Fr: Apprentice	06/75	Apps.	23	6
			To: Leicester City	01/78	Goals		
RAMSEY, Chris	Birmingham	28/04/62	Fr: Swindon Town	08/87	Apps.	8+5	4+2
					Goals		
RANDLE, Harry	Stonebroom	31/07/06	Fr: Birmingham	05/32	Apps.	40	7
			To: Gillingham	07/34	Goals		
REDFERN, Leslie	Burton-on-Trent	06/12/11	Fr: Wolverhampton Wanderers	07/33	Apps.	3	
					Goals		
REID, David	Glasgow		Fr: Aston Villa	06/21	Apps.	39	3
			To: Barrow	08/23	Goals		
REID, Robert	Midlothian		Fr: Burnley	06/19	Apps.	28	2
					Goals		
REILLY, William	Lanark		Fr: Chester	08/32	Apps.	2	
			To: Hartlepools United	08/33	Goals		
RHODES, Brian	Marylebone	23/10/37	Fr: West Ham United	09/63	Apps.	11	
			To: Australia	06/64	Goals		
RILEY, Ian	Tollesbury	08/02/47	Fr: Maldon Town	11/67	Apps.	3+1	
					Goals		
ROBERTS, John	Australia	24/03/44	Fr: Bradford City	01/71	Apps.	47	4
			To: Northampton Town	07/72	Goals		

ROBERTS, Paul	West Ham	27/04/62	Fr: Swindon Town	07/86	Apps.	91+1	18
			To: Aldershot	08/87	Goals		
			Fr: Exeter City	01/89			
			To: Fisher Athletic	07/90			
ROBERTS, Trevor	Caernarfon	25/02/42	Fr: Liverpool	01/66	Apps.	171	17
			To: Cambridge United	03/70	Goals		
ROBERTSON, George	Farnworth		Fr: Cambuslang Rangers	06/33	Apps.	43	4
					Goals		
ROBINSON, Billy	Darlington	24/08/03	Fr: Darlington	07/27	Apps.	4	
			To: Torquay United	06/28	Goals		
ROBINSON, Dave	Longton		Fr: Leeds United	05/28	Apps.	317	31
			To: Assistant trainer after war		Goals	(1)	
ROBINSON, Jack	Blackburn	23/04/18	Fr: Bury	08/47	Apps.	6	
					Goals		
ROBINSON, Martin	Ilford	17/07/57	Fr: Gillingham	07/87	Apps.	43+13	13
			To: Cambridge United	06/89	Goals	(14)	(1)
ROBINSON, Peter	St. Ives	11/04/44	Fr: Cambridge United	03/69	Apps.	1+3	
			To: Margate	02/70	Goals		
ROBSON, Bert	Hill Wheatley	19/10/00	Fr: Leeds United	06/26	Apps.	5	2
			To: Hartlepools United	08/27	Goals	(1)	
ROBSON, John	Sunderland		Fr: South Shields	07/23	Apps.	5	1
			To: Durham City	06/24	Goals		
ROBSON, John C.	Birtley	24/03/06	Fr: Derby County	06/32	Apps.	24	3
			To: Rochdale	08/33	Goals	(5)	(1)
ROGERS, Alan	Plymouth	06/07/54	Fr: Portsmouth	03/84	Apps.	84+3	8
			To: Cardiff City	08/86	Goals	(4)	
ROGERS, Andy	Chatteris	01/12/56	Fr: Reading	10/86	Apps.	40+5	9
			To: Carshalton Athletic	08/88	Goals	(2)	
RONSON, Brian	Durham	07/08/35	Fr: Fulham	08/56	Apps.	30	2
			To: Norwich City	08/59	Goals		
ROSIER, Bertie	Hanwell	21/03/93	Fr: Clapton Orient	06/27	Apps.	41	1
			To: Fulham	08/28	Goals		
ROYCE, Simon			Fr: Heybridge Swifts		Apps.	1	
			Still with club		Goals		
RUARK, Tony	West Ham	23/03/33	Fr: Local	05/56	Apps.	9	
			To: Tonbridge	06/57	Goals		
RUDDOCK, Bill	Ryhope Colliery		Fr: The Wednesday	07/21	Apps.	8	
					Goals	(4)	
RUSSELL, Harry	Burton		Fr: Burton All Saints	06/24	Apps.	3	
			To: Burnley	06/25	Goals	(1)	

S

SAMUEL, Dan	Swansea		Fr: Llanelly	08/32	Apps.	7	
			To: Reading	05/33	Goals	(3)	
SANSOME, Paul	New Addington	06/10/61	Fr: Millwall	03/88	Apps.	187	31
			Still with club		Goals		
SARGENT, Fred	London		Fr: Fulham	11/20	Apps.	2	
					Goals		
SAYER, Stan	Chatham	02/02/95	Fr: Lincoln City	07/27	Apps.	32	1
			To: Dartford	06/29	Goals	(1)	
SAYLES, Tommy	Worksop	1892	Fr: Barnsley	05/23	Apps.	94	8
			To: Worksop	06/27	Goals	(2)	
SCANNELL, Tommy	Youghal, Ireland	03/06/25	Fr: Tilbury	12/49	Apps.	98	4
			To: Folkestone Town	06/55	Goals		
SCHNEIDER, Danny	Rochford	30/03/70	Fr: Trainee	08/88	Apps.	1	
					Goals		
SCULLY, Pat	Dublin	23/06/70	Fr: Arsenal	03/91	Apps.	65	4
			Still with club		Goals	(3)	
SEADEN, John	Southend	04/06/67	Fr: Apprentice	03/85	Apps.	18+1	2
			To: Chelmsford City	07/87	Goals		
SHANKLY, Jimmy	Glenbuck		Fr: Sheffield United	06/28	Apps.	147	5
			To: Barrow	05/33	Goals	(97)	(3)
SHAW, Tom	London		Fr: Local (amateur)	08/20	Apps.	1	
					Goals		

Name	Birthplace	DOB	Movement	Date		
SHAW, William	Swinton		Fr: Scunthorpe	05/25	Apps. 34	5
			To: Gainsborough Trinity	06/26	Goals (19)	(2)
SHEARD, Frank	Spilsby	29/01/22	Fr: Leicester City	05/46	Apps. 180	12
			To: Gravesend & Northfleet	06/56	Goals (1)	
SHEPHERD, Greig	Edinburgh	29/09/60	Fr: Eastern Athletic (Hong Kong)	08/83	Apps. 47+6	8
			To: Peterborough United	12/84	Goals (11)	(5)
SHIELS, Jimmy	Derry	24/02/38	Fr: Manchester United	06/61	Apps. 25	1
			To: Ballymena	06/62	Goals	
SHIRES, Alan	Leigh	29/06/48	Fr: Apprentice	08/65	Apps. 0+1	
			To: Colchester United	07/66	Goals	
SHORT, Russell	Ilford	04/09/68	Fr: YTS	06/87	Apps. 0+1	1+1
			To: Dagenham	08/89	Goals	
SIBLEY, Joe	Southend	06/10/19	Fr: Juniors	08/37	Apps. 213	13
			To: Newcastle United	02/47	Goals (39)	(5)
			Fr: Newcastle United	07/50		
			Retired	05/56		
SILKMAN, Barry	Stepney	29/06/52	Fr: Leyton Orient	07/85	Apps. 38+2	3
			To: Crewe Alexandra	09/86	Goals (1)	
SILVESTER, Peter	Wokingham	19/02/48	Fr: Norwich City	02/74	Apps. 79+2	10
			To: Reading (loan)	03/75	Goals (32)	(5)
			To: Blackburn Rovers (loan)	10/76		
			To: Washington Diplomats (USA)	03/77		
SIMPSON, Owen	Stocksfield	18/09/43	Fr: Colchester United	08/69	Apps. 64	9
			To: Darlington	03/71	Goals (1)	
SINGLETON, Ted	London	27/11/19	Fr: Local (amateur)	08/38	Apps. 2	
			Retired during war		Goals	
SKIVINGTON, Glen	Barrow	19/01/62	Fr: Derby County	08/83	Apps. 2+1	1
			To: Barrow	03/84	Goals	
SLACK, Mel	Bishop Auckland	07/03/44	Fr: Sunderland	08/65	Apps. 107+4	9
			To: Cambridge United	07/69	Goals (5)	(1)
SLATER, Jackie	Sheffield		Fr: Swansea Town	07/22	Apps. 92	7
			To: Grays Thurrock	07/25	Goals (15)	(3)
SLATER, Malcolm	Buckie	22/10/39	Fr: Montrose	11/63	Apps. 82	11+1
			To: Leyton Orient	01/67	Goals (6)	(1)
SMILLIE, Andy	Ilford	15/03/41	Fr: Scunthorpe United	09/64	Apps. 164	16
			To: Gillingham	10/68	Goals (29)	
SMIRK, Alf	Pershore	14/03/17	Fr: Sunderland Bus Company	06/38	Apps. 100	14
			To: Gateshead	03/48	Goals (26)	(6)
SMITH, Alex	Dewsbury	11/05/47	Fr: Huddersfield Town	04/70	Apps. 129+1	10
			To: Colchester United	01/73	Goals (1)	
SMITH, Herbert	Birmingham	17/12/22	Fr: Aston Villa	06/54	Apps. 5	
			To: Corby Town	07/55	Goals	
SMITH, Nicky	Berkeley	28/01/69	Fr: YTS	07/87	Apps. 49+11	6+6
			To: Dartford (loan)	02/90	Goals (6)	
			To: Colchester United			
SMITH, Paul	Lenham	18/09/71	Fr: YTS	08/89	Apps. 10+2	
			Still with club		Goals (1)	
SMITH, Ray J.	Islington	18/04/43	Fr: Basildon United	12/61	Apps. 150	12
			To: Wrexham	07/67	Goals (55)	(2)
SMITH, Ray S.	Evenwood	14/04/29	Fr: Luton Town	08/57	Apps. 46	6
			To: Hastings United	10/66	Goals (1)	
SMITH, Stephen	Hednesford	27/03/96	Fr: Charlton Athletic	05/25	Apps. 79	7
			To: Clapton Orient	05/27	Goals (10)	(1)
SMITH, William	Aberaman		Fr: Wolverhampton Wanderers	07/33	Apps. 16	3
					Goals	
SPELMAN, Isaac (Taffy)	Newcastle		Fr: Leeds United	05/35	Apps. 43	7
			To: Tottenham Hotspur	05/37	Goals (3)	
SPENCE, Derek	Belfast	18/01/52	Fr: Blackpool	12/79	Apps. 100+4	9
			To: See Bee (Hong Kong)	07/82	Goals (32)	(2)
STANNARD, Jim	Harold Hill	06/10/62	Fr: Fulham (loan)	09/84	Apps. 109	15
			Fr: Fulham	03/85	Goals	
			To: Fulham	08/87		
STEAD, Micky	West Ham	28/02/57	Fr: Tottenham Hotspur	09/78	Apps. 297+1	43
			To: Doncaster Rovers	11/85	Goals (5)	
STEBBING, Gary	Croydon	11/08/65	Fr: Crystal Palace (loan)	01/86	Apps. 5	1
					Goals	

Name	Birthplace	DOB	Transfer	Date		Apps	Goals
STEELE, Eric	Newcastle	14/05/54	Fr: Derby County	07/87	Apps.	27	8
			To: Mansfield Town (loan)	03/88	Goals		
			To: Notts. County	08/88			
STEGGLES, Kevin	Bungay	19/03/61	Fr: Ipswich Town (loan)	02/84	Apps.	3	1
					Goals		
STENHOUSE, Alec	Stirling	01/01/33	Fr: Portsmouth	11/58	Apps.	84	5
			To: Bedford Town	06/61	Goals	(7)	(2)
STEVENS, Leo	Wallasey	18/03/10	Fr: Everton	06/33	Apps.	72	9
			To: Stockport County	06/36	Goals	(45)	(2)
STEVENSON, Alex	Airdrie		Fr: Brentford	05/34	Apps.	11	1
			To: Ards	06/35	Goals		
STEVENSON, Jimmy	Bellshill	04/08/46	Fr: Hibernian	07/67	Apps.	33+1	3
			To: Brentwood Town	07/68	Goals		
STEWART, Duncan	Dundee		Fr: Sunderland	06/24	Apps.	1	
					Goals		
STIRLING, Jim	Airdrie	23/07/25	Fr: Birmingham City	12/50	Apps.	218	15
			To: Poole Town	06/60	Goals	(2)	
STOKER, Robert	Bearpark	17/04/08	Fr: Huddersfield Town	05/33	Apps.	2	1
					Goals		
STOKES, Ernie	Hull		Fr: Torquay United	03/38	Apps.	11	1
			Retired during war		Goals		
STONE, David	Bristol	29/12/42	Fr: Bristol Rovers	07/68	Apps.	6	1
			To: Hastings United	07/69	Goals		
STUBBS, Les	Great Wakering	18/02/29	Fr: Great Wakering	05/48	Apps.	105	6
			To: Chelsea	11/52	Goals	(43)	(5)
			Fr: Chelsea	11/58			
			To: Bedford Town	06/60			
SULLIVAN, Con	Tynemouth	06/03/03	Fr: Swansea Town	08/24	Apps.	1	
			To: Hull City	06/25	Goals		
SURTEES, Albert	Willington Quay	1902	Fr: North-East League	09/26	Apps.	5	1
			To: Clapton Orient	06/27	Goals		
SUSSEX, Andy	Enfield	23/11/64	Fr: Crewe Alexandra	07/91	Apps.	12+3	3
			Still with club		Goals	(3)	(1)

T

Name	Birthplace	DOB	Transfer	Date		Apps	Goals
TAYLOR, Ernie	Mansfield		Fr: Mansfield Town	06/23	Apps.	5	
			To: Frickley Colliery	08/24	Goals		
TAYLOR, Peter	Southend	03/01/53	Fr: Apprentice	01/71	Apps.	57+18	2+1
			To: Crystal Palace	10/73	Goals	(12)	(1)
TAYLOR, Tony	Glasgow	06/09/46	Fr: Crystal Palace	08/74	Apps.	56	7
			To: Swindon Town	08/76	Goals	(1)	
TENNANT, John	Darlington	01/08/39	Fr: Chelsea	10/59	Apps.	2	2
			To: Ashford Town	12/62	Goals		
TERNANT, Ray	Blyth	09/09/48	Fr: Burnley	06/71	Apps.	82	7
			To: Doncaster Rovers	08/73	Goals	(1)	
THARME, Derek	Brighton	19/08/38	Fr: Tottenham Hotspur	05/62	Apps.	7	
			To: Hastings United	07/63	Goals		
THIRLAWAY, Bill	Washington	01/10/96	Fr: West Ham United	06/24	Apps.	8	
			To: Luton Town	05/25	Goals		
THOMAS, Martin	Senghenydd	28/11/59	Fr: Bristol Rovers (loan)	02/83	Apps.	6	
					Goals		
THOMPSON, Charlie	Kimberworth		Fr: West Ham United	06/26	Apps.	1	
					Goals	(1)	
THOMPSON, Cyril	Southend	18/12/18	Fr: Local	08/45	Apps.	66	4
			To: Derby County	07/48	Goals	(36)	(5)
THOMPSON, Dennis	Sheffield	02/06/25	Fr: Sheffield United	07/51	Apps.	51	1
			To: Clacton Town	06/54	Goals	(11)	(1)
THOMSON, Arthur	West Stanley		Fr: Manchester United	07/31	Apps.	14	2
			To: Coventry City	05/32	Goals	(6)	
THOMSON, Jimmy	Govan	17/03/31	Fr: Raith Rovers	05/56	Apps.	40	4
			To: Headington United	03/59	Goals	(10)	(3)
THORNHILL, Dennis	Draycott	05/07/23	Fr: Wolverhampton Wanderers	03/48	Apps.	11	
					Goals		
THREADGOLD, Harry	Tattenhall	06/11/24	Fr: Sunderland	07/53	Apps.	320	23
			Retired	05/63	Goals		

Name	Birthplace	DOB		Date		Apps	
TIBBS, Jimmy			Fr:		Apps.	1	
			To:		Goals		
TILSON, Steve	Wickford	27/07/66	Fr: Witham Town	02/89	Apps.	103+13	17+2
			Still with club		Goals	(17)	(4)
TIPPETT, Tommy	Gateshead	04/08/24	Fr: Army	05/46	Apps.	92	1
			To: Bournemouth	09/51	Goals	(20)	
TODD, ?			Fr:		Apps.	2	
			To:		Goals		
TOWNSEND, John	Ebbw Vale		Fr: Ebbw Vale	06/28	Apps.	6	
			To: Grays Thurrock	07/29	Goals	(1)	
TOWNSEND, Neil	Long Buckby	01/02/50	Fr: Northampton Town	07/73	Apps.	156+1	21
			To: Bournemouth	07/79	Goals	(7)	(1)
TRAINER, Jack	Athlone		Fr: Leeds United	05/38	Apps.	25	5
			Retired during war		Goals	(6)	(1)
TRAVIS, Don	Manchester	21/01/24	Fr: West Ham United	05/48	Apps.	1	
			To: Accrington Stanley	12/48	Goals		
TULLOCH, Ron	Haddington	05/06/33	Fr: Heart Of Midlothian	05/56	Apps.	11	
			To: Carlisle United	07/57	Goals	(3)	
TUNBRIDGE, Alec	Burnham-on-Crouch		Fr: Burnham-on-Crouch (am.)	07/28	Apps.	3	
					Goals		
TUOHY, Micky	West Bromwich	28/03/56	Fr: Redditch United	06/79	Apps.	20+1	7
			To: Worcester City	07/80	Goals	(4)	(2)
TURNBULL, Bob	Dumbarton	22/06/94	Fr: Clapton Orient	11/29	Apps.	2	2
			To: Chatham	08/30	Goals	(1)	
TURNER, Charlie	Athlone		Fr: Leeds United	06/35	Apps.	99	15
			To: West Ham United	06/38	Goals		
TURNER, Chris	St. Neots	03/04/51	Fr: Cambridge United	10/83	Apps.	22	4
			Retired through injury	05/84	Goals	(2)	(1)

U,V,W

Name	Birthplace	DOB		Date		Apps	
UPRICHARD, Norman	Moyraverty,Ireland	20/04/28	Fr: Portsmouth	07/59	Apps.	12	
			To: Hastings United	06/60	Goals		
VICKERY, Paul	Chelmsford	20/05/53	Fr: Apprentice	07/69	Apps.	0+1	
			To: Barking	08/70	Goals		
WAKEFIELD, Albert	Pudsey	19/11/21	Fr: Leeds United	08/49	Apps.	109	10
			To: Clacton Town	06/53	Goals	(58)	(11)
WALKER, John	Rochford	10/12/58	Fr: Apprentice	12/76	Apps.	38+13	6+2
			Joined Police	06/83	Goals	(1)	
WALL, Billy	Taunton	28/10/39	Fr: Chelsea	03/60	Apps.	56	
			To: Cambridge City	06/63	Goals	(5)	
WALLBANKS, Choppy	Chopwell	27/07/21	Fr: Fulham	10/49	Apps.	39	4
			To: Workington	08/52	Goals	(2)	
WALSH, Mario	Paddington	19/01/66	Fr: Colchester United	07/89	Apps.	10+1	4+3
			To: Colchester United	08/90	Goals	(2)	(1)
WALSH, Roy	Dedham	15/01/47	Fr: Ipswich Town	07/67	Apps.	1	
			To: Chelmsford City	01/68	Goals		
WALTERS, Joe	Prestwich	1886	Fr: Accrington Stanley	09/20	Apps.	27	4
			To: Millwall	05/21	Goals	(5)	(2)
WALTON, Frank	Southend	09/04/18	Fr: School	08/34	Apps.	144	10
			To: Dartford	07/51	Goals		
WALTON, Harry	Manchester	01/04/24	Fr: Local	05/46	Apps.	1	
					Goals		
WARD, Bob	Manchester		Fr: Manchester United	05/29	Apps.	39	2
			To: Crewe Alexandra	06/31	Goals	(2)	
WARING, Bernard	Sheffield		Fr: Kiveton Park	02/29	Apps.	1	
			To: Worksop Town	07/29	Goals		
WATKINS, Ernie	Finchley	03/04/98	Fr: Birmingham	02/24	Apps.	32	2
			To: Brentford	01/26	Goals	(15)	(2)
WATSON, Peter	Stapleford	15/04/34	Fr: Nottingham Forest	07/59	Apps.	247	16
			Retired through injury	05/66	Goals	(3)	
WEBSTER, Malcolm	Rossington	12/11/50	Fr: Fulham	01/74	Apps.	96	12
			To: Cambridge United	09/76	Goals		

Name	Birthplace	DOB	Transfer	Date		Apps	Goals
WELCH, Micky	Barbados	21/05/58	Fr: Grays Athletic	02/85	Apps.	4	1
			To: Grays Athletic	07/85	Goals		
WESTLEY, Shane	Canterbury	16/06/65	Fr: Charlton Athletic	03/85	Apps.	142+2	22+1
			To: Wolverhampton Wanderers	07/89	Goals	(10)	(2)
WHALE, Ray	West Bromwich	23/02/37	Fr: West Bromwich Albion	04/59	Apps.	29	3
					Goals		
WHALLEY, Arthur	Prestwich	1886	Fr: Manchester United	09/20	Apps.	30	4
			To: Charlton Athletic	08/21	Goals	(5)	(1)
WHELAN, Billy	Airdrie	20/02/06	Fr: Sunderland	05/32	Apps.	8	
			To: Darlington	06/33	Goals		
WHITCHURCH, Charlie	Grays	29/10/20	Fr: Tottenham Hotspur	07/47	Apps.	17	1
			To: Folkestone Town	07/48	Goals	(5)	
WHITE, Harry	Leyton		Fr: Leigh Ramblers	06/21	Apps.	4	
					Goals		
WHITE, Ray	Rochford	14/01/48	Fr: Apprentice	01/66	Apps.	10	
			To: Bristol Rovers	07/68	Goals		
WHITELAW, Dave	Glasgow		Fr: Bristol City	07/31	Apps.	92	11
			To: Gillingham	07/35	Goals		
WHITFIELD, Frank	Anston		Fr: Local (amateur)	06/25	Apps.	2	
					Goals		
WHITHAM, Victor	Burnley	1894	Fr: Scunthorpe	05/23	Apps.	20	2
			To: Boston Town	08/24	Goals	(10)	
WHYMARK, Trevor	Diss	04/05/50	Fr: Grimsby Town	01/84	Apps.	37+2	5+1
			To: Peterborough United	08/85	Goals	(6)	(2)
WHYTE, Jimmy	Glasgow	19/01/30	Fr: Third Lanark	05/54	Apps.	33	2
			To: Sittingbourne	06/57	Goals	(8)	
WIGGINS, Steve			Fr:		Apps.	0+1	
			To:		Goals		
WILEMAN, Henage	Burton		Fr: Chelsea	07/11	Apps.	58	4
			Retired	05/22	Goals	(2)	
WILKINS, Graham	Hillingdon	28/06/55	Fr: Brentford (loan)	03/84	Apps.	3	1
					Goals		
WILLIAMS, Billy	Sheffield		Fr: Sheffield Wednesday	07/34	Apps.	1	
					Goals		
WILLIAMS, Owen	Ryhope	23/09/96	Fr: Middlesbrough	07/30	Apps.	16	
			To: Shildon	09/31	Goals	(4)	
WILLIAMSON, Arthur	Ardblae	26/07/30	Fr: Clyde	05/55	Apps.	269	18
					Goals	(2)	
WILLIAMSON, Charlie	Sheffield	16/03/62	Fr: Sheffield Wednesday (loan)	03/85	Apps.	10	
					Goals		
WILLSHAW, George	London		Fr: Southall	02/36	Apps.	28	4
			To: Bristol City	06/38	Goals	(6)	(1)
WILSON, Joe	Tow Law	10/12/11	Fr: Newcastle United	07/30	Apps.	164	11
			To: Brentford	06/35	Goals	(4)	
WILSON, John	Chilton		Fr: Middlesbrough	06/27	Apps.	3	
					Goals		
WILSON, Tom	Lambeth	09/12/02	Fr: Charlton Athletic	06/32	Apps.	12	1
			Retired	03/36	Goals		
WOLFE, Tom	Barry Dock	07/03/00	Fr: Coventry City	06/24	Apps.	11	
			To: Fulham	03/25	Goals		
WOODLAND, Arthur	Nottingham		Fr: Notts. County	07/22	Apps.	30	1
					Goals	(1)	
WOODLEY, Derek	Isleworth	02/03/42	Fr: West Ham United	08/62	Apps.	167+4	10+1
			To: Charlton Athletic	06/67	Goals	(23)	
			Fr: Charlton Atheltic	10/67			
			To: Gillingham	01/68			
WOODS, Peter	Sale	21/01/50	Fr: Luton Town	02/72	Apps.	25	0+1
			To: Doncaster Rovers	07/73	Goals		
WOODS, Ray	Peterborough	27/04/30	Fr: Peterborough United	05/48	Apps.	3	
			To: Crystal Palace	06/53	Goals	(1)	
WOODWARD, Harry	Bromley	29/08/19	Fr: Chelmsford City	05/46	Apps.	14	1
			To: Tonbridge	06/52	Goals		

Name	Birthplace	DOB	Transfer	Date			
WOODWARD, John	Catford		Fr: Local	08/27	Apps.	2	
			To: Clapton Orient	10/27	Goals		
WOOLHOUSE, Ben	Sheffield		Fr: Birmingham	05/28	Apps.	2	1
			To: Loughborough Corinthians	08/29	Goals	(1)	
WOOTTON, Billy	Longton		Fr: Port Vale	08/32	Apps.	2	
					Goals		
WORTHINGTON, Bob	Halifax	22/04/47	Fr: Notts. County	08/74	Apps.	20	3
			To: Hartlepool (loan)	03/75	Goals	(1)	
			Retired – Rugby Union	06/75			
WORTHINGTON, Dave	Halifax	28/03/45	Fr: Grimsby Town	12/73	Apps.	92+3	12
			To: Cambridge City (play/man)	06/77	Goals		
WORTHY, Albert	Pilsley	01/11/05	Fr: Lincoln City	06/33	Apps.	28	2
			To: Rochdale	06/34	Goals		
WRIGHT, Doug	Southend	29/04/17	Fr: Local	07/36	Apps.	31	3
			To: Newcastle United	05/38	Goals	(2)	
WRIGHT, Pat	Oldbury	17/11/40	Fr: Derby County (loan)	03/70	Apps.	11	
					Goals		

Y

Name	Birthplace	DOB	Transfer	Date			
YATES, Steve	Burton	08/12/53	Fr: Leicester City	11/77	Apps.	223+1	30
			To: Doncaster Rovers	12/83	Goals	(8)	(1)
YOUNG, Dave	Newcastle	12/11/45	Fr: Charlton Athletic	09/76	Apps.	56+4	7
			To: Dartford	12/79	Goals		
YOUNG, Doug	Croydon	02/02/27	Fr: Walthamstow Avenue	06/53	Apps.	38	2
			To: Folkestone Town	06/56	Goals		
YOUNG, Richard	Nottingham	18/10/68	Fr: Notts. County	08/87	Apps.	5+4	2
			To: Wimbledon (loan)	02/89	Goals	(1)	
			To: Exeter City	03/89			
YOUNG, R.H.	Southend		Fr: Grays Thurrock (amateur)	08/22	Apps.	1	
					Goals		
YOUNG, ?			Fr:		Apps.	0+1	
			To:		Goals		

Long serving 1920s half back Stan Sayer has been credited with setting the great Dixie Dean on the road to stardom. Sayer, who spent most of his time in Southend's reserves, played alongside Dean in his fledgling days at Tranmere, where, according to the Sheffield Sports Special of 1928 'he taught the youngster most of his first principles'.

In March 1936, 33 year old Southend player Thomas Wilson, who lost 90% of the sight in his left eye after being struck in the face by a ball during a reserve match against Leicester, was awarded £1 7s 6d a week compensation by Southend County Court – for the rest of his life.

Southend have had two appalling runs of penalty misses. They missed six consecutive spot kicks in the 1936/7 season, then missed seven in a row during 1991 before Dean Austin scored against Charlton on 26 October.

Goalkeeper Ray White played five league games for Southend during the 1965/6 season and conceded 16 goals, including nine against Brighton.

Manchester United & England star Gordon Hill, Wimbledon striker John Fashanu, pre war legend Bryn Jones, and Scotland favourite Bruce Rioch were all given trials with Southend as youngsters. All were rejected.

Southend's amateur centre forward Ron Fogg was picked for the 20 strong Great Britain olympic soccer squad in November 1959, even though he'd only made one first team appearance during the season.

Centre forward Jim Fryatt, who played for Southend in 1962 and 1963, later retired from the game to become a Las Vegas casino croupier.

Season 1920/21 – League Division Three (South)

No.	Date	Opposition	Venue	Score	H.T.	Res.	Att.	Goalscorers	1	2	3	4	5	6	7	8	9	10	11
1	28 Aug	Brighton	(H)	2-0	(1-0)	W	10000	Fairclough(2)	Capper	Reid	Newton	Wileman	Henderson	Martin	Nicholls	Nuttall	Fairclough	Myers	Dorsett
2	30	Grimsby Town	(A)	0-1	(0-1)	L	10000		Capper	Reid	Newton	Wileman	Henderson	Martin	Nicholls	Nuttall	Fairclough	MyersD	orsett
3	4 Sep	Brighton	(A)	0-1	(0-1)	L	11000		Capper	Reid	Newton	Bollington	Henderson	Martin	Nicholls	Nuttall	Wileman	Evans	Dorsett
4	6	Grimsby Town	(H)	3-1	(2-0)	W	7000	Fairclough(3)	Capper	Reid	Newton	Wileman	Henderson	Martin	Nicholls	Myers	Fairclough	Evans	Dorsett
5	11	Swindon Town	(H)	1-3	(0-2)	L	8000	Nuttall	Capper	Reid	Newton	Wileman	Henderson	Martin	Nicholls	Nuttall	Fairclough	Allen E	Dorsett
6	18	Swindon Town	(A)	0-3	(0-)	L	9500		Capper	Reid	Evans	Wileman	Henderson	Martin	Nuttall	Myers	Fairclough	Allen E	Dorsett
7	25	Watford	(A)	0-3	(0-2)	L	9000		Capper	Reid	Evans	Wileman	Henderson	Martin	Nuttall	Myers	Fairclough	Allen E	Dorsett
8	2 Oct	Watford	(H)	4-1	(3-0)	W		Fairclough(3),Walters	Capper	Newton	Evans	Wileman	Henderson	Martin	Nicholls	Nuttall	Fairclough	Walters	Dorsett
9	9	Queens Park Rangers	(A)	0-2	(0-1)	L	14500		Capper	Newton	Evans	Wileman	Henderson	Whalley	Nicholls	Nuttall	Fairclough	Myers	Newton
10	16	Queens Park Rangers	(H)	1-0	(1-0)	W	8000	Fairclough	Capper	Reid	Evans	Whalley	Henderson	Martin	Newton	Nuttall	Fairclough	Walters	Dorsett
11	20	Exeter City	(A)	0-0	(0-0)	D	3000		Capper	Reid	Evans	Whalley	Henderson	Martin	Myers	Wileman	Fairclough	Nuttall	Newton
12	23	Northampton Town	(H)	1-2	(0-1)	L	8000	Whalley	Capper	Reid	Evans	Whalley	Henderson	Martin	Newton	Wileman	Fairclough	Nuttall	Dorsett
13	30	Northampton Town	(A)	0-1	(0-1)	L	9000		Capper	Reid	Evans	Wileman	Whalley	Martin	Nicholls	Wileman	Fairclough	Walters	Dorsett
14	3 Nov	Crystal Palace	(A)	3-2	(2-1)	W	9000	Fairclough(2),Dorsett	Capper	Reid	Evans	Newton	Whalley	Martin	Nicholls	Nuttall	Fairclough	Walters	Dorsett
15	6	Portsmouth	(H)	2-1	(1-1)	W	8000	Fairclough,Nuttall	Capper	Reid	Evans	Wileman	Whalley	Martin	Nicholls	Nuttall	Fairclough	Walters	Dorsett
16	13	Portsmouth	(A)	0-3	(0-2)	L	15000		Capper	Reid	Evans	Wileman	Whalley	Martin	Nicholls	Nuttall	Fairclough	Walters	Dorsett
17	22	Merthyr Town	(A)	0-2	(0-1)	L	7000		Capper	Evans	Reid	Wileman	Whalley	Martin	Allen E	Nuttall	Fairclough	Walters	Dorsett
18	27	Merthyr Town	(H)	0-1	(0-0)	L	6000		Capper	Newton	Evans	Henderson	Whalley	Henderson	Sargent	Nuttall	Fairclough	Walters	Dorsett
19	4 Dec	Plymouth Argyle	(H)	2-1	(1-1)	W	3750	Fairclough,Logan(O.G.)	Barnes	Newton	Evans	Henderson	Whalley	Martin	Allen E	Walters	Fairclough	Haynes	Dorsett
20	11	Plymouth Argyle	(A)	0-0	(0-0)	D	12500		Capper	Newton	Evans	Wileman	Whalley	Martin	Ford	Nuttall	Fairclough	Walters	Ford
21	25	Newport County	(A)	1-1	(0-0)	D	7500	Walters	Capper	Reid	Newton	Wileman	Whalley	Henderson	Nicholls	Myers	Nuttall	Walters	Ford
22	27	Newport County	(H)	2-1	(1-0)	W	10000	Whalley(2)(1 pen)	Capper	Reid	Newton	Wileman	Whalley	Henderson	Nicholls	Myers	Nuttall	Walters	Dorsett
23	1 Jan	Exeter City	(H)	0-0	(0-0)	D	4000		Capper	Reid	Newton	Wileman	Whalley	Henderson	Ford	Myers	Nuttall	Walters	Ford
24	15	Swansea Town	(H)	1-2	(0-2)	L	6500	Whalley	Capper	Reid	Newton	Wileman	Whalley	Martin	Nuttall	Myers	Fairclough	Walters	Sargent
25	22	Swansea Town	(A)	0-2	(0-2)	L	12000		Capper	Reid	Newton	Myers	Whalley	Henderson	Ford	Myers	Fairclough	Walters	Dorsett
26	5 Feb	Millwall Athletic	(A)	2-4	(1-1)	L	20000	Fairclough(2)	Capper	Wileman	Newton	Wileman	Henderson	Martin	Nicholls	Nuttall	Fairclough	Walters	Dorsett
27	12	Luton Town	(H)	1-1	(1-1)	D	6000	Nuttall	Capper	Lawson	Newton	Wileman	Henderson	Martin	Nicholls	Nuttall	Fairclough	Walters	Dorsett
28	26	Southampton	(H)	1-0	(1-0)	W	11000	Myers	Capper	Lawson	Evans	Wileman	Whalley	Martin	Nicholls	Allen H	Nuttall	Myers	Dorsett
29	5 Mar	Southampton	(A)	0-3	(0-1)	L	12000		Capper	Lawson	Evans	Wileman	Whalley	Martin	Nicholls	Ford	Myers	Allen H	Dorsett
30	12	Reading	(H)	1-0	(1-0)	W	6000	Walters	Capper	Lawson	Evans	Wileman	Whalley	Martin	Allen H	Nuttall	Fairclough	Walters	Newton
31	19	Reading	(A)	1-1	(0-1)	D	5000	Newton	Capper	Reid	Evans	Wileman	Whalley	Martin	Allen H	Nuttall	Dickinson	Walters	Newton
32	25	Gillingham	(A)	1-1	(0-1)	D	4000	Nuttall	Capper	Reid	Evans	Wileman	Whalley	Martin	Allen H	Newton	Dickinson	Myers	Dorsett
33	26	Bristol Rovers	(A)	1-2	(0-0)	L	14000	Nuttall	Capper	Reid	Evans	Wileman	Whalley	Martin	Nicholls	Myers	Nuttall	Myers	Dorsett
34	28	Gillingham	(H)	1-0	(1-0)	W	10000	Nuttall	Capper	Reid	Evans	Wileman	Henderson	Martin	Nicholls	Newton	Nuttall	Walters	Dorsett
35	2 Apr	Bristol Rovers	(H)	1-0	(1-0)	W	7000	Nuttall	Capper	Reid	Evans	Henderson	Whalley	Martin	Baldwin	Newton	Dickinson	Walters	Dorsett
36	6	Millwall Athletic	(H)	1-2	(0-0)	L	6000	Dorsett	Capper	Reid	Evans	Myers	Whalley	Martin	Baldwin	Newton	Nuttall	Walters	Dorsett
37	9	Brentford	(A)	2-2	(2-1)	D	4000	Nuttall,Hodson(O.G.)	Capper	Newton	Evans	Wileman	Whalley	Martin	Baldwin	Myers	Nuttall	Walters	Dorsett
38	16	Brentford	(H)	4-1	(2-1)	W	6000	Walters(2),Baldwin,Nuttall	Capper	Newton	Evans	Wileman	Whalley	Martin	Baldwin	Myers	Nuttall	Walters	Dorsett
39	23	Norwich City	(A)	1-3	(0-2)	L	4000	Myers	Capper	Lawson	Evans	Wileman	Whalley	Martin	Baldwin	Myers	Nuttall	Walters	Dorsett
40	30	Norwich City	(H)	3-1	(1-1)	W	6000	Mather E,Dorsett,Whalley	Capper	Lawson	Evans	Wileman	Shaw	Martin	Baldwin	Myers	Mather E	Walters	Dorsett
41	2 May	Luton Town	(A)	0-4	(0-2)	L			Mather J	Lawson	Evans	Wileman	Whalley	Martin	Baldwin	Myers	Mather E	Walters	Dorsett
42	7	Crystal Palace	(H)	0-2	(0-1)	L	6500		Mather J	Reid	Evans	Wileman	Whalley	Martin	Baldwin	Nuttall	Mather E	Walters	Dorsett

Major Cup Competitions

Rd.	Date	Opposition	Venue	Score	H.T.	Res.	Att.	Goalscorers	1	2	3	4	5	6	7	8	9	10	11
			F.A.Cup																
Q6	18 Dec	Hednesford Town	(H)	3-1	(1-0)	W	4445	Walters, Whaley(pen), Dorsett	Capper	Newton	Evans	Henderson	Whaley	Martin	Ford	Nuttall	Wileman	Walters	Dorsett
R1	8 Jan	Eccles United	(H)	5-1	(3-1)	W	7063	Myers(2), Nuttall(2), Walters	Capper	Reid	Evans	Wileman	Whaley	Martin	Ford	Myers	Nuttall	Walters	Newton
R2	29	Blackpool	(H)	1-0	(0-0)	W	9250	Dorsett	Capper	Reid	Newton	Wileman	Whaley	Henderson	Ford	Nuttall	Fairclough	Walters	Dorsett
R3	19 Feb	Tottenham H.	(H)	1-4	(1-1)	L	11661	Nicholls	Capper	Newton	Evans	Wileman	Whaley	Martin	Nicholls	Nuttall	Fairclough	Walters	Dorsett

SOUTHEND UNITED 1st XI — 1906

Morris, Mitchell, Johnson, Owen, Perry, Cotton, Molyneur (Captain), Freeman, Thompson (Trainer), Holden, Cotgrove, Halse, Watkins, Axcell, R. Jack (Secretary/Manager).

(The first) team group from 1906 and the first programme issued, on the 12th of September 1908.

Appearances and Goals

Name	Appearances Lge.	FAC	Total	Goals Lge.	FAC	Total
ALLEN, Edward	5		5			
ALLEN, Henry	5		5			
BALDWIN, Harry	7		7	1		1
BARNES, Edward	1		1			
BOLLINGTON, John	1		1			
CAPPER, Tom	39	4	43			
DICKINSON, Harold	3		3			
DORSETT, Joe	35	3	38	3	2	5
EVANS, Jimmy	32	3	35			
FAIRCLOUGH, Albert	24	2	26	15		15
FORD, Arthur	7	3	10			
HAYNES, Robert	1		1			
HENDERSON, Jim	23	2	25			
LAWSON, James	6		6			
MARTIN, Blakey	36	3	39			
MATHER, E	3		3	1		1
MATHER, Stan J.	2		2			
MYERS, Colin	23	1	24	2	2	4
NEWTON, Andrew	29	4	33	1		1
NICHOLLS, George	20	1	21		1	1
NUTTALL, Tommy	35	4	39	9	2	11
REID, Robert	28	2	30			
SARGENT, Fred	2		2			
SHAW, Tom	1		1			
WALTERS, Joe	27	4	31	5	2	7
WHALEY, Arthur	30	4	34	5	1	6
WILEMAN, Harry	37	4	41			
Own Goal				2		2

	Ps	P	W	D	L	F	A	W	D	L	F	A	Pts.
1920/21	17	42	13	2	6	32	20	1	6	14	12	41	36

Season 1921/22 – League Division Three (South)

No.	Date	Opposition	Venue	Score	H.T.	Res.	Att.	Goalscorers	1	2	3	4	5	6	7	8	9	10	11
1	27 Aug	Brighton	(A)	0-0	(0-0)	D	9000		Capper	Lawson	Evans J	Wileman	Halstead	Martin	Baldwin	Nuttall	Ruddock	Howard	Elliott
2	29	Brentford	(H)	1-1	(1-0)	D	7000	Ruddock	Capper	Lawson	Evans J	Wileman	Halstead	Martin	Baldwin	Nuttall	Ruddock	Howard	Elliott
3	3 Sep	Brighton	(H)	1-2	(0-1)	L	8000	Baldwin	Capper	Lawson	Evans J	Wileman	Halstead	Martin	Baldwin	Nuttall	Ruddock	Howard	Elliott
4	5	Brentford	(A)	0-1	(0-0)	L	10000		Capper	Lawson	Evans J	Wileman	Halstead	Martin	Harris F	Reid	Flowers	Logan	Kettle
5	10	Swansea Town	(A)	1-1	(1-0)	D	14500	Wileman	Capper	Lawson	Evans J	Wileman	Lawrence	Martin	Harris F	Reid	Nuttall	Logan	Elliott
6	12	Newport County	(A)	1-2	(1-2)	L	5500	Martin	Capper	Lawson	Evans J	Wileman	Lawrence	Martin	Baldwin	Reid	Nuttall	Logan	Elliott
7	17	Swansea Town	(H)	1-0	(0-0)	W	6250	Howard	Capper	Lawson	Evans J	Wileman	Lawrence	Martin	Harris F	Allen	Nuttall	Howard	Elliott
8	24	Exeter City	(A)	1-4	(0-1)	L	4500	Evans J(pen)	Capper	Lawson	Evans J	Wileman	Lawrence	Martin	Harris F	Allen	Nuttall	Howard	Elliott
9	1 Oct	Exeter City	(H)	0-1	(0-0)	L	6000		Capper	Dellow	Evans J	Dellow	Lawrence	Martin	Harris F	Jones	Nuttall	Flowers	Elliott
10	8	Millwall Athletic	(A)	0-0	(0-0)	D	16000		Capper	Dellow	Evans J	Harris G	Lawrence	Martin	Harris F	Nuttall	Wileman	Hawarden	Kettle
11	15	Millwall Athletic	(H)	1-1	(1-1)	D	7000	Harris F	Capper	Dellow	Evans J	Harris G	Lawrence	Martin	Harris F	Nuttall	Wileman	Hawarden	Kettle
12	22	Gillingham	(A)	0-1	(0-0)	L	10000		Capper	Dellow	Evans J	Wileman	Harris G	Martin	Harris F	Reid	Nuttall	Hawarden	Kettle
13	29	Gillingham	(H)	2-0	(2-0)	W	6000	Wileman,Evans J(pen)	Capper	Dellow	Evans J	Wileman	Lawrence	Martin	Harris F	Reid	White	Hawarden	Kettle
14	5 Nov	Luton Town	(A)	0-3	(0-1)	L	8000		Capper	Dellow	Evans J	Wileman	Lawrence	Martin	Harris F	Reid	White	Hawarden	Kettle
15	12	Luton Town	(H)	0-1	(0-0)	L	6000		Capper	Dellow	Evans J	Jones	Lawrence	Martin	Baldwin	Wileman	Harris F	Hawarden	Kettle
16	19	Aberdare Athletic	(H)	3-2	(2-1)	W	7000	Hawarden,Pidgeon,Evans J(pen)	Capper	Dellow	Evans J	Wileman	Lawrence	Martin	Harris F	Reid	Pidgeon	Hawarden	Kettle
17	26	Aberdare Athletic	(A)	1-1	(0-0)	D	8000	Pidgeon	Capper	Dellow	Evans J	Wileman	Lawrence	Martin	Baldwin	Buddery	Pidgeon	Hawarden	Kettle
18	10 Dec	Newport County	(H)	0-1	(0-0)	L	7000		Capper	Dellow	Evans J	Wileman	Lawrence	Martin	Harris F	Buddery	Pidgeon	Hawarden	Kettle
19	17	Plymouth Argyle	(A)	0-4	(0-3)	L	14000		Capper	Dellow	Evans J	Wileman	Halstead	Martin	Harris F	Nuttall	Pidgeon	Buddery	Kettle
20	24	Plymouth Argyle	(H)	1-0	(1-0)	W		Pidgeon	Capper	Dellow	Evans J	Wileman	Lawrence	Martin	Harris F	Nuttall	Pidgeon	Buddery	Kettle
21	26	Portsmouth	(H)	1-2	(0-1)	L	8000	Evans J(pen)	Capper	Dellow	Evans J	Wileman	Lawrence	Martin	Baldwin	Nuttall	Pidgeon	Buddery	Kettle
22	27	Portsmouth	(A)	0-6	(0-3)	L	23000		Capper	Lawson	Evans J	Dellow	Lawrence	Martin	Allen	Reid	Pidgeon	Buddery	Kettle
23	31	Merthyr Town	(H)	2-1	(1-1)	W	5000	Halstead,Pidgeon	Capper	Dellow	Evans J	Reid	Halstead	Martin	Allen	Nuttall	Pidgeon	Buddery	Kettle
24	14 Jan	Merthyr Town	(A)	2-2	(0-0)	D	4000	Evans J(pen),Harris F	Capper	Dellow	Evans J	Reid	Halstead	Martin	Harris F	Nuttall	Pidgeon	Buddery	Kettle
25	21	Watford	(A)	1-4	(1-2)	L	4000	Evans J(pen)	Capper	Lawson	Evans J	Halstead	Lawrence	Martin	Harris F	Nuttall	Pidgeon	Hawarden	Kettle
26	4 Feb	Charlton Athletic	(A)	0-4	(0-1)	L	7000		Capper	Jones	Evans W	Reid	Halstead	Martin	Harris F	Buddery	Pidgeon	Gibbons	Kettle
27	11	Charlton Athletic	(H)	1-1	(0-0)	D	4500	Evans J(pen)	Capper	Evans W	Evans J	Reid	Halstead	Martin	Harris F	Buddery	Pidgeon	Gibbons	Kettle
28	18	Northampton Town	(A)	2-0	(0-0)	W	5500	Evans J(pen),Gibbons	Jeffries	Evans W	Evans J	Reid	Halstead	Martin	Pidgeon	Allen	Buddery	Gibbons	Kettle
29	25	Northampton Town	(H)	1-1	(1-0)	D	6000	Evans J(pen)	Capper	Evans W	Evans J	Reid	Halstead	Martin	Allen	Dobson	Buddery	Buddery	Kettle
30	4 Mar	Southampton	(A)	0-5	(0-1)	L	11000		Capper	Evans W	Evans J	Reid	Halstead	Howard	Allen	Dobson	Pidgeon	Buddery	Kettle
31	11	Southampton	(H)	0-0	(0-0)	D	7000		Capper	Evans W	Evans J	Reid	Halstead	Howard	Allen	Dobson	Nuttall	Buddery	Kettle
32	18	Queens Park Rangers	(H)	1-2	(1-0)	L	7000	Nuttall	Capper	Evans W	Evans J	Howard	Halstead	Howard	Allen	Dobson	Nuttall	Buddery	Kettle
33	25	Queens Park Rangers	(A)	0-1	(0-0)	L	12000		Capper	Evans W	Evans J	Howard	Halstead	Martin	Harris F	Dobson	Nuttall	Buddery	Flowers
34	1 Apr	Norwich City	(H)	0-1	(0-1)	L	4000		Capper	Lawson	Evans J	Howard	Lawrence	Martin	Allen	Dobson	Nuttall	Buddery	Flowers
35	8	Norwich City	(A)	1-1	(1-0)	D	6500	Kettle	Capper	Evans W	Evans J	Howard	Halstead	Martin	Allen	Dobson	Pidgeon	Buddery	Kettle
36	14	Swindon Town	(A)	1-2	(1-2)	L	8000	Halstead	Capper	Evans W	Evans J	Howard	Halstead	Martin	Allen	Dobson	Pidgeon	Buddery	Kettle
37	15	Reading	(H)	2-0	(1-0)	W	4000	Halstead,Evans J(pen)	Capper	Lawson	Evans J	Howard	Halstead	Martin	Allen	Dobson	Ruddock	Buddery	Kettle
38	17	Swindon Town	(H)	1-6	(0-2)	L	5000	Ruddock	Hall	Lawson	Evans J	Howard	Halstead	Martin	Allen	Dobson	Ruddock	Buddery	Flowers
39	22	Reading	(A)	0-4	(0-3)	L	4500		Capper	Evans W	Evans J	Reid	Halstead	White	Allen	Buddery	Ruddock	Gibbons	Kettle
40	26	Watford	(H)	1-4	(0-0)	L	1500	Ruddock	Capper	Evans W	Evans J	Reid	Halstead	Martin	Allen	Buddery	Ruddock	Gibbons	Kettle
41	29	Bristol Rovers	(H)	3-0	(2-0)	W	3000	Dobson(2),Ruddock	Jeffries	Evans J	Evans J	Howard	Halstead	Martin	Allen	Dobson	Ruddock	Gibbons	Kettle
42	6 May	Bristol Rovers	(A)	0-1	(0-0)	L	6000		Capper	Evans J	Evans J	Howard	Halstead	Martin	Allen	Dobson	Nuttall	Buddery	Kettle

Major Cup Competitions

Rd.	Date	Opposition	Venue	Score	H.T.	Res.	Att.	Goalscorers
				F.A.Cup				
R1	7 Jan	Worksop Town	(A)	2-1	(1-1)	W	5560	Kettle.Buddery
R2	28	Swansea Town	(H)	0-1	(0-1)	L	10200	

1	2	3	4	5	6	7	8	9	10	11
Capper	Dellow	Evans J	Reid	Halstead	Martin	Allen H	Nuttall	Pidgeon	Buddery	Kettle
Capper	Evans W	Evans J	Reid	Lawrence	Martin	Harris	Nuttall	Pidgeon	Buddery	Kettle

Team Group of the 1913/14 Season.

EMERY BARNES ROBSON Councillor H. WARD (Director) Mr O. TRIGG (Director) STEEL KEBBELL LIDDELL J. BYFORD (Director) PROBERT Councillor G. RADFORD (Chairman) AXCELL

KITTO (Trainer) WILSON FROST L. A. LOUCH WILEMAN BRADSHAW G. A. WESTON (Director)

Copyright Photo.   *A. Wilkes, 46, Legge Street, West Bromwich.*

Appearances and Goals

Name	Appearances Lge.	FAC	Total	Goals Lge.	FAC	Total
ALLEN, Henry	18	1	19			
BALDWIN, Harry	7		7	1		1
BUDDERY, Harry	25	2	27		1	1
CAPPER, Tom	39	2	41			
DELLOW, Stan	16	1	17			
DOBSON, Harry	13		13	2		2
ELLIOTT, Alex	8		8			
EVANS, Billy	15	1	16			
EVANS, Jimmy	40	2	42	10		10
FLOWERS, Alf	5		5			
GIBBONS, A S	5		5	1		1
HALL, Joe	1		1			
HALSTEAD, Fred	24	1	25	3		3
HARRIS, Fred	20	1	21	2		2
HARRIS, George	3		3			
HAWARDEN, Andrew	10		10	1		1
HOWARD, Stephen	15		15	1		1
JEFFRIES, Syd	2		2			
JONES, Tommy	3		3			
KETTLE, Billy	31	2	33	1	1	2
LAWRENCE, George	18	1	19			
LAWSON, James	13		13			
LOGAN, James	3		3			
MARTIN, Blakey	39	2	41	1		1
NUTTALL, Tommy	22	2	24	1		1
PIDGEON, Henry	16	2	18	4		4
REID, David	19	2	21			
RUDDOCK, Bill	8		8	4		4
WHITE, Harry	3		3			
WILEMAN, Harry	21		21	2		2

	Ps	P	W	D	L	F	A	W	D	L	F	A	Pts.
1921/22	22	42	7	5	9	23	23	1	6	14	11	51	27

Season 1922/23 – League Division Three (South)

No.	Date	Opposition	Venue	Score	H.T.	Res.	Att.	Goalscorers	1	2	3	4	5	6	7	8	9	10	11
1	26 Aug	Newport County	(A)	2-0	(2-0)	W	10215	Goodwin,Slater	Jennings	Bissett	Evans J	Reid	Woodland	Booth	Firth	Dobson	Goodwin	Slater	Davies
2	2 Sep	Newport County	(H)	3-1	(2-0)	W	11000	Goodwin,Booth,Dobson	Jennings	Bissett	Evans J	Reid	Humph'ys	Booth	Firth	Dobson	Goodwin	Slater	Davies
3	9	Swansea Town	(A)	0-1	(0-0)	L	14000		Jennings	Bissett	Evans J	Reid	Humph'ys	Booth	Firth	Dobson	Goodwin	Slater	Davies
4	11	Aberdare Athletic	(A)	1-1	(1-0)	D	5000	Goodwin	Jennings	Bissett	Evans J	Reid	Humph'ys	Booth	Firth	Dobson	Goodwin	Slater	Davies
5	16	Swansea Town	(H)	0-1	(0-0)	L	10000		Jennings	Bissett	Evans J	Woodland	Humph'ys	Booth	Firth	Dobson	Goodwin	Slater	Davies
6	23	Norwich City	(A)	1-2	(0-0)	L	10000	Slater	Jennings	Bissett	Evans J	Reid	Humph'ys	Booth	Firth	Dobson	Goodwin	Slater	Davies
7	25	Aberdare Athletic	(H)	4-0	(4-0)	W	6000	Goodwin(3),Slater	Jennings	Bissett	Evans J	Reid	Humph'ys	Booth	Firth	Dobson	Goodwin	Slater	Davies
8	30	Norwich City	(H)	3-1	(2-0)	W	8700	Goodwin,Evans J(pen),Slater	Jennings	Bissett	Evans J	Reid	Humph'ys	Booth	Firth	Dobson	Goodwin	Slater	Davies
9	7 Oct	Bristol Rovers	(A)	0-2	(0-1)	L	9000		Jennings	Bissett	Evans W	Reid	Humph'ys	Booth	Firth	Dobson	Goodwin	Slater	Davies
10	14	Bristol Rovers	(H)	0-0	(0-0)	D	9000		Jennings	Bissett	Evans W	Reid	Woodland	Humph'ys	Firth	Dobson	Goodwin	Slater	Davies
11	21	Bristol City	(A)	0-5	(0-4)	L	10000		Jennings	Evans W	Evans J	Reid	Humph'ys	Woodland	Firth	Dobson	Goodwin	Slater	Davies
12	28	Bristol City	(H)	0-3	(0-1)	L	5300		Jennings	Evans W	Evans J	Reid	Humph'ys	White	Firth	Dobson	Goodwin	Slater	Davies
13	4 Nov	Northampton Town	(H)	1-2	(0-1)	L	7000	Goodwin	Jennings	Bissett	Evans J	Woodland	Dorey	Booth	Firth	Dobson	Goodwin	Lievesley	Davies
14	11	Northampton Town	(A)	2-5	(0-2)	L	8000	Slater,Goodwin	Jennings	Bissett	Evans J	Woodland	Dorey	Booth	Firth	Dobson	Goodwin	Slater	Davies
15	25	Plymouth Argyle	(A)	1-1	(1-1)	D	10000	Goodwin	Hall	Bissett	Dellow	Booth	Halley	Price	Firth	Dobson	Goodwin	Slater	Davies
16	9 Dec	Exeter City	(A)	1-2	(1-0)	L	5000	Goodwin	Hall	Bissett	Dellow	Woodland	Halley	Booth	Firth	Barnes	Goodwin	Lievesley	Davies
17	16	Exeter City	(H)	5-0	(3-0)	W	3000	Davies(2),Slater,Woodland,Evans J	Hall	Bissett	Evans J	Woodland	Halley	Booth	Firth	Dobson	Goodwin	Slater	Davies
18	23	Charlton Athletic	(H)	0-0	(0-0)	D			Hall	Bissett	Halley	Reid	Woodland	Humph'ys	Firth	Barnes	Goodwin	Slater	Davies
19	25	Reading	(A)	3-1	(2-0)	W	8900	Goodwin,Halley(pen),Slater	Hall	Bissett	Dellow	Woodland	Halley	Humph'ys	Firth	Reid	Goodwin	Lievesley	Davies
20	26	Reading	(H)	1-1	(0-1)	D	9000	Goodwin	Hall	Bissett	Dellow	Reid	Halley	Humph'ys	Cox	Slater	Goodwin	Lievesley	Davies
21	30	Merthyr Town	(A)	1-2	(0-2)	L	4000	Lievesley	Hall	Bissett	Dellow	Woodland	Halley	Humph'ys	Firth	Slater	Goodwin	Lievesley	Davies
22	6 Jan	Merthyr Town	(H)	1-1	(1-1)	D	5890	Slater	Hall	Bissett	Evans W	Woodland	Halley	Humph'ys	Firth	Slater	Goodwin	Lievesley	Davies
23	20	Watford	(H)	2-1	(0-1)	W	4000	Dobson,Davies	Hall	Bissett	Evans W	Halley	Dorey	Woodland	Bradshaw	Dobson	Goodwin	Slater	Davies
24	27	Watford	(A)	1-1	(1-1)	D	7000	Dobson	Hall	Bissett	Evans W	Halley	Dorey	Woodland	Firth	Dobson	Goodwin	Slater	Davies
25	3 Feb	Portsmouth	(A)	0-0	(0-0)	D	9000		Hall	Bissett	Evans W	Halley	Dorey	Woodland	Firth	Dobson	Goodwin	Slater	Davies
26	10	Portsmouth	(H)	0-0	(0-0)	D	6200		Hall	Bissett	Evans J	Halley	Dorey	Woodland	Firth	Dobson	Goodwin	Slater	Davies
27	17	Millwall Athletic	(A)	1-1	(1-1)	D	16000	Goodwin	Hall	Bissett	Evans J	Halley	Dorey	Woodland	Firth	Dobson	Goodwin	Slater	Davies
28	24	Millwall Athletic	(H)	4-0	(3-0)	W	9000	Goodwin(4)	Hall	Bissett	Evans J	Halley	Dorey	Woodland	Firth	Dobson	Goodwin	Slater	Davies
29	3 Mar	Luton Town	(A)	0-2	(0-0)	L	7000		Hall	Evans J	Evans W	Halley	Dorey	Woodland	Firth	Dobson	Goodwin	Slater	Davies
30	10	Luton Town	(H)	1-3	(0-3)	L	7296	Goodwin	Hall	Bissett	Evans J	Halley	Dorey	Booth	Firth	Dobson	Goodwin	Slater	Davies
31	12	Charlton Athletic	(A)	1-5	(0-1)	L		Firth	Jennings	Bissett	Evans J	Halley	Dorey	Booth	Firth	Dobson	Goodwin	Slater	Davies
32	17	Queens Park Rangers	(H)	2-0	(1-0)	W	7000	Slater,Halley	Hall	Bissett	Evans W	Woodland	Dorey	Booth	Halley	Dobson	Goodwin	Slater	Davies
33	24	Queens Park Rangers	(A)	0-1	(0-0)	L	8000		Hall	Bissett	Evans J	Woodland	Dorey	Booth	Halley	Barnes	Goodwin	Slater	Davies
34	30	Brentford	(H)	0-0	(0-0)	D	8000		Hall	Evans J	Evans W	Woodland	Dorey	Booth	Firth	Dobson	Goodwin	Slater	Davies
35	31	Gillingham	(H)	1-1	(1-1)	D	8000	Goodwin(pen)	Hall	Bissett	Evans W	Woodland	Dorey	Booth	Firth	Dobson	Goodwin	Slater	Davies
36	2 Apr	Brentford	(A)	1-2	(0-1)	L	10000	Evans J(pen)	Hall	Evans J	Evans W	Woodland	Dorey	Booth	Firth	Dobson	Goodwin	Slater	Davies
37	7	Gillingham	(A)	0-1	(0-1)	L	6000		Hall	Evans J	Evans W	Reid	Woodland	Booth	Pidgeon	Dobson	Goodwin	Slater	Davies
38	9	Plymouth Argyle	(H)	2-1	(0-1)	W		Goodwin,Evans J(pen)	Hall	Evans J	Evans W	Reid	Booth	Woodland	Firth	Dobson	Goodwin	Slater	Davies
39	14	Brighton	(H)	0-1	(0-1)	L	6200		Hall	Bissett	Evans J	Reid	Booth	Woodland	Firth	Dobson	Goodwin	Slater	Davies
40	21	Brighton	(A)	1-0	(0-0)	W	8000	Jenkins(O.G.)	Hall	Halley	Evans J	Reid	Booth	Woodland	Firth	Dobson	Goodwin	Slater	Lievesley
41	28	Swindon Town	(H)	2-0	(1-0)	W	6000	Davies(pen),Dobson	Hall	Halley	Evans J	Reid	Booth	Woodland	Firth	Dobson	Lievesley	Slater	Davies
42	5 May	Swindon Town	(A)	0-3	(0-2)	L	3000		Hall	Barnes	Halley	Reid	Booth	Woodland	Firth	Dobson	Lievesley	Slater	Davies

Abbrev.: Humph'ys = Humphreys.

Major Cup Competitions

Rd.	Date	Opposition	Venue	Score	H.T.	Res.	Att.	1	2	3	4	5	6	7	8	9	10	11	Goalscorers
			F.A.Cup																
Q4	18 Nov	Sittingbourne	(A)	0-0	(0-0)	D	5000	Hall	Bissett	Evans J	Reid	Booth	Price	Firth	Dobson	Goodwin	Slater	Davies	
Q4r	22	Sittingbourne	(H)	4-2	(3-0)	W	5000	Hall	Bissett	Evans J	Booth	Dorey	Price	Firth	Dobson	Goodwin	Slater	Davies	Slater(2),Firth,Evans J(pen)
Q5	2 Dec	Norwich City	(H)	2-2	(1-1)	D	8030	Hall	Bissett	Dellow	Halley	Dorey	Booth	Firth	Dobson	Goodwin	Slater	Davies	Goodwin,Slater
Q5r	7	Norwich City	(A)	1-2	(0-2)	L	10113	Hall	Bissett	Dellow	Woodland	Halley	Booth	Firth	Barnes	Goodwin	Slater	Davies	Halley(pen)

Unnamed Team Group – believed to be 1922/23 season.

Appearances and Goals

Name	Appearances Lge.	FAC	Total	Goals Lge.	FAC	Total
BARNES, Harold	5	1	6			
BISSETT, James	33	4	37			
BOOTH, Robert	27	4	31	1		1
BRADSHAW, John	1		1			
COX, Arthur	1		1			
DAVIES, George	41	4	45	4		4
DELLOW, Stan	5	2	7			
DOBSON, Harry	35	3	38	5		5
DOREY, Charles	15	2	17			
EVANS, Billy	15		15			
EVANS, Jimmy	27	2	29	4	1	5
FIRTH, Robert	37	4	41	1	1	2
GOODWIN, Billy	40	4	44	21	1	22
HALL, Joe	27	4	31			
HALLEY, George	21	2	23	2	1	3
HUMPHREYS, Joe	16		16			
JENNINGS, Walter	15		15			
LIEVESLEY, Wilf	7		7	1		1
PIDGEON, Henry	1		1			
PRICE, Arthur	1	2	3			
REID, David	20	1	21			
SLATER, Jackie	41	4	45	8	3	11
WHITE, Harry	1		1			
WOODLAND, Arthur	30	1	31	1		1
Own Goal				1		1

	Ps	P	W	D	L	F	A	W	D	L	F	A	Pts.
1922/23	15	42	10	6	5	35	18	2	7	12	14	36	37

Season 1923/24 – League Division Three (South)

No.	Date	Opposition	Venue	Score	H.T.	Res.	Att.	Goalscorers	No.	1	2	3	4	5	6	7	8	9	10	11
1	25 Aug	Merthyr Town	(A)	2-3	(0-1)	L	8000	Whitham(2)	1	Hall	Sayles	Gibson	Kay	Edwards	Dreyer	Middleton	Whitham	Goodwin	Slater	Davies
2	27	Charlton Athletic	(H)	2-2	(1-0)	D	8000	Whitham,Davies	2	Hall	Sayles	Gibson	Evans T	Edwards	Dreyer	Middleton	Whitham	Goodwin	Slater	Davies
3	1 Sep	Merthyr Town	(H)	3-1	(1-1)	W	8500	Whitham(2),Slater	3	Hall	Taylor	Gibson	Evans T	Edwards	Dreyer	Middleton	Whitham	Goodwin	Slater	Davies
4	3	Charlton Athletic	(A)	1-4	(0-3)	L	4000	Goodwin	4	Hall	Taylor	Gibson	Evans T	Edwards	Dreyer	Middleton	Whitham	Goodwin	Slater	Davies
5	8	Newport County	(A)	0-5	(0-4)	L	8000		5	Hall	Taylor	Gibson	Evans T	Kay	Edwards	Middleton	Whitham	Goodwin	Slater	Davies
6	15	Newport County	(H)	2-0	(1-0)	W	8000	Maycock,Whitham	6	Maidment	Evans W	Robson	Evans T	Dorey	Edwards	Middleton	Whitham	Goodwin	Slater	Maycock
7	19	Portsmouth	(H)	0-1	(0-)	L	6000		7	Maidment	Evans W	Robson	Evans T	Dorey	Edwards	Middleton	Whitham	Goodwin	Slater	Maycock
8	22	Bristol Rovers	(A)	1-3	(1-2)	L	9000	Whitham	8	Maidment	Evans W	Robson	Evans T	Dorey	Edwards	Middleton	McClelland	Goodwin	Whitham	Davies
9	29	Bristol Rovers	(H)	1-0	(1-0)	W	7500	Goodwin	9	Hall	Evans W	Robson	Evans T	Dorey	Edwards	Middleton	Whitham	Goodwin	Slater	Davies
10	6 Oct	Millwall Athletic	(H)	0-0	(0-0)	D	8500		10	Hall	Evans W	Hodge	Evans T	Dorey	Edwards	Middleton	Dobson	Goodwin	Whitham	Davies
11	13	Millwall Athletic	(A)	0-0	(0-0)	D	20000		11	Hall	Evans W	Hodge	Evans T	Dorey	Edwards	Middleton	Dobson	Goodwin	Slater	Davies
12	20	Brentford	(H)	3-1	(1-1)	W	7000	Slater(2),Davies(pen)	12	Hall	Evans W	Hodge	Evans T	Dorey	Edwards	Middleton	Dobson	Goodwin	Slater	Davies
13	27	Brentford	(A)	1-3	(0-2)	L	5000	Davies	13	Hall	Hodge	Robson	Evans T	Dreyer	Edwards	Middleton	Dobson	Goodwin	Slater	Davies
14	3 Nov	Bournemouth	(H)	1-1	(1-1)	D	6200	Slater	14	Hall	Evans W	Hodge	Evans T	Edwards	Dreyer	Middleton	Dobson	Goodwin	Slater	Davies
15	10	Bournemouth	(A)	1-0	(1-0)	W	5000	Edwards	15	Hall	Evans W	Hodge	Evans T	Edwards	Dreyer	Middleton	Whitham	Goodwin	Slater	Davies
16	24	Portsmouth	(A)	0-3	(0-1)	L	9000		16	Hall	Evans W	Hodge	Dreyer	Edwards	Slater	Middleton	Whitham	Kay	Goodwin	Slater
17	8 Dec	Reading	(H)	2-1	(2-0)	W	5000	Davies(pen),Goodwin	17	Hall	Evans W	Hodge	Dorey	Edwards	Dreyer	Johnson	Whitham	Goodwin	Slater	Davies
18	22	Exeter City	(H)	0-0	(0-0)	D	3000		18	Hall	Evans W	Hodge	Dorey	Edwards	Dreyer	Johnson	Goodwin	McClelland	Slater	Davies
19	25	Aberdare Athletic	(H)	1-1	(0-1)	D	7000	McClelland(pen)	19	Hall	Evans W	Taylor	Dorey	Edwards	Dreyer	Johnson	Dobson	McClelland	Slater	Maycock
20	26	Aberdare Athletic	(A)	2-5	(1-4)	L	8000	Kay,Davies	20	Hall	Taylor	Evans W	Kay	Edwards	Dorey	Johnson	Dobson	Goodwin	Slater	Davies
21	29	Luton Town	(A)	4-4	(3-2)	D		Davies(2),Goodwin,Dobson	21	Hall	Evans W	Dreyer	Kay	Edwards	Slater	Johnson	Dobson	Goodwin	Davies	Middleton
22	5 Jan	Luton Town	(H)	1-1	(0-0)	D	7000	Dobson	22	Hall	Evans W	Hodge	Kay	Edwards	Slater	Johnson	Dobson	Goodwin	Davies	Middleton
23	12	Reading	(A)	0-1	(0-)	L			23	Hall	Evans W	Hodge	Kay	Edwards	Dreyer	Johnson	Dobson	Goodwin	Lunn	Slater
24	19	Norwich City	(A)	1-3	(0-1)	L	5000	Whitham	24	Hall	Evans W	Hodge	Kay	Edwards	Slater	Johnson	Whitham	Lunn	Slater	Harvey
25	26	Norwich City	(H)	3-1	(1-1)	W	6000	Dobson,Whitham,Goodwin	25	Hall	Evans W	Hodge	Kay	Edwards	Slater	Johnson	Whitham	Lunn	Dobson	Goodwin
26	9 Feb	Swindon Town	(H)	0-2	(0-0)	L	4000		26	Hall	Evans T	Hodge	Kay	Edwards	Slater	Johnson	Whitham	Lunn	Dobson	Goodwin
27	16	Watford	(A)	1-4	(1-1)	L		Lunn	27	Maidment	Evans T	Hodge	Kay	Edwards	Slater	Johnson	Davies	Lunn	Dobson	Goodwin
28	23	Exeter City	(A)	0-2	(0-1)	L	4000		28	Maidment	Evans T	Hodge	Jewhurst	Edwards	Slater	Johnson	Davies	Watkins	Dobson	Goodwin
29	1 Mar	Swansea Town	(A)	1-2	(0-0)	L	12000	Lunn	29	Maidment	Evans W	Hodge	Evans T	Edwards	Slater	Johnson	Whitham	Watkins	Lunn	Goodwin
30	8	Swansea Town	(H)	0-0	(0-0)	D	9000		30	Maidment	Evans W	Hodge	Evans T	Edwards	Slater	Middleton	Whitham	Watkins	Lunn	Goodwin
31	15	Northampton Town	(H)	5-1	(3-0)	W	7000	Watkins(3),Goodwin,Johnson	31	Maidment	Evans T	Evans W	Dreyer	Edwards	Slater	Johnson	Dobson	Watkins	Goodwin	Middleton
32	19	Watford	(H)	3-0	(-0)	W		Whitham,Goodwin,Edwards	32	Maidment	Evans T	Evans W	Dreyer	Edwards	Slater	Johnson	Whitham	Watkins	Goodwin	Middleton
33	22	Northampton Town	(A)	0-8	(0-5)	L			33	Maidment	Evans T	Evans W	Dreyer	Edwards	Slater	Johnson	Whitham	Watkins	Goodwin	Middleton
34	29	Gillingham	(H)	3-2	(1-2)	W	5000	Dobson(2),Johnson	34	Maidment	Evans T	Evans W	Dreyer	Edwards	Slater	Johnson	Dobson	Watkins	Goodwin	Middleton
35	2 Apr	Swindon Town	(A)	0-3	(0-)	L			35	Maidment	Evans T	Evans W	Dreyer	Edwards	Slater	Johnson	Dobson	Watkins	Goodwin	Middleton
36	5	Gillingham	(A)	2-3	(2-2)	L	6000	Johnson,Dobson	36	Hall	Sayles	Evans W	Jewhurst	Edwards	Slater	Johnson	Dobson	Watkins	Goodwin	Davies
37	12	Queens Park Rangers	(H)	4-2	(1-0)	W		Goodwin(2),Johnson,Watkins	37	Hall	Evans W	Sayles	Evans T	Edwards	Slater	Johnson	Dobson	Watkins	Goodwin	Middleton
38	18	Brighton	(A)	0-2	(0-0)	L	9000		38	Hall	Sayles	Evans W	Jewhurst	Dorey	Dreyer	Johnson	Dobson	Watkins	Goodwin	Middleton
39	19	Queens Park Rangers	(A)	0-0	(0-0)	D			39	Hall	Sayles	Evans W	Jewhurst	Edwards	Dreyer	Johnson	Dobson	Watkins	Slater	Middleton
40	21	Brighton	(H)	1-0	(1-0)	W	9000	Jenkins(O.G.)	40	Hall	Sayles	Evans W	Jewhurst	Edwards	Dreyer	Johnson	Dobson	Watkins	Slater	Middleton
41	26	Plymouth Argyle	(H)	0-2	(0-0)	L			41	Hall	Sayles	Evans W	Jewhurst	Edwards	Dreyer	Johnson	Dobson	Watkins	Slater	Middleton
42	3 May	Plymouth Argyle	(A)	1-7	(1-4)	L		Slater	42	Maidment	Sayles	Evans W	Jewhurst	Edwards	Young	Johnson	Dobson	Watkins	Slater	Middleton

Rd.	Date	Opposition	Venue Score	H.T. Res.	Att.	Goalscorers
			F.A.Cup			
Q4	17 Nov	Kings Lynn	(H) 1-0	(0-0) W	6577	Davies(pen)
Q5	1 Dec	Clapton	(A) 3-1	(2-0) W		Goodwin(2),Davies
Q6	15	Llanelly	(A) 1-2	(0-1) L	7276	Edwards

1	2	3	4	5	6	7	8	9	10	11
Hall	Evans W	Hodge	Dreyer	Edwards	Robson	Middleton	Whitham	Goodwin	Slater	Davies
Hall	Evans W	Hodge	Dorey	Edwards	Dreyer	Johnson	Whitham	Goodwin	Slater	Davies
Hall	Evans W	Hodge	Dorey	Edwards	Dreyer	Johnson	Dobson	Goodwin	Slater	Davies

Typical programme cover of the season.

Appearances and Goals

Name	Appearances Lge.	FAC	Total	Goals Lge.	FAC	Total
DAVIES, George	22	3	25	7	2	9
DOBSON, Harry	23	1	24	6		6
DOREY, Charles	12	2	14			
DREYER, Henry	22	3	25			
EDWARDS, Ernest	41	3	44	2	1	3
EVANS, Billy	32	3	35			
EVANS, Tommy	27		27			
GIBSON, Tommy	5		5			
GOODWIN, Billy	36	3	39	9	2	11
HALL, Joe	29	3	32			
HARVEY, Albert	1		1			
HODGE, James	18	3	21			
JEWHURST, Fred	7		7			
JOHNSON, George	25	2	27	4		4
KAY, Harold	11		11	1		1
LUNN, Fred	7		7	2		2
MAIDMENT, Jimmy	13		13	1		1
MAYCOCK, Harry	3		3			
MIDDLETON, Billy	30	1	31	1		1
McCLELLAND, Jim	3		3			
ROBSON, John	5	1	6			
SAYLES, Tommy	9		9			
SLATER, Jackie	40	3	43	5		5
TAYLOR, Ernie	5		5			
WATKINS, Ernie	15		15	4		4
WHITHAM, Victor	20	2	22	10		10
YOUNG, R H	1		1	1		1
Own Goal						1

	Ps	P	W	D	L	F	A	W	D	L	F	A	Pts.
1923/24	19	42	11	7	3	35	19	1	3	17	18	65	34

Season 1924/25 – League Division Three (South)

No.	Date	Opposition	Venue	Score	H.T.	Res.	Att.	Goalscorers	1	2	3	4	5	6	7	8	9	10	11
1	30 Aug	Charlton Athletic	(H)	0-3		L	10000		Hayes	Stewart	Donnelly	Bennett	O'Rawe	Edwards	Thirl(A)	Bissett	Watkins	Wolfe	MacDonald
2	1 Sep	Merthyr Town	(A)	0-1		L			Hayes	Sayles	Donnelly	Bennett	O'Rawe	Edwards	Thirl(A)	Bissett	Phillips	Wolfe	MacDonald
3	6	Northampton Town	(A)	1-0		W	7000	Watson(O.G.)	Hayes	Sayles	Donnelly	Bennett	O'Rawe	Edwards	Thirl(A)	Bissett	Phillips	Wolfe	MacDonald
4	10	Merthyr. Town	(H)	2-1		W		Phillips,Edwards	Hayes	Sayles	Donnelly	Bennett	O'Rawe	Edwards	Johnson	Dobson	Phillips	Wolfe	MacDonald
5	13	Watford	(A)	0-4		L	8000		Hayes	Sayles	Donnelly	Bennett	O'Rawe	Edwards	Johnson	Dobson	Watkins	Wolfe	Thirl(A)
6	17	Queens Park Rangers	(H)	1-0		W		Bissett	Hayes	Sayles	Donnelly	Jewhurst	O'Rawe	Edwards	Thirl(A)	Bissett	Phillips	Wolfe	MacDonald
7	20	Bournemouth	(A)	0-1		L			Hayes	Sayles	Donnelly	Jewhurst	O'Rawe	Edwards	Thirl(A)	Bissett	Phillips	Wolfe	MacDonald
8	24	Swindon Town	(A)	0-3		L	3000		Hayes	Sayles	Donnelly	Jewhurst	O'Rawe	Edwards	Thirl(A)	Bissett	Phillips	Wolfe	MacDonald
9	27	Newport County	(A)	1-1		D	9000	Russell	Hayes	Sayles	Donnelly	Jewhurst	O'Rawe	Edwards	Johnson	Dobson	Russell	Bissett	MacDonald
10	4 Oct	Bristol Rovers	(H)	2-1		W	8000	McClelland,Dobson	Hayes	Sayles	Donnelly	Jewhurst	O'Rawe	Edwards	Johnson	Dobson	McClelland	Bissett	MacDonald
11	11	Exeter City	(A)	1-0	(0-0)	W	6000	McClelland	Hayes	Sayles	Donnelly	Jewhurst	O'Rawe	Edwards	Johnson	Bissett	McClelland	Dobson	MacDonald
12	18	Swansea Town	(H)	1-0	(0-0)	W	10000	McClelland	Hayes	Sayles	Donnelly	Jewhurst	O'Rawe	Edwards	Johnson	Bissett	McClelland	Dobson	MacDonald
13	25	Brighton	(H)	2-0		W		McClelland,Johnson	Hayes	Sayles	Donnelly	Jewhurst	O'Rawe	Edwards	Johnson	Bissett	McClelland	Dobson	MacDonald
14	8 Nov	Bristol City	(H)	2-0	(1-0)	W	8000	Bissett,Dobson	Hayes	Sayles	Donnelly	Jewhurst	O'Rawe	Edwards	Johnson	Bissett	McClelland	Dobson	MacDonald
15	22	Aberdare Athletic	(H)	2-1		W		O'Rawe,McClelland	Hayes	Sayles	Donnelly	Jewhurst	O'Rawe	Edwards	Johnson	Bissett	McClelland	Dobson	MacDonald
16	6 Dec	Brentford	(H)	6-1		W	4000	Dobson(4),McClelland(2)	Hayes	Donnelly	Sayles	Jewhurst	Dorey	Edwards	Johnson	Bissett	McClelland	Dobson	Wolfe
17	13	Millwall Athletic	(A)	0-2		L	15000		Hayes	Sayles	Donnelly	Jewhurst	O'Rawe	Edwards	Johnson	Bissett	McClelland	Dobson	Wolfe
18	20	Luton Town	(A)	2-1		W		Johnson,Bissett	Hayes	Sayles	Donnelly	Jewhurst	O'Rawe	Edwards	Johnson	Bissett	McClelland	Dobson	Wolfe
19	25	Gillingham	(H)	1-3		L	8000	Bissett	Hayes	Sayles	Donnelly	Jewhurst	O'Rawe	Edwards	Johnson	Bissett	McClelland	Dobson	MacDonald
20	26	Gillingham	(H)	4-0		W	9000	Edwards,Johnson,McClelland,Bissett	Hayes	Sayles	Donnelly	Jewhurst	Dorey	Edwards	Johnson	Bissett	McClelland	Slater	MacDonald
21	27	Charlton Athletic	(A)	0-0	(0-0)	D			Hayes	Sayles	Donnelly	Jewhurst	Dorey	Edwards	Johnson	Bissett	McClelland	Slater	MacDonald
22	3 Jan	Northampton Town	(H)	0-1		L			Hayes	Sayles	Donnelly	Jewhurst	Dorey	Edwards	Johnson	Bissett	McClelland	Slater	Brooks
23	10	Brentford	(A)	2-2	(0-0)	D	7000	McClelland(2)	Hayes	Sayles	Donnelly	Jewhurst	Dorey	Edwards	Brooks	Bissett	McClelland	Dobson	MacDonald
24	17	Watford	(H)	3-0	(0-0)	W	5000	Bissett,McClelland,Brooks	Hayes	Sayles	Donnelly	Jewhurst	Dorey	Edwards	Brooks	Bissett	McClelland	Dobson	MacDonald
25	24	Bournemouth	(H)	3-0		W		Bissett(2),Dobson	Hayes	Russell	Donnelly	Jewhurst	Dorey	Edwards	Brooks	Bissett	McClelland	Dobson	MacDonald
26	31	Newport County	(A)	0-1	(0-0)	L	9000		Hayes	Sayles	Donnelly	Jewhurst	Dorey	Edwards	Brooks	Bissett	McClelland	Dobson	MacDonald
27	7 Feb	Bristol Rovers	(A)	3-1	(1-0)	W	7000	McClelland(2),Brooks	Hayes	Sayles	Donnelly	Jewhurst	Dorey	Edwards	Brooks	Bissett	McClelland	Dobson	MacDonald
28	14	Exeter City	(H)	3-0	(1-0)	W	3000	McClelland(3)	Hayes	Sayles	Donnelly	Jewhurst	Dorey	Edwards	Brooks	Bissett	McClelland	Dobson	MacDonald
29	21	Swansea Town	(A)	0-4		L			Hayes	Sayles	Donnelly	Jewhurst	Dorey	Edwards	Brooks	Bissett	McClelland	Dobson	MacDonald
30	28	Brighton	(A)	1-2	(0-0)	L	10000	Sayles(pen)	Hayes	Sayles	Donnelly	Jewhurst	Dorey	Edwards	Brooks	Bissett	McClelland	Dobson	MacDonald
31	7 Mar	Plymouth Argyle	(H)	0-3		L	9000		Hayes	Sayles	Donnelly	Jewhurst	Dorey	Edwards	Brooks	Bissett	McClelland	Dobson	MacDonald
32	14	Bristol City	(A)	0-5	(0-1)	L	8000		Hayes	Sayles	Donnelly	Jewhurst	Dorey	Edwards	Brooks	Bissett	McClelland	Slater	MacDonald
33	21	Swindon Town	(H)	0-0	(0-0)	D			Hayes	Sayles	Donnelly	Jewhurst	Dorey	Edwards	Johnson	Dobson	McClelland	MacDonald	Brooks
34	28	Aberdare Athletic	(A)	0-3		L			Hayes	Gates	Sayles	Jewhurst	Dorey	Edwards	Johnson	Bennett	Hick	Donnelly	MacDonald
35	4 Apr	Norwich City	(H)	0-1		L	7000		Hayes	Sayles	Donnelly	Jewhurst	Dorey	Edwards	Johnson	Phillips	Hick	Russell	MacDonald
36	10	Reading	(A)	2-2		D	10000	O'Rawe,Sayles	Hayes	Sayles	Donnelly	Jewhurst	Dorey	Edwards	Johnson	Dobson	Hick	Slater	MacDonald
37	13	Reading	(H)	3-0		W		Slater(2),Hick	Hayes	Sayles	Donnelly	Jewhurst	Dorey	Edwards	Johnson	Dobson	Hick	Slater	MacDonald
38	14	Norwich City	(A)	1-0		W	6000	Hick	Hayes	Sayles	Donnelly	Jewhurst	Dorey	Edwards	Johnson	Dobson	Hick	Slater	MacDonald
39	18	Millwall Athletic	(H)	1-0		W	7000	MacDonald	Hayes	Sayles	Donnelly	Jewhurst	Dorey	Edwards	Johnson	Dobson	Hick	Slater	MacDonald
40	25	Luton Town	(A)	0-4		L			Hayes	Sayles	Donnelly	Jewhurst	Dorey	Edwards	Johnson	Dobson	Hick	Slater	MacDonald
41	29	Plymouth Argyle	(A)	0-6		L	7000		Hayes	Sayles	Donnelly	Jewhurst	Dorey	Edwards	Johnson	Dobson	Hick	Slater	MacDonald
42	2 May	Queens Park Rangers	(A)	1-3		L		Hick	Hayes	Sayles	Donnelly	Jewhurst	Dorey	Sullivan	Phillips	Dobson	Hick	Slater	MacDonald

Major Cup Competitions

Rd.	Date	Opposition	Venue Score	H.T.	Res.	Att.	Goalscorers	1	2	3	4	5	6	7	8	9	10	11
			F.A.Cup															
Q4	15 Nov	London Caledonians	(H) 3-3		D	8097	Johnson,Bissett,McClelland	Hayes	Donnelly	Sayles	Jewhurst	O'Rawe	Edwards	Johnson	Bissett	McClelland	Dobson	MacDonald
Q4r	20	London Caledonians	(A) 4-1		W		McClelland(3),Bissett	Hayes	Sayles	Donnelly	Jewhurst	O'Rawe	Edwards	Johnson	Bissett	McClelland	Dobson	MacDonald
Q5	19	Reading	(A) 1-2	(0-2)	L	10457	McClelland	Hayes	Donnelly	Sayles	Jewhurst	O'Rawe	Edwards	Johnson	Bissett	McClelland	Dobson	MacDonald

Unnamed Team Group.

Appearances and Goals

Name	Appearances			Goals		
	Lge.	FAC	Total	Lge.	FAC	Total
BENNETT, Walter	7		7			
BISSETT, George	29	3	32	8	2	10
BROOKS, Sammy	12		12	2		2
DOBSON, Harry	31	3	34	7		7
DONNELLY, Jim	42	3	45			
DOREY, Charles	24		24			
EDWARDS, Ernest	41	3	44	2		2
GATES, B	1		1			
HAYES, William	42	3	45			
HICK, Billy	10		10	3		3
JEWHURST, Fred	36	3	39			
JOHNSON, George	24	3	27	3	1	4
MacDONALD, Elias	37	3	40	1		1
McCLELLAND, Jim	23	3	26	16	5	21
O'RAWE, Frank	18	3	21	2		2
PHILLIPS, Jack	8		8	1		1
RUSSELL, Harry	3		3	1		1
SAYLES, Tommy	40	3	43	2		2
SLATER, Jackie	11		11	2		2
STEWART, Duncan	1		1			
SULLIVAN, Con	1		1			
THIRLAWAY, Bill	8		8			
WATKINS, Ernie	2		2			
WOLFE, Tom	11		11			
Own Goal						1

	Ps	P	W	D	L	F	A	W	D	L	F	A	Pts.
1924/25	10	42	14	1	6	34	18	5	4	12	17	43	43

Season 1925/26 – League Division Three (South)

No.	Date	Opposition	Venue	Score	H.T.	Res.	Att.	Goalscorers	1	2	3	4	5	6	7	8	9	10	11
1	29 Aug	Plymouth Argyle	(A)	2-6		L	13936	Smith,Russell(O.G.)	Hayes	Dixon	Bell	Jewhurst	O'Rawe	Edwards	Hind	Bissett	Shaw	Graver	Smith
2	2 Sep	Brentford	(H)	3-1		W	8224	Watkins(3)	Hayes	Dixon	Bell	Jewhurst	O'Rawe	Edwards	Hind	Bissett	Watkins	Graver	Smith
3	5	Reading	(H)	2-2		D	8450	Watkins(2)	Hayes	Dixon	Bell	Jewhurst	O'Rawe	Edwards	Hind	Watkins	Graver	Donoven	Smith
4	7	Brentford	(A)	3-1		W	6409	Donoven,Hind,Graver	Hayes	Sayles	Lamb	Jewhurst	O'Rawe	Edwards	Hind	Watkins	Donoven	Graver	Smith
5	12	Norwich City	(H)	0-1		L	8764		Hayes	Sayles	Bell	Jewhurst	O'Rawe	Edwards	Johnson	Bissett	Shaw	Watkins	Smith
6	16	Watford	(H)	0-1		L	4799		Hayes	Sayles	Bell	Jewhurst	Purdy	Andrews	Cooke	Bissett	Watkins	Shaw	Smith
7	19	Millwall Athletic	(A)	1-8		L	9731	Shaw	Moore	Sayles	Bell	Jewhurst	Purdy	Andrews	Hind	Bissett	Watkins	Shaw	Smith
8	25	Watford	(H)	4-1		W	4780	Watkins(2),Hind,Bell	Moore	Sayles	Bell	Jewhurst	Purdy	Bayliss	Hind	Bissett	Watkins	Shaw	Smith
9	26	Northampton Town	(H)	6-1		W	7332	Watkins(2),Shaw,Bissett,Morris,Bell	Moore	Sayles	Bell	Jewhurst	Purdy	Edwards	Morris	Bissett	Watkins	Shaw	Smith
10	3 Oct	Aberdare Athletic	(A)	0-2		L	6074		Moore	Sayles	Bell	Jewhurst	Purdy	Edwards	Morris	Bissett	Hick	Shaw	Smith
11	10	Brighton	(H)	4-0		W	8276	Watkins(2),Shaw,Bissett	Moore	Sayles	Bell	Jewhurst	Purdy	Edwards	Morris	Bisett	Watkins	Shaw	Smith
12	17	Bournemouth	(A)	2-1		W	5725	Smith,Shaw	Moore	Sayles	Bell	Jewhurst	Purdy	Edwards	Morris	Bissett	Watkins	Shaw	Smith
13	24	Charlton Athletic	(H)	1-2		L	8804	Shaw	Moore	Sayles	Bell	Jewhurst	Purdy	Edwards	Morris	Bissett	Watkins	Shaw	Smith
14	31	Swindon Town	(A)	0-2		L	6658		Moore	Sayles	Bell	Jewhurst	O'Rawe	Andrews	Morris	Bissett	Watkins	Shaw	Smith
15	7 Nov	Exeter City	(H)	3-1	(0-0)	W	6845	Shaw(2),Hick	Moore	French	Sayles	Jewhurst	O'Rawe	Andrews	Morris	Bissett	Hick	Shaw	Smith
16	14	Newport County	(A)	0-1		L	4503		Moore	French	Sayles	Jewhurst	O'Rawe	Andrews	Morris	Bissett	Hick	Shaw	Smith
17	21	Luton Town	(H)	2-0		W	6706	Shaw(2)	Moore	French	Sayles	Jewhurst	O'Rawe	Andrews	Morris	Bissett	Watkins	Shaw	Smith
18	5 Dec	Bristol Rovers	(H)	3-1		W	5661	Morris(2),Shaw	Moore	French	Sayles	Jewhurst	O'Rawe	Andrews	Morris	Bissett	Watkins	Shaw	Smith
19	19	Merthyr Town	(A)	5-1		W	6142	Bissett(2),Smith,Morris,Hick	Moore	French	Sayles	Jewhurst	O'Rawe	Andrews	Morris	Bissett	Hick	Shaw	Smith
20	25	Bristol City	(A)	4-1		W	13841	Shaw(2),Hick(2)	Moore	French	Sayles	Jewhurst	O'Rawe	Andrews	Morris	Bissett	Hick	Shaw	Smith
21	26	Bristol City	(H)	1-2	(1-1)	L	13438	Hick	Moore	French	Sayles	Graver	O'Rawe	Andrews	Morris	Bissett	Hick	Shaw	Smith
22	2 Jan	Plymouth Argyle	(H)	2-0	(2-0)	W	7545	Hick,Shaw	Moore	French	Sayles	Purdy	O'Rawe	Andrews	Morris	Bissett	Hick	Shaw	Smith
23	16	Reading	(A)	0-1		L	5711		Moore	French	Sayles	Purdy	O'Rawe	Andrews	Morris	Bissett	Hick	Shaw	Smith
24	20	Gillingham	(A)	1-3		L	3493	Smith	Moore	Bell	Sayles	Jewhurst	O'Rawe	Andrews	Morris	Bissett	Hick	Shaw	Smith
25	23	Norwich City	(A)	2-1		W	5248	Bissett,Bradbrook(O.G.)	Moore	Bell	Sayles	Jewhurst	O'Rawe	Andrews	Morris	Bissett	Hick	Donoven	Smith
26	6 Feb	Northampton Town	(A)	3-3	(0-1)	D	7414	Morris(2),Shaw	Moore	French	Sayles	Jewhurst	O'Rawe	Andrews	Morris	Graver	Hick	Shaw	Smith
27	13	Aberdare Athletic	(H)	0-1	(0-1)	L	8030		Moore	French	Sayles	Jewhurst	O'Rawe	Andrews	Morris	Graver	Hick	Shaw	Smith
28	27	Bournemouth	(H)	3-0	(1-0)	W	6417	Shaw(3)	Moore	French	Sayles	Jewhurst	O'Rawe	Andrews	Bissett	Morris	Hick	Shaw	Smith
29	4 Mar	Queens Park Rangers	(A)	2-2	(0-0)	D	3377	Hick,Shaw	Moore	French	Sayles	Jewhurst	O'Rawe	Andrews	Bissett	Graver	Hick	Shaw	Smith
30	6	Charlton Athletic	(A)	0-5		L	7243		Moore	French	Sayles	Jewhurst	O'Rawe	Andrews	Johnson	Graver	Hick	Shaw	Smith
31	13	Swindon Town	(H)	3-0		W	6796	Hick(2),Donoven	Moore	French	Sayles	Jewhurst	O'Rawe	Andrews	Bissett	Donoven	Hick	Shaw	Smith
32	17	Millwall Athletic	(H)	0-2		L	4222		Moore	Bell	Sayles	Jewhurst	Whitfield	Andrews	Johnson	Bissett	Hick	Donoven	Smith
33	20	Exeter City	(A)	1-0	(0-0)	W	4868	Bissett	Moore	Bell	Sayles	Jewhurst	O'Rawe	Andrews	Johnson	Bissett	Hick	Shaw	Smith
34	27	Newport County	(H)	4-1	(1-0)	W	6124	Hick(3),Johnson	Moore	Bell	Sayles	Jewhurst	O'Rawe	Andrews	Johnson	Bissett	Hick	Shaw	Smith
35	2	Crystal Palace	(A)	0-3		L	17260		Moore	Bell	Sayles	Jewhurst	O'Rawe	Andrews	Johnson	Shaw	Hick	Donoven	Smith
36	3	Luton Town	(A)	0-2	(0-1)	L	7239		Hayes	Bell	Sayles	Jewhurst	O'Rawe	Andrews	Johnson	Graver	Hick	Donoven	Smith
37	5	Crystal Palace	(H)	5-1	(3-0)	W	10908	Johnson(3),Hick,Cross(O.G.)	Moore	Bell	Sayles	Jewhurst	O'Rawe	Andrews	Johnson	Shaw	Hick	Donoven	Smith
38	10	Queens Park Rangers	(H)	2-1		W	6398	Johnson,Donoven	Moore	Bell	Sayles	Jewhurst	Whitfield	Andrews	Johnson	Shaw	Hick	Donoven	Smith
39	17	Bristol Rovers	(A)	0-2		L	3726		Moore	Bell	Sayles	Jewhurst	O'Rawe	Andrews	Johnson	Shaw	Hick	Donoven	Cooke
40	21	Brighton	(A)	2-3		L	3722	Johnson,Donoven	Moore	Bell	Sayles	Purdy	O'Rawe	Andrews	Johnson	Shaw	Hick	Donoven	Smith
41	24	Gillingham	(H)	1-1		D	6083	Hick	Moore	Bell	Sayles	Purdy	O'Rawe	Andrews	Johnson	Shaw	Hick	Donoven	Smith
42	1 May	Merthyr Town	(A)	1-5	(1-3)	L	3171	Shaw	Hayes	Dixon	Bell	Jewhurst	O'Rawe	Andrews	Johnson	Shaw	Hick	Donoven	Smith

F.A.Cup

Rd.	Date	Opposition	Venue	Score	H.T.	Res.	Att.	1	2	3	4	5	6	7	8	9	10	11	Goalscorers
R1	28 Nov	Dulwich Hamlet	(H)	5-1	(1-0)	W	11864	Moore	French	Sayles	Jewhurst	O'Rawe	Andrews	Morris	Bissett	Watkins	Shaw	Smith	Morris,Shaw,Bissett,Watkins,Goodliffe(O.G.)
R2	12 Dec	Gillingham	(H)	1-0	(0-0)	W	10500	Moore	French	Sayles	Jewhurst	O'Rawe	Andrews	Morris	Bissett	Watkins	Shaw	Smith	Watkins
R3	9 Jan	Southport	(H)	5-2		W		Moore	French	Sayles	Purdy	O'Rawe	Andrews	Morris	Bissett	Hick	Shaw	Smith	Hick(2),Smith,Shaw,Bissett
R4	30	Derby County	(H)	4-1		W	14225	Moore	French	Sayles	Jewhurst	O'Rawe	Andrews	Morris	Graver	Hick	Shaw	Smith	Hick(2),Andrews,Graver
R5	20 Feb	Nottingham For.	(H)	0-1	(0-0)	L	18153	Moore	French	Sayles	Jewhurst	O'Rawe	Andrews	Morris	Bissett	Hick	Shaw	Smith	

Unnamed team group

Appearances and Goals

Name	Appearances Lge.	FAC	Total	Goals Lge.	FAC	Total
ANDREWS, Jack	31	5	36		1	1
BAYLISS, Len	1		1			
BELL, Tommy	27		27	2		2
BISSETT, George	29	4	33	6	2	8
COOKE, George	2		2			
DIXON, David	4		4			
DONOVEN, Dickie	15		15	4		4
EDWARDS, Ernest	10		10			
FRENCH, Jack	14	5	19			
GRAVER, Fred	10	1	11	1	1	2
HAYES, William	9		9			
HICK, Billy	26	3	29	14	4	18
HIND, Billy	6		6	2		2
JEWHURST, Fred	38	4	42			
JOHNSON, George	13		13	6		6
LAMB, Walter	1		1			
MOORE, Billy	33	5	38			
MORRIS, Hugh	20	5	25	6	1	7
O'RAWE, Frank	32	5	37			
PURDY, Albert	11	1	12			
SAYLES, Tommy	38	5	43			
SHAW, William	34	5	39	19	2	21
SMITH, Stephen	41	5	46	4	1	5
WATKINS, Ernie	15	2	17	11	2	13
WHITFIELD, Frank	2		2			
Own Goal				3	1	4

	Ps	P	W	D	L	F	A	W	D	L	F	A	Pts.
1925/26	10	42	13	2	6	50	20	6	2	13	28	53	42

Season 1926/27 – League Division Three (South)

No.	Date	Opposition	Venue	Score	H.T.	Res.	Att.	Goalscorers	No.	1	2	3	4	5	6	7	8	9	10	11
1	28 Aug	Swindon Town	(A)	1-5	(1-2)	L	8943	Hick	1	Moore	French	Sayles	Jewhurst	Murphy	Andrews	Dennis	Morris	Hick	Donoven	Smith
2	30	Millwall	(H)	1-1		D	8000	Hick	2	Moore	French	Sayles	Jewhurst	Murphy	Andrews	Robson	Morris	Hick	Donoven	Smith
3	4 Sep	Exeter City	(H)	1-2	(1-2)	L	9029	Robson	3	Moore	French	Sayles	Jewhurst	Murphy	Andrews	Robson	Morris	Hick	Donoven	Smith
4	6	Brentford	(A)	1-3		L	7996	Thompson	4	Moore	French	Sayles	Jewhurst	Purdy Alb.	Bayliss	Robson	Clenshaw	Andrews	Donoven	Thompson
5	11	Merthyr Town	(A)	1-0		W	2507	Clenshaw	5	Moore	French	Bell	Jewhurst	Purdy Alb.	Bayliss	Morris	Clenshaw	Hick	Donoven	Smith
6	15	Brentford	(H)	3-1		W	6512	Brayshaw(2),Donoven	6	Moore	French	Bell	Jewhurst	Purdy Alb.	Bayliss	Dennis	Brayshaw	Hick	Donoven	Smith
7	18	Aberdare Athletic	(H)	5-1	(0-0)	W	8058	Donoven(2),Dennis(2),Brayshaw	7	Moore	French	Bell	Jewhurst	Purdy Alb.	Bayliss	Dennis	Brayshaw	Hick	Donoven	Smith
8	25	Luton Town	(A)	2-1	(2-1)	W	9211	Donoven,Hick	8	Moore	French	Bell	Jewhurst	Purdy Alb.	Bayliss	Dennis	Brayshaw	Hick	Donoven	Smith
9	2 Oct	Norwich City	(H)	1-1	(0-1)	D	8980	Hick	9	Moore	French	Bell	Jewhurst	Purdy Alb.	Bayliss	Dennis	Brayshaw	Hick	Donoven	Smith
10	9	Brighton	(H)	0-1		L	7369		10	Moore	French	Bell	Jewhurst	Purdy Alb.	Beaumont	Dennis	Brayshaw	Hick	Donoven	Smith
11	16	Plymouth Argyle	(A)	1-2		L	9435	Smith	11	Moore	French	Bell	Jewhurst	Purdy Alb.	Beaumont	Dennis	Brayshaw	Hick	Donoven	Smith
12	23	Newport County	(H)	5-0		W	6481	Brayshaw(2),Hick(2),Donoven	12	Moore	French	Bell	Jewhurst	Purdy Alb.	Beaumont	Dennis	Brayshaw	Hick	Donoven	Smith
13	30	Gillingham	(A)	3-2	(3-1)	W	4809	Smith,Hick,Donoven	13	Moore	French	Bell	Jewhurst	Purdy Alb.	Beaumont	Morris	Brayshaw	Hick	Donoven	Smith
14	6 Nov	Watford	(H)	2-0		W	7109	Smith,Hick	14	Purdy Art.	French	Bell	Jewhurst	Purdy Alb.	Beaumont	Morris	Brayshaw	Hick	Donoven	Smith
15	13	Crystal Palace	(A)	3-5		L	4101	Hick(2),Orr(O.G.)	15	Moore	French	Bell	Jewhurst	Purdy Alb.	Beaumont	Morris	Harvey	Hick	Donoven	Smith
16	20	Coventry City	(H)	3-1		W	3681	Smith,Donoven,Hick	16	Moore	French	Bell	Jewhurst	Purdy Alb.	Beaumont	Morris	Surtees	Hick	Donoven	Smith
17	4 Dec	Charlton Athletic	(H)	5-0		W	7255	Hick(3),Donoven,Smith	17	Moore	French	Bell	Jewhurst	Purdy Alb.	Beaumont	Robson	Surtees	Hick	Donoven	Smith
18	18	Bournemouth	(H)	0-3		L	6058		18	Moore	French	Bell	Jewhurst	Purdy Alb.	Beaumont	Robson	Surtees	Hick	Morris	Smith
19	25	Bristol Rovers	(A)	1-5		L	8555	Morris	19	Moore	French	Bell	Jewhurst	Purdy Alb.	Beaumont	Morris	Surtees	Hick	Donoven	Smith
20	27	Bristol Rovers	(H)	2-1	(1-0)	W	11091	Goodwin(2)	20	Moore	Hope	Bell	Jewhurst	Purdy Alb.	Beaumont	Morris	Goodwin	Hick	Donoven	Smith
21	1 Jan	Millwall	(A)	0-2		L	17472		21	Moore	Sayles	Bell	Jewhurst	Purdy Alb.	Beaumont	Morris	Goodwin	Hick	Donoven	Smith
22	8	Queens Park Rangers	(A)	2-3		L	6726	Hick(2)	22	Moore	Sayles	Bell	Purdy Alb.	Jewhurst	Beaumont	Morris	Goodwin	Hick	Harvey	Smith
23	15	Swindon Town	(H)	2-2	(0-2)	D	7118	Donoven,Smith	23	Moore	Sayles	Bell	Jewhurst	Purdy Alb.	Beaumont	Morris	Goodwin	Hick	Donoven	Smith
24	22	Exeter City	(A)	0-2	(0-1)	L	5676		24	Moore	French	Bell	Jewhurst	Purdy Alb.	Beaumont	Morris	Goodwin	Hick	Donoven	Smith
25	29	Merthyr Town	(H)	3-1	(0-0)	W	4763	Hick(3)	25	Moore	French	Bell	Jewhurst	Purdy Alb.	Beaumont	Morris	Goodwin	Hick	Donoven	Smith
26	5 Feb	Aberdare Athletic	(A)	0-1		L	1114		26	Purdy Art.	French	Bell	Jewhurst	Purdy Alb.	Andrews	Morris	Brayshaw	Goodwin	Donoven	Smith
27	12	Luton Town	(A)	0-0	(0-0)	D	4334		27	Moore	Hogg	Bell	Jewhurst	Beaumont	Andrews	Morris	Brayshaw	Hick	Donoven	Smith
28	19	Norwich City	(H)	3-3	(0-0)	D	6517	Donoven(2),Hick	28	Moore	Hogg	Bell	Jewhurst	Beaumont	Andrews	Morris	Brayshaw	Hick	Donoven	Smith
29	23	Bristol City	(A)	1-5		L	8533	Hick	29	Moore	Hope	Bell	Purdy Alb.	Beaumont	Andrews	Morris	Clenshaw	Hick	Donoven	Smith
30	26	Brighton	(A)	1-2		L	10676	Hick	30	Moore	Hope	Bell	Jewhurst	Beaumont	Andrews	Morris	Brayshaw	Hick	Donoven	Smith
31	5 Mar	Plymouth Argyle	(H)	1-2		L	5936	Hick	31	Moore	Hope	Bell	Jewhurst	Beaumont	Andrews	Morris	Goodwin	Hick	Donoven	Smith
32	12	Newport County	(A)	0-3	(0-2)	L	4725		32	Moore	Hope	Bell	Jewhurst	Beaumont	Andrews	Morris	Baron	Hick	Donoven	Smith
33	19	Gillingham	(H)	1-0		W	6605	Hick	33	Moore	French	Bell	Jewhurst	Beaumont	Andrews	Morris	Baron	Hick	Donoven	Smith
34	26	Watford	(A)	2-4	(0-1)	L	5127	Hick,Donoven	34	Moore	French	Bell	Jewhurst	Beaumont	Andrews	Morris	Baron	Hick	Donoven	Smith
35	2 Apr	Crystal Palace	(H)	3-1		W	6270	Bailey,Hick,Donoven	35	Moore	French	Bell	Jewhurst	Beaumont	Andrews	Morris	Bailey	Hick	Donoven	Smith
36	9	Coventry City	(A)	1-1		D	8762	Baron	36	Moore	French	Bell	Jewhurst	Beaumont	Andrews	Morris	Baron	Hick	Donoven	Smith
37	16	Queens Park Rangers	(H)	0-3		L	7813		37	Moore	French	Bell	Jewhurst	Beaumont	Andrews	Morris	Bailey	Hick	Donoven	Smith
38	18	Northampton Town	(H)	2-0		W	7809	Hick,Donoven	38	Moore	French	Bell	Purdy Alb.	Beaumont	Andrews	Morris	Bailey	Hick	Donoven	Smith
39	19	Northampton Town	(A)	1-2		L	6710	Clenshaw	39	Moore	Hope	Bell	Purdy Alb.	Beaumont	Andrews	Morris	Baron	Hick	Clenshaw	Dennis
40	23	Charlton Athletic	(A)	0-1		L	5172		40	Moore	Hope	Bell	Purdy Alb.	Beaumont	Andrews	Morris	Bailey	Hick	Donoven	Dennis
41	30	Bristol City	(H)	0-1		L	6608		41	Moore	Hope	Bell	Purdy Alb.	Beaumont	Andrews	Morris	Bailey	Hick	Donoven	Dennis
42	7 May	Bournemouth	(A)	0-3		L	3269		42	Moore	Hope	Bell	Purdy Alb.	Beaumont	Andrews	Morris	Surtees	Baron	Donoven	Smith

Major Cup Competitions

Rd.	Date	Opposition	Venue	Score	H.T.	Res.	Att.	Goalscorers	1	2	3	4	5	6	7	8	9	10	11
				F.A.Cup															
R1	27 Nov	Dulwich Hamlet	(A)	4-1		W		Donoven(3),Hick	Moore	French	Bell	Jewhurst	Purdy	Beaumont	Robson	Morris	Hick	Donoven	Smith
R2	11 Dec	Reading	(A)	2-3	(1-0)	L	17000	Hick,Purdy Alb.	Moore	French	Bell	Jewhurst	Purdy	Beaumont	Robson	Surtees	Hick	Donoven	Smith

Dulwich Hamlet Football Club.
CHAMPION HILL GROUND.
Price — ONE PENNY
F.A. CUP — 1st Round Proper
Dulwich Hamlet
v
Southend United
SATURDAY NOV. 27th, 1926.
K.O. 2.15
EVERY ISSUE OF THE
Sunday Pictorial
contains a coupon of special interest to all Football enthusiasts.
ORDER YOUR COPY TO-DAY.
LYDALL & SON. Sports Printers. 73 Park Road. Dulwich. S.E.21 6351E

Appearances and Goals

Name	Appearances Lge.	FAC	Total	Goals Lge.	FAC	Total
ANDREWS, Jack	22		22			
BAILEY, Jack	5		5	1		1
BARON, Fred	6		6	1		1
BAYLISS, Len	7		7			
BEAUMONT, Percy	30	2	32			
BELL, Tommy	38	2	40			
BRAYSHAW, Walter	13		13	5		5
CLENSHAW, Les	4		4	2		2
DENNIS, Harold	11		11	2		2
DONOVEN, Dickie	39	2	41	14	3	17
FRENCH, Jack	28	2	30			
GOODWIN, Billy	8		8	2		2
HARVEY, Albert	2		2			
HICK, Billy	39	2	41	27	2	29
HOGG, George	2		2			
HOPE, Phil	9		9			
JEWHURST, Fred	36	2	38			
MOORE, Billy	40	2	42			
MORRIS, Hugh	33	1	34	1		1
MURPHY, John	3		3			
PURDY, Albert	29	2	31		1	1
PURDY, Arthur	2		2			
ROBSON, Bert	5	2	7	1		1
SAYLES, Tommy	7		7	1		1
SMITH, Stephen	38	2	40	6		6
SURTEES, Albert	5	1	6			
THOMPSON, Charlie	1		1	1		1
Own Goal				1		1

	Ps	P	W	D	L	F	A	W	D	L	F	A	Pts.
1926/27	19	42	12	3	6	44	25	2	3	16	20	52	34

Season 1927/28 – League Division Three (South)

No.	Date	Opposition	Venue	Score	H.T.	Res.	Att.	Goalscorers	No.	1	2	3	4	5	6	7	8	9	10	11
1	27 Aug	Luton Town	(H)	1-0		W	11186	Hick	1	Boyce	Rosier	Bell	Dixon	Frew	Plum	Home	Bailey	Hick	Donoven	Fell
2	31	Bournemouth	(A)	3-2		W	5874	Hick(2),Bailey	2	Boyce	Rosier	Bell	Dixon	Frew	Plum	Home	Bailey	Hick	Donoven	Fell
3	3	Millwall	(A)	1-5		L	15690	Home	3	Boyce	Rosier	Bell	Dixon	Frew	Plum	Home	Bailey	Hick	Donoven	Fell
4	7	Bournemouth	(H)	3-0		W	5631	Hick(3)	4	Woodward	Rosier	Bell	Dixon	Frew	Plum	Home	Bailey	Hick	Donoven	Fell
5	10	Crystal Palace	(H)	6-1		W	6808	Donoven(4),Hick,Home	5	Woodward	Rosier	Brophy	Dixon	Frew	Plum	Home	Bailey	Hick	Donoven	Fell
6	17	Exeter City	(A)	2-3	(2-0)	L	6309	Hick,Bailey	6	Boyce	Rosier	Bell	Dixon	Frew	Plum	Home	Bailey	Hick	Donoven	Fell
7	24	Torquay United	(H)	1-0	(0-0)	W	8546	Donoven	7	Moore	Rosier	Brophy	Dixon	Frew	Plum	Home	Bailey	Hick	Donoven	Fell
8	1 Oct	Norwich City	(A)	1-2		L	9079	Home	8	Moore	Rosier	Bell	Dixon	Frew	Plum	Home	Bailey	Hick	Donoven	Fell
9	8	Northampton Town	(H)	2-0		W	8768	Sayer,Home	9	Moore	Rosier	Brophy	Dixon	Frew	Plum	Home	Sayer	Hick	Donoven	Fell
10	15	Coventry City	(A)	1-6		L	11059	Hick	10	Moore	Rosier	Bell	Dixon	Frew	Plum	Home	Sayer	Hick	Donoven	Fell
11	22	Merthyr Town	(H)	2-1		W	3774	Fell,Hick	11	Moore	Rosier	Bell	Dixon	Frew	Brophy	Home	Sayer	Hick	Falconbridge	Fell
12	29	Walsall	(A)	1-0		W	7897	Hick	12	Moore	Rosier	Bell	Dixon	Frew	Brophy	Home	Sayer	Hick	Falconbridge	Fell
13	5 Nov	Gillingham	(H)	1-2		L	6756	Hick	13	Moore	Rosier	Bell	Dixon	Frew	Brophy	Home	Sayer	Hick	Falconbridge	Fell
14	12	Plymouth Argyle	(A)	2-3	(1-1)	L	10624	Hick(2)	14	Moore	Rosier	Bell	Morris	Frew	Brophy	Home	Sayer	Hick	Falconbridge	Fell
15	19	Bristol Rovers	(H)	2-1	(1-1)	W	4421	Hick,Falconbridge	15	Moore	Rosier	Bell	Morris	Frew	Brophy	Home	Sayer	Hick	Falconbridge	Fell
16	3 Dec	Watford	(H)	3-0		W	5320	Donoven,Hick,Fell	16	Moore	Rosier	Bell	Morris	Robinson	Dixon	Home	Falconbridge	Hick	Donoven	Fell
17	24	Newport County	(A)	2-3	(1-1)	L	3837	Bailey,Baron	17	Moore	Rosier	Bell	Dixon	Frew	Donoven	Home	Bailey	Baron	Falconbridge	Fell
18	26	Brentford	(H)	3-2		W	3540	Home,Baron,Fell	18	Moore	Rosier	Bell	Dixon	Robinson	Donoven	Home	Bailey	Baron	Falconbridge	Fell
19	31	Luton Town	(A)	0-0	(0-0)	D	5402		19	Moore	Rosier	Bell	Brophy	Frew	Donoven	Home	Bailey	Hick	Falconbridge	Fell
20	7 Jan	Millwall	(H)	0-1	(0-1)	L	9767		20	Moore	Rosier	Bell	Brophy	Robinson	Donoven	Home	Bailey	Hick	Falconbridge	Fell
21	14	Queens Park Rangers	(A)	2-3		L	7294	Donoven,Hick	21	Boyce	Rosier	Bell	Dixon	Purdy	Donoven	Home	Bailey	Hick	Falconbridge	Fell
22	21	Crystal Palace	(A)	1-4	(1-2)	L	10606	Home	22	Moore	French	Bell	Morris	Purdy	Andrews	Home	Bailey	Baron	Falconbridge	Fell
23	4 Feb	Torquay United	(A)	3-3		D	3419	Hick(2),Bailey	23	Moore	Rosier	Bell	Morris	Purdy	Andrews	Home	Bailey	Baron	Donoven	Fell
24	11	Norwich City	(H)	1-1		D	4671	Home	24	Moore	Rosier	Bell	Morris	Frew	Andrews	Home	Bailey	Hick	Donoven	Fell
25	15	Exeter City	(H)	1-2	(1-2)	L	2603	Home	25	Moore	Rosier	Bell	Morris	Frew	Dixon	Home	Bailey	Hick	Sayer	Fell
26	18	Northampton Town	(A)	1-2		L	13133	Hick	26	Moore	French	Rosier	Morris	Frew	Dixon	Home	Bailey	Hick	Sayer	Fell
27	25	Coventry City	(H)	3-2	(0-1)	W	5979	Baron(2),Home	27	Moore	Rosier	Bell	Morris	Frew	Dixon	Home	Bailey	Baron	Falconbridge	Fell
28	3 Mar	Merthyr Town	(A)	3-2		W	2289	Baron(2),Home	28	Boyce	Rosier	Bell	Morris	Frew	Dixon	Home	Sayer	Baron	Donoven	Fell
29	10	Walsall	(H)	2-1		W	4736	Baron,Donoven	29	Boyce	Rosier	Bell	Morris	Frew	Dixon	Home	Sayer	Baron	Donoven	Fell
30	14	Swindon Town	(H)	1-1		D	3159	Dixon	30	Jarvie	Rosier	Bell	Morris	Frew	Dixon	Home	Falconbridge	Baron	Donoven	Fell
31	17	Gillingham	(A)	0-1		L	6240		31	Jarvie	French	Rosier	Dixon	Frew	Andrews	Morris	Sayer	Baron	Donoven	Daykin
32	24	Plymouth Argyle	(H)	3-0		W	5187	Baron(2),Morris	32	Jarvie	French	Rosier	Dixon	Frew	Andrews	Morris	Sayer	Baron	Donoven	Clenshaw
33	26	Charlton Athletic	(A)	2-1		W	2210	Donoven,Morris	33	Jarvie	French	Rosier	Dixon	Frew	Andrews	Morris	Sayer	Hick	Donoven	Clenshaw
34	31	Bristol Rovers	(A)	3-1		W	4764	Baron(2),Morris	34	Jarvie	French	Rosier	Dixon	Frew	Andrews	Morris	Sayer	Baron	Donoven	Clenshaw
35	6 Apr	Brighton	(A)	0-1		L	11742		35	Jarvie	French	Rosier	Dixon	Frew	Andrews	Morris	Sayer	Baron	Donoven	Clenshaw
36	7	Queens Park Rangers	(H)	7-0		W	8126	Hick(3),Donoven,Morris,Dixon,Clenshaw	36	Jarvie	French	Rosier	Dixon	Frew	Andrews	Morris	Sayer	Hick	Donoven	Clenshaw
37	9	Brighton	(H)	0-1		L	10407		37	Jarvie	French	Rosier	Dixon	Frew	Andrews	Morris	Sayer	Hick	Donoven	Clenshaw
38	14	Watford	(A)	1-1		D	5048	Hick	38	Jarvie	French	Rosier	Dixon	Robinson	Andrews	Morris	Sayer	Baron	Falconbridge	Clenshaw
39	21	Charlton Athletic	(H)	1-2		L	4501	Donoven	39	Jarvie	French	Rosier	Dixon	Frew	Andrews	Morris	Sayer	Baron	Donoven	Clenshaw
40	23	Brentford	(A)	2-2		D	4889	Clenshaw,Baron	40	Jarvie	Wilson	Rosier	Dixon	Frew	Sayer	Morris	Hick	Baron	Donoven	Clenshaw
41	28	Swindon Town	(A)	1-0		W	4899	Andrews	41	Jarvie	Wilson	Rosier	Dixon	Sayer	Andrews	Morris	Bailey	Hick	Donoven	Clenshaw
42	5 May	Newport County	(H)	5-1		W	4796	Morris(2),Bailey,Clenshaw,Hick	42	Jarvie	Wilson	Rosier	Dixon	Sayer	Andrews	Morris	Bailey	Hick	Donoven	Clenshaw

Major Cup Competitions

Rd.	Date	Opposition	Venue	Score	H.T. Res.	Att.	Goalscorers	1	2	3	4	5	6	7	8	9	10	11
				F.A.Cup														
R1	26 Nov	Wellington Town	(H)	1-0	(0-0)	W 5000	Hick	Moore	Brophy	Bell	Morris	Frew	Andrews	Horne	Sayer	Hick	Falconbridge	Fell
R2	10 Dec	Gillingham	(A)	0-2	(0-1)	L		Moore	Rosier	Bell	Morris	Frew	Dixon	Horne	Falconbridge	Hick	Donoven	Fell

LEAGUE COLOURS

SOUTHEND UNITED

B.D.V. CIGARETTES

Appearances and Goals

Name	Appearances Lge.	FAC	Total	Goals Lge.	FAC	Total
ANDREWS, Jack	13	1	14	1		1
BAILEY, Jack	21		21	5		5
BARON, Fred	12		12	12		12
BELL, Tommy	26	2	28			
BOYCE, Tommy	7		7			
BROPHY, Tom	10	1	11			
CLENSHAW, Les	11		11	3		3
DAYKIN, Harry	1		1			
DIXON, Tom	36	1	37	2		2
DONOVEN, Dickie	31	1	32	11		11
FALCONBRIDGE, George	17	2	19	1		1
FELL, John	30	2	32	3		3
FRENCH, Jack	11		11			
FREW, Jimmy	33	2	35			
HICK, Billy	31	2	33	25	1	26
HORNE, Alf	30	2	32	10		10
JARVIE, John	13		13			
MOORE, Billy	20	2	22			
MORRIS, Hugh	23	2	25	6		6
PLUM, Seth	10		10			
PURDY, Albert	3		3			
ROBINSON, William	4		4			
ROSIER, Bertie	41	1	42			
SAYER, Stan	23	1	24	1		1
WILSON, John	3		3			
WOODWARD, John	2		2			

	Ps	P	W	D	L	F	A	W	D	L	F	A	Pts.
1927/28	7	42	14	2	5	48	19	6	4	11	32	45	46

Season 1928/29 – League Division Three (South)

No.	Date	Opposition	Venue	Score	H.T.	Res.	Att.	Goalscorers	1	2	3	4	5	6	7	8	9	10	11
1	25 Aug	Bournemouth	(A)	2-2		D	9042	Shankly(2)	Moore	French	Robinson	Dixon	Binks	Sayer	Morris	Townsend	Shankly	Donoven	Clenshaw
2	27	Exeter City	(H)	1-0	(0-0)	W	6355	Shankly	Moore	French	Robinson	Dixon	Binks	Sayer	Morris	Townsend	Shankly	Donoven	Clenshaw
3	1 Sep	Brentford	(H)	1-1		D	8082	Shankly	Moore	French	Robinson	Dixon	Binks	Sayer	Morris	Townsend	Shankly	Donoven	Clenshaw
4	5	Exeter City	(A)	2-1		W	5818	Shankly(2)	Moore	French	Robinson	Dixon	Binks	Sayer	Morris	Townsend	Shankly	Donoven	Clenshaw
5	8	Luton Town	(A)	2-4		L	10600	Shankly,Townsend	Moore	French	Robinson	Dixon	Frew	Sayer	Morris	Townsend	Shankly	Donoven	Clenshaw
6	15	Coventry City	(H)	0-0	(0-0)	D	7243		Moore	Robinson	Brophy	Dixon	Binks	Sayer	Morris	Townsend	Shankly	Donoven	Clenshaw
7	22	Northampton Town	(A)	3-2		W	10711	Shankly(2),Donoven	Moore	Robinson	Brophy	Dixon	Binks	Donoven	Morris	Bailey	Shankly	Baron	Clenshaw
8	29	Charlton Athletic	(H)	1-3		L	8144	Shankly	Moore	Robinson	Brophy	Dixon	Binks	Morris	Morris	Bailey	Shankly	Baron	Clenshaw
9	6 Oct	Norwich City	(A)	5-2		W	7472	Shankly(3),Clenshaw,Bailey	Moore	Robinson	Brophy	Dixon	Binks	Morris	Woolhouse	Bailey	Baron	Donoven	Clenshaw
10	13	Brighton	(H)	1-1		D	7746	Shankly	Moore	Robinson	Brophy	Dixon	Binks	Johnson	Morris	Bailey	Shankly	Donoven	Clenshaw
11	20	Plymouth Argyle	(A)	1-1		D	12063	Shankly	Moore	Robinson	Brophy	Dixon	Binks	Johnson	Morris	Bailey	Shankly	Donoven	Clenshaw
12	27	Fulham	(H)	0-1		L	8843		Moore	Robinson	Brophy	Dixon	Binks	Johnson	Morris	Bailey	Baron	Donoven	Clenshaw
13	3 Nov	Queens Park Rangers	(A)	1-3		L	12701	Baron	Moore	Robinson	Brophy	Dixon	Frew	Johnson	Morris	Bailey	Baron	Donoven	Clenshaw
14	10	Bristol Rovers	(H)	1-0		W	5764	Bailey	Moore	Robinson	Brophy	Dixon	Frew	Johnson	Morris	Bailey	Shankly	Donoven	Clenshaw
15	17	Watford	(A)	1-4		L	7593	Shankly	Moore	Lloyd	Robinson	Dixon	Frew	Morris	Oxley	Bailey	Shankly	Donoven	Clenshaw
16	1 Dec	Newport County	(A)	2-2		D	3725	Clenshaw,Oxley	Moore	Robinson	Andrews	Dixon	Frew	Morris	Oxley	Bailey	Baron	Binks	Clenshaw
17	15	Swindon Town	(A)	1-3		L	2879	Bailey	Moore	Robinson	Andrews	Dixon	Frew	Morris	Oxley	Bailey	Shankly	Binks	Clenshaw
18	22	Torquay United	(H)	3-0		W	4096	Shankly,Donoven,Clenshaw	Moore	Robinson	Andrews	Dixon	Frew	Morris	Oxley	Bailey	Shankly	Donoven	Clenshaw
19	25	Merthyr Town	(A)	1-2		L	2627	Donoven	Moore	Robinson	Andrews	Dixon	Frew	Morris	Oxley	Bailey	Shankly	Donoven	Clenshaw
20	26	Merthyr Town	(H)	5-1	(3-1)	W	3579	Oxley,Donoven,Shankly,Bailey,Clenshaw	Moore	French	Andrews	Dixon	Frew	Morris	Oxley	Bailey	Shankly	Donoven	Clenshaw
21	29	Bournemouth	(H)	4-4		D	5432	Shankly(2),Clenshaw,Oxley	Moore	French	Binks	Dixon	Frew	Morris	Oxley	Bailey	Shankly	Donoven	Clenshaw
22	5 Jan	Brentford	(A)	0-1		L	4588		Moore	French	Brophy	Dixon	Frew	Morris	Oxley	Bailey	Shankly	Donoven	Clenshaw
23	19	Luton Town	(H)	5-0	(1-0)	W	6153	Oxley(2),Bailey,Donoven,Shankly	Moore	French	Brophy	Dixon	Johnson	Morris	Oxley	Bailey	Shankly	Donoven	Clenshaw
24	26	Coventry City	(A)	1-1	(0-0)	D	15231	Shankly	Moore	French	Brophy	Dixon	Johnson	Morris	Oxley	Bailey	Shankly	Donoven	Clenshaw
25	2 Feb	Northampton Town	(H)	2-2		D	5944	Bailey(2)	Moore	French	Brophy	Dixon	Frew	Morris	Oxley	Bailey	Shankly	Donoven	Clenshaw
26	9	Charlton Athletic	(A)	2-3	(1-1)	L	11099	Shankly,Donoven	Moore	Robinson	Brophy	Dixon	Johnson	Morris	Oxley	Bailey	Shankly	Donoven	Clenshaw
27	16	Norwich City	(H)	5-3		W	3459	Shankly(2),Clenshaw(2),Oxley	Moore	Robinson	Brophy	Dixon	Johnson	Morris	Oxley	Bailey	Shankly	Donoven	Clenshaw
28	20	Walsall	(H)	3-1		W	2905	Shankly(3)	Moore	Robinson	Brophy	Dixon	Frew	Morris	Oxley	Bailey	Shankly	Donoven	Clenshaw
29	23	Brighton	(H)	1-2	(0-2)	L	4964	Morris	Moore	Robinson	Brophy	Dixon	Frew	Andrews	Morris	Bailey	Shankly	Donoven	Clenshaw
30	2 Mar	Plymouth Argyle	(H)	1-1		D	6486	Bailey	Moore	Robinson	Brophy	Dixon	Frew	Andrews	Morris	Bailey	Shankly	Donoven	Waring
31	9	Fulham	(A)	4-2	(0-2)	W	16189	Shankly(2),Bailey,Donoven	Moore	Robinson	Brophy	Dixon	Frew	Andrews	Oxley	Bailey	Shankly	Donoven	Waring
32	16	Queens Park Rangers	(H)	0-3		L	6259		Moore	Robinson	Brophy	Dixon	Frew	Johnson	Morris	Bailey	Shankly	Donoven	Clenshaw
33	23	Bristol Rovers	(A)	1-4		L	5553	Clenshaw	Moore	French	Brophy	Dixon	Johnson	Johnson	Morris	Bailey	Shankly	Donoven	Clenshaw
34	29	Gillingham	(A)	2-0		W	7643	Shankly,Martin	Moore	French	Brophy	Dixon	Sayer	Sayer	Morris	Bailey	Shankly	Martin	Clenshaw
35	30	Watford	(H)	1-3		L	7688	Woolhouse	Moore	French	Brophy	Dixon	Johnson	Donoven	Morris	Bailey	Shankly	Martin	Woolhouse
36	1 Apr	Gillingham	(H)	2-0		W	7773	Falconbridge,Bailey	Moore	French	Brophy	Dixon	Johnson	Donoven	Morris	Bailey	Shankly	Falconbridge	Martin
37	6	Walsall	(A)	1-4	(1-1)	L	4233	Shankly	Moore	French	Brophy	Dixon	Frew	Donoven	Morris	Bailey	Shankly	Falconbridge	Donoven
38	10	Crystal Palace	(H)	3-0		W	3084	Bailey(2),Donoven	Moore	French	Brophy	Dixon	Frew	Johnson	Morris	Bailey	Shankly	Donoven	Baron
39	13	Newport County	(H)	4-2		W	4820	Donoven(3),Bailey	Moore	French	Brophy	Dixon	Frew	Johnson	Morris	Bailey	Shankly	Donoven	Baron
40	20	Crystal Palace	(A)	2-3		L	16327	Clenshaw,Bailey	Moore	French	Brophy	Dixon	Frew	Johnson	Morris	Bailey	Shankly	Donoven	Clenshaw
41	27	Swindon Town	(H)	1-1		D	5312	Shankly	Moore	French	Brophy	Dixon	Frew	Johnson	Morris	Bailey	Shankly	Donoven	Clenshaw
42	4 May	Torquay United	(A)	1-2	(0-0)	L	4937	Shankly	Moore	French	Brophy	Dixon	Frew	Johnson	Morris	Bailey	Shankly	Donoven	Clenshaw

Major Cup Competitions

Rd.	Date	Opposition	Venue	Score	H.T.	Res.	Att.	Goalscorers
				F.A.Cup				
R1	24 Nov	Luton Town	(A)	1-5	(1-3)	L	10000	Shankly

Appearances and Goals

Name	Appearances			Goals		
	Lge.	FAC	Total	Lge.	FAC	Total
ANDREWS, Jack	8	1	9			
BAILEY, Jack	36		36	14		14
BARON, Fred	6		6	1		1
BINKS, Sid	14		14			
BROPHY, Tom	30		30			
CLENSHAW, Les	36	1	37	9		9
DAVIES, Baden	1		1			
DIXON, Tom	42	1	43			
DONOVEN, Dickie	40		40	11		11
FALCONBRIDGE, George	2		2	1		1
FRENCH, Jack	21		21			
FREW, Jimmy	23	1	24			
JOHNSON, Joe	19		19			
LLOYD, Charlie	1		1			
MARTIN, Jimmy	3		3	1		1
MOORE, Billy	42	1	43			
MORRIS, Hugh	41	1	42	1		1
OXLEY, Cyril	15	1	16	6		6
ROBINSON, Dave	26	1	27			
SAYER, Stan	9		9			
SHANKLY, Jimmy	39	1	40	34	1	35
TOWNSEND, John	6		6	1		1
WARING, Bernard	1		1			
WOOLHOUSE, Ben	2	1	3	1		1

	Ps	P	W	D	L	F	A	W	D	L	F	A	Pts.
1928/29	12	42	10	7	4	44	27	5	4	12	36	48	41

Typical programme cover of the season.

Season 1929/30 – League Division Three (South)

No.	Date	Opposition	Venue	Score	H.T.	Res.	Att.	Goalscorers	No.	1	2	3	4	5	6	7	8	9	10	11
1	31 Aug	Newport County	(H)	2-1	(2-0)	W	8186	Armitage(pen),Donoven	1	Moore	French	Brophy	Dixon	Armitage	Campbell	Barnett	Jones	Shankly	Donoven	Clenshaw
2	2 Sep	Crystal Palace	(H)	3-2		W	6954	Baron,Armitage,Donoven	2	Moore	French	Robinson	Dixon	Armitage	Campbell	Barnett	Jones	Baron	Donoven	Clenshaw
3	7	Luton Town	(A)	3-0	(1-0)	W	9992	Borland(2),Baron	3	Moore	French	Brophy	Dixon	Armitage	Johnson	Barnett	Jones	Baron	Donoven	Borland
4	11	Crystal Palace	(A)	2-1		W	13279	Baron(2)	4	Moore	French	Robinson	Dixon	Armitage	Johnson	Barnett	Jones	Baron	Donoven	Borland
5	14	Bournemouth	(H)	4-1	(2-0)	W	9577	Donoven(2),Baron,Borland	5	Moore	French	Robinson	Dixon	Armitage	Johnson	Barnett	Jones	Baron	Donoven	Borland
6	16	Northampton Town	(H)	1-2		L	8145	Baron	6	Moore	French	Robinson	Dixon	Armitage	Johnson	Barnett	Jones	Baron	Donoven	Borland
7	21	Walsall	(A)	3-1	(2-0)	W	7929	Donoven,Jones,Baron	7	Moore	French	Robinson	Dixon	Ward	Johnson	Barnett	Jones	Baron	Donoven	Borland
8	28	Queens Park Rangers	(H)	1-0	(1-0)	W	10867	Donoven	8	Moore	French	Robinson	Dixon	Armitage	Campbell	Barnett	Jones	Shankly	Donoven	Borland
9	5 Oct	Fulham	(A)	2-2	(2-0)	D	21578	Donoven,Baron	9	Moore	French	Robinson	Dixon	Armitage	Campbell	Barnett	Jones	Baron	Donoven	Borland
10	12	Norwich City	(H)	1-1	(0-1)	D	8981	Baron	10	Moore	French	Robinson	Dixon	Ward	Campbell	Barnett	Jones	Baron	Donoven	Clenshaw
11	19	Torquay United	(H)	1-1	(1-1)	D	8269	Baron	11	Moore	French	Robinson	Dixon	Ward	Campbell	Barnett	Jones	Baron	Donoven	Borland
12	26	Merthyr Town	(A)	2-2	(0-1)	D	3989	Bailey,Baron	12	Moore	French	Robinson	Davies	Ward	Donoven	Barnett	Bailey	Baron	Jones	Borland
13	2 Nov	Plymouth Argyle	(H)	1-1	(0-0)	D	10966	Baron	13	Moore	French	Robinson	Davies	Ward	Donoven	Barnett	Bailey	Baron	Jones	Borland
14	9	Swindon Town	(A)	1-5	(0-3)	L	6638	Baron	14	Moore	French	Robinson	Davies	Ward	Davies	Barnett	Jones	Baron	Donoven	Borland
15	16	Brighton	(H)	0-0	(0-0)	D	3553		15	Moore	French	Robinson	Dixon	Ward	Davies	Barnett	Jones	Baron	Donoven	Borland
16	23	Bristol Rovers	(A)	2-4	(1-2)	L	5197	Donoven,Barnett	16	Moore	French	Robinson	Dixon	Ward	Davies	Barnett	Jones	Baron	Donoven	Clenshaw
17	7 Dec	Clapton Orient	(H)	1-1	(1-1)	D	7622	Clenshaw	17	Moore	Turnbull	Robinson	Dixon	Ward	Davies	Barnett	Jones	Shankly	Donoven	Clenshaw
18	21	Watford	(A)	1-2	(0-1)	L	3327	Barnett	18	Moore	French	Robinson	Dixon	Ward	Lloyd	Barnett	Jones	Shankly	Jones	Borland
19	25	Exeter City	(H)	1-0	(1-0)	W	6154	Jones	19	Moore	French	Robinson	Crewe	Ward	Lloyd	Barnett	Bailey	Shankly	Jones	Borland
20	26	Exeter City	(A)	1-3	(0-3)	L	11502	Bailey	20	Moore	French	Robinson	Dixon	Ward	Lloyd	Barnett	Bailey	Shankly	Jones	Borland
21	4 Jan	Luton Town	(H)	1-1	(0-1)	D	5859	Jones	21	McKenna	French	Robinson	Johnson	Ward	Lloyd	Barnett	Bailey	Baron	Jones	Borland
22	11	Brentford	(H)	2-0	(0-0)	W	6456	Baron,Jones	22	McKenna	French	Robinson	Dixon	Ward	Donoven	Barnett	Jones	Baron	Bryant	Borland
23	18	Bournemouth	(A)	0-0	(0-0)	D	5623		23	McKenna	French	Robinson	Dixon	Ward	Donoven	Barnett	Jones	Shankly	Bryant	Borland
24	25	Newport County	(A)	0-0	(0-0)	D	4945		24	McKenna	French	Robinson	Dixon	Ward	Donoven	Barnett	Jones	Shankly	Bailey	Borland
25	1 Feb	Queens Park Rangers	(A)	5-2	(5-1)	W	8187	Shankly(4),Jones	25	McKenna	French	Robinson	Dixon	Ward	Donoven	Barnett	Jones	Shankly	Bailey	Borland
26	8	Fulham	(H)	1-2	(0-2)	L	6204	Jones	26	McKenna	French	Robinson	Dixon	Ward	Donoven	Barnett	Jones	Shankly	Bailey	Borland
27	15	Norwich City	(A)	1-2	(0-1)	L	9816	Dixon	27	McKenna	French	Robinson	Dixon	Ward	Donoven	Barnett	Jones	Shankly	Bailey	Burke
28	19	Walsall	(H)	1-0	(-0)	W	3006	Barnett	28	Moore	French	Robinson	Dixon	Ward	Donoven	Barnett	Jones	Shankly	Bailey	Clenshaw
29	22	Torquay United	(A)	1-1	(1-1)	D	3429	Donoven	29	Moore	French	Robinson	Dixon	Ward	Johnson	Barnett	Jones	Shankly	Donoven	Clenshaw
30	1 Mar	Merthyr Town	(H)	6-0	(2-0)	W	5583	Shankly(5),Donoven	30	Moore	French	Robinson	Dixon	Ward	Johnson	Barnett	Jones	Shankly	Donoven	Clenshaw
31	8	Plymouth Argyle	(A)	0-1	(0-0)	L	13998		31	Moore	French	Robinson	Dixon	Ward	Johnson	Barnett	Jones	Shankly	Donoven	Clenshaw
32	15	Swindon Town	(H)	3-1	(0-0)	W	6106	Clenshaw,Donoven,Barnett	32	Moore	French	Robinson	Dixon	Ward	Johnson	Barnett	Jones	Shankly	Donoven	Clenshaw
33	22	Brighton	(A)	0-1	(0-1)	L	10223		33	Moore	French	Robinson	Dixon	Ward	Johnson	Barnett	Jones	Shankly	Donoven	Clenshaw
34	29	Bristol Rovers	(H)	6-0	(4-0)	W	5903	Baron(3),Jones,Clenshaw,Ward	34	Moore	French	Robinson	Dixon	Ward	Johnson	Barnett	Jones	Baron	Donoven	Clenshaw
35	5 Apr	Brentford	(A)	1-2	(1-0)	L	13255	Baron	35	Moore	French	Robinson	Dixon	Ward	Johnson	Barnett	Jones	Baron	Donoven	Clenshaw
36	12	Clapton Orient	(H)	4-1	(4-0)	W	6282	Baron(2),Ward,Barnett	36	Moore	French	Robinson	Dixon	Ward	Johnson	Barnett	Jones	Baron	Donoven	Clenshaw
37	18	Gillingham	(A)	0-1	(0-0)	L	7964		37	Moore	French	Robinson	Johnson	Ward	Dixon	Clenshaw	Donoven	Baron	Jones	Barnett
38	19	Coventry City	(A)	1-5	(0-1)	L	9259	Baron	38	McKenna	French	Robinson	Dixon	Ward	Johnson	Barnett	Jones	Baron	Donoven	Clenshaw
39	21	Gillingham	(H)	0-0	(0-0)	D	9036		39	McKenna	French	Robinson	Dixon	Ward	Johnson	Barnett	Jones	Baron	Donoven	Clenshaw
40	26	Watford	(H)	1-3	(0-2)	L	4459	Donoven	40	McKenna	French	Robinson	Dixon	Ward	Johnson	Barnett	Jones	Baron	Donoven	Clenshaw
41	30	Coventry City	(H)	1-2		L	2667	Donoven	41	James	French	Robinson	Dixon	Ward	Johnson	Barnett	Jones	Baron	Donoven	Clenshaw
42	3 May	Northampton Town	(A)	1-5	(1-0)	L	3454	Baron	42	Moore	Robinson	Turnbull	Dixon	Armitage	Johnson	Barnett	Jones	Baron	Donoven	Clenshaw

Major Cup Competitions

F.A.Cup

Rd.	Date	Opposition	Venue	Score	H.T.	Res.	Att.	Goalscorers	1	2	3	4	5	6	7	8	9	10	11
R1	30 Nov	Brentford	(H)	1-0	(1-0)	W	7000	Barnett	Moore	Turnbull	Robinson	Dixon	Ward	Davies	Barnett	Jones	Baron	Donoven	Clenshaw
R2	14 Dec	York City	(H)	1-4	(1-1)	L	9000	Turnbull(pen)	Moore	Turnbull	Robinson	Dixon	Ward	Davies	Barnett	Jones	Baron	Donoven	Clenshaw

Appearances and Goals

Name	Appearances			Goals		
	Lge.	FAC	Total	Lge.	FAC	Total
ARMITAGE, John	9		9	2		2
BAILEY, Jack	11		11	2		2
BARNETT, Fred	42	2	44	5	1	6
BARON, Fred	25	2	27	22		22
BORLAND, John	21		21	3		3
BROPHY, Tom	2		2			
BRYANT, John	2		2			
BURKE, John	1		1			
CAMPBELL, Joe	7		7			
CLENSHAW, Les	20	2	22	3		3
CREWE, Billy	1		1			
DAVIES, Haydn	7	2	9			
DIXON, Tom	37	2	39	1		1
DONOVEN, Dickie	38	2	40	13		13
FRENCH, Jack	40		40			
JAMES, Charlie	1		1			
JOHNSON, Joe	19		19			
JONES, Mickey	42	2	44	7		7
LLOYD, Jack	4		4			
MOORE, Billy	31	2	33			
McKENNA, Tom	10		10			
ROBINSON, Dave	40	2	42			
SHANKLY, Jimmy	17		17	9		9
TURNBULL, Bob	2	2	4		1	1
WARD, Bob	33	2	35	2		2

	Ps	P	W	D	L	F	A	W	D	L	F	A	Pts.
1929/30	11	42	11	6	4	41	19	4	7	10	28	40	43

This season saw the departure of Merthyr Town from the League. 1930/31 – from which the above programme comes – saw the London team Thames Association make a brief appearance in the division, for just two seasons.

Season 1930/31 – League Division Three (South)

No.	Date	Opposition	Venue	Score	H.T.	Res.	Att.	Goalscorers	1	2	3	4	5	6	7	8	9	10	11
1	30 Aug	Crystal Palace	(H)	2-4	(0-2)	L	7413	Shankly,Barnett	Moore	French	Robinson	Dixon	Ward	Powell	Barnett	Jones	Shankly	Donoven	Williams
2	3 Sep	Brighton	(A)	2-1	(0-0)	W	7035	Shankly,Jones	Moore	French	Robinson	Dixon	Ward	Donoven	Barnett	Jones	Shankly	Pike	Williams
3	6	Bournemouth	(A)	0-0	(0-0)	D	7719		Moore	French	Robinson	Dixon	Ward	Donoven	Barnett	Jones	Shankly	Bailey	Williams
4	8	Torquay United	(H)	6-3	(3-2)	W	5656	Shankly(3),Williams(2),Barnett	Moore	French	Robinson	Dixon	Ward	Donoven	Barnett	Jones	Shankly	Bailey	Williams
5	13	Luton Town	(A)	1-2	(0-0)	L	6347	Shankly	Moore	French	Robinson	Dixon	Ward	Donoven	Barnett	Jones	Shankly	Bailey	Williams
6	17	Torquay United	(A)	1-3		L	3077	Williams	Moore	French	Robinson	Johnson	Wilson	Donoven	Barnett	Jones	Shankly	Crompton	Williams
7	20	Bristol Rovers	(H)	4-0	(3-0)	W	6442	Crompton(2),Shankly(2)	Moore	French	Robinson	Dixon	Wilson	Donoven	Barnett	Jones	Shankly	Crompton	Clenshaw
8	27	Newport County	(A)	1-3	(1-2)	L	2711	Shankly	Moore	French	Robinson	Dixon	Wilson	Donoven	Barnett	Jones	Shankly	Crompton	Williams
9	4 Oct	Gillingham	(H)	3-2	(1-2)	W	7476	Shankly(2),Crompton	Moore	Gibson	Robinson	Dixon	Wilson	Donoven	Barnett	Jones	Shankly	Crompton	Williams
10	11	Exeter City	(A)	1-1	(0-0)	D	5212	Barnett	Moore	French	Robinson	Dixon	Wilson	Donoven	Barnett	Jones	Shankly	Crompton	Williams
11	18	Swindon Town	(H)	5-3	(2-3)	W	7532	Jones(3),Barnett,Shankly	Moore	French	Robinson	Dixon	Wilson	Donoven	Barnett	Jones	Shankly	Crompton	Williams
12	25	Fulham	(A)	0-1	(0-0)	L	10837		Moore	French	Robinson	Dixon	Wilson	Donoven	Barnett	Jones	Shankly	Crompton	Clenshaw
13	1 Nov	Coventry City	(H)	2-0	(1-0)	W	4019	Barnett(2)	Moore	Gibson	Robinson	Dixon	Wilson	Donoven	Barnett	Jones	Shankly	Crompton	Clenshaw
14	8	Walsall	(A)	3-1	(2-0)	W	4610	Shankly,Crompton,Barnett	Moore	Gibson	Robinson	Dixon	Wilson	Donoven	Barnett	Jones	Shankly	Crompton	Clenshaw
15	15	Queens Park Rangers	(H)	2-0	(2-0)	W	5060	Jones,Shankly	Moore	Gibson	Robinson	Dixon	Wilson	Donoven	Barnett	Jones	Shankly	Crompton	Clenshaw
16	22	Norwich City	(A)	1-0	(1-0)	W	7485	Williams	Moore	French	Robinson	Dixon	Wilson	Donoven	Barnett	Jones	Shankly	Crompton	Williams
17	6 Dec	Clapton Orient	(A)	1-3	(1-1)	L	1916	Jones	Moore	French	Robinson	Ward	Wilson	Johnson	Barnett	Jones	Shankly	Donoven	Crompton
18	13	Bournemouth	(H)	4-0	(3-0)	W	4635	Nicol(2),Shankly(2)	Moore	French	Robinson	Dixon	Wilson	Donoven	Barnett	Jones	Shankly	Nicol	Williams
19	17	Notts County	(H)	2-1		W	4827	Dixon,Nicol	Moore	French	Robinson	Dixon	Wilson	Donoven	Barnett	Jones	Shankly	Nicol	Crompton
20	20	Watford	(A)	3-1	(1-0)	W	5750	Nicol(2),Barnett	Moore	French	Robinson	Dixon	Wilson	Donoven	Barnett	Jones	Shankly	Nicol	Clenshaw
21	25	Northampton Town	(H)	2-1	(1-0)	W	10068	Shankly,Allon(O.G.)	Moore	French	Gibson	Dixon	Wilson	Donoven	Barnett	Jones	Shankly	Nicol	Clenshaw
22	26	Northampton Town	(A)	0-4		L	9976		Moore	French	Gibson	Dixon	Wilson	Donoven	Barnett	Jones	Shankly	Nicol	Williams
23	27	Crystal Palace	(H)	1-3	(0-2)	L	16466	Shankly(pen)	Moore	French	Clenshaw	Dixon	Wilson	Donoven	Barnett	Jones	Shankly	Nicol	Williams
24	10 Jan	Thames Association	(H)	1-0	(0-0)	W	1830	Wilson	Moore	French	Gibson	Dixon	Wilson	Donoven	Barnett	Jones	Shankly	Nicol	Williams
25	17	Luton Town	(H)	0-2	(0-1)	L	4857		Moore	French	Gibson	Dixon	Wilson	Donoven	Barnett	Jones	Shankly	Nicol	Crompton
26	28	Bristol Rovers	(A)	3-2	(3-1)	W	3441	Shankly(3)	Moore	French	Tunbridge	Dixon	Wilson	Donoven	Barnett	Jones	Shankly	Nicol	Crompton
27	31	Newport County	(H)	6-2	(3-1)	W	5536	Barnett(2),Crompton(2),Shankly,Nicol	Moore	French	Tunbridge	Dixon	Wilson	Donoven	Barnett	Jones	Shankly	Nicol	Crompton
28	7 Feb	Gillingham	(A)	0-1	(0-0)	L	4223		Moore	French	Robinson	Dixon	Wilson	Donoven	Barnett	Jones	Shankly	Pike	Crompton
29	21	Swindon Town	(A)	1-1	(1-0)	D	4994	Pike	Moore	French	Robinson	Dixon	Wilson	Donoven	Barnett	Jones	Shankly	Pike	Crompton
30	28	Fulham	(H)	2-4	(1-2)	L	5353	Crompton,Shankly	Moore	French	Robinson	Dixon	Wilson	Donoven	Barnett	Jones	Shankly	Pike	Crompton
31	7 Mar	Coventry City	(A)	0-0	(0-0)	D	6396		Moore	French	Robinson	Dixon	Wilson	Donoven	Barnett	Jones	Shankly	Pike	Crompton
32	14	Walsall	(H)	2-0	(2-0)	W	6460	Pike,Shankly	Moore	French	Robinson	Dixon	Wilson	Donoven	Barnett	Jones	Shankly	Pike	Crompton
33	18	Exeter City	(H)	5-1	(2-0)	W	4097	Shankly(2),Pike,Jones,Barnett	Moore	French	Robinson	Dixon	Wilson	Johnson	Barnett	Jones	Shankly	Pike	Crompton
34	21	Queens Park Rangers	(A)	2-0	(2-0)	W	7114	Jones,Pike	Moore	French	Robinson	Dixon	Wilson	Donoven	Barnett	Jones	Shankly	Pike	Crompton
35	28	Norwich City	(H)	2-0	(2-0)	W	5638	Baron,Donoven	Moore	French	Robinson	Dixon	Wilson	Johnson	Barnett	Jones	Baron	Donoven	Williams
36	3 Apr	Brentford	(A)	1-3	(0-1)	L	6027	Shankly	Moore	French	Robinson	Dixon	Wilson	Donoven	Barnett	Jones	Shankly	Bailey	Crompton
37	4	Thames Association	(A)	0-3	(0-0)	L	3201		Moore	French	Robinson	Dixon	Wilson	Donoven	Barnett	Jones	Shankly	Nicol	Crompton
38	6	Brentford	(H)	0-1	(0-0)	L	9969		Moore	French	Robinson	Dixon	Wilson	Donoven	Barnett	Jones	Shankly	Nicol	Crompton
39	11	Clapton Orient	(H)	2-0	(0-0)	W	5791	Nicol,Dixon	Moore	French	Robinson	Dixon	Wilson	Donoven	Barnett	Jones	Shankly	Nicol	Crompton
40	18	Notts County	(A)	1-1	(0-0)	D	11919	Shankly	Moore	French	Robinson	Dixon	Wilson	Donoven	Barnett	Jones	Shankly	-Nicol	Crompton
41	25	Watford	(H)	1-0	(1-0)	W	3459	Shankly	Moore	French	Robinson	Dixon	Wilson	Johnson	Barnett	Jones	Shankly	Pike	Crompton
42	2 May	Brighton	(H)	0-2	(0-1)	L	5758	Crompton	Moore	Gibson	Robinson	Dixon	Wilson	Johnson	Barnett	Jones	Shankly	Pike	Crompton

Rd.	Date	Opposition	Venue Score	H.T. Res.	Att.	Goalscorers
			F.A.Cup			
R1	29 Nov	Torquay United	(A) 0–1	(0–0)	L 10000	

1	2	3	4	5	6	7	8	9	10	11
Moore	French	Robinson	Dixon	Wilson	Donoven	Barnett	Jones	Shankly	Crompton	Clenshaw

Appearances and Goals

Name	Appearances			Goals		
	Lge.	FAC	Total	Lge.	FAC	Total
BAILEY, Jack	5		5			
BARNETT, Fred	42	1	43	11		11
BARON, Fred	1		1	1		1
CLENSHAW, Les	7	1	8			
CROMPTON, Arthur	30	1	31	8		8
DIXON, Tom	40	1	41	2		2
DONOVEN, Dickie	39	1	40	1		1
FRENCH, Jack	36	1	37			
GIBSON, William	10		10			
JOHNSON, Joe	6		6			
JONES, Mickey	42	1	43	8		8
MOORE, Billy	42	1	43			
NICOL, Jim	15		15	7		7
PIKE, Tot	9		9	4		4
POWELL, Billy	1		1			
ROBINSON, Dave	35	1	36			
SHANKLY, Jimmy	41	1	42	28		28
TUNBRIDGE, Alec	2		2			
WARD, Bob	6		6			
WILLIAMS, Owen	16		16	4		4
WILSON, Joe	37	1	38	1		1
Own Goal				1		1

	Ps	P	W	D	L	F	A	W	D	L	F	A	Pts.
1930/31	5	42	16	0	5	53	26	6	5	10	23	34	49

Season 1931/32 – League Division Three (South)

No.	Date	Opposition	Venue	Score	H.T.	Res.	Att.	Goalscorers	No.	1	2	3	4	5	6	7	8	9	10	11
1	29 Aug	Gillingham	(H)	2-0	(2-0)	W	10665	Shankly,Crompton(pen)	1	Moore	French	Robinson	Dixon	Wilson	Donoven	Barnett	Jones	Shankly	Pike	Crompton
2	31	Coventry City	(A)	2-0		W	12483	Crompton,Baron	2	Moore	French	Robinson	Dixon	Wilson	Donoven	Barnett	Jones	Baron	Pike	Crompton
3	5 Sep	Luton Town	(A)	3-1		W	9179	Barnett,Baron,Wilson	3	Moore	French	Robinson	Dixon	Wilson	Donoven	Barnett	Jones	Baron	Pike	Crompton
4	7	Thames	(H)	1-1		D	7461	Crompton	4	Whitelaw	French	Robinson	Dixon	Wilson	Donoven	Barnett	Jones	Baron	Pike	Crompton
5	12	Cardiff City	(H)	1-1	(1-0)	D	7494	Pike	5	Moore	French	Robinson	Dixon	Wilson	Donoven	Barnett	Jones	Shankly	Pike	Crompton
6	17	Thames	(A)	3-1		W	3848	French,Crompton,Shankly	6	Moore	French	Robinson	Dixon	Wilson	Donoven	Barnett	Jones	Shankly	Pike	Crompton
7	19	Northampton Town	(A)	2-1		W	8779	Shankly,French(pen)	7	Moore	French	Robinson	Dixon	Wilson	Donoven	Barnett	Jones	Shankly	Pike	Crompton
8	26	Reading	(H)	1-1	(0-0)	D	9633	Shankly	8	Moore	French	Robinson	Dixon	Wilson	Donoven	Barnett	Jones	Shankly	Pike	Crompton
9	3 Oct	Clapton Orient	(A)	4-2	(0-0)	W	17072	Shankly(3),Barnett	9	Whitelaw	French	Robinson	Dixon	Wilson	Donoven	Barnett	Jones	Shankly	Pike	Crompton
10	10	Fulham	(A)	1-1	(1-0)	D	28757	Thomson	10	Whitelaw	French	Robinson	Dixon	Wilson	Donoven	Barnett	Jones	Shankly	Thomson	Crompton
11	17	Swindon Town	(H)	3-0	(1-0)	W	10430	Jones,Barnett,Thomson	11	Whitelaw	French	Robinson	Dixon	Wilson	Donoven	Barnett	Jones	Shankly	Thomson	Crompton
12	24	Norwich City	(A)	1-1	(0-0)	D	16764	Crompton	12	Whitelaw	French	Robinson	Dixon	Wilson	Donoven	Barnett	Jones	Shankly	Thomson	Crompton
13	31	Brighton	(H)	2-0		W	10488	Thomson,Crompton	13	Whitelaw	French	Robinson	Dixon	Wilson	Donoven	Barnett	Jones	Shankly	Thomson	Crompton
14	7 Nov	Mansfield Town	(A)	4-4	(2-4)	D	8833	Shankly(2),Crompton(2)	14	McKenna	French	Robinson	Dixon	Wilson	Donoven	Barnett	Jones	Shankly	Thomson	Crompton
15	14	Watford	(H)	3-0	(0-0)	W	10692	Crompton(2),Shankly	15	McKenna	French	Robinson	Dixon	Wilson	Donoven	Barnett	Jones	Shankly	Thomson	Crompton
16	21	Crystal Palace	(A)	2-3	(2-2)	L	29335	Shankly,Crompton	16	Whitelaw	French	Robinson	Dixon	Wilson	Donoven	Barnett	Jones	Shankly	Thomson	Crompton
17	5 Dec	Queens Park Rangers	(A)	1-2	(0-1)	L	17898	Wilson	17	Moore	French	Robinson	Dixon	Wilson	nDonoven	Barnett	Jones	Shankly	Thomson	Crompton
18	19	Torquay United	(H)	1-2	(1-1)	L	2900	Barnett	18	Moore	French	Robinson	Dixon	Wiso	Donoven	Barnett	Jones	Shankly	Thomson	Crompton
19	25	Exeter City	(A)	0-1	(0-1)	L	9845		19	Moore	French	Robinson	Dixon	Wilson	Donoven	Barnett	Jones	Shankly	Fitton	Crompton
20	26	Exeter City	(A)	0-3	(0-2)	L	12393		20	Moore	French	Robinson	Dixon	Wilson	Donoven	Barnett	Jones	Shankly	Fitton	Crompton
21	2 Jan	Gillingham	(A)	0-4		L	5353		21	Whitelaw	Tunbridge	Robinson	Dixon	Wilson	Oakes	Hall	Jones	Shankly	Mayes	Crompton
22	9	Bristol Rovers	(H)	4-1	(1-1)	W	6220	Shankly(2),Thomson,Barnett	22	Whitelaw	Robinson	Hatfield	Dixon	Wilson	Pike	Barnett	Jones	Shankly	Thomson	Crompton
23	13	Bournemouth	(A)	1-3		L	4227	Mayes	23	Whitelaw	Hatfield	Robinson	Dixon	Wilson	Pike	Thomson	Jones	Shankly	Mayes	Crompton
24	16	Luton Town	(H)	1-1		D	5508	Jones	24	Whitelaw	French	Robinson	Johnson	Wilson	Pike	Crompton	Jones	Shankly	Donoven	Clenshaw
25	23	Cardiff City	(A)	3-2	(0-1)	W	6831	Hatfield,Fitton,Crompton	25	Whitelaw	French	Hatfield	Pike	Wilson	Donoven	Crompton	Jones	Shankly	Fitton	Clenshaw
26	30	Northampton Town	(H)	0-1	(0-1)	L	6465		26	Whitelaw	Hatfield	Robinson	Mayes	Wilson	Donoven	Barnett	Jones	Shankly	Crompton	Clenshaw
27	6 Feb	Reading	(A)	1-3	(1-2)	L	9874	Jones	27	Whitelaw	Hatfield	Robinson	Mayes	Wilson	Donoven	Barnett	Jones	Baron	Pike	Clenshaw
28	13	Clapton Orient	(H)	1-3	(1-0)	L	4714	Baron	28	Whitelaw	Hatfield	Robinson	Pike	Wilson	Donoven	Barnett	Jones	Baron	Shankly	Clenshaw
29	20	Fulham	(H)	4-1	(3-1)	W	6330	Clenshaw,Barnett,Dixon,Shankly	29	Whitelaw	French	Robinson	Dixon	Wilson	Donoven	Barnett	Jones	Shankly	Pike	Clenshaw
30	27	Swindon Town	(A)	2-1	(1-1)	W	4480	Barnett,Shankly	30	Whitelaw	French	Robinson	Dixon	Wilson	Donoven	Barnett	Jones	Shankly	Pike	Clenshaw
31	5 Mar	Norwich City	(H)	2-0	(2-0)	W	7262	Shankly,Pike	31	Whitelaw	Hatfield	Robinson	Dixon	Wilson	Donoven	Barnett	Jones	Shankly	Pike	Clenshaw
32	12	Brighton	(A)	2-1	(1-1)	W	7021	Shankly(2)	32	Whitelaw	Hatfield	Robinson	Dixon	Wilson	Donoven	Barnett	Jones	Shankly	Pike	Clenshaw
33	19	Mansfield Town	(H)	5-2	(3-0)	W	6710	Clenshaw(4),Pike	33	Whitelaw	Hatfield	Robinson	Dixon	Wilson	Donoven	Barnett	Jones	Shankly	Pike	Clenshaw
34	25	Brentford	(A)	3-2	(1-1)	W	15237	Pike(2),Baron	34	Whitelaw	Hatfield	Robinson	Dixon	Wilson	Donoven	Barnett	Jones	Baron	Pike	Clenshaw
35	26	Watford	(A)	1-1	(1-0)	D	8409	Dixon	35	Whitelaw	Hatfield	Robinson	Dixon	Wilson	Donoven	Barnett	Jones	Baron	Pike	Clenshaw
36	28	Brentford	(H)	1-0	(1-0)	W	17025	Baron	36	Whitelaw	Hatfield	Robinson	Dixon	Wilson	Donoven	Barnett	Jones	Baron	Pike	Clenshaw
37	2 Apr	Crystal Palace	(H)	1-0		W	8745	Clenshaw	37	Whitelaw	Hatfield	Robinson	Dixon	Wilson	Donoven	Barnett	Jones	Baron	Pike	Clenshaw
38	9	Bournemouth	(A)	0-0	(0-0)	D	3549		38	Whitelaw	Hatfield	Robinson	Dixon	Wilson	Donoven	Barnett	Jones	Baron	Pike	Clenshaw
39	16	Queens Park Rangers	(H)	0-0	(0-0)	D	5669		39	Whitelaw	Hatfield	Robinson	Dixon	Wilson	Mayes	Barnett	Jones	Baron	Pike	Clenshaw
40	23	Bristol Rovers	(A)	0-0	(0-0)	D	3847		40	Whitelaw	Hatfield	Robinson	Dixon	Wilson	Donoven	Barnett	Jones	Baron	Pike	Clenshaw
41	30	Torquay United	(H)	4-2	(2-0)	W	5471	Pike(2),Clenshaw,Jones	41	Whitelaw	Hatfield	Robinson	Dixon	Wilson	Donoven	Barnett	Jones	Thomson	Pike	Clenshaw
42	7 May	Coventry City	(H)	4-0	(2-0)	W	6356	Thomson(2),Fryar,Barnett	42	Whitelaw	Hatfield	Robinson	Dixon	Wilson	Donoven	Barnett	Jones	Thomson	Fryar	Clenshaw

Major Cup Competitions

F.A.Cup

Rd.	Date	Opposition	Venue Score	H.T.	Res.	Att.	Goalscorers
R1	28 Nov	Torquay United	(A) 3-1	(1-0)	W	5000	Shankly(2),Fowler(O.G.)
R2	12 Dec	Northampton T.	(A) 0-3		L		

	1	2	3	4	5	6	7	8	9	10	11
	Moore	French	Robinson	Dixon	Wilson	Donoven	Barnett	Jones	Shankly	Thomson	Crompton
	Moore	French	Robinson	Dixon	Wilson	Donoven	Barnett	Jones	Shankly	Thomson	Clenshaw

Photo by W. P. DOBBS Southend.

Presented with the compliments of the "News Chronicle."

SOUTHEND UNITED F.C. 1931-32.

BACK ROW.—G. IRWIN, A. TUNBRIDGE, J. FRENCH, W. MOORE, D. WHITELAW, E. HATFIELD, D. ROBINSON, J. FUCH, (Ass. Trainer), (Groundsman).

MIDDLE ROW.— MR. E. L. BIRNIE MR. C. J. WARD W. CARTWRIGHT J. WILSON, T. DIXON, J. OAKES, L. BUTLER, W. JOHNSON, A. DONOVAN, MR. DR. F. MOORHOUSE MR. W. G. KIRBY (Sec. Manager), (Director), (Trainer), (Chairman), (Director).

FRONT ROW.—F. FITTON, F. FRYER, F. BARNETT, A. CROMPTON, E. JONES, J. SHANKLY, F. BARON, A. THOMSON, I. PIKE, L. CLENSHAW, W. HALL.

Appearances and Goals

Name	Appearances Lge.	FAC	Total	Goals Lge.	FAC	Total
BARNETT, Fred	38	2	40	8		8
BARON, Fred	12		12	5		5
CLENSHAW, Les	19	1	20	7		7
CROMPTON, Arthur	26	1	27	12		12
DIXON, Tom	37	2	39	2		2
DONOVEN, Dickie	37	2	39			
FITTON, Fred	3		3	1		1
FRENCH, Jack	24	2	26	2		2
FRYAR, Buck	1		1	1		1
HALL, Billy	1		1			
HATFIELD, Ernie	18		18	1		1
JOHNSON, Joe	1		1			
JONES, Mickey	42	2	44	4		4
MAYES, Ken	5		5	1		1
MOORE, Billy	11	2	13			
McKENNA, Peter	2		2			
OAKES, Jack	2		2			
PIKE, Tot	27		27	7		7
ROBINSON, Dave	41	2	43			
SHANKLY, Jimmy	29	2	31	18	2	20
THOMSON, Arthur	14	2	16	6		6
TUNBRIDGE, Alec	1		1			
WHITELAW, Dave	29		29			
WILSON, Joe	42	2	44	2		2
Own Goal					1	1

	Ps	P	W	D	L	F	A	W	D	L	F	A	Pts.
1931/32	3	42	12	5	4	41	18	9	6	6	36	35	53

Season 1932/33 – League Division Three (South)

No.	Date	Opposition	Venue	Score	H.T.	Res.	Att.	Goalscorers	1	2	3	4	5	6	7	8	9	10	11
1	27 Aug	Aldershot	(A)	2-1	(1-1)	W	8022	Pike(2)	Whitelaw	Hatfield	Robinson	Dixon	Wilson J	Donoven	Barnett	Jones	Shankly	Pike	Clenshaw
2	29	Bristol Rovers	(H)	2-2		D	8677	Barnett(2)	Whitelaw	Hatfield	Robinson	Dixon	Wilson J	Randle	Barnett	Jones	Shankly	Pike	Clenshaw
3	3 Sep	Queens Park Rangers	(H)	0-1		L	7408		Whitelaw	Hatfield	Robinson	Dixon	Wilson J	Donoven	Barnett	Lewis	Morfitt	Pike	Robson
4	7	Bristol Rovers	(A)	1-3		L	6987	Shankly	Whitelaw	Hatfield	Robinson	Dixon	Wilson J	Donoven	Barnett	Jones	Shankly	Pike	Robson
5	10	Torquay United	(A)	1-8	(1-3)	L	4488	Shankly	Whitelaw	Hatfield	Robinson	Dixon	Wilson J	Donoven	Barnett	Jones	Shankly	Pike	Robson
6	14	Newport County	(H)	3-0		W	5687	Barnett,Shankly,Robson	Moore	Wootton	Robinson	Dixon	Hall	Pike	Barnett	Samuel	Shankly	Lewis	Robson
7	17	Crystal Palace	(A)	1-4		L	19419	Samuel	Moore	Hatfield	Robinson	Dixon	Hall	Pike	Clenshaw	Samuel	Shankly	Lewis	Robson
8	24	Gillingham	(H)	2-2		D	5278	Lewis,Shankly	Moore	Hatfield	Robinson	Dixon	Wilson J	Reilly	Barnett	Jones	Shankly	Lewis	Robson
9	1 Oct	Watford	(A)	2-2		D	6019	Lewis,Morfitt	Moore	Hatfield	Robinson	Dixon	Wilson J	Donoven	Curran	Jones	Morfitt	Lewis	Robson
10	8	Cardiff City	(H)	2-2	(0-0)	D	3590	Jones,Morfitt	Moore	Hatfield	Robinson	Dixon	Wilson J	Donoven	Pike	Jones	Morfitt	Lewis	Robson
11	15	Reading	(A)	1-1	(0-1)	D	10412	Morfitt	Whitelaw	Hatfield	Robinson	Dixon	Randle	Donoven	Pike	Jones	Morfitt	Lewis	Robson
12	22	Brentford	(H)	0-1	(0-0)	L	9453		Whitelaw	Hatfield	Robinson	Dixon	Randle	Donoven	Pike	Jones	Morfitt	Lewis	Robson
13	29	Coventry City	(A)	3-2	(1-0)	W	9706	Morfitt(2),Lewis	Whitelaw	Hatfield	Robinson	Dixon	Randle	Donoven	Pike	Jones	Morfitt	Lewis	Robson
14	5 Nov	Bristol City	(H)	3-1	(2-0)	W	7017	Morfitt,Pike,Robson	Whitelaw	Hatfield	Robinson	Dixon	Randle	Donoven	Pike	Jones	Morfitt	Lewis	Robson
15	12	Northampton Town	(A)	0-0	(0-0)	D	6474		Whitelaw	Hatfield	Robinson	Dixon	Randle	Donoven	Pike	Jones	Morfitt	Lewis	Robson
16	19	Clapton Orient	(H)	3-3	(1-3)	D	4901	Hatfield(pen),Morfitt,Lewis	Whitelaw	Hatfield	Robinson	Dixon	Randle	Donoven	Barnett	Jones	Morfitt	Lewis	Robson
17	3 Dec	Bournemouth	(A)	2-1		W	6014	Robson,Lewis	Whitelaw	Hatfield	Robinson	Dixon	Randle	Donoven	Barnett	Jones	Morfitt	Lewis	Robson
18	17	Luton Town	(H)	2-1	(2-1)	W	6057	Hatfield(pen),Barnett	Whitelaw	Hatfield	Robinson	Dixon	Randle	Donoven	Barnett	Jones	Morfitt	Lewis	Robson
19	24	Exeter City	(A)	0-3	(0-3)	L	6315		Whitelaw	Hatfield	Wootton	Dixon	Randle	Donoven	Barnett	Jones	Morfitt	Lewis	Robson
20	26	Norwich City	(H)	2-1	(1-1)	W	8342	Pike,Robson	Whitelaw	Hatfield	Robinson	Dixon	Randle	Donoven	Barnett	Jones	Morfitt	Lewis	Robson
21	27	Norwich City	(A)	0-1	(0-0)	L	17161		Whitelaw	Hatfield	Robinson	Dixon	Randle	Donoven	Barnett	Jones	Morfitt	Lewis	Robson
22	31	Aldershot	(H)	5-1		W	6087	Pike(2),Clenshaw,Morfitt,Jones	Whitelaw	Hatfield	Robinson	Dixon	Randle	Donoven	Barnett	Jones	Morfitt	Pike	Robson
23	7 Jan	Queens Park Rangers	(A)	1-6	(0-5)	L	5588	Clenshaw	Moore	Hatfield	Wilson T	Dixon	Randle	Reilly	Barnett	Jones	Shankly	Morfitt	Clenshaw
24	21	Torquay United	(H)	2-1	(2-1)	W	5570	Samuel,Jones	Whitelaw	Hatfield	Robinson	Pike	Randle	Donoven	Barnett	Jones	Morfitt	Samuel	Clenshaw
25	1 Feb	Crystal Palace	(H)	1-2		L	3008	Morfitt	Whitelaw	Hatfield	Shankly	Dixon	Randle	Donoven	Barnett	Jones	Morfitt	Pike	Clenshaw
26	4	Gillingham	(A)	2-3		L	5816	Samuel,Morfitt	Whitelaw	Hatfield	Shankly	Pike	Randle	Donoven	Barnett	Jones	Morfitt	Samuel	Clenshaw
27	9	Newport County	(A)	3-1		W	1769	Morfitt,Barnett,Robson	Whitelaw	Hatfield	Shankly	Pike	Randle	Donoven	Barnett	Samuel	Morfitt	Clenshaw	Robson
28	11	Watford	(H)	2-1	(1-1)	W	5048	Clenshaw,Barnett	Whitelaw	Hatfield	Shankly	Dixon	Randle	Donoven	Barnett	Samuel	Morfitt	Clenshaw	Robson
29	18	Cardiff City	(A)	0-2	(0-1)	L	5275		Whitelaw	Hatfield	Shankly	Dixon	Randle	Donoven	Barnett	Samuel	Morfitt	Pike	Clenshaw
30	25	Reading	(H)	3-1		W	4384	Morfitt(2),Barnett	Whitelaw	Hatfield	Shankly	Dixon	Randle	Donoven	Barnett	Jones	Morfitt	Pike	Clenshaw
31	1 Mar	Swindon Town	(A)	2-2		D	2201	Morfitt,Curran	Whitelaw	Hatfield	Cox	Dixon	Randle	Donoven	Curran	Jones	Morfitt	Pike	Clenshaw
32	4	Brentford	(A)	1-3		L	14288	Barnett	Whitelaw	Hatfield	Shankly	Dixon	Randle	Donoven	Barnett	Jones	Morfitt	Pike	Clenshaw
33	11	Coventry City	(H)	1-3	(1-1)	L	5958	Barnett	Whitelaw	Hatfield	Shankly	Dixon	Randle	Donoven	Barnett	Jones	Morfitt	Pike	Clenshaw
34	18	Bristol City	(A)	1-5		L	7467	Donoven	Moore	Hatfield	Cox	Dixon	Randle	Donoven	Barnett	Jones	Shankly	Pike	Clenshaw
35	25	Northampton Town	(H)	1-0	(1-0)	W	5670	Wilson J(pen)	Moore	Whelan	Wilson T	Dixon	Wilson J	Donoven	Barnett	Jones	Morfitt	Pike	Clenshaw
36	1 Apr	Clapton Orient	(A)	0-0	(0-0)	D	4677		Moore	Whelan	Wilson T	Dixon	Wilson J	Donoven	Barnett	Jones	Fryar	Pike	Robson
37	8	Swindon Town	(H)	0-0	(0-0)	D	5383		Moore	Whelan	Robinson	Randle	Wilson J	Donoven	Barnett	Jones	Fryar	Pike	Robson
38	14	Brighton	(A)	2-1	(2-0)	W	8996	Pike,Shankly	Moore	Whelan	Robinson	Randle	Wilson J	Donoven	Barnett	Jones	Shankly	Pike	Clenshaw
39	15	Bournemouth	(A)	0-4		L	4549		Moore	Whelan	Robinson	Randle	Wilson J	Donoven	Barnett	Jones	Shankly	Pike	Clenshaw
40	17	Brighton	(H)	2-1		W	8372	Pike,Shankly	Moore	Whelan	Robinson	Randle	Wilson J	Donoven	Barnett	Jones	Shankly	Pike	Clenshaw
41	29	Luton Town	(H)	3-3	(1-1)	D	2969	Shankly(2),Clenshaw	Moore	Whelan	Robinson	Dixon	Wilson J	Donoven	Barnett	Jones	Shankly	Lewis	Clenshaw
42	6 May	Exeter City	(H)	1-2	(0-1)	L	5848	Lewis	Moore	Whelan	Robinson	Dixon	Wilson J	Donoven	Barnett	Jones	Bungay	Lewis	Clenshaw

Major Cup Competitions

F.A.Cup

Rd.	Date	Opposition	Venue Score	H.T. Res.	Att.	Goalscorers	1	2	3	4	5	6	7	8	9	10	11
R1	26 Nov	Exeter City	(H) 1-1	(0-1) D	8565	Morfitt	Whitelaw	Hatfield	Robinson	Dixon	Randle	Donoven	Barnett	Jones	Morfitt	Lewis	Robson
R1r	30	Exeter City	(A) 1-0	(0-0) W	6500	Morfitt	Whitelaw	Hatfield	Robinson	Dixon	Randle	Donoven	Barnett	Jones	Morfitt	Lewis	Robson
R2	10 Dec	Scarborough	(H) 4-1	W	8000	Morfitt(3),Robson	Whitelaw	Hatfield	Robinson	Dixon	Randle	Donoven	Barnett	Jones	Morfitt	Lewis	Robson
R3	14 Jan	Watford	(A) 1-1	(1-1) D	11403	Clenshaw	Whitelaw	Hatfield	Robinson	Dixon	Randle	Donoven	Barnett	Jones	Morfitt	Pike	Clenshaw
R3r	18	Watford	(H) 2-0	W	8036	Morfitt,Clenshaw	Whitelaw	Hatfield	Robinson	Dixon	Randle	Donoven	Barnett	Jones	Morfitt	Pike	Clenshaw
R4	28	Derby County	(H) 2-3	L	15188	Pike,Morfitt	Whitelaw	Hatfield	Shankly	Dixon	Randle	Donoven	Barnett	Jones	Morfitt	Pike	Clenshaw

SOUTHEND UNITED F.C. 1932—3

H. Footman (Ass. Trainer), Hatfield, Wootton, Moore, Whitelaw, Robinson,
Dixon, Randle, Reiley, T. Wilson, Hall, Donovan, W. Cartwright (Trainer),
E. L. Birnie (Man.), Curran, Barnett, Jones, Samuel, Pike, Lewis, Robson, Clenshaw, A. L. A. Woodhouse (Dir.),
Morfitt, Shankley, Bennett

Appearances and Goals

Name	Appearances Lge.	FAC	Total	Goals Lge.	FAC	Total
BARNETT, Fred	32	6	38	9		9
BUNGAY, Frank	1		1			
CLENSHAW, Les	21	3	24	4	2	6
COX, Charlie	2		2			
CURRAN, Jimmy	2		2	1		1
DIXON, Tom	34	6	40			
DONOVEN, Dickie	37	6	43	1		1
FRYAR, Buck	2		2			
HALL, John	2		2			
HATFIELD, Ernie	33	6	39	2		2
JONES, Mickey	36	6	42	3		3
LEWIS, Harry	18	3	21	6		6
MOORE, Billy	15		15			
MORFITT, Jack	27	6	33	14	7	21
PIKE, Tot	33	3	36	8	1	9
RANDLE, Herbert	29	6	35			
REILLY, William	2		2			
ROBINSON, Dave	28	5	33			
ROBSON, John Cecil	24	3	27	5	1	6
SAMUEL, Dan	7		7	3		3
SHANKLY, Jimmy	21	1	22	8		8
WHELAN, William	8		8			
WHITELAW, Dave	27	6	33			
WILSON, Joe	16		16	1		1
WILSON, Tom	3		3			
WOOTTON, Billy	2		2			

	Ps	P	W	D	L	F	A	W	D	L	F	A	Pts.
1932/33	13	42	11	5	5	39	27	4	6	11	26	55	41

Season 1933/34 – League Division Three (South)

No.	Date	Opposition	Venue	Score	H.T.	Res.	Att.	Goalscorers	1	2	3	4	5	6	7	8	9	10	11
1	26 Aug	Crystal Palace	(H)	0-4	(0-2)	L	10285		Moore	Robertson	Robinson	Smith	Wilson	Donoven	Stoker	Redfern	Morfitt	Lane	Clenshaw
2	30	Gillingham	(A)	0-0	(0-0)	D	8416		Moore	Robertson	Robinson	Smith	Wilson	Donoven	Barnett	Jones	Morfitt	Lane	Clenshaw
3	2 Sep	Bristol Rovers	(A)	1-3	(0-2)	L	12207	Lane	Whitelaw	Robertson	Robinson	Smith	Wilson	Donoven	Barnett	Jones	Morfitt	Lane	Clenshaw
4	6	Gillingham	(H)	1-2		L	7208	Morfitt	Whitelaw	Robertson	Robinson	Randle	Wilson	Donoven	Barnett	Jones	Morfitt	Lane	Clenshaw
5	9	Clapton Orient	(H)	2-1	(0-0)	W	8927	Lane(2)	Whitelaw	Worthy	Bateman	Robertson	Wilson	Donoven	Barnett	Jones	Bungay	Redfern	Lane
6	16	Coventry City	(H)	2-1	(2-1)	W	7666	Barnett,Jones	Whitelaw	Worthy	Bateman	Robertson	Wilson	Donoven	Barnett	Jones	Fryar	Redfern	Lane
7	23	Reading	(A)	0-5	(0-2)	L	9442		Whitelaw	Worthy	Bateman	Robertson	Wilson	Donoven	Barnett	Jones	Fryar	Lane	McMahon
8	30	Watford	(H)	1-1	(0-0)	D	6799	Fryar	Whitelaw	Worthy	Bateman	Robertson	Wilson	Donoven	Barnett	Jones	Fryar	Lane	McMahon
9	7 Oct	Charlton Athletic	(A)	3-1	(1-1)	W	14914	Fryar,Barnett,Lane	Whitelaw	Worthy	Bateman	Robertson	Randle	Donoven	Barnett	Jones	Fryar	Proudfoot	McMahon
10	14	Bournemouth	(H)	1-2	(1-1)	L	4809	Fryar	Whitelaw	Worthy	Bateman	Robertson	Randle	Donoven	Barnett	Lane	Fryar	Proudfoot	McMahon
11	21	Swindon Town	(A)	4-1	(2-1)	W	10943	McMahon(3),Lane(pen)	Whitelaw	Worthy	Bateman	Robertson	Randle	Donoven	Barnett	Lane	Morfitt	Lane	McMahon
12	28	Brighton	(H)	0-0	(0-0)	D	5803		Whitelaw	Worthy	Bateman	Robertson	Randle	Donoven	Barnett	Jones	Wilson	Lane	McMahon
13	4 Nov	Aldershot	(A)	0-2	(0-1)	L	4368		Whitelaw	Worthy	Bateman	Robertson	Randle	Donoven	Barnett	Jones	Stevens	Lane	McMahon
14	11	Luton Town	(H)	0-1	(0-1)	L	5828		Whitelaw	Robertson	Bateman	Wilson	Randle	Donoven	Barnett	Jones	Stevens	Morfitt	Lane
15	18	Northampton Town	(A)	0-2	(0-1)	L	3520		Whitelaw	Worthy	Bateman	Robertson	Randle	Morfitt	Stoker	Lane	Stevens	Fryar	McMahon
16	2 Dec	Queens Park Rangers	(A)	0-4	(0-3)	L	8191		Whitelaw	Robertson	Bateman	Dixon	Wilson	Morfitt	Barnett	Jones	Stevens	Lane	Clenshaw
17	16	Norwich City	(A)	0-0	(0-0)	D	9139		Whitelaw	Robertson	Bateman	Dixon	Wilson	Morfitt	Barnett	Jones	Stevens	Lane	Clenshaw
18	23	Bristol City	(H)	3-0	(2-0)	W	4549	Stevens(3)	Whitelaw	Robertson	Bateman	Dixon	Wilson	Morfitt	Barnett	Jones	Stevens	Lane	Clenshaw
19	25	Exeter City	(A)	0-2	(0-1)	L	8234		Whitelaw	Robertson	Bateman	Dixon	Wilson	Morfitt	Barnett	Jones	Stevens	Lane	Clenshaw
20	26	Exeter City	(H)	3-1	(1-0)	W	4828	Stevens(2),Jones	Whitelaw	Robertson	Bateman	Dixon	Wilson	Donoven	Mustard	Jones	Stevens	Proudfoot	Lane
21	30	Crystal Palace	(A)	1-1	(0-1)	D	8383	Jones	Whitelaw	Robertson	Bateman	Dixon	Wilson	Morfitt	Mustard	Jones	Stevens	Proudfoot	Lane
22	6 Jan	Bristol Rovers	(H)	2-2	(2-2)	D	5960	Mustard,Stevens	Whitelaw	Robertson	Bateman	Dixon	Wilson	Morfitt	Mustard	Jones	Stevens	Proudfoot	Lane
23	17	Torquay United	(H)	3-1	(1-0)	W	2732	Stevens(2),Lane	Whitelaw	Robertson	Bateman	Randle	Wilson	Donoven	Mustard	Jones	Stevens	Lane	McMahon
24	20	Clapton Orient	(A)	2-5	(1-2)	L	8091	Jones,Stevens	Whitelaw	Worthy	Robertson	Randle	Wilson	Donoven	Mustard	Jones	Stevens	Lane	Clenshaw
25	27	Coventry City	(A)	0-2	(0-0)	L	13861		Moore	Worthy	Robertson	Dixon	Wilson	Donoven	Mustard	Jones	Stevens	Lane	Clenshaw
26	3 Feb	Reading	(H)	2-2	(0-0)	D	3054	Stevens(2)	Moore	Worthy	Robertson	Dixon	Wilson	Donoven	Mustard	Jones	Stevens	Lane	Clenshaw
27	10	Watford	(A)	1-2	(0-1)	L	5984	Lane	Moore	Worthy	Robertson	Dixon	Wilson	Donoven	Mustard	Jones	Stevens	Lane	Barnett
28	17	Charlton Athletic	(H)	1-0	(0-0)	W	5655	Lane	Moore	Worthy	Robertson	Dixon	Wilson	Donoven	Mustard	Jones	Stevens	Lane	McMahon
29	24	Bournemouth	(H)	4-1	(1-1)	W	4145	Stevens(2),Mustard,Lane	Moore	Worthy	Robertson	Dixon	Wilson	Donoven	Mustard	Jones	Stevens	Proudfoot	Barrow
30	3 Mar	Swindon Town	(H)	4-1	(0-1)	W	5869	Stevens(2),Proudfoot,Barrow	Moore	Worthy	Robertson	Dixon	Wilson	Donoven	Mustard	Lane	Stevens	Proudfoot	Barrow
31	10	Brighton	(A)	0-1	(0-0)	L	5400		Moore	Worthy	Robertson	Dixon	Wilson	Donoven	Mustard	Lane	Stevens	Proudfoot	Barrow
32	14	Newport County	(A)	3-5	(1-2)	L	2580	Barrow,Stevens,Mustard	Moore	Worthy	Robertson	Dixon	Wilson	Donoven	Mustard	Lane	Stevens	Proudfoot	Barrow
33	17	Aldershot	(H)	1-0	(0-0)	W	4865	Jones	Moore	Worthy	Robinson	Dixon	Wilson	Donoven	Mustard	Jones	Stevens	Jones	Barrow
34	24	Luton Town	(A)	1-3	(0-1)	L	6313	Stevens	Moore	Worthy	Robinson	Dixon	Wilson	Donoven	Mustard	Lane	Stevens	Lane	Barrow
35	30	Cardiff City	(A)	1-1	(1-0)	D	7890	Jones	Moore	Worthy	Robinson	Randle	Wilson	Donoven	Mustard	Lane	Stevens	Jones	Barrow
36	31	Northampton Town	(H)	2-0	(1-0)	W	6513	Stevens,Jones	Moore	Worthy	Robinson	Dixon	Wilson	Donoven	Mustard	Jones	Stevens	Clenshaw	Barrow
37	2 Apr	Cardiff City	(H)	1-1	(0-1)	D	9303	Stevens	Moore	Worthy	Robinson	Dixon	Wilson	Donoven	Lyman	Jones	Stevens	Clenshaw	Barrow
38	7	Torquay United	(A)	0-3	(0-2)	L	2634		Moore	Worthy	Robinson	Dixon	Wilson	Donoven	Mustard	Proudfoot	Stevens	Jones	Barrow
39	14	Queens Park Rangers	(H)	0-2	(0-1)	L	5249		Moore	Worthy	Robinson	Morfitt	Wilson	Donoven	Mustard	Lane	Stevens	Jones	Barrow
40	21	Newport County	(A)	0-3	(0-0)	L	4728		Moore	Worthy	Robinson	Dixon	Wilson	Donoven	Barnett	Lane	Stevens	Jones	Barrow
41	28	Norwich City	(H)	0-0	(0-0)	D	4700		Moore	Robertson	Robinson	Dixon	Wilson	Donoven	Mustard	Barnett	Stevens	Jones	Barrow
42	5 May	Bristol City	(A)	1-5	(0-3)	L	4323	Stevens	Moore	Worthy	Robinson	Dixon	Wilson	Donoven	Lane	Barnett	Stevens	Jones	Barrow

Major Cup Competitions

F.A.Cup

Rd.	Date	Opposition	Venue Score	H.T.	Res.	Att.	Goalscorers	1	2	3	4	5	6	7	8	9	10	11
R1	25 Nov	London Paper Mills	(A) 1-0		W		Fryar	Whitelaw	Worthy	Bateman	Dixon	Randle	Robertson	Stoker	Lane	Stevens	Fryar	McMahon
R2	9 Dec	Chester	(H) 2-1		W	6524	Stevens,Barnett	Whitelaw	Robertson	Bateman	Dixon	Wilson J	Morfitt	Barnett	Jones	Stevens	Lane	Clenshaw
R3	13 Jan	Tranmere Rovers	(A) 0-3		L	13533		Whitelaw	Robertson	Bateman	Dixon	Wilson J	Morfitt	Mustard	Jones	Stevens	Proudfoot	Lane

Third Division South Cup

Rd.	Date	Opposition	Venue Score	H.T.	Res.	Att.	Goalscorers	1	2	3	4	5	6	7	8	9	10	11
R1		Bye																
R2	22 Feb	Coventry City	(A) 1-3 (0-2)		L		Barnett	Moore	Worthy	Robinson	Morfitt	Wilson J	Smith	Barnett	Jones	Stevens	Lane	Barrow

Appearances and Goals

Name	Appearances Lge.	FAC	L.C.	Total	Goals Lge.	FAC	L.C.	Total
BARNETT, Fred	20	1	1	22	2	1	1	4
BARROW, Billy	14		1	15	2			2
BATEMAN, Arthur	19	3		22				
BUNGAY, Frank	1			1				
CLENSHAW, Les	13	1		14				
DIXON, Tom	23	3		26				
DONOVEN, Dickie	35			35				
FRYAR, Buck	6	1		7	3	1		4
JONES, Mickey	34	2	1	37	7			7
LANE, Harry	39	3	1	43	9			9
LYMAN, Colin	1			1				
MOORE, Billy	20		1	21				
MORFITT, Jack	14	2	1	17	1			1
MUSTARD, John	20	1		21	3			3
McMAHON, Hugh	11			11	3			3
PROUDFOOT, James	10	1		11	1			1
RANDLE, Herbert	11		1	12				
REDFERN, Leslie	3			3				
ROBERTSON, George	34	3		37				
ROBINSON, Dave	13		1	14				
SMITH, William	3		1	4				
STEVENS, Leo	30	3	1	34	20		1	21
STOKER, Robert	2	1		3				
WHITELAW, Dave	22	3		25				
WILSON, Joe	37	2	1	40				
WORTHY, Albert	28	1	1	30				

	Ps	P	W	D	L	F	A	W	D	L	F	A	Pts.
1933/34	16	42	9	6	6	32	27	3	4	14	19	47	34

Season 1934/35 – League Division Three (South)

No.	Date	Opposition	Venue	Score	H.T.	Res.	Att.	Goalscorers	1	2	3	4	5	6	7	8	9	10	11
1	25 Aug	Luton Town	(A)	1-1		D	12255	Johnson	Whitelaw	Stevenson	Robinson	Williams	Wilson J	Smith	Oswald	Jones E	Johnson	Cheesmur	Clark
2	29	Aldershot	(H)	2-1		W	7456	Johnson,Cheesmur	Whitelaw	Stevenson	Robinson	Robertson	Wilson J	Donoven	Oswald	Jones E	Johnson	Cheesmur	Clark
3	1 Sep	Exeter City	(H)	1-2	(1-1)	L	11389	Clark	Whitelaw	Stevenson	Robinson	Robertson	Wilson J	Donoven	Oswald	Jones E	Stevens	Johnson	Clark
4	5	Aldershot	(A)	2-3		L	3903	Johnson(2)	Whitelaw	Stevenson	Wilson T	Jackson	Wilson J	Smith	Lane	Jones E	Johnson	Oswald	Clark
5	8	Bristol Rovers	(H)	5-1	(3-1)	W	8878	Lane(2),Johnson(2),Clark	Whitelaw	Stevenson	Robinson	Jones G	Wilson J	Donoven	Lane	Jones E	Johnson	Cheesmur	Clark
6	10	Cardiff City	(A)	0-2		L	11922		Whitelaw	Stevenson	Robinson	Jones G	Wilson J	Donoven	Lane	Jones E	Johnson	Cheesmur	Clark
7	15	Charlton Athletic	(A)	0-3		L	11306		Whitelaw	Stevenson	Robinson	Jones G	Wilson J	Donoven	Lane	Jones E	Johnson	Cheesmur	Clark
8	22	Crystal Palace	(H)	1-4		L	7032	Lane	Whitelaw	Stevenson	Robinson	Mackay	Wilson J	Smith	Lane	Jones E	Johnson	Oswald	Clark
9	29	Queens Park Rangers	(A)	1-1	(1-1)	D	9989	Johnson	Whitelaw	Stevenson	Kelly	Mackay	Wilson J	Morfitt	Lane	Stevens	Johnson	Jones E	Oswald
10	6 Oct	Torquay United	(H)	2-3		L	7994	Johnson,Barrow	Whitelaw	Stevenson	Kelly	Mackay	Wilson J	Carr	Barrow	Stevens	Johnson	Jones E	Oswald
11	13	Swindon Town	(A)	0-5		L	9122		Whitelaw	Robertson	Kelly	Mackay	Jackson	Carr	Barrow	Deacon	Johnson	Cheesmur	Oswald
12	20	Bristol City	(A)	0-2		L	10235		Whitelaw	Morfitt	Kelly	Mackay	Wilson J	Carr	Barrow	Deacon	Stevens	Jones E	Clark
13	27	Millwall	(H)	2-1		W	7858	Clark,Deacon	Whitelaw	Morfitt	Kelly	Mackay	Wilson J	Carr	Barrow	Deacon	Johnson	Jones E	Clark
14	3 Nov	Watford	(A)	1-3	(1-1)	L	6596	Johnson	Whitelaw	Morfitt	Kelly	Mackay	Wilson J	Carr	Barrow	Deacon	Johnson	Jones E	Clark
15	10	Newport County	(H)	0-1	(0-0)	L	5498		Moore	Morfitt	Kelly	Mackay	Wilson J	Carr	Oswald	Deacon	Johnson	Johnson	Clark
16	17	Gillingham	(A)	2-2	(1-1)	D	4168	Cheesmur(2)	Moore	Morfitt	Kelly	Mackay	Wilson J	Carr	Oswald	Johnson	Cheesmur	Deacon	Clark
17	1 Dec	Northampton Town	(A)	1-1	(0-1)	D	5933	Dawes(O.G.)	Moore	Morfitt	Kelly	Mackay	Wilson J	Carr	Lane	Johnson	Cheesmur	Deacon	Oswald
18	15	Coventry City	(A)	3-6	(1-3)	L	13022	Cheesmur(2),Johnson	Moore	Robertson	Robinson	Mackay	Wilson J	Carr	Lane	Johnson	Cheesmur	Deacon	Oswald
19	22	Clapton Orient	(H)	0-2	(0-1)	L	5586		Moore	Stevenson	Robinson	Carr	Wilson J	Carr	Barrow	Cheesmur	Johnson	Deacon	Oswald
20	26	Cardiff City	(H)	2-1	(1-1)	W	9438	Oswald,Stevens	Moore	Wilson T	Robinson	Carr	Wilson J	Morfitt	Barrow	Cheesmur	Stevens	Deacon	Oswald
21	29	Luton Town	(H)	3-3	(2-0)	D	5394	Stevens(3,1 pen)	Moore	Smith	Robinson	Carr	Wilson J	Morfitt	Barrow	Cheesmur	Stevens	Deacon	Oswald
22	5 Jan	Exeter City	(A)	3-4	(1-1)	L	4887	Stevens(2),Deacon	Moore	Smith	Robinson	Mackay	Wilson J	Morfitt	Barrow	Cheesmur	Stevens	Deacon	Oswald
23	19	Bristol Rovers	(A)	1-2	(0-1)	L	7074	Clark	Moore	Smith	Robinson	Mackay	Wilson J	Carr	Barrow	Jones E	Stevens	Oswald	Clark
24	26	Charlton Athletic	(H)	0-3	(0-0)	L	5151		Moore	Smith	Robinson	Mackay	Wilson T	Carr	Barrow	Bushby	Stevens	Deacon	Oswald
25	2 Feb	Crystal Palace	(A)	0-1	(0-1)	L	13313		Moore	Smith	Robinson	Mackay	Wilson T	Carr	Barrow	Stevens	Cheesmur	Wilson J	Clark
26	9	Queens Park Rangers	(H)	2-0	(1-0)	W	5681	Lane,Clark	Moore	Smith	Robinson	Mackay	Wilson T	Carr	Barrow	Lane	Stevens	Johnson	Clark
27	16	Torquay United	(A)	0-2	(0-2)	L	2434		Moore	Robertson	Robinson	Mackay	Wilson T	Carr	Barrow	Bushby	Stevens	Lane	Clark
28	23	Swindon Town	(H)	2-0	(1-0)	W	5756	Bushby,Stevens	Moore	Robertson	Robinson	Mackay	Wilson T	Carr	Barrow	Bushby	Stevens	Lane	Clark
29	2 Mar	Bristol City	(H)	6-0	(4-0)	W	6581	Stevens(3),Clark,Bushby,Lane	Moore	Robertson	Robinson	Mackay	Wilson T	Morfitt	Barrow	Bushby	Stevens	Lane	Clark
30	9	Millwall	(A)	0-1	(0-1)	L	5681		Moore	Robertson	Robinson	Mackay	Wilson T	Morfitt	Barrow	Bushby	Stevens	Lane	Clark
31	16	Watford	(H)	0-2	(0-2)	L	7055		Moore	Robertson	Robinson	Mackay	Wilson T	Morfitt	Barrow	Bushby	Stevens	Lane	Clark
32	23	Newport County	(A)	5-0	(1-0)	W	3005	Fryar(3),Stevens(2)	Moore	Robinson	Kelly	Mackay	Morfitt	Donoven	Lane	Cheesmur	Stevens	Fryar	Clark
33	30	Gillingham	(H)	0-0	(0-0)	D	5936		Moore	Robinson	Kelly	Mackay	Morfitt	Donoven	Lane	Cheesmur	Stevens	Fryar	Clark
34	6 Apr	Reading	(A)	2-3	(1-0)	L	4799	Stevens(2)	Moore	Robinson	Kelly	Mackay	Wilson J	Morfitt	Lane	Jones E	Stevens	Fryar	Clark
35	10	Bournemouth	(H)	0-0	(0-0)	D	3479		Moore	Robinson	Kelly	Mackay	Wilson J	Morfitt	Lane	Jones E	Stevens	Fryar	Oswald
36	13	Northampton Town	(H)	2-1	(1-1)	W	5992	Cheesmur,Fryar	Moore	Robinson	Kelly	Mackay	Wilson J	Morfitt	Lane	Jones E	Cheesmur	Fryar	Clark
37	19	Brighton	(A)	2-2	(0-2)	D	4594	Lane,Cheesmur	Moore	Robinson	Kelly	Mackay	Wilson J	Morfitt	Lane	Jones E	Cheesmur	Fryar	Clark
38	20	Bournemouth	(A)	1-2	(1-1)	L	5192	Johnson	Moore	Robinson	Kelly	Mackay	Wilson J	Morfitt	Lane	Deacon	Johnson	Fryar	Clark
39	22	Brighton	(H)	3-2		W	9692	Lane,Fryar,Jones E	Moore	Robinson	Holborn	Mackay	Wilson J	Jackson	Lane	Lane	Fryar	Jones E	Oswald
40	27	Coventry City	(H)	1-1	(0-1)	D	5401	Lane	Moore	Robinson	Kelly	Mackay	Wilson J	Morfitt	Jones B	Lane	Fryar	Jones E	Oswald
41	1 May	Reading	(H)	6-1		W	4057	Johnson(4),Oswald,O.G.	Moore	Robertson	Robinson	Mackay	Wilson J	Morfitt	Barrow	Lane	Johnson	Jones E	Oswald
42	4	Clapton Orient	(A)	0-3	(0-2)	L	6560		Moore	Robertson	Robinson	Mackay	Morfitt	Carr	Barrow	Lane	Johnson	Jones E	Oswald

Major Cup Competitions

F.A. Cup

Rd.	Date	Opposition	Venue	Score	H.T.	Res.	Att.	Goalscorers	1	2	3	4	5	6	7	8	9	10	11
R1	24 Nov	Golders Green	(H)	10-1	(3-0)	W	8500	Johnson(5),Cheesmur(2),Deacon,Carr,Lane	Moore	Morfitt	Kelly	Mackay	Wilson J	Carr	Lane	Johnson	Cheesmur	Deacon	Oswald
R2	8 Dec	Wimbledon	(A)	5-1	(3-1)	W	10869	Cheesmur(3),Johnson,Deacon	Moore	Morfitt	Kelly	Mackay	Wilson J	Carr	Lane	Johnson	Cheesmur	Deacon	Oswald
R3	12	Sheffield United	(H)	0-4		L	13712		Moore	Smith	Robinson	Carr	Wilson J	Morfitt	Barrow	Cheesmur	Stevens	Deacon	Oswald

Third Division South Cup

Rd.	Date	Opposition	Venue	Score	H.T.	Res.	Att.	Goalscorers	1	2	3	4	5	6	7	8	9	10	11
R1	19 Sep	Brighton & H.A.	(H)	1-1	(0-0)	D	4442	Lane(pen)	Whitelaw	Stevenson	Robertson	Todd	Wilson J	Smith	Lane	Jones	Johnson	Oswald	Clark
R1r	26	Brighton & H.A.	(A)	1-3	(1-1)	L	2000	Johnson	Whitelaw	Wilson T	Kelly	Todd	Wilson J	Morfitt	Lane	Jones	Johnson	Cheesmur	Oswald

Left to Right (Back Row): A. Footman, Stevenson, Moore, Kelly, Whitelaw, Robertson, Woods and Robinson.
Standing: W. Cartwright (Trainer), Cheesmur, Jackson, Gulliver, Williams, Wilson (T.), Wilson (J.) (capt.), Smith and Todd, Mr. S. Gibson.
Mr. David Jack (Secretary and Manager).
Sitting: Barrow, Stevens, Rogers, Johnson, Jones (B.), Clark, Morfitt, Donovan.
Front Row: Oswald, Jones (Bertram), Jones (E.) and Lane.

Appearances and Goals

Name	Appearances Lge.	FAC	L.C.	Total	Goals Lge.	FAC	L.C.	Total
BARROW, Billy	20	1		21	1			1
BUSHBY, Billy	6			6	2			2
CARR, Billy	20	3		23		1		1
CHEESMUR, Fred	19	3	1	23	7	5		12
CLARK, Jimmy	23		1	24	6			6
DEACON, Jimmy	14	3		17	2	2		4
DONOVEN, Dickie	7			7				
FRYAR, Buck	9			9	5			5
HOLBORN, Harry	1			1				
JACKSON, Wilbert	3			3				
JOHNSON, Harry	22	2	2	26	15	6	1	22
JONES, Benny	3			3				
JONES, Bertram	1			1				
KELLY, Mickey	23		2	25	1			1
LANE, Harry	18	2	1	21	8	1	1	10
MACKAY, Norman	32	2		34				
MOORE, Billy	28	3		31				
MORFITT, Jack	23	3	1	27				
OSWALD, Robert	27	3	2	32	2			2
ROBERTSON, George	9		1	10				
ROBINSON, Dave	31		1	32				
SMITH, William	11	1	1	13				
STEVENS, Leo	20		1	21	14			14
STEVENSON, Alex	11		1	12				
TODD, ?			2	2				
WHITELAW, Dave	14		2	16	2			2
WILLIAMS, Billy	1			1				
WILSON, Joe	32	3	2	37				
WILSON, Tom	9		1	10				
Own Goal					2			2

	Ps	P	W	D	L	F	A	W	D	L	F	A	Pts.
1934/35	21	42	10	4	7	40	29	1	5	15	25	49	31

Season 1935/36 – League Division Three (South)

No.	Date	Opposition	Venue	Score	H.T.	Res.	Att.	Goalscorers	1	2	3	4	5	6	7	8	9	10	11
1	31 Aug	Bournemouth	(H)	3-3	(2-1)	D	11487	Stevens(2),Firth	Moore	Nelson	Kelly	Spelman	Turner	Carr	Deacon	Firth	Stevens	Lane	Oswald
2	4 Sep	Crystal Palace	(H)	7-1		W	7580	Stevens(3),Firth(2),Oswald,Lane	Moore	Nelson	Robinson	Spelman	Turner	Carr	Demelweek	Firth	Stevens	Lane	Oswald
3	7	Luton Town	(A)	2-1	(1-1)	W	14379	Stevens(2)	Moore	Nelson	Robinson	Spelman	Turner	Carr	Demelweek	Firth	Stevens	Lane	Oswald
4	11	Crystal Palace	(A)	0-3		L	11954		MacKenzie	Nelson	Robinson	Spelman	Turner	Carr	Demelweek	Firth	Stevens	Lane	Oswald
5	14	Notts County	(H)	0-0	(0-0)	D	11948		MacKenzie	Nelson	Robinson	Spelman	Turner	Carr	Demelweek	Firth	Stevens	Lane	Oswald
6	18	Reading	(H)	1-2		L	7501	Lane	MacKenzie	Nelson	Robinson	Spelman	Turner	Carr	Demelweek	Firth	Stevens	Lane	Oswald
7	21	Bristol Rovers	(A)	2-3	(2-1)	L	9737	Firth(2)	MacKenzie	Nelson	Robinson	Spelman	Turner	Carr	Lane	Firth	Cheesmur	Deacon	Oswald
8	28	Clapton Orient	(H)	2-1	(1-1)	W	10148	Stevens(2)	MacKenzie	Nelson	Robinson	Spelman	Turner	Carr	Deacon	Firth	Stevens	Lane	Oswald
9	5 Oct	Torquay United	(H)	1-1	(0-0)	D	4662	Spelman	MacKenzie	Nelson	Robinson	Spelman	Turner	Carr	Deacon	Firth	Stevens	Lane	Oswald
10	12	Northampton Town	(A)	0-2	(0-1)	L	6991		MacKenzie	Nelson	Robinson	Deacon	Turner	Carr	Demelweek	Spelman	Stevens	Lane	Oswald
11	19	Millwall	(H)	6-0	(2-0)	W	8138	Lane(3),Oswald,Cheesmur,Firth	MacKenzie	Nelson	Robinson	Spelman	Turner	Carr	Deacon	Firth	Cheesmur	Lane	Oswald
12	26	Bristol City	(A)	1-2	(0-1)	L	8891	Oswald	MacKenzie	Nelson	Robinson	Deacon	Turner	Carr	Bolan	Firth	Cheesmur	Lane	Oswald
13	2 Nov	Watford	(A)	1-1	(0-1)	D	7667	Bolan	MacKenzie	Nelson	Robinson	Deacon	Turner	Carr	Bolan	Firth	Johnson	Lane	Oswald
14	9	Aldershot	(A)	1-1	(1-1)	D	4807	Firth	MacKenzie	Nelson	Robinson	Deacon	Turner	Carr	Bolan	Firth	Stevens	Lane	Oswald
15	16	Brighton	(H)	0-0	(0-0)	D	6403		MacKenzie	Nelson	Robinson	Spelman	Turner	Carr	Bolan	Deacon	Stevens	Lane	Oswald
16	23	Exeter City	(A)	0-1	(0-0)	L	5045		MacKenzie	Nelson	Robinson	Deacon	Turner	Carr	Bolan	Jones E	Stevens	Lane	Oswald
17	7 Dec	Coventry City	(A)	0-3	(0-1)	L	8390		MacKenzie	Nelson	Robinson	Deacon	Turner	Carr	Bolan	Cheesmur	Johnson	Lane	Oswald
18	21	Queens Park Rangers	(A)	1-2	(0-1)	L	8252	Bolan	MacKenzie	Nelson	Robinson	Deacon	Turner	Carr	Bolan	Cheesmur	Stevens	Lane	Oswald
19	25	Cardiff City	(A)	3-1		W	8478	Oswald,Lane,Morfitt	MacKenzie	Nelson	Robinson	Deacon	Turner	Carr	Bolan	Cheesmur	Morfitt	Lane	Oswald
20	26	Cardiff City	(H)	1-1	(1-0)	D	11574	Lane	MacKenzie	Nelson	Robinson	Deacon	Turner	Carr	Bolan	Cheesmur	Morfitt	Lane	Oswald
21	28	Bournemouth	(A)	1-2	(0-1)	L	7768	Oswald	MacKenzie	Nelson	Robinson	Deacon	Turner	Spelman	Bolan	Cheesmur	Johnson	Lane	Oswald
22	4 Jan	Luton Town	(H)	0-1	(0-1)	L	8585		MacKenzie	Nelson	Robinson	Deacon	Turner	Carr	Bolan	Cheesmur	Stevens	Lane	Oswald
23	18	Notts County	(A)	2-1	(0-1)	W	6840	Stevens,Spelman	MacKenzie	Nelson	Robinson	Spelman	Turner	Carr	Lane	Bolan	Stevens	Deacon	Oswald
24	22	Newport County	(H)	1-2	(1-0)	L	3328	Bolan	MacKenzie	Nelson	Robinson	Spelman	Turner	Deacon	Bolan	Stevens	Fryar	Lane	Oswald
25	25	Bristol Rovers	(H)	1-1	(1-0)	D	6005	Stevens	MacKenzie	Nelson	Robinson	Deacon	Turner	Carr	Bolan	Firth	Stevens	Lane	Oswald
26	1 Feb	Clapton Orient	(A)	0-3	(0-1)	L	9960		MacKenzie	Nelson	Robinson	Deacon	Turner	Carr	Bolan	Cheesmur	Stevens	Lane	Oswald
27	8	Torquay United	(H)	2-1	(2-0)	W	5513	Fryar(2)	MacKenzie	Nelson	Robinson	Deacon	Turner	Carr	Bolan	Stevens	Fryar	Cheesmur	Oswald
28	22	Millwall	(A)	2-1	(1-0)	W	5274	Lane,Bushby	MacKenzie	Nelson	Robinson	Deacon	Turner	Carr	Bolan	Bushby	Fryar	Lane	Oswald
29	29	Aldershot	(H)	2-2	(1-0)	D	5557	Bushby,Lane	MacKenzie	Nelson	Robinson	Deacon	Turner	Carr	Bolan	Bushby	Fryar	Lane	Oswald
30	7 Mar	Swindon Town	(A)	3-1	(1-0)	W	5721	Willshaw,Lane(pen),Shanks(O.G.)	MacKenzie	Nelson	Robinson	Deacon	Turner	Carr	Oswald	Firth	Fryar	Lane	Willshaw
31	14	Bristol City	(H)	0-1	(0-1)	L	6233		MacKenzie	Nelson	Robinson	Deacon	Turner	Carr	Oswald	Firth	Fryar	Lane	Willshaw
32	21	Brighton	(A)	3-1	(2-0)	W	8260	Willshaw,Lane,Goddard	MacKenzie	Nelson	Robinson	Deacon	Turner	Carr	Bolan	Firth	Goddard	Lane	Willshaw
33	28	Exeter City	(H)	4-0	(1-0)	W	7238	Bolan(2),Goddard,Firth	MacKenzie	Nelson	Robinson	Deacon	Turner	Carr	Bolan	Firth	Goddard	Lane	Willshaw
34	4 Apr	Newport County	(A)	1-3	(1-2)	L	3445	Goddard	MacKenzie	Nelson	Robinson	Deacon	Turner	Carr	Bolan	Firth	Goddard	Lane	Willshaw
35	10	Gillingham	(A)	1-2	(0-1)	L	7763	Firth	MacKenzie	Nelson	Robinson	Spelman	Turner	Carr	Bolan	Firth	Goddard	Lane	Willshaw
36	11	Coventry City	(H)	0-0	(0-0)	D	8382		MacKenzie	Nelson	Robinson	Spelman	Turner	Deacon	Bolan	Firth	Goddard	Lane	Willshaw
37	13	Gillingham	(H)	4-2	(2-2)	W	10568	Willshaw(2),Goddard,Firth	MacKenzie	Nelson	Robinson	Spelman	Turner	Deacon	Bolan	Firth	Goddard	Lane	Willshaw
38	18	Watford	(H)	0-5	(0-3)	L	6467		MacKenzie	Johnson	Robinson	Spelman	Smith	Deacon	Bolan	Firth	Goddard	Lane	Willshaw
39	22	Northampton Town	(A)	0-1	(0-0)	L	4134		MacKenzie	Robinson	Kelly	Spelman	Carr	Deacon	Bolan	Stevens	Goddard	Cheesmur	Willshaw
40	25	Queens Park Rangers	(H)	0-1	(0-0)	L	4969		MacKenzie	Smith	Robinson	Deacon	Carr	Jackson	Bolan	Stevens	Goddard	Lane	Willshaw
41	29	Swindon Town	(H)	1-0	(0-0)	W	3072	Willshaw	Kane	Turner	Robinson	Spelman	Carr	Deacon	Bolan	Lane	Stevens	Oswald	Willshaw
42	2 May	Reading	(A)	1-2	(0-1)	L	4439	Lane	Kane	Corbett	Robinson	Spelman	Turner	Deacon	Bolan	Lane	Graham	Willshaw	Oswald

Major Cup Competitions

F.A.Cup

Rd.	Date	Opposition	Venue Score	H.T. Res.	Att.	Goalscorers	1	2	3	4	5	6	7	8	9	10	11
R1	30 Nov	Newport County	(A) 1-0	(1-0) W	5000	Lane	MacKenzie	Nelson	Robinson	Morfitt	Turner	Carr	Bolan	Cheesmur	Johnson	Lane	Oswald
R2	14 Dec	Burton Town	(H) 5-0	W		Oswald(3),Bolan,Cheesmur	MacKenzie	Nelson	Robinson	Deacon	Turner	Carr	Bolan	Firth	Cheesmur	Lane	Oswald
R3	11 Jan	Tottenham H.	(A) 4-4	D	48839	Bolan(3),Lane	MacKenzie	Nelson	Robinson	Deacon	Turner	Carr	Bolan	Cheesmur	Stevens	Lane	Oswald
R3r	15	Tottenham H.	(H) 1-2	L	23634	Bolan	MacKenzie	Nelson	Robinson	Deacon	Turner	Carr	Bolan	Cheesmur	Stevens	Lane	Oswald

Third Divison South Cup

Rd.	Date	Opposition	Venue Score	H.T. Res.	Att.	Goalscorers	1	2	3	4	5	6	7	8	9	10	11
R1	2 Oct	Newport County	(H) 3-0	(2-0) W		Stevens,Lane,Firth	MacKenzie	Robinson	Kelly	Spelman	Turner	Carr	Deacon	Firth	Stevens	Lane	Oswald
R2		Bye															
R3	11 Nov	Crystal Palace	(A) 2-3	(0-0) L		Lane(2)	MacKenzie	Nelson	Robinson	Spelman	Turner	Carr	Stevens	Deacon	Morfitt	Lane	Oswald

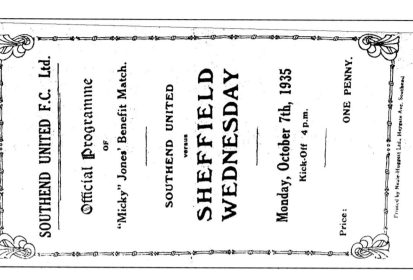

Appearances and Goals

Name	Appearances				Goals			
	Lge.	FAC	L.C.	Total	Lge.	FAC	L.C.	Total
BOLAN, Len	29	4		33	5	5		10
BUSHBY, Billy	2			2	2			2
CARR, Billy	36	4	2	42				
CHEESMUR, Fred	12	4		16	1	1		2
CORBETT, Vic	1			1				
DEACON, Jimmy	37	3	2	42				
DEMELWEEK, Johnny	6			6				
FIRTH, Joe	23	1	1	25	10	1		11
FRYAR, Buck	6			6	2			2
GODDARD, George	9			9	4			4
GRAHAM, Jimmy	1			1				
JACKSON, Bob	1			1				
JOHNSON, Harry	4	1		5				
JONES, Mickey	1			1				
KANE, Sid	2			2				
KELLY, Lawrie	2		1	3				
LANE, Harry	40	4	2	46	12	2	3	17
MOORE, Billy	3			3				
MORFITT, Jack	2	1	1	4	1			1
MACKENZIE, George	37	4	2	43				
NELSON, Jimmy	37	4	1	42				
OSWALD, Robert	33	4	2	39	5	3		8
ROBINSON, Dave	41	4	2	47				
SMITH, William	2			2				
SPELMAN, Taffy	21		2	23	2			2
STEVENS, Leo	22	2	2	26	11	1		12
TURNER, Charlie	39	4	2	45				
WILLSHAW, George	13			13	5			5
Own Goal					1			1

	Ps	P	W	D	L	F	A	W	D	L	F	A	Pts.
1935/36	18	42	8	7	6	38	21	5	3	13	23	41	36

Season 1936/37 – League Division Three (South)

No.	Date	Opposition	Venue	Score	H.T.	Res.	Att.	Goalscorers	1	2	3	4	5	6	7	8	9	10	11
1	29 Aug	Luton Town	(A)	0-1	(0-1)	L	14461		MacKenzie	Nelson	Everest	Deacon	Turner	Carr	Bolan	Firth	Graham	Egan	Willshaw
2	2 Sep	Watford	(H)	1-1		D	7372	Everest	MacKenzie	Nelson	Everest	Deacon	Turner	Carr	Bolan	Firth	Graham	Egan	Willshaw
3	5	Newport County	(H)	9-2	(4-1)	W	7346	Godd'd(3),Lane(2),Dick'son,Bolan,Oswald,Ev'est(p)	MacKenzie	Nelson	Everest	Deacon	Turner	Carr	Bolan	Lane	Goddard	Dickinson	Oswald
4	9	Watford	(A)	3-1		W	9356	Dickinson,Deacon,Goddard	MacKenzie	Nelson	Everest	Deacon	Turner	Carr	Bolan	Lane	Goddard	Dickinson	Oswald
5	12	Gillingham	(A)	0-1	(0-1)	L	7873		MacKenzie	Nelson	Everest	Deacon	Turner	Carr	Bolan	Lane	Goddard	Dickinson	Oswald
6	16	Northampton Town	(H)	2-0	(2-0)	W	6627	Dickinson(2)	MacKenzie	Nelson	Everest	Deacon	Turner	Carr	Bolan	Lane	Goddard	Dickinson	Oswald
7	19	Aldershot	(H)	2-2	(0-2)	D	10052	Dickinson,Goddard	MacKenzie	Nelson	Everest	Deacon	Turner	Carr	Kirkaldie	Lane	Goddard	Dickinson	Oswald
8	26	Swindon Town	(A)	0-4	(0-2)	L	9701		MacKenzie	Robinson	Everest	Deacon	Turner	Carr	Bolan	Egan	Goddard	Dickinson	Willshaw
9	28	Cardiff City	(A)	1-1		D	26094	Goddard	MacKenzie	Nelson	Everest	Deacon	Turner	Carr	Bolan	Lane	Goddard	Dickinson	Oswald
10	3 Oct	Millwall	(H)	0-0	(0-0)	D	11525		MacKenzie	Nelson	Everest	Deacon	Turner	Carr	Bolan	Lane	Goddard	Dickinson	Egan
11	10	Bristol Rovers	(A)	2-1	(2-0)	W	9981	Dickinson,Lane	MacKenzie	Nelson	Everest	Deacon	Turner	Carr	Bolan	Lane	Goddard	Dickinson	Bird
12	24	Crystal Palace	(H)	2-1	(1-1)	W	10281	Bird,Dickinson	MacKenzie	Nelson	Everest	Deacon	Turner	Carr	Bolan	Lane	Goddard	Dickinson	Bird
13	31	Exeter City	(A)	2-2	(1-1)	D	5162	Lane,Goddard	MacKenzie	Nelson	Robinson	Deacon	Turner	Carr	Bolan	Lane	Goddard	Dickinson	Bird
14	7 Nov	Reading	(H)	1-1	(1-0)	D	6644	Dickinson	MacKenzie	Nelson	Everest	Deacon	Turner	Carr	Bolan	Lane	Goddard	Dickinson	Bird
15	14	Queens Park Rangers	(A)	2-7	(1-1)	L	11446	Dickinson,Willshaw	MacKenzie	Nelson	Everest	Deacon	Turner	Carr	Bolan	Lane	Goddard	Dickinson	Willshaw
16	21	Bristol City	(H)	3-0	(3-0)	W	7069	Dickinson(2),Spelman	MacKenzie	Brook	Robinson	Spelman	Turner	Deacon	Bolan	Lane	Goddard	Dickinson	Willshaw
17	5 Dec	Notts County	(H)	2-3	(2-1)	L	6838	Lane,Goddard	MacKenzie	Brook	Robinson	Spelman	Turner	Deacon	Bolan	Lane	Goddard	Dickinson	Willshaw
18	19	Walsall	(H)	3-0	(1-0)	W	5492	Goddard,Lane,Oswald	MacKenzie	Nelson	Everest	Spelman	Turner	Deacon	Oswald	Lane	Dickinson	Goddard	Bird
19	25	Bournemouth	(H)	0-0	(0-0)	D	10550		MacKenzie	Nelson	Everest	Spelman	Turner	Deacon	Bird	Lane	Dickinson	Goddard	Oswald
20	26	Luton Town	(H)	3-0	(1-0)	W	11869	Lane,Dickinson,Goddard	MacKenzie	Nelson	Robinson	Harris	Turner	Spelman	Bird	Lane	Dickinson	Goddard	Oswald
21	28	Bournemouth	(A)	0-1	(0-0)	L	5905		MacKenzie	Nelson	Robinson	Harris	Turner	Spelman	Bird	Lane	Dickinson	Goddard	Oswald
22	2 Jan	Newport County	(A)	2-6	(1-2)	L	4574	Oswald,Webb(O.G.)	MacKenzie	Nelson	Robinson	Spelman	Turner	Deacon	Bird	Firth	Bolan	Lane	Oswald
23	9	Gillingham	(H)	0-2	(0-1)	L	6456		MacKenzie	Nelson	Everest	Spelman	Hague	Deacon	Lane	Goddard	Fryar	Dickinson	Willshaw
24	16	Torquay United	(A)	4-1	(1-0)	W	3043	Fryar(2),Bolan,Lane	MacKenzie	Adams	Everest	Harris	Turner	Wright	Bolan	Bushby	Fryar	Deacon	Lane
25	23	Aldershot	(A)	2-1	(2-1)	W	3004	Fryar,Lane	MacKenzie	Adams	Everest	Spelman	Turner	Wright	Bolan	Harris	Fryar	Deacon	Lane
26	30	Swindon Town	(H)	2-0	(1-0)	W	4793	Fryar(2)	Bryan	Adams	Everest	Spelman	Turner	Wright	Lane	Harris	Fryar	Dickinson	Dickinson
27	6 Feb	Millwall	(A)	2-1	(2-0)	W	26081	Dickinson,Oswald	MacKenzie	Adams	Everest	Spelman	Turner	Wright	Lane	Dickinson	Martin	Egan	Oswald
28	13	Bristol Rovers	(H)	2-3	(1-2)	L	6664	Dickinson,Preece(O.G.)	MacKenzie	Adams	Everest	Spelman	Turner	Wright	Lane	Dickinson	Martin	Egan	Oswald
29	20	Cardiff City	(H)	8-1	(5-1)	W	7504	Lane(3),Martin(2),Wright(2),Oswald	MacKenzie	Adams	Everest	Spelman	Turner	Wright	Bolan	Deacon	Martin	Oswald	Oswald
30	27	Crystal Palace	(A)	1-1	(1-0)	D	8830	Martin	MacKenzie	Adams	Robinson	Spelman	Turner	Wright	Bolan	Dickinson	Martin	Oswald	Lane
31	6 Mar	Exeter City	(H)	4-4	(2-1)	D	6707	Bolan(2),Dickinson,Lane	MacKenzie	Adams	Everest	Deacon	Turner	Wright	Bolan	Dickinson	Martin	Oswald	Lane
32	13	Reading	(A)	3-2	(1-2)	W	7684	Martin(2),Dickinson	MacKenzie	Nelson	Robinson	Harris	Turner	Carr	Dickinson	Lane	Martin	Oswald	Lane
33	20	Queens Park Rangers	(H)	3-2	(2-1)	W	8675	Lane(3)	MacKenzie	Adams	Robinson	Deacon	Turner	Wright	Bolan	Dickinson	Martin	Oswald	Lane
34	26	Brighton	(A)	0-1	(0-1)	L	17227		MacKenzie	Adams	Robinson	Deacon	Turner	Wright	Firth	Dickinson	Martin	Oswald	Lane
35	27	Bristol City	(H)	1-0	(0-0)	W	10130	Martin	MacKenzie	Adams	Everest	Spelman	Turner	Carr	Dickinson	Firth	Martin	Oswald	Lane
36	29	Brighton	(H)	2-1	(0-1)	W	14551	Carr,Firth	MacKenzie	Nelson	Robinson	Spelman	Turner	Carr	Dickinson	Firth	Martin	Oswald	Lane
37	3 Apr	Torquay United	(H)	0-0	(0-0)	D	7255		Bryan	Nelson	Robinson	Spelman	Turner	Carr	Dickinson	Firth	Fryar	Oswald	Willshaw
38	10	Notts County	(A)	1-2	(1-1)	L	15295	Fryar	Bryan	Nelson	Robinson	Spelman	Turner	Carr	Dickinson	Firth	Fryar	Oswald	Lane
39	17	Clapton Orient	(H)	0-0	(0-0)	D	5166		Bryan	Brook	Everest	Spelman	Turner	Wright	Bolan	Firth	Martin	Oswald	Willshaw
40	24	Walsall	(A)	0-3	(0-0)	L	4148		Bryan	Adams	Robinson	Spelman	Turner	Carr	Bird	Harris	Martin	Oswald	Lane
41	29	Clapton Orient	(A)	0-3		L	2541		Bryan	Turner	Robinson	Spelman	Hague	Carr	Lane	Harris	Martin	Fryar	Willshaw
42	1 May	Northampton Town	(A)	3-4	(1-3)	L	3751	Graham(2),Firth	Bryan	Adams	Everest	Spelman	Turner	Carr	Bolan	Firth	Graham	Oswald	Willshaw

Major Cup Competitions

F.A.Cup

Rd.	Date	Opposition	Venue	Score	H.T. Res.	Att.	Goalscorers	1	2	3	4	5	6	7	8	9	10	11
R1	28 Nov	Crystal Palace	(A)	1-1	D	15932	Dickinson	MacKenzie	Brook	Robinson	Spelman	Turner	Deacon	Bolan	Jack	Goddard	Dickinson	Willshaw
R1r	2 Dec	Crystal Palace	(H)	2-0	W	8500	Bolan,Goddard	MacKenzie	Brook	Robinson	Spelman	Turner	Deacon	Bolan	Lane	Goddard	Dickinson	Willshaw
R2	12 Dec	York City	(H)	3-3	(1-1) D	11200	Lane,Willshaw,Dickinson	MacKenzie	Nelson	Robinson	Spelman	Turner	Deacon	Bolan	Lane	Goddard	Dickinson	Willshaw
R2r	16	York City	(A)	1-2	(1-1) L	6789	Dickinson	MacKenzie	Nelson	Everest	Spelman	Turner	Deacon	Bolan	Lane	Goddard	Dickinson	Willshaw

(After extra time. 1-1 at 90 mins.)

Third Division South Cup

Rd.	Date	Opposition	Venue	Score	H.T. Res.	Att.	Goalscorers	1	2	3	4	5	6	7	8	9	10	11
R1		Bye																
R2	28 Oct	Clapton Orient	(H)	0-2	(0-1) L	2068		MacKenzie	Robinson	Everest	Spelman	Turner	Jackson	Oswald	Firth	Goddard	Lane	Bird

SOUVENIR PROGRAMME   N? 1051

ANNUAL
CHARITY MATCH

SOUTHEND UNITED F.C. — WEST HAM UNITED F.C.

THE JOHN MOSS CUP

WEDNESDAY APRIL 21st. 1937

ORGANISED BY THE SOUTHEND UNITED SUPPORTERS' CLUB

Appearances and Goals

Name	Appearances				Goals			
	Lge.	FAC	L.C.	Total	Lge.	FAC	L.C.	Total
ADAMS, William	13			13				
BIRD, Dickie	10		1	11	1			1
BOLAN, Len	25	4		29	4	1		5
BROOK, Reg	3	2		5				
BRYAN, William	7			7				
BUSHBY, Billy	1			1				
CARR, Billy	23			23	1			1
DEACON, Jimmy	27	4		31	1			1
DICKINSON, Billy	33	4		37	16	3		19
EGAN, Harry	6			6				
EVEREST, Jack	27	1	1	29	2			2
FIRTH, Joe	10		1	11	2			2
FRYAR, Buck	8			8	6			6
GODDARD, George	20	4	1	25	10	1		11
GRAHAM, Jimmy	3			3	2			2
HAGUE, Keith	2			2				
HARRIS, Arthur	8			8				
JACK, David	1			1				
JACKSON, Bob			1	1				
KIRKALDIE, Jack	1			1				
LANE, Harry	36	3	1	40	16	1		17
MARTIN, Tudor	11			11	6			6
MacKenzie, George	35	4	1	40				
NELSON, Jimmy	24	2		26				
OSWALD, Robert	27		1	28	5			5
ROBINSON, Dave	16	3	1	20				
SPELMAN, Taffy	22	4	1	27	1			1
TURNER, Charlie	41	4	1	46				
WILLSHAW, George	12	4		16	1	1		2
WRIGHT, Doug	11			11	2			2
Own Goal					2			2

Ps	P	W	D	L	F	A	W	D	L	F	A	Pts.
1936/37	10	42	10	8	3	49	23	7	3	11	29	44 45

Season 1937/38 – League Division Three (South)

No.	Date	Opposition	Venue	Score	H.T.	Res.	Att.	Goalscorers	No.	1	2	3	4	5	6	7	8	9	10	11
1	28 Aug	Bournemouth	(H)	1-0	(1-0)	W	10830	Bolan	1	Mackenzie	Milne	Everest	Deacon	Turner	Carr	Bolan	Hall	Martin	Bell	Lane
2	1 Sep	Brighton	(A)	1-3	(0-2)	L	9492	Hall	2	Mackenzie	Milne	Everest	Deacon	Hague	Carr	Bolan	Hall	Martin	Bell	Lane
3	4	Cardiff City	(A)	0-5	(0-3)	L	22912		3	Mackenzie	Milne	Everest	Deacon	Turner	Carr	Bolan	Harris	Martin	Bell	Oswald
4	8	Brighton	(H)	2-1	(2-0)	W	5460	Bolan,Harris	4	Mackenzie	Milne	Everest	Deacon	Hague	Carr	Bolan	Harris	Fryar	Bell	Lane
5	11	Walsall	(H)	1-0	(0-0)	W	7540	Lane	5	Mackenzie	Milne	Everest	Deacon	Jones	Carr	Bolan	Harris	Fryar	Bell	Lane
6	15	Clapton Orient	(H)	1-2	(1-2)	L	5587	Bolan	6	Higgs	Milne	Everest	Deacon	Hague	Wright	Bolan	Hall	Bell	Hall	Lane
7	18	Northampton Town	(A)	2-0	(0-0)	W	7680	Bell,Hall	7	Higgs	Milne	Everest	Harris	Hague	Wright	Bolan	Hall	Martin	Bell	Lane
8	25	Bristol Rovers	(H)	1-1	(1-0)	D	7035	Dickinson	8	Mackenzie	Milne	Everest	Harris	Turner	Wright	Bolan	Lane	Dickinson	Bell	Oswald
9	2 Oct	Mansfield Town	(A)	2-2	(1-0)	D	8330	Martin,Jones	9	Mackenzie	Milne	Everest	Harris	Jones	Wright	Bolan	Hall	Martin	Dickinson	Lane
10	9	Torquay United	(H)	5-1	(3-1)	W	7120	Dickinson(2),Martin(2),Bolan	10	Higgs	Milne	Everest	Harris	Jones	Wright	Bolan	Hall	Martin	Dickinson	Willshaw
11	16	Millwall	(A)	0-1	(0-0)	L	31804		11	Mackenzie	Milne	Everest	Deacon	Turner	Wright	Bolan	Hall	Martin	Dickinson	Bell
12	23	Reading	(H)	4-2	(2-1)	W	6858	Martin(2),Bell,Bolan	12	Mackenzie	Milne	Everest	Harris	Turner	Wright	Bolan	Bell	Martin	Dickinson	Oswald
13	30	Crystal Palace	(A)	1-2	(0-2)	L	15324	Martin	13	Mackenzie	Milne	Everest	Harris	Turner	Jackson	Bolan	Bell	Martin	Bell	Oswald
14	6 Nov	Notts County	(H)	2-1	(1-1)	W	8674	Lane,Martin	14	Mackenzie	Milne	Everest	Harris	Turner	Jackson	Bolan	Hall	Martin	Dickinson	Lane
15	13	Newport County	(A)	0-2	(0-1)	L	9295		15	Mackenzie	Milne	Everest	Harris	Turner	Wright	Bolan	Bell	Fryar	Dickinson	Lane
16	20	Bristol City	(H)	5-0	(3-0)	W	6682	Martin(3,1 pen),Dickinson,Bolan	16	Mackenzie	Milne	Everest	Harris	Turner	Jackson	Bolan	Bell	Martin	Dickinson	Willshaw
17	4 Dec	Gillingham	(H)	2-0	(1-0)	W	6770	Bell,Martin	17	Mackenzie	Milne	Everest	Harris	Turner	Jackson	Bolan	Bell	Martin	Dickinson	Lane
18	18	Swindon Town	(H)	0-0	(0-0)	D	6785		18	Mackenzie	Milne	Everest	Harris	Turner	Jackson	Bolan	Bell	Martin	Dickinson	Hall
19	25	Queens Park Rangers	(H)	0-1	(0-0)	L	17934		19	Mackenzie	Milne	Everest	Harris	Turner	Wright	Bolan	Bell	Martin	Dickinson	Hall
20	27	Queens Park Rangers	(A)	2-1	(1-1)	W	16531	Bell,Hall	20	Mackenzie	Milne	Everest	Harris	Turner	Wright	Bolan	Bell	Martin	Dickinson	Hall
21	1 Jan	Bournemouth	(A)	1-7	(0-2)	L	5726	Martin	21	Mackenzie	Milne	Jackson	Wright	Turner	Turner	Bolan	Bell	Martin	Hall	Lane
22	15	Cardiff City	(H)	3-1	(2-0)	W	6061	Martin,Bell,Dickinson	22	Mackenzie	Nelson	Everest	Turner	Jones	Carr	Hall	Bell	Martin	Dickinson	Walton
23	19	Watford	(A)	1-3		L	5424	Oswald	23	Mackenzie	Nelson	Robinson	Deacon	Turner	Carr	Hall	Bell	Dickinson	Oswald	Walton
24	22	Walsall	(A)	5-1	(2-1)	W	3536	Goddard(2),Oswald(2),Dickinson(pen)	24	Hankey	Milne	Robinson	Harris	Turner	Wright	Bolan	Hall	Goddard	Dickinson	Oswald
25	29	Northampton Town	(H)	4-2	(0-1)	W	5933	Dickinson(2),Goddard,Oswald	25	Mackenzie	Milne	Robinson	Harris	Turner	Wright	Bolan	Hall	Goddard	Dickinson	Oswald
26	5 Feb	Bristol Rovers	(A)	1-2	(1-2)	L	7519	Oswald	26	Mackenzie	Milne	Everest	Harris	Turner	Wright	Bolan	Hall	Martin	Dickinson	Oswald
27	12	Mansfield Town	(A)	0-1	(0-1)	L	5375		27	Mackenzie	Milne	Robinson	Harris	Jones	Wright	Harris	Hall	Martin	Dickinson	Oswald
28	19	Torquay United	(A)	3-3	(1-1)	D	2909	Lane(2),McAdam	28	Mackenzie	Milne	Robinson	Harris	Jones	Wright	McAdam	Hall	Martin	Lane	Oswald
29	26	Millwall	(H)	1-2	(0-0)	L	9145	Lane	29	Mackenzie	Milne	Robinson	Harris	Jones	Wright	Bolan	Bell	Martin	Lane	Oswald
30	5 Mar	Reading	(A)	2-3	(0-0)	L	8234	Bell(2)	30	Mackenzie	Milne	Robinson	Deacon	Jones	Jackson	Willshaw	Bell	Martin	Lane	Oswald
31	12	Crystal Palace	(H)	2-2	(1-0)	D	6300	Martin,Oswald	31	Mackenzie	Milne	Robinson	Deacon	Jones	Jackson	McAdam	Harris	Martin	Bell	Oswald
32	19	Notts County	(A)	2-0	(1-0)	W	12878	Goddard,Jones(pen)	32	Mackenzie	Milne	Stokes	Deacon	Jones	Jackson	Hall	Bell	Goddard	Dickinson	Oswald
33	26	Newport County	(H)	0-2	(0-0)	L	5570		33	Mackenzie	Milne	Stokes	Deacon	Jones	Jackson	Harris	Bell	Goddard	Hall	Oswald
34	30	Exeter City	(A)	1-1	(1-0)	D	2620	Hall	34	Mackenzie	Milne	Stokes	Deacon	Jones	Jackson	Hall	Goddard	Martin	Bell	Oswald
35	2 Apr	Bristol City	(A)	2-4	(1-2)	L	19632	Martin,Hague(pen)	35	Mackenzie	Milne	Stokes	Deacon	Hague	Jackson	Hall	Bell	Martin	Dickinson	Oswald
36	9	Watford	(H)	2-2	(1-0)	D	6760	Martin,Oswald	36	Hankey	Nelson	Robinson	Deacon	Carr	Jackson	Hall	Bell	Martin	Dickinson	Oswald
37	15	Aldershot	(A)	0-1	(0-0)	L	5988		37	Hankey	Nelson	Robinson	Deacon	Carr	Jackson	Bolan	Harris	Martin	Hall	Oswald
38	16	Gillingham	(A)	1-2	(1-1)	L	6822	Hartley(O.G.)	38	Hankey	Nelson	Robinson	Deacon	Carr	Wright	Dickinson	Harris	Fryar	Bell	Bell
39	18	Aldershot	(H)	4-1	(2-0)	W	6996	Fryar(2),Hall,Oswald	39	Hankey	Nelson	Robinson	Harris	Hague	Wright	Dickinson	Bell	Fryar	Hall	Hall
40	23	Exeter City	(H)	1-1	(0-1)	D	4921	Hall	40	Hankey	Nelson	Stokes	Harris	Carr	Wright	Dickinson	Bell	Fryar	Hall	Hall
41	30	Swindon Town	(A)	1-1	(0-0)	D	5028	Dickinson	41	Mackenzie	Nelson	Robinson	Deacon	Carr	Jackson	Dickinson	Bushby	Martin	Bell	Walton
42	7 May	Clapton Orient	(A)	1-1	(0-0)	D	5560	Dickinson	42	Mackenzie	Nelson	Robinson	Deacon	Carr	Wright	Dickinson	Bushby	Martin	Bell	Oswald

Major Cup Competitions

Rd.	Date	Opposition	Venue	Score	H.T.	Res.	Att.	Goalscorers
				F.A.Cup				
R1	27 Nov	Corinthians	(A)	2-0		W		Dickinson,Martin
R2	10 Dec	Walthamstow A.	(A)	1-0		W	11850	Bolan
R3	8 Jan	Barnsley	(H)	2-2	(2-0)	D	15236	Martin,Dickinson
R3r	12	Barnsley	(A)	1-2	(1-0)	L	18910	Bell
				Third Division South Cup				
R1	22 Sep	Exeter City	(H)	1-2	(1-0)	L	2680	Bell

	1	2	3	4	5	6	7	8	9	10	11
R1	MacKenzie	Milne	Everest	Harris	Turner	Jackson	Bolan	Bell	Martin	Dickinson	Lane
R2	MacKenzie	Milne	Everest	Harris	Turner	Jackson	Bolan	Bell	Martin	Dickinson	Oswald
R3	MacKenzie	Milne	Everest	Harris	Turner	Wright	Bolan	Hall	Martin	Dickinson	Lane
R3r	MacKenzie	Milne	Everest	Turner	Jones	Wright	Hall	Bell	Martin	Dickinson	Lane
R1	MacKenzie	Nelson	Robinson	Deacon	Hague	Wright	McAdam	Harris	Dickinson	Bell	Lane

(Back) Higgs, Everest, Nelson, Milne, Robinson, MacKenzie.
(Front) Cartwright (Trainer) MacAdams, Jackson, Wright, Hague, Jones,Dickinson, Footman.
(Seated back) Jack (Manager), Bell, Firth, Oswald, Willshaw, Harris, Deacon, Carr.
(Seated front) Bolan, Hall, Martin, Bushby, Lane

Appearances and Goals

Name	Appearances Lge.	FAC	L.C.	Total	Goals Lge.	FAC	L.C.	Total
BELL, Sid	32	3	1	36	7	1	1	9
BOLAN, Len	27	3		30	6	1		7
BUSHBY, Billy	2			2				
CARR, Billy	15			15				
DEACON, Jimmy	19		1	20				
DICKINSON, Billy	26	4	1	31	10	2		12
EVEREST, Jack	22	4		26				
FRYAR, Buck	6			6	2			2
GODDARD, George	5			5	4			4
HAGUE, Keith	6		1	7	1			1
HALL, Almer	29	2		31	6			6
HANKEY, Ted	6			6				
HARRIS, Arthur	29	3	1	33	1			1
HIGGS, Frank	2			2				
JACKSON, Bob	15	2		17	2			2
JONES, Charlie	12	1		13	5			5
LANE, Harry	15	3	1	19				
MARTIN, Tudor	29	4		33	16	2		18
MILNE, Johnny	33	4		37				
McADAM, Tom	2		1	3	1			1
MACKENZIE, George	34	4	1	39				
NELSON, Jimmy	9		1	10				
OSWALD, Robert	23		1	24	8			8
ROBINSON, Dave	13		1	14				
STOKES, Ernie	6			6				
TURNER, Charlie	19	4		23				
WALTON, Frank	3			3				
WILLSHAW, George	3			3				
WRIGHT, Doug	20	2	1	23				
Own Goal					1			1

	Ps	P	W	D	L	F	A	W	D	L	F	A	Pts.
1937/38	12	42	12	5	4	43	23	3	5	13	27	45	40

Season 1938/39 – League Division Three (South)

No.	Date	Opposition	Venue	Score	H.T.	Res.	Att.	Goalscorers	No.	1	2	3	4	5	6	7	8	9	10	11
1	27 Aug	Ipswich Town	(A)	2-4	(0-2)	L	19242	Bushby(2)	1	Mackenzie	Milne	Forster	Leighton	Trainer	Carr	Bolan	Bushby	Martin	Bell	Oswald
2	31	Torquay United	(H)	1-1	(0-0)	D	6022	Smirk	2	Hillam	Nelson	Forster	Leighton	Jones	Jackson	Smirk	Bushby	Martin	Bell	Walton
3	3 Sep	Reading	(H)	2-0	(0-0)	W	8725	Muncie,Bushby	3	Hillam	Nelson	Forster	Leighton	Jones	Jackson	Smirk	Bushby	Broadhurst	Hall	Muncie
4	7	Queens Park Rangers	(H)	2-1	(2-1)	W	6999	Hall(2)	4	Hillam	Robinson	Stokes	Harris	Hague	Leighton	Smirk	Hall	Trainer	Bell	Muncie
5	10	Bristol Rovers	(A)	1-4	(1-2)	L	8967	Muncie	5	Hillam	Milne	Stokes	Harris	Hague	Leighton	Smirk	Hall	Trainer	Bell	Muncie
6	17	Brighton	(H)	1-1	(0-1)	D	8274	Smirk	6	Hillam	Milne	Robinson	Leighton	Hague	Muncie	Smirk	Davis	Trainer	Bushby	Oswald
7	24	Bournemouth	(A)	4-0	(3-0)	W	7975	Trainer,Davis,Smirk,Hall	7	Hillam	Milne	Robinson	Harris	Hague	Bushby	Smirk	Davis	Trainer	Hall	Muncie
8	1 Oct	Walsall	(H)	2-0	(2-0)	W	7326	Davis,Hall	8	Hillam	Milne	Robinson	Harris	Hague	Bushby	Smirk	Davis	Trainer	Hall	Muncie
9	8	Mansfield Town	(A)	1-3	(1-3)	L	5472	Davis	9	Hillam	Milne	Robinson	Harris	Hague	Bushby	Smirk	Davis	Trainer	Hall	Muncie
10	15	Swindon Town	(H)	2-3	(1-2)	L	7619	Bell,Bushby	10	Mackenzie	Milne	Robinson	Harris	Hague	Leighton	Smirk	Bushby	Trainer	Bell	Oswald
11	22	Clapton Orient	(A)	0-5	(0-4)	L	9744		11	Mackenzie	Milne	Stokes	Harris	Jones	Leighton	Smirk	Bushby	Martin	Bell	Oswald
12	29	Watford	(H)	3-0	(0-0)	W	6385	Smirk(3)	12	Hankey	Milne	Robinson	Harris	Jones	Jackson	Smirk	Bushby	Trainer	Bell	Oswald
13	5 Nov	Crystal Palace	(A)	3-4	(2-2)	L	17685	Trainer,Bell(pen),Oswald	13	Hankey	Nelson	Robinson	Harris	Jones	Jackson	Bolan	Smirk	Trainer	Bell	Oswald
14	12	Bristol City	(H)	2-0	(1-0)	W	5957	Bell(2)	14	Hankey	Milne	Robinson	Harris	Jones	Jackson	Smirk	Bolan	Trainer	Bell	Oswald
15	19	Aldershot	(A)	0-1	(0-1)	L	5583		15	Hankey	Milne	Robinson	Harris	Jones	Jackson	Smirk	Bolan	Trainer	Bell	Muncie
16	3 Dec	Northampton Town	(A)	2-2	(2-0)	D	5568	Bushby,Smirk	16	Mackenzie	Milne	Robinson	Harris	Jones	Jackson	Smirk	Bolan	Bushby	Bell	Oswald
17	17	Port Vale	(A)	2-2	(1-1)	D	4209	Bolan,Smirk	17	Mackenzie	Milne	Robinson	Harris	Hague	Bushby	Smirk	Bolan	Trainer	Bell	Muncie
18	27	Exeter City	(A)	3-3		D	9601	Bell,Trainer,Smirk	18	Mackenzie	Milne	Robinson	Harris	Hague	Bushby	Smirk	Bolan	Trainer	Bell	Muncie
19	31	Reading	(A)	0-3	(0-0)	L	6272		19	Mackenzie	Milne	Stokes	Harris	Hague	Bushby	Smirk	Bolan	Trainer	Bell	Muncie
20	14 Jan	Bristol Rovers	(H)	3-2	(1-0)	W	5610	Trainer,Martin,Davis	20	Mackenzie	Forster	Robinson	Harris	Jones	Jackson	Smirk	Davis	Trainer	Bell	Martin
21	28	Bournemouth	(H)	2-2	(0-0)	D	5845	Bolan,Bell	21	Hankey	Milne	Robinson	Harris	Hague	Jackson	Smirk	Bolan	Bushby	Bell	Martin
22	4 Feb	Walsall	(A)	2-0	(1-0)	W	8459	Bolan,Trainer	22	Hankey	Milne	Robinson	Harris	Hague	Leighton	Smirk	Bolan	Trainer	Bell	Martin
23	8	Brighton	(H)	0-3		L	5408		23	Hankey	Milne	Robinson	Deacon	Hague	Leighton	Smirk	Harris	Martin	Bell	Muncie
24	11	Mansfield Town	(H)	2-0	(1-0)	W	6195	Bushby(2)	24	Hankey	Milne	Robinson	Harris	Hague	Jackson	Smirk	Leighton	Bushby	Bell	Oswald
25	18	Swindon Town	(A)	1-2	(0-1)	L	8270	Smirk	25	Hankey	Milne	Robinson	Harris	Hague	Jackson	Smirk	Bolan	Bushby	Bell	Martin
26	25	Clapton Orient	(H)	1-0	(0-0)	W	4497	Bushby	26	Hankey	Forster	Robinson	Harris	Hague	Jackson	Smirk	Bolan	Bushby	Bell	Oswald
27	4 Mar	Watford	(A)	0-3	(0-1)	L	5708		27	Hankey	Milne	Robinson	Harris	Hague	Jackson	Smirk	Bolan	Bushby	Bell	Martin
28	11	Crystal Palace	(H)	3-1	(1-0)	W	6244	Martin(2),Bolan	28	Hankey	Milne	Robinson	Harris	Hague	Bushby	Smirk	Bolan	Martin	Bell	Walton
29	18	Bristol City	(A)	0-1	(0-0)	L	7747		29	Hankey	Milne	Trainer	Harris	Hague	Bushby	Smirk	Bolan	Martin	Bell	Walton
30	25	Aldershot	(H)	2-1	(0-0)	W	5563	Bolan,Bell	30	Hankey	Milne	Stokes	Harris	Hague	Jackson	Smirk	Bolan	Bushby	Bell	Martin
31	1 Apr	Notts County	(A)	1-4	(1-1)	L	9467	Martin	31	Hankey	Milne	Robinson	Harris	Hague	Jackson	Smirk	Bolan	Bushby	Bell	Martin
32	7	Cardiff City	(H)	2-0	(1-0)	W	9299	Martin(2)	32	Hillam	Milne	Robinson	Harris	Hague	Jackson	Smirk	Bolan	Bushby	Bell	Martin
33	8	Northampton Town	(H)	2-0	(2-0)	W	7031	Smirk,Bell	33	Hillam	Milne	Robinson	Harris	Hague	Leighton	Smirk	Bolan	Bushby	Bell	Martin
34	10	Cardiff City	(A)	0-1	(0-1)	L	8220		34	Hillam	Milne	Trainer	Harris	Hague	Jackson	Smirk	Bolan	Singleton	Bushby	Martin
35	12	Exeter City	(H)	0-1		L	3218		35	Hillam	Trainer	Robinson	Harris	Hague	Jackson	Smirk	Bell	Fryar	Oswald	Martin
36	15	Newport County	(A)	0-3	(0-2)	L	11397		36	Hillam	Forster	Robinson	Harris	Hague	Jackson	Smirk	Bushby	Trainer	Bell	Oswald
37	19	Ipswich Town	(H)	0-0	(0-0)	D	3984		37	Mackenzie	Harris	Robinson	Leighton	Hague	Jackson	Smirk	Bushby	Singleton	Bell	Oswald
38	22	Port Vale	(H)	0-0	(0-0)	D	4239		38	Mackenzie	Milne	Robinson	Leighton	Hague	Jackson	Smirk	Harris	Bushby	Bell	Walton
39	25	Notts County	(H)	1-0	(0-0)	W	2270	Smirk	39	Mackenzie	Milne	Robinson	Harris	Hague	Leighton	Smirk	Hall	Trainer	Walton	Bell
40	29	Torquay United	(A)	0-2	(0-1)	L	2704		40	Mackenzie	Milne	Robinson	Harris	Hague	Leighton	Smirk	Bolan	Trainer	Hall	Bell
41	2 May	Newport County	(H)	5-0	(4-0)	W	2815	Smirk(2),Robinson,Trainer,Bell	41	Mackenzie	Milne	Robinson	Deacon	Hague	Jackson	Smirk	Bolan	Trainer	Bell	Muncie
42	6	Queens Park Rangers	(A)	1-1	(0-1)	D	5702	Milne	42	Mackenzie	Milne	Robinson	Deacon	Hague	Jackson	Smirk	Bolan	Trainer	Bell	Muncie

Major Cup Competitions

Rd.	Date	Opposition	Venue	Score	H.T.	Res.	Att.	Goalscorers	1	2	3	4	5	6	7	8	9	10	11
F.A.Cup																			
R1	26 Nov	Corinthians	(H)	3-0	(1-0)	W	10068	Smirk(3)	MacKenzie	Milne	Robinson	Harris	Jones	Jackson	Smirk	Bolan	Trainer	Bell	Oswald
R2	10 Dec	Port Vale	(A)	1-0	(0-0)	W	7933	Trainer	MacKenzie	Milne	Robinson	Harris	Hague	Bushby	Smirk	Bolan	Trainer	Bell	Muncie
R3	7 Jan	Chesterfield	(A)	1-1	(0-1)		8149	Hague	MacKenzie	Milne	Robinson	Harris	Hague	Jackson	Smirk	Bolan	Bushby	Bell	Muncie
				(Abandoned after 73 minutes)															
R3	11	Chesterfield	(A)	1-1		D	6121	Bushby	MacKenzie	Milne	Robinson	Harris	Hague	Jackson	Smirk	Bolan	Bushby	Bell	Muncie
R3r	16	Chesterfield	(H)	4-3		W	11393	Bell(2),Bushby,Bolan	MacKenzie	Milne	Stokes	Harris	Hague	Jackson	Smirk	Bolan	Bushby	Bell	Martin
				(After Extra Time, 90 mins 2-2)															
R4	21	Blackburn Rovers	(A)	2-4		L	21200	Bushby,Bell	MacKenzie	Milne	Robinson	Harris	Hague	Downey	Smirk	Bolan	Bushby	Bell	Martin
Third Division South Cup																			
R1	28 Sep	Northampton T.	(H)	1-1	(0-1)	D	1000	Smirk	Hankey	Milne	Robinson	Harris	Hague	Bushby	Smirk	Davis	Trainer	Hall	Muncie
R1r	5 Oct	Northampton T.	(A)	2-3	(0-1)	L		Davis(2)	Hillam	Milne	Robinson	Harris	Hague	Bushby	Smirk	Davis	Trainer	Hall	Muncie
				(After Extra Time - 90 mins. 2-2)															

SOUTHEND UNITED F.C. 1938-39.

W. CARTWRIGHT (Trainer), W. FORSTER, A. HALL, J. MILNE, C. MACKENZIE, E. STOKES, T. MARTIN, S. BELL and H. FOOTMAN (Asst. Trainer)

Mr. DAVID B N JACK (Sec. Manager) I. F. WALTON, J TRAINER, H. DOWNEY, J. BROADHURST, T. SHALLCROSS, T. W. BUSHBY, E. BOLAN, W. LEIGHTON, A. SMIR...

C. WINKFIELD, Esq (Dir.), E GRANT, Esq (Dir.), W. CARR, R. G. JACKSON and ? NELSON, C. N. NEWITT, Esq (Chairman), C. JONES, J K. HAGUE, J DEACON...

A. J. HAY, Esq (Dir.) Grant H SMITH, Dir

A. HARRIS, W. MUNCIE, H. SCAIFE, R. R. OSWALD and D. ROBINSON.

Appearances and Goals

Name	Appearances Lge.	FAC	L.C.	Total	Goals Lge.	FAC	L.C.	Total
BELL, Sid	36	6		42	9			9
BOLAN, Len	23	6		29	5			5
BROADHURST, Jack	1			1				
BUSHBY, Billy	29	4	2	35	8			8
CARR, Billy	1			1				
DAVIS, Edward	5		2	7	4		2	6
DEACON, Jimmy	3			3				
DOWNEY, ?		1		1				
FORSTER, Billy	6			6				
FRYAR, Buck	1			1				
HAGUE, Keith	31	5	2	38				
HALL, Almer	8		2	10	4			4
HANKEY, Ted	15		1	16				
HARRIS, Arthur	36	6	2	44				
HILLAM, Charlie	13		1	14				
JACKSON, Bob	23	4		27				
JONES, Charlie	10	1		11				
LEIGHTON, Billy	16			16				
MARTIN, Tudor	17	2		19	6			6
MILNE, Johnny	33	6	2	41	1			1
MUNCIE, Bill	14	3	2	19	2			2
MACKENZIE, George	14	6		20				
NELSON, Jimmy	3			3				
OSWALD, Robert	13	1		14	1			1
ROBINSON, Dave	33	5	2	40	1			1
SINGLETON, Ted	2			2				
SMIRK, Alf	41	6	2	49	14	3	1	18
STOKES, Ernie	5	1		6				
TRAINER, Jack	25	3	2	30	6		1	7
WALTON, Frank	5			5				

	Ps	P	W	D	L	F	A	W	D	L	F	A	Pts.
1938/39	12	42	14	5	2	38	13	2	4	15	23	51	41

Season 1946/47 – League Division (Three South)

No.	Date	Opposition	Venue	Score	H.T.	Res.	Att.	Goalscorers	1	2	3	4	5	6	7	8	9	10	11
1	31 Aug	Walsall	(H)	3-1		W	10991	Lane(2),Dudley	Hankey	Jackson	Bell	Harris	Sheard	Walton F	Smirk	Hamilton	Dudley	Thompson	Lane
2	4 Sep	Leyton Orient	(A)	1-1		D	6799	Dudley	Hankey	Jackson	Bell	Harris	Sheard	Walton F	Smirk	Hamilton	Dudley	Thompson	Lane
3	7	Reading	(A)	2-7	(0-1)	L	15064	Dudley(2)	Hankey	Jackson	Bell	Harris	Sheard	Walton F	Smirk	Hamilton	Dudley	Thompson	Lane
4	12	Ipswich Town	(H)	1-1	(1-0)	D	7438	Smirk	Hankey	Humphreys	Linton	Harris	Jackson	Bennett	Smirk	Smirk	Dudley	Lane	Tippett
5	14	Crystal Palace	(H)	2-0	(2-0)	W	9288	Dudley(2)	Hankey	Humphreys	Linton	Harris	Jackson	Linton	Smirk	Lane	Dudley	Gibson	Tippett
6	19	Leyton Orient	(H)	0-0	(0-0)	D	7610		Hankey	Humphreys	Linton	Harris	Jackson	Mont'ery	Sibley	Hamilton	Dudley	Gibson	Lane
7	21	Torquay United	(A)	1-0	(0-0)	W	6798	Lane	Hankey	Bell	Linton	Harris	Sheard	Mont'ery	Sibley	Smirk	Dudley	Thompson	Lane
8	28	Mansfield Town	(H)	1-1	(1-0)	D	10994	Smirk	Hankey	Jackson	Linton	Harris	Sheard	Mont'ery	Sibley	Smirk	Dudley	Thompson	Tippett
9	5 Oct	Bristol Rovers	(A)	3-1	(3-1)	W	9925	Thompson(2),Smirk	Jackson	Mont'ery	Linton	Harris	Jackson	Walton F	Sibley	Smirk	Dudley	Thompson	Lane
10	12	Swindon Town	(H)	2-0	(2-0)	W	11275	Dudley,Thompson	Hankey	Linton	Walton F	Walton H	Mont'ery	Mont'ery	Sibley	Smirk	Thompson	Gardiner	Lane
11	19	Bournemouth	(A)	1-3	(0-1)	L	9621	Smirk	Hankey	Linton	Walton F	Harris	Jackson	Mont'ery	Sibley	Smirk	Dudley	Thompson	Lane
12	26	Cardiff City	(H)	0-2	(0-1)	L	12973		Hankey	Linton	Walton F	Harris	Mont'ery	Bennett	Sibley	Smirk	Dudley	Thompson	Lane
13	2 Nov	Norwich City	(H)	5-1		W	19836	Thompson(3),Bennett,Lane	Hankey	Linton	Walton F	Harris	Jackson	Mont'ery	Sibley	Smirk	Thompson	Bennett	Lane
14	9	Notts County	(H)	3-0	(1-0)	W	10100	Thompson,Smirk,Lane	Hankey	Linton	Walton F	Harris	Jackson	Mont'ery	Sibley	Smirk	Thompson	Bennett	Lane
15	16	Northampton Town	(A)	3-2	(2-1)	W	11338	Thompson(2),Lane	Hankey	Linton	Walton F	Harris	Jackson	Mont'ery	Sibley	Smirk	Thompson	Bennett	Lane
16	23	Aldershot	(H)	2-1	(1-0)	W	10437	Smirk,Lane	Hankey	Linton	Walton F	Harris	Jackson	Mont'ery	Sibley	Smirk	Thompson	Bennett	Lane
17	7 Dec	Exeter City	(H)	2-2	(1-1)	D	7360	Lane,Mont'ery	Hankey	Linton	Walton F	Harris	Jackson	Mont'ery	Sibley	Smirk	Thompson	Bennett	Lane
18	21	Bristol City	(H)	4-1	(2-1)	W	8007	Thompson(3),Sibley(pen)	Hankey	Linton	Walton F	Harris	Jackson	Mont'ery	Sibley	Smirk	Thompson	Bennett	Lane
19	25	Watford	(A)	0-4	(0-2)	L	6849		Hankey	Linton	Walton F	Harris	Jackson	Mont'ery	Sibley	Smirk	Thompson	Bennett	Lane
20	26	Watford	(H)	5-0	(2-0)	W	15254	Sibley(2),Lane(2),Thompson	Hankey	Linton	Walton F	Harris	Jackson	Mont'ery	Sibley	Smirk	Thompson	Bennett	Lane
21	28	Walsall	(A)	2-2	(2-0)	D	14966	Thompson,Smirk	Hankey	Linton	Walton F	Harris	Jackson	Mont'ery	Sibley	Smirk	Thompson	Bennett	Lane
22	4 Jan	Reading	(A)	0-2	(0-0)	L	11407		Hankey	Jackson	Linton	Harris	Sheard	Mont'ery	Sibley	Smirk	Thompson	Bennett	Lane
23	15	Brighton	(A)	1-2	(1-1)	L	4146	Smirk	Hankey	Linton	Walton F	Harris	Jackson	Mont'ery	Sibley	Smirk	Thompson	Bennett	Lane
24	18	Crystal Palace	(A)	3-0	(0-0)	W	18968	Thompson(2),Bennett	Hankey	Linton	Walton F	Harris	Jackson	Mont'ery	Sibley	Smirk	Thompson	Bennett	Bennett
25	25	Torquay United	(H)	0-2	(0-1)	L	5492		Hankey	Linton	Walton F	Harris	Jackson	Mont'ery	Sibley	Smirk	Thompson	Bennett	Bennett
26	1 Feb	Mansfield Town	(A)	1-0	(1-0)	W	4411	Mont'ery	Hankey	Linton	Walton F	Harris	Jackson	Mont'ery	Sibley	Smirk	Thompson	Bennett	Lane
27	8	Bristol Rovers	(H)	2-3	(2-3)	L	5986	Thompson,Pritchard	Hankey	Linton	Walton F	Harris	Jackson	Mont'ery	Smirk	French	Thompson	Lane	Pritchard
28	1 Mar	Cardiff City	(A)	1-3	(1-1)	L	33698	Dudley	Hankey	Linton	Walton F	Harris	Jackson	Mont'ery	Pritchard	Smirk	Dudley	Thompson	Lane
29	8	Norwich City	(H)	3-0	(1-0)	W	6810	Dudley(2),Thompson	Hankey	Jackson	Walton F	Harris	Sheard	Mont'ery	Bennett	Smirk	Dudley	Thompson	Lane
30	22	Northampton Town	(H)	4-0	(1-0)	W	8465	Dudley(3),Thompson	Hankey	Jackson	Walton F	Harris	Sheard	Mont'ery	Pritchard	Smirk	Dudley	Thompson	Bennett
31	29	Aldershot	(H)	0-0	(0-0)	D	4118		Hankey	Jackson	Walton F	Harris	Sheard	Mont'ery	Pritchard	Smirk	Dudley	Thompson	Bennett
32	4 Apr	Queens Park Rangers	(A)	0-1	(0-1)	L	20307		Hankey	Jackson	Walton F	Harris	Sheard	Mont'ery	Pritchard	Smirk	Dudley	Thompson	Lane
33	5	Brighton	(H)	0-0	(0-0)	D	10594		Hankey	Jackson	Walton F	Harris	Mont'ery	Linton	Pritchard	Smirk	Thompson	Bennett	Lane
34	7	Queens Park Rangers	(H)	1-3	(0-1)	L	17295	Lane	Hankey	Jackson	Walton F	Harris	Mont'ery	Linton	Pritchard	Smirk	Dudley	Thompson	Lane
35	12	Exeter City	(A)	5-1	(1-0)	W	7269	Dudley(3),Thompson(2)	Hankey	Jackson	Walton F	Harris	Mont'ery	Linton	Pritchard	Smirk	Dudley	Thompson	Lane
36	19	Port Vale	(H)	1-1	(1-1)	D	8762	Smirk	Hankey	Jackson	Bell	Harris	Mont'ery	Linton	Pritchard	Smirk	Dudley	Thompson	Lane
37	26	Bristol City	(A)	0-2	(0-0)	L	12816		Hankey	Jackson	Walton F	Harris	Mont'ery	Linton	Pritchard	Smirk	Dudley	Thompson	Lane
38	3 May	Ipswich Town	(A)	0-1	(0-0)	L	12436		Hankey	Jackson	Walton F	Harris	Mont'ery	Linton	Bennett	Smirk	Dudley	Brown	Lane
39	10	Swindon Town	(A)	1-2	(1-2)	L	13498	Smirk	Davies	Bell	Walton F	Harris	Mont'ery	Jackson	Smirk	Thompson	Dudley	Brown	Pritchard
40	17	Bournemouth	(H)	2-2	(1-0)	D	6951	Lane,Smirk	Davies	Bell	Walton F	Harris	Mont'ery	Jackson	Pritchard	Smirk	Dudley	Brown	Lane
41	24	Notts County	(H)	2-0	(1-0)	W	14041	Lane,Pritchard	Davies	Jackson	Bell	Harris	Sheard	Mont'ery	Pritchard	Smirk	Dudley	Thompson	Lane
42	31	Port Vale	(A)	1-5	(1-0)	L	8879	Thompson	Hankey	Jackson	Bell	Harris	Sheard	Mont'ery	Pritchard	Smirk	Dudley	Thompson	Lane

Abbrev.: Mont'ery = Montgomery.

Major Cup Competitions

F.A.Cup

Rd.	Date	Opposition	Venue	Score	H.T.	Res.	Att.	1	2	3	4	5	6	7	8	9	10	11	Goalscorers
R1	30 Nov	Brush Sports	(A)	6-1	(2-1)	W	8000	Hankey	Linton	Walton F	Harris	Jackson	Mont'ery	Sibley	Smirk	Thompson	Bennett	Lane	Thompson(3),Sibley,Bennett,Smirk
R2	14 Dec	Barnet	(A)	9-2	(5-1)	W	8065	Hankey	Linton	Walton F	Harris	Sheard	Mont'ery	Sibley	Smirk	Thompson	Bennett	Lane	Lane(3),Siby(2),Bentt(2),Thomp'n,Bunker(O.G.)
R3	11 Jan	Everton	(A)	2-4	(1-2)	L	50124	Hankey	Linton	Walton F	Harris	Jackson	Mont'ery	Sibley	Smirk	Thompson	Bennett	Lane	Thompson,Bennett

Abbrev.: Mont'ery = Montgomery. Siby = Sibley. Benntt = Bennett. Thomp'n = Thompson.

Appearances and Goals

Name	Appearances			Goals		
	Lge.	FAC	Total	Lge.	FAC	Total
BELL, Sid	10		10			
BENNETT, Ken	21	3	24	2	4	6
BROWN, Ernest	3		3			
DAVIES, Len	3		3			
DUDLEY, Frank	25		25	16		16
FRENCH, Jack	1		1			
GARDINER, John	1		1			
GIBSON, Bob	2		2			
HAMILTON, David	4		4			
HANKEY, Ted	38	3	41			
HARRIS, Arthur	41	3	44			
HUMPHREYS, Ron	3		3			
JACKSON, Bob	41	2	43			
LANE, Harry	38	3	41	13	3	16
LINTON, Tommy	31	3	34			
MONTGOMERY, Stan	37	3	40	2		2
PRITCHARD, Harvey	14		14	2		2
SHEARD, Frank	12	1	13			
SIBLEY, Joe	21	3	24	3	3	6
SMIRK, Alf	42	3	45	11	1	12
THOMPSON, Cyril	37	3	40	22	5	27
TIPPETT, Tommy	3		3			
WALTON, Frank	33	3	36			
WALTON, Harry	1		1			
Own Goal					1	1

	Ps	P	W	D	L	F	A	W	D	L	F	A	Pts.
1946/47	8	42	9	7	5	38	22	8	3	10	33	38	44

(Middle) Warren (Manager), Benson (Dir.), H.Walton, F.Walton, Woodward, Bennett, Savage, Linton, O'Brien, Sheard, Copping (Trainer), Robinson, (Asst. Trainer), Hogan (Coach). (Front) Bewes (Doctor), Smirk, Gibson, Hamilton, Jones, Hewitt (Chair), Jackson, Thompson, Dudley, Tippett, Hays (Vicer.Chair). (Kneeling) Sibley, Gardener, Lane.

(Back) Humphries, Harris, Hankey, Davis, Middleton, Bell.

1945/46 Season: F.A.Cup

Rd.	Date	Opposition	Venue	Score	H.T.	Res.	Att.	1	2	3	4	5	6	7	8	9	10	11	Goalscorers
R1L1	17 Nov	Watford	(A)	1-1	(0-1)	D	5808	Conway	Jackson	Harvey J	Leighton	Jones	Walton	Smirk	Thompson C	Gardiner J	Dudley	Peters	Smirk
R1L2	24	Watford	(H)	0-3	(0-2)	L	8000	Conway	Humphreys	Harvey J	Jackson	Jones C	Leighton	Dudley	Hockey E	Gardiner J	Smirk	Walton	

Season 1947/48 – League Division Three (South)

No.	Date	Opposition	Venue	Score	H.T.	Res.	Att.	Goalscorers	No.	1	2	3	4	5	6	7	8	9	10	11
1	23 Aug	Bristol City	(A)	0-6	(0-3)	L	23874		1	Hankey	Beach	Walton	Goodyear	Sheard	Mont'ery	Pritchard	Smirk	Dudley	Thompson	Whit'ch
2	27	Ipswich Town	(H)	3-2	(2-1)	W	10106	Whit'ch,Thompson,Dudley	2	Hankey	Beach	Walton	Goodyear	Sheard	Mont'ery	Pritchard	Thompson	Dudley	Smirk	Whit'ch
3	30	Reading	(H)	1-1	(1-1)	D	11710	Pritchard	3	Hankey	Beach	Walton	Goodyear	Mont'ery	Jackson	Pritchard	Thompson	Dudley	Smirk	Whit'ch
4	3 Sep	Ipswich Town	(A)	0-4	(0-4)	L	12410		4	Hankey	Jackson	Walton	French	Mont'ery	Goodyear	Pritchard	Lane	Dudley	Pryde	Lane
5	6	Walsall	(A)	0-6	(0-4)	L	18285		5	Robinson	Linton	Walton	Goodyear	Mont'ery	Bennett	Dudley	Smirk	Thompson	Pryde	Lane
6	10	Swansea Town	(H)	1-1	(1-1)	D	8483	Pritchard	6	Hankey	Linton	Bell	Goodyear	Mont'ery	Pritchard	Smirk	French	Dudley	Pryde	Whit'ch
7	13	Leyton Orient	(H)	2-1	(2-0)	W	10019	Whit'ch,Dudley	7	Hankey	Linton	Bell	Goodyear	Mont'ery	Pritchard	Smirk	Lane	Dudley	Bennett	Whit'ch
8	18	Swansea Town	(A)	0-3	(0-2)	L	14356		8	Hankey	Jackson	Bell	Goodyear	Mont'ery	Pritchard	Bennett	Thompson	Dudley	Lane	Whit'ch
9	20	Exeter City	(A)	0-0	(0-0)	D	9295		9	Hankey	Jackson	Bell	Goodyear	Mont'ery	Pritchard	Bennett	Thompson	Dudley	Lane	Whit'ch
10	27	Newport County	(H)	1-0	(1-0)	W	11447	Thompson	10	Hankey	Jackson	Bell	Goodyear	Mont'ery	Pritchard	Bennett	Lane	Thompson	Brown	Whit'ch
11	2 Oct	Queens Park Rangers	(A)	2-3	(1-2)	L	17585	Whit'ch,Thompson	11	Hankey	Jackson	Bell	Goodyear	Mont'ery	Pritchard	Smirk	Dudley	Thompson	Lane	Whit'ch
12	4	Port Vale	(A)	1-2	(1-1)	L	15100	Whit'ch	12	Hankey	Linton	Walton	Goodyear	Mont'ery	Pritchard	Smirk	Dudley	Thompson	Lane	Whit'ch
13	11	Swindon Town	(H)	1-0	(0-0)	W	11605	Thompson	13	Hankey	Jackson	Linton	Goodyear	Mont'ery	Pritchard	Smirk	Dudley	Thompson	Lane	Whit'ch
14	18	Torquay United	(A)	1-4	(1-2)	L	7432	Thompson	14	Hankey	Jackson	Linton	Goodyear	Mont'ery	Pritchard	Pritchard	Dudley	Thompson	Lane	Whit'ch
15	25	Crystal Palace	(H)	2-1	(1-1)	W	10560	Whit'ch,Pritchard	15	Robinson	Beach	Linton	Goodyear	Sheard	Pritchard	Pritchard	Smirk	Dudley	Bennett	Whit'ch
16	1 Nov	Aldershot	(A)	1-1	(0-1)	D	7593	Scott(O.G.)	16	Robinson	Beach	Linton	Goodyear	Sheard	Mont'ery	Pritchard	Smirk	Dudley	Bennett	Whit'ch
17	8	Northampton Town	(H)	3-1	(1-0)	W	10481	Dudley(2),Smirk	17	Robinson	Beach	Linton	Goodyear	Sheard	Mont'ery	Pritchard	Smirk	Dudley	Bennett	Whit'ch
18	15	Bristol Rovers	(A)	2-1	(0-0)	W	12607	Bennett,Watkins(O.G.)	18	Robinson	Beach	Linton	Goodyear	Sheard	Mont'ery	Pritchard	Dudley	Dudley	Bennett	Whit'ch
19	22	Norwich City	(H)	0-0	(0-0)	D	10231		19	Robinson	Beach	Linton	Goodyear	Sheard	Mont'ery	Pritchard	Smirk	Dudley	Bennett	Whit'ch
20	20 Dec	Bristol City	(H)	4-0	(1-0)	W	7717	Bennett(2),Pritchard,Thompson	20	Nash	Beach	Linton	Goodyear	Sheard	Mont'ery	Pritchard	Dudley	Thompson	Bennett	Lane
21	26	Bournemouth	(H)	0-2	(0-0)	L	15091		21	Nash	Beach	Linton	Goodyear	Sheard	Mont'ery	Pritchard	Dudley	Thompson	Bennett	Lane
22	27	Bournemouth	(A)	1-0	(0-0)	W	15985	Dudley	22	Nash	Beach	Linton	Goodyear	Sheard	Mont'ery	Pritchard	Dudley	Thompson	Bennett	Lane
23	3 Jan	Reading	(A)	3-1	(1-1)	W	12149	Thompson(2),Bennett	23	Nash	Beach	Linton	Goodyear	Sheard	Mont'ery	Pritchard	Dudley	Thompson	Bennett	Lane
24	17	Walsall	(H)	1-1	(1-0)	D	9218	Thompson	24	Nash	Beach	Linton	Goodyear	Sheard	Mont'ery	Pritchard	Dudley	Thompson	Bennett	Lane
25	24	Watford	(H)	1-1	(1-0)	D	8178	Mont'ery	25	Nash	Beach	Linton	Jackson	Sheard	Mont'ery	Pritchard	Smirk	Dudley	Bennett	Lane
26	31	Leyton Orient	(A)	0-2	(0-1)	L	13306		26	Nash	Beach	Linton	Jackson	Sheard	Mont'ery	Smirk	Dudley	Thompson	Bennett	Lane
27	7 Feb	Exeter City	(H)	2-0	(1-0)	W	8618	Lane,Thompson	27	Hankey	Beach	Linton	Goodyear	Sheard	Mont'ery	Tippett	Dudley	Thompson	Bennett	Lane
28	14	Newport County	(A)	5-1	(4-1)	W	10640	Bennett(3),Pritchard,Thompson	28	Nash	Beach	Linton	Goodyear	Sheard	Mont'ery	Tippett	Dudley	Thompson	Bennett	Pritchard
29	21	Port Vale	(H)	1-1	(0-0)	D	3961	Tippett	29	Nash	Beach	Linton	Goodyear	Sheard	Mont'ery	Tippett	Dudley	Thompson	Bennett	Pritchard
30	28	Swindon Town	(A)	0-0	(0-0)	D	14858		30	Nash	Beach	Linton	Goodyear	Sheard	Mont'ery	Tippett	Dudley	Thompson	Bennett	Pritchard
31	6 Mar	Torquay United	(H)	1-0	(0-0)	W	9165	Thompson	31	Nash	Beach	Linton	Goodyear	Sheard	Mont'ery	Tippett	Lane	Thompson	Bennett	Pritchard
32	13	Crystal Palace	(A)	0-0	(0-0)	D	14458		32	Nash	Beach	Linton	Goodyear	Sheard	Mont'ery	Tippett	Lane	Thompson	Bennett	Pritchard
33	20	Aldershot	(H)	4-0	(1-0)	W	9837	Thompson,Edwards,Grant,Tippett	33	Hankey	Beach	Linton	Mont'ery	Sheard	Pryde	Tippett	Bennett	Grant	Thompson	Edwards
34	26	Notts County	(A)	1-2	(1-0)	L	35689	Thompson	34	Hankey	Beach	Linton	Mont'ery	Sheard	Pryde	Tippett	Bennett	Grant	Thompson	Edwards
35	27	Northampton Town	(A)	0-2	(0-2)	L	9104		35	Hankey	Beach	Linton	Mont'ery	Sheard	Pryde	Tippett	Bennett	Grant	Thompson	Edwards
36	29	Notts County	(H)	1-2	(1-2)	L	17613	Goodyear	36	Hankey	Beach	Linton	Mont'ery	Sheard	Pryde	Tippett	Goodyear	Grant	Thompson	Lane
37	3 Apr	Bristol Rovers	(H)	1-0	(0-0)	W	8410	Grant	37	Hankey	Beach	Linton	Jackson	Sheard	Pryde	Tippett	Thompson	Grant	Brown	Edwards
38	7	Brighton	(A)	0-1	(0-1)	L	10194		38	Hankey	Beach	Linton	Jackson	Sheard	Pryde	Tippett	Bennett	Grant	Brown	Edwards
39	10	Norwich City	(A)	0-1	(0-1)	L	22734		39	Hankey	Linton	Walton	Jackson	Sheard	Pryde	Tippett	Thompson	Grant	Mont'ery	Pritchard
40	17	Brighton	(H)	2-2	(0-1)	D	6428	Pritchard,Tippett	40	Hankey	Linton	Walton	Jackson	Sheard	Mont'ery	Tippett	Pryde	Grant	Lane	Pritchard
41	24	Watford	(A)	2-2	(0-2)	D	9964	Mont'ery(pen),Bennett	41	Hankey	Linton	Walton	Goodyear	Sheard	Mont'ery	Tippett	Pryde	Grant	Bennett	Pritchard
42	1 May	Queens Park Rangers	(H)	0-0	(0-0)	D	13827		42	Hankey	Linton	Walton	Goodyear	Sheard	Mont'ery	Tippett	Pryde	Grant	Bennett	Pritchard

Abbrev.: Mont'ery = Montgomery. Whit'ch = Whitchurch.

Major Cup Competitions

Rd.	Date	Opposition	Venue	Score	H.T. Res.	Att.	Goalscorers
				F.A.Cup			
R1	29 Nov	Newport County	(A)	2–3	L		Bennett(2)

Abbrev.: Mont'ery = Montgomery

1	2	3	4	5	6	7	8	9	10	11
Hankey	Beach	Linton	Goodyear	Sheard	Mont'ery	Pritchard	Smirk	Dudley	Bennett	Whitchurch

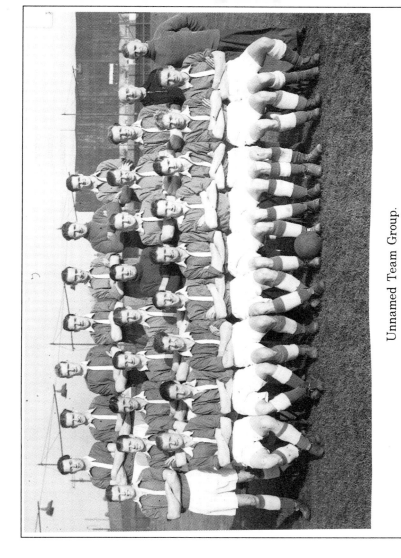

Unnamed Team Group.

Appearances and Goals

Name	Appearances Lge.	FAC	Total	Goals Lge.	FAC	Total
BEACH, Doug	27	1	28			
BELL, Sid	6		6			
BENNETT, Ken	29	1	30	8	2	10
BROWN, Ernie	3		3			
DUDLEY, Frank	29	1	30	5		5
EDWARDS, Tommy	5		5	1		1
FRENCH, Jack	2		2			
GOODYEAR, George	33	1	34	1		1
GRANT, Cyril	10		10	2		2
HANKEY, Ted	24	1	25			
JACKSON, Bob	13		13			
LANE, Harry	23		23	1		1
LINTON, Tommy	34	1	35			
MONTGOMERY, Stan	41	1	42	2		2
NASH, Paddy	12		12			
PRITCHARD, Harvey	33	1	34	6		6
PRYDE, Bill	13		13			
ROBINSON, Jack	6		6			
SHEARD, Frank	30	1	31			
SMIRK, Alf	17	1	18	1		1
THOMPSON, Cyril	29		29	14		14
TIPPETT, Tommy	16		16	3		3
WALTON, Frank	10		10			
WHITCHURCH, Charles	17	1	18	5		5
Own Goal				2		2

	Ps	P	W	D	L	F	A	W	D	L	F	A	Pts.
1947/48	9	42	11	8	2	32	16	4	5	12	19	42	43

Season 1948/49 – League Division (Three South)

No.	Date	Opposition	Venue	Score	H.T.	Res.	Att.	Goalscorers	1	2	3	4	5	6	7	8	9	10	11
1	21 Aug	Bristol City	(H)	1–0	(1–0)	W	15000	Grant	Nash	Beach	Walton	French	Sheard	Mont'ery	Tippett	Gray	Grant	Dudley	Edwards
2	25	Exeter City	(A)	0–0	(0–0)	D	11000		Nash	Beach	Walton	French	Sheard	Mont'ery	Tippett	Gray	Grant	Dudley	Edwards
3	28	Swindon Town	(A)	1–2	(1–1)	L	20000	Grant	Nash	Beach	Walton	French	Sheard	Mont'ery	Tippett	Brown	Grant	Osmond	Edwards
4	31	Exeter City	(H)	0–0	(0–0)	D	14000		Nash	Lindsay	Walton	French	Sheard	Mont'ery	Tippett	Grant	Dudley	Osmond	Edwards
5	4 Sep	Leyton Orient	(H)	2–2	(1–1)	D	16000	Mont'ery(2)	Nash	Beach	Walton	French	Thornhill	Pritchard	Tippett	Dudley	Mont'ery	Brown	Bell
6	7	Northampton Town	(H)	0–1	(0–1)	L	12500		Nash	Beach	Walton	French	Thornhill	Pritchard	Tippett	Dudley	Mont'ery	Brown	Bell
7	11	Port Vale	(A)	2–0	(2–0)	W	18000	Dudley,Grant	Nash	Beach	Walton	Goodyear	Sheard	Mont'ery	Tippett	Dudley	Grant	French	Bell
8	16	Northampton Town	(A)	2–2	(1–2)	D	8850	Dudley(2)	Nash	Beach	Walton	Goodyear	Sheard	Mont'ery	Tippett	Dudley	Grant	French	Lane
9	18	Millwall	(H)	2–1	(1–0)	W	20000	Grant(2)	Nash	Beach	Walton	Goodyear	Sheard	Mont'ery	Tippett	Dudley	Grant	French	Lane
10	25	Aldershot	(A)	0–1	(0–0)	L	8000		Nash	Beach	Walton	Goodyear	Sheard	Mont'ery	Tippett	Dudley	Grant	French	Lane
11	2 Oct	Brighton	(H)	0–0	(0–0)	D	16000		Nash	Beach	Walton	Goodyear	Sheard	Mont'ery	Tippett	Dudley	Grant	Brown	Edwards
12	9	Bournemouth	(A)	0–0	(0–0)	D	15000		Nash	Beach	Walton	Goodyear	Sheard	Mont'ery	Tippett	Gray	Grant	Dudley	Edwards
13	16	Watford	(A)	0–0	(0–0)	D	11000		Nash	Beach	Walton	Goodyear	Sheard	Mont'ery	Tippett	McAlinden	Dudley	Grant	Edwards
14	23	Bristol Rovers	(H)	0–1	(0–0)	L	17000		Nash	Beach	Walton	Goodyear	Sheard	Mont'ery	Grant	McAlinden	Dudley	Gray	Pritchard
15	30	Torquay United	(A)	3–0	(0–0)	W	7500	Dudley(2),Grant	Nash	Lindsay	Walton	Goodyear	Sheard	Pritchard	Dudley	McAlinden	Grant	Mont'ery	Tippett
16	6 Nov	Swansea Town	(H)	0–0	(0–0)	D	17000		Nash	Lindsay	Pritchard	Goodyear	Thornhill	French	Dudley	McAlinden	Grant	Mont'ery	Tippett
17	13	Newport County	(A)	2–4	(1–2)	L	12000	Dudley,Mont'ery	Nash	Lindsay	Pritchard	Goodyear	Sheard	French	Butler	McAlinden	Grant	Mont'ery	Dudley
18	20	Crystal Palace	(H)	0–0	(0–0)	L	13000		Nash	Lindsay	Pritchard	French	Sheard	Mont'ery	Butler	McAlinden	Travis	Grant	Dudley
19	18 Dec	Bristol City	(A)	1–2	(1–1)	L	13358	Tippett	Nash	Lindsay	Beach	Goodyear	Sheard	Pryde	Butler	McAlinden	Dudley	French	Tippett
20	25	Norwich City	(A)	0–3	(0–1)	L	22202		Nash	Lindsay	Beach	Pryde	Sheard	Pritchard	Grant	McAlinden	Dudley	French	Tippett
21	26	Norwich City	(H)	2–2	(2–0)	D	14000	Grant,Tippett	Hankey	Lindsay	Linton	Pryde	Sheard	Pritchard	Grant	McAlinden	Dudley	French	Tippett
22	1 Jan	Swindon Town	(H)	3–4	(3–3)	L	10000	Morris,Tippett,Dudley	Hankey	Lindsay	Linton	French	Sheard	Pritchard	Grant	McAlinden	Dudley	Morris	Tippett
23	15	Leyton Orient	(A)	0–2	(0–1)	L	8500		Nash	Lindsay	Walton	Pryde	Sheard	Pritchard	Tippett	McAlinden	Dudley	Morris	Lane
24	22	Port Vale	(H)	0–0	(0–0)	D	12000		Nash	Lindsay	Walton	Goodyear	Sheard	French	Tippett	McAlinden	Brown	Lawler	Morris
25	5 Feb	Millwall	(A)	0–1	(0–0)	L	24200		Nash	Lindsay	Walton	Goodyear	Sheard	French	Tippett	McAlinden	Brown	Lawler	Morris
26	12	Notts County	(A)	1–0	(0–0)	W	29290	French	Nash	Lindsay	Walton	Goodyear	Sheard	French	Tippett	McAlinden	Brown	Lawler	Morris
27	19	Aldershot	(H)	0–1	(0–1)	L	14001		Nash	Lindsay	Walton	Goodyear	Sheard	French	Dudley	McAlinden	Brown	Lawler	Morris
28	26	Brighton	(A)	2–3	(1–3)	L	12300	Lawler,Morris	Nash	Lindsay	Walton	Goodyear	Sheard	French	Dudley	McAlinden	Grant	Lawler	Morris
29	5 Mar	Bournemouth	(H)	0–1	(0–0)	L	10500		Nash	Lindsay	Walton	Goodyear	Sheard	French	Pritchard	McAlinden	Dudley	Lawler	Morris
30	12	Watford	(H)	0–0	(0–0)	D	16040		Nash	Lindsay	Walton	Goodyear	Thornhill	French	Butler	McAlinden	Dudley	Lawler	Tippett
31	19	Bristol Rovers	(H)	1–1	(0–0)	D	8500	Butler	Nash	Lindsay	Walton	Goodyear	Thornhill	French	Butler	McAlinden	Dudley	Lawler	Tippett
32	26	Torquay United	(A)	2–2	(0–0)	D	20000	French,Grant	Nash	Lindsay	Walton	Goodyear	Sheard	French	Butler	McAlinden	Grant	Lawler	Tippett
33	2 Apr	Swansea Town	(H)	2–0	(2–0)	W	9000	Butler,Lawler	Nash	Pritchard	Walton	Goodyear	Thornhill	French	Butler	McAlinden	Grant	Lawler	Tippett
34	6	Walsall	(A)	0–1	(0–1)	L	11000		Hankey	Pritchard	Walton	Goodyear	Sheard	French	Butler	McAlinden	Grant	Lawler	Tippett
35	9	Newport County	(H)	1–1	(1–1)	D	17000	Grant	Hankey	Lindsay	Walton	Goodyear	Sheard	French	Butler	McAlinden	Grant	Lawler	Tippett
36	15	Ipswich Town	(H)	1–2	(0–1)	L	14250	French	Hankey	Lindsay	Walton	Goodyear	Sheard	French	Butler	McAlinden	Grant	Dudley	Tippett
37	16	Crystal Palace	(A)	3–1	(1–1)	W	16000	Dudley(2),Lawler	Hankey	Pritchard	Walton	Goodyear	Sheard	French	Tippett	Lawler	Grant	Dudley	Morris
38	18	Ipswich Town	(A)	0–0	(0–0)	D	14000		Hankey	Lindsay	Walton	Gray	Sheard	French	Butler	McAlinden	Dudley	Lawler	Morris
39	23	Reading	(H)	1–2	(1–2)	L	12164	Morris	Hankey	Lindsay	Walton	Gray	Sheard	French	Butler	McAlinden	Dudley	Lawler	Brown
40	27	Reading	(A)	3–0	(0–0)	W	7000	Morris,Dudley,McAlinden	Hankey	Lindsay	Walton	Gray	Sheard	French	Butler	McAlinden	Dudley	Lawler	Morris
41	30	Walsall	(H)	3–2	(2–1)	W	15000	McAlinden(pen),Dudley,Morris	Hankey	Lindsay	Walton	Gray	Sheard	French	Butler	McAlinden	Dudley	Lawler	Morris
42	7 May	Notts County	(H)	3–2	(2–1)	W	15000		Hankey	Lindsay	Walton	Gray	Sheard	French	Butler	McAlinden	Dudley	Morris	Brown

Major Cup Competitions

Rd.	Date	Opposition	Venue	Score	H.T.	Res.	Att.	Goalscorers
				F.A.Cup				
R1	4 Dec	Swansea Town	(H)	1-2	(1-0)	L	13000	Dudley
					(After Extra Time – 90 minutes 1-1)			

	1	2	3	4	5	6	7	8	9	10	11
	Nash	Lindsay	Pritchard	Goodyear	Sheard	French	Butler	McAlinden	Dudley	Brown	Edwards

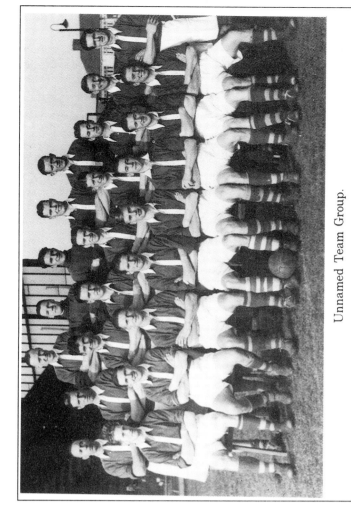

Unnamed Team Group.

Appearances and Goals

Name	Appearances			Goals		
	Lge.	FAC	Total	Lge.	FAC	Total
BEACH, Doug	14		14			
BELL, Stan	3		3			
BROWN, Ernie	10	1	11			
BUTLER, Ernie	14	1	15	2		2
DUDLEY, Frank	34	1	35	11	1	12
EDWARDS, Tommy	7	1	8			
FRENCH, Jack	36	1	37	3		3
GOODYEAR, George	26	1	27			
GRANT, Cyril	26		26	9		9
GRAY, Harry	9		9			
HANKEY, Ted	11		11			
LANE, Harry	4		4			
LAWLER, Jimmy	17		17	3		3
LINDSAY, David	26	1	27			
LINTON, Tommy	2		2			
MONTGOMERY, Stan	18		18	3		3
MORRIS, Freddie	14		14	5		5
McALINDEN, Jimmy	29	1	30	2		2
NASH, Paddy	31	1	32			
OSMOND, Avery	2		2			
PRITCHARD, Harvey	16	1	17			
PRYDE, Bill	4		4			
SHEARD, Frank	36	1	37			
THORNHILL, Dennis	6		6			
TIPPETT, Tommy	31		31	3		3
TRAVIS, Don	1		1			
WALTON, Frank	35		35			

	Ps	P	W	D	L	F	A	W	D	L	F	A	Pts.
1948/49	18	42	5	10	6	18	18	4	6	11	23	28	34

Season 1949/50 – League Division Three (South)

No.	Date	Opposition	Venue	Score	H.T.	Res.	Att.	Goalscorers	1	2	3	4	5	6	7	8	9	10	11
1	20 Aug	Notts County	(A)	0-2	(0-1)	L	33490		Hankey	Lindsay	Walton	Gray	Sheard	French	Jones	McAlinden	Brown	Lawler	Clough
2	23	Port Vale	(H)	1-0	(1-0)	W	12000	Butler(O.G.)	Hankey	Lindsay	Walton	Gray	Sheard	French	Jones	McAlinden	Wakefield	Lawler	Clough
3	27	Newport County	(H)	6-0	(1-0)	W	14500	Clough(2),Wakefield(2),McAlinden(pen),Lawler	Hankey	Lindsay	Walton	Gray	Sheard	French	Jones	McAlinden	Wakefield	Lawler	Clough
4	29	Port Vale	(A)	0-0	(0-0)	D	15000		Hankey	Lindsay	Walton	Gray	Sheard	Pritchard	Jones	McAlinden	Wakefield	Lawler	Clough
5	3 Sep	Bristol Rovers	(H)	3-1	(3-0)	W	16000	Clough,Wakefield,Lawler	Hankey	Lindsay	Walton	Gray	Sheard	French	Jones	McAlinden	Wakefield	Lawler	Clough
6	6	Leyton Orient	(H)	2-0	(0-0)	W	12000	Lawler,Wakefield	Hankey	Lindsay	Walton	Gray	Sheard	French	Jones	McAlinden	Wakefield	Lawler	Clough
7	10	Bournemouth	(A)	0-3	(0-2)	L	17115		Hankey	Lindsay	Walton	Gray	Sheard	Pritchard	Jones	McAlinden	Wakefield	Lawler	Clough
8	17	Crystal Palace	(H)	0-0	(0-0)	D	18000		Hankey	Lindsay	Walton	Gray	Sheard	French	Jones	McAlinden	Wakefield	Lawler	Clough
9	24	Watford	(A)	0-1	(0-0)	L	11000		Hankey	Lindsay	Walton	Gray	Sheard	French	Jones	McAlinden	Wakefield	Lawler	Clough
10	1 Oct	Reading	(H)	3-2	(1-1)	W	20000	Morris(2),Wakefield	Hankey	Loughran	Walton	Gray	Sheard	French	Jones	McAlinden	Wakefield	Morris	Clough
11	8	Bristol City	(A)	1-1	(0-0)	D	17535	Wakefield	Hankey	Loughran	Walton	Wallbanks	Sheard	French	Jones	McAlinden	Wakefield	Morris	Tippett
12	15	Brighton	(H)	3-2	(1-1)	W	18000	Morris(2),Tippett	Hankey	Lindsay	Walton	Wallbanks	Sheard	French	Jones	McAlinden	Wakefield	Morris	Tippett
13	22	Walsall	(A)	1-1	(1-0)	D	11000	Wakefield	Hankey	Lindsay	Walton	Wallbanks	Sheard	French	Jones	McAlinden	Wakefield	Morris	Tippett
14	29	Millwall	(H)	3-0	(2-0)	W	15000	French,Wakefield,Morris	Hankey	Lindsay	Walton	Wallbanks	Sheard	French	Jones	McAlinden	Wakefield	Morris	Clough
15	5 Nov	Swindon Town	(A)	2-2	(1-1)	D	12000	Clough,Wakefield	Hankey	Lindsay	Walton	Wallbanks	Sheard	French	Jones	McAlinden	Wakefield	Morris	Clough
16	12	Torquay United	(H)	2-0	(2-0)	W	12000	Morris(2)	Hankey	Lindsay	Walton	Wallbanks	Sheard	French	Jones	McAlinden	Wakefield	Morris	Clough
17	3 Dec	Northampton Town	(A)	0-2	(0-1)	L	12009		Hankey	Loughran	Walton	Wallbanks	Sheard	French	Jones	McAlinden	Wakefield	Morris	Clough
18	17	Notts County	(H)	2-0	(0-0)	W	13000	Davies,Morris	Hankey	Loughran	Walton	Wallbanks	Sheard	French	Tippett	Davies	Grant	Morris	Clough
19	26	Exeter City	(A)	1-1	(1-1)	D	14105	Davies	Hankey	Lindsay	Walton	Wallbanks	Sheard	French	Clough	McAlinden	Wakefield	Davies	Morris
20	27	Exeter City	(H)	1-0	(0-0)	W	20000	Morris	Hankey	Loughran	Walton	Wallbanks	Sheard	French	Clough	McAlinden	Wakefield	Davies	Morris
21	31	Bristol Rovers	(A)	1-1	(0-1)	D	15406	Wakefield	Hankey	Loughran	Walton	Wallbanks	Sheard	French	Morris	McAlinden	Wakefield	Davies	Clough
22	14 Jan	Bournemouth	(H)	1-0	(0-0)	W	14000	Sheard	Hankey	Loughran	Walton	Wallbanks	Sheard	French	Pritchard	McAlinden	Wakefield	Morris	Clough
23	21	Crystal Palace	(A)	1-2	(1-2)	L	12846	Gawler	Hankey	Loughran	Walton	Gawler	Thornhill	French	Jones	McAlinden	Wakefield	Davies	Clough
24	28	Nottingham Forest	(H)	2-3	(1-1)	L	9000	Wakefield(2)	Hankey	Loughran	Walton	Wallbanks	Sheard	French	Jones	McAlinden	Wakefield	Morris	Clough
25	4 Feb	Watford	(H)	1-1	(1-0)	D	14000	Clough	Hankey	Loughran	Walton	Wallbanks	Sheard	French	McAlinden	Davies	Wakefield	Morris	Clough
26	11	Norwich City	(H)	1-0	(0-0)	W	11000	Loughran	Hankey	Loughran	Walton	Wallbanks	Sheard	French	Jones	McAlinden	Wakefield	Davies	Clough
27	18	Reading	(A)	0-5	(0-4)	L	13005		Hankey	Loughran	Walton	Wallbanks	Sheard	French	Jones	McAlinden	Wakefield	Lawler	Clough
28	25	Bristol City	(H)	2-0	(2-0)	W	10000	Wallbanks,Lawler	Hankey	Loughran	Walton	Wallbanks	Sheard	French	Jones	McAlinden	Wakefield	Lawler	Clough
29	4 Mar	Brighton	(A)	1-2	(0-0)	L	11000	Wakefield	Hankey	Loughran	Walton	Wallbanks	Sheard	French	Jones	McAlinden	Wakefield	Lawler	Clough
30	11	Walsall	(H)	2-2	(0-0)	D	10000	Wakefield,Lindsay	Hankey	Lindsay	Walton	Gawler	Thornhill	French	Brown	McAlinden	Wakefield	Clough	Tippett
31	18	Millwall	(A)	2-1	(1-0)	W	18513	Wakefield(2)	Nash	Loughran	Walton	Gawler	Thornhill	French	Jones	McAlinden	Wakefield	Morris	Clough
32	25	Swindon Town	(H)	2-0	(1-0)	W	10000	Morris,Wakefield	Nash	Lindsay	Walton	Gawler	Thornhill	French	Jones	McAlinden	Wakefield	Morris	Clough
33	30	Newport County	(A)	1-2	(1-2)	L	7779	Wakefield	Nash	Loughran	Walton	Gawler	Thornhill	French	Jones	McAlinden	Wakefield	Morris	Clough
34	1 Apr	Torquay United	(A)	4-2	(1-1)	W	8000	Stubbs(2),Clough,Wakefield	Nash	Loughran	Walton	Gawler	Sheard	French	Jones	McAlinden	Wakefield	Stubbs	Clough
35	7	Ipswich Town	(H)	2-2	(1-1)	D	17000	Stubbs,Clough	Nash	Loughran	Walton	Gawler	Sheard	French	Jones	McAlinden	Wakefield	Stubbs	Clough
36	8	Aldershot	(H)	3-0	(1-0)	W	12000	Davies(2),Wakefield	Nash	Lindsay	Walton	Wallbanks	Sheard	French	Butler	Davies	Wakefield	Stubbs	Clough
37	10	Ipswich Town	(A)	3-1	(1-0)	W	14000	Morris,Grant,Wallbanks	Nash	Lindsay	Walton	Wallbanks	Sheard	French	Davies	McAlinden	Grant	Stubbs	Morris
38	15	Nottingham Forest	(A)	2-1	(0-0)	W	25316	Davies,Wakefield	Nash	Lindsay	Walton	Wallbanks	Sheard	French	Davies	McAlinden	Wakefield	Stubbs	Morris
39	22	Northampton Town	(H)	1-2	(1-2)	L	15000	Wakefield(pen)	Hankey	Lindsay	Walton	Wallbanks	Sheard	French	Davies	McAlinden	Wakefield	Stubbs	Clough
40	29	Norwich City	(A)	0-0	(0-0)	D	10153		Nash	Lindsay	Walton	Wallbanks	Sheard	French	Grant	Davies	Wakefield	Stubbs	Tippett
41	2 May	Aldershot	(A)	1-1	(0-0)	D	10000	Tippett	Nash	Lindsay	Walton	Wallbanks	Sheard	French	Butler	Davies	Grant	Lawler	Tippett
42	6	Leyton Orient	(A)	2-2	(0-0)	D	13197	Davies,Wakefield	Nash	Lindsay	Horsfall	Wallbanks	Sheard	French	Butler	McAlinden	Wakefield	Lawler	Davies

Major Cup Competitions

Rd.	Date	Opposition	Venue	Score	H.T.	Res.	Att.	Goalscorers
			F.A.Cup					
R1	26 Nov	Leyton Orient	(A)	2-0	(1-0)	W	17632	Wakefield(2)
R2	10 Dec	Wrexham	(A)	2-2	(1-0)	D	12435	Wakefield(2)
R2r	14	Wrexham	(H)	2-0	(1-0)	W	11153	Wakefield,Clough
R3	7 Jan	Blackpool	(A)	0-4	(0-2)	L	24532	

	1	2	3	4	5	6	7	8	9	10	11
	Hankey	Loughran	Walton	Wallbanks	Sheard	French	Jones	McAlinden	Wakefield	Morris	Clough
	Hankey	Loughran	Walton	Wallbanks	Sheard	French	Jones	McAlinden	Wakefield	Harris	Tippett
	Hankey	Loughran	Walton	Wallbanks	Sheard	French	Jones	McAlinden	Wakefield	Harris	Clough
	Hankey	Loughran	Walton	Wallbanks	Sheard	French	Jones	McAlinden	Wakefield	Morris	Clough

(Back) Copping (Trainer) Wallbanks, Lindsay, Hankey, Walton, French, Sheard.
(Front) L.Jones, Wakefield, McAlinden, Morris, Clough.

Appearances and Goals

	Appearances			Goals		
Name	Lge.	FAC	Total	Lge.	FAC	Total
BROWN, Ernie	2		2			
BUTLER, Ernie	2		2			
CLOUGH, James	34	3	37	7	1	8
DAVIES, Reg	14		14	6		6
FRENCH, Jack	40	4	44	1		1
GAWLER, Ron	7		7	1		1
GRANT, Cyril	4		4	1		1
GRAY, Harry	10		10			
HANKEY, Ted	31	4	35			
HARRIS, ?	0	2	2			
HORSFALL, George	1		1			
JONES, Les	29	4	33			
LAWLER, Jimmy	14		14	4		4
LINDSAY, David	24		24	1		1
LOUGHRAN, Joe	18	4	22	1		1
MORRIS, Freddie	20	2	22	11		11
McALINDEN, Jimmy	38	4	42	1		1
NASH, Paddy	11		11			
PRITCHARD, Harvey	3		3			
SHEARD, Frank	37	4	41	1		1
STUBBS, Les	7		7	3		3
THORNHILL, Dennis	5		5			
TIPPETT, Tommy	7	1	8	2		2
WAKEFIELD, Albert	38	4	42	23	5	28
WALLBANKS, Choppy	25	4	29	2		2
WALTON, Frank	41	4	45			
Own Goals				1		1

	Ps	P	W	D	L	F	A	W	D	L	F	A	Pts.
1949/50	3	42	15	4	2	43	15	4	9	8	23	33	51

Season 1950/51 – League Division Three South

No.	Date	Opposition	Venue	Score	H.T.	Res.	Att.	Goalscorers	1	2	3	4	5	6	7	8	9	10	11
1	19 Aug	Watford	(H)	5-1	(2-0)	W	18000	Davies(2),Wakefield(2),Lawler	Coombs	Loughran	Walton	Wallbanks	Sheard	French	Sibley	Davies	Wakefield	Lawler	Harper
2	21	Millwall	(A)	1-1	(0-1)	D	27989	Wakefield	Coombs	Loughran	Walton	Wallbanks	Sheard	French	Sibley	Davies	Wakefield	Lawler	Harper
3	26	Walsall	(A)	2-1	(2-0)	W	11178	Wakefield,Lawler	Coombs	Loughran	Walton	Wallbanks	Sheard	French	Sibley	Stubbs	Wakefield	Lawler	Harper
4	29	Millwall	(H)	0-3	(0-2)	L	20000		Coombs	Loughran	Walton	Wallbanks	Sheard	French	Davies	Stubbs	Wakefield	Lawler	Harper
5	2 Sep	Leyton Orient	(H)	0-1	(0-0)	L	18000		Coombs	Loughran	Walton	Wallbanks	Sheard	Lawler	Stubbs	Butter	Wakefield	Davies	Harper
6	6	Aldershot	(A)	2-2	(0-2)	D	6500	Wakefield,Stubbs	Coombs	Loughran	Anderson	Wallbanks	Woodward	Lawler	Stubbs	Davies	Wakefield	French	Davies
7	9	Ipswich Town	(A)	0-1	(0-1)	L	12955		Coombs	Loughran	Walton	Wallbanks	Woodward	Lawler	Sibley	Davies	Wakefield	French	Tippett
8	12	Aldershot	(H)	4-2	(3-0)	W	9800	Davies(2),French,Wakefield	Coombs	Loughran	Walton	Wallbanks	Woodward	Lawler	Sibley	Davies	Wakefield	French	Tippett
9	16	Plymouth Argyle	(H)	1-0	(0-0)	W	14000	Tippett	Coombs	Loughran	Walton	Wallbanks	Woodward	Lawler	Sibley	Davies	Wakefield	French	Tippett
10	23	Reading	(H)	2-0	(1-0)	W	14744	Wakefield(2)	Coombs	Loughran	Walton	Wallbanks	Woodward	Lawler	Sibley	Davies	Wakefield	French	Tippett
11	30	Torquay United	(H)	3-0	(1-0)	W	12500	Wakefield(2),Sibley	Coombs	Loughran	Walton	Wallbanks	Woodward	Lawler	Sibley	Davies	Wakefield	French	Tippett
12	7 Oct	Swindon Town	(A)	1-4	(0-1)	L	12623	Kaye(O.G.)	Coombs	Loughran	Walton	Wallbanks	Woodward	Lawler	Sibley	Davies	Wakefield	French	Tippett
13	14	Colchester United	(H)	4-2	(2-0)	W	21000	Davies(2),Wakefield(2)	Coombs	Loughran	Walton	French	Woodward	Lawler	Sibley	McAlinden	Wakefield	Stubbs	Davies
14	21	Bristol Rovers	(A)	1-4	(1-1)	L	19614	Sibley	Coombs	Loughran	Walton	French	Woodward	Lawler	Sibley	McAlinden	Wakefield	Stubbs	Davies
15	28	Crystal Palace	(H)	5-2	(3-1)	W	11500	Grant(2),Wakefield,Davies,Murphy(O.G.)	Coombs	Loughran	Walton	French	Woodward	Lawler	Sibley	McAlinden	Wakefield	Grant	Davies
16	4 Nov	Brighton	(A)	1-2	(1-0)	L	11283	Grant	Nash	Loughran	Walton	Woods	Woodward	Lawler	Butter	McAlinden	Wakefield	McAlinden	Davies
17	11	Newport County	(H)	3-0	(1-0)	W	10000	Butter,Davies,Woods	Nash	Loughran	Walton	Woods	Woodward	Lawler	Butter	Grant	Wakefield	Grant	Davies
18	18	Norwich City	(A)	0-3	(0-3)	L	24328		Nash	Loughran	Walton	French	Gawler	Lawler	Butter	McAlinden	Wakefield	Davies	Tippett
19	2 Dec	Port Vale	(H)	1-3	(1-2)	L	8400	McAlinden	Coombs	Loughran	Anderson	French	Stirling	Lawler	Butter	McAlinden	Wakefield	Stubbs	Tippett
20	16	Watford	(A)	3-1	(2-1)	W	5646	Stubbs(2),Tippett	Scannell	Loughran	Anderson	French	Stirling	Lawler	Sibley	McAlinden	Wakefield	Stubbs	Tippett
21	23	Walsall	(H)	0-1	(0-0)	L	8000		Scannell	Loughran	Anderson	French	Stirling	Lawler	Sibley	McAlinden	Wakefield	Stubbs	Tippett
22	25	Bournemouth	(H)	6-1	(4-1)	W	12000	Wakefield(2),Stubbs(2),Sibley,Tippett	Scannell	Lindsay	Anderson	French	Stirling	Lawler	Sibley	McAlinden	Wakefield	Stubbs	Tippett
23	25	Bournemouth	(A)	1-3	(1-2)	L	14366	Stubbs	Scannell	Lindsay	Anderson	French	Stirling	Lawler	Sibley	Davies	Wakefield	Stubbs	Tippett
24	30	Leyton Orient	(A)	1-1	(1-1)	D	9000	French	Scannell	Pritchard	Anderson	French	Stirling	Lawler	Lockhart	McAlinden	Wakefield	Stubbs	Tippett
25	30	Ipswich Town	(H)	1-0	(1-0)	W	8000	Stubbs	Scannell	Loughran	Anderson	French	Stirling	Wallbanks	Sibley	McAlinden	Grant	Stubbs	Tippett
26	13 Jan	Bristol City	(A)	3-0	(2-0)	W	6719	Stubbs(2),Tippett	Scannell	Loughran	Anderson	French	Stirling	Lawler	Sibley	McAlinden	Grant	Stubbs	Tippett
27	17	Plymouth Argyle	(A)	0-2	(0-1)	L	14187		Scannell	Anderson	Walton	Walton	Stirling	Wallbanks	Lockhart	McAlinden	Grant	Stubbs	Tippett
28	20	Bristol City	(H)	1-1	(1-0)	D	5500	Sibley	Scannell	Loughran	Anderson	French	Stirling	Lawler	Sibley	McAlinden	Grant	Stubbs	Davies
29	31	Reading	(A)	3-3	(2-0)	D	6900	Grant(2),Stubbs	Scannell	Pritchard	Anderson	French	Stirling	Lawler	Sibley	McAlinden	Grant	Stubbs	Davies
30	3 Feb	Northampton Town	(H)	3-0	(2-0)	W	11000	McAlinden,Grant,Stubbs	Coombs	Loughran	Anderson	French	Stirling	Lawler	Sibley	McAlinden	Grant	Stubbs	Davies
31	10	Torquay United	(A)	2-2	(1-1)	D	6000	Grant,Lawler	Scannell	Loughran	Anderson	French	Stirling	Lawler	Sibley	McAlinden	Grant	Stubbs	Davies
32	17	Swindon Town	(H)	8-2	(5-2)	W	10000	Tippett(3),Davies(2),Grant(2),Lawler	Scannell	Loughran	Anderson	French	Stirling	Lawler	Sibley	McAlinden	Grant	Davies	Tippett
33	24	Colchester United	(A)	3-1	(0-1)	W	12360	Tippett(2),Stubbs	Scannell	Loughran	Anderson	French	Stirling	Lawler	Sibley	McAlinden	Grant	Stubbs	Tippett
34	3 Mar	Bristol Rovers	(H)	1-1	(1-1)	D	12000	Stubbs	Scannell	Loughran	Anderson	French	Stirling	Lawler	Sibley	McAlinden	Grant	Stubbs	Tippett
35	10	Crystal Palace	(A)	2-0	(1-0)	W	12898	Grant,Stubbs	Scannell	Loughran	Anderson	French	Stirling	Lawler	Sibley	McAlinden	Grant	Stubbs	Tippett
36	17	Gillingham	(A)	0-0	(0-0)	D	15000		Scannell	Loughran	Anderson	French	Stirling	Lawler	Sibley	McAlinden	Grant	Stubbs	Tippett
37	23	Brighton	(H)	3-1	(2-0)	W	7500	Stubbs(2),Tippett	Scannell	Loughran	Anderson	French	Stirling	Lawler	Sibley	McAlinden	Grant	Stubbs	Tippett
38	24	Gillingham	(H)	4-0	(1-0)	W	14500	Davies(2),Tippett,Stubbs	Scannell	Loughran	Anderson	French	Stirling	Lawler	Sibley	Davies	Grant	Stubbs	Tippett
39	26	Newport County	(A)	1-6	(1-3)	L	12000	Tippett	Scannell	Loughran	Anderson	French	Stirling	Lawler	Sibley	McAlinden	Grant	Stubbs	Tippett
40	31	Norwich City	(H)	0-2	(0-0)	L	18000		Scannell	Loughran	Anderson	French	Stirling	Lawler	Sibley	Davies	Stubbs	McAlinden	Tippett
41	7 Apr	Nottingham Forest	(H)	3-2	(2-0)	W	12500	Grant,French,Anderson	Coombs	Loughran	Anderson	French	Stirling	Lawler	Sibley	McAlinden	Grant	Stubbs	Tippett
42	14	Northampton Town	(A)	1-1	(0-1)	D	6000	Sibley	Coombs	Loughran	Anderson	French	Stirling	Lawler	Sibley	McAlinden	Grant	Stubbs	Tippett
43	18	Exeter City	(A)	0-1	(0-1)	L	6500		Coombs	Loughran	Anderson	French	Stirling	Lawler	Sibley	McAlinden	Grant	Stubbs	Tippett
44	21	Port Vale	(H)	1-1	(1-0)	D	8554	French	Scannell	Loughran	Anderson	French	Sheard	Lawler	Sibley	McAlinden	Grant	Stubbs	Tippett
45	28	Nottingham Forest	(A)	0-3	(0-1)	L	17596		Scannell	Loughran	Anderson	French	Sheard	Lawler	Sibley	McAlinden	Grant	Stubbs	Tippett
46	5 May	Exeter City	(H)	5-1	(1-1)	W	10850	Stubbs(2),French,Grant,Warren(O.G.)	Scannell	Loughran	Anderson	French	Stirling	Lawler	Sibley	McAlinden	Grant	Stubbs	Tippett

Major Cup Competitions

Rd.	Date	Opposition	Venue	Score	H.T.	Res.	Att.	Goalscorers
				F.A.Cup				
R1	29 Nov	Swindon Town	(H)	0-3	(0-0)	L	10000	

1	2	3	4	5	6	7	8	9	10	11
Nash	Loughran	Walton	French	Woodward	Lawler	Butler	McAlinden	Wakefield	Grant	Davies

(Back) Tippett, Woods, Acton, Nash, Scannell, Coombs, Gawler, Thornhill, Woodward.
(Middle) Copping (Trainer), Anderson, Stubbs, Grant, French, Sheard, Walton, Lindsay, Gray, Pritchard, Robinson (Trainer). (Front) Sibley, Davies, Wallbanks, Wakefield, Lawler, Harper, Butler, Bridge.

SOUTHEND UNITED F.C. 1950-51

Appearances and Goals

Name	Appearances Lge.	FAC	Total	Goals Lge.	FAC	Total
ANDERSON, Sandy	30		30	1		1
BUTLER, Ernie	5	1	6	1		1
COOMBS, Frank	20		20			
DAVIES, Reg	27	1	28	12		12
FRENCH, Jack	42	1	43	5		5
GAWLER, Ron	1		1			
GRANT, Cyril	25	1	26	12		12
HARPER, Robert	6		6			
LAWLER, Jimmy	44	1	45	4		4
LINDSAY, David	2		2			
LOCKHART, Crighton	2		2			
LOUGHRAN, Joe	41	1	42			
McALINDEN, Jimmy	31	1	32	2		2
NASH, Paddy	3	1	4			
PRITCHARD, Harvey	2		2			
SCANNELL, Tommy	23		23			
SHEARD, Frank	8		8			
SIBLEY, Joe	39		39	5		5
STIRLING, Jimmy	26		26			
STUBBS, Les	31		31	19		19
TIPPETT, Tommy	30		30	12		12
WAKEFIELD, Albert	24	1	25	15		15
WALLBANKS, Choppy	14		14			
WALTON, Frank	17	1	18			
WOODS, Ray	2		2			
WOODWARD, Harry	11	1	12	1		1
Own Goals				3		3

Ps	P	W	D	L	F	A	W	D	L	F	A	Pts.
1950/51	7	46	15	4	4	64	27	6	6	11	28	42	52

Season 1951/52 – League Division Three South

No.	Date	Opposition	Venue	Score	H.T.	Res.	Att.	Goalscorers	No.	1	2	3	4	5	6	7	8	9	10	11
1	18 Aug	Ipswich Town	(A)	1-4	(1-4)	L	15828	Sibley	1	Scannell	Loughran	Anderson	French	Stirling	Lawler	Sibley	McAinden	Wakefield	Stubbs	Tippett
2	21	Port Vale	(H)	0-0	(0-0)	D	10000		2	Scannell	Loughran	Anderson	French	Stirling	Lawler	Sibley	McAinden	Grant	Stubbs	Tippett
3	25	Torquay United	(H)	2-2	(2-2)	D	10000	McAinden,Grant	3	Scannell	Loughran	Anderson	French	Stirling	Lawler	Sibley	McAinden	Grant	Stubbs	Tippett
4	27	Port Vale	(A)	0-0	(0-0)	D	10000		4	Scannell	Loughran	Anderson	French	Stirling	Lawler	Thompson	McAinden	Grant	Stubbs	Tippett
5	1 Sep	Gillingham	(A)	0-2	(0-2)	L	15000		5	Scannell	Loughran	Anderson	French	Stirling	Lawler	Sibley	McAinden	Grant	Grant	Thompson
6	8	Brighton	(H)	2-0	(1-0)	W	9500	Wakefield(2)	6	Scannell	Loughran	Anderson	French	Stirling	Lawler	Thompson	McAinden	Wakefield	Grant	Tippett
7	11	Northampton Town	(H)	2-0	(2-0)	W	8000	French,Grant	7	Scannell	Loughran	Anderson	French	Sheard	Lawler	Thompson	McAinden	Wakefield	Grant	Loukes
8	15	Millwall	(A)	0-2	(0-2)	L	17918		8	Scannell	Loughran	Anderson	French	Sheard	Lawler	Butter	Thompson	Wakefield	Grant	Loukes
9	20	Northampton Town	(A)	3-4	(3-1)	L	10395	Stubbs,Thompson,Lawler	9	Scannell	Loughran	Anderson	French	Stirling	Lawler	Thompson	McAinden	Stubbs	Grant	Butter
10	22	Bournemouth	(H)	1-0	(0-0)	W	11000	Stubbs	10	Scannell	Loughran	Anderson	French	Woodward	Lawler	Thompson	McAinden	Stubbs	Stubbs	Butter
11	29	Leyton Orient	(H)	1-0	(0-0)	W	11700	French	11	Scannell	Loughran	Anderson	French	Woodward	Lawler	Thompson	McAinden	Grant	Stubbs	Butter
12	6 Oct	Shrewsbury Town	(A)	1-0	(0-0)	W	11636	Grant	12	Scannell	Loughran	Anderson	French	Woodward	Lawler	Thompson	McAinden	Grant	Stubbs	Butter
13	13	Aldershot	(H)	7-1	(3-1)	W	11500	McAinden(2),1(pen),Grant(2),French,Sibley,Wfield	13	Scannell	Loughran	Anderson	French	Sheard	Lawler	Sibley	McAinden	Wakefield	Grant	Butter
14	20	Watford	(A)	0-0	(0-0)	D	13748		14	Heathcote	Loughran	Anderson	French	Sheard	Lawler	Sibley	McAinden	Wakefield	Grant	Butter
15	27	Bristol Rovers	(H)	2-1	(1-0)	W	12000	French(2)	15	Scannell	Loughran	Anderson	French	Sheard	Lawler	Sibley	McAinden	Wakefield	Grant	Butter
16	3 Nov	Plymouth Argyle	(A)	0-2	(0-1)	L	18000		16	Scannell	Loughran	Anderson	French	Sheard	Lawler	Sibley	McAinden	Wakefield	Grant	Butter
17	10	Norwich City	(H)	2-1	(0-1)	W	13000	Sibley,Grant	17	Scannell	Loughran	Anderson	French	Sheard	Lawler	Sibley	McAinden	Wakefield	Grant	Butter
18	17	Exeter City	(A)	2-2	(0-1)	D	7200	Wakefield(2)	18	Scannell	Loughran	Anderson	French	Sheard	Lawler	Sibley	McAinden	Wakefield	Grant	Butter
19	1 Dec	Crystal Palace	(H)	0-1	(0-1)	L	15940		19	Scannell	Loughran	Anderson	French	Sheard	Lawler	Sibley	McAinden	Wakefield	Grant	Stubbs
20	8	Swindon Town	(A)	2-2	(0-2)	D	9000	Grant,Stubbs	20	Scannell	Loughran	Anderson	French	Sheard	Lawler	Sibley	McAinden	Wakefield	Grant	Stubbs
21	22	Torquay United	(A)	3-1	(1-0)	W	6997	Wakefield(2),Grant	21	Scannell	Loughran	Anderson	French	Sheard	Lawler	Sibley	McAinden	Wakefield	Grant	Stubbs
22	25	Walsall	(A)	0-2	(0-0)	L	7484		22	Scannell	Pritchard	Anderson	French	Sheard	Lawler	Sibley	Grant	Wakefield	Thompson	Stubbs
23	26	Walsall	(H)	3-0	(1-0)	W	15000	Grant(2),Stubbs	23	Scannell	Loughran	Anderson	French	Sheard	Lawler	Sibley	McAinden	Wakefield	Grant	Stubbs
24	29	Gillingham	(A)	3-1	(3-1)	W	9000	Stubbs,Anderson,Wakefield	24	Scannell	Loughran	Anderson	French	Stirling	Lawler	Sibley	McAinden	Wakefield	Grant	Butter
25	5 Jan	Brighton	(H)	0-5	(0-3)	L	19400		25	Scannell	Loughran	Anderson	French	Stirling	Lawler	Sibley	McAinden	Wakefield	Grant	Stubbs
26	17	Newport County	(A)	0-3	(0-2)	L	4897		26	Scannell	Pritchard	Anderson	French	Stirling	Lawler	Sibley	Thompson	Grant	Butter	Stubbs
27	19	Millwall	(A)	0-1	(0-1)	L	9000		27	Heathcote	Loughran	Anderson	French	Stirling	Lawler	Sibley	McAinden	Grant	Thompson	Thompson
28	26	Bournemouth	(H)	1-2	(1-1)	L	10018	Sibley	28	Scannell	Loughran	Anderson	French	Sheard	Lawler	Sibley	McAinden	Wakefield	Grant	Stubbs
29	6 Feb	Bristol City	(A)	0-6	(0-2)	L	6912		29	Scannell	Pritchard	Anderson	French	Sheard	Lawler	Sibley	Thompson	Wakefield	Thompson	Stubbs
30	9	Leyton Orient	(A)	4-1	(2-1)	W	16900	Stubbs(2),Anderson,Sibley	30	Morton	Loughran	Anderson	French	Sheard	Lawler	Sibley	McAinden	Grant	Thompson	Stubbs
31	16	Shrewsbury Town	(H)	2-2	(2-0)	D	9500	Grant,French	31	Morton	Loughran	Anderson	French	Sheard	Lawler	Sibley	McAinden	Wakefield	Grant	Stubbs
32	27	Bristol City	(H)	5-1	(1-0)	W	5000	Sibley,Grant,French,Thompson,Stubbs	32	Morton	Loughran	Anderson	French	Sheard	Lawler	Sibley	McAinden	Grant	Thompson	Thompson
33	1 Mar	Aldershot	(A)	2-2	(1-1)	D	7500	Grant,Stubbs	33	Morton	Loughran	Anderson	French	Sheard	Lawler	Sibley	McAinden	Grant	Thompson	Stubbs
34	8	Watford	(H)	5-1	(5-0)	W	11000	McAinden,Sibley,Stubbs,Thompson,French	34	Morton	Loughran	Anderson	French	Sheard	Lawler	Sibley	McAinden	Grant	Thompson	Stubbs
35	15	Bristol Rovers	(A)	0-2	(0-1)	L	14519		35	Morton	Loughran	Anderson	French	Sheard	Lawler	Sibley	McAinden	Grant	Thompson	Stubbs
36	22	Plymouth Argyle	(H)	1-1	(1-0)	D	15000	Stubbs	36	Morton	Loughran	Anderson	French	Sheard	Lawler	Sibley	McAinden	Grant	Thompson	Stubbs
37	2 Apr	Norwich City	(A)	0-1	(0-1)	L	10903		37	Morton	Loughran	Anderson	French	Sheard	Lawler	Sibley	McAinden	Grant	Thompson	Stubbs
38	5	Exeter City	(H)	0-0	(0-0)	D	6000		38	Morton	Loughran	Anderson	French	Sheard	Lawler	Sibley	McAinden	Grant	Thompson	Stubbs
39	11	Reading	(H)	2-0	(1-0)	W	18000	Wakefield,Stubbs	39	Morton	Loughran	Anderson	French	Sheard	Lawler	Sibley	McAinden	Wakefield	Stubbs	Butter
40	12	Colchester United	(A)	0-1	(0-0)	L	11967		40	Morton	Loughran	Anderson	French	Sheard	Lawler	Sibley	McAinden	Wakefield	Stubbs	Butter
41	14	Reading	(A)	2-5	(0-3)	L	16245	Wakefield,Thompson	41	Morton	Loughran	Anderson	French	Sheard	Lawler	Sibley	McAinden	Wakefield	Stubbs	Thompson
42	19	Crystal Palace	(H)	4-0	(3-0)	W	11500	Grant(2),Lawler,Thompson	42	Morton	Loughran	Anderson	French	Sheard	Lawler	Sibley	McAinden	Wakefield	Grant	Thompson
43	22	Colchester United	(H)	3-2	(3-1)	W	7500	Wakefield(2),Grant	43	Morton	Loughran	Anderson	French	Sheard	Lawler	Sibley	McAinden	Wakefield	Grant	Thompson
44	26	Swindon Town	(A)	0-1	(0-0)	L	7469		44	Morton	Loughran	Anderson	Woods	Sheard	Lawler	Sibley	McAinden	Wakefield	Grant	Thompson
45	29	Ipswich Town	(H)	5-0	(2-0)	W	6500	Wakefield(2),Thompson,Sibley,Grant	45	Morton	Loughran	Anderson	French	Sheard	Lawler	Sibley	McAinden	Wakefield	Grant	Thompson
46	3 May	Newport County	(H)	2-1	(1-1)	W	7000	Wakefield,Stubbs	46	Morton	Loughran	Anderson	French	Sheard	Lawler	Sibley	McAinden	Wakefield	Grant	Stubbs

Abbrev.: Wfield = Wakefield.

Major Cup Competitions

F.A.Cup

Rd.	Date	Opposition	Venue Score	H.T.	Res.	Att.	Goalscorers	1	2	3	4	5	6	7	8	9	10	11
R1	24 Nov	Bournemouth	(H) 6-1	(2-0)	W	12581	Stubbs(2),Wakefield(2),French,Bird(O.G.)	Scannell	Loughran	Anderson	French	Sheard	Lawler	Sibley	McAlinden	Wakefield	Grant	Stubbs
R2	15 Dec	Oldham Athletic	(H) 5-0	(2-0)	W	13300	Wakefield(3),Grant,Stubbs	Scannell	Loughran	Anderson	French	Sheard	Lawler	Sibley	McAlinden	Wakefield	Grant	Stubbs
R3	12 Jan	Southampton	(H) 3-0	(1-0)	W	18920	Sibley,Stubbs,French	Scannell	Loughran	Pritchard	French	Stirling	Lawler	Sibley	McAlinden	Wakefield	Grant	Stubbs
R4	2 Feb	Bristol Rovers	(H) 2-1	(0-0)	W	22429	Stubbs,French	Scannell	Loughran	Anderson	French	Sheard	Lawler	Sibley	McAlinden	Wakefield	Grant	Stubbs
R5	23	Sheffield United	(H) 1-2	(1-0)	L	21887	Wakefield	Morton	Loughran	Anderson	French	Sheard	Lawler	Sibley	McAlinden	Wakefield	Grant	Stubbs

(SOUTHEND. UNITED. F.C. 1951-2.)
25 PLAYERS

(Back) Thornhill, Sheard, French, Woods, Heathcote, Scannell, Turnbull, Woodward, Tippett, Pritchard, Tirling, Andrews, Lockhart. (Front) Grant, Thompson, Wallbanks, Sibley, Butler, McAlinden, Wakefield, Lawler, Stubbs, Robertson. (Seated foreground) Anderson, Loukes.

Appearances and Goals

Name	Appearances Lge.	FAC	Total	Goals Lge.	FAC	Total
ANDERSON, Sandy	46	4	50	2		2
BUTLER, Ernie	15		15			
FRENCH, Jack	45	5	50	8	3	11
GRANT, Cyril	42	5	47	17	1	18
HEATHCOTE, Peter	2		2			
LAWLER, Jimmy	46	5	51	2		2
LOUGHRAN, Joe	43	5	48			
LOUKES, Gordon	2		2			
MORTON, Geoff	17	1	18			
McALINDEN, Jimmy	42	5	47	4		4
PRITCHARD, Harvey	3	1	4			
SCANNELL, Tommy	27	4	31			
SHEARD, Frank	33	4	37			
SIBLEY, Joe	38	5	43	8	1	9
STIRLING, Jimmy	10	1	11			
STUBBS, Les	31	5	36	13	5	18
THOMPSON, Dennis	27		27	6		6
TIPPETT, Tommy	5		5			
WAKEFIELD, Albert	28	5	33	15	6	21
WOODS, Ray	1		1			
WOODWARD, Harry	3		3			
Own Goals					1	1

	Ps	P	W	D	L	F	A	W	D	L	F	A	Pts.
1951/52	9	46	16	6	1	56	17	3	4	16	19	49	48

Season 1952/53 – League Division Three South

No.	Date	Opposition	Venue	Score	H.T.	Res.	Att.	Goalscorers	No.	1	2	3	4	5	6	7	8	9	10	11
1	23 Aug	Torquay United	(H)	3-1	(1-0)	W	8500	French,Wakefield,Sibley	1	Scannell	Loughran	Anderson	French	Sheard	Lawler	Sibley	McAlinden	Wakefield	Grant	Stubbs
2	27	Swindon Town	(A)	3-1	(1-1)	W	14276	Anderson(pen),Grant,Stubbs	2	Scannell	Loughran	Anderson	French	Sheard	Lawler	Sibley	McAlinden	Wakefield	Grant	Stubbs
3	30	Northampton Town	(A)	3-4	(1-1)	L	13928	Wakefield,Grant,Southam(O.G.)	3	Scannell	Loughran	Anderson	French	Sheard	Lawler	Sibley	McAlinden	Wakefield	Grant	Stubbs
4	2 Sep	Swindon Town	(H)	3-0	(2-0)	W	10500	Wakefield(2),Grant	4	Scannell	Loughran	Anderson	French	Sheard	Lawler	Sibley	McAlinden	Wakefield	Grant	Stubbs
5	6	Leyton Orient	(H)	1-0	(0-0)	W	14200	Stubbs	5	Scannell	Loughran	Anderson	French	Sheard	Lawler	Sibley	McAlinden	Wakefield	Grant	Stubbs
6	9	Brighton	(H)	1-2	(0-1)	L	13200	French	6	Scannell	Loughran	Anderson	French	Sheard	Lawler	Sibley	McAlinden	Wakefield	Grant	Stubbs
7	13	Ipswich Town	(A)	0-0	(0-0)	D	11200		7	Scannell	Loughran	Anderson	French	Sheard	Lawler	Sibley	McAlinden	Wakefield	Grant	Stubbs
8	17	Brighton	(A)	2-2	(1-1)	D	17000	Grant,Stubbs	8	Scannell	Loughran	Anderson	French	Sheard	Lawler	Sibley	McAlinden	Wakefield	Grant	Stubbs
9	20	Reading	(H)	3-1	(2-0)	W	15300	McAlinden(2),Wakefield	9	Scannell	Loughran	Anderson	French	Sheard	Lawler	Sibley	McAlinden	Wakefield	Grant	Stubbs
10	23	Millwall	(H)	2-1	(1-0)	W	14000	Sibley,Thompson	10	Scannell	Loughran	Anderson	French	Sheard	Lawler	Sibley	McAlinden	Wakefield	Grant	Thompson
11	27	Bournemouth	(A)	1-5	(1-2)	L	12819	Sibley	11	Scannell	Loughran	Anderson	French	Sheard	Lawler	Sibley	McAlinden	Wakefield	Grant	Thompson
12	30	Watford	(H)	1-0	(1-0)	W	6500	Thompson	12	Scannell	Loughran	Anderson	French	Sheard	Lawler	Sibley	McAlinden	Wakefield	Grant	Thompson
13	4 Oct	Queens Park Rangers	(A)	2-3	(0-2)	L	14675	Thompson,Stubbs	13	Scannell	Loughran	Anderson	French	Sheard	Lawler	Sibley	McAlinden	Grant	Stubbs	Stubbs
14	11	Aldershot	(H)	1-1	(0-1)	D	12500	Burns	14	Scannell	Loughran	Anderson	Burns	Sheard	Lawler	Sibley	McAlinden	Grant	French	Stubbs
15	18	Colchester United	(A)	3-3	(0-1)	D	10589	Marsden(2),Stubbs	15	Scannell	Loughran	Anderson	French	Sheard	Lawler	Sibley	McAlinden	Marsden	Burns	Stubbs
16	25	Norwich City	(H)	1-2	(1-2)	L	15500	Grant	16	Morton	Loughran	Anderson	Burns	Sheard	Lawler	Sibley	McAlinden	Marsden	Grant	Thompson
17	1 Nov	Coventry City	(A)	1-1	(1-1)	D	12623	Marsden	17	Morton	Loughran	Anderson	Burns	Sheard	Lawler	Sibley	McAlinden	Marsden	Wakefield	Mansfield
18	8	Exeter City	(H)	1-1	(1-0)	D	9500	Marsden	18	Morton	Loughran	Anderson	Burns	Sheard	Lawler	Sibley	McAlinden	Marsden	Wakefield	Mansfield
19	15	Bristol Rovers	(A)	1-2	(1-0)	L	20227	Grant	19	Morton	Loughran	Anderson	Burns	Sheard	Lawler	Sibley	Grant	Marsden	Thompson	Mansfield
20	29	Gillingham	(A)	1-1	(0-0)	D	11537	Mansfield	20	Morton	Loughran	Anderson	Burns	Sheard	Lawler	Sibley	McAlinden	Marsden	Grant	Mansfield
21	6 Dec	Walsall	(H)	2-1	(2-0)	W	8000	Sibley,Marsden	21	Morton	Loughran	Anderson	Burns	Stirling	Lawler	Sibley	McAlinden	Marsden	Wakefield	Mansfield
22	13	Shrewsbury Town	(A)	1-7	(0-1)	L	6095	Mansfield	22	Morton	Loughran	Anderson	Burns	Stirling	Lawler	Sibley	McAlinden	Marsden	Wakefield	Mansfield
23	20	Torquay United	(A)	2-4	(0-1)	L	6559	McAlinden,Thompson	23	Morton	Loughran	Duggins	Anderson	Stirling	Lawler	Sibley	McAlinden	Marsden	Thompson	Mansfield
24	26	Bristol City	(A)	0-5	(0-2)	L	30100		24	Scannell	Loughran	Duggins	O'Neil	Sheard	Lawler	Sibley	McAlinden	Marsden	Grant	Thompson
25	3 Jan	Northampton Town	(H)	3-1	(0-1)	W	7000	Sibley(2),Grant	25	Scannell	Loughran	Duggins	Burns	Stirling	Lawler	Sibley	McAlinden	Marsden	Grant	Thompson
26	10	Newport County	(A)	1-0	(0-0)	W	3000	Marsden	26	Scannell	Loughran	Duggins	Burns	Stirling	Lawler	Sibley	McAlinden	Marsden	Grant	Thompson
27	17	Leyton Orient	(A)	0-3	(0-0)	L	9178		27	Scannell	Loughran	Duggins	Burns	Sheard	Lawler	Sibley	McAlinden	Marsden	Grant	Thompson
28	24	Ipswich Town	(H)	2-0	(1-0)	W	6500	Mansfield,Sibley	28	Scannell	Loughran	Duggins	Burns	Stirling	Lawler	Sibley	McAlinden	Marsden	Grant	Mansfield
29	31	Newport County	(H)	1-0	(0-0)	W	6000	Stirling	29	Scannell	Loughran	Duggins	Burns	Stirling	Lawler	Sibley	McAlinden	Grant	Bridge	Mansfield
30	7 Feb	Reading	(A)	0-1	(0-0)	L	13197		30	Scannell	Loughran	Duggins	Burns	Stirling	Lawler	Sibley	McAlinden	Grant	Bridge	Mansfield
31	14	Bournemouth	(H)	0-0	(0-0)	D	6000		31	Scannell	Loughran	Duggins	Burns	Stirling	Lawler	Sibley	McAlinden	Wakefield	Grant	Bainbridge
32	21	Queens Park Rangers	(H)	2-0	(0-0)	W	12000	Sibley,O'Neil	32	Scannell	Loughran	Duggins	Burns	Stirling	O'Neil	Sibley	McAlinden	Wakefield	O'Neil	Bainbridge
33	28	Aldershot	(A)	1-1	(0-1)	D	6852	Lawler	33	Scannell	Loughran	Duggins	Burns	Sheard	Lawler	Sibley	McAlinden	Wakefield	O'Neil	Bainbridge
34	7 Mar	Colchester United	(H)	4-0	(2-0)	W	10250	Bainbridge(2),Grant,Thompson	34	Scannell	Loughran	Duggins	Burns	Stirling	O'Neil	Sibley	McAlinden	Grant	Thompson	Bainbridge
35	14	Norwich City	(A)	1-3	(1-1)	L	16890	O'Neil	35	Scannell	Loughran	Duggins	Burns	Stirling	Lawler	Sibley	Thompson	Grant	O'Neil	Bainbridge
36	21	Coventry City	(H)	1-0	(1-0)	W	10000	Burns	36	Scannell	Loughran	Duggins	Burns	Stirling	Bridge	Sibley	McAlinden	Grant	O'Neil	Bainbridge
37	28	Exeter City	(A)	2-0	(1-0)	W	7000	O'Neil,Grant	37	Scannell	Loughran	Duggins	Burns	Stirling	Bridge	Sibley	McAlinden	Grant	O'Neil	Bainbridge
38	3 Apr	Crystal Palace	(H)	2-2	(0-2)	D	13000	Burns,Grant	38	Scannell	Loughran	Duggins	Burns	Stirling	Bridge	Sibley	McAlinden	Grant	O'Neil	Bainbridge
39	4	Bristol Rovers	(H)	2-1	(1-0)	W	16000	Grant(2)	39	Scannell	Loughran	Duggins	Burns	Stirling	Bridge	Sibley	McAlinden	Grant	O'Neil	Bainbridge
40	6	Crystal Palace	(A)	0-0	(0-0)	D	12845		40	Scannell	Loughran	Duggins	Burns	Stirling	Bridge	Sibley	McAlinden	Grant	O'Neil	Bainbridge
41	11	Millwall	(A)	1-4	(1-4)	L	21564	O'Neil	41	Scannell	Loughran	Duggins	Burns	Stirling	Bridge	Sibley	McAlinden	Grant	O'Neil	Bainbridge
42	18	Gillingham	(H)	3-1	(2-0)	W	7390	O'Neil(2),Sibley	42	Scannell	Loughran	Duggins	Burns	Stirling	Bridge	Sibley	McAlinden	Grant	O'Neil	Bainbridge
43	23	Watford	(A)	1-1	(0-0)	D	10042	Sibley	43	Scannell	Loughran	Duggins	Burns	Stirling	Bridge	Sibley	McAlinden	Grant	O'Neil	Bainbridge
44	25	Walsall	(A)	1-1	(1-0)	D	5044	Bainbridge	44	Scannell	Loughran	Duggins	Burns	Stirling	Bridge	Sibley	McAlinden	Grant	O'Neil	Bainbridge
45	29	Bristol City	(H)	0-4	(0-2)	L	7500		45	Scannell	Lawer	Duggins	Burns	Stirling	Bridge	Sibley	McAlinden	Grant	Thompson	Bainbridge
46	2 May	Shrewsbury Town	(H)	2-2	(2-2)	D	3000	Grant,O'Neil	46	Scannell	Loughran	Duggins	Burns	Stirling	Bridge	Sibley	Thompson	Grant	O'Neil	Bainbridge

Major Cup Competitions

Rd.	Date	Opposition	Venue	Score	H.T.	Res.	Att.	Goalscorers
				F.A.Cup				
R1	22 Nov	Bath City	(A)	1-3	(1-1)	L	16000	Thompson

1	2	3	4	5	6	7	8	9	10	11
Morton	Loughran	Anderson	Burns	Sheard	Lawler	Sibley	McAlinden	Marsden	Grant	Thompson

SOUTHEND UNITED F.C 1952-53
29 PLAYERS

(Back) Warren (Manager), Woods, Wakefield, Grant, Sheard, Heathcote, Morton, Scannell, Wilson, Duggins, Woodward, Burns, Quanton, Kilworth, Copping (Coach). (Middle) Benson & Newitt (Dirs.), French, Thompson, Anderson, McAlinden, Hay (Chair), Lawler, Stubbs, Costello, Young, Smith & Bewes (Dirs.). (Front) Medlow, Loughran, Sibley, Foots, Beith, Hope, Harris, Oakley, Robins (Asst. Train.).

Appearances and Goals

Name	Appearances			Goals		
	Lge.	FAC	Total	Lge.	FAC	Total
ANDERSON, Sandy	23	1	24	1		1
BAINBRIDGE, Ken	16		16	3		3
BRIDGE, Jackie	13		13			
BURNS, Frank	30	1	31	3		3
DUGGINS, Eric	23		23			
FRENCH, Jack	16		16	2		2
GRANT, Cyril	38	1	39	13		13
LAWLER, Jimmy	35	1	36	1		1
LOUGHRAN, Joe	45	1	46			
MANSFIELD, Ron	8		8	3		3
MARSDEN, Eric	14	1	15	6		6
MORTON, Geoff	8	1	9			
McALINDEN, Jimmy	43	1	44	3		3
O'NEIL, Joe	16		16	7		7
SCANNELL, Tommy	38		38			
SHEARD, Frank	24	1	25			
SIBLEY, Joe	46	1	47	10		10
STIRLING, Jimmy	22		22	1		1
STUBBS, Les	14		14	5		5
THOMPSON, Dennis	15	1	16	5	1	6
WAKEFIELD, Albert	19		19	5		5
Own Goals				1		1

	Ps	P	W	D	L	F	A	W	D	L	F	A	Pts.
1952/53	8	46	15	5	3	41	21	3	8	12	28	53	49

Season 1953/54 – League Division Three South

No.	Date	Opposition	Venue	Score	H.T.	Res.	Att.	Goalscorers	No.	1	2	3	4	5	6	7	8	9	10	11
1	19 Aug	Norwich City	(A)	0-1	(0-1)	L	27523		1	Threadgold	Anderson	Duggins	Duthie	Pavitt	Lawler	Sibley	McAlinden	McDonald	Dicker	Bainbridge
2	22	Northampton Town	(H)	2-0	(2-0)	W	15000	Sibley(2)	2	Threadgold	Anderson	Duggins	Duthie	Pavitt	Lawler	Sibley	McAlinden	McDonald	Grant	Bainbridge
3	26	Reading	(A)	0-2	(0-0)	L	12538		3	Threadgold	Anderson	Duggins	Duthie	Pavitt	Lawler	Sibley	McAlinden	McDonald	Grant	Bainbridge
4	29	Gillingham	(H)	1-1	(0-0)	D	10905	Sibley	4	Threadgold	Young	Anderson	Burns	Pavitt	Bridge	Sibley	McAlinden	Lowder	O'Neil	Bainbridge
5	1 Sep	Reading	(H)	1-2	(1-1)	L	7661	O'Neil	5	Threadgold	Young	Anderson	Burns	Pavitt	Bridge	Sibley	McAlinden	Lowder	O'Neil	Dicker
6	5	Coventry City	(A)	0-1	(0-0)	L	13069		6	Threadgold	Young	Anderson	Burns	Pavitt	Bridge	Sibley	O'Neil	Lowder	Dicker	McDonald
7	9	Brighton	(A)	2-3	(1-1)	L	17790	Lowder,Dicker	7	Threadgold	Young	Anderson	Burns	Pavitt	Bridge	Sibley	O'Neil	Grant	Dicker	McDonald
8	12	Bournemouth	(H)	2-1	(2-0)	W	12000	Bainbridge,Grant	8	Threadgold	Anderson	Duggins	Duthie	Pavitt	Bridge	Sibley	McAlinden	Grant	Bainbridge	Lowder
9	15	Brighton	(H)	2-0	(1-0)	W	6980	Bainbridge,Grant	9	Scannell	Anderson	Duggins	Lawler	Pavitt	Bridge	Sibley	McAlinden	Grant	Bainbridge	Lowder
10	19	Ipswich Town	(A)	1-1	(0-0)	D	14479	Sibley	10	Threadgold	Young	Anderson	Lawler	Pavitt	Bridge	Sibley	McAlinden	Grant	Bainbridge	Lowder
11	23	Torquay United	(A)	1-1	(1-1)	D	6005	Grant	11	Threadgold	Young	Anderson	Lawler	Pavitt	Bridge	Sibley	McAlinden	Grant	Bainbridge	Lowder
12	26	Millwall	(H)	1-2	(1-2)	L	15000	Grant	12	Threadgold	Young	Anderson	Lawler	Pavitt	Bridge	Sibley	McAlinden	Grant	Bainbridge	Lowder
13	30	Torquay United	(H)	1-0	(1-0)	W	4700	Norman(O.G.)	13	Threadgold	Young	Anderson	Lawler	Pavitt	Bridge	Sibley	McAlinden	Grant	Bainbridge	Dicker
14	3 Oct	Leyton Orient	(A)	1-1	(0-1)	D	16986	Sibley	14	Threadgold	Young	Anderson	Lawler	Pavitt	Bridge	Sibley	McAlinden	Grant	Dicker	Bainbridge
15	10	Shrewsbury Town	(A)	1-2	(0-1)	L	9500	Bainbridge	15	Threadgold	Young	Anderson	Duthie	Pavitt	Burns	Sibley	McAlinden	Grant	Dicker	Bainbridge
16	17	Exeter City	(H)	0-1	(0-0)	L	7500		16	Threadgold	Young	Anderson	Duthie	Pavitt	Burns	Sibley	McAlinden	Grant	Thompson	Bainbridge
17	24	Newport County	(A)	2-3	(0-2)	L	6958	Bridge,O'Neil	17	Threadgold	Young	Anderson	Duthie	Pavitt	O'Neil	Lockhart	Grant	Lowder	Bridge	Thompson
18	31	Norwich City	(H)	5-2	(5-1)	W	10000	Lockhart(3),Grant,O'Neil	18	Threadgold	Young	Anderson	Pavitt	Stirling	Bridge	Lockhart	McAlinden	Grant	O'Neil	Lowder
19	7 Nov	Queens Park Rangers	(A)	0-1	(0-1)	L	9894		19	Threadgold	Young	Anderson	Pavitt	Stirling	Bridge	Lockhart	McAlinden	Grant	O'Neil	Lowder
20	14	Southampton	(A)	2-1	(1-0)	W	11000	Dicker,O'Neil	20	Threadgold	Young	McDonald	Pavitt	Stirling	Bridge	Sibley	McAlinden	Dicker	Bainbridge	Lowder
21	28	Crystal Palace	(H)	1-2	(1-2)	L	10500	Dicker	21	Threadgold	Young	McDonald	Pavitt	Stirling	Bridge	Sibley	McAlinden	Dicker	Bainbridge	Lowder
22	5 Dec	Bristol City	(A)	1-4	(1-2)	L	14342	Dicker	22	Threadgold	Young	Anderson	Pavitt	Stirling	Lawler	Lockhart	McAlinden	Grant	Dicker	Lowder
23	19	Northampton Town	(A)	0-5	(0-0)	L	9081		23	Threadgold	Young	Anderson	Lawler	Pavitt	Bridge	Lockhart	McAlinden	Grant	Thompson	Bainbridge
24	25	Watford	(A)	2-2	(1-0)	D	11292	Lockhart,Dicker	24	Threadgold	Young	Anderson	Duthie	Pavitt	Burns	Lockhart	Bridge	Lowder	Dicker	Bainbridge
25	26	Watford	(H)	3-0	(1-0)	W	10000	Lowder(2),Bainbridge	25	Scannell	Anderson	McDonald	Duthie	Pavitt	Burns	Lockhart	McAlinden	Lowder	Dicker	Bainbridge
26	2 Jan	Gillingham	(A)	1-3	(0-2)	L	7557	Dicker	26	Scannell	Anderson	McDonald	Duthie	Pavitt	Burns	Lockhart	McAlinden	Lowder	Dicker	Bainbridge
27	9	Swindon Town	(A)	0-3	(0-2)	L	8217		27	Scannell	Anderson	McDonald	Duthie	Pavitt	Burns	Lockhart	McAlinden	Lowder	Dicker	Bainbridge
28	16	Coventry City	(H)	2-2	(2-2)	D	6700	Dicker,Sibley	28	Threadgold	Young	Anderson	Duthie	Stirling	Burns	Sibley	McAlinden	Lowder	Dicker	McDonald
29	23	Bournemouth	(A)	1-0	(1-0)	W	9263	Duthie	29	Threadgold	Pavitt	Anderson	Duthie	Stirling	Burns	Sibley	McAlinden	Lowder	Dicker	McDonald
30	30	Swindon Town	(H)	3-1	(0-1)	W	4000	McDonald(2),Burns	30	Threadgold	Pavitt	Anderson	Duthie	Stirling	Burns	Sibley	McAlinden	Grant	Bainbridge	McDonald
31	6 Feb	Ipswich Town	(H)	3-1	(2-0)	W	7500	Bainbridge,Grant,Sibley	31	Threadgold	Pavitt	Anderson	Duthie	Stirling	Burns	Sibley	McAlinden	Grant	Bainbridge	McDonald
32	13	Millwall	(A)	1-2	(0-2)	L	13021	Bainbridge	32	Threadgold	Pavitt	Anderson	Duthie	Stirling	Burns	Sibley	McAlinden	Grant	Bainbridge	McDonald
33	24	Leyton Orient	(H)	2-1	(0-1)	W	4500	Bainbridge,McDonald	33	Threadgold	Pavitt	Anderson	Duthie	Stirling	Burns	Sibley	McAlinden	Grant	Bainbridge	McDonald
34	27	Shrewsbury Town	(H)	3-0	(1-0)	W	8110	Hollis,Bainbridge,McDonald	34	Threadgold	Pavitt	Anderson	Duthie	Stirling	Burns	Sibley	McAlinden	Hollis	Bainbridge	McDonald
35	6 Mar	Exeter City	(A)	1-1	(0-0)	D	8392	Sibley	35	Threadgold	Pavitt	Anderson	Duthie	Stirling	Burns	Sibley	McAlinden	Hollis	Bainbridge	McDonald
36	13	Colchester United	(H)	3-0	(3-0)	W	8100	Hollis(2),Bainbridge	36	Threadgold	Pavitt	Anderson	Duthie	Stirling	Burns	Sibley	McAlinden	Hollis	Bainbridge	McDonald
37	20	Crystal Palace	(A)	2-4	(2-3)	L	9275	McDonald,Bainbridge	37	Threadgold	Pavitt	Anderson	Duthie	Stirling	Burns	Sibley	McAlinden	Hollis	Bainbridge	McDonald
38	27	Queens Park Rangers	(H)	4-1	(2-1)	W	10000	Duthie,Bainbridge,McDonald,Hollis	38	Threadgold	Pavitt	Anderson	Duthie	Stirling	Burns	Sibley	McAlinden	Hollis	Bainbridge	McDonald
39	3 Apr	Southampton	(H)	5-3	(2-3)	W	13224	Hollis(2),Burns,Sibley,Duthie	39	Threadgold	Pavitt	Anderson	Duthie	Stirling	Burns	Sibley	Thompson	Hollis	Bainbridge	McDonald
40	10	Bristol City	(H)	0-1	(0-1)	L	10000		40	Threadgold	Pavitt	Anderson	Duthie	Stirling	Burns	Sibley	Thompson	Hollis	Bainbridge	McDonald
41	13	Aldershot	(H)	2-1	(1-1)	W	5000	Burns,Hollis	41	Threadgold	Pavitt	Anderson	Duthie	Stirling	Burns	Sibley	Thompson	Hollis	Bainbridge	McDonald
42	16	Walsall	(H)	3-1	(3-0)	W	8500	Hollis(3)	42	Threadgold	Pavitt	Anderson	Duthie	Stirling	Burns	Sibley	Thompson	Hollis	Bainbridge	McDonald
43	17	Aldershot	(A)	0-4	(0-2)	L	6687		43	Threadgold	Pavitt	Anderson	Duthie	Stirling	Burns	Sibley	Thompson	Hollis	Bainbridge	McDonald
44	19	Walsall	(A)	0-2	(0-1)	L	6987		44	Threadgold	Young	Anderson	Duthie	Stirling	Burns	Sibley	Thompson	Hollis	Bainbridge	McDonald
45	24	Newport County	(H)	0-1	(0-0)	L	5993		45	Threadgold	Pavitt	Anderson	Duthie	Stirling	Burns	Sibley	Grant	Hollis	Bridge	Bainbridge
46	29	Colchester United	(A)	1-0	(0-0)	W	6035	Bainbridge	46	Threadgold	Pavitt	Anderson	Duthie	Stirling	Burns	Lockhart	Grant	Hollis	Bridge	Bainbridge

Major Cup Competitions

Rd.	Date	Opposition	Venue	Score	H.T. Res.	Att.		Goalscorers
				F.A.Cup				
R1	21 Nov	Finchley	(A)	3-1	(2-1)	W	9000	O'Neil, Sibley, McAlinden
R2	12 Dec	Chesterfield	(H)	1-2	(0-0)	L	14000	Dicker

1	2	3	4	5	6	7	8	9	10	11
Threadgold	Young	Anderson	Pavitt	Stirling	Bridge	Sibley	McAlinden	Dicker	O'Neil	Lowder
Threadgold	Young	Anderson	Lawler	Pavitt	Bridge	Lockhart	McAlinden	Grant	Dicker	Bainbridge

SOUTHEND UNITED
Blue Shirts (White Collars and Cuffs); White Shorts.

RIGHT WING — LEFT WING

Threadgold

Anderson 2 — Duggins 3

Duthie 4 — Lawler 6

Sibley 7 — McAlinden 8 — Grant 10 — Bainbridge 11

Pavitt 5 — McDonald 9

REFEREE Mr. F. C. WILLIS

LINESMEN Mr. S. J. Dowse (Red Flag) — Mr. D. W. Markham (Yellow Flag)

Fowler 11 — Ramscar 10 — Edelston 8 — English 7

McLean 6 — Hughes 4

Paterson 3 — Marston 2

Walsh 5 — O'Donnell 9

Wood

LEFT WING — RIGHT WING

NORTHAMPTON TOWN

Line-ups from the match programme.

Appearances and Goals

Name	Appearances Lge	FAC	Total	Goals Lge	FAC	Total
ANDERSON, Sandy	45	2	47			
BAINBRIDGE, Ken	37	1	38	12		12
BRIDGE, Jackie	20	2	22	1		1
BURNS, Frank	29		29	3		3
DICKER, Leslie	16	2	18	7	1	8
DUGGINS, Eric	5		5			
DUTHIE, Jim	30		30	3		3
GRANT, Cyril	23	1	24	6		6
HOLLIS, Roy	13		13	10		10
LAWLER, Jimmy	11	1	12			
LOCKHART, Crichton	10	1	11	4		4
LOWDER, Thomas	21	1	22	3		3
McALINDEN, Jimmy	34	2	36		1	1
McDONALD, Jack	24		24	6		6
O'NEIL, Joe	8	1	9	4	1	5
PAVITT, Bill	45	2	47			
SCANNELL, Tommy	4		4			
SIBLEY, Joe	36	1	37	9	1	10
STIRLING, Jimmy	23	1	24			
THOMPSON, Dennis	9		9			
THREADGOLD, Harry	42	2	44			
YOUNG, Doug	21	2	23			
Own Goals				1		1

	Ps	P	W	D	L	F	A	W	D	L	F	A	Pts.
1953/54	16	46	15	2	6	46	22	3	5	15	23	49	43

Season 1954/55 – League Division Three South

No.	Date	Opposition	Venue	Score	H.T.	Res.	Att.	Goalscorers	No.	1	2	3	4	5	6	7	8	9	10	11
1	21 Aug	Shrewsbury Town	(H)	4-1	(3-1)	W	14000	Baron(2),Bainbridge,Hollis	1	Threadgold	Pavitt	Anderson A	Duthie	Stirling	Burns	Sibley	Anders'n W	Hollis	Baron	Bainbridge
2	24	Queens Park Rangers	(H)	2-2	(0-1)	D	10500	Baron(2)	2	Threadgold	Pavitt	Anderson A	Duthie	Stirling	Burns	Sibley	Anders'n W	Hollis	Baron	Bainbridge
3	28	Aldershot	(A)	0-1	(0-1)	L	7019		3	Threadgold	Pavitt	Anderson A	Duthie	Stirling	Burns	Sibley	Anders'n W	Hollis	Baron	Bainbridge
4	30	Queens Park Rangers	(A)	1-1	(0-1)	D	10904	Baron	4	Threadgold	Pavitt	Anderson A	Duthie	Stirling	Burns	Sibley	Anders'n W	Hollis	Baron	Bainbridge
5	4 Sep	Swindon Town	(H)	4-1	(1-1)	W	10500	Burns,Bainbridge,Hollis,Baron	5	Threadgold	Pavitt	Anderson A	Duthie	Stirling	Burns	Sibley	Anders'n W	Hollis	Baron	Bainbridge
6	7	Newport County	(H)	1-1	(0-1)	D	12000	Burns	6	Threadgold	Pavitt	Anderson A	Duthie	Howe	Burns	Sibley	Baron	Hollis	Bainbridge	McDonald
7	11	Crystal Palace	(A)	2-2	(2-0)	D	11418	Baron(2)	7	Threadgold	Pavitt	Anderson A	Duthie	Howe	Burns	Sibley	Anders'n W	Hollis	Baron	Bainbridge
8	16	Newport County	(A)	2-3	(0-2)	L	8050	Burns,Bainbridge	8	Threadgold	Pavitt	Anderson A	Duthie	Howe	Burns	Smith	Anders'n W	Hollis	Baron	Bainbridge
9	18	Northampton Town	(H)	4-1	(1-1)	W	10519	Hollis(2),Bainbridge(2)	9	Threadgold	Pavitt	Anderson A	Duthie	Howe	Burns	Smith	Anders'n W	Hollis	Baron	Bainbridge
10	21	Exeter City	(H)	0-0	(0-0)	D	12000		10	Threadgold	Pavitt	Anderson A	Duthie	Howe	Burns	Smith	Anders'n W	Hollis	Baron	Bainbridge
11	25	Watford	(H)	1-1	(0-1)	D	13724	Bainbridge	11	Threadgold	Pavitt	Anderson A	Duthie	Howe	Lawler	Smith	Whyte	Hollis	Baron	Bainbridge
12	29	Exeter City	(A)	1-2	(0-1)	L	7142	Bainbridge	12	Threadgold	Pavitt	Anderson A	Duthie	Howe	Lawler	Smith	Whyte	Hollis	Baron	Bainbridge
13	2 Oct	Bournemouth	(A)	2-2	(1-2)	D	12500	Baron,Burns	13	Threadgold	Pavitt	Anderson A	Burns	Howe	Lawler	Sibley	Whyte	Hollis	Baron	Bainbridge
14	9	Bristol City	(H)	3-2	(1-1)	W	18000	Burns,Bainbridge,Sibley	14	Threadgold	Pavitt	Anderson A	Burns	Howe	Lawler	Sibley	Bridge	Hollis	Baron	Bainbridge
15	16	Torquay United	(A)	1-4	(1-2)	L	7500	Hollis	15	Threadgold	Pavitt	Anderson A	Burns	Howe	Lawler	Sibley	Bridge	Hollis	Baron	Bainbridge
16	23	Brighton	(H)	4-0	(3-0)	W	11500	Burns,Bridge,Anders'n W,Hollis	16	Threadgold	Pavitt	Anderson A	Burns	Howe	Lawler	Sibley	Bridge	Hollis	Anders'n W	Bainbridge
17	30	Reading	(A)	1-1	(0-0)	D	9948	Bainbridge	17	Threadgold	Pavitt	Anderson A	Burns	Howe	Lawler	Sibley	Bridge	Hollis	Anders'n W	Bainbridge
18	6 Nov	Coventry City	(H)	1-0	(0-0)	W	11000	Bainbridge	18	Scannell	Pavitt	Anderson A	Burns	Howe	Lawler	Sibley	Bridge	Hollis	Baron	Dicker
19	13	Southampton	(A)	0-3	(0-1)	L	15965		19	Threadgold	Pavitt	Anderson A	Burns	Howe	Lawler	Sibley	Bridge	Hollis	Baron	Lockhart
20	27	Leyton Orient	(A)	1-5	(0-3)	L	16061	Burns	20	Threadgold	Pavitt	Anderson A	Burns	Howe	Lawler	Sibley	Bridge	Hollis	Baron	Lockhart
21	4 Dec	Gillingham	(H)	3-1	(1-1)	W	7500	Sibley(2),Hollis	21	Threadgold	Pavitt	Anderson A	Burns	Howe	Lawler	Sibley	Whyte	Hollis	Baron	Whyte
22	18	Shrewsbury Town	(H)	3-2	(2-1)	W	8000	Hollis(2),Baron	22	Threadgold	Pavitt	Anderson A	Burns	Howe	Lawler	Sibley	Whyte	Hollis	Baron	Barker
23	25	Norwich City	(H)	4-1	(2-1)	W	12000	Baron(3),Hollis	23	Threadgold	Pavitt	Anderson A	Burns	Howe	Lawler	Sibley	Whyte	Hollis	Baron	Bridge
24	27	Norwich City	(A)	3-3	(1-1)	D	21963	Hollis(3)	24	Threadgold	Pavitt	Anderson A	Burns	Howe	Lawler	Sibley	Whyte	Hollis	Baron	Bridge
25	1 Jan	Aldershot	(H)	0-1	(0-0)	L	7500		25	Threadgold	Pavitt	Anderson A	Burns	Howe	Lawler	Sibley	Whyte	Hollis	Baron	Bridge
26	22	Crystal Palace	(H)	3-2	(2-2)	W	5000	Hollis(2),Whyte	26	Threadgold	Pavitt	Anderson A	Burns	Howe	Lawler	Sibley	Whyte	Hollis	Baron	
27	29	Walsall	(H)	2-1	(0-1)	W	8000	Hollis(2)	27	Threadgold	Pavitt	Anderson A	Burns	Howe	Lawler	Sibley	Whyte	Hollis	Baron	
28	5 Feb	Northampton Town	(A)	2-6	(0-1)	L	7709	Hollis,Burns	28	Threadgold	Pavitt	Anderson A	Burns	Howe	Lawler	Sibley	Anders'n W	Hollis	Baron	
29	12	Watford	(A)	1-3	(0-2)	L	6188	Whyte	29	Threadgold	Pavitt	Anderson A	Burns	Howe	Lawler	Sibley	Bridge	Hollis	Baron	
30	19	Bournemouth	(H)	1-2	(0-0)	L	7086	Baron	30	Threadgold	Pavitt	Anderson A	Burns	Howe	Lawler	Sibley	Bridge	Hollis	Baron	
31	26	Bristol City	(A)	2-3	(2-1)	L	20616	Bridge,Hollis	31	Scannell	Pavitt	Anderson A	Burns	Howe	Lawler	Sibley	Duthie	Hollis	Baron	
32	5 Mar	Torquay United	(H)	1-2	(0-1)	L	4000	Hollis	32	Scannell	Pavitt	Young	Burns	Howe	Lawler	Sibley	Duthie	Hollis	Baron	
33	12	Brighton	(A)	1-2	(0-1)	L	9585	Whyte	33	Threadgold	Pavitt	Anderson A	Duthie	Howe	Duffy	Sibley	Baron	Hollis	Whyte	
34	19	Reading	(H)	0-0	(0-0)	D	7000		34	Threadgold	Pavitt	Anderson A	Duthie	Howe	Duffy	Sibley	Baron	Hollis	Whyte	McDonald
35	2 Apr	Southampton	(H)	0-1	(0-1)	L	10000		35	Threadgold	Young	Anderson A	Duthie	Howe	Duffy	Lockhart	Baron	Hollis	Whyte	McDonald
36	8	Colchester United	(A)	0-2		L	10809		36	Threadgold	Young	Anderson A	Duthie	Howe	Duffy	Lockhart	Baron	Hollis	Whyte	McDonald
37	9	Millwall	(A)	4-1	(2-1)	W	11399	Whyte,Grant,Hollis,Baron	37	Threadgold	Young	Anderson A	Duffy	Howe	Lawler	Whyte	Grant	Hollis	Baron	Barker
38	11	Colchester United	(H)	4-2		W	8478	Grant(2),Hollis(2)	38	Threadgold	Young	Anderson A	Duffy	Howe	Lawler	Whyte	Grant	Hollis	Baron	Barker
39	16	Leyton Orient	(H)	1-2	(1-1)	L	9013	Hollis	39	Threadgold	Young	Anderson A	Duffy	Howe	Lawler	Whyte	Grant	Hollis	Baron	Barker
40	20	Swindon Town	(H)	1-0	(0-0)	W	4230	Anderson A	40	Threadgold	Young	Anderson A	Bridge	Howe	Lawler	Whyte	Grant	Hollis	Baron	Barker
41	23	Gillingham	(A)	1-1	(0-0)	D	9830	Baron	41	Threadgold	Young	Anderson A	Duffy	Howe	Lawler	Whyte	Grant	Hollis	Baron	Barker
42	26	Millwall	(H)	1-0	(0-0)	W	6000	Hollis	42	Threadgold	Young	Anderson A	Duffy	Howe	Lawler	Whyte	Grant	Hollis	Baron	Barker
43	30	Brentford	(H)	3-2	(1-1)	W	8000	Anderson A,Hollis,Barker	43	Threadgold	Young	Anderson A	Duffy	Howe	Lawler	Barker	Grant	Hollis	Baron	Barker
44	2 May	Walsall	(A)	1-4		L	12856	Duthie	44	Scannell	Howe	Anderson A	Duthie	Stirling	Lawler	Sibley	Anders'n W	Hollis	Baron	Lockhart
45	4	Coventry City	(A)	4-1		W	7303	Lockhart(3),Hollis	45	Scannell	Duffy	Anderson A	Duthie	Stirling	Bridge	Sibley	Anders'n W	Hollis	Baron	Lockhart
46	5	Brentford	(A)	2-2	(1-1)	D	7000	Sibley,Baron	46	Scannell	Duffy	Anderson A	Duthie	Stirling	Bridge	Sibley	Anders'n W	Hollis	Baron	Lockhart

Abbrev.: Anders'n W = Anderson W

Major Cup Competitions

Rd.	Date	Opposition	Venue	Score	H.T.	Res.	Att.	Goalscorers	1	2	3	4	5	6	7	8	9	10	11
								F.A.Cup											
R1	20 Nov	Bristol City	(A)	2-1	(1-1)	W	20594	Hollis(2)	Threadgold	Pavitt	Anderson A	Burns	Howe	Lawler	Sibley	Bridge	Hollis	Baron	Bainbridge
R2	11 Dec	Bradford P.A.	(A)	3-2	(1-0)	W	12094	Hollis(3)	Threadgold	Pavitt	Anderson A	Burns	Howe	Lawler	Sibley	Whyte	Hollis	Baron	Bainbridge
R3	8 Jan	Everton	(A)	1-3	(1-2)	L	53043	Baron	Threadgold	Pavitt	Anderson A	Burns	Howe	Lawler	Sibley	Whyte	Hollis	Baron	Bainbridge

Appearances and Goals

Name	Appearances			Goals		
	Lge.	FAC	Total	Lge.	FAC	Total
ANDERSON, Sandy	45	3	48	2		2
ANDERSON, William	15		15	1		1
BAINBRIDGE, Ken	25	3	28	10		10
BARKER, Gordon	8		8	1		1
BARON, Kevin	44	3	47	17	1	18
BRIDGE, Jackie	16	1	17	2		2
BURNS, Frank	30	3	33	8		8
DICKER, Leslie	1		1			
DUFFY, John	12		12	1		1
DUTHIE, Jim	21		21	3		3
GRANT, Cyril	7		7			
HOLLIS, Roy	46	3	49	27	5	32
HOWE, Denis	38	3	41			
LAWLER, Jimmy	30	3	33			
LOCKHART, Crichton	8		8	3		3
McDONALD, Jack	4		4			
PAVITT, Bill	34	3	37			
SCANNELL, Tommy	6		6			
SIBLEY, Joe	32	3	35	4		4
SMITH, Herbert	5		5			
STIRLING, Jimmy	9		9			
THREADGOLD, Harry	40	3	43			
WHYTE, James	20	2	22	4		4
YOUNG, Doug	10		10			

	Ps	P	W	D	L	F	A	W	D	L	F	A	Pts.
1954/55	10	46	13	5	5	48	28	4	7	12	35	52	46

Season 1955/56 – League Division Three South

No.	Date	Opposition	Venue	Score	H.T.	Res.	Att.	Goalscorers	1	2	3	4	5	6	7	8	9	10	11
1	20 Aug	Norwich City	(H)	3-1	(1-0)	W	17700	McCrory,Hollis,Dowsett	Threadgold	Young	Anderson A	Duthie	Howe	Lawler	Dowsett	McCrory	Hollis	Baron	McGuigan
2	24	Reading	(H)	1-0	(0-0)	W	13261	McCrory	Threadgold	Young	Anderson A	Duthie	Howe	Lawler	Dowsett	McCrory	Hollis	Baron	McGuigan
3	27	Colchester United	(A)	6-3	(1-0)	W	8900	Hollis(4),Baron,McGuigan	Threadgold	Young	Anderson A	Duthie	Howe	Lawler	Dowsett	McCrory	Hollis	Baron	McGuigan
4	31	Reading	(A)	1-4	(1-1)	L	6553	Hollis	Threadgold	Young	Anderson A	Duthie	Howe	Lawler	Dowsett	McCrory	Hollis	Baron	McGuigan
5	3 Sep	Leyton Orient	(H)	0-0	(0-0)	D	21000		Threadgold	Young	Williamson	Duthie	Howe	Lawler	Dowsett	McCrory	Hollis	Baron	McGuigan
6	7	Bournemouth	(A)	1-4	(0-1)	L	9048	McCrory	Threadgold	Young	Williamson	Duthie	Howe	Lawler	Dowsett	McCrory	Hollis	Baron	McGuigan
7	10	Exeter City	(A)	1-0	(0-0)	W	9231	McGuigan	Threadgold	Young	Williamson	Duthie	Howe	Lawler	Dowsett	McCrory	Hollis	Baron	McGuigan
8	14	Bournemouth	(H)	4-1	(1-1)	W	10000	Hollis(3),McCrory	Threadgold	Williamson	May	Duthie	Howe	Lawler	Dowsett	McCrory	Hollis	Baron	McGuigan
9	17	Newport County	(H)	4-1	(1-1)	W	14000	Hollis(2),McGuigan,McCrory	Threadgold	Williamson	May	Duthie	Howe	Lawler	Dowsett	McCrory	Hollis	Baron	McGuigan
10	21	Millwall	(H)	3-1	(2-0)	W	9600	Dowsett,Baron,McCrory	Threadgold	Williamson	May	Duthie	Howe	Lawler	Dowsett	McCrory	Hollis	Baron	McGuigan
11	24	Coventry City	(H)	3-0	(1-0)	W	14000	Lawler,McCrory,Baron	Threadgold	Williamson	May	Duthie	Howe	Lawler	Dowsett	McCrory	Hollis	Baron	McGuigan
12	27	Watford	(A)	2-3	(1-1)	L	6000	Baron,McCrory	Threadgold	Williamson	May	Duthie	Howe	Lawler	Dowsett	McCrory	Hollis	Baron	McGuigan
13	1 Oct	Brentford	(A)	1-2	(0-0)	L	14300	Hollis	Threadgold	Williamson	May	Duthie	Howe	Lawler	Lockhart	McCrory	Hollis	Baron	McGuigan
14	8	Queens Park Rangers	(A)	2-1	(2-0)	W	11945	McCrory,Baron	Threadgold	Williamson	May	Duthie	Howe	Lawler	Whyte	McCrory	Hollis	Baron	McGuigan
15	15	Northampton Town	(H)	2-0	(1-0)	W	15009	Whyte,Hollis	Brewster	Williamson	May	Duthie	Howe	Lawler	Lockhart	McCrory	Hollis	Whyte	McGuigan
16	22	Aldershot	(A)	3-3	(2-2)	D	5697	Whyte,McCrory,Billington(O.G.)	Brewster	Williamson	May	Duthie	Howe	Lawler	Lockhart	McCrory	Hollis	Whyte	McGuigan
17	29	Crystal Palace	(H)	4-3	(3-1)	W	15000	Hollis(2),May,McCrory	Threadgold	Williamson	May	Duthie	Howe	Lawler	Lockhart	McCrory	Hollis	Whyte	McGuigan
18	5 Nov	Brighton	(A)	0-4	(0-2)	L	17708		Threadgold	Williamson	May	Duthie	Howe	Lawler	Barker	McCrory	Hollis	Baron	McGuigan
19	12	Southampton	(H)	2-1	(0-1)	W	14000	Baron,McGuigan	Threadgold	Williamson	May	Duthie	Howe	Lawler	Barker	McCrory	Hollis	Baron	McGuigan
20	26	Ipswich Town	(H)	2-3	(0-0)	L	13340	Hollis,Baron	Threadgold	Williamson	May	Duthie	Howe	Lawler	Barker	McCrory	Hollis	Baron	McGuigan
21	3 Dec	Walsall	(A)	1-3	(0-2)	L	11874	Baron	Threadgold	Williamson	May	Duthie	Howe	Lawler	Barker	McCrory	Hollis	Baron	McGuigan
22	17	Norwich City	(A)	2-7	(2-4)	L	11219	McGuigan(2)	Threadgold	Williamson	May	Duthie	Stirling	Lawler	Lockhart	McCrory	Hollis	Baron	McGuigan
23	24	Colchester United	(H)	4-0	(1-0)	W	8404	McGuigan(2),Baron;Hollis	Threadgold	Williamson	Anderson A	Duthie	Stirling	Lawler	Lockhart	McCrory	Hollis	Baron	McGuigan
24	26	Gillingham	(H)	2-2	(1-1)	D	9643	Baron,McCrory	Threadgold	Williamson	Anderson A	Duthie	Stirling	Lawler	Lockhart	McCrory	Hollis	Baron	McGuigan
25	27	Gillingham	(A)	3-2	(0-1)	W	10563	Hollis,McGuigan,Mansell(O.G.)	Threadgold	Howe	Anderson A	Duthie	Stirling	Lawler	Lockhart	McCrory	Anderson W	Baron	McGuigan
26	31	Leyton Orient	(A)	0-3	(0-2)	L	17760		Threadgold	Howe	Anderson A	Duthie	Stirling	Lawler	Lockhart	McCrory	Hollis	Baron	McGuigan
27	14 Jan	Exeter City	(H)	6-0	(1-0)	W	8033	Baron(2),Hollis,McCrory,Lockhart,Lawler	Threadgold	Williamson	Howe	Duthie	Stirling	Lawler	Lockhart	McCrory	Hollis	Baron	McGuigan
28	11 Feb	Brentford	(H)	2-2	(1-1)	D	5124	Baron,McCrory	Threadgold	Williamson	Howe	Duthie	Stirling	Lawler	Lockhart	McCrory	Hollis	Baron	McGuigan
29	18	Queens Park Rangers	(H)	5-1	(4-1)	W	5000	Lockhart(3),McGuigan(2)	Threadgold	Williamson	Howe	Duthie	Stirling	Lawler	Lockhart	McCrory	Hollis	Baron	McGuigan
30	25	Northampton Town	(A)	1-1	(1-0)	D	9535	Baron	Threadgold	Williamson	Howe	Duthie	Stirling	Lawler	Lockhart	McCrory	Hollis	Baron	McGuigan
31	3 Mar	Aldershot	(H)	3-2	(3-2)	W	7500	McGuigan,Hollis,McCrory	Threadgold	Williamson	Howe	Duthie	Stirling	Lawler	Lockhart	McCrory	Hollis	Baron	McGuigan
32	10	Crystal Palace	(A)	2-1	(1-0)	W	13092	McCrory(2)	Threadgold	Williamson	Howe	Duthie	Stirling	Lawler	Lockhart	McCrory	Hollis	Baron	McGuigan
33	17	Brighton	(H)	1-2	(0-1)	L	15000	Baron	Threadgold	Williamson	Howe	Duthie	Stirling	Lawler	Lockhart	McCrory	Hollis	Baron	McGuigan
34	19	Coventry City	(A)	0-0	(0-0)	D	12873		Threadgold	Williamson	Howe	Duthie	Stirling	Bridge	Whyte	McCrory	Hollis	Baron	McGuigan
35	24	Southampton	(A)	0-0	(0-0)	D	9329		Threadgold	Williamson	Howe	Duthie	Stirling	Bridge	Whyte	McCrory	Hollis	Barker	McGuigan
36	30	Swindon Town	(H)	0-0	(0-0)	D	12500		Threadgold	Williamson	Howe	Duthie	Stirling	Bridge	Whyte	McCrory	Hollis	Duffy	McGuigan
37	31	Shrewsbury Town	(H)	1-0	(1-0)	W	8500	Duffy	Threadgold	Williamson	Howe	Duthie	Stirling	Lawler	Whyte	McCrory	Hollis	Duffy	McGuigan
38	2 Apr	Swindon Town	(A)	1-1	(0-1)	D	8728	Dowsett	Threadgold	Williamson	Howe	Duthie	Stirling	Lawler	Barker	McCrory	Hollis	Dowsett	McGuigan
39	7	Ipswich Town	(A)	0-3	(0-2)	L	13484		Threadgold	Williamson	Howe	Duthie	Stirling	Lawler	Dowsett	McCrory	Hollis	Barker	McGuigan
40	14	Walsall	(H)	3-2	(2-0)	W	5488	Hollis(2),Barker	Threadgold	Williamson	Howe	Duthie	Stirling	Lawler	Dowsett	McCrory	Hollis	Barker	McGuigan
41	19	Newport County	(A)	0-2	(0-0)	L	4286		Threadgold	Williamson	May	Duthie	Stirling	Lawler	Dowsett	McCrory	Hollis	Barker	McGuigan
42	21	Torquay United	(A)	2-2	(2-1)	D	6070	Hollis,Dowsett	Threadgold	Williamson	May	Duthie	Stirling	Lawler	Dowsett	McCrory	Hollis	Barker	McGuigan
43	23	Shrewsbury Town	(A)	1-1	(0-0)	D	6560	McCrory	Threadgold	Williamson	May	Duthie	Stirling	Bridge	Dowsett	McCrory	Hollis	Barker	McGuigan
44	25	Watford	(H)	1-0	(0-0)	W	6500	Whyte	Threadgold	Williamson	Anderson A	Duthie	Stirling	Lawler	Dowsett	McCrory	Hollis	Whyte	McGuigan
45	28	Millwall	(A)	0-5	(0-1)	L	9213		Threadgold	Williamson	May	Duthie	Stirling	Lawler	Dowsett	McCrory	Hollis	Whyte	McGuigan
46	2 May	Torquay United	(H)	2-3	(1-1)	L	5870	McGuigan,Whyte	Threadgold	Williamson	Howe	Duthie	Stirling	Lawler	Sibley	McCrory	Hollis	Whyte	McGuigan

Major Cup Competitions

Rd.	Date	Opposition	Venue	Score	H.T.	Res.	Att.	Goalscorers
			F.A.Cup					
R1	19 Nov	Q.P.Rangers	(H)	2-0	(1-0)	W	15000	Barker,Hollis
R2	10 Dec	Weymouth	(A)	1-0	(0-0)	W	10000	Lockhart
R3	7 Jan	Lincoln City	(A)	3-2	(3-2)	W	11238	Hollis(2),McCrory
R4	28	Manchester City	(H)	0-1	(0-1)	L	29500	

	1	2	3	4	5	6	7	8	9	10	11
	Threadgold	Williamson	May	Duthie	Howe	Lawler	Barker	McCrory	Hollis	Baron	McGuigan
	Threadgold	Williamson	May	Duthie	Howe	Lawler	Lockhart	McCrory	Hollis	Baron	McGuigan
	Threadgold	Williamson	Howe	Duthie	Stirling	Lawler	Lockhart	McCrory	Hollis	Baron	McGuigan
	Threadgold	Williamson	Howe	Duthie	Stirling	Lawler	Lockhart	McCrory	Hollis	Baron	McGuigan

SOUTHEND UNITED F.C., 1955-56. Back Row (left to right): A. Anderson, H. Threadgold, J. Bridge, A. Phillips, A. Oakley. Middle Row: J. Lawler, F. Burnt, A. Williamson, J. Duthie, J. Duffy, D. Young, J. McGuigan, J. Stirling, D. Howe. Front Row: C. Lockhart, J. Sibley, W. Anderson, K. Baron, R. Hollis, R. Dowsett, J. Whyte. Absent: McGrory. C. Grant, F. Sheard, G. Barker, W. Brewster.

Appearances and Goals

Name	Appearances Lge.	FAC	Total	Goals Lge.	FAC	Total
ANDERSON, Sandy	9		9			
ANDERSON, William	1		1			
BARKER, Gordon	11	1	12	1	1	2
BARON, Kevin	30	4	34	15		15
BREWSTER, Bill	2		2			
BRIDGE, Jackie	4		4			
DOWSETT, Dickie	20		20	4		4
DUFFY, John	2		2	1		1
DUTHIE, Jim	46	4	50			
HOLLIS, Roy	45	4	49	23	3	26
HOWE, Dennis	38	4	42			
LAWLER, Jimmy	42	4	46	2		2
LOCKHART, Crichton	16	3	19	4	1	5
MAY, Harry	19	2	21	1		1
McCRORY, Sammy	46	4	50	18	1	19
McGUIGAN, John	46	4	50	13		13
SIBLEY, Joe	1		1			
STIRLING, Jimmy	25	2	27			
THREADGOLD, Harry	44	4	48			
WHYTE, James	12		12	4		4
WILLIAMSON, Arthur	40	4	44			
YOUNG, Doug	7		7			
Own Goals				2		2

	Ps	P	W	D	L	F	A	W	D	L	F	A	Pts.
1955/56	4	46	16	4	3	58	25	5	7	11	30	55	53

Season 1956/57 – League Division Three South

No.	Date	Opposition	Venue	Score	H.T.	Res.	Att.	Goalscorers	1	2	3	4	5	6	7	8	9	10	11	No.
1	18 Aug	Colchester United	(A)	2-3	(1-3)	L	11484	Duthie,Tulloch	Threadgold	Williamson	Howe	Duthie	Stirling	Lawler	Lockhart	McCrory	Hollis	Tulloch	McGuigan	1
2	22	Newport County	(H)	3-3	(1-2)	D	12000	McCrory,Lawler,Hollis	Threadgold	Williamson	Howe	Duthie	Stirling	Lawler	Lockhart	McCrory	Hollis	Tulloch	McGuigan	2
3	25	Norwich City	(H)	0-0	(0-0)	D	12500		Threadgold	Williamson	Howe	Duthie	Stirling	Lawler	Lockhart	McCrory	Hollis	Tulloch	McGuigan	3
4	30	Newport County	(A)	1-2	(0-0)	L	12224	McGuigan	Threadgold	Williamson	Howe	Duthie	Stirling	Lawler	Lockhart	McCrory	Hollis	Thomson	McGuigan	4
5	1 Sep	Coventry City	(A)	0-2	(0-0)	L	20365		Threadgold	Williamson	Howe	Duthie	Stirling	Lawler	Lockhart	French	Hollis	Thomson	McGuigan	5
6	5	Plymouth Argyle	(H)	0-1	(0-0)	L	8000		Threadgold	Williamson	Howe	Duthie	Stirling	Lawler	Lockhart	French	Hollis	Thomson	McGuigan	6
7	8	Southampton	(H)	1-2	(0-1)	L	12500	Tulloch	Threadgold	Williamson	Howe	Duthie	Stirling	French	Tulloch	McCrory	D'Arcy	Thomson	Duchart	7
8	10	Plymouth Argyle	(A)	0-2	(0-0)	L	14000		Threadgold	Williamson	Howe	Duthie	Ruark	French	Tulloch	McCrory	D'Arcy	Thomson	Duchart	8
9	15	Exeter City	(A)	1-6	(1-2)	L	9000	Duthie	Threadgold	Williamson	Howe	Duthie	Ruark	French	Tulloch	Whyte	Hollis	Thomson	Duchart	9
10	19	Reading	(H)	4-0	(2-0)	W	6500	Barker,Duthie,Hollis,Thomson	Threadgold	Williamson	Howe	Duthie	Ruark	Lawler	Barker	Tulloch	Hollis	Thomson	Duchart	10
11	22	Crystal Palace	(H)	1-1	(1-0)	D	14000	Duchart	Threadgold	Williamson	Howe	French	Ruark	Lawler	Barker	Tulloch	Hollis	Thomson	Duchart	11
12	26	Reading	(A)	2-3	(1-1)	L	10659	McGuigan,Tulloch	Threadgold	Williamson	Howe	Duthie	Ruark	Lawler	Barker	Tulloch	Hollis	McCrory	McGuigan	12
13	29	Brighton	(H)	3-1	(2-0)	W	12000	Hollis(2),Barker	Ronson	Williamson	Howe	Duthie	Ruark	Lawler	Barker	Tulloch	Hollis	McCrory	McGuigan	13
14	6 Oct	Swindon Town	(A)	2-3	(1-1)	L	7572	McGuigan,McCrory	Ronson	Williamson	Howe	Duthie	Ruark	Lawler	Barker	Tulloch	Hollis	McCrory	Duchart	14
15	13	Brentford	(H)	1-0	(1-0)	W	14000	Hollis	Threadgold	Williamson	Howe	Duthie	Ruark	Lawler	Lockhart	McCrory	Hollis	McGuigan	McGuigan	15
16	20	Aldershot	(A)	3-5	(3-4)	L	5000	Hollis(2),McCrory	Threadgold	Williamson	Howe	Duthie	Ruark	Lawler	Barker	McCrory	Hollis	McGuigan	McGuigan	16
17	27	Watford	(H)	2-0	(2-0)	W	10000	Duchart,McCrory	Threadgold	Williamson	Howe	Duthie	Stirling	Lawler	Barker	McCrory	Hollis	McGuigan	McGuigan	17
18	3 Nov	Shrewsbury Town	(A)	0-0	(0-0)	D	7978		Threadgold	Williamson	Howe	Duthie	Stirling	Lawler	Barker	McCrory	Hollis	McGuigan	Duchart	18
19	10	Walsall	(H)	2-0	(2-0)	W	8000	Thomson,McCrory	Threadgold	Williamson	Howe	Duthie	Stirling	Lawler	Barker	McCrory	Hollis	Thomson	McGuigan	19
20	24	Bournemouth	(H)	2-1	(1-1)	W	8000	Hollis,McGuigan	Threadgold	Williamson	Anderson	Duthie	Stirling	Lawler	Barker	McCrory	Hollis	Thomson	McGuigan	20
21	1 Dec	Torquay United	(A)	3-3	(0-1)	D	8000	Barker(2),McCrory	Threadgold	Williamson	Anderson	Duthie	Stirling	Lawler	Barker	McCrory	Hollis	Thomson	Lockhart	21
22	15	Colchester United	(H)	3-2	(2-0)	W	8100	Barker,Thomson,McGuigan	Threadgold	Williamson	Anderson	Duthie	Stirling	Lawler	Barker	McCrory	Hollis	Thomson	McGuigan	22
23	22	Norwich City	(A)	2-1	(2-0)	W	8945	Hollis,McCrory	Threadgold	Williamson	Anderson	Duthie	Stirling	Lawler	Barker	McCrory	Hollis	Thomson	McGuigan	23
24	25	Northampton Town	(A)	2-2	(0-0)	D	4156	McCrory,Barker	Threadgold	Williamson	Anderson	Duthie	Stirling	Lawler	Barker	McCrory	Hollis	Thomson	McGuigan	24
25	26	Northampton Town	(H)	0-1	(0-0)	L	11000		Threadgold	Williamson	Anderson	Duthie	Stirling	Lawler	Barker	McCrory	Hollis	Thomson	McGuigan	25
26	29	Coventry City	(H)	1-2	(0-2)	L	11000	Hollis	Threadgold	Williamson	Anderson	Duthie	Stirling	Lawler	Barker	McCrory	Hollis	Thomson	McGuigan	26
27	12 Jan	Southampton	(A)	2-1	(2-0)	W	18231	McGuigan,Thomson	Threadgold	Williamson	Anderson	Duthie	Stirling	Lawler	Barker	McCrory	Hollis	Thomson	McGuigan	27
28	19	Exeter City	(H)	2-0	(2-0)	W	9500	Baron,Hollis	Threadgold	Williamson	Anderson	Duthie	Stirling	Lawler	Barker	Baron	Hollis	Thomson	McGuigan	28
29	2 Feb	Crystal Palace	(A)	0-2	(0-0)	L	9545		Threadgold	Williamson	Anderson	Duthie	Stirling	Lawler	Barker	McCrory	Hollis	Thomson	McGuigan	29
30	9	Brighton	(A)	1-1	(0-0)	D	11179	McCrory	Threadgold	Williamson	Anderson	Duthie	Stirling	Lawler	Hollis	McCrory	Thomson	Baron	McGuigan	30
31	16	Swindon Town	(H)	1-0	(1-0)	W	8000	McCrory	Threadgold	Williamson	Anderson	Duthie	Stirling	Lawler	Hollis	McCrory	Thomson	Baron	McGuigan	31
32	2 Mar	Aldershot	(H)	2-4	(2-2)	L	8000	Hollis,McGuigan	Threadgold	Williamson	Anderson	Duthie	Stirling	Lawler	Hollis	McCrory	Thomson	Baron	McGuigan	32
33	9	Millwall	(A)	0-0	(0-0)	D	11441		Threadgold	Williamson	Anderson	Duthie	Stirling	Duffy	Barker	McCrory	Hollis	Thomson	McGuigan	33
34	12	Brentford	(A)	2-3	(1-1)	L	11950	McCrory,Hollis	Threadgold	Williamson	Anderson	Duthie	Stirling	Duffy	Barker	McCrory	Hollis	Thomson	McGuigan	34
35	16	Shrewsbury Town	(H)	1-2	(1-1)	L	8500	Thomson	Threadgold	Williamson	Anderson	Duthie	Stirling	Duffy	Lockhart	McCrory	Hollis	Thomson	McGuigan	35
36	23	Walsall	(A)	1-0	(0-0)	W	15312	Hollis	Threadgold	Williamson	Anderson	Duthie	Stirling	Duffy	Baron	McCrory	Hollis	Thomson	McGuigan	36
37	25	Queens Park Rangers	(A)	0-3	(0-2)	L	6371		Threadgold	Williamson	Anderson	Duthie	Stirling	Duffy	Baron	McCrory	Hollis	Baron	McGuigan	37
38	30	Ipswich Town	(H)	2-0	(1-0)	W	7500	Baron(2)	Threadgold	Williamson	Anderson	Duthie	Stirling	Duffy	Barker	McCrory	Hollis	Baron	McGuigan	38
39	6 Apr	Bournemouth	(A)	1-1	(0-1)	D	10777	McCrory	Threadgold	Williamson	Anderson	Duthie	Stirling	Duffy	Barker	McCrory	Hollis	Baron	McGuigan	39
40	13	Torquay United	(H)	2-0	(1-0)	W	8000	McCrory,McGuigan	Threadgold	Williamson	Anderson	Duthie	Stirling	Duffy	Barker	McCrory	Hollis	Baron	McGuigan	40
41	15	Queens Park Rangers	(H)	3-0	(0-0)	W	6000	McGuigan,McCrory,Baron	Ronson	Williamson	Anderson	Duthie	Stirling	Duffy	Barker	McCrory	Hollis	Baron	McGuigan	41
42	19	Gillingham	(A)	2-0	(1-0)	W	7589	Baron,Hollis	Threadgold	Williamson	Anderson	Duthie	Stirling	Duffy	Barker	McCrory	Hollis	Baron	McGuigan	42
43	20	Watford	(A)	1-1	(0-1)	D	7398	Williamson	Threadgold	Williamson	Anderson	Duthie	Stirling	Duffy	Thomson	McCrory	Hollis	Baron	McGuigan	43
44	22	Gillingham	(H)	5-0	(0-0)	W	10000	Hollis(2),Thomson(2),McCrory	Threadgold	Williamson	Anderson	Duthie	Stirling	Duffy	Thomson	McCrory	Hollis	Baron	McGuigan	44
45	27	Ipswich Town	(A)	3-3	(2-1)	D	20012	McGuigan,Baron,Hollis	Threadgold	Williamson	Anderson	Duthie	Stirling	Duffy	Thomson	McCrory	Hollis	Baron	McGuigan	45
46	1 May	Millwall	(H)	1-0	(0-0)	W	8000	Baron	Threadgold	Williamson	Anderson	Duthie	Stirling	Duffy	Barker	McCrory	Hollis	Baron	McGuigan	46

Major Cup Competitions

Rd.	Date	Opposition	Venue Score	H.T.	Res.	Att.	1	2	3	4	5	6	7	8	9	10	11	Goalscorers
		F.A.Cup																
R1	17 Nov	Colchester United	(A) 4-1	(1-1)	W	11280	Threadgold	Williamson	Anderson	Duthie	Stirling	Lawler	Lockhart	McCrory	Hollis	Thomson	McGuigan	McCrory(3),Hollis
R2	8 Dec	Hereford United	(A) 3-2	(0-1)	W	10838	Threadgold	Williamson	Anderson	Duthie	Stirling	Lawler	Barker	McCrory	Hollis	Thomson	McGuigan	Thomson(2),McGuigan
R3	5 Jan	Liverpool	(H) 2-1	(1-1)	W	18253	Threadgold	Williamson	Anderson	Duthie	Stirling	Lawler	Barker	McCrory	Hollis	Thomson	McGuigan	Duthie,Thomson
R4	26	Birmingham City	(H) 1-6	(0-4)	L	28964	Threadgold	Williamson	Anderson	Duthie	Stirling	Lawler	Barker	McCrory	Hollis	Thomson	McGuigan	Hollis

SOUTHEND UNITED 1st XI — September 5th, 1956

W. Dixon (Trainer), D. Howe, J. Thomson, A. Williamson, H. Threadgold, R. Hollis.
J. Stirling, C. Lockhart, J. French, J. Duthie (Captain), J. Lawler, J. McGuigan.

Appearances and Goals

Name	Appearances			Goals		
	Lge.	FAC	Total	Lge.	FAC	Total
ANDERSON, Sandy	27	4	31			
BARKER, Gordon	27	3	30	6		6
BARON, Kevin	15		15	7		7
D'ARCY, Thomas	2		2			
DUCHART, Alex	8		8	2		2
DUFFY, John	14		14			
DUTHIE, Jim	45	4	49	3	1	4
FRENCH, Jack	5		5			
HOLLIS, Roy	44	4	48	18	2	20
HOWE, Dennis	19		19			
LAWLER, Jimmy	30	4	34	1		1
LOCKHART, Crichton	9	1	10			
McCRORY, Sammy	40	4	44	15	3	18
McGUIGAN, John	41	4	45	10	1	11
RONSON, Brian	3		3			
RUARK, Tony	9		9			
STIRLING, Jimmy	37	4	41			
THOMSON, Jimmy	30	4	34	7	3	10
THREADGOLD, Harry	43	4	47			
TULLOCH, Ron	11		11	3		3
WHYTE, James	1		1			
WILLIAMSON, Arthur	46	4	50	1		1

	Ps	P	W	D	L	F	A	W	D	L	F	A	Pts.
1956/57	7	46	14	3	6	42	20	4	9	10	31	45	48

Season 1957/58 – League Division Three South

No.	Date	Opposition	Venue	Score	H.T.	Res.	Att.	Goalscorers	1	2	3	4	5	6	7	8	9	10	11
1	24 Aug	Exeter City	(A)	5-0	(2-0)	W	10000	Hollis(3),McCrory,McGuigan	Threadgold	Williamson	Howe	Duthie	Stirling	Duffy	Crossan	McCrory	Hollis	Baron	McGuigan
2	28	Norwich City	(H)	5-2	(4-1)	W	13911	McCrory(2),McGuigan,Hollis(pen),Duthie	Threadgold	Williamson	Howe	Duthie	Stirling	Duffy	Crossan	McCrory	Hollis	Baron	McGuigan
3	31	Queens Park Rangers	(H)	6-0	(2-0)	W	15883	Crossan(2),McCrory(2),Hollis,McGuigan	Threadgold	Williamson	Howe	Duthie	Stirling	Duffy	Crossan	McCrory	Hollis	Baron	McGuigan
4	4 Sep	Norwich City	(A)	2-0	(1-0)	W	21748	McCrory(2)	Threadgold	Williamson	Howe	Duthie	Stirling	Duffy	Crossan	McCrory	Hollis	Baron	McGuigan
5	7	Colchester United	(H)	3-1	(1-2)	L	18125	Crossan(2)	Threadgold	Williamson	Howe	Duthie	Stirling	Duffy	Crossan	McCrory	Hollis	Baron	McGuigan
6	11	Aldershot	(H)	1-2	(0-1)	L	10886	Hollis	Threadgold	Williamson	Howe	Smith	Stirling	Duffy	Crossan	McCrory	Hollis	Baron	McGuigan
7	14	Brighton	(A)	1-3	(0-0)	L	20390	Hollis	Threadgold	Williamson	Anderson	Smith	Stirling	Duffy	Crossan	McCrory	Hollis	Baron	McGuigan
8	18	Aldershot	(A)	2-0	(2-0)	W	4093	Hollis(2)	Threadgold	Williamson	Anderson	Smith	Stirling	Duffy	Barker	McCrory	Hollis	Baron	McGuigan
9	21	Southampton	(H)	3-2	(1-0)	W	14583	McCrory,Baron,McGuigan	Threadgold	Williamson	Anderson	Smith	Stirling	Duffy	D'Arcy	McCrory	Hollis	Baron	McGuigan
10	25	Swindon Town	(H)	2-3	(1-2)	L	8716	McCrory,Duffy	Threadgold	Williamson	Anderson	Duthie	Stirling	Duffy	D'Arcy	McCrory	Hollis	Baron	Barker
11	28	Newport County	(A)	0-1	(0-0)	L	8023		Threadgold	Williamson	Anderson	Duthie	Stirling	Duffy	Costello	McCrory	Hollis	Baron	Barker
12	2 Oct	Swindon Town	(A)	1-2	(1-1)	L	8035	McCrory	Threadgold	Williamson	Anderson	Duthie	Stirling	Smith	Crossan	McCrory	Hollis	Baron	McGuigan
13	5	Port Vale	(H)	1-1	(0-1)	D	11941	McCrory	Threadgold	Williamson	Anderson	Duthie	Stirling	Smith	Duffy	McCrory	Hollis	Baron	McGuigan
14	12	Bournemouth	(H)	1-2	(1-1)	L	12605	McGuigan	Threadgold	Williamson	Anderson	Duthie	Stirling	Duffy	Crossan	McCrory	Hollis	Baron	McGuigan
15	19	Walsall	(H)	4-1	(1-0)	W	10692	McCrory(3),Hollis	Threadgold	Williamson	Anderson	Duthie	Stirling	Smith	Crossan	McCrory	Hollis	Baron	McGuigan
16	26	Coventry City	(A)	0-1	(0-1)	L	13371		Threadgold	Williamson	Anderson	Smith	Stirling	Duffy	Crossan	McCrory	Hollis	Baron	McGuigan
17	2 Nov	Shrewsbury Town	(H)	5-1	(1-1)	W	10887	Hollis(2),Middleton,Anderson(pen),Baron	Threadgold	Williamson	Anderson	Costello	Stirling	Smith	Crossan	Baron	Hollis	Middleton	McGuigan
18	9	Reading	(A)	1-1	(0-0)	D	12998	Hollis	Threadgold	Williamson	Anderson	Costello	Stirling	Smith	Crossan	McCrory	Hollis	Middleton	McGuigan
19	23	Watford	(A)	1-1	(0-0)	D	7790	Costello	Threadgold	Williamson	Anderson	Costello	Stirling	Smith	Crossan	McCrory	Hollis	Middleton	McGuigan
20	30	Crystal Palace	(H)	1-1	(1-1)	D	10706	Crossan	Threadgold	Williamson	Anderson	Costello	Stirling	Smith	Crossan	Baron	Hollis	Baron	McGuigan
21	14 Dec	Brentford	(H)	0-0	(0-0)	D	7952		Ronson	Williamson	Anderson	Duthie	Stirling	Smith	Crossan	McCrory	Hollis	Middleton	McGuigan
22	21	Exeter City	(H)	2-0	(1-0)	W	7512	McCrory(2)	Ronson	Williamson	Anderson	Duthie	Stirling	Smith	Crossan	McCrory	Hollis	Baron	McGuigan
23	25	Millwall	(H)	2-0	(1-1)	W	9543	McCrory,Hollis	Threadgold	Williamson	Anderson	Duthie	Stirling	Smith	Crossan	McCrory	Hollis	Baron	McGuigan
24	26	Millwall	(A)	2-1	(1-0)	W	8193	McCrory,Crossan	Threadgold	Williamson	Anderson	Duthie	Stirling	Smith	Crossan	McCrory	Hollis	Baron	McGuigan
25	28	Queens Park Rangers	(A)	1-1	(0-0)	D	10072	Stirling	Threadgold	Williamson	Anderson	Duthie	Stirling	Smith	Barker	McCrory	Middleton	Baron	McGuigan
26	11 Jan	Colchester United	(A)	0-1	(0-0)	L	9357		Threadgold	Williamson	Anderson	Smith	Stirling	Duffy	Crossan	Price	Hollis	Baron	McGuigan
27	18	Brighton	(H)	0-2	(0-1)	L	11665		Threadgold	Williamson	Anderson	Duffy	Stirling	Smith	Crossan	McCrory	Hollis	Price	Barker
28	1 Feb	Southampton	(A)	2-2	(1-1)	D	15306	Price,McCrory	Threadgold	Williamson	Anderson	Morrison	Stirling	Smith	Crossan	McCrory	Hollis	Baron	Price
29	8	Newport County	(H)	1-1	(1-1)	D	10103	Costello	Threadgold	Williamson	Anderson	Morrison	Stirling	Smith	Crossan	McCrory	Hollis	Baron	Price
30	15	Port Vale	(H)	3-1	(3-1)	W	7642	McCrory(3)	Threadgold	Williamson	Anderson	Morrison	Stirling	Smith	Crossan	McCrory	Costello	Baron	Price
31	22	Bournemouth	(H)	2-0	(2-0)	W	11131	McCrory(2)	Threadgold	Williamson	Anderson	Morrison	Stirling	Smith	Crossan	McCrory	Costello	Baron	Price
32	1 Mar	Walsall	(H)	1-1	(1-1)	D	7658	Price	Threadgold	Williamson	Anderson	Morrison	Stirling	Smith	Crossan	McCrory	Costello	Baron	Price
33	8	Coventry City	(H)	5-1	(2-0)	W	9881	McGuigan(2),Price(2),Baron	Threadgold	Williamson	Anderson	Morrison	Stirling	Smith	Price	McCrory	Hollis	Baron	McGuigan
34	15	Shrewsbury Town	(A)	1-1	(0-1)	D	5527	Hollis	Threadgold	Williamson	Anderson	Morrison	Stirling	Smith	Price	Price	Hollis	Baron	McGuigan
35	22	Watford	(H)	2-1	(1-0)	W	9883	McGuigan(2)	Threadgold	Williamson	Anderson	Morrison	Stirling	Smith	Price	Price	Hollis	Baron	McGuigan
36	29	Brentford	(A)	2-4	(0-2)	L	12870	Morrison,McGuigan	Threadgold	Williamson	Anderson	Morrison	Stirling	Smith	Price	McCrory	Costello	Baron	McGuigan
37	4 Apr	Gillingham	(A)	0-2	(0-0)	L	7450		Threadgold	Williamson	Anderson	Morrison	Stirling	Smith	Price	McCrory	Hollis	Baron	McGuigan
38	5	Reading	(H)	2-1	(0-0)	W	10278	Hollis(2)	Threadgold	Williamson	Anderson	Morrison	Stirling	Smith	Crossan	Price	Hollis	Baron	McGuigan
39	7	Gillingham	(H)	2-0	(0-0)	W	12224	Baron,Hollis	Threadgold	Williamson	Anderson	Morrison	Stirling	Smith	Crossan	Price	Hollis	Baron	McGuigan
40	12	Crystal Palace	(A)	0-2	(0-2)	L	12843		Threadgold	Williamson	Anderson	Morrison	Stirling	Smith	Price	McCrory	Hollis	Baron	McGuigan
41	16	Plymouth Argyle	(H)	2-1	(0-1)	W	9828	Price,Morrison	Threadgold	Williamson	Anderson	Morrison	Stirling	Smith	Crossan	Price	Hollis	Baron	McGuigan
42	19	Torquay United	(H)	0-0	(0-0)	D	11691		Threadgold	Williamson	Anderson	Morrison	Stirling	Smith	Crossan	Price	Hollis	Baron	McGuigan
43	21	Plymouth Argyle	(A)	3-2	(1-1)	W	22416	Crossan,Morrison,Baron	Threadgold	Williamson	Anderson	Duthie	Stirling	Smith	Crossan	Price	Hollis	Baron	McGuigan
44	26	Northampton Town	(A)	3-1	(1-1)	W	10975	McCrory(2),McGuigan	Threadgold	Williamson	Anderson	Duthie	Stirling	Smith	Crossan	McCrory	Hollis	Baron	McGuigan
45	29	Torquay United	(A)	2-2	(1-1)	D	5635	Crossan,McCrory	Ronson	Williamson	Anderson	Duthie	Stirling	Smith	Crossan	McCrory	Price	Baron	McGuigan
46	2 May	Northampton Town	(H)	6-3	(0-2)	W	9391	McCrory(3),Price(2),Smith	Ronson	Williamson	Anderson	Morrison	Stirling	Smith	Crossan	McCrory	Price	Baron	McGuigan

Major Cup Competitions

Rd.	Date	Opposition	Venue	Score	H.T.	Res.	Att.	1	2	3	4	5	6	7	8	9	10	11	Goalscorers
		F.A.Cup																	
R1	16 Nov	Trowbridge Town	(A)	2-0	(1-0)	W	6063	Threadgold	Williamson	Anderson	Costello	Stirling	Smith	Crossan	McCrory	Hollis	Baron	McGuigan	Hollis(2)
R2	7 Dec	Torquay United	(A)	1-1	(0-1)	D	8638	Threadgold	Williamson	Anderson	Costello	Stirling	Smith	Crossan	McCrory	Hollis	Baron	McGuigan	McCrory
R2r	11	Torquay United	(H)	2-1	(0-0)	W	6090	Ronson	Williamson	Anderson	Costello	Stirling	Smith	Crossan	McCrory	Hollis	Baron	McGuigan	Hollis,McCrory
R3	4 Jan	Liverpool	(A)	1-1	(0-1)	D	43454	Threadgold	Williamson	Anderson	Duthie	Stirling	Smith	Crossan	McCrory	Hollis	Baron	McGuigan	McGuigan
R3r	8	Liverpool	(H)	2-3	(2-1)	L	16655	Threadgold	Williamson	Anderson	Duthie	Stirling	Smith	Crossan	McCrory	Hollis	Baron	McGuigan	McCrory,Molyneux(O.G.)

SOUTHEND UNITED F.C. 1957-58 PLAYERS

(Back) Swan, French, Smith, Threadgold, Ronson, Young, Duffy, Williamson, Anderson, Dixon (Trainer).
(Middle) Crossan, Baron, Riches, Howe, Perry (Manager), Duthie, Thomson, Wilson, Sterling.
(Front) McGuigan, McCrory, Costello, Hollis, D'Arcy.

Appearances and Goals

	Appearances			Goals			
Name	Lge.	FAC	Total	Lge.	FAC	Total	
ANDERSON, Sandy	40	5	45	1		1	
BARKER, Gordon	5		5				
BARON, Kevin	43	5	48	5		5	
COSTELLO, Lou	9	3	12	2		2	
CROSSAN, Errol	34	5	39	8		8	
D'ARCY, Thomas	2		2				
DUFFY, John	16		16	1		1	
DUTHIE, Jim	18	2	20	1		1	
HOLLIS, Roy	38	5	43	18	3	21	
HOWE, Dennis	6		6				
MIDDLETON, Ray	5		5	1		1	
MORRISON, Willie	17		17	3		3	
McCRORY, Sammy	38	5	43	30	3	33	
McGUIGAN, John	38	5	43	11	1	12	
PRICE, Duggie	21		21	7		7	
RONSON, Brian	4	1	5				
SMITH, Ray S	38	5	43				
STIRLING, Jimmy	46	5	51	1		1	
THREADGOLD, Harry	42	4	46	1		1	
WILLIAMSON, Arthur	46	5	51				
Own Goals					1	1	

	Ps	P	W	D	L	F	A	W	D	L	F	A	Pts.
1957/58	7	46	14	5	4	56	26	7	7	9	34	32	54

Season 1958/59 – League Division Three

No.	Date	Opposition	Venue	Score	H.T.	Res.	Att.	Goalscorers	No.	1	2	3	4	5	6	7	8	9	10	11
1	23 Aug	Bournemouth	(A)	4-1	(1-1)	W	14219	Hollis(2),Crossan,McCrory	1	Threadgold	Williamson	Anderson	Morrison	Stirling	Smith	Crossan	McCrory	Hollis	Baron	Punton
2	27	Reading	(H)	2-2	(1-1)	D	15479	Punton,Crossan	2	Threadgold	Williamson	Anderson	Morrison	Stirling	Smith	Crossan	McCrory	Hollis	Baron	Punton
3	30	Norwich City	(H)	1-0	(0-0)	W	15661	Crossan	3	Threadgold	Williamson	Anderson	Morrison	Stirling	Smith	Crossan	McCrory	Hollis	Baron	Punton
4	3 Sep	Reading	(A)	0-3	(0-2)	L	13605		4	Threadgold	Williamson	Anderson	Morrison	Stirling	Smith	Crossan	McCrory	Hollis	Price	Punton
5	6	Chesterfield	(A)	0-4	(0-2)	L	11057		5	Threadgold	Williamson	Anderson	Morrison	Stirling	Smith	Crossan	McCrory	Hollis	Price	Punton
6	10	Tranmere Rovers	(H)	1-3	(1-1)	L	11057	Price	6	Threadgold	Williamson	Anderson	Costello	Stirling	Duffy	Crossan	Price	Hollis	Cairns	Punton
7	13	Bury	(A)	3-2	(1-1)	W	11505	McCrory(2),Hollis	7	Threadgold	Williamson	Anderson	Costello	Stirling	Duffy	Price	McCrory	Hollis	Baron	Punton
8	15	Tranmee Rovers	(A)	1-1	(0-1)	D	12963	Hollis	8	Threadgold	Williamson	Anderson	Costello	Stirling	Duffy	Price	McCrory	Hollis	Baron	Punton
9	20	Queens Park Rangers	(H)	4-0	(1-0)	W	13534	Hollis,Baron,Price,Punton	9	Threadgold	Williamson	Anderson	Costello	Stirling	Duffy	Price	McCrory	Hollis	Baron	Punton
10	24	Colchester United	(H)	1-1	(0-0)	D	11471	Punton	10	Threadgold	Williamson	Anderson	Costello	Stirling	Duffy	Price	McCrory	Hollis	Thomson	Punton
11	27	Rochdale	(H)	1-1	(1-0)	D	5196	Hollis	11	Threadgold	Williamson	Anderson	Costello	Stirling	Duffy	Price	McCrory	Hollis	Thomson	Punton
12	29	Colchester United	(A)	1-0	(0-0)	W	6833	Thomson	12	Threadgold	Williamson	Anderson	Costello	Stirling	Duffy	Price	McCrory	Hollis	Thomson	Punton
13	4 Oct	Doncaster Rovers	(H)	5-0	(4-0)	W	11889	Hollis(2),Thomson(2),McCrory	13	Threadgold	Williamson	Anderson	Morrison	Costello	Duffy	Price	McCrory	Hollis	Thomson	Punton
14	8	Plymouth Argyle	(A)	1-3	(0-1)	L	25349	McCrory(pen)	14	Threadgold	Williamson	Anderson	Morrison	Costello	Duffy	Price	McCrory	Hollis	Thomson	Punton
15	11	Halifax Town	(H)	3-2	(1-0)	W	12307	McCrory(2),Price	15	Threadgold	Williamson	Anderson	Morrison	Costello	Duffy	Price	McCrory	Hollis	Thomson	Punton
16	17	Accrington Stanley	(A)	0-3	(0-1)	L	8113		16	Ronson	Williamson	Anderson	Morrison	Costello	Duffy	Price	McCrory	Hollis	Thomson	Punton
17	20	Stockport County	(A)	1-0	(1-0)	W	11900	McCrory	17	Ronson	Williamson	Anderson	Morrison	Costello	Duffy	Price	McCrory	Hollis	Thomson	Punton
18	25	Southampton	(A)	1-1	(1-1)	D	13289	Price	18	Ronson	Williamson	Anderson	Morrison	Costello	Duffy	Price	McCrory	Hollis	Thomson	Punton
19	1 Nov	Wrexham	(A)	1-3	(1-3)	L	13172	Punton	19	Ronson	Williamson	Anderson	Morrison	Costello	Duffy	Price	McCrory	Houghton	Thomson	Punton
20	8	Bradford City	(H)	1-1	(1-0)	D	14176	Hollis	20	Threadgold	Williamson	Anderson	Costello	Dicks	Duffy	Barker	McCrory	Hollis	Stubbs	Price
21	22	Mansfield Town	(H)	5-1	(2-0)	W	9337	McCrory(2),Duffy,Costello,Houghton	21	Ronson	Williamson	Anderson	Costello	Stirling	Duffy	Stenhouse	McCrory	Houghton	Stubbs	Punton
22	29	Swindon Town	(A)	1-2	(0-1)	L	10000	Costello	22	Ronson	Williamson	Anderson	Costello	Stirling	Duffy	Stenhouse	McCrory	Houghton	Stubbs	Punton
23	13 Dec	Notts County	(A)	4-1	(1-1)	W	7121	Houghton(2),Stubbs,Punton	23	Threadgold	Williamson	Anderson	Costello	Dicks	Duffy	Stenhouse	McCrory	Houghton	Stubbs	Punton
24	20	Bournemouth	(H)	2-0	(1-0)	W	10082	Punton,Nelson(O.G.)	24	Threadgold	Williamson	Anderson	Costello	Dicks	Duffy	Stenhouse	McCrory	Houghton	Stubbs	Punton
25	27	Stockport County	(H)	3-1	(2-1)	W	15315	McCrory,Costello,Houghton	25	Threadgold	Williamson	Anderson	Costello	Dicks	Duffy	Stenhouse	McCrory	Houghton	Stubbs	Punton
26	3 Jan	Norwich City	(A)	0-4	(0-4)	L	19077		26	Threadgold	Williamson	Anderson	Costello	Dicks	Duffy	Price	McCrory	Houghton	Stubbs	Punton
27	10	Hull City	(A)	2-3	(1-1)	L	12908	McCrory,Stubbs	27	Threadgold	Williamson	Anderson	Costello	Dicks	Duffy	Price	McCrory	Hollis	Stubbs	Punton
28	17	Chesterfield	(H)	2-5	(1-1)	L	9895	Price,McCrory(pen)	28	Threadgold	Williamson	Anderson	Costello	Dicks	Duffy	Price	McCrory	Hollis	Stubbs	Punton
29	24	Plymouth Argyle	(H)	0-0	(0-0)	D	12430		29	Ronson	Williamson	Anderson	Morrison	Dicks	Duffy	Price	McCrory	Houghton	Stubbs	Punton
30	31	Bury	(H)	1-0	(1-0)	W	10885	Houghton	30	Ronson	Williamson	Anderson	Morrison	Stirling	Duffy	Price	McCrory	Houghton	Stubbs	Punton
31	7 Feb	Queens Park Rangers	(A)	3-1	(3-0)	W	6099	Hollis(2),Price	31	Ronson	Williamson	Anderson	Morrison	Stirling	Duffy	Price	McCrory	Hollis	Stubbs	Punton
32	14	Rochdale	(A)	3-1	(1-0)	W	8766	Hollis,Houghton,McCrory	32	Threadgold	Williamson	Anderson	Morrison	Stirling	Duffy	Price	McCrory	Houghton	Houghton	Stubbs
33	21	Doncaster Rovers	(A)	1-2	(0-1)	L	5727	Houghton	33	Ronson	Williamson	Anderson	Morrison	Stirling	Duffy	Price	McCrory	Hollis	Houghton	Punton
34	28	Halifax Town	(A)	0-1	(0-1)	L	6861		34	Ronson	Williamson	Duffy	Morrison	Dicks	Costello	Stenhouse	McCrory	Stubbs	Houghton	Punton
35	7 Mar	Accrington Stanley	(H)	4-2	(3-2)	W	9343	Houghton(3),McCrory	35	Ronson	Williamson	Duffy	Morrison	Dicks	Costello	Stenhouse	McCrory	Hollis	Houghton	Punton
36	14	Southampton	(A)	2-3	(1-2)	L	9251	Houghton,Stenhouse	36	Ronson	Williamson	Duffy	Morrison	Dicks	Costello	Stenhouse	McCrory	Hollis	Houghton	Punton
37	21	Wrexham	(H)	4-1	(2-0)	W	8699	McCrory(2),Hollis,Houghton	37	Ronson	Williamson	Duffy	Morrison	Dicks	Costello	Stenhouse	McCrory	Houghton	Houghton	Punton
38	28	Bradford City	(A)	1-6	(0-2)	L	9783	Stenhouse	38	Ronson	Williamson	Duffy	Morrison	Stirling	Costello	Stenhouse	McCrory	Houghton	Houghton	Punton
39	30	Newport County	(H)	1-0	(1-0)	W	9672	Houghton	39	Ronson	Williamson	Anderson	Morrison	Costello	Duffy	Stenhouse	McCrory	Hollis	Houghton	Punton
40	4 Apr	Hull City	(A)	1-1	(1-1)	D	12231	Hollis(2)	40	Ronson	Williamson	Anderson	Morrison	Costello	Duffy	Stenhouse	McCrory	Hollis	Houghton	Barker
41	8	Brentford	(A)	2-0	(1-0)	W	8824	Hollis(2)	41	Ronson	Williamson	Anderson	Morrison	Costello	Duffy	Stenhouse	McCrory	Hollis	Houghton	Barker
42	11	Mansfield Town	(A)	4-1	(1-1)	W	7143	Houghton(4)	42	Ronson	Williamson	Anderson	Morrison	Costello	Duffy	Stenhouse	McCrory	Hollis	Houghton	Barker
43	13	Newport County	(A)	1-3	(1-2)	L	5070	Morrison	43	Ronson	Williamson	Anderson	Morrison	Costello	Duffy	Stenhouse	McCrory	Hollis	Houghton	Barker
44	18	Swindon Town	(H)	0-2	(0-1)	L	7384		44	Ronson	Williamson	Anderson	Morrison	Costello	Duffy	Stenhouse	McCrory	Hollis	Houghton	Barker
45	25	Brentford	(A)	1-6	(0-4)	L	11260	Barker	45	Ronson	Williamson	Anderson	Morrison	Costello	Duffy	Stenhouse	Cairns	Price	Houghton	Barker
46	29	Notts County	(H)	5-2	(2-2)	W	5774	Hollis(2),Houghton(2),McCrory	46	Ronson	Williamson	Anderson	Dicks	Costello	Duffy	Stenhouse	McCrory	Hollis	Houghton	Kent

Major Cup Competitions

Rd.	Date	Opposition	Venue	Score	H.T.	Res.	Att.	Goalscorers
			F.A.Cup					
R1	15 Nov	Yeovil	(H)	0-0	(0-0)	D	15265	
R1r	20	Yeovil	(A)	0-1	(0-0)	L	11000	

	1	2	3	4	5	6	7	8	9	10	11
	Threadgold	Williamson	Anderson	Smith	String	Duffy	Price	McCrory	Hollis	Houghton	Punton
	Ronson	Williamson	Anderson	Costello	String	Duffy	Price	McCrory	Hollis	Houghton	Punton

(Back) Knight, Wright, Ferguson, O'Hara, Cairns, Dobson, Smith, Walker, Costello, Fletcher, Edmunds
(Middle) Jefferson, Duffy, Ronson, Anderson, Williamson, Threadgold, Punton, Walker.
(Front) Kellard, Morrison, Crossan, Barron, Stirling, McCrory, Hollis, Price, Thomson, Ayres.

Appearances and Goals

Name	Appearances Lge.	FAC	Total	Goals Lge.	FAC	Total
ANDERSON, Sandy	41	2	43			
BARKER, Gordon	6		6	1		1
BARON, Kevin	6		6	1		1
CAIRNS, Colin	2		2			
COSTELLO, Lou	35	1	36	3		3
CROSSAN, Errol	6		6	3		3
DICKS, Alan	14		14			
DUFFY, John	41	2	43	1		1
HOLLIS, Roy	35	2	37	17		17
HOUGHTON, Bud	25	2	27	20		20
KENT, Terry	1		1			
MORRISON, Willie	29		29	1		1
McCRORY, Sammy	44	2	46	18		18
PRICE, Duggie	27	2	29	6		6
PUNTON, Bill	38	2	40	6		6
RONSON, Brian	23	1	24			
SMITH, Ray	5	1	6			
STENHOUSE, Alec	17		17	2		2
STIRLING, Jimmy	19	2	21			
STUBBS, Les	13		13	2		2
THOMSON, Jimmy	10		10	3		3
THREADGOLD, Harry	23	1	24			
WILLIAMSON, Arthur	46	2	48	1		1
Own Goals				1		1

	Ps	P	W	D	L	F	A	W	D	L	F	A	Pts.
1958/59	8	46	14	6	3	52	26	7	2	14	33	54	50

Season 1959/60 – League Division Three

No.	Date	Opposition	Venue	Score	H.T.	Res.	Att.	Goalscorers	No.	1	2	3	4	5	6	7	8	9	10	11
1	22 Aug	Halifax Town	(A)	1-2	(0-1)	L	7665	Houghton	1	Uprichard	Williamson	Anderson	Costello	Watson	Smith	Stenhouse	McCrory	Hollis	Houghton	Price
2	24	Queens Park Rangers	(H)	3-2	(3-1)	W	12197	Price(2),Hollis	2	Uprichard	Williamson	Anderson	Costello	Watson	Smith	Stenhouse	McCrory	Hollis	Houghton	Price
3	29	Bury	(H)	0-4	(0-1)	L	12973		3	Uprichard	Williamson	Anderson	Morrison	Watson	Duffy	Stenhouse	McCrory	Hollis	Houghton	Price
4	31	Queens Park Rangers	(A)	0-0	(0-0)	D	13360		4	Uprichard	Williamson	Anderson	Costello	Watson	Duffy	Stenhouse	McCrory	Hollis	Houghton	Price
5	5 Sep	Barnsley	(A)	1-4	(0-2)	L	5391	McCrory	5	Uprichard	Williamson	Anderson	Costello	Watson	Duffy	Stenhouse	McCrory	Hollis	Houghton	Price
6	7	Mansfield Town	(H)	0-2	(0-0)	L	11416		6	Uprichard	Williamson	Anderson	Smith	Watson	Duffy	Forrester	McCrory	Fogg	Costello	Stenhouse
7	12	Southampton	(A)	2-4	(1-3)	L	10751	Costello(2)	7	Uprichard	Williamson	Anderson	Costello	Watson	Duffy	Forrester	McCrory	Hollis	Houghton	Stenhouse
8	14	Mansfield Town	(H)	1-1	(0-0)	D	7000	Houghton	8	Threadgold	Williamson	Anderson	Costello	Watson	Duffy	Forrester	McCrory	Hollis	Houghton	Price
9	19	Reading	(A)	1-4	(0-0)	L	10211	Forrester	9	Uprichard	Williamson	Anderson	Costello	Watson	Duffy	Forrester	McCrory	Fogg	Houghton	Price
10	21	Bradford City	(H)	2-1	(1-0)	W	10186	McCrory,Price	10	Threadgold	Williamson	Anderson	Morrison	Watson	Duffy	Forrester	McCrory	Houghton	Costello	Price
11	26	Shrewsbury Town	(H)	2-1	(2-0)	W	10669	McCrory,Costello	11	Threadgold	Williamson	Anderson	Morrison	Watson	Duffy	Forrester	McCrory	Houghton	Costello	Stenhouse
12	29	Bradford City	(A)	1-3	(1-3)	L	8569	Houghton	12	Threadgold	Williamson	Anderson	Morrison	Watson	Duffy	Stenhouse	McCrory	Houghton	Costello	Kellard
13	3 Oct	Port Vale	(A)	1-3	(0-1)	L	12008	Duffy	13	Threadgold	Williamson	Anderson	Morrison	Watson	Duffy	Stenhouse	McCrory	Houghton	Costello	Kellard
14	5	Norwich City	(H)	1-0	(1-0)	W	16568	McCrory	14	Threadgold	Williamson	Anderson	Morrison	Watson	Duffy	Stenhouse	McCrory	Costello	Price	Kellard
15	10	Grimsby Town	(H)	3-0	(1-0)	W	10462	Price(2),Costello	15	Threadgold	Williamson	Anderson	Morrison	Watson	Duffy	Stenhouse	McCrory	Costello	Price	Kellard
16	17	Wrexham	(A)	1-3	(0-3)	L	9232	Kellard	16	Threadgold	Williamson	Anderson	Morrison	Watson	Duffy	Stenhouse	McCrory	Costello	Price	Kellard
17	24	Tranmere Rovers	(H)	7-1	(3-0)	W	9533	McCrory(2),Hollis(2),Price(2),Stenhouse	17	Threadgold	Williamson	Anderson	Morrison	Watson	Duffy	Stenhouse	McCrory	Hollis	Price	Kellard
18	31	Coventry City	(A)	0-2	(0-1)	L	14144		18	Threadgold	Williamson	Anderson	Morrison	Watson	Duffy	Stenhouse	McCrory	Hollis	Price	Kellard
19	7 Nov	Accrington Stanley	(H)	6-1	(5-1)	W	9338	Price(2),McCrory,Kellard,Stenhouse,Garrity(O.G.)	19	Threadgold	Williamson	Anderson	Morrison	Watson	Duffy	Stenhouse	McCrory	Hollis	Price	Kellard
20	21	Chesterfield	(A)	1-2	(0-1)	L	10115	Price	20	Threadgold	Williamson	Anderson	Costello	Watson	Duffy	Stenhouse	McCrory	Hollis	Price	Kellard
21	28	Swindon Town	(A)	0-2	(0-0)	L	8822		21	Threadgold	Williamson	Anderson	Costello	Watson	Morrison	Stenhouse	McCrory	Hollis	Stubbs	Kellard
22	12 Dec	Bournemouth	(A)	0-0	(0-0)	D	10000		22	Threadgold	Williamson	Anderson	Costello	Watson	Duffy	Price	McCrory	Hollis	Stubbs	Kellard
23	19	Halifax Town	(H)	3-0	(1-0)	W	5722	Hollis(3)	23	Threadgold	Williamson	Anderson	Costello	Watson	Duffy	Price	McCrory	Hollis	Stubbs	Kellard
24	26	Brentford	(A)	2-0	(1-0)	W	11771	Price,Stubbs	24	Threadgold	Williamson	Anderson	Costello	Watson	Duffy	Price	McCrory	Hollis	Stubbs	Kellard
25	28	Brentford	(A)	1-3	(0-2)	L	11750	Price	25	Threadgold	Williamson	Anderson	Costello	Watson	Duffy	Price	McCrory	Hollis	Stubbs	Kellard
26	2 Jan	Bury	(A)	0-3	(0-2)	L	12049		26	Threadgold	Williamson	Anderson	Costello	Watson	Duffy	Stenhouse	McCrory	Hollis	Stubbs	Price
27	23	Southampton	(A)	1-3	(0-2)	L	13535	Hollis	27	Threadgold	Williamson	Anderson	Costello	Watson	Duffy	Stenhouse	McCrory	Hollis	Price	Kellard
28	30	York City	(H)	1-1	(1-1)	D	8636	Price	28	Threadgold	Williamson	Anderson	Dicks	Watson	Duffy	Stenhouse	Costello	Hollis	Price	Kellard
29	6 Feb	Reading	(H)	2-0	(0-0)	W	8153	Price(2)	29	Threadgold	Williamson	Anderson	Costello	Watson	Dicks	Stenhouse	McCrory	Hollis	Price	Kellard
30	13	Shrewsbury Town	(A)	3-1	(3-1)	W	6263	Houghton,McCrory,Pountney(O.G.)	30	Threadgold	Williamson	Anderson	Costello	Watson	Dicks	Stenhouse	McCrory	Houghton	Price	Kellard
31	20	Port Vale	(H)	2-1	(1-0)	W	6500	Price,Houghton	31	Threadgold	Williamson	Anderson	Costello	Watson	Dicks	Stenhouse	McCrory	Houghton	Price	Duffy
32	27	Grimsby Town	(A)	1-1	(1-0)	D	8860	McCrory	32	Threadgold	Williamson	Anderson	Costello	Watson	Dicks	Stenhouse	McCrory	Houghton	Price	Forrester
33	29	Barnsley	(H)	2-2	(1-2)	D	10941	Costello,Price	33	Threadgold	Williamson	Anderson	Costello	Watson	Dicks	Stenhouse	McCrory	Houghton	Price	Forrester
34	5 Mar	Wrexham	(H)	1-1	(1-1)	D	9296	Price	34	Threadgold	Williamson	Anderson	Duffy	Watson	Dicks	Stenhouse	McCrory	Houghton	Price	Forrester
35	12	Tranmere Rovers	(A)	0-1	(0-0)	L	8715		35	Threadgold	Williamson	Anderson	Dicks	Watson	Duffy	Stenhouse	McCrory	Stubbs	Price	Forrester
36	19	Swindon Town	(H)	1-3	(1-1)	L	8451	Price	36	Threadgold	Williamson	Anderson	Dicks	Watson	Duffy	Stenhouse	McCrory	Houghton	Price	Forrester
37	21	Newport County	(A)	1-1	(0-0)	D	5652	Corthine	37	Threadgold	Williamson	Anderson	Costello	Watson	Dicks	Stenhouse	Corthine	Houghton	Price	Wall
38	26	Accrington Stanley	(H)	4-0	(1-0)	W	2052	Corthine(2),Dicks,Houghton	38	Threadgold	Williamson	Whale	Costello	Watson	Dicks	Stenhouse	Corthine	Houghton	Price	Wall
39	2 Apr	Newport County	(H)	3-2	(2-1)	W	8632	Corthine,Stenhouse,Houghton	39	Threadgold	Williamson	Whale	Costello	Stirling	Dicks	Stenhouse	Corthine	Houghton	Price	Wall
40	9	Chesterfield	(A)	0-1	(0-1)	L	5423		40	Threadgold	Williamson	Anderson	Costello	Watson	Dicks	Stenhouse	Corthine	Houghton	Price	Wall
41	15	Colchester United	(A)	3-2	(0-1)	W	10317	Price(2),Corthine	41	Uprichard	Williamson	Whale	Costello	Watson	Dicks	Stenhouse	Corthine	Houghton	Price	Wall
42	16	Coventry City	(H)	1-0	(1-0)	W	12152	Price	42	Uprichard	Williamson	Whale	Costello	Watson	Dicks	Stenhouse	Corthine	Houghton	Price	Wall
43	18	Colchester United	(H)	1-0	(1-0)	W	12664	Corthine	43	Uprichard	Williamson	Whale	Costello	Watson	Dicks	Stenhouse	Corthine	Stubbs	McCrory	Wall
44	23	York City	(A)	3-2	(0-1)	W	4883	Price(2),McCrory	44	Uprichard	Williamson	Whale	Costello	Watson	Dicks	Stenhouse	Corthine	McCrory	Price	Wall
45	27	Norwich City	(A)	3-4	(2-3)	L	34908	Price(2),Stenhouse	45	Threadgold	Williamson	Whale	Costello	Watson	Dicks	Stenhouse	Corthine	Houghton	Price	Kellard
46	30	Bournemouth	(H)	3-0	(0-0)	W	8971	Price(2),Corthine	46	Threadgold	Williamson	Whale	Costello	Watson	Dicks	Stenhouse	Corthine	Houghton	Price	Kellard

Major Cup Competitions

Rd.	Date	Opposition	Venue	Score	H.T.	Res.	Att.	Goalscorers	1	2	3	4	5	6	7	8	9	10	11
				F.A.Cup															
R1	14 Nov	Oswestry Town	(H)	6-0	(1-0)	W	11710	Hollis(2),Price,Kellard,McCrory,O.G.	Threadgold	Williamson	Anderson	Morrison	Watson	Duffy	Stenhouse	McCrory	Hollis	Price	Kellard
R2	5 Dec	Southampton	(A)	0-3		L	21692		Threadgold	Williamson	Anderson	Costello	Watson	Duffy	Stenhouse	McCrory	Hollis	Stubbs	Kellard

Appearances and Goals

Name	Appearances			Goals		
	Lge.	FAC	Total	Lge.	FAC	Total
ANDERSON, Sandy	38	2	40	7		7
CORTHINE, Peter	10		10			
COSTELLO, Lou	38	1	39	5		5
DICKS, Alan	19		19	1		1
DUFFY, John	29	2	31	1		1
FOGG, Ron	2		2			
FORRESTER, Anthony	10		10	1		1
HOLLIS, Roy	19	2	21	7	2	9
HOUGHTON, Bud	27		27	7		7
KELLARD, Bobby	18	2	20	2	1	3
MORRISON, Willie	14	1	15			
McCRORY, Sammy	37	2	39	10	1	11
PRICE, Duggie	41	1	42	28	1	29
SMITH, Ray	3		3			
STENHOUSE, Alec	37	2	39	4		4
STIRLING, Jimmy	1		1			
STUBBS, Les	9	1	10	1		1
THREADGOLD, Harry	34	2	36			
UPRICHARD, Norman	12		12			
WALL, Billy	9		9			
WATSON, Peter	45	2	47			
WHALE, Ray	8		8			
WILLIAMSON, Arthur	46	2	48			
Own Goals				2	1	3

	Ps	P	W	D	L	F	A	W	D	L	F	A	Pts.
1959/60	12	46	15	3	5	49	28	4	5	14	27	46	46

Southend United Football Club Limited

FOOTBALL LEAGUE DIVISION III

MONDAY, 24th AUGUST 1959   KICK OFF 6.30 p.m.

SOUTHEND UNITED
VERSUS
QUEENS PARK RANGERS

Next Home Match   Football League Div III
SOUTHEND UNITED   SATURDAY
29th AUGUST
BURY   KICK off 3.15 p.m.

Official Programme Price 3d.

The first home game of the season.

Season 1960/61 – League Division Three

No.	Date	Opposition	Venue	Score	H.T.	Res.	Att.	Goalscorers	1	2	3	4	5	6	7	8	9	10	11
1	20 Aug	Bury	(H)	0-3	(0-0)	L	11538		Threadgold	Williamson	Whale	Costello	Watson	Dicks	Stenhouse	Corthine	Houghton	Price	Wall
2	23	Walsall	(A)	1-5	(1-1)	L	11032	Wall	Threadgold	Williamson	Whale	Costello	Watson	Dicks	Stenhouse	Corthine	Houghton	Price	Wall
3	27	Chesterfield	(A)	3-0	(2-0)	W	4393	Laverty,Fryatt,Wall	Threadgold	Williamson	Anderson	Costello	Watson	Dicks	Wall	Stenhouse	Fryatt	Laverty	Kellard
4	29	Walsall	(H)	1-2	(0-1)	L	10977	Laverty	Threadgold	Williamson	Anderson	Costello	Watson	Dicks	Stenhouse	Corthine	Fryatt	Laverty	Wall
5	3 Sep	Hull City	(A)	3-1	(2-0)	W	8434	Corthine(2),Laverty	Threadgold	Williamson	Anderson	Costello	Watson	Dicks	Stenhouse	Corthine	Fryatt	Laverty	Wall
6	5	Tranmere Rovers	(A)	1-2	(1-2)	L	10665	Fryatt	Threadgold	Williamson	Anderson	Costello	Watson	Dicks	Stenhouse	Corthine	Fryatt	Laverty	Wall
7	10	Port Vale	(H)	2-1	(1-0)	W	8693	Corthine,Fryatt	Threadgold	Williamson	Anderson	Costello	Watson	Dicks	Stenhouse	Corthine	Fryatt	Laverty	Wall
8	12	Tranmere Rovers	(H)	1-2	(1-1)	L	9531	Corthine	Tennant	Williamson	Anderson	Costello	Watson	Dicks	Stenhouse	Corthine	Fryatt	Laverty	Houghton
9	17	Torquay United	(A)	1-2	(1-1)	L	6175	Stenhouse	Threadgold	Williamson	Anderson	Costello	Watson	Dicks	Wall	Corthine	Fryatt	Laverty	Kellard
10	21	Shrewsbury Town	(A)	2-2	(1-0)	D	6959	Corthine(2)	Threadgold	Williamson	Anderson	Costello	Watson	Dicks	Wall	Corthine	Houghton	Laverty	Kellard
11	24	Swindon Town	(H)	0-2	(0-1)	L	9242		Threadgold	Williamson	Anderson	Costello	Watson	Dicks	Wall	Corthine	Houghton	Houghton	Kellard
12	26	Shrewsbury Town	(H)	1-1	(1-0)	D	6891	Corthine	Threadgold	Anderson	Holton	Whale	Watson	Costello	Stenhouse	Corthine	Houghton	McKinven	McKinven
13	1 Oct	Brentford	(A)	1-1	(0-1)	D	7700	McKinven	Threadgold	Anderson	Holton	Costello	Watson	Dicks	Stenhouse	Corthine	Houghton	Laverty	McKinven
14	3	Watford	(H)	6-1	(1-1)	W	11540	Houghton(3),Corthine(2),Laverty	Threadgold	Anderson	Holton	Costello	Dicks	Whale	Stenhouse	Corthine	Houghton	Laverty	McKinven
15	8	Coventry City	(A)	0-3	(0-2)	L	7412		Threadgold	Anderson	Holton	Costello	Dicks	Whale	Stenhouse	Corthine	Houghton	Laverty	Nutt
16	15	Bristol City	(H)	1-0	(0-0)	W	8848	Laverty	Threadgold	Anderson	Holton	Watson	Dicks	Whale	Stenhouse	Corthine	Houghton	Laverty	Nutt
17	22	Queens Park Rangers	(A)	1-2	(0-1)	L	6006	Laverty	Threadgold	Anderson	Holton	Watson	Dicks	Whale	Stenhouse	Corthine	Houghton	Laverty	Nutt
18	29	Notts County	(H)	3-1	(1-0)	W	5369	Houghton,Nutt,Anderson	Threadgold	Anderson	Holton	Watson	Dicks	Whale	Stenhouse	Costello	Houghton	Laverty	Nutt
19	12 Nov	Bradford City	(H)	0-0	(0-0)	D	7475		Threadgold	Anderson	Holton	Watson	Dicks	Whale	Stenhouse	Corthine	Houghton	Laverty	Nutt
20	19	Barnsley	(A)	1-2	(0-0)	L	4525	Houghton	Threadgold	Anderson	Holton	Watson	Dicks	Whale	Stenhouse	Corthine	Houghton	Laverty	Nutt
21	3 Dec	Colchester United	(A)	0-2	(0-1)	L	5007		Threadgold	Anderson	Holton	Kellard	Dicks	Whale	Stenhouse	Corthine	Houghton	Fryatt	Nutt
22	10	Grimsby Town	(H)	1-1	(1-0)	D	5991	Williamson	Threadgold	Williamson	Anderson	Kellard	Watson	Dicks	Stenhouse	Corthine	Houghton	McKinven	Nutt
23	24	Halifax Town	(A)	2-6	(0-3)	L	6007	Costello,McKinven	Threadgold	Williamson	Anderson	Kellard	Watson	Whale	Stenhouse	Corthine	Costello	McKinven	Duncan
24	26	Halifax Town	(H)	2-2	(1-0)	D	8534	Duncan(2)	Goy	Holton	Anderson	Kellard	Dicks	Whale	Wall	Jones	Costello	McKinven	Duncan
25	31	Chesterfield	(H)	1-1	(0-0)	D	6975	Corthine	Goy	Williamson	Anderson	Kellard	Dicks	Whale	Wall	Corthine	Costello	McKinven	Duncan
26	7 Jan	Newport County	(H)	4-2	(4-2)	W	6037	Fryatt(2),Wall,Corthine	Goy	Williamson	Anderson	Kellard	Dicks	Whale	Wall	Corthine	Fryatt	McKinven	Duncan
27	14	Hull City	(A)	1-0	(1-0)	W	9774	Fryatt	Goy	Williamson	Anderson	Kellard	Dicks	Whale	Wall	Corthine	Fryatt	McKinven	Duncan
28	21	Port Vale	(A)	0-4	(0-4)	L	9571		Goy	Watson	Anderson	Kellard	Dicks	Whale	Wall	Corthine	Fryatt	McKinven	Nutt
29	28	Bournemouth	(H)	2-3	(1-2)	L	5508	Fryatt,Nutt	Goy	Williamson	Whale	Kellard	Watson	Dicks	Wall	Corthine	Fryatt	McKinven	Nutt
30	4 Feb	Torquay United	(H)	3-2	(2-2)	W	6885	Fryatt(3)	Goy	Williamson	Anderson	Kellard	Dicks	Whale	Wall	Laverty	Fryatt	McKinven	Nutt
31	11	Swindon Town	(A)	1-1	(0-0)	D	8746	Kellard	Goy	Williamson	Anderson	Costello	Dicks	Whale	Wall	Kellard	Fryatt	Laverty	Nutt
32	18	Brentford	(A)	1-1	(0-1)	D	7678	Watson	Goy	Williamson	Anderson	Dicks	Watson	Whale	Corthine	Kellard	Fryatt	Laverty	Nutt
33	25	Colchester United	(H)	2-1	(1-0)	W	6042	Fryatt,McKinven	Goy	Williamson	Anderson	Kellard	Watson	Dicks	Wall	Laverty	Fryatt	McKinven	Corthine
34	4 Mar	Bristol City	(A)	0-2	(0-1)	L	11173		Goy	Williamson	Anderson	Kellard	Watson	Dicks	Corthine	Laverty	Fryatt	McKinven	Duncan
35	11	Queens Park Rangers	(H)	0-0	(0-0)	D	10987		Goy	Williamson	Anderson	Costello	Watson	Dicks	Stenhouse	Corthine	Fryatt	Kellard	McKinven
36	18	Notts County	(A)	2-1	(1-0)	W	10530	Corthine,Fryatt	Goy	Williamson	Anderson	Costello	Watson	Dicks	Stenhouse	Corthine	Fryatt	Kellard	McKinven
37	21	Bury	(A)	0-2	(0-0)	L	11819		Goy	Williamson	Anderson	Costello	Watson	Dicks	Stenhouse	Corthine	Fryatt	Kellard	McKinven
38	25	Bournemouth	(H)	0-0	(0-0)	D	7555		Goy	Williamson	Anderson	Costello	Watson	Dicks	Stenhouse	Corthine	Fryatt	Kellard	McKinven
39	1 Apr	Bradford City	(A)	1-2	(1-0)	L	6011	McKinven	Goy	Williamson	Anderson	Costello	Watson	Dicks	Wall	Corthine	Fryatt	McKinven	Nutt
40	3	Reading	(A)	0-3	(0-1)	L	4875		Goy	Williamson	Anderson	Costello	Watson	Dicks	Wall	Corthine	Fryatt	Kellard	Nutt
41	5	Reading	(H)	0-1	(0-1)	L	6689		Goy	Williamson	Anderson	Costello	Watson	Whale	Corthine	Jones	Fryatt	Jones	Wall
42	8	Barnsley	(H)	2-0	(0-0)	W	7153	Jones,Fryatt	Goy	Williamson	Anderson	Costello	Watson	Dicks	Corthine	Jones	Fryatt	Corthine	Jones
43	15	Newport County	(A)	2-1	(2-0)	W	2917	Fryatt,Dicks	Goy	Williamson	Anderson	Costello	Watson	Dicks	Wall	Stenhouse	Fryatt	Corthine	Jones
44	22	Coventry City	(H)	4-1	(1-1)	W	7700	Corthine(3),Fryatt	Goy	Williamson	Anderson	Costello	Watson	Dicks	Wall	Stenhouse	Fryatt	Corthine	McKinven
45	25	Watford	(A)	0-3	(0-2)	L	7084		Goy	Williamson	Anderson	Costello	Watson	Dicks	Nutt	Stenhouse	Fryatt	Corthine	Nutt
46	29	Grimsby Town	(A)	0-1	(0-1)	L	3629		Goy	Williamson	Anderson	Costello	Watson	Dicks	Wall	Stenhouse	Fryatt	Corthine	Nutt

Major Cup Competitions

Rd.	Date	Opposition	Venue	Score	H.T.	Res.	Att.	Goalscorers	1	2	3	4	5	6	7	8	9	10	11
F.A.Cup																			
R1	5 Nov	Clacton Town	(A)	3-1	(2-0)	W	3185	Corthine,Stenhouse,Kellard	Threadgold	Anderson	Holton	Watson	Dicks	Whale	Stenhouse	Corthine	Houghton	Kellard	Nutt
R2	26	Gillingham	(A)	2-3	(0-0)	L	10220	Fryatt,Stenhouse	Threadgold	Anderson	Whale	Watson	Dicks	Kellard	Stenhouse	Fryatt	Houghton	Laverty	Nutt
League Cup																			
R1	Bye																		
R2	25 Oct	Rochdale	(A)	2-5	(2-2)	L	3591	Houghton,Laverty	Tennant	Anderson	Holton	Watson	Dicks	Whale	Stenhouse	Corthine	Houghton	Laverty	Duncan

(Back) Whale, Houghton, Threadgold, Williamson, Dicks, Costello.
(Front) Stenhouse, Corthine, Watson, Price, Wall.

Appearances and Goals

Name	Appearances				Goals			
	Lge.	FAC	L.C.	Total	Lge.	FAC	L.C.	Total
ANDERSON, Sandy	43	2	1	46	1			1
CORTHINE, Peter	40	1	1	42	15	1		16
COSTELLO, Lou	33			33	1			1
DICKS, Alan	44	2	1	47	1			1
DUNCAN, Bob	6		1	7	2			2
FRYATT, Jim	30	1		31	15	1		16
GOY, Peter	23			23				
HOLTON, Pat	11	1	1	13				
HOUGHTON, Bud	16	2	1	19	5		1	6
JONES, Ken	5			5	1			1
KELLARD, Bobby	24	2		26	1	1		2
LAVERTY, Pat	21	1	1	23	6		1	7
McKINVEN, John	22			22	4			4
NUTT, Gordon	16	2		18	2			2
PRICE, Duggie	2			2				
STENHOUSE, Alec	30	2	1	33	1	2		3
TENNANT, John	1		1	2				
THREADGOLD, Harry	22	2		24				
WALL, Billy	26			26	3			3
WATSON, Peter	36	2	1	39	1			1
WHALE, Ray	21	2	1	24				
WILLIAMSON, Arthur	34			34	1			1

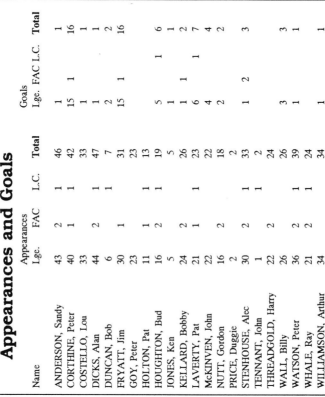

	Ps	P	W	D	L	F	A	W	D	L	F	A	Pts.
1960/61	20	46	10	8	5	38	26	4	3	16	22	50	39

Season 1961/62 – League Division Three

No.	Date	Opposition	Venue	Score	H.T.	Res.	Att.	Goalscorers	1	2	3	4	5	6	7	8	9	10	11
1	19 Aug	Bradford Park Avenue	(H)	2-1	(1-1)	W	13049	Corthine(pen),Scoular(O.G.)	Goy	Shiels	Anderson	Costello	Watson	Dicks	Bentley	Corthine	Bleanch	Goulden	Kellard
2	23	Portsmouth	(A)	0-1	(0-0)	L	18893		Goy	Shiels	Anderson	Costello	Watson	Dicks	Bentley	Corthine	Bleanch	Goulden	Kellard
3	26	Grimsby Town	(A)	1-3	(1-0)	L	8834	Kellard	Goy	Shiels	Anderson	Costello	Watson	Dicks	Bentley	Corthine	Bleanch	Goulden	Kellard
4	28	Portsmouth	(H)	2-2	(1-0)	D	12935	Fryatt,McKinven	Goy	Shiels	Anderson	Costello	Watson	Grieveson	Wall	Corthine	Fryatt	McKinven	Kellard
5	2 Sep	Coventry City	(H)	2-0	(0-0)	W	9372	Corthine,Fryatt	Goy	Shiels	Anderson	Costello	Watson	Grieveson	Bentley	Corthine	Fryatt	McKinven	Kellard
6	4	Port Vale	(A)	0-0	(0-0)	D	10317		Goy	Shiels	Anderson	Costello	Watson	Grieveson	Bentley	Corthine	Fryatt	McKinven	Kellard
7	9	Brentford	(A)	0-0	(0-0)	D	7100		Goy	Shiels	Anderson	Costello	Watson	Grieveson	Bentley	Corthine	Fryatt	McKinven	Kellard
8	16	Reading	(H)	0-2	(0-1)	L	10240		Goy	Shiels	Anderson	Costello	Watson	Grieveson	Bentley	Corthine	Jones	McKinven	Kellard
9	18	Bristol City	(H)	1-0	(1-0)	W	9316	Kellard	Goy	Shiels	Anderson	Costello	Watson	Grieveson	Bentley	Jones	Brand	McKinven	Kellard
10	23	Newport County	(A)	3-0	(1-0)	W	6817	Jones,Brand,Kellard	Goy	Shiels	Anderson	Costello	Watson	Grieveson	Bentley	Jones	Brand	McKinven	Kellard
11	26	Bristol City	(A)	2-3	(1-2)	L	10376	Jones,Brand	Goy	Shiels	Anderson	Costello	Watson	Grieveson	Bentley	Jones	Brand	McKinven	Kellard
12	30	Crystal Palace	(A)	2-2	(2-0)	D	15388	Brand(2)	Goy	Shiels	Anderson	Costello	Watson	Grieveson	Bentley	Jones	Brand	McKinven	Kellard
13	2 Oct	Shrewsbury Town	(H)	1-1	(1-1)	D	10744	Brand	Goy	Shiels	Anderson	Costello	Watson	Grieveson	Bentley	Jones	Brand	McKinven	Kellard
14	7	Barnsley	(H)	1-2	(0-0)	L	8823	Houghton(O.G.)	Goy	Shiels	Anderson	Costello	Watson	Grieveson	Wall	Jones	Brand	Goulden	Kellard
15	14	Queens Park Rangers	(A)	3-5	(3-2)	L	10519	Jones,Brand,Goulden	Goy	Shiels	Anderson	Costello	Watson	Grieveson	Wall	Jones	Brand	Goulden	Kellard
16	16	Port Vale	(H)	4-1	(1-0)	W	8419	Fryatt(2),Goulden,Kellard	Goy	Williamson	Anderson	Dicks	Brand	Grieveson	Wall	Jones	Fryatt	Goulden	Kellard
17	21	Watford	(H)	0-1	(0-0)	L	9478		Goy	Williamson	Anderson	Dicks	Brand	Kerrins	Wall	Jones	Fryatt	Goulden	Kellard
18	25	Shrewsbury Town	(A)	1-1	(0-0)	D	5262	Kellard	Goy	Williamson	Anderson	Dicks	Brand	Kerrins	Bentley	Goulden	Fryatt	McKinven	Kellard
19	28	Bournemouth	(A)	0-3	(0-2)	L	11572		Goy	Williamson	Anderson	Dicks	Brand	Kerrins	Wall	Jones	Fryatt	Goulden	Kellard
20	11 Nov	Lincoln City	(A)	0-2	(0-1)	L	3831		Goy	Shiels	Anderson	Costello	Watson	Kerrins	Wall	Corthine	Bentley	Kellard	McKinven
21	18	Northampton Town	(H)	1-3	(0-2)	L	5974	Fryatt	Goy	Watson	Anderson	Costello	Brand	Dicks	Bentley	Corthine	Fryatt	Kerrins	Kellard
22	2 Dec	Halifax Town	(A)	2-1	(1-1)	W	4754	Grieveson,Stanley(O.G.)	Goy	Williamson	Anderson	Grieveson	Watson	Kerrins	Bentley	Corthine	Costello	McKinven	Kellard
23	9	Swindon Town	(A)	0-0	(0-0)	D	6634		Goy	Williamson	Anderson	Grieveson	Watson	Kerrins	Bentley	Corthine	Costello	McKinven	Kellard
24	23	Grimsby Town	(H)	2-0	(0-0)	W	4365	Kellard(2)	Goy	Williamson	Anderson	Grieveson	Watson	Kerrins	Bentley	Corthine	Costello	McKinven	Kellard
25	26	Peterborough United	(H)	1-4	(1-3)	L	8237	Costello	Goy	Williamson	Anderson	Grieveson	Watson	Kerrins	Bentley	Corthine	Costello	McKinven	Kellard
26	30	Peterborough United	(A)	1-1	(0-0)	D	6687	McKinven	Goy	Williamson	Anderson	Grieveson	Watson	Kerrins	Bentley	Corthine	Costello	McKinven	Kellard
27	6 Jan	Torquay United	(A)	2-1	(0-0)	W	5998	Costello(2)	Threadgold	Williamson	Duncan	Grieveson	Watson	Kerrins	Bentley	Jones	Costello	McKinven	Kellard
28	13	Coventry City	(A)	3-3	(3-1)	D	9360	Jones(2),Kellard	Goy	Shiels	Anderson	Bentley	Watson	Grieveson	Wall	Jones	Costello	McKinven	Kellard
29	20	Brentford	(H)	0-0	(0-0)	D	6818		Goy	Shiels	Anderson	Bentley	Watson	Grieveson	Wall	Jones	Costello	McKinven	Kellard
30	27	Hull City	(A)	0-0	(0-0)	D	4517		Goy	Shiels	Anderson	Bentley	Watson	Grieveson	Wall	Jones	Costello	McKinven	Kellard
31	2 Feb	Reading	(A)	1-3	(0-2)	L	8479	Bentley	Goy	Williamson	Anderson	Bentley	Watson	Grieveson	Corthine	Jones	Costello	McKinven	Kellard
32	10	Newport County	(H)	1-0	(1-0)	W	6175	Jones	Threadgold	Shiels	Anderson	Bentley	Watson	Grieveson	Corthine	Jones	Costello	Goulden	Kellard
33	17	Crystal Palace	(H)	2-2	(2-1)	D	8733	Jones,Kellard	Threadgold	Shiels	Anderson	Bentley	Watson	Costello	Corthine	Jones	Costello	McKinven	Kellard
34	24	Barnsley	(A)	1-1	(0-1)	D	4666	Brand	Threadgold	Shiels	Anderson	Bentley	Watson	Costello	Corthine	Jones	Brand	McKinven	Kellard
35	3 Mar	Queens Park Rangers	(H)	2-3	(0-1)	L	8324	Watson,Brand	Threadgold	Shiels	Anderson	Bentley	Watson	Costello	Corthine	Jones	Brand	McKinven	Kellard
36	9	Watford	(A)	3-1	(2-1)	W	8243	Jones(2),Smith	Threadgold	Shiels	Anderson	Bentley	Watson	Lee	Corthine	Smith	Jones	McKinven	Kellard
37	14	Bradford Park Avenue	(A)	0-4	(0-1)	L	2818		Threadgold	Shiels	Anderson	Bentley	Watson	Lee	Corthine	Smith	Jones	McKinven	Kellard
38	17	Bournemouth	(H)	0-0	(0-0)	D	8245		Threadgold	Shiels	Anderson	Bentley	Brand	Lee	Corthine	Smith	Costello	Jones	Kellard
39	24	Torquay United	(A)	2-2	(0-2)	D	4024	Fryatt,Jones	Threadgold	Fryatt	Anderson	Bentley	Watson	Lee	Wall	Smith	Jones	McKinven	Kellard
40	31	Lincoln City	(H)	0-0	(0-0)	D	5402		Threadgold	Fryatt	Anderson	Bentley	Watson	Lee	Wall	Smith	Jones	McKinven	Kellard
41	7 Apr	Northampton Town	(A)	1-3	(1-2)	L	7452	Bentley	Threadgold	Fryatt	Anderson	Bentley	Watson	Lee	Wall	Jones	Jones	McKinven	Kellard
42	14	Hull City	(H)	2-1	(1-0)	W	5366	Jones,Kellard	Threadgold	Fryatt	Anderson	Bentley	Watson	Lee	Wall	Jones	Brand	Goulden	Kellard
43	20	Notts County	(H)	3-2	(0-0)	W	8310	Jones,Brand,McKinven	Threadgold	Fryatt	Anderson	Bentley	Watson	Lee	Wall	Jones	Brand	McKinven	Kellard
44	21	Halifax Town	(A)	2-0	(1-0)	W	1557	Jones,Kellard	Threadgold	Fryatt	Anderson	Bentley	Watson	Lee	Wall	Jones	Brand	McKinven	Kellard
45	23	Notts County	(A)	0-2	(0-1)	L	5158		Threadgold	Fryatt	Anderson	Bentley	Watson	Lee	Wall	Jones	Brand	McKinven	Kellard
46	28	Swindon Town	(H)	0-2	(0-1)	L	5764		Threadgold	Fryatt	Anderson	Bentley	Watson	Lee	Wall	Jones	Brand	McKinven	Kellard

Major Cup Competitions

Rd.	Date	Opposition	Venue	Score	H.T.	Res.	Att.	Goalscorers	1	2	3	4	5	6	7	8	9	10	11
F.A.Cup																			
R1	4 Nov	Watford	(H)	0-2	(0-1)	L	12460		Goy	Williamson	Anderson	Costello	Watson	Kerrins	Bentley	Fryatt	Brand	Goulden	Kellard
League Cup																			
R1	13 Sep	Stoke City	(H)	0-1	(0-1)	L	7553		Goy	Shiels	Anderson	Costello	Watson	Grieveson	Wall	Bentley	Fryatt	McKinven	Kellard

(Back) Goy, Kerrins, Costello, Bleanch, Dicks, Brand, Watson, Britton, Jones, Threadgold.
(Middle) French (Trainer), Leaper (Sec.), Shiels, Anderson, McKinney, Fryatt, Tennant, Grieveson, Duncan, Williamson, McKinven, Fenton (Manager), Robinson (Groundsman), Shepherd (Trainer)
(Front) Cox & Smith (Directors), Wall, Corthine, Goulden, Bentley, Hay (Chair.), Scott, Gallagher, Curran, Kellard.
Directors – Bates, Nelson, Mitchell.

Appearances and Goals

Name	Appearances Lge.	FAC	L.C.	Total	Goals Lge.	FAC	L.C.	Total
ANDERSON, Sandy	45	1	1	47				
BENTLEY, Tony	41	1	1	43	2			2
BLEANCH, Norman	3			3				
BRAND, Ray	19	1		20	9			9
CORTHINE, Peter	23			23	2			2
COSTELLO, Lou	31	1	1	33	3			3
DICKS, Alan	8			8				
DUNCAN, Bob	1			1				
FRYATT, Jim	18	1	1	20	6			6
GOULDEN, Roy	9	1		10	2			2
GOY, Peter	30	1	1	32				
GRIEVESON, Harry	24		1	25	1			1
JONES, Ken	31			31	13			13
KELLARD, Bobby	46	1	1	48	11			11
KERRINS, Pat	11	1		12				
LEE, Norman	11			11				
McKINVEN, John	36		1	37	3			3
SHIELS, Jimmy	25		1	26				
SMITH, Ray J	8			8	1			1
THREADGOLD, Harry	16			16				
WALL, Billy	17		1	18				
WATSON, Peter	42	1	1	44	1			1
WILLIAMSON, Arthur	11	1		12	1			1
Own Goals					3			3

	Ps	P	W	D	L	F	A	W	D	L	F	A	Pts.
1961/62	16	46	10	7	6	31	26	3	9	11	26	43	42

Season 1962/63 – League Division Three

No.	Date	Opposition	Venue	Score	H.T.	Res.	Att.	Goalscorers	No.	1	2	3	4	5	6	7	8	9	10	11
1	18 Aug	Watford	(A)	1-3	(0-1)	L	11492	Beesley	1	Threadgold	Tharme	Anderson	Bentley	Watson	Lee	Woodley	Jones	Beesley	McNeill	Kellard
2	20	Reading	(H)	2-0	(0-0)	W	9665	Beesley,Woodley	2	Goy	Tharme	Anderson	Bentley	Watson	Lee	Woodley	Jones	Beesley	McNeill	Kellard
3	25	Bradford Park Avenue	(H)	3-1	(2-1)	W	8084	Jones(2),Beesley	3	Goy	Tharme	Anderson	Bentley	Watson	Lee	Woodley	McNeill	Beesley	Jones	Kellard
4	29	Reading	(A)	4-1	(0-0)	W	8381	Beesley(3),McNeill	4	Goy	Tharme	Anderson	Bentley	Watson	Lee	Woodley	McNeill	Beesley	Jones	Kellard
5	1 Sep	Coventry City	(A)	4-3	(1-1)	W	17949	Beesley(3),Woodley	5	Goy	Tharme	Anderson	Bentley	Watson	Lee	Woodley	Jones	Beesley	McNeill	Kellard
6	3	Shrewsbury Town	(H)	3-1	(1-0)	W	14449	Jones(2),Lee	6	Goy	Tharme	Anderson	Bentley	Watson	Lee	Woodley	McNeill	Beesley	Jones	Kellard
7	8	Bournemouth	(H)	0-1	(0-1)	L	13614		7	Threadgold	Tharme	Anderson	Bentley	Watson	Lee	Woodley	McNeill	Beesley	Jones	Kellard
8	12	Shrewsbury Town	(A)	0-6	(0-4)	L	5558		8	Threadgold	Fryatt	Anderson	Bentley	Watson	Lee	Woodley	McNeill	Beesley	Jones	McKinven
9	15	Notts County	(A)	1-2	(0-1)	L	7229	McKinven	9	Threadgold	Bentley	Anderson	Costello	Watson	Lee	Woodley	Jones	Beesley	Jones	McKinven
10	17	Port Vale	(H)	2-0	(2-0)	W	11000	Woodley,Smith	10	Threadgold	Bentley	Anderson	Costello	Watson	Lee	Woodley	Jones	Beesley	Smith	McKinven
11	22	Colchester United	(H)	2-3	(1-3)	L	11632	Beesley,Smith	11	Threadgold	Bentley	Anderson	Costello	Watson	Lee	Woodley	Kellard	Beesley	Smith	McKinven
12	24	Port Vale	(A)	1-5	(1-1)	L	9618	Kellard	12	Tennant	Costello	Anderson	Bentley	Watson	Bradbury	Woodley	Kellard	Beesley	Smith	McKinven
13	29	Queens Park Rangers	(H)	1-3	(1-1)	L	12565	Beesley	13	Threadgold	Watson	Anderson	Bentley	Brand	Bradbury	Woodley	Kellard	Beesley	Smith	McKinven
14	1 Oct	Millwall	(A)	1-3	(0-2)	L	14726	Beesley	14	Threadgold	Costello	Anderson	Bentley	Brand	Bradbury	Woodley	Beesley	Fryatt	Kellard	McKinven
15	6	Crystal Palace	(A)	3-2	(0-1)	W	13236	Jones(2),Werge(O.G.)	15	Threadgold	Costello	Anderson	Bentley	Brand	Bradbury	Woodley	Jones	Fryatt	Kellard	McKinven
16	13	Wrexham	(H)	2-0	(1-0)	W	9548	Woodley,Jones	16	Threadgold	Costello	Anderson	Bentley	Watson	Bradbury	Woodley	Jones	Beesley	McNeill	McKinven
17	19	Halifax Town	(A)	1-0	(0-0)	W	5708	Jones	17	Threadgold	Costello	Anderson	Bentley	Watson	Bradbury	Woodley	Jones	Beesley	McNeill	McKinven
18	27	Bristol Rovers	(H)	3-2	(2-1)	W	9180	McKinven(3)	18	Threadgold	Costello	Anderson	Bentley	Watson	Bradbury	Woodley	Jones	Smith	McNeill	McKinven
19	10 Nov	Carlisle United	(H)	2-0	(0-0)	W	8851	Woodley,Beesley	19	Threadgold	Costello	Anderson	Bentley	Watson	Bradbury	Woodley	Jones	Beesley	McNeill	McKinven
20	17	Swindon Town	(A)	1-4	(0-2)	L	10296	Beesley	20	Threadgold	Costello	Anderson	Bentley	Watson	Bradbury	Woodley	Jones	Beesley	McNeill	McKinven
21	1 Dec	Barnsley	(A)	2-2	(1-2)	D	9280	McKinven,Jones	21	Goy	Costello	Neal	Bentley	Watson	Bradbury	Woodley	Jones	Beesley	McNeill	McKinven
22	8	Northampton Town	(H)	5-1	(3-0)	W	8203	McKinven(2),Woodley(2),Beesley	22	Goy	Costello	Neal	Bentley	Watson	Bradbury	Woodley	Jones	Beesley	McNeill	McKinven
23	15	Watford	(H)	2-1	(1-0)	W	9252	McKinven(pen)	23	Goy	Costello	Neal	Bentley	Watson	Bradbury	Woodley	Jones	Beesley	McNeill	McKinven
24	26	Hull City	(A)	0-1	(0-1)	L	9783		24	Goy	Costello	Neal	Bentley	Watson	Bradbury	Woodley	Jones	Fryatt	McNeill	McKinven
25	29	Hull City	(H)	2-1	(1-1)	W	9577	Fryatt,McMillan(O.G.)	25	Goy	Costello	Neal	Bentley	Watson	Bradbury	Woodley	Smith	Fryatt	McNeill	McKinven
26	26 Jan	Brighton	(A)	0-0	(0-0)	D	11814		26	Goy	Costello	Neal	Bentley	Watson	Bradbury	Woodley	Jones	Fryatt	McNeill	McKinven
27	2 Mar	Wrexham	(H)	1-1	(1-1)	D	10344	Bradbury	27	Goy	Costello	Neal	Bentley	Watson	Bradbury	Woodley	Jones	Fryatt	McNeill	McKinven
28	9	Halifax Town	(H)	1-1	(1-1)	D	6989	Fryatt	28	Goy	Costello	Neal	Bentley	Watson	Bradbury	Woodley	Jones	Fryatt	McNeill	McKinven
29	16	Bristol Rovers	(A)	2-1	(1-1)	W	7213	Fryatt,Hillard(O.G.)	29	Goy	Costello	Neal	Bentley	Watson	Bradbury	Woodley	Jones	Fryatt	McNeill	McKinven
30	19	Bradford Park Avenue	(A)	2-2	(1-0)	D	7136	Jones(2)	30	Goy	Costello	Neal	Bentley	Watson	Bradbury	Woodley	Jones	Fryatt	McNeill	McKinven
31	23	Brighton	(H)	1-1	(1-1)	D	8990	Jones	31	Goy	Costello	Neal	Bentley	Watson	Bradbury	Woodley	Jones	Fryatt	McNeill	McKinven
32	30	Carlisle United	(A)	2-1	(0-1)	W	5435	McKinven,McNeill	32	Goy	Costello	Neal	Bentley	Watson	Bradbury	Woodley	Jones	Fryatt	McNeill	McKinven
33	6 Apr	Swindon Town	(H)	1-1	(0-1)	D	11705	McKinven	33	Goy	Costello	Neal	Bentley	Watson	Bradbury	Woodley	Jones	Fryatt	McNeill	McKinven
34	8	Queens Park Rangers	(A)	0-1	(0-1)	L	7540		34	Goy	Costello	Neal	Bentley	Watson	Bradbury	Woodley	Jones	Beesley	Kellard	McKinven
35	13	Peterborough United	(A)	3-1	(2-0)	W	11620	Jones(2),Beesley	35	Goy	Costello	Neal	Bentley	Watson	Bradbury	Wall	Jones	Beesley	Kellard	McKinven
36	15	Bristol City	(A)	2-2	(1-0)	D	12570	Wall,Bradbury	36	Goy	Costello	Neal	Bentley	Watson	Bradbury	Wall	Jones	Fryatt	Kellard	McKinven
37	16	Bristol City	(H)	3-6	(1-4)	L	9815	Wall,McNeill,Jones	37	Goy	Costello	Neal	Bentley	Watson	Bradbury	Wall	Jones	Fryatt	McNeill	McKinven
38	20	Barnsley	(H)	0-0	(0-0)	D	6901		38	Goy	Costello	Neal	Bentley	Liggitt	Bradbury	Woodley	Jones	Beesley	McNeill	McKinven
39	22	Millwall	(H)	2-1	(2-1)	W	10290	Smith,Jones	39	Goy	Costello	Neal	Bentley	Watson	Bradbury	Woodley	Jones	Smith	McNeill	Kellard
40	27	Northampton Town	(A)	3-5	(2-4)	L	13562	Smith,Bentley,McKinven	40	Goy	Costello	Neal	Bentley	Watson	Bradbury	Woodley	Jones	Smith	McNeill	McKinven
41	4 May	Colchester United	(A)	1-3	(1-0)	L	7244	Jones	41	Goy	Costello	Neal	Bentley	Watson	Bradbury	Woodley	Jones	Smith	McNeill	McKinven
42	6	Peterborough United	(H)	2-1	(0-1)	W	10763	Bradbury,Smith	42	Goy	Costello	Neal	Bentley	Watson	Bradbury	Woodley	Jones	Smith	McNeill	McKinven
43	11	Coventry City	(H)	1-1	(1-1)	D	9275	Smith	43	Goy	Costello	Neal	Bentley	Watson	Bradbury	Woodley	Jones	Smith	Kellard	McKinven
44	13	Notts County	(H)	1-2	(1-1)	L	8210	McKinven	44	Goy	Costello	Neal	Bentley	Watson	Bradbury	Woodley	Jones	Smith	McNeill	McKinven
45	18	Bournemouth	(A)	0-0	(0-0)	D	7074		45	Goy	Costello	Neal	Bentley	Watson	Bradbury	Woodley	Jones	Smith	McNeill	Kellard
46	20	Crystal Palace	(H)	1-0	(1-0)	W	8017	Smith	46	Goy	Costello	Neal	Bentley	Watson	Bradbury	Woodley	Jones	Smith	McNeill	McKinven

Major Cup Competitions

F.A.Cup

Rd.	Date	Opposition	Venue	Score	H.T.	Res.	Att.	Goalscorers
R1	3 Nov	Brighton & H.A.	(H)	2-1	(2-0)	W	8695	Jones(2)
R2	24	Watford	(H)	0-2	(0-1)	L	16892	

1	2	3	4	5	6	7	8	9	10	11
Threadgold	Costello	Anderson	Bentley	Watson	Bradbury	Woodley	Jones	Beesley	McNeill	McKinven
Goy	Costello	Anderson	Bentley	Watson	Bradbury	Woodley	Jones	Beesley	McNeill	McKinven

League Cup

Rd.	Date	Opposition	Venue	Score	H.T.	Res.	Att.	Goalscorers
R1		Bye						
R2	26 Sep	Notts County	(H)	2-3	(1-1)	L	5500	Beesley, Smith

1	2	3	4	5	6	7	8	9	10	11
Tennant	Watson	Anderson	Bentley	Brand	Costello	Woodley	Kellard	Beesley	Smith	McKinven

Southend United F.C.—Season 1962-63. REAR: Lee, Costello, Tennant, Goy, Threadgold, Fryatt, McKinven.   CENTRE: Jack French (assistant trainer), Smith, Jones, McNeill, Anderson, Manager Ted Fenton, Brand, Tharme, Palmer, Ernie Shepherd (trainer-coach). FRONT: Kellard, Wall, Banks, Liggitt, Watson, Donovan, Bentley, Barnard, Faulkner.

Appearances and Goals

Name	Appearances Lge.	FAC	L.C.	Total	Goals Lge.	FAC	L.C.	Total
ANDERSON, Sandy	20	2	1	23				
BEESLEY, Micky	26	2	1	29	15	1		16
BENTLEY, Tony	46	2	1	49	1			1
BRADBURY, Terry	35	2		37	3			3
BRAND, Ray	3		1	4				
COSTELLO, Lou	37	2	1	40				
FRYATT, Jim	13			13	3			3
GOY, Peter	31	1		32				
JONES, Ken	41	2		43	17	2		19
KELLARD, Bobby	18		1	19	1			1
LEE, Norman	11			11	1			1
LIGGETT, Norman	1			1				
McKINVEN, John	37	2	1	40	12			12
McNEILL, Ian	36	2		38	3			3
NEAL, John	26			26				
SMITH, Ray J	14		1	15	7	1		8
TENNANT, John	1		1	2				
THARME, Derek	7			7				
THREADGOLD, Harry	14	1		15				
WALL, Billy	4			4	2			2
WATSON, Peter	43	2	1	46	7			7
WOODLEY, Derek	42	2	1	45	7			7
Own Goals					3			3

	Ps	P	W	D	L	F	A	W	D	L	F	A	Pts.
1962/63	8	46	11	7	5	38	24	8	5	10	37	53	50

Season 1963/64 – League Division Three

No.	Date	Opposition	Venue	Score	H.T.	Res.	Att.	Goalscorers	1	2	3	4	5	6	7	8	9	10	11
1	24 Aug	Bournemouth	(H)	1-1	(0-0)	D	10257	Beesley	Goy	Neal	King	Bentley	Watson	Bradbury	Woodley	Jones	Smith	Beesley	McKinven
2	27	Barnsley	(A)	1-0	(0-0)	W	6203	McKinven	Goy	Neal	King	Bentley	Watson	Bradbury	Woodley	Jones	Smith	Beesley	McKinven
3	31	Wrexham	(A)	3-1	(1-0)	W	8939	Woodley,Beesley,Jones	Goy	Neal	King	Bentley	Watson	Bradbury	Woodley	Jones	Smith	Beesley	McKinven
4	7 Sep	Queens Park Rangers	(H)	1-3	(1-2)	L	14069	McKinven	Goy	Neal	King	Bentley	Watson	Bradbury	Woodley	Ashworth	Smith	Beesley	McKinven
5	9	Barnsley	(H)	4-1	(2-0)	W	10441	Ashworth(2),Beesley(2)	Goy	Neal	King	Bentley	Watson	Bradbury	Woodley	Ashworth	Beesley	McNeill	McKinven
6	14	Bristol Rovers	(A)	1-3	(1-2)	L	8613	Beesley	Goy	Neal	King	Bentley	Watson	Bradbury	Woodley	Ashworth	Beesley	McNeill	McKinven
7	16	Hull City	(H)	1-1	(0-1)	D	11764	Smith	Goy	Costello	King	Bentley	Watson	Bradbury	Woodley	Smith	Smith	Beesley	McKinven
8	21	Oldham Athletic	(H)	2-2	(1-2)	D	9968	Beesley,Gilfillan	Goy	Costello	King	Bentley	Watson	Bradbury	Woodley	Smith	Gilfillan	Beesley	McKinven
9	28	Peterborough United	(A)	0-3	(0-1)	L	11173		Goy	Costello	Neal	Bentley	Watson	Bradbury	Woodley	Jones	Gilfillan	Beesley	McKinven
10	2 Oct	Hull City	(A)	0-1	(0-1)	L	10706		Goy	Costello	Neal	Bentley	Watson	Bradbury	Woodley	Smith	Smith	McNeill	McKinven
11	5	Crewe Alexandra	(H)	1-1	(1-1)	D	8339	Smith	Rhodes	Costello	Neal	Bentley	Watson	Bradbury	Gilfillan	Cameron	Smith	McNeill	McKinven
12	7	Colchester United	(H)	0-0	(0-0)	D	8829		Rhodes	Costello	Neal	Bentley	Watson	Bradbury	Woodley	Cameron	Gilfillan	Beesley	McKinven
13	12	Port Vale	(A)	1-4	(0-2)	L	10306	McKinven	Rhodes	Neal	King	Bentley	Costello	Bradbury	Woodley	Friel	Gilfillan	Beesley	McKinven
14	14	Colchester United	(A)	3-3	(2-2)	D	6610	Smith(2),Ashworth	Rhodes	Neal	King	Bentley	Costello	Bradbury	Banks	Smith	Ashworth	Friel	McKinven
15	19	Reading	(H)	2-0	(0-0)	W	8325	Friel(2)	Rhodes	Neal	King	Bentley	Costello	Bradbury	Jones	Smith	Ashworth	Friel	McKinven
16	21	Watford	(H)	3-0	(1-0)	W	9827	Smith,Bradbury(pen),Friel	Rhodes	Neal	King	Bentley	Costello	Bradbury	Woodley	Smith	Ashworth	Friel	McKinven
17	26	Luton Town	(A)	1-4	(0-1)	L	5337	Bradbury(pen)	Rhodes	Neal	King	Bentley	Costello	Bradbury	Woodley	Smith	Ashworth	Friel	McKinven
18	29	Watford	(A)	1-3	(0-1)	L	9262	Smith	Rhodes	Neal	Neal	Bentley	Costello	Bradbury	Woodley	Smith	Conway	Friel	McKinven
19	2 Nov	Coventry City	(H)	1-2	(0-1)	L	12003	Bradbury(pen)	Rhodes	Costello	Neal	Bentley	Watson	Bradbury	Slater	Smith	Conway	Beesley	Woodley
20	9	Mansfield Town	(A)	1-4	(0-3)	L	8125	Jones	Goy	Costello	Neal	Bentley	Watson	Bradbury	Slater	Jones	Cameron	Cameron	McKinven
21	23	Shrewsbury Town	(A)	2-2	(0-2)	D	5151	McKinven(2)	Goy	Costello	Neal	Bentley	Watson	Ashworth	Slater	Gilfillan	Conway	Beesley	McKinven
22	30	Bristol City	(H)	1-1	(1-0)	D	6801	McKinven	Goy	Costello	Neal	Bentley	Watson	Ashworth	Slater	Gilfillan	Conway	Beesley	McKinven
23	7 Dec	Walsall	(A)	0-2	(0-1)	L	4566		Goy	Costello	Neal	Bentley	Watson	Ashworth	Slater	McNeill	Conway	Beesley	McKinven
24	14	Bournemouth	(A)	0-1	(0-0)	L	6034		Goy	Costello	Neal	Bentley	Watson	Ashworth	Woodley	Jones	Conway	Smith	McKinven
25	21	Wrexham	(H)	1-1	(0-0)	D	4829	Jones	Goy	Costello	King	Bentley	Watson	Ashworth	Woodley	Jones	Conway	Friel	McKinven
26	26	Crystal Palace	(H)	2-1	(0-1)	W	8392	Conway,Friel	Goy	Costello	King	Bentley	Watson	Ashworth	Woodley	Jones	Conway	Friel	McKinven
27	28	Crystal Palace	(A)	0-3	(0-2)	L	16168		Goy	Costello	King	Bentley	Watson	Ashworth	Woodley	Jones	Conway	Friel	McKinven
28	11 Jan	Queens Park Rangers	(A)	5-4	(3-1)	W	4674	Conway(2),Woodley,Smith,Brady(O.G.)	Rhodes	Costello	King	Bentley	Watson	Bradbury	Woodley	Smith	Conway	Beesley	McKinven
29	18	Bristol Rovers	(H)	3-4	(2-1)	L	6737	Smith,Beesley,Woodley	Rhodes	Costello	King	Bentley	Watson	Bradbury	Woodley	Smith	Conway	Beesley	McKinven
30	1 Feb	Oldham Athletic	(A)	2-0	(0-0)	W	12149	Conway,Beesley,Smith	Goy	Costello	King	Bentley	Watson	Bradbury	Woodley	Smith	Conway	Beesley	Slater
31	8	Peterborough United	(H)	2-0	(2-0)	W	8096	Conway(2)	Goy	Costello	King	Ashworth	Watson	Bradbury	Woodley	Smith	Conway	Beesley	McKinven
32	14	Crewe Alexandra	(A)	2-1	(1-1)	W	5926	Conway,Woodley	Goy	Costello	King	Bentley	Watson	Bradbury	Woodley	Smith	Conway	Beesley	McKinven
33	22	Port Vale	(H)	1-1	(0-0)	D	7612	Bradbury(pen)	Goy	Costello	King	Bentley	Watson	Bradbury	Woodley	Smith	Conway	Beesley	McKinven
34	29	Notts County	(A)	1-1	(0-0)	D	3610	Bradbury	Goy	Costello	King	Bentley	Bradbury	Slater	Smith	Watson	Conway	Beesley	Slater
35	7 Mar	Luton Town	(H)	0-1	(0-0)	L	5486		Goy	Costello	King	Bentley	Watson	Bradbury	Woodley	Gilfillan	Conway	Beesley	Gilfillan
36	13	Coventry City	(A)	5-2	(3-0)	W	28887	Beesley(2),Gilfillan,Bradbury,Woodley	Goy	Costello	King	Bentley	Watson	Bradbury	Woodley	Gilfillan	Conway	Beesley	McKinven
37	16	Brentford	(A)	2-1	(1-1)	W	6814	Beesley(2)	Goy	Costello	King	Bentley	Watson	Bradbury	Woodley	Gilfillan	Conway	Beesley	McKinven
38	20	Notts County	(H)	3-1	(2-1)	W	7575	Gilfillan,Conway,Hampton(O.G.)	Goy	Neal	King	Bentley	Watson	Bradbury	Woodley	Gilfillan	Conway	Beesley	McKinven
39	27	Millwall	(A)	1-1	(1-1)	D	18418	Smith	Goy	Costello	King	Bentley	Watson	Bradbury	Woodley	Smith	Conway	Beesley	McKinven
40	28	Brentford	(A)	0-3	(0-0)	L	9250		Goy	Neal	King	Bentley	Watson	Bradbury	Woodley	Smith	Conway	Beesley	Slater
41	30	Millwall	(H)	1-1	(0-1)	D	10173	Gilfillan	Goy	Neal	King	Bentley	Watson	Bradbury	Woodley	Smith	Conway	Beesley	Gilfillan
42	4 Apr	Shrewsbury Town	(H)	7-1	(4-0)	W	4668	Gilfillan(4),Smith(2),Bradbury	Goy	Neal	King	Bentley	Watson	Bradbury	Woodley	Smith	Gilfillan	Beesley	McKinven
43	11	Bristol City	(A)	2-2	(0-0)	D	7314	Bradbury(2)	Goy	Neal	King	Bentley	Watson	Bradbury	Slater	Smith	Gilfillan	Beesley	McKinven
44	18	Walsall	(H)	1-1	(1-0)	D	7467	Gilfillan	Goy	Neal	King	Bentley	Costello	Bradbury	Slater	Smith	Gilfillan	Beesley	McKinven
45	20	Mansfield Town	(H)	2-1	(2-1)	W	6562	Friel(2)	Goy	Neal	King	Bentley	Costello	Ashworth	Woodley	Friel	Gilfillan	Beesley	McKinven
46	25	Reading	(A)	2-4	(0-3)	L	5973	Ashworth,Beesley	White	Neal	King	Bentley	Watson	Ashworth	Woodley	Friel	Gilfillan	Beesley	McKinven

Major Cup Competitions

Rd.	Date	Opposition	Venue	Score	H.T.	Res.	Att.	Goalscorers	1	2	3	4	5	6	7	8	9	10	11
F.A.Cup																			
R1	16 Nov	Yeovil Town	(A)	0-1	(0-0)	L	7631		Goy	Costello	Neal	Bentley	Watson	Bradbury	Slater	Jones	Conway	Ashworth	McKinven
League Cup																			
R1		Bye																	
R2	25 Sep	Port Vale	(H)	2-1	(0-0)	W	7209	Gilfillan,McKinven	Goy	Costello	Neal	Bentley	Watson	Bradbury	Woodley	Jones	Gilfillan	Beesley	McKinven
R3	16 Oct	Swindon Town	(A)	0-3	(0-2)	L	12046		Goy	Neal	King	Bentley	Costello	Bradbury	Jones	Smith	Ashworth	Friel	McKinven

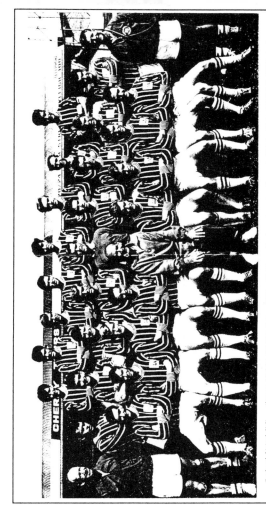

Southend United F.C. — Season 1963-64. REAR: Ewing, White, Matthews, Harrison, Langston, Barnard, Wright, Watts. MIDDLE ROW: Assistant trainer Jack French, Bradbury, King, Liggitt, Smith, Goy, Costello, McKinven, Beesley, Ashworth, trainer-coach Ernie Shepherd. FRONT ROW (seated): Friel, McNeill, Jones, Neal, Manager Ted Fenton, Woodley, Bentley, Watson, Gilfillan.

Appearances and Goals

Name	Appearances Lge.	FAC	L.C.	Total	Goals Lge.	FAC	L.C.	Total
ASHWORTH, Barry	18	1	1	20	4			4
BANKS, Frank	1			1				
BEESLEY, Micky	34		1	35	13			13
BENTLEY, Tony	45	1	2	48	9			9
BRADBURY, Terry	37	1	2	40	9			9
CAMERON, Bobby	3			3				
CONWAY, James	24	1		25	8			8
COSTELLO, Lou	33	1	2	36				
FRIEL, Benny	11	1		12	6			6
GILFILLAN, Bobby	18	1		19	9		1	10
GOY, Peter	34	1	2	37				
JONES, Ken	10	1	2	13	3			3
KING, Bobby	36		1	37				
McKINVEN, John	42	1	2	45	6	1		7
McNEILL, Ian	5			5				
NEAL, John	30	1	2	33				
RHODES, Brian	11			11				
SLATER, Malcolm	10	1		11				
SMITH, Ray J	28		1	29	12			12
WATSON, Peter	39	1	1	41				
WHITE, Ray	1			1				
WOODLEY, Derek	36		1	37	5			5
Own Goals					2			2

Ps	P	W	D	L	F	A	W	D	L	F	A	Pts.
14	46	9	10	4	42	26	6	5	12	35	52	45

1963/64

Season 1964/65 – League Division Three

No.	Date	Opposition	Venue	Score	H.T.	Res.	Att.	Goalscorers	1	2	3	4	5	6	7	8	9	10	11
1	22 Aug	Shrewsbury Town	(H)	1-0	(1-0)	W	10777	Beesley	McKechnie	Costello	King	Bentley	Watson	Bradbury	Woodley	Ashworth	Gilfillan	Beesley	McKinven
2	24	Queens Park Rangers	(A)	0-2	(0-1)	L	6709		McKechnie	Costello	King	Bentley	Watson	Bradbury	Woodley	Ashworth	Gilfillan	Beesley	McKinven
3	29	Reading	(A)	0-2	(0-1)	L	7558		McKechnie	Costello	King	Bentley	Watson	Bradbury	Woodley	Ashworth	Gilfillan	Beesley	McKinven
4	31	Queens Park Rangers	(H)	0-0	(0-0)	D	10862		McKechnie	Costello	King	Bentley	Watson	Bradbury	Slater	Friel	Gilfillan	Beesley	Howe
5	5 Sep	Peterborough United	(A)	2-4	(1-2)	L	10404	Friel(2)	McKechnie	Hutton	King	Bentley	Bradbury	Ashworth	Slater	Friel	Gilfillan	Beesley	Howe
6	8	Bristol City	(A)	0-4	(0-1)	L	11737		McKechnie	Neal	King	Banks	Bradbury	Ashworth	Woodley	Friel	Gilfillan	Beesley	Slater
7	12	Barnsley	(H)	2-0	(1-0)	W	6131	Conway,Ashworth	McKechnie	Neal	King	Ashworth	Metcalf	Bradbury	Slater	Smith	Conway	Beesley	Woodley
8	14	Bristol City	(H)	0-2	(0-1)	L	8780		McKechnie	Neal	King	Banks	Metcalf	Bradbury	Slater	Friel	Conway	Beesley	Woodley
9	18	Scunthorpe United	(A)	1-2	(1-1)	L	6171	Beesley	McKechnie	Neal	King	Bentley	Metcalf	Bradbury	Slater	Gilfillan	Conway	Beesley	Woodley
10	29	Walsall	(H)	0-0	(0-0)	D	5847		McKechnie	Neal	King	Bentley	Watson	Bradbury	Woodley	Slater	Conway	Beesley	McKinven
11	30	Gillingham	(A)	0-1	(0-1)	L	13109		McKechnie	Neal	King	Bentley	Watson	Bradbury	Woodley	Friel	Conway	Beesley	Slater
12	3 Oct	Watford	(A)	1-2	(1-1)	L	8402	Slater	McKechnie	Neal	King	Bentley	Watson	Bradbury	Woodley	Beesley	Smith	Smillie	Slater
13	5	Gillingham	(H)	3-1	(1-0)	W	9001	Woodley(2),Gilfillan	McKechnie	Costello	Neal	Ashworth	Watson	Bradbury	Woodley	Slater	Bentley	Gilfillan	McKinven
14	10	Exeter City	(A)	0-0	(0-0)	D	6521		McKechnie	Costello	Neal	Ashworth	Watson	Bradbury	Woodley	Slater	Bentley	Gilfillan	McKinven
15	12	Workington	(H)	3-0	(2-0)	W	6397	Gilfillan(3)	McKechnie	Costello	Neal	Ashworth	Watson	Bradbury	Woodley	Smillie	Bentley	Gilfillan	McKinven
16	17	Oldham Athletic	(A)	2-0	(1-0)	W	8166	Gilfillan(2)	McKechnie	Costello	Neal	Ashworth	Watson	Bradbury	Smith	Smillie	Bentley	Gilfillan	McKinven
17	19	Workington	(A)	1-3	(1-2)	L	5229	Gilfillan	McKechnie	Costello	Neal	Bentley	Watson	Bradbury	Slater	Smillie	Smith	Gilfillan	McKinven
18	24	Bristol Rovers	(H)	6-3	(4-1)	W	6343	McKinven(3),Smith(2),Smillie	McKechnie	Costello	Neal	Bentley	Watson	Bradbury	Slater	Smillie	Smith	Gilfillan	McKinven
19	28	Grimsby Town	(A)	0-1	(0-0)	L	5729		McKechnie	Costello	Neal	Bentley	Watson	Bradbury	Slater	Smillie	Smith	Gilfillan	McKinven
20	31	Brentford	(A)	1-2	(1-2)	L	11215	Smith	McKechnie	Costello	Neal	Bentley	Watson	Bradbury	Slater	Smillie	Smith	Gilfillan	McKinven
21	7 Nov	Colchester United	(H)	6-3	(4-1)	W	6915	Gilfillan(4),McKinven(2)	McKechnie	Costello	Neal	Bentley	Watson	Bradbury	Slater	Smillie	Smith	Gilfillan	McKinven
22	21	Carlisle United	(A)	1-0	(1-0)	W	6422	Neal	McKechnie	Costello	Neal	Ashworth	Watson	Bradbury	Slater	Smillie	Smith	Gilfillan	McKinven
23	28	Luton Town	(H)	1-0	(1-0)	W	5020	Smillie	McKechnie	Costello	Neal	Bentley	Watson	Bradbury	Slater	Smillie	Smith	Gilfillan	McKinven
24	12 Dec	Shrewsbury Town	(A)	3-1	(1-0)	W	4047	Smillie(2),Smith	McKechnie	Costello	Neal	Bentley	Watson	Bradbury	Slater	Smillie	Smith	Gilfillan	McKinven
25	19	Reading	(H)	2-2	(2-0)	D	5326	Gilfillan(2)	McKechnie	Costello	Neal	Bentley	Watson	Bradbury	Slater	Smillie	Smith	Gilfillan	McKinven
26	26	Bournemouth	(A)	1-2	(0-0)	L	6863	Smillie	McKechnie	Costello	Neal	Bentley	Watson	Bradbury	Slater	Smillie	Smith	Gilfillan	McKinven
27	28	Bournemouth	(H)	2-1	(0-0)	W	6219	Gilfillan,Smillie	McKechnie	Costello	Neal	Bentley	Watson	Bradbury	Slater	Smillie	Ashworth	Gilfillan	McKinven
28	2 Jan	Peterborough United	(H)	2-0	(0-0)	W	6786	Costello,Gilfillan	McKechnie	Costello	Neal	Bentley	Watson	Bradbury	Slater	Smillie	Beesley	Gilfillan	McKinven
29	8	Port Vale	(A)	2-2	(1-1)	D	4852	Beesley,Bradbury	McKechnie	Costello	Neal	Bentley	Watson	Bradbury	Slater	Smillie	Beesley	Gilfillan	McKinven
30	16	Barnsley	(A)	4-1	(4-0)	W	2898	Bradbury,Smillie,Beesley,Gilfillan	McKechnie	Costello	Neal	Bentley	Watson	Bradbury	Slater	Smillie	Beesley	Gilfillan	McKinven
31	23	Scunthorpe United	(H)	0-1	(0-0)	L	7630		McKechnie	Costello	Neal	Bentley	Watson	Bradbury	Slater	Smillie	Beesley	Gilfillan	McKinven
32	30	Mansfield Town	(H)	1-4	(1-4)	L	5360	McKinven	McKechnie	Costello	Neal	Bentley	Watson	Bradbury	Slater	Smillie	Beesley	Gilfillan	McKinven
33	6 Feb	Walsall	(A)	3-2	(0-0)	W	5916	Beesley(2),Smith	McKechnie	Costello	Neal	Bentley	Watson	Bradbury	Slater	Smith	Beesley	Gilfillan	McKinven
34	13	Watford	(H)	0-1	(0-1)	L	7272		McKechnie	Costello	Neal	Bentley	Watson	Bradbury	Slater	Smillie	Bullock	Gilfillan	McKinven
35	20	Exeter City	(H)	1-1	(0-0)	D	4946	Smillie	McKechnie	Costello	Neal	Bentley	Watson	Bradbury	Slater	Smillie	Bullock	Gilfillan	McKinven
36	27	Oldham Athletic	(H)	6-1	(3-1)	W	5584	Bradbury(2),Gilfillan(2),Woodley,Smillie	McKechnie	Costello	Neal	Bentley	Watson	Bradbury	Woodley	Smillie	Bullock	Gilfillan	McKinven
37	13 Mar	Brentford	(H)	0-1	(0-1)	L	7888		McKechnie	Neal	May	Bentley	Watson	Bradbury	Woodley	Smillie	Bullock	Gilfillan	McKinven
38	20	Colchester United	(A)	1-3	(1-2)	L	2923	Bullock	McKechnie	Neal	May	Bentley	Watson	Bradbury	Woodley	Beesley	Bullock	Gilfillan	McKinven
39	26	Port Vale	(H)	2-1	(1-0)	W	6017	McKinven,King	McKechnie	Neal	May	Bentley	Watson	Bradbury	Woodley	Bullock	King	Gilfillan	McKinven
40	2 Apr	Carlisle United	(A)	3-4	(1-3)	L	12050	Bradbury,Slater,Bullock	McKechnie	Costello	Neal	Bentley	Conway	Bradbury	Slater	Bullock	King	Smillie	McKinven
41	5	Mansfield Town	(A)	1-6	(0-1)	L	11850	Gilfillan	McKechnie	Bentley	King	Bradbury	Conway	Beesley	Gilfillan	Smillie	Smith	Bullock	McKinven
42	10	Luton Town	(H)	5-0	(2-0)	W	4968	McKinven(2),Gilfillan,Bentley,Reid(O.G.)	McKechnie	Costello	King	Bentley	Watson	Bradbury	Woodley	Smillie	Smith	Gilfillan	McKinven
43	16	Hull City	(H)	2-1	(1-1)	W	11023	Bentley,King	McKechnie	Costello	King	Bentley	Watson	Bradbury	Woodley	Smillie	Smith	Gilfillan	McKinven
44	17	Bristol Rovers	(A)	2-2	(0-0)	D	5578	McKinven,Watson	McKechnie	King	Costello	Bentley	Watson	Bradbury	McKinven	Smillie	Smith	Gilfillan	Woodley
45	19	Hull City	(A)	0-0	(0-0)	D	20984		McKechnie	Costello	King	Bentley	Watson	Bradbury	Woodley	Smillie	Gilfillan	Smith	McKinven
46	24	Grimsby Town	(H)	4-0	(4-0)	W	6529	Gilfillan(2),Smith,McKinven	McKechnie	Costello	King	Bentley	Watson	Bradbury	Woodley	Smillie	Smith	Gilfillan	McKinven

Major Cup Competitions

									1	2	3	4	5	6	7	8	9	10	11
Rd.	Date	Opposition	Venue	Score	H.T.	Res.	Att.	Goalscorers											
			F.A.Cup																
R1	14 Nov	Luton Town	(A)	0-1	(0-1)	L	6892		McKechnie	Costello	Neal	Ashworth	Watson	Bradbury	Slater	Smillie	Smith	Gilfillan	McKinven
			League Cup																
R1	2 Sep	Brentford	(A)	2-0	(1-0)	W	5380	Gilfillan, Beesley	McKechnie	Hutton	King	Bentley	Bradbury	Ashworth	Slater	Friel	Gilfillan	Beesley	Howe
R2	22	Hull City	(A)	0-0	(0-0)	D	4012		McKechnie	Neal	King	Bentley	Watson	Bradbury	Woodley	Slater	Conway	Beesley	McKinven
R2r	28	Hull City	(H)	3-1	(2-0)	W	5420	Bentley, Conway, Slater	McKechnie	Neal	King	Bentley	Watson	Bradbury	Woodley	Friel	Conway	Beesley	Slater
R3	14 Oct	Stoke City	(A)	1-3	(1-2)	L	8284	Ashworth	McKechnie	Costello	Neal	Bentley	Watson	Ashworth	Woodley	Smillie	Gilfillan	Beesley	McKinven

Southend United F.C., 1964/65. BACK ROW: Smith, Neal, Shires, Barnard, White, McKechnie, Watson, Conway. MIDDLE ROW: Bradbury, Ashworth, Woodley, Howe, Mathews, Ewing, Day, McKinven, Costello, Beesley. FRONT ROW: King, Hutton, Gilfillan, Friel, Slater, Bentley, Banks, Wright.

Appearances and Goals

Name	Appearances Lge	FAC	L.C.	Total	Goals Lge	FAC	L.C.	Total
ASHWORTH, Barry	13	1	2	16	1	1		2
BANKS, Frank	2		2					
BEESLEY, Micky	19		4	23	6		1	7
BENTLEY, Tony	42		4	46	2		1	3
BRADBURY, Terry	46	1	3	50	5			5
BULLOCK, Peter	8			8	2			2
CONWAY, James	7		2	9	1		1	2
COSTELLO, Lou	35	1	1	37	1			1
FRIEL, Benny	6		2	8	2			2
GILFILLAN, Bobby	39	1	2	42	22	1		23
HOWE, Tony	2		1	3				
HUTTON, Alec	1		1	2				
KING, Bobby	20		3	23	2			2
MAY, Eddie	2			2				
METCALF, Colin	3			3				
McKECHNIE, Ian	46	1	4	51				
McKINVEN, John	38	1	2	41	11			11
NEAL, John	35	1	3	39	1			1
SLATER, Malcolm	31	1	3	35	2		1	3
SMILLIE, Andy	30	1	1	32	9			9
SMITH, Ray J	20	1		21	6			6
WATSON, Peter	39	1	3	43	1			1
WOODLEY, Derek	22		3	25	3			3
Own Goals					1			1

	Ps	P	W	D	L	F	A	W	D	L	F	A	Pts.
1964/65	12	46	14	4	5	48	24	5	4	14	30	47	46

Season 1965/66 – League Division Three

No.	Date	Opposition	Venue	Score	H.T.	Res.	Att.	Goalscorers	No.	1	2	3	4	5	6	7	8	9	10	11	12
1	21 Aug	Swansea Town	(H)	2-0	(1-0)	W	11141	McKinven,Smith	1	McKechnie	Neal	King	Bentley	Bradbury	Smillie	Slater	Smith	Firmani	Bullock	McKinven	
2	25	Oxford United	(A)	2-3	(0-2)	L	10992	Slater,Firmani	2	McKechnie	Neal	King	Bentley	Bradbury	Smillie	Slater	Smith	Firmani	Bullock	McKinven	
3	28	Walsall	(A)	0-3	(0-2)	L	8450		3	McKechnie	Bentley	King	Slack	Bradbury	Smillie	Slater	Smith	Firmani	Bullock	McKinven	Gilfillan(3)
4	11 Sep	Bournemouth	(A)	0-0	(0-0)	D	5586		4	McKechnie	Neal	King	Bentley	Bradbury	Slack	Slater	Smith	Firmani	Smillie	McKinven	
5	13	York City	(H)	2-3	(1-2)	L	10530	Firmani,Slater	5	McKechnie	Neal	King	Bentley	Bradbury	Slack	Slater	Smith	Firmani	Smillie	McKinven	
6	17	Oldham Athletic	(A)	0-1	(0-0)	L	7548		6	McKechnie	Neal	King	Bentley	Bradbury	Slack	Slater	Smith	Firmani	Smillie	McKinven	Barnard(10)
7	24	Swindon Town	(H)	4-2	(3-1)	W	9748	Firmani(2),Gilfillan,Nurse(O.G.)	7	McKechnie	Bentley	King	Slack	Watson	Bradbury	Slater	Smith	Firmani	Gilfillan	McKinven	
8	1 Oct	Shrewsbury Town	(A)	0-3	(0-1)	L	5334		8	McKechnie	Bentley	King	Slack	Watson	Bradbury	Slater	Smillie	Firmani	Gilfillan	McKinven	Barnard(8)
9	4	York City	(A)	3-0	(1-0)	W	9751	Slater,Smillie,Slack	9	White	Bentley	King	Slack	Watson	Bradbury	Slater	Smith	Firmani	Gilfillan	Smillie	Barnard(8)
10	8	Millwall	(H)	0-2	(0-1)	L	15197		10	White	Bentley	King	Slack	Bradbury	Smillie	Slater	Smith	Firmani	Gilfillan	McKinven	
11	16	Peterborough United	(A)	0-4	(0-1)	L	9623		11	White	Neal	King	Bentley	Bradbury	Slack	Woodley	Barnard	Smith	Bullock	Smillie	Shires(3)
12	23	Exeter City	(H)	4-2	(1-1)	W	7249	McKinven(2),Gilfillan,Smith	12	McKechnie	King	Bentley	Slack	May	Smillie	Slater	Smith	Firmani	Gilfillan	McKinven	
13	25	Workington	(H)	3-1	(0-1)	W	8138	Firmani(2),Smillie	13	McKechnie	Bentley	King	Slack	May	Bradbury	Slater	Smith	Firmani	Gilfillan	Smillie	
14	30	Reading	(A)	0-1	(0-0)	L	8048		14	McKechnie	Bentley	King	Slack	May	Bradbury	Slater	Smith	Firmani	Gilfillan	Smillie	
15	6 Nov	Hull City	(H)	0-2	(0-2)	L	8088		15	McKechnie	Bentley	King	Slack	May	Bradbury	Slater	Smith	Firmani	Gilfillan	McKinven	
16	20	Queens Park Rangers	(H)	1-3	(1-2)	L	6690	Firmani	16	White	Bentley	Neal	Slack	May	Bradbury	Slater	Smith	Firmani	Smillie	McKinven	King(4)
17	22	Oxford United	(H)	2-1	(1-0)	W	4556	Firmani,Slater	17	White	Bentley	Neal	Slack	May	Bradbury	Slater	Barnard	Firmani	Smillie	McKinven	
18	27	Brighton	(A)	1-9	(0-3)	L	11124	Slack	18	White	Bentley	Neal	Slack	May	Bradbury	Slater	Barnard	Woodley	Smillie	McKinven	King(6)
19	11 Dec	Watford	(A)	1-4	(0-1)	L	5923	Firmani	19	McKechnie	Bentley	King	Slack	May	Bradbury	Slater	Smith	Firmani	Smillie	McKinven	
20	18	Peterborough United	(H)	2-0	(2-0)	W	5478	Firmani,Smith	20	McKechnie	Bentley	King	Slack	May	Bradbury	Slater	Smith	Firmani	Smillie	McKinven	
21	1 Jan	Millwall	(A)	0-2	(0-2)	L	15748		21	McKechnie	Bentley	King	Slack	May	Bradbury	Woodley	Slater	Smith	Smillie	McKinven	Mathews(5)
22	8	Mansfield Town	(H)	1-0	(1-0)	W	7155	Birks	22	Roberts	Bentley	Birks	Slack	May	Bradbury	Slater	Smith	Firmani	Smillie	McKinven	
23	15	Exeter City	(A)	1-1	(0-0)	D	4845	Smith	23	Roberts	Bentley	Birks	Slack	May	Bradbury	Slater	Smith	Firmani	Smillie	McKinven	Mathews(7)
24	29	Swansea Town	(A)	0-5	(0-2)	L	7500		24	Roberts	Bentley	Birks	Slack	May	Bradbury	Banks	Smith	Firmani	Smillie	McKinven	
25	5 Feb	Walsall	(H)	5-3	(3-2)	W	6310	Bentley,Bradbury,Smith,Firmani,Atthey(O.G.)	25	Roberts	Bentley	Birks	Slack	May	Bradbury	Woodley	Smith	Firmani	Smillie	McKinven	
26	12	Bristol Rovers	(H)	2-0	(0-0)	W	6311	Slack,Smillie	26	Roberts	Bentley	Birks	Slack	May	Bradbury	Woodley	Smith	Firmani	Smillie	McKinven	
27	19	Workington	(A)	1-3	(0-1)	L	3505	McKinven	27	Roberts	Bentley	Birks	Slack	May	Bradbury	Woodley	Smith	Firmani	Smillie	McKinven	
28	26	Bournemouth	(H)	1-2	(1-2)	L	5422	Smillie	28	Roberts	Bentley	Birks	Slack	May	Bradbury	Woodley	Smith	Firmani	Smillie	McKinven	
29	1 Mar	Brentford	(A)	0-2	(0-2)	L	9007		29	Roberts	Bentley	Birks	Slack	May	Bradbury	Woodley	Slater	Smith	Smillie	Barnard	
30	5	Bristol Rovers	(A)	1-3	(1-1)	L	7844	McKinven	30	Roberts	Bentley	Birks	Slack	May	Bradbury	Woodley	Slater	Smith	Smillie	McKinven	Barnard(3)
31	7	Brentford	(H)	1-0	(1-0)	W	7029	Firmani	31	Roberts	Bentley	Mathews	Slack	May	Smillie	Woodley	Slater	Firmani	King	McKinven	
32	11	Oldham Athletic	(H)	0-2	(0-1)	L	5145		32	Roberts	Bentley	Mathews	Slack	May	Smillie	Woodley	Slater	Firmani	King	McKinven	Bradbury(11)
33	14	Shrewsbury Town	(H)	2-0	(2-0)	W	5046	Smillie,Firmani	33	Roberts	Bentley	Mathews	Slack	May	Bradbury	Woodley	Slater	Firmani	Beanland	Slater	
34	19	Swindon Town	(A)	0-4	(0-3)	L	12352		34	Roberts	Bentley	Mathews	Slack	May	Bradbury	Slater	Smith	Firmani	Beanland	Smillie	Woodley(8)
35	8 Apr	Gillingham	(H)	5-2	(1-2)	W	7975	Firmani(3),Smith(2)	35	Roberts	Bentley	Birks	Slack	Bradbury	Beanland	Woodley	Smith	Firmani	Smillie	Slater	
36	11	Gillingham	(A)	0-1	(0-0)	L	6613		36	Roberts	Bentley	Birks	Slack	May	Beanland	Woodley	Smith	Firmani	Smillie	Slater	
37	16	Queens Park Rangers	(A)	1-2	(0-2)	L	7028	Bradbury	37	Roberts	Bentley	Birks	Beanland	May	Beanland	Woodley	Smith	Firmani	Smillie	McKinven	
38	22	Brighton	(H)	0-0	(0-0)	D	6660		38	Roberts	Bentley	Birks	Slack	May	Bradbury	Woodley	Smith	Firmani	Smillie	McKinven	
39	25	Grimsby Town	(A)	3-1	(3-1)	W	7000	Woodley,Smith,Smillie	39	Roberts	Bentley	Birks	Beanland	May	Beanland	Woodley	Slater	Smith	Smillie	Mathews	
40	30	Scunthorpe United	(H)	0-0	(0-0)	D	4233		40	Roberts	Bentley	Birks	Firmani	Bradbury	Beanland	Woodley	Slater	Smith	Firmani	Slater	
41	6 May	Watford	(H)	1-0	(1-0)	W	6400	Smillie	41	Roberts	Bentley	Birks	Firmani	Bradbury	Beanland	Woodley	Slater	Smith	Smillie	Slater	
42	9	Mansfield Town	(A)	0-2	(0-1)	L	6545		42	Roberts	Bentley	Birks	Beanland	May	Bradbury	Woodley	Slack	Firmani	Firmani	Slater	
43	13	Scunthorpe United	(A)	0-1	(0-0)	L	7120		43	Roberts	Bentley	Birks	Firmani	Bradbury	Beanland	Woodley	Slack	Smith	Smillie	Slater	
44	17	Grimsby Town	(H)	0-0	(0-0)	L	4340		44	Roberts	Bentley	Birks	Beanland	May	Bradbury	Woodley	Slack	Smith	Smith	Slater	
45	20	Hull City	(A)	0-1	(0-0)	L	30371		45	Roberts	Bentley	Birks	Beanland	May	Bradbury	Woodley	Slack	Firmani	Smith	Smillie	
46	27	Reading	(H)	2-1	(1-1)	W	3600	Smith(2)	46	Roberts	Bentley	Birks	Beanland	May	Bradbury	Woodley	Slack	Smith	Lumsden	Smillie	

Major Cup Competitions

Rd.	Date	Opposition	Venue	Score	H.T.	Res.	Att.	Goalscorers
		F.A.Cup						
R1	13 Nov	Notts County	(A)	3-1	(2-0)	W	8408	Slack,McKinven,Bentley
R2	4 Dec	Watford	(H)	2-1	(2-0)	W	10583	Firmani(2)
R3	22 Jan	Rotherham United	(A)	2-3	(2-2)	L	11000	Banks,Bentley
		League Cup						
R1	1 Sep	Newport County	(A)	2-2	(1-1)	D	3500	Barnard(2)
R1r	6	Newport County	(H)	3-1	(2-1)	W	8644	Smith,Firmani,Barnard
R2	22	Reading	(A)	1-5	(1-0)	L	7664	Firmani

1	2	3	4	5	6	7	8	9	10	11	12
McKech'	Bentley	Neal	Slack	May	Bradbury	Slater	Smith	Firmani	Smillie	McKinven	
McKech'	Bentley	King	Slack	May	Bradbury	Slater	Smith	Firmani	Smillie	McKinven	
Roberts	Bentley	Neal	Slack	May	Bradbury	Banks	Smith	Firmani	Smillie	McKinven	
McKech'	Mathews	Neal	Bentley	Bradbury	Smillie	Woodley	Smith	Firmani	Barnard	Slater	
McKech'	Neal	King	Bentley	Bradbury	Smillie	Slater	Smith	Firmani	Barnard	McKinven	
McKech'	Bradbury	King	Bentley	Smith	Slack	Slater	Barnard	Firmani	Smillie	McKinven	

Abbrev.: McKech' = McKechnie

SOUTHEND UNITED FOOTBALL CLUB. LIMITED

OFFICIAL PROGRAMME 6d.

Typical 1965/66 Programme Cover

Appearances and Goals

Name	Appearances				Goals			
	Lge.	FAC	L.C.	Total	Lge.	FAC	L.C.	Total
BANKS, Frank	1	1		2		1		1
BARNARD, Chris	4+4		3	7+4			3	3
BEANLAND, Tony	13			13				
BENTLEY, Tony	46	3	3	52	1	2		3
BIRKS, Graham	21			21	1			1
BRADBURY, Terry	42+1	3	3	48+1	2			2
BULLOCK, Peter	4			4				
FIRMANI, Eddie	36	3	3	42	16	2	2	20
GILFILLAN, Bobby	8+1			8+1	2			2
KING, Bobby	21+2	1	2	24+2				
LUMSDEN, Alex	1			1				
MATHEWS, Frank	5+2		1	6+2				
MAY, Eddie	30	3		33				
McKECHNIE, Ian	16	2	3	21				
McKINVEN, John	29	3	2	34	5	1		6
NEAL, John	9	2	2	13				
ROBERTS, Trevor	25	1		26				
SHIRES, Alan	0+1			0+1				
SLACK, Mel	44	3	1	48	3	1		4
SLATER, Malcolm	35	2	3	40	4			4
SMILLIE, Andy	43	3	3	49	7			7
SMITH, Ray J	41	3	3	47	10		1	11
WATSON, Peter	3			3				
WHITE, Ray	5			5				
WOODLEY, Derek	24+1		1	25+1	1			1
Own Goal					2			2

	Ps	P	W	D	L	F	A	W	D	L	F	A	Pts.
1965/66	21	46	15	1	7	43	28	1	3	19	11	55	36

Season 1966/67 – League Division Four

No.	Date	Opposition	Venue	Score	H.T.	Res.	Att.	Goalscorers	No.	1	2	3	4	5	6	7	8	9	10	11	12
1	20 Aug	Bradford City	(H)	2-1	(1-1)	W	4596	Beanland,Firmani	1	Roberts	Bentley	Birks	Slack	May	Beanland	Smillie	Slater	Firmani	Flatt	Baber	
2	27	Exeter City	(A)	1-0	(1-0)	W	4346	Baber	2	Roberts	Bentley	Mathews	Slack	May	Beanland	Smillie	Woodley	Smith	Flatt	Baber	
3	2 Sep	Hartlepools United	(H)	2-0	(1-0)	W	6689	Woodley,Firmani	3	Roberts	Bentley	Birks	Slack	May	Beanland	Smillie	Woodley	Firmani	Smith	Baber	
4	7	Chester	(A)	1-1	(0-0)	D	6123	Smith	4	Roberts	Bentley	Birks	Slack	May	Beanland	Smillie	Woodley	Firmani	Smith	Baber	
5	9	Halifax Town	(A)	2-2	(0-2)	D	2835	Firmani,Baber	5	Roberts	Bentley	Birks	Slack	May	Beanland	Smillie	Woodley	Firmani	Smith	Baber	
6	17	Brentford	(H)	3-0	(3-0)	W	8200	Woodley,Bentley,Firmani	6	Roberts	Bentley	Mathews	Slack	May	Beanland	Smillie	Woodley	Firmani	Smith	Baber	Flatt(9)
7	24	Newport County	(A)	0-3	(0-2)	L	2994		7	Roberts	Bentley	Birks	Slack	May	Beanland	Smillie	Woodley	Firmani	Smith	Baber	
8	26	Chester	(H)	5-1	(4-0)	W	8822	Smith(3),Baber,Firmani	8	Roberts	Bentley	Birks	Slack	May	Beanland	Smillie	Woodley	Firmani	Smith	Baber	
9	30	Barnsley	(H)	3-0	(1-0)	W	9576	Smith(2),Baber	9	Roberts	Bentley	Birks	Slack	May	Beanland	Smillie	Woodley	Firmani	Smith	Baber	
10	8 Oct	Bradford Park Avenue	(A)	2-1	(2-1)	W	5391	Woodley,Smith	10	Roberts	Bentley	Birks	Slack	May	Beanland	Smillie	Woodley	Smith	McKinven	Baber	
11	14	Port Vale	(H)	4-1	(4-0)	W	12609	Firmani(2),Beanland,Baber	11	Roberts	Bentley	Birks	Slack	Haddrick	Beanland	Smillie	Woodley	Firmani	Smith	Baber	
12	17	Wrexham	(A)	0-2	(0-2)	L	14050		12	Roberts	Bentley	Birks	Slack	Firmani	Beanland	Smillie	Woodley	Smith	McKinven	Baber	
13	22	Crewe Alexandra	(A)	0-1	(0-0)	L	4063		13	Roberts	Bentley	Birks	Slack	Haddrick	Beanland	Smillie	Woodley	Smith	Flatt	Slater	
14	28	Barrow	(H)	1-3	(0-1)	L	9063	Baber	14	Roberts	Bentley	Birks	Slack	May	Beanland	Smillie	Woodley	Firmani	Smith	Baber	
15	4 Nov	York City	(A)	1-2	(1-0)	L	4079	Baber	15	Roberts	Bentley	Birks	Slack	May	Beanland	Smillie	Woodley	Firmani	Smith	Baber	
16	12	Lincoln City	(H)	3-0	(1-0)	W	6761	Smith(2),Woodley	16	Roberts	Bentley	Birks	Slack	May	Beanland	Smillie	Woodley	Firmani	Smith	Baber	
17	14	Wrexham	(H)	1-1	(1-0)	D	9221	Smith	17	Roberts	Bentley	Birks	Slack	May	Beanland	Smillie	Woodley	Firmani	Smith	Baber	
18	19	Chesterfield	(A)	1-2	(1-0)	L	5007	Woodley	18	Roberts	Bentley	Birks	Slack	May	Beanland	Smillie	Woodley	Firmani	Flatt	Baber	
19	3 Dec	Rochdale	(A)	2-1	(1-0)	W	1733	Flatt,Slack	19	Roberts	Bentley	Birks	Slack	May	Beanland	Smillie	Slater	Smith	Smith	Baber	
20	10	Southport	(A)	0-1	(0-1)	L	7466		20	Roberts	Bentley	Birks	Slack	May	Beanland	Smillie	Slater	Firmani	Flatt	Baber	
21	17	Bradford City	(A)	1-2	(0-1)	L	3010	Bentley	21	Roberts	Bentley	Birks	Slack	May	Beanland	Smillie	Slater	Smith	Smith	Baber	
22	26	Aldershot	(H)	2-5	(1-2)	L	6049	Baber,Flatt	22	Roberts	Bentley	Birks	Slack	May	Beanland	Smillie	Slater	Smith	Flatt	Baber	Mathews(9)
23	27	Aldershot	(A)	4-0	(2-0)	W	6864	Beanland,May,Firmani,Slack	23	Roberts	Bentley	Birks	Slack	May	Beanland	Smillie	Woodley	Firmani	Flatt	Baber	
24	31	Exeter City	(H)	0-0	(0-0)	D	6534		24	Roberts	Bentley	Birks	Slack	May	Beanland	Smillie	Woodley	Firmani	McKinven	Baber	
25	6 Jan	Hartlepools United	(A)	2-1	(1-0)	W	9574	Bentley,Baber	25	Roberts	Bentley	Birks	Slack	May	Beanland	Smillie	Woodley	Flatt	Baber	McKinven	
26	14	Halifax Town	(H)	1-0	(0-0)	W	6905	Flatt	26	Roberts	Bentley	Birks	Slack	May	Beanland	Smillie	Woodley	Flatt	Lumsden	McKinven	Mathews(10)
27	21	Brentford	(A)	1-1	(1-0)	D	10646	Flatt	27	Roberts	Bentley	Birks	Slack	May	Beanland	Smillie	Baber	Ingle	Flatt	McKinven	Woodley(8)
28	4 Feb	Newport County	(H)	1-0	(1-0)	W	7476	May	28	Roberts	Bentley	Birks	Slack	May	Beanland	Smillie	Woodley	Ingle	Flatt	Firmani	
29	11	Barnsley	(A)	2-1	(1-1)	W	7648	Ingle(2)	29	Roberts	Bentley	Birks	Slack	May	Beanland	Smillie	Woodley	Ingle	Smith	McKinven	
30	18	Notts County	(H)	1-0	(0-0)	W	8476	Smith	30	Roberts	Bentley	Birks	Slack	May	Beanland	Smillie	Baber	Ingle	Smith	McKinven	Flatt(8)
31	25	Bradford Park Avenue	(H)	4-0	(1-0)	W	7749	Smith(3),Ingle	31	Roberts	Bentley	Birks	Slack	May	Beanland	Smillie	Woodley	Ingle	Smith	McKinven	
32	4 Mar	Port Vale	(A)	3-1	(2-1)	W	4695	Woodley,Smith,McKinven	32	Roberts	Bentley	Birks	Slack	May	Beanland	Baber	Woodley	Ingle	Smith	McKinven	
33	11	Notts County	(A)	0-1	(0-1)	L	3858		33	Roberts	Bentley	Birks	Slack	May	Beanland	Smillie	Woodley	Ingle	Smith	McKinven	
34	17	Crewe Alexandra	(H)	1-1	(1-1)	D	9453	McKinven	34	Roberts	Bentley	Birks	Slack	May	Beanland	Smillie	Woodley	Ingle	Smith	McKinven	
35	17	Tranmere Rovers	(A)	2-1	(0-1)	W	12701	Flatt(2)	35	Roberts	Bentley	Birks	Slack	May	Beanland	Smillie	Flatt	Ingle	Smith	McKinven	
36	25	Stockport County	(A)	1-4	(0-3)	L	9024	Bentley	36	Roberts	Bentley	Birks	Slack	May	Beanland	Smillie	Flatt	Ingle	Smith	McKinven	
37	27	Tranmere Rovers	(H)	0-0	(0-0)	D	10049		37	Roberts	Bentley	Birks	Slack	May	Beanland	Smillie	Woodley	Smith	Flatt	McKinven	
38	31	York City	(A)	2-1	(1-0)	W	8513	McKinven,Flatt	38	Roberts	Bentley	Birks	Slack	May	Beanland	Smillie	Woodley	Smith	Smith	McKinven	
39	8 Apr	Lincoln City	(A)	2-2	(1-1)	D	3116	Smith(2)	39	Roberts	Bentley	Birks	Slack	May	Ingle	Woodley	Flatt	Ingle	McKinven	Baber	
40	13	Luton Town	(A)	0-1	(0-0)	L	4666		40	Roberts	Bentley	Mathews	Slack	May	Beanland	Smillie	Woodley	Ingle	Smith	McKinven	
41	15	Chesterfield	(H)	4-1	(0-0)	W	6895	Smillie,Smith,Woodley,Flatt	41	Roberts	Bentley	Mathews	Slack	May	Beanland	Smillie	Woodley	Flatt	Smith	McKinven	
42	22	Barrow	(A)	0-1	(0-1)	L	5847		42	Roberts	Mathews	Birks	Bentley	May	Beanland	Baber	Flatt	Smith	Smillie	McKinven	
43	24	Luton Town	(H)	2-0	(2-0)	W	7249	Smith,Smillie	43	Roberts	Mathews	Birks	Bentley	May	Beanland	Woodley	Slack	Smith	Smillie	McKinven	
44	29	Rochdale	(H)	0-0	(0-0)	D	8236		44	Roberts	Mathews	Birks	Bentley	May	Beanland	Woodley	Slack	Smith	Smillie	McKinven	
45	6 May	Southport	(A)	0-1	(0-0)	L	8999		45	Roberts	Ingle	Birks	Bentley	May	Beanland	Woodley	Slack	Smith	Smillie	McKinven	Ingle(11)
46	13	Stockport County	(H)	0-1	(0-0)	L	6581		46	Roberts	Ingle	Birks	Bentley	May	Smillie	Woodley	Slack	Smith	Flatt	McKinven	Baber(9)

Major Cup Competitions

Rd.	Date	Opposition	Venue Score	H.T.	Res.	Att.	Goalscorers	1	2	3	4	5	6	7	8	9	10	11	12
F.A.Cup																			
R1	26 Nov	Watford	(A) 0-1	(0-0)	L	8797		Roberts	Bentley	Birks	Slack	May	Beanland	Woodley	Smillie	Firmani	Smith	Baber	
League Cup																			
R1	24 Aug	Gillingham	(H) 0-0	(0-0)	D	5661		Roberts	Bentley	Mathews	Slack	May	Beanland	Smillie	Slater	Smith	Flatt	Baber	Woodley(3)
R1r	31	Gillingham	(A) 0-2	(0-0)	L	7010		Roberts	Mathews	Birks	Slack	May	Beanland	Smillie	Woodley	Smith	Flatt	Baber	Slater(10)

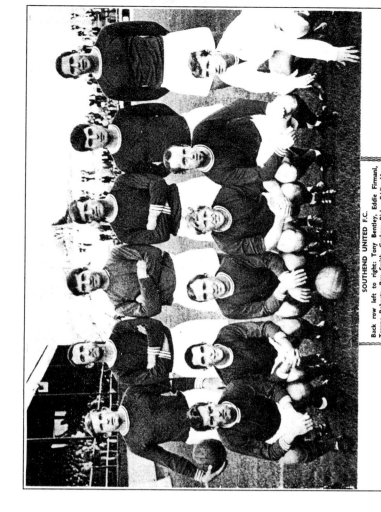

SOUTHEND UNITED F.C.

Back row left to right: Tony Bentley, Eddie Firmani, Trevor Roberts, Ray Smith, Graham Birks, Eddie May. Front: Derek Woodley, John Baber, Andy Smillie, Mel Slack, Tony Beanland, Malcolm Slater. (Prov. l.)

Appearances and Goals

Name	Appearances				Goals			
	Lge.	FAC	L.C.	Total	Lge.	FAC	L.C.	Total
BABER, John	28+1	1	2	31+1	9			9
BEANLAND, Tony	44	1	2	47	3			3
BENTLEY, Tony	46	1	1	48	4			4
BIRKS, Graham	42	1	1	44				
FIRMANI, Eddie	19			20	8			8
FLATT, Colin	20+2		2	22+2	8			8
HADDRICK, Bobby	2			2				
INGLE, Steve	14+1			14+1	3			3
LUMSDEN, Alex	1			1				
MATHEWS, Frank	7+2		2	9+2				
MAY, Eddie	42	1	2	45	2			2
McKINVEN, John	24			24	3			3
ROBERTS, Trevor	46	1	2	49				
SLACK, Mel	45	1	2	48	2			2
SLATER, Malcolm	6		1+1	7+1				
SMILLIE, Andy	45	1	2	48	2			2
SMITH, Ray J	39	1	2	42	19			19
WOODLEY, Derek	36+1	1	1+1	38+2	7			7

	Ps	P	W	D	L	F	A	W	D	L	F	A	Pts.
1966/67	6	46	15	5	3	44	12	7	4	12	26	37	53

Season 1967/68 – League Division Four

No.	Date	Opposition	Venue	Score	H.T.	Res.	Att.	Goalscorers	1	2	3	4	5	6	7	8	9	10	11	12
1	19 Aug	Port Vale	(A)	2-1	(0-1)	W	7451	McKinven(pen),Chisnall	Roberts	Bentley	Birks	Stevenson	May	Ashworth	Ferguson	Chisnall	Smillie	Baber	McKinven	
2	25	Wrexham	(H)	3-1	(1-1)	W	11596	McKinven(2),Showell(O.G.)	Roberts	Bentley	Birks	Beesley	Ashworth	Stevenson	Baber	Chisnall	Smillie	Slack	McKinven	Beesley(3)
3	2 Sep	Barnsley	(A)	1-1	(0-0)	D	6797	Baber	Roberts	Bentley	Birks	Ashworth	May	Stevenson	Ferguson	Chisnall	Beesley	Slack	McKinven	McMillan(7)
4	4	Luton Town	(H)	3-0	(1-0)	W	11083	Smillie(2),Baber	Roberts	Bentley	Birks	Ashworth	May	Stevenson	Ferguson	Chisnall	Smillie	Baber	McKinven	Beesley(8)
5	8	Swansea Town	(H)	1-0	(0-0)	W	13502	Smillie	Roberts	Bentley	Birks	Ashworth	May	Stevenson	Ferguson	Chisnall	Smillie	Baber	McKinven	Slack(8)
6	16	Hartlepools United	(A)	1-0	(1-0)	W	5906	Baber	Roberts	Bentley	Birks	Ashworth	May	Stevenson	Ferguson	Chisnall	Smillie	Baber	McKinven	May
7	22	Newport County	(H)	2-2	(1-0)	D	15389	McKinven(pen),Wood(O.G.)	Roberts	Bentley	Birks	Ashworth	May	Stevenson	Ferguson	Chisnall	Smillie	Baber	McKinven	Ferguson
8	27	Luton Town	(A)	1-3	(0-1)	L	13332	Ferguson	Roberts	Bentley	Birks	Beesley	Ashworth	Stevenson	Ferguson	Chisnall	Smillie	McMillan	McKinven	Ferguson(8)
9	30	York City	(A)	2-2	(1-0)	D	4170	Smillie,Chisnall	Roberts	Bentley	Birks	Beesley	Ashworth	Stevenson	Ferguson	Chisnall	Smillie	McMillan	McKinven	Woodley(7)
10	2 Oct	Bradford Park Avenue	(H)	2-1	(0-0)	W	11732	McKinven,Chisnall	Roberts	Bentley	Birks	Ashworth	May	Stevenson	Ferguson	Chisnall	Smillie	McMillan	McKinven	May(3)
11	7	Chesterfield	(A)	1-3	(1-2)	L	8618	Chisnall	Roberts	Bentley	Birks	Ashworth	Ashworth	Stevenson	Beesley	Chisnall	Smillie	McMillan	McKinven	Riley
12	14	Exeter City	(H)	1-0	(0-0)	W	9528	Beesley	Roberts	Bentley	Birks	Beesley	May	Stevenson	Woodley	Chisnall	Smillie	McMillan	McKinven	Ferguson
13	16	Wrexham	(A)	1-4	(0-1)	L	6625	McKinven	Roberts	Bentley	Birks	Ashworth	Ashworth	Stevenson	Woodley	Chisnall	Smillie	McMillan	McKinven	Ferguson(8)
14	21	Darlington	(A)	1-1	(0-1)	D	4296	Beesley	Roberts	Bentley	Birks	Beesley	May	Stevenson	Ferguson	Chisnall	Smillie	McMillan	McKinven	May(3)
15	23	Bradford Park Avenue	(A)	1-0	(1-0)	W	3917	Chisnall	Roberts	Bentley	Mathews	Ashworth	Ashworth	Stevenson	Woodley	Chisnall	Smillie	Beesley	McKinven	Riley
16	27	Aldershot	(H)	1-1	(1-0)	D	12101	Chisnall	Roberts	Bentley	Mathews	Ashworth	May	Stevenson	Woodley	Chisnall	Smillie	Beesley	McKinven	Ferguson
17	4 Nov	Workington	(A)	2-2	(2-1)	D	1742	McKinven(2)	Roberts	Bentley	Birks	Smillie	Ashworth	Stevenson	Woodley	Chisnall	Beesley	Baber	McKinven	Mathews(10)
18	11	Lincoln City	(H)	2-1	(2-0)	W	8943	Chisnall(2)	Roberts	Bentley	Birks	Smillie	Ashworth	Stevenson	Baber	Chisnall	Howlett	Beesley	McKinven	Mathews(9)
19	13	Barnsley	(H)	4-1	(3-1)	W	10513	Chisnall,Baber,Bentley,McKinven(pen)	Roberts	Mathews	Birks	Beesley	Ashworth	Stevenson	Woodley	Chisnall	Smillie	Baber	McKinven	May(2)
20	18	Halifax Town	(A)	2-1	(1-0)	W	4884	McKinven,Chisnall	Roberts	Howlett	May	Beesley	Ashworth	Stevenson	Woodley	Chisnall	Baber	McMillan	McKinven	Riley(7)
21	25	Bradford City	(H)	1-1	(1-1)	D	10850	Ferguson	Roberts	Bentley	Birks	Beesley	Ashworth	Stevenson	Ferguson	Chisnall	Smillie	Baber	McKinven	May(6)
22	2 Dec	Crewe Alexandra	(A)	0-1	(0-1)	L	6227		Roberts	Bentley	Birks	Beesley	Ashworth	Stevenson	Baber	Chisnall	Smillie	McMillan	McKinven	May(7)
23	15	Port Vale	(H)	1-1	(1-0)	D	8543	Baber	Roberts	Bentley	Birks	Beesley	May	Stevenson	Baber	Beesley	Smillie	Howlett	McKinven	Woodley(7)
24	26	Brentford	(A)	2-1	(2-0)	W	8360	Beesley(2)	Roberts	Bentley	Birks	Ashworth	May	Stevenson	Smillie	Beesley	McMillan	Chisnall	McKinven	Slack(11)
25	30	Brentford	(H)	1-0	(0-0)	W	9181	Chisnall	Roberts	Bentley	Birks	Ashworth	May	Stevenson	Woodley	Beesley	McMillan	Chisnall	Smillie	
26	20 Jan	Hartlepools United	(H)	2-1	(2-0)	W	8452	Chisnall,Ashworth	Roberts	Bentley	Birks	Ashworth	May	Stevenson	Smillie	Best	McMillan	Chisnall	McKinven	Baber(8)
27	27	Chester	(A)	0-0	(0-0)	D	4623		Roberts	Mathews	Birks	Ashworth	May	Stevenson	Smillie	Chisnall	Smillie	Beesley	McKinven	McMillan
28	6 Feb	Newport County	(A)	0-2	(0-1)	L	2850		Roberts	Mathews	Birks	Beesley	May	Stevenson	Moore	Chisnall	McMillan	Best	McKinven	
29	10	York City	(H)	0-1	(0-1)	L	9134		Roberts	Beesley	Birks	Beesley	May	Stevenson	Moore	Chisnall	Baber	Best	McKinven	Stevenson(7)
30	17	Rochdale	(A)	1-0	(1-0)	W	2370	McKinven	Roberts	Beesley	Birks	Ashworth	May	Slack	Moore	Chisnall	Ashworth	Best	McKinven	Mathews
31	24	Halifax Town	(H)	2-2	(2-1)	D	6973	Best,Chisnall	Roberts	Beesley	Birks	Stevenson	May	Slack	Baber	Chisnall	Chisnall	Baber	McKinven	Howlett
32	2 Mar	Exeter City	(A)	2-1	(1-0)	W	3716	Best(2)	White	Beesley	Birks	McMillan	May	Ashworth	Baber	Slack	Smillie	Baber	McKinven	Stevenson
33	8	Chester	(H)	5-1	(2-0)	W	9437	Best(3),Smillie,Ashworth	Roberts	Beesley	Birks	McMillan	May	Slack	Slack	Best	Smillie	Baber	McKinven	Stevenson
34		Darlington	(H)	2-1	(1-0)	W	10586	Smillie,Chisnall	Roberts	Beesley	Birks	McMillan	May	Slack	Chisnall	Best	Smillie	Baber	McKinven	Baber(4)
35	19	Swansea Town	(A)	2-2	(0-1)	D	4076	McKinven,Smillie	Roberts	Beesley	Birks	McMillan	May	Slack	Chisnall	Clayton	Smillie	Best	McKinven	Baber
36	23	Aldershot	(A)	3-1	(1-0)	W	5166	Chisnall,Clayton,McKinven(pen)	Roberts	Beesley	Mathews	McMillan	May	Slack	Chisnall	Best	Smillie	Clayton	McKinven	Baber
37	29	Workington	(H)	7-0	(4-0)	W	13871	Clayton(2),McKinven(2),Smillie,May,Best	Roberts	Beesley	Birks	McMillan	May	Slack	Chisnall	Best	Clayton	Clayton	McKinven	Stevenson
38	6 Apr	Lincoln City	(A)	2-4	(0-3)	L	4764	Best(2)	Roberts	Beesley	Birks	McMillan	May	Slack	Chisnall	Best	Clayton	Baber	McKinven	Bentley(10)
39	8	Doncaster Rovers	(H)	1-2	(0-0)	L	13634	Chisnall	Roberts	Bentley	Birks	McMillan	May	Stevenson	Clayton	Best	Beesley	Clayton	McKinven	Ashworth
40	13	Chesterfield	(H)	1-1	(1-0)	D	11437	Best	White	Bentley	May	Ashworth	Ashworth	Stevenson	Best	Clayton	Beesley	Chisnall	McKinven	Baber(4)
41	16	Doncaster Rovers	(A)	1-2	(0-2)	L	8724	Best	White	Bentley	Birks	Ashworth	May	Stevenson	Best	Clayton	Chisnall	Slack	McKinven	Beesley(3)
42	20	Bradford City	(A)	1-2	(0-2)	L	8051	Best	Roberts	Bentley	Riley	McMillan	May	Slack	Best	Clayton	Chisnall	Slack	Moore	Baber(11)
43	22	Notts County	(H)	0-1	(0-0)	L	10518		Roberts	Bentley	Birks	McMillan	Ashworth	Slack	Best	Smillie	Chisnall	Clayton	McKinven	Baber
44	26	Crewe Alexandra	(H)	3-4	(2-3)	L	10478	McKinven,McMillan,Baber	Roberts	Bentley	Mathews	McMillan	May	Slack	Baber	Clayton	Smillie	Chisnall	McKinven	Baber(6)
45	4 May	Notts County	(A)	0-1	(0-0)	L	3848		Roberts	Bentley	Mathews	McMillan	Howlett	Slack	Baber	Clayton	Best	Chisnall	McKinven	Howlett(3)
46	10	Rochdale	(H)	3-1	(2-0)	W	5572	Best(2),Chisnall	White	Bentley	Riley	McMillan	Howlett	Slack	Baber	Clayton	Chisnall	Best	McKinven	Moore

Major Cup Competitions

Rd.	Date	Opposition	Venue Score	H.T.	Res.	Att.	Goalscorers
			F.A.Cup				
R1	13 Dec	Brighton & H.A.	(A) 0-1		L	12296	
			League Cup				
R1	23 Aug	Brentford	(H) 1-0	(0-0)	W	8089	McKinven
R2	13 Sep	Darlington	(H) 1-2	(1-0)	L	11727	Baber

1	2	3	4	5	6	7	8	9	10	11	12
Roberts	Bentley	Birks	Beesley	Ashworth	Stevenson	Baber	Chisnall	Smillie	Howlett	McKinven	
Roberts	Bentley	Birks	Beesley	Ashworth	Stevenson	Baber	Chisnall	Smillie	Slack	McKinven	
Roberts	Bentley	Birks	May	Ashworth	Stevenson	Ferguson	Chisnall	Smillie	Baber	Walsh	Beesley(6)

● Taken during a training session at Roots Hall this week, the photograph shows the senior players the United are relying upon to get them promotion this season. They are (back row, left to right): Ray White, Phil Chisnall, Mike Beesley, Joe Ashworth, Jimmy Stevenson, John McKinven, Graham Birks, Eddie May and Trevor Roberts. Front row (left to right): Jackie Ferguson, Micky Judge, Tony Bentley, John Baber, Andy Smillie, Mel Slack, Ray Walsh and Frank Mathews.

Appearances and Goals

	Appearances				Goals			
Name	Lge.	FAC	L.C.	Total	Lge.	FAC	L.C.	Total
ASHWORTH, Joe	36	1	2	39	2			2
BABER, John	21+6	1	2	24+6	6	1		7
BEESLEY, Micky	34+3		1+1	36+4	4			4
BENTLEY, Tony	33+1	1	2	36+1	1			1
BEST, Billy	20			20	14			14
BIRKS, Graham	37	1	2	40				
CHISNALL, Phil	44	1	2	47	17			17
CLAYTON, Eddie	12			12	3			3
FERGUSON, Jackie	13+1		1	14+1	2			2
HOWLETT, Robert	4+1	1		5+1				
MATHEWS, Frank	8+2			8+2				
MAY, Eddie	32+4		1	33+4	1			1
MOORE, Howard	4			4				
McKINVEN, John	44	1	1	46	16	1		17
McMILLAN, Sammy	25+1			25+1	1			1
RILEY, Ian	2+1			2+1				
ROBERTS, Trevor	42	1	2	45				
SLACK, Mel	18+2	1	1	19+2				
SMILLIE, Andy	33	1	2	36	8			8
STEVENSON, Jimmy	33+1	1	2	36+1				
WALSH, Roy	0		1	1				
WHITE, Ray	4			4				
WOODLEY, Derek	7+2			7+2				
Own Goal					2			2

	Ps	P	W	D	L	F	A	W	D	L	F	A	Pts.
1967/68	6	46	12	8	3	45	21	8	6	9	32	37	54

Season 1968/69 – League Division Four

No.	Date	Opposition	Venue	Score	H.T.	Res.	Att.	Goalscorers	No.	1	2	3	4	5	6	7	8	9	10	11	12
1	16 Aug	Halifax Town	(H)	2-1	(0-1)	W	10401	McKinven,Smillie	1	Leslie	Bentley	Birks	McMillan	Stone	Kurila	Clayton	Best	Smillie	Chisnall	McKinven	Beesley(11)
2	17	Notts County	(A)	2-2	(1-2)	D	5149	Smillie,Clayton	2	Leslie	Bentley	Birks	McMillan	Stone	Kurila	Clayton	Best	Smillie	Chisnall	McKinven	Beesley(4)
3	23	Darlington	(H)	1-1	(0-1)	D	12404	Best	3	Leslie	Bentley	Birks	McMillan	Stone	Kurila	Clayton	Best	Smillie	Chisnall	McKinven	Beesley(4)
4	28	Lincoln City	(A)	1-2	(1-1)	L	10078	Clayton	4	Leslie	Bentley	Birks	McMillan	Stone	Kurila	Clayton	Best	Beesley	Chisnall	McKinven	Slack
5	31	Newport County	(A)	1-4	(0-2)	L	2801	Bentley	5	Leslie	Bentley	Birks	McMillan	Stone	Kurila	Clayton	Best	Smillie	Chisnall	McKinven	Beesley(5)
6	6 Sep	Wrexham	(H)	1-0	(1-0)	W	11832	Clayton	6	Roberts	Bentley	Birks	Beesley	McMillan	Kurila	Clayton	Hamilton	Smillie	Chisnall	McKinven	Slack(11)
7	14	Swansea Town	(A)	2-2	(0-1)	D	7668	Hamilton,McKinven	7	Leslie	Bentley	Birks	McMillan	Beesley	Kurila	Best	Clayton	Smillie	Chisnall	Hamilton	McKinven(10)
8	18	Aldershot	(A)	1-2	(0-1)	L	5166	Best	8	Leslie	Bentley	Birks	McMillan	Beesley	Kurila	Clayton	Best	Smillie	Chisnall	McKinven	Chisnall
9	20	Workington	(H)	1-0	(0-0)	W	10105	Hamilton	9	Leslie	Bentley	Birks	McMillan	Beesley	Kurila	Clayton	Best	Smillie	Hamilton	McKinven	Chisnall(6)
10	28	Grimsby Town	(A)	0-0	(0-0)	D	2177		10	Leslie	Bentley	Birks	McMillan	Beesley	Kurila	Clayton	Hamilton	Baber	Chisnall	McKinven	Slack(11)
11	5 Oct	Peterborough United	(A)	0-1	(0-0)	L	5905		11	Leslie	Bentley	Birks	McMillan	Beesley	Kurila	Clayton	Best	Smillie	Chisnall	Hamilton	McKinven(1)
12	7	Lincoln City	(H)	3-0	(1-0)	W	9886	Baber,Hamilton,Smillie	12	Roberts	Bentley	Birks	McMillan	Beesley	Kurila	Clayton	Best	Smillie	Hamilton	McKinven	Baber(11)
13	11	Exeter City	(H)	6-1	(2-0)	W	9860	Best(3),Hamilton(2),Clayton	13	Roberts	Bentley	Birks	McMillan	Beesley	Kurila	Clayton	Best	Smillie	Hamilton	Baber	Moore G
14	19	York City	(A)	1-1	(0-0)	D	3760	Hamilton	14	Roberts	Bentley	Birks	McMillan	Beesley	Kurila	Clayton	Best	Smillie	Hamilton	Baber	Moore G(4)
15	26	Rochdale	(H)	1-3	(0-0)	L	9341	Best	15	Roberts	Bentley	Riley	McMillan	Beesley	Kurila	Clayton	Best	Smillie	Hamilton	Baber	Chisnall(9)
16	2 Nov	Chester	(A)	2-1	(1-1)	W	5311	Chisnall,Hamilton	16	Roberts	Bentley	Birks	McMillan	Beesley	Kurila	Clayton	Chambers	Chisnall	Best	Hamilton	Baber
17	4	Port Vale	(A)	1-1	(0-1)	D	3572	McMillan	17	Roberts	Bentley	Birks	McMillan	Beesley	Kurila	Clayton	Chambers	Moore G	Best	Hamilton	Chisnall
18	9	Doncaster Rovers	(H)	2-0	(1-0)	W	8531	Moore G,Chambers	18	Roberts	Bentley	Birks	Kurila	Beesley	Chisnall	Clayton	Chambers	Moore G	Best	Hamilton	Baber
19	22	Bradford City	(H)	2-0	(1-0)	W	11111	Clayton,Chisnall	19	Roberts	Bentley	Birks	McMillan	Beesley	Kurila	Clayton	Chisnall	Moore G	Best	Hamilton	Chambers(3)
20	29	Colchester United	(A)	0-4	(0-1)	L	10604		20	Roberts	Bentley	Stone	Kurila	McMillan	Chisnall	Clayton	Chambers	Moore G	Best	Hamilton	Slack
21	14 Dec	Exeter City	(A)	2-1	(1-1)	W	12475	Moore G,Clayton	21	Roberts	Bentley	Birks	McMillan	Beesley	Kurila	Clayton	Chisnall	Moore G	Best	Hamilton	Chambers(11)
22	20	York City	(H)	1-2	(1-1)	L	9095	Clayton	22	Roberts	Bentley	Birks	McMillan	Beesley	Kurila	Clayton	Chisnall	Moore G	Best	Hamilton	Chambers(6)
23	26	Peterborough United	(H)	2-1	(2-1)	W	11124	McMillan,Moore G	23	Roberts	Bentley	Birks	McMillan	Beesley	Kurila	Clayton	Chisnall	Moore G	Best	Chambers	Hamilton(4)
24	10 Jan	Chester	(H)	1-2	(0-2)	L	11149	Best	24	Roberts	Bentley	Birks	McMillan	Beesley	Kurila	Clayton	Chisnall	Moore G	Best	Chambers	Chambers(11)
25	18	Doncaster Rovers	(A)	0-2	(0-1)	L	7230		25	Roberts	Bentley	Birks	McMillan	Beesley	Kurila	Clayton	Best	Moore G	Chisnall	Chambers	Hamilton(8)
26	31	Brentford	(H)	4-0	(3-0)	W	10954	Moore G(2),Clayton,Haydock	26	Roberts	Lindsey	Birks	Bentley	Haydock	Kurila	Chambers	Best	Moore G	Hamilton	Clayton	Baber(8)
27	14 Feb	Colchester United	(H)	3-1	(1-0)	W	12849	Best(2),Moore G	27	Roberts	Bentley	Lindsey	Beesley	Haydock	Kurila	Clayton	Best	Moore G	Hamilton	Chambers	McMillan
28	24	Port Vale	(A)	1-1	(1-1)	D	10725	Best	28	Roberts	Lindsey	Birks	Bentley	Beesley	Kurila	Clayton	Best	Moore G	Best	Chambers	Beesley(5)
29	1 Mar	Halifax Town	(H)	1-1	(0-0)	D	3522	Best	29	Roberts	Lindsey	Birks	Bentley	Beesley	Kurila	Clayton	Best	Moore G	Best	Chambers	Chisnall
30	3	Chesterfield	(H)	2-2	(0-2)	D	10243	Chisnall,Bell(O.G.)	30	Roberts	Bentley	Chisnall	Chisnall	Beesley	Kurila	Clayton	Best	Moore G	Hamilton	Chambers	Moore H(10)
31	7	Notts County	(H)	4-0	(3-0)	W	11029	Best,Bentley,Clayton,Chambers	31	Roberts	Lindsey	Birks	Bentley	Beesley	Kurila	Chambers	Best	Moore G	Clayton	Baber	Moore H
32	10	Brentford	(A)	1-1	(1-0)	D	6030	Chambers	32	Roberts	Lindsey	Birks	Bentley	Beesley	Kurila	Chambers	Best	Moore G	Clayton	Baber	Beesley(11)
33	17	Scunthorpe United	(A)	0-3	(0-1)	L	9942		33	Roberts	Bentley	Birks	McMillan	Haydock	Kurila	Chambers	Best	Moore G	Clayton	Clayton	Chisnall(10)
34	28	Wrexham	(A)	3-3	(2-1)	D	4166	Best(2),Moore G	34	Roberts	Lindsey	Birks	Bentley	Beesley	Kurila	Chambers	Best	Moore G	Clayton	Clayton	Robinson(10)
35	5 Apr	Grimsby Town	(H)	0-1	(0-0)	L	9740		35	Leslie	Lindsey	Birks	Bentley	McMillan	Kurila	Chambers	Best	Moore G	Hamilton	Clayton	Beesley(11)
36	7	Aldershot	(H)	4-2	(2-1)	W	8400	Best(3),Lindsey	36	Leslie	Bentley	Lindsey	Beesley	McMillan	Kurila	Moore H	Best	Moore G	Chisnall	Moore H	Robinson(7)
37	8	Bradford Park Avenue	(A)	3-0	(1-0)	W	2543	Hamilton(2),Moore G	37	Leslie	Bentley	Lindsey	Beesley	McMillan	Kurila	Chisnall	Best	Moore G	Hamilton	Chisnall	Robinson
38	12	Workington	(A)	0-0	(0-0)	D	1411		38	Roberts	Bentley	Lindsey	Beesley	McMillan	Kurila	Baber	Best	Moore G	Hamilton	Baber	Howlett
39	14	Bradford Park Avenue	(H)	5-0	(1-0)	W	7525	Best(2),Moore G(2),Baber	39	Roberts	Bentley	Lindsey	Beesley	McMillan	Kurila	Baber	Best	Moore G	Hamilton	Chisnall	Howlett
40	18	Swansea Town	(H)	4-0	(1-0)	W	10647	Moore G(3),Best	40	Roberts	Bentley	Lindsey	Beesley	McMillan	Kurila	Baber	Best	Moore G	Hamilton	Chisnall	Haydock
41	25	Chesterfield	(A)	0-0	(0-0)	D	3000		41	Roberts	Bentley	Lindsey	Beesley	McMillan	Kurila	Baber	Best	Moore G	Hamilton	Chisnall	Haydock(4)
42	28	Newport County	(H)	1-0	(0-0)	W	11905	Kurila	42	Roberts	Bentley	Birks	McMillan	Robinson	Kurila	Baber	Best	Moore G	Hamilton	Chisnall	Barnett
43	2 May	Bradford City	(A)	2-3	(2-0)	L	11128	Moore G,Hamilton	43	Roberts	Bentley	Birks	McMillan	Haydock	Kurila	Baber	Best	Moore G	Hamilton	Chisnall	Barnett
44	5	Darlington	(A)	3-2	(0-2)	W	6624	Bentley,Hamilton,Chisnall	44	Roberts	Lindsey	Birks	Bentley	McMillan	Kurila	Baber	Best	Moore G	Hamilton	Chisnall	Barnett(5)
45	10	Rochdale	(A)	0-3	(0-1)	L	9095		45	Roberts	Lindsey	Birks	Bentley	Haydock	Kurila	Baber	Best	Moore G	Hamilton	Chisnall	Barnett(4)
46	12	Scunthorpe United	(A)	1-4	(0-1)	L	1950	Chisnall	46	Roberts	Bentley	Lindsey	McMillan	Barnett	Kurila	Hunt	Best	Moore G	Hamilton	Chisnall	Howlett(10)

Major Cup Competitions

Rd.	Date	Opposition	Venue Score	H.T. Res.	Att.	Goalscorers	1	2	3	4	5	6	7	8	9	10	11	12
			F.A.Cup															
R1	16 Nov	Kings Lynn	(H) 9-0	(4-0) W	9983	Best(3),Moore G(3),Chisnall(2),Haskins(O.G.)	Roberts	Bentley	Birks	McMillan	Beesley	Kurila	Clayton	Best	Moore G	Chisnall	Hamilton	
R2	7 Dec	Brentwood	(H) 10-1	(3-1) W	13107	Best(5),Moore G(4),McMillan	Roberts	Bentley	Birks	McMillan	Beesley	Kurila	Clayton	Best	Moore G	Hamilton	Chisnall	
R3	4 Jan	Swindon Town	(A) 2-0	(1-0) W	18828	Best,Hamilton	Roberts	Bentley	Birks	Slack	Beesley	Kurila	Clayton	Best	Moore G	Hamilton	Chisnall	
R4	25	Mansfield Town	(A) 1-2	(1-0) L	16160	Best	Roberts	Bentley	Birks	McMillan	Kurila	Clayton	Chisnall	Baber	Hamilton	Moore G	Best	Beesley(11)
			League Cup															
R1	13 Aug	Bournemouth	(A) 6-1		W 7182	Clayton(2),McKinven,Chisnall,Kurila,Best	Leslie	Bentley	Birks	McMillan	Stone	Kurila	Clayton	Best	Smillie	Chisnall	McKinven	
R2	4 Sep	Wolverhampton W.	(A) 0-1		L 18667		Leslie	Bentley	Birks	Beesley	McMillan	Kurila	Clayton	Best	Smillie	Chisnall	McKinven	

SOUTHEND UNITED 1968/69

Back row, left to right: Geoff Hudson (Trainer), Graham Birks, Sammy McMillan, David Stone, John Kurila, Trevor Roberts, Gary Moore, Ian Hamilton, Eddie Clayton, Mike Beesley, Ernie Shepherd (Manager). Front row: Mel Slack, David Chambers, Tony Bentley, Billy Best, Phil Chisnall, John Baber (Mel anes).

Appearances and Goals

Name	Appearances Lge.	FAC	L.C.	Total	Goals Lge.	FAC	L.C.	Total
BABER, John	16+2	1		17+2	2			2
BARNETT, Dave	1+2			1+2				
BEESLEY, Micky	30+6	3	1+1	34+7				3
BENTLEY, Tony	45	4	2	51				
BEST, Billy	44	4	2	50	20	10	1	31
BIRKS, Graham	36	4	2	42				
CHAMBERS, David	17+4			17+4	3			3
CHISNALL, Phil	31+3	4	2	37+3	5	2	1	8
CLAYTON, Eddie	34	4	2	40	9		2	11
HAMILTON, Chico	34+2	4		38+2	11	1		12
HAYDOCK, Frank	6+1			6+1	1			1
HOWLETT, Robert	0+1			0+1				
HUNT, Peter	1			1				
KURILA, John	46	4	2	52	1		1	2
LESLIE, Lawrie	13		2	15				
LINDSEY, Keith	18			18	1			1
MOORE, Gary	30+1	4		34+1	14	7		21
MOORE, Howard	2+1			2+1				
McKINVEN, John	10+2		2	12+2	2		1	3
McMILLAN, Sammy	38	3	2	43	2	1		3
RILEY, Ian	1			1				
ROBERTS, Trevor	33	4		37				
ROBINSON, Peter	1+2			1+2				
SLACK, Mel	0+2	1		1+2				
SMILLIE, Andy	13		2	15	3			3
STONE, David	6		1	7				
Own Goal					1	1		2

	Ps	P	W	D	L	F	A	W	D	L	F	A	Pts.
1968/69	7	46	15	3	5	51	21	4	10	9	27	40	51

Season 1969/70 – League Division Four

No.	Date	Opposition	Venue	Score	H.T.	Res.	Att.	Goalscorers	No.	1	2	3	4	5	6	7	8	9	10	11	12
1	9 Aug	Darlington	(A)	2-0	(2-0)	W	3904	Best,McMillan	1	Roberts	Lindsey	Simpson	Beesley	Haydock	Kurila	Bentley	Best	McMillan	Chisnall	Baber	Barnett(4)
2	15	Scunthorpe United	(A)	3-0	(2-0)	W	8763	Best(3)	2	Roberts	Lindsey	Simpson	Beesley	Haydock	Kurila	Bentley	Best	McMillan	Hunt	Chisnall	Clayton(10)
3	23	Lincoln City	(A)	3-3	(1-3)	D	6956	Best,Beesley,Haydock	3	Roberts	Lindsey	Birks	Beesley	Haydock	Kurila	Bentley	Best	Moore	McMillan	Simpson	Chisnall(8)
4	25	Grimsby Town	(H)	1-3	(1-2)	L	11703	Haydock	4	Roberts	Lindsey	Birks	Beesley	Haydock	Kurila	Bentley	Hunt	Moore	McMillan	Simpson	Chisnall(7)
5	30	Crewe Alexandra	(H)	2-0	(1-0)	W	8691	Moore,Baber	5	Roberts	Lindsey	Simpson	Beesley	Haydock	Kurila	Bentley	Hunt	Moore	McMillan	Chisnall	Baber(10)
6	6 Sep	Swansea Town	(A)	0-2	(0-0)	L	5009		6	Roberts	Bentley	Simpson	Beesley	Haydock	Kurila	Barnett	Baber	Moore	McMillan	Chisnall	Clayton
7	13	Hartlepool	(H)	0-2	(0-1)	L	8146		7	Roberts	Bentley	Simpson	Beesley	Haydock	Kurila	Clayton	Hunt	Moore	Hunt	Chisnall	Chamb's.D(7)
8	15	Brentford	(A)	1-3	(0-2)	L	7440	Chamb's.D	8	Roberts	Lindsey	Simpson	Beesley	Haydock	Kurila	Chamb's.J	Chamb's.D	Moore	Hunt	Chisnall	Birks(2)
9	20	Newport County	(A)	0-4	(0-3)	L	2905		9	Roberts	Simpson	Birks	Beesley	McMillan	Kurila	McMillan	Chamb's.D	Moore	McMillan	Chisnall	Clayton(6)
10	27	Bradford Park Avenue	(H)	1-1	(1-0)	D	5891	Beesley	10	Roberts	Lindsey	Simpson	Beesley	Barnett	Barnett	Barnett	Hunt	Moore	McMillan	Chisnall	Chamb's.J(10)
11	29	Port Vale	(H)	1-1	(1-1)	D	7526	Moore	11	Lloyd	Lindsey	Simpson	Beesley	Barnett	McKinven	Clayton	Chamb's.D	Moore	Hunt	Chisnall	Robinson(9)
12	4 Oct	Wrexham	(A)	0-4	(0-2)	L	9876		12	Lloyd	Lindsey	Simpson	Beesley	Haydock	McKinven	Clayton	Chamb's.D	Moore	Chisnall	Baber	Hunt(8)
13	7	Scunthorpe United	(H)	0-2	(0-1)	L	3007		13	Lloyd	Lindsey	Simpson	Barnett	Haydock	Kurila	Chamb's.D	Beesley	Beesley	McMillan	Chisnall	Hunt
14	11	Workington	(H)	3-1	(1-0)	W	5320	Beesley(2),Lindsey	14	Lloyd	Lindsey	Simpson	Barnett	Haydock	Kurila	Chamb's.J	Beesley	Clayton	Hunt	Chisnall	McKinven
15	18	Exeter City	(A)	1-1	(1-1)	D	6172	Clayton	15	Lloyd	Lindsey	Simpson	Barnett	Haydock	Kurila	Chamb's.J	Beesley	Clayton	Clayton	Chisnall	Chamb's.D
16	25	Northampton Town	(A)	0-2	(0-1)	L	5154		16	Lloyd	Lindsey	Simpson	Beesley	Barnett	Kurila	Barnett	Best	Moore	Hunt	Chisnall	McMillan
17	1 Nov	Chesterfield	(H)	0-0	(0-0)	D	6374		17	Lloyd	Lindsey	Simpson	Beesley	Barnett	Kurila	Haydock	Best	Moore	Hunt	Chisnall	Hunt(4)
18	8	Colchester United	(A)	2-0	(1-0)	W	6021	Clayton,McMillan	18	Lloyd	Lindsey	Simpson	Beesley	Barnett	Kurila	Jacques	Best	McMillan	Clayton	Chamb's.D	McKinven
19	22	York City	(A)	0-1	(0-0)	L	3018		19	Lloyd	Lindsey	Simpson	Beesley	Barnett	Kurila	Jacques	Best	Garner	Clayton	Chamb's.D	McKinven
20	26	Chester	(A)	0-2	(0-1)	L	4501		20	Roberts	Lindsey	Simpson	Beesley	Barnett	Kurila	Jacques	Best	Garner	Clayton	Chamb's.D	Hunt(9)
21	29	Aldershot	(H)	2-2	(1-0)	D	2887	Best,Clayton	21	Roberts	Lindsey	Simpson	Jacques	Barnett	Kurila	Chamb's.D	Best	Garner	Hunt	McKinven	Beesley(2)
22	13 Dec	Hartlepool	(A)	1-2	(0-2)	L	1834	Moore	22	Lloyd	Lindsey	Simpson	Hunt	Barnett	Kurila	Chamb's.D	Best	Moore	Garner	Clayton	Beesley
23		Swansea City	(H)	2-1	(1-0)	W	3206	Moore,Best	23	Lloyd	Lindsey	Simpson	Hunt	Barnett	Kurila	Chamb's.D	Best	Moore	Garner	Clayton	
24	26	Lincoln City	(H)	2-2	(1-1)	D	7563	Garner(2)	24	Lloyd	Jacques	Lindsey	Hunt	Barnett	Kurila	Chamb's.D	Haydock	Moore	Chamb's.J	O'Connor	Vickery(11)
25	10 Jan	Newport County	(H)	3-2	(1-1)	W	4147	Best(2),Garner	25	Lloyd	Jacques	Simpson	Hunt	Barnett	Kurila	Clayton	Best	Moore	Garner	Chamb's.D	Beesley(4)
26	17	Bradford Park Avenue	(A)	0-1	(0-0)	L	4524		26	Lloyd	Chamb's.D	Simpson	Beesley	Barnett	Kurila	Hunt	Best	Moore	Garner	Clayton	Haydock(11)
27	24	Notts County	(H)	2-5	(2-1)	L	5094	Best,Moore	27	Lloyd	Lindsey	Simpson	Jacques	Barnett	Kurila	Chamb's.D	Clayton	Moore	Best	Chisnall	Beesley(10)
28	28	Crewe Alexandra	(A)	3-5	(1-3)	L	3142	Chisnall(2),Clayton	28	Roberts	Beesley	Simpson	Jacques	Barnett	Kurila	Chamb's.D	Moore	Chisnall	Garner	Clayton	
29	31	Wrexham	(H)	1-0	(0-0)	W	5133	Moore	29	Roberts	Lindsey	Simpson	Beesley	Haydock	Kurila	Chamb's.D	Best	Chisnall	Garner	Clayton	Moore(7)
30	7 Feb	Workington	(A)	0-5	(0-2)	L	1790		30	Roberts	Lindsey	Simpson	Beesley	Haydock	Kurila	Chisnall	Best	Moore	Garner	Clayton	Jacques
31	21	Colchester United	(H)	2-1	(1-1)	W	6799	Best,Beesley	31	Roberts	Lindsey	Simpson	Beesley	Haydock	Kurila	Chisnall	Best	Moore	Garner	Clayton	Jacques(10)
32	23	Port Vale	(A)	0-3	(0-2)	L	6333		32	Roberts	Chamb's.D	Simpson	Beesley	Haydock	Kurila	Chisnall	Best	Moore	Garner	Clayton	Jacques(5)
33	28	Exeter City	(A)	0-3	(0-0)	L	4343		33	Roberts	Jacques	Simpson	Beesley	Barnett	Kurila	Chamb's.D	Hunt	Chisnall	Best	Clayton	Haydock(8)
34	3 Mar	Oldham Athletic	(A)	0-3	(0-1)	L	3584		34	Roberts	Barnett	Simpson	Jacques	Beesley	Kurila	Chamb's.D	Hunt	Moore	Best	Chisnall	Chamb's.J
35	9	Peterborough United	(H)	2-0	(1-0)	W	4716	Beesley,Haydock	35	Roberts	Wright	Simpson	Clayton	Haydock	Jacques	Chamb's.D	Beesley	Chamb's.J	Kurila	Chisnall	Hunt(9)
36	14	Aldershot	(A)	1-2	(1-1)	L	6559	Best	36	Roberts	Wright	Simpson	Beesley	Haydock	Jacques	Chamb's.D	Best	Garner	Kurila	Clayton	Chisnall
37	18	Notts County	(A)	0-2	(0-1)	L	5828		37	Roberts	Wright	Simpson	Beesley	Kyle	Jacques	Chamb's.D	Best	Moore	Lindsey	Clayton	
38	21	Oldham Athletic	(H)	1-0	(0-0)	W	4590	Thompson(O.G.)	38	Roberts	Wright	Simpson	Lindsey	Kyle	Jacques	Chamb's.D	Best	Moore	Kurila	Chisnall	Beesley
39	27	Northampton Town	(H)	2-2	(2-1)	D	7204	Best,Beesley	39	Roberts	Wright	Simpson	Lindsey	Kyle	Jacques	Chamb's.D	Best	Garner	Chisnall	Beesley	Hunt(7)
40	28	Peterborough United	(A)	0-3	(0-2)	L	4911		40	Roberts	Wright	Simpson	Kurila	Kyle	Jacques	Hunt	Best	Moore	Chisnall	Beesley	Chamb's.D(11)
41	31	Chesterfield	(A)	4-3	(1-0)	W	11074	Best(4)	41	Lloyd	Wright	Simpson	Lindsey	Kyle	Jacques	Hunt	Best	Garner	Best	Kurila	Garner(11)
42	4 Apr	Grimsby Town	(H)	2-2	(0-1)	D	2891	Best,Moore	42	Lloyd	Wright	Simpson	Kurila	Kyle	Jacques	Chamb's.D	Best	Garner	Best	Chisnall	Hunt
43	6	Chester	(H)	4-2	(2-0)	W	5357	Best(2),Garner(2)	43	Lloyd	Wright	Lindsey	Chisnall	Kyle	Jacques	Hunt	Best	Garner	Moore	Simpson	Kurila(6)
44	10	Darlington	(H)	2-0	(1-0)	W	5662	Best(2)	44	Lloyd	Wright	Lindsey	Chisnall	Haydock	Kurila	Hunt	Moore	Garner	Chisnall	Simpson	Chamb's.D
45	13	Brentford	(A)	2-2	(1-0)	D	6433	Chisnall,Garner	45	Lloyd	Wright	Lindsey	Chisnall	Kyle	Kurila	Chamb's.D	Best	Garner	Moore	Simpson	Hunt
46	1 May	York City	(H)	1-0	(1-0)	W	5546	Best	46	Lloyd	Lindsey	Simpson	Chisnall	Barnett	Kurila	Baber	Best	Beesley	Moore	Chamb's.D	Hunt(7)

Abbrev.: Chamb's.D = Chambers D. Chamb's.J = Chambers J.

Major Cup Competitions

F.A.Cup

Rd.	Date	Opposition	Venue Score	H.T.	Res.	Att.	Goalscorers	1	2	3	4	5	6	7	8	9	10	11	12
R1	15 Nov	Gillingham	(H) 0-0	(0-0)	D	8114		Lloyd	Lindsey	Simpson	Beesley	Barnett	Kurila	Jacques	Best	McMillan	Clayton	Chambers D	
R1r	19	Gillingham	(A) 1-2		L	6919	Best	Lloyd	Lindsey	Simpson	Beesley	Barnett	Kurila	Jacques	Best	McMillan	Clayton	Chambers D	Clayton(11)

League Cup

Rd.	Date	Opposition	Venue Score	H.T.	Res.	Att.	Goalscorers	1	2	3	4	5	6	7	8	9	10	11	12
R1	12 Aug	Brentford	(H) 2-2	(0-2)	D	8366	Chisnall,McMillan	Roberts	Lindsey	Barnett	Clayton	Haydock	Kurila	Bentley	Best	McMillan	Chisnall	Baber	
R1r	18	Brentford	(A) 0-0	(0-0)	D	7941		Roberts	Bentley	Birks	Barnett	Haydock	Kurila	Beesley	Best	Moore	McMillan	Chisnall	
R1r2	21		* 3-2	(1-0)	W	2068	McMillan(3)	Roberts	Lindsey	Birks	Beesley	Haydock	Kurila	Bentley	Hunt	Moore	McMillan	Chisnall	
R2	3 Sep	Shrewsbury Town	(A) 2-2	(1-1)	D	4969	Moore,Beesley	Roberts	Lindsey	Simpson	Beesley	Haydock	Kurila	Bentley	Baber	Moore	McMillan	Chisnall	Hunt(7)
R2r	8	Shrewsbury Town	(H) 2-0	(1-0)	W	10924	Beesley,McMillan	Roberts	Bentley	Simpson	Beesley	Haydock	Kurila	Barnett	Clayton	Moore	McMillan	Chisnall	
R3	24	Bradford City	(A) 1-2	(1-0)	L	9904	Moore	Roberts	Bentley	Simpson	Beesley	Haydock	Kurila	Barnett	Clayton	Moore	Hunt	Chisnall	Chambers J(2)

* At Millwall.

SOUTHEND UNITED 1st TEAM JANUARY, 1970

Back row, left to right: Geoff Hudson (Team Manager), Dave Barnett, Brian Lloyd, Gary Moore, John Kurila, Bill Garner, Joe Jacques, Laurie Leslie (Trainer).
Front row, left to right: Eddie Clayton, Billy Best, Dave Chambers, Peter Hunt, Owen Simpson.

Appearances and Goals

Name	Appearances Lge.	FAC	L.C.	Total	Goals Lge.	FAC	L.C.	Total
BABER, John	4+1		2	6+1	1			1
BARNETT, Dave	24+1	2	4	30+1				
BEESLEY, Micky	34+3	2	5	41+3	6	2		8
BENTLEY, Tony	7		6	13				
BEST, Billy	31	2	2	35	23	1		24
BIRKS, Graham	3+1		2	5+1				
CHAMBERS, David	28+2	2		30+2	1			1
CHAMBERS, John	6+1		0+1	6+2				
CHISNALL, Phil	33+2		6	39+2	3		1	4
CLAYTON, Eddie	23+2	2	3+1	28+3	4			4
GARNER, Bill	19+1			19+1	6			6
HAYDOCK, Frank	22+2		6	28+2	3			3
HUNT, Peter	22+6	0+1	2+1	24+8				
JACQUES, Joe	19+2	2		21+2				
KURILA, John	41+1	2	6	49+1				
KYLE, Maurice	8			8				
LINDSEY, Keith	33	2	3	38	1			1
LLOYD, Brian	21	2		23				
MOORE, Gary	31+1		5	36+1	8		2	10
McKINVEN, John	2	0+1		2+1				
McMILLAN, Sammy	13	2	5	20	2		5	7
O'CONNOR, Phil	1			1				
ROBERTS, Trevor	25		6	31				
ROBINSON, Peter	0+1			0+1				
SIMPSON, Owen	45	2	3	50				
VICKERY, Paul	0+1			0+1				
WRIGHT, Pat	11			11				
Own Goal							1	1

	Ps	P	W	D	L	F	A	W	D	L	F	A	Pts.
1969/70	17	46	12	8	3	40	28	3	2	18	19	57	40

Season 1970/71 – League Division Four

No.	Date	Opposition	Venue	Score	H.T.	Res.	Att.	Goalscorers	No.	1	2	3	4	5	6	7	8	9	10	11	12
1	15 Aug	Southport	(H)	1-1	(1-0)	D	8728	Best	1	Lloyd	Lindsey	Simpson	Chisnall	Smith	Fallon	Cowan	Best	Garner	Bentley	Chambers	
2	22	Scunthorpe United	(A)	0-3	(0-2)	L	3930		2	Lloyd	Lindsey	Simpson	Bentley	Smith	Fallon	Cowan	Best	Garner	Chisnall	Beesley	Beesley(10)
3	28	Darlington	(H)	0-0	(0-0)	D	7548		3	Lloyd	Lindsey	Simpson	Hunt	Smith	Bentley	Baber	Best	Garner	Chisnall	Beesley	Barnett(7)
4	2 Sep	Exeter City	(A)	0-2	(0-2)	L	5190		4	Lloyd	Lindsey	Simpson	Chisnall	Smith	Bentley	Baber	Best	Garner	Chambers	Beesley	
5	5	Notts County	(A)	1-2	(0-2)	L	9025	Best	5	Lloyd	Lindsey	Simpson	Chisnall	Smith	Bentley	Baber	Fallon	McMahon	Garner	Best	Beesley(10)
6	11	Bournemouth	(H)	1-2	(0-2)	L	7339	Best	6	Lloyd	Lindsey	Simpson	Chisnall	Smith	Bentley	Cowan	McMahon	Beesley	Best	Lewis	Barnett(7)
7	19	Lincoln City	(A)	2-1	(2-1)	W	7011	Garner,Best	7	Lloyd	Bentley	McMahon	Lindsey	Smith	Chisnall	Beesley	Best	Garner	Barnett	Lewis	Chambers(6)
8	21	Hartlepool	(A)	1-0	(0-0)	W	3755	Beesley	8	Lloyd	Bentley	McMahon	Lindsey	Smith	Chisnall	Beesley	Best	Garner	Barnett	Lewis	
9	25	Northampton Town	(H)	1-0	(0-0)	W	9431	Simpson	9	Lloyd	Bentley	Simpson	Beesley	Smith	Lumsden	Chisnall	Best	Garner	Barnett	Lewis	Chambers(7)
10	29	Grimsby Town	(A)	0-2	(0-2)	L	4102		10	Lloyd	Bentley	Simpson	Lumsden	Smith	Chisnall	Beesley	Best	Garner	Barnett	Lewis	
11	3 Oct	Oldham Athletic	(H)	0-2	(0-2)	L	7726		11	Lloyd	Bentley	Simpson	Lindsey	Smith	Lumsden	Chisnall	Best	Garner	Barnett	Lewis	Chambers(7)
12	9	Crewe Alexandra	(H)	0-2	(0-2)	L	7517		12	Lloyd	Lindsey	Simpson	Chisnall	Smith	Lumsden	Hunt	Best	Garner	Barnett	Lewis	
13	16	Southport	(A)	0-3	(0-1)	L	3352		13	Bellotti	Lindsey	Simpson	Hunt	Smith	Lumsden	Chisnall	Best	Garner	Barnett	Lewis	Taylor(8)
14	21	Newport County	(H)	3-0	(2-0)	W	4349	Garner,Moore,Best	14	Bellotti	Smith	Bentley	Lumsden	Fallon	Lindsay	Moore	Best	Garner	Beesley	Lewis	
15	24	Brentford	(H)	4-3	(2-1)	W	5881	Best,Moore,Garner,Lewis	15	Bellotti	Bentley	Simpson	Chisnall	Beesley	Smith	Moore	Best	Garner	Hunt	Lewis	
16	31	Cambridge United	(A)	3-0	(3-0)	W	5701	Best(2),Chisnall	16	Lloyd	Bentley	Simpson	Lumsden	Smith	Barnett	Chisnall	Best	Garner	Moore	Lewis	Lindsey(11)
17	6 Nov	Barrow	(H)	2-3	(1-1)	L	6923	Best(2)	17	Lloyd	Bentley	Simpson	Lumsden	Smith	Barnett	Chisnall	Best	Garner	Taylor	Lewis	
18	9	Stockport County	(H)	2-1	(1-0)	W	4685	Chisnall,Garner	18	Lloyd	Bentley	Simpson	Lumsden	Smith	Barnett	Chisnall	Best	Garner	Moore	Chambers	Lindsey(4)
19	13	Colchester United	(A)	1-1	(1-1)	D	7777	Moore	19	Lloyd	Bentley	Simpson	Lumsden	Smith	Beesley	Chisnall	Best	Garner	Moore	Chambers	
20	27	York City	(A)	0-3	(0-2)	L	3088		20	Lloyd	Bentley	Simpson	Lindsey	Beesley	Smith	Moore	Chambers	Garner	Barnett	Lewis	Taylor(8)
21	4 Dec	Workington	(H)	1-1	(0-0)	D	5490	Chisnall	21	Lloyd	Bentley	Barnett	Lindsey	Beesley	Smith	Chisnall	Best	Garner	Beesley	Barnett	Chambers(4)
22	18	Scunthorpe United	(H)	2-2	(1-1)	D	4609	Best,Chambers	22	Lloyd	Smith	Barnett	Lumsden	Barker	Beesley	Chisnall	Best	Garner	Bentley	Lewis	Chambers(11)
23	26	Peterborough United	(A)	0-4	(0-1)	L	4396		23	Lloyd	Lindsey	Smith	Jacques	Barker	Bentley	Chisnall	Best	Garner	Beesley	Lewis	
24	8 Jan	Grimsby Town	(H)	1-1	(0-0)	D	6802	Lindsey	24	Lloyd	Lindsey	Harmston	Lumsden	Barker	Jacques	Chisnall	Beesley	Best	Barnett	Chambers	Beesley(9)
25	15	Newport County	(A)	0-3	(0-2)	L	2308		25	Lloyd	Lindsey	Simpson	Hunt	Barker	Jacques	Chambers	Best	Garner	Beesley	Lewis	
26	29	York City	(H)	1-0	(0-0)	W	5125	Johnson	26	Lloyd	Lindsey	Bentley	Chisnall	Barker	Jacques	Johnson	Best	Garner	Hunt	Lewis	Beesley(9)
27	6 Feb	Workington	(A)	1-1	(0-0)	D	2026	Johnson	27	Lloyd	Lindsey	Smith	Barker	Jacques	Hunt	Chisnall	Johnson	Best	Garner	Lewis	Bentley(11)
28	12	Aldershot	(H)	2-2	(0-0)	D	5895	Garner,Best	28	Lloyd	Lindsey	Smith	Chisnall	Barker	Beesley	Johnson	Best	Garner	Hunt	Lewis	
29	19	Stockport County	(A)	0-0	(0-0)	D	1734		29	Roberts J	Bentley	Smith	Elliott	Barker	Beesley	Johnson	Best	Garner	Hunt	Lewis	Barnett(9)
30	22	Chester	(H)	1-1	(0-1)	D	5550	Best	30	Roberts J	Bentley	Smith	Elliott	Barker	Beesley	Johnson	Best	Chisnall	Hunt	Taylor	
31	26	Cambridge United	(H)	1-1	(0-1)	D	6654	Best	31	Roberts J	Lindsey	Smith	Elliott	Barker	Jacques	Johnson	Best	Garner	Hunt	Taylor	
32	6 Mar	Brentford	(A)	2-4	(1-1)	L	6200	Taylor,Best	32	Roberts J	Lindsey	Smith	Elliott	Barker	Jacques	Johnson	Best	Garner	Hunt	Taylor	Barnett(2)
33	10	Hartlepool	(H)	2-0	(1-0)	W	3681	Johnson,Best	33	Roberts J	Lindsey	Smith	Elliott	Barker	Jacques	Johnson	Best	Garner	Hunt	Taylor	
34	12	Colchester United	(H)	1-1	(0-1)	D	9396	Smith	34	Roberts J	Lindsey	Smith	Elliott	Barker	Jacques	Johnson	Best	Garner	Hunt	Lewis	
35	17	Chester	(A)	0-2	(0-1)	L	3870		35	Roberts J	Lindsey	Smith	Elliott	Barker	Jacques	Hunt	Best	Johnson	Garner	Taylor	Barnett(2)
36	20	Barrow	(A)	0-2	(0-1)	L	1452		36	Roberts J	Lindsey	Smith	Elliott	Barker	Jacques	Johnson	Best	Garner	Hunt	Lewis	
37	26	Notts County	(H)	1-0	(1-0)	W	6745	Johnson	37	Roberts J	Bentley	Smith	Hunt	Barker	Jacques	Johnson	Best	Chisnall	Moore	Lewis	Barnett(2)
38	29	Aldershot	(A)	2-2	(2-1)	D	3847	Moore,Best	38	Roberts J	Lindsey	Smith	Hunt	Barker	Jacques	Johnson	Best	Garner	Moore	Lewis	
39	3 Apr	Darlington	(A)	4-0	(3-0)	W	2111	Johnson(2),Garner(2)	39	Roberts J	Smith	Bentley	Hunt	Barker	Jacques	Johnson	Best	Garner	Moore	Chisnall	
40	5	Peterborough United	(H)	1-2	(1-0)	L	5812	Best	40	Roberts J	Lindsey	Smith	Elliott	Barker	Jacques	Johnson	Best	Lewis	Moore	Hunt	
41	9	Bournemouth	(A)	0-4	(0-1)	L	11330		41	Roberts J	Lindsey	Smith	Elliott	Barker	Jacques	Johnson	Best	Moore	Moore	Hunt	
42	12	Oldham Athletic	(H)	3-0	(3-0)	W	6022	Johnson,Taylor,Hunt	42	Roberts J	Lindsey	Smith	Elliott	Barker	Jacques	Johnson	Best	Taylor	Hunt	Lewis	
43	17	Crewe Alexandra	(A)	2-1	(1-0)	W	3675	Garner,Johnson	43	Roberts J	Lindsey	Smith	Elliott	Barker	Beesley	Johnson	Best	Garner	Moore	Lewis	
44	28	Exeter City	(H)	0-0	(0-0)	D	4471		44	Roberts J	Lindsey	Smith	Elliott	Barker	Jacques	Johnson	Best	Garner	Moore	Lewis	
45	1 May	Northampton Town	(A)	2-0	(0-0)	W	3713	Moore,Taylor	45	Roberts J	Lindsey	Smith	Elliott	Barker	Jacques	Johnson	Best	Moore	Hunt	Lewis	Taylor(2)
46	3	Lincoln City	(H)	1-1	(0-0)	D	4523	Best	46	Roberts J	Lindsey	Bentley	Elliott	Piek'tis	Jacques	Lewis	Best	Johnson	Hunt	Taylor	

Abbrev.: Piek'tis = Piekalnietis.

Major Cup Competitions

Rd.	Date	Opposition	Venue	Score	H.T.	Res.	Att.	1	2	3	4	5	6	7	8	9	10	11	12	Goalscorers
F.A.Cup																				
R1	21 Nov	Weymouth	(H)	7-0	(3-0)	W	7188	Lloyd	Bentley	Simpson	Lindsey	Beesley	Smith	Chisnall	Best	Garner	Moore	Lewis	Chambers(11)	Garner(4),Best(2),Lewis
R2	12 Dec	Dagenham	(H)	1-0	(1-0)	W	10900	Lloyd	Smith	Simpson	Lindsey	Beesley	Barnett	Chisnall	Best	Garner	Bentley	Lewis	Beesley(4)	Best
R3	11 Jan	Carlisle United	(H)	0-3	(0-2)	L	16668	Lloyd	Lindsey	Simpson	Barnett	Barker	Jacques	Chambers	Hunt	Best	Chisnall	Lewis	Beesley(10)	
League Cup																				
R1	18 Aug	Charlton Athletic	(A)	0-3	(0-2)	L	7221	Lloyd	Lindsey	Simpson	Chisnall	Smith	Barnett	Cowan	Best	Garner	Bentley	Hunt		

SOUTHEND UNITED PROFESSIONAL STAFF 1970/71 — Back Row (left to right): Lawrie Leslie (coach), Bill Garner, Brian Lloyd, Gary Steel, Mike Beesley, Keith Lindsey. Second Row (left to right): Phil Chisnall, Joe Jaques, Gary Moore, Kevin Fallon, Owen Simpson, Alec Smith, Ken Reynolds. Front Row (left to right): Ian Cowan, Billy Best, Dave Chambers, Arthur Rowley (manager), Tony Bentley, John Baber, Peter Hunt.

Appearances and Goals

Name	Appearances				Goals			
	Lge.	FAC	L.C.	Total	Lge.	FAC	L.C.	Total
BABER, John	3			3				
BARKER, Geoff	25	1		26				
BARNETT, Dave	14+4	2	1	17+4				
BEESLEY, Micky	21+2	2+1	0+1	23+4	1			1
BELLOTTI, Derek	3			3				
BENTLEY, Tony	28+1	2	1	31+1				
BEST, Billy	45	3	1	49	19	3		22
CHAMBERS, David	7+4	1+1		8+5	1			1
CHISNALL, Phil	29	3	1	33	3			3
COWAN, Ian	3		1	4				
ELLIOTT, Dave	15			15				
FALLON, Kevin	4			4				
GARNER, Bill	37	2	1	40	8	4		12
HARMSTON, Michael	1			1				
HUNT, Peter	26	1	1	28	1			1
JACQUES, Joe	20	1		21				
JOHNSON, Terry	21			21	8			8
LEWIS, Bernard	31	3		34	1	1		2
LINDSEY, Keith	33+2	3	1	37+2	1			1
LLOYD, Brian	25	3	1	29				
LUMSDEN, Jimmy	12			12				
MOORE, Gary	11	1		12	5			5
McMAHON, John	4			4				
PIEKALNIETIS, John	1			1				
ROBERTS, John	18			18				
SIMPSON, Owen	19	3	1	23	1			1
SMITH, Alex	42	2	1	45	1			1
TAYLOR, Peter	8+2			8+2	3			3

	Ps	P	W	D	L	F	A	W	D	L	F	A	Pts.
1970/71	18	46	8	11	4	32	24	6	4	13	21	42	43

Season 1971/72 – League Division Four

No.	Date	Opposition	Venue	Score	H.T.	Res.	Att.	Goalscorers	No.	1	2	3	4	5	6	7	8	9	10	11	12
1	14 Aug	Peterborough United	(A)	0-2	(0-0)	L	4557		1	Roberts	Lindsey	Smith	Elliott	Albeson	Barnett	Johnson	Best	Garner	Duck	Ternent	Moore(2)
2	20	Darlington	(H)	3-0	(2-0)	W	6360	Lindsey, Moore, Best	2	Roberts	Lindsey	Smith	Elliott	Albeson	Jacques	Johnson	Best	Garner	Moore	Ternent	Taylor(9)
3	28	Hartlepool	(A)	2-2	(1-1)	D	5437	Best,Johnson	3	Roberts	Lindsey	Smith	Elliott	Albeson	Jacques	Johnson	Best	Garner	Moore	Ternent	Taylor(10)
4	30	Scunthorpe United	(H)	2-3	(1-2)	L	6704	Garner(2)	4	Roberts	Lindsey	Smith	Elliott	Albeson	Jacques	Johnson	Best	Garner	Moore	Ternent	
5	4 Sep	Bury	(H)	0-0	(0-0)	D	5222		5	Roberts	Lindsey	Smith	Elliott	Albeson	Jacques	Johnson	Best	Garner	Ternent	Lewis	Taylor(10)
6	11	Aldershot	(A)	0-0	(0-0)	D	4611		6	Roberts	Ternent	Smith	Elliott	Albeson	Jacques	Johnson	Best	Garner	Duck	Lewis	
7	17	Grimsby Town	(H)	3-1	(0-1)	W	6211	Best(3)	7	Roberts	Ternent	Smith	Elliott	Albeson	Jacques	Johnson	Best	Garner	Moore	Lewis	
8	25	Doncaster Rovers	(A)	2-0	(1-0)	W	3884	Garner,Best	8	Roberts	Ternent	Smith	Elliott	Albeson	Jacques	Johnson	Best	Garner	Moore	Lewis	
9	27	Newport County	(H)	3-1	(1-0)	W	7145	Lewis,Johnson,Moore	9	Roberts	Smith	Ternent	Elliott	Albeson	Jacques	Johnson	Best	Garner	Moore	Lewis	
10	1 Oct	Southport	(H)	2-1	(1-1)	W	10316	Garner,Albeson	10	Roberts	Ternent	Smith	Elliott	Albeson	Jacques	Johnson	Best	Garner	Moore	Lewis	
11	9	Chester	(A)	1-1	(1-1)	D	4092	Garner(pen)	11	Roberts	Smith	Ternent	Elliott	Albeson	Barnett	Johnson	Best	Garner	Moore	Lewis	
12	15	Peterborough United	(H)	2-1	(1-1)	W	10594	Garner(2)	12	Roberts	Ternent	Smith	Elliott	Albeson	Jacques	Johnson	Best	Garner	Moore	Lewis	Barnett(8)
13	18	Colchester United	(A)	0-1	(0-0)	L	9609		13	Roberts	Ternent	Smith	Elliott	Albeson	Jacques	Johnson	Duck	Garner	Moore	Lewis	
14	23	Brentford	(A)	2-1	(1-0)	W	14000	Garner,Nelmes(O.G.)	14	Roberts	Ternent	Smith	Elliott	Albeson	Jacques	Johnson	Best	Garner	Moore	Lewis	
15	29	Barrow	(H)	1-0	(1-0)	W	12426	Johnson	15	Roberts	Ternent	Smith	Elliott	Albeson	Jacques	Johnson	Best	Garner	Moore	Lewis	
16	6 Nov	Workington	(A)	1-3	(1-1)	L	3849	Johnson	16	Roberts	Ternent	Smith	Elliott	Albeson	Jacques	Johnson	Best	Hunt	Moore	Lewis	Taylor(8)
17	12	Exeter City	(H)	3-0	(2-0)	W	10107	Garner(2),Moore	17	Roberts	Ternent	Smith	Elliott	Albeson	Jacques	Johnson	Best	Garner	Moore	Lewis	
18	26	Stockport County	(H)	4-2	(3-2)	W	9299	Best(2),Garner(2)	18	Roberts	Ternent	Smith	Elliott	Albeson	Barnett	Johnson	Best	Garner	Moore	Lewis	
19	4 Dec	Cambridge United	(A)	1-1	(0-1)	D	6260	Lewis	19	Roberts	Smith	Ternent	Elliott	Albeson	Jacques	Johnson	Best	Garner	Moore	Lewis	Myton(11)
20	18	Bury	(A)	0-2	(0-0)	L	3077		20	Roberts	Smith	Ternent	Elliott	Albeson	Jacques	Johnson	Best	Garner	Moore	Lewis	
21	27	Lincoln City	(H)	2-1	(1-1)	W	15434	Lewis(2)	21	Roberts	Ternent	Smith	Elliott	Albeson	Jacques	Johnson	Best	Garner	Moore	Lewis	
22	1 Jan	Grimsby Town	(A)	1-4	(1-1)	L	9137	Garner	22	Roberts	Ternent	Smith	Elliott	Albeson	Jacques	Johnson	Best	Garner	Moore	Taylor	Lewis(9)
23	7	Hartlepool	(H)	3-1	(1-0)	W	6327	Johnson,Best,Parry(O.G.)	23	Roberts	Ternent	Smith	Barnett	Albeson	Jacques	Johnson	Best	Garner	Elliott	Taylor	
24	15	Crewe Alexandra	(A)	2-1	(0-1)	W	1493	Johnson,Taylor	24	Roberts	Ternent	Smith	Elliott	Albeson	Jacques	Johnson	Best	Garner	Moore	Taylor	Lewis(11)
25	22	Newport County	(A)	0-2	(0-1)	L	3535		25	Roberts	Ternent	Smith	Elliott	Albeson	Jacques	Johnson	Best	Garner	Moore	Taylor	
26	28	Colchester United	(H)	1-4	(1-2)	L	8971	Taylor	26	Roberts	Ternent	Smith	Elliott	Albeson	Jacques	Johnson	Best	Garner	Barnett	Lewis	Taylor(11)
27	12 Feb	Brentford	(H)	3-1	(2-0)	W	9658	Johnson,Moore,Taylor	27	Roberts	Ternent	Smith	Elliott	Albeson	Jacques	Johnson	Best	Moore	Barnett	Taylor	
28	19	Barrow	(A)	1-2	(1-1)	L	2068	Johnson	28	Bellotti	Smith	Ternent	Elliott	Albeson	Jacques	Johnson	Best	Moore	Barnett	Lewis	
29	25	Workington	(A)	2-0	(0-0)	W	7335	Moore,Best	29	Bellotti	Ternent	Smith	Elliott	Albeson	Jacques	Johnson	Best	Moore	Woods	Lewis	
30	4 Mar	Exeter City	(H)	0-0	(0-0)	D	3336		30	Bellotti	Ternent	Smith	Elliott	Albeson	Jacques	Best	Moore	Garner	Woods	Lewis	Taylor(11)
31	10	Chester	(H)	4-2	(3-2)	W	8189	Garner(3),Moore	31	Bellotti	Ternent	Smith	Booth	Albeson	Jacques	Johnson	Best	Garner	Moore	Woods	Lewis(7)
32	13	Crewe Alexandra	(H)	4-1	(2-0)	W	8148	Moore,Lewis,Albeson(pen),Best	32	Bellotti	Ternent	Smith	Booth	Albeson	Jacques	Woods	Best	Garner	Moore	Lewis	Taylor(11)
33	18	Darlington	(A)	3-2	(1-0)	W	2280	Garner,Best,Peddelty(O.G.)	33	Bellotti	Ternent	Smith	Booth	Albeson	Jacques	Lewis	Best	Garner	Moore	Woods	
34	22	Reading	(A)	4-1	(2-1)	W	6045	Best(3),Garner	34	Bellotti	Smith	Ternent	Booth	Albeson	Jacques	Lewis	Best	Garner	Moore	Woods	
35	24	Aldershot	(H)	1-0	(1-0)	W	12181	Moore	35	Bellotti	Ternent	Smith	Booth	Albeson	Jacques	Lewis	Best	Garner	Moore	Woods	Elliott(9)
36	31	Doncaster Rovers	(H)	2-1	(1-0)	W	15814	Garner,Best	36	Bellotti	Ternent	Smith	Booth	Albeson	Jacques	Johnson	Best	Garner	Moore	Woods	
37	1 Apr	Lincoln City	(A)	0-0	(0-0)	D	12199		37	Bellotti	Ternent	Smith	Booth	Albeson	Jacques	Elliott	Best	Johnson	Woods	Lewis	Taylor(10)
38	3	Southport	(H)	1-0	(1-0)	W	3320	Moore	38	Bellotti	Ternent	Smith	Elliott	Albeson	Jacques	Johnson	Best	Garner	Moore	Woods	Taylor(11)
39	7	Reading	(H)	4-1	(1-1)	W	13252	Johnson(2),Garner(2)	39	Bellotti	Ternent	Smith	Elliott	Albeson	Jacques	Johnson	Best	Garner	Booth	Woods	Taylor(11)
40	11	Northampton Town	(A)	1-1	(0-0)	D	3604	Best	40	Bellotti	Ternent	Smith	Elliott	Albeson	Jacques	Johnson	Best	Garner	Booth	Woods	
41	14	Stockport County	(A)	2-2	(0-0)	D	2513	Johnson,Garner	41	Bellotti	Ternent	Smith	Elliott	Albeson	Jacques	Johnson	Best	Garner	Moore	Booth	
42	17	Northampton Town	(H)	4-1	(1-1)	W	13399	Garner(2),Ternent,Best	42	Bellotti	Ternent	Smith	Elliott	Albeson	Jacques	Johnson	Best	Garner	Moore	Booth	Taylor(1)
43	21	Cambridge United	(H)	1-2	(0-0)	L	17059	Garner	43	Bellotti	Ternent	Smith	Elliott	Albeson	Jacques	Johnson	Best	Garner	Moore	Booth	
44	25	Scunthorpe United	(A)	1-1	(1-1)	D	8540	Best	44	Roberts	Ternent	Smith	Elliott	Albeson	Jacques	Taylor	Best	Garner	Moore	Booth	
45	29	Gillingham	(A)	0-0	(0-0)	D	6092		45	Roberts	Ternent	Smith	Elliott	Albeson	Jacques	Johnson	Best	Garner	Moore	Booth	
46	3 May	Gillingham	(H)	2-2	(2-1)	D	15854	Johnson,Elliott	46	Roberts	Ternent	Smith	Elliott	Albeson	Jacques	Johnson	Best	Garner	Moore	Booth	

Major Cup Competitions

F.A.Cup

Rd.	Date	Opposition	Venue	Score	H.T.	Res.	Att.	Goalscorers	1	2	3	4	5	6	7	8	9	10	11	12
R1	20 Nov	Aston Villa	(H)	1-0	(1-0)	W	16929	Best	Roberts	Ternent	Smith	Elliott	Albeson	Jacques	Johnson	Best	Garner	Moore	Lewis	12
R2	11 Dec	Bournemouth	(A)	0-2	(0-0)	L	14643		Roberts	Ternent	Smith	Elliott	Jacques	Albeson	Johnson	Best	Garner	Moore	Lewis	

League Cup

Rd.	Date	Opposition	Venue	Score	H.T.	Res.	Att.	Goalscorers	1	2	3	4	5	6	7	8	9	10	11	12
R1	18 Aug	Aldershot	(A)	1-1	(1-0)	D	5159	Johnson	Roberts	Lindsey	Smith	Elliott	Albeson	Jacques	Johnson	Best	Garner	Moore	Ternent	
R1r	23	Aldershot	(H)	1-2	(0-0)	L	7729	Garner	Roberts	Lindsey	Smith	Elliott	Albeson	Jacques	Johnson	Best	Garner	Moore	Ternent	Taylor(11)

SAVE AS

Back Row (left to right) : John Piekalmitis, Bill Garner, Dave Elliott, Dave Barnett, John Roberts, Alex Smith, Brian Albeson, Joe Jacques, George Duck.

Front Row (left to right) : Peter Taylor, Ray Ternent, Terry Johnson, Bernie Lewis, Billy Best, Peter Hunt, Keith Lindsey.

Appearances and Goals

Name	Appearances Lge.	FAC	L.C.	Total	Goals Lge.	FAC	L.C.	Total
ALBESON, Brian	46	2	2	50	2			2
BARNETT, Dave	5+1			5+1				
BELLOTTI, Derek	17			17				
BEST, Billy	45	2	2	49	19	1		20
BOOTH, Dennis	16			16				
DUCK, George	3			3				
ELLIOTT, Dave	41+1	2	2	45+1	1			1
GARNER, Bill	40	2	2	44	25		1	26
HUNT, Peter	1			1				
JACQUES, Joe	43	2	2	47				
JOHNSON, Terry	40	2	2	44	12		1	13
LEWIS, Bernard	24+3	2		26+3	5			5
LINDSEY, Keith	5		2	7	1			1
MOORE, Gary	40+1	2	2	44+1	9			9
MYTON, Brian	0+1			0+1				
ROBERTS, John	29	2	2	33				
SMITH, Alex	46	2	2	50				
TAYLOR, Peter	7+11		0+1	7+12	3			3
TERNENT, Ray	46	2	2	50	1			1
WOODS, Peter	12			12				
Own Goal					3			3

	Ps	P	W	D	L	F	A	W	D	L	F	A	Pts.
1971/72	2	46	18	2	3	56	26	6	10	7	25	29	60

Season 1972/73 – League Division Three

No.	Date	Opposition	Venue	Score	H.T.	Res.	Att.	Goalscorers	1	2	3	4	5	6	7	8	9	10	11	12
1	12 Aug	Wrexham	(H)	0-1	(0-1)	L	9345		Bellotti	Terrent	Smith	Elliott	Albeson	Jacques	Johnson T	Best	Garner	Moore	Booth	Harrison
2	19	Plymouth Argyle	(A)	0-2	(0-1)	L	6969		Bellotti	Smith	Terrent	Elliott	Albeson	Jacques	Johnson T	Best	Garner	Moore	Booth	Harrison
3	25	Swansea City	(H)	3-1	(1-0)	W	11062	Garner(2),Taylor	Bellotti	Smith	Terrent	Woods	Albeson	Harrison	Johnson T	Best	Garner	Taylor	Booth	Elliott
4	28	Rochdale	(H)	1-2	(0-2)	L	8657	Moore	Bellotti	Smith	Terrent	Woods	Albeson	Jacques	Johnson T	Best	Garner	Taylor	Booth	Moore(4)
5	1 Sep	Tranmere Rovers	(A)	1-3	(1-0)	L	2830	Johnson T	Bellotti	Smith	Terrent	Elliott	Albeson	Jacques	Johnson T	Best	Garner	Moore	Booth	Harrison
6	9	Notts. County	(H)	2-1	(1-0)	W	5886	Moore,Albeson	Bellotti	Terrent	Smith	Elliott	Albeson	Woods	Johnson T	Best	Moore	Harrison	Booth	Taylor(11)
7	16	Bournemouth	(A)	0-2	(0-1)	L	10311		Bellotti	Terrent	Smith	Elliott	Albeson	Mathews	Johnson T	Best	Moore	Harrison	Booth	Barnett(6)
8	19	Walsall	(A)	1-3	(0-1)	L	5545	Best	Bellotti	Terrent	Smith	Elliott	Albeson	Woods	Johnson T	Best	Moore	Harrison	Taylor	Bennett
9	22	Charlton Athletic	(H)	1-1	(1-0)	D	9743	Johnson T	Bellotti	Terrent	Smith	Elliott	Albeson	Harrison	Johnson T	Best	Moore	Booth	Taylor	Smith
10	25	Scunthorpe United	(H)	1-0	(0-0)	W	6391	Johnson T	Bellotti	Terrent	Woods	Elliott	Albeson	Harrison	Johnson T	Best	Moore	Booth	Taylor	Smith(10)
11	30	Port Vale	(A)	1-3	(0-1)	L	4005	Albeson	Bellotti	Terrent	Woods	Elliott	Albeson	Harrison	Johnson T	Best	Moore	Booth	Taylor	Barnett
12	6 Oct	Shrewsbury Town	(H)	2-0	(1-0)	W	7252	Elliott,Best	Bellotti	Terrent	Woods	Elliott	Albeson	Harrison	Johnson T	Best	Moore	Booth	Taylor	Johnson K
13	9	Oldham Athletic	(A)	0-1	(0-0)	L	7343		Bellotti	Terrent	Woods	Elliott	Albeson	Harrison	Johnson T	Best	Moore	Booth	Taylor	Johnson K(3)
14	14	Watford	(A)	0-1	(0-0)	L	7860		Bellotti	Terrent	Moody	Elliott	Albeson	Harrison	Johnson T	Best	Moore	Booth	Taylor	Johnson K(6)
15	21	Brentford	(H)	4-0	(2-0)	W	7010	Taylor(2),Best,Gelson(O.G.)	Bellotti	Booth	Terrent	Elliott	Albeson	Barnett	Johnson T	Best	Moore	Moody	Taylor	Bennett
16	24	Grimsby Town	(A)	1-3	(1-1)	L	9964	Johnson T	Bellotti	Booth	Terrent	Elliott	Albeson	Barnett	Johnson T	Best	Moore	Moody	Taylor	Bennett
17	28	Bolton Wanderers	(A)	1-1	(1-1)	D	7342	Elliott	Bellotti	Booth	Terrent	Elliott	Albeson	Barnett	Johnson T	Best	Moore	Moody	Taylor	Bennett
18	4 Nov	Scunthorpe United	(A)	0-0	(0-0)	D	3147		Bellotti	Booth	Terrent	Elliott	Albeson	Harrison	Johnson T	Best	Moore	Moody	Taylor	Woods
19	10	Walsall	(H)	2-0	(1-0)	W	6973	Johnson T,Best	Bellotti	Booth	Terrent	Elliott	Albeson	Harrison	Johnson T	Best	Bennett	Moody	Taylor	Moore(9)
20	24	Bristol Rovers	(H)	0-0	(0-0)	D	5859		Bellotti	Booth	Terrent	Elliott	Albeson	Harrison	Johnson T	Best	Guthrie	Moody	Taylor	Moore
21	2 Dec	York City	(A)	0-2	(0-0)	L	2572		Bellotti	Booth	Terrent	Elliott	Albeson	Harrison	Johnson T	Best	Guthrie	Moody	Taylor	Moore
22	16	Blackburn Rovers	(H)	1-2	(1-2)	L	5710	Guthrie	Bellotti	Booth	Terrent	Elliott	Albeson	Harrison	Johnson T	Best	Guthrie	Taylor	Moody	Horsfall(3)
23	22	Halifax Town	(A)	1-1	(0-1)	D	4162	Best	Bellotti	Booth	Terrent	Elliott	Albeson	Woods	Johnson T	Best	Guthrie	Taylor	Moody	Harrison
24	26	Charlton Athletic	(A)	0-0	(0-0)	D	7071		Bellotti	Booth	Smith	Elliott	Albeson	Moody	Johnson T	Best	Guthrie	Moore	Woods	Taylor
25	29	Plymouth Argyle	(H)	3-1	(2-1)	W	4790	Moore(2),Johnson T	Bellotti	Booth	Smith	Elliott	Albeson	Moody	Johnson T	Best	Guthrie	Moore	Woods	Taylor(11)
26	6 Jan	Swansea City	(A)	1-1	(0-1)	D	2306	Taylor	Bellotti	Booth	Smith	Elliott	Albeson	Moody	Johnson T	Best	Guthrie	Moore	Woods	Taylor(11)
27	20	Tranmere Rovers	(H)	1-0	(0-0)	W	4507	Guthrie	Bellotti	Booth	Smith	Elliott	Albeson	Moody	Johnson T	Best	Guthrie	Moore	Taylor	Woods
28	27	Notts. County	(A)	0-2	(0-0)	L	7717		Bellotti	Booth	Smith	Elliott	Albeson	Moody	Johnson T	Best	Guthrie	Moore	Taylor	Woods
29	3 Feb	Oldham Athletic	(A)	1-0	(0-0)	W	11124	Moore	Bellotti	Booth	Smith	Elliott	Albeson	Moody	Johnson K	Best	Guthrie	Moore	Taylor	Johnson K
30	9	Bournemouth	(H)	2-2	(0-1)	D	9435	Taylor,Guthrie	Bellotti	Booth	Smith	Elliott	Albeson	Moody	Johnson T	Best	Guthrie	Moore	Taylor	Johnson K(10)
31	17	Wrexham	(H)	2-4	(0-2)	L	3583	Guthrie,Johnson T	Bellotti	Booth	Smith	Elliott	Albeson	Moody	Johnson T	Best	Guthrie	Moore	Taylor	Ternent
32	24	Blackburn Rovers	(A)	0-1	(0-0)	L	6599		Bellotti	Booth	Smith	Elliott	Albeson	Moody	Johnson T	Best	Guthrie	Moore	Taylor	Ternent
33	2 Mar	Shrewsbury Town	(A)	0-2	(0-0)	L	2542		Mackay	Booth	Smith	Elliott	Albeson	Moody	Johnson T	Best	Guthrie	Johnson K	Taylor	Best
34	7	Chesterfield	(A)	4-2	(1-0)	W	3508	Guthrie(2),Moore,Johnson T	Mackay	Booth	Smith	Elliott	Albeson	Moody	Johnson T	Ternent	Guthrie	Moore	Taylor	Best(6)
35	9	Watford	(H)	0-0	(0-0)	D	6354		Mackay	Ternent	Smith	Elliott	Albeson	Moody	Johnson T	Ternent	Guthrie	Moore	Taylor	Best
36	12	Grimsby Town	(H)	2-0	(0-0)	W	4803	Johnson T,Hickman((O.G.))	Mackay	Ternent	Dyer	Elliott	Albeson	Moody	Johnson T	Booth	Guthrie	Moore	Taylor	Best
37	17	Brentford	(A)	2-1	(1-1)	W	8050	Guthrie,Moore	Mackay	Booth	Smith	Elliott	Albeson	Moody	Johnson T	Ternent	Guthrie	Moore	Taylor	Best
38	19	Rotherham United	(H)	1-0	(1-0)	W	6170	Guthrie	Mackay	Booth	Smith	Elliott	Albeson	Moody	Johnson T	Ternent	Guthrie	Moore	Taylor	Best
39	24	Bolton Wanderers	(H)	1-1	(0-0)	D	8032	Taylor	Mackay	Booth	Smith	Elliott	Albeson	Moody	Johnson T	Ternent	Guthrie	Moore	Taylor	Norris
40	31	Bristol Rovers	(A)	2-1	(1-0)	W	6374	Guthrie(2)	Mackay	Booth	Smith	Elliott	Albeson	Moody	Johnson T	Ternent	Guthrie	Moore	Taylor	Woods
41	6 Apr	York City	(H)	3-0	(1-0)	W	7346	Albeson,Best,Horsfall	Bellotti	Booth	Smith	Elliott	Albeson	Moody	Horsfall	Ternent	Guthrie	Moore	Best	Woods
42	14	Rotherham United	(A)	0-1	(0-0)	L	3389		Bellotti	Dyer	Smith	Elliott	Albeson	Moody	Horsfall	Ternent	Guthrie	Norris	Best	Moore(11)
43	20	Port Vale	(H)	5-0	(2-0)	W	9146	Guthrie(3),Best(2)	Bellotti	Ternent	Smith	Elliott	Albeson	Moody	Horsfall	Best	Guthrie	Best	Taylor	Booth(7)
44	21	Chesterfield	(H)	5-1	(3-0)	W	7167	Best(2),Guthrie(2),Moore	Bellotti	Johnson T	Johnson T	Elliott	Albeson	Moody	Horsfall	Ternent	Guthrie	Taylor	Horsfall	Horsfall(5)
45	24	Halifax Town	(A)	1-2	(0-2)	L	2887	Moore	Bellotti	Smith	Smith	Elliott	Albeson	Moody	Horsfall	Best	Moore	Best	Taylor	
46	28	Rochdale	(A)	2-3	(1-0)	L	2081	Best,Johnson T	Bellotti	Smith	Ternent	Elliott	Barnett	Moody	Johnson T	Booth	Moore	Best	Taylor	

Major Cup Competitions

Rd.	Date	Opposition	Venue Score	H.T. Res.	Att.	Goalscorers	1	2	3	4	5	6	7	8	9	10	11	12
F.A.Cup																		
R1	18 Nov	Aldershot	(H) 0-2		L 7377		Bellotti	Booth	Ternent	Elliott	Albeson	Harrison	Johnson T	Best	Bennett	Moody	Taylor	Johnson K(9)
League Cup																		
R1	16 Aug	Aldershot	(H) 2-1	(1-1)	W 5861	Garner,Best	Bellotti	Smith	Ternent	Elliott	Albeson	Jacques	Johnson T	Best	Garner	Moore	Booth	Harrison
R2	6 Sep	Chelsea	(H) 0-1	(0-1)	L 24160		Bellotti	Ternent	Smith	Elliott	Albeson	Harrison	Johnson T	Best	Garner	Bennett	Booth	Woods(10)

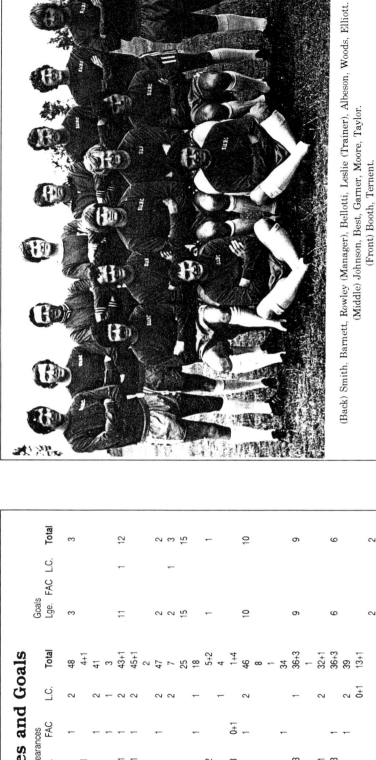

(Back) Smith, Barnett, Rowley (Manager), Bellotti, Leslie (Trainer), Albeson, Woods, Elliott.
(Middle) Johnson, Best, Garner, Moore, Taylor.
(Front) Booth, Ternent.

Appearances and Goals

Name	Appearances Lge	FAC	L.C.	Total	Goals Lge	FAC	L.C.	Total
ALBESON, Brian	45	1	2	48	3			3
BARNETT, Dave	4+1			4+1				
BELLOTTI, Derek	38	1	2	41				
BENNETT, Bobby	1	1	1	3				
BEST, Billy	40+1	1	2	43+1	11		1	12
BOOTH, Dennis	42+1	1	2	45+1				
DYER, Steve	2			2				
ELLIOTT, Dave	44	1	2	47	2			2
GARNER, Bill	5		2	7	2		1	3
GUTHRIE, Chris	25			25	15			15
HARRISON, Mike	16	1	1	18	1			1
HORSFALL, Tommy	5+2			5+2				
JACQUES, Joe	3		1	4				
JOHNSON, Kevin	1+3	0+1		1+4				
JOHNSON, Terry	43	1	2	46	10			10
MACKAY, Don	8			8				
MATTHEWS, Paul	1			1				
MOODY, Alan	33	1		34				
MOORE, Gary	35+3		1	36+3	9			9
NORRIS, Graham	1			1				
SMITH, Alex	30+1		2	32+1				
TAYLOR, Peter	35+3	1		36+3	6			6
TERNENT, Ray	36	1	2	39				
WOODS, Peter	13		0+1	13+1	2			2
Own Goal					2			2

	Ps	P	W	D	L	F	A	W	D	L	F	A	Pts.
1972/73	14	46	13	6	4	40	14	4	4	15	21	40	44

Season 1973/74 – League Division Three

No.	Date	Opposition	Venue	Score	H.T.	Res.	Att.	Goalscorers	No.	1	2	3	4	5	6	7	8	9	10	11	12
1	25 Aug	Blackburn Rovers	(A)	0-1	(0-1)	L	8504		1	Mackay	Smith	Ford	Elliott	Albeson	Moody	Booth	Johnson T	Moore	Townsend	Taylor	Dyer
2	31	Watford	(H)	2-3	(1-1)	L	7583	Booth,Johnson T	2	Mackay	Smith	Ford	Elliott	Albeson	Moody	Johnson T	Moore	Guthrie	Booth	Taylor	Townsend
3	8 Sep	Halifax Town	(A)	0-0	(0-0)	D	2604		3	Mackay	Smith	Ford	Elliott	Townsend	Moody	Johnson T	Moore	Guthrie	Booth	Taylor	Johnson K(4)
4	11	Oldham Athletic	(A)	0-2	(0-1)	L	6038		4	Mackay	Smith	Ford	Elliott	Townsend	Moody	Johnson T	Moore	Guthrie	Booth	Taylor	Albeson(11)
5	14	Cambridge United	(H)	3-1	(1-1)	W	6413	Guthrie,Moore,Johnson K	5	Mackay	Smith	Albeson	Elliott	Townsend	Moody	Johnson T	Moore	Guthrie	Booth	Johnson K	Horsfall(11)
6	17	Southport	(H)	0-1	(0-0)	L	4592		6	Bellotti	Smith	Albeson	Elliott	Townsend	Moody	Johnson T	Moore	Guthrie	Booth	Johnson K	Taylor(2)
7	22	Port Vale	(A)	0-0	(0-0)	D	4323		7	Bellotti	Smith	Albeson	Elliott	Townsend	Moody	Johnson T	Moore	Guthrie	Booth	Johnson K	Taylor(7)
8	29	Rochdale	(H)	1-2	(1-1)	L	4860	Johnson T	8	Bellotti	Smith	Albeson	Elliott	Townsend	Albeson	Johnson T	Moore	Taylor	Booth	Johnson K	Guthrie(11)
9	1 Oct	Southport	(A)	0-0	(0-0)	D	2293		9	Bellotti	Smith	Albeson	Elliott	Townsend	Albeson	Johnson T	Taylor	Guthrie	Booth	Johnson K	Horsfall(2)
10	6	Wrexham	(A)	1-5	(0-1)	L	4220	Elliott	10	Bellotti	Moody	Booth	Elliott	Townsend	Albeson	Johnson T	Booth	Guthrie	Smith	Johnson K	Dyer(3)
11	13	Aldershot	(H)	2-1	(1-0)	W	3821	Albeson,Townsend	11	Bellotti	Moody	Smith	Elliott	Townsend	Albeson	Johnson T	Booth	Guthrie	Horsfall	Johnson K	Dyer
12	19	Hereford United	(H)	2-1	(1-0)	W	6066	Albeson,Brace	12	Bellotti	Moody	Ford	Elliott	Townsend	Albeson	Johnson T	Brace	Guthrie	Coulson	Johnson K	Smith
13	22	Oldham Athletic	(H)	2-2	(2-2)	D	5537	Brace(2)	13	Bellotti	Moody	Ford	Elliott	Townsend	Albeson	Johnson T	Brace	Guthrie	Coulson	Johnson K	Smith
14	27	Shrewsbury Town	(A)	2-1	(1-0)	W	1815	Moody,Guthrie	14	Bellotti	Moody	Ford	Elliott	Townsend	Albeson	Johnson T	Brace	Guthrie	Coulson	Cunn'ham	Johnson T(11)
15	3 Nov	Huddersfield Town	(H)	5-2	(2-2)	W	7032	Brace(3),Albeson,Elliott	15	Bellotti	Moody	Ford	Elliott	Townsend	Albeson	Booth	Brace	Guthrie	Coulson	Johnson K	Moore
16	10	York City	(A)	0-1	(0-1)	L	8433		16	Bellotti	Moody	Ford	Elliott	Townsend	Albeson	Booth	Brace	Guthrie	Coulson	Johnson K	Moore
17	14	Chesterfield	(A)	0-0	(0-0)	D	4087		17	Bellotti	Moody	Ford	Elliott	Townsend	Albeson	Booth	Brace	Guthrie	Coulson	Johnson T	Moore
18	17	Walsall	(H)	2-1	(1-1)	W	6235	Brace,Albeson	18	Bellotti	Moody	Ford	Elliott	Townsend	Albeson	Booth	Brace	Guthrie	Coulson	Johnson T	Dyer
19	1 Dec	Tranmere Rovers	(H)	1-1	(0-1)	D	4760	Townsend	19	Bellotti	Moody	Ford	Elliott	Townsend	Worth'ton	Booth	Brace	Guthrie	Coulson	Johnson T	Dyer
20	8	Bristol Rovers	(A)	0-4	(0-0)	L	10778		20	Bellotti	Moody	Ford	Elliott	Townsend	Worth'ton	Booth	Brace	Guthrie	Coulson	Johnson T	Cunn'ham(11)
21	22	Rochdale	(H)	1-1	(1-1)	D	1011	Guthrie	21	Bellotti	Worth'ton	Ford	Elliott	Townsend	Dyer	Moody	Brace	Guthrie	Coulson	Johnson T	Moore(8)
22	26	Charlton Athletic	(H)	2-0	(0-0)	W	8888	Moody,Johnson T	22	Bellotti	Worth'ton	Ford	Elliott	Townsend	Dyer	Moody	Brace	Guthrie	Coulson	Johnson T	Moore
23	29	Halifax Town	(H)	1-2	(0-2)	L	6369	Guthrie	23	Bellotti	Worth'ton	Ford	Elliott	Townsend	Dyer	Moody	Brace	Guthrie	Coulson	Johnson T	Booth
24	1 Jan	Watford	(A)	0-1	(0-0)	L	8044		24	Bellotti	Worth'ton	Booth	Elliott	Townsend	Dyer	Moody	Brace	Moore	Coulson	Johnson T	Booth
25	12	Cambridge United	(A)	2-3	(1-2)	L	4255	Coulson,Ford	25	Webster	Worth'ton	Albeson	Johnson K	Townsend	Dyer	Moody	Brace	Moore	Coulson	Ford	Moore(5)
26	19	Blackburn Rovers	(H)	1-1	(1-0)	D	5338	Brace	26	Webster	Worth'ton	Ford	Elliott	Townsend	Dyer	Moody	Brace	Horsfall	Coulson	Johnson K	Elliott(5)
27	25	Bournemouth	(A)	3-1	(1-0)	W	9676	Brace(2),Guthrie	27	Webster	Worth'ton	Ford	Elliott	Townsend	Dyer	Horsfall	Brace	Guthrie	Coulson	Johnson K	Cunn'ham(7)
28	2 Feb	Plymouth Argyle	(A)	1-1	(1-1)	D	6955	Johnson T	28	Webster	Worth'ton	Ford	Elliott	Townsend	Dyer	Horsfall	Brace	Guthrie	Coulson	Johnson K	Johnson K
29	9	Port Vale	(H)	1-0	(1-0)	W	4187	Brace	29	Webster	Worth'ton	Ford	Elliott	Townsend	Moody	Horsfall	Brace	Guthrie	Coulson	Johnson K	Moody(7)
30	16	Aldershot	(A)	3-3	(0-1)	D	6677	Johnson T,Coulson,Silvester	30	Webster	Worth'ton	Ford	Elliott	Townsend	Moody	Silvester	Brace	Guthrie	Coulson	Johnson T	Booth
31	24	Wrexham	(H)	1-1	(0-0)	D	10054	Guthrie	31	Webster	Worth'ton	Dyer	Elliott	Townsend	Moody	Coulson	Brace	Guthrie	Silvester	Johnson T	Dyer(2)
32	3 Mar	Charlton Athletic	(A)	1-2	(0-1)	L	4449	Silvester	32	Webster	Worth'ton	Dyer	Elliott	Townsend	Moody	Coulson	Brace	Guthrie	Silvester	Johnson T	Ford
33	10	Shrewsbury Town	(H)	2-0	(1-0)	W	5038	Moody,Brace	33	Webster	Worth'ton	Dyer	Elliott	Albeson	Moody	Coulson	Brace	Guthrie	Silvester	Johnson T	Ford
34	16	Hereford United	(A)	2-1	(1-1)	W	7138	Moody,Silvester	34	Webster	Worth'ton	Dyer	Elliott	Townsend	Moody	Coulson	Brace	Guthrie	Silvester	Johnson T	Ford
35	18	Plymouth Argyle	(H)	2-0	(0-0)	W	5271	Silvester,Brace	35	Webster	Worth'ton	Dyer	Elliott	Townsend	Moody	Coulson	Brace	Guthrie	Silvester	Johnson T	Ford
36	24	York City	(H)	3-3	(2-2)	D	7025	Brace(2),Elliott	36	Webster	Worth'ton	Dyer	Elliott	Townsend	Moody	Coulson	Brace	Guthrie	Silvester	Johnson T	Ford(3)
37	26	Grimsby Town	(A)	1-2	(0-1)	L	5933	Brace	37	Webster	Worth'ton	Ford	Elliott	Townsend	Moody	Coulson	Brace	Guthrie	Silvester	Johnson T	Horsfall
38	30	Huddersfield Town	(H)	1-0	(0-0)	W	4453	Moody	38	Webster	Worth'ton	Ford	Elliott	Townsend	Moody	Coulson	Brace	Guthrie	Silvester	Johnson T	Dyer
39	1 Apr	Bournemouth	(H)	2-2	(1-2)	D	6385	Silvester,Guthrie	39	Webster	Worth'ton	Ford	Elliott	Townsend	Moody	Coulson	Brace	Guthrie	Silvester	Johnson T	Dyer
40	5	Chesterfield	(H)	1-3	(1-2)	L	6222	Moody	40	Webster	Worth'ton	Ford	Elliott	Townsend	Moody	Coulson	Brace	Dyer	Silvester	Johnson T	Horsfall(7)
41	12	Brighton	(H)	0-2	(0-0)	L	9772		41	Webster	Worth'ton	Ford	Elliott	Townsend	Moody	Coulson	Brace	Horsfall	Silvester	Johnson T	Dyer(9)
42	13	Walsall	(A)	2-1	(1-1)	W	3165	Brace(2)	42	Webster	Worth'ton	Ford	Elliott	Townsend	Moody	Coulson	Brace	Guthrie	Silvester	Johnson T	Dyer(5)
43	15	Brighton	(A)	2-0	(2-0)	W	12943	Silvester,Guthrie	43	Webster	Worth'ton	Ford	Elliott	Townsend	Moody	Coulson	Brace	Guthrie	Silvester	Johnson T	Dyer
44	19	Bristol Rovers	(H)	0-0	(0-0)	D	8323		44	Webster	Worth'ton	Ford	Elliott	Townsend	Moody	Coulson	Brace	Guthrie	Silvester	Johnson T	
45	22	Grimsby Town	(H)	4-1	(3-1)	W	5335	Brace(2),Coulson,Elliott	45	Webster	Worth'ton	Ford	Elliott	Townsend	Moody	Coulson	Brace	Guthrie	Silvester	Johnson T	
46	26	Tranmere Rovers	(A)	0-2	(0-0)	L	4227		46	Webster	Worth'ton	Ford	Elliott	Townsend	Moody	Coulson	Brace	Guthrie	Silvester	Johnson T	

Abbrev.: Worth'ton = Worthington. Cunn'ham = Cunningham.

Major Cup Competitions

F.A.Cup

Rd.	Date	Opposition	Venue	Score	H.T.	Res.	Att.	Goalscorers	1	2	3	4	5	6	7	8	9	10	11	12
R1	24 Nov	Boreham Wood	(H)	3-0	(0-0)	W	6937	Johnson T,Albeson,Brace	Bellotti	Moody	Ford	Elliott	Townsend	Albeson	Booth	Brace	Guthrie	Coulson	Johnson T	Cunningham
R2	15 Dec	Reading	(H)	2-0	(1-0)	W	5768	Brace,Johnson T	Bellotti	Worthington	Ford	Elliott	Townsend	Albeson	Moody	Brace	Guthrie	Coulson	Johnson T	Dyer
R3	5 Jan	Peterborough Utd.	(A)	1-3	(0-2)	L	11661	Moody	Bellotti	Worthington	Booth	Elliott	Townsend	Dyer	Moody	Brace	Guthrie	Coulson	Johnson T	Moore(8)

League Cup

Rd.	Date	Opposition	Venue	Score	H.T.	Res.	Att.	Goalscorers	1	2	3	4	5	6	7	8	9	10	11	12
R1	28 Aug	Portsmouth	(A)	1-2	(0-1)	L	9652	Taylor	MacKay	Smith	Ford	Elliott	Albeson	Moody	Booth	Johnson T	Moore	Guthrie	Taylor	Townsend

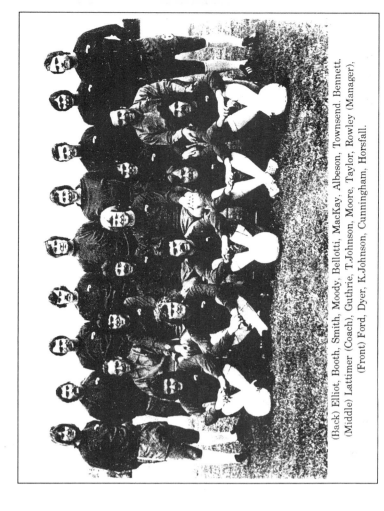

(Back) Elliot, Booth, Smith, Moody, Bellotti, MacKay, Albeson, Townsend, Bennett.
(Middle) Lattimer (Coach), Guthrie, T.Johnson, Moore, Taylor, Rowley (Manager),
(Front) Ford, Dyer, K.Johnson, Cunningham, Horsfall.

Appearances and Goals

Name	Appearances Lge.	FAC	L.C.	Total	Goals Lge.	FAC	L.C.	Total
ALBESON, Brian	18+1	2	1	21+1	4	1		5
BELLOTTI, Derek	18	3		21				
BOOTH, Dennis	19	2	1	22	1			1
BRACE, Stuart	35	3		38	20	2		22
COULSON, Willie	35	3		38	3			3
CUNNINGHAM, Dave	1+2			1+2				
DYER, Steve	15+4	1		16+4				
ELLIOTT, Dave	45+1	3	1	49+1	4			4
FORD, Andy	32+1	2	1	35+1	1			1
GUTHRIE, Chris	40+1	3	1	44+1	8			8
HORSFALL, Tommy	6+3			6+3				
JOHNSON, Kevin	11+1			11+1	1			1
JOHNSON, Terry	43+1	3	1	47+1	5	2		7
MACKAY, Don	6		1	7				
MOODY, Alan	44+1	3	1	48+1	6	1		7
MOORE, Gary	9+2	0+1	1	10+3	1			1
SILVESTER, Peter	17			17	6			6
SMITH, Alex	11		1	12				
TAYLOR, Peter	7+2		1	8+2			1	1
TOWNSEND, Neil	44	3		47	2			2
WEBSTER, Malcolm	22			22				
WORTHINGTON, Dave	28	2		30				

	Ps	P	W	D	L	F	A	W	D	L	F	A	Pts.
1973/74	12	46	10	7	6	40	30	6	7	10	.22	32	46

Season 1974/75 – League Division Three

No.	Date	Opponents	Venue	Score	H.T.	Res.	Att.	Goalscorers	1	2	3	4	5	6	7	8	9	10	11	12
1	17 Aug	Chesterfield	H	2-1	(1-1)	W	6158	Coulson,Brace	Webster	Dyer	Worth' R	Elliott	Townsend	Moody	Coulson	Brace	Guthrie	Taylor	Cunn'ham	Worth' D
2	24	Bury	A	1-0	(1-0)	W	5871	Cunn'ham	Cawston	Dyer	Worth' R	Elliott	Townsend	Moody	Coulson	Brace	Guthrie	Taylor	Cunn'ham	Worth' D
3	30	Plymouth Argyle	H	2-1	(1-1)	W	8600	Worth' R,Cunn'ham	Cawston	Dyer	Worth' R	Elliott	Townsend	Moody	Coulson	Brace	Guthrie	Taylor	Cunn'ham	Worth' D
4	2 Sep	Halifax Town	H	4-0	(1-0)	W	7973	Guthrie(3),Brace	Cawston	Dyer	Worth' R	Elliott	Townsend	Moody	Coulson	Brace	Guthrie	Taylor	Cunn'ham	Worth' D(7)
5	7	Bournemouth	A	0-0	(0-0)	D	6582		Cawston	Dyer	Worth' R	Elliott	Townsend	Moody	Coulson	Brace	Guthrie	Taylor	Cunn'ham	Worth' D
6	13	Crystal Palace	H	0-1	(0-1)	L	17394		Cawston	Dyer	Worth' R	Elliott	Townsend	Moody	Coulson	Brace	Guthrie	Johnson	Cunn'ham	Silvester
7	16	Walsall	H	3-0	(2-0)	W	6966	Brace,Guthrie,Cunn'ham	Webster	Dyer	Worth' R	Elliott	Townsend	Moody	Coulson	Brace	Guthrie	Johnson	Cunn'ham	Silvester(11)
8	21	Watford	A	0-2	(0-0)	L	6955		Cawston	Dyer	Worth' R	Elliott	Townsend	Moody	Coulson	Brace	Guthrie	Johnson	Taylor	Silvester
9	25	Blackburn Rovers	A	0-1	(0-0)	L	9159		Cawston	Dyer	Worth' R	Elliott	Townsend	Moody	Coulson	Brace	Guthrie	Johnson	Taylor	Johnson(7)
10	27	Charlton Athletic	H	2-1	(2-0)	W	7252	Moody,Brace	Cawston	Dyer	Worth' R	Elliott	Townsend	Moody	Johnson	Brace	Guthrie	Taylor	Cunn'ham	Silvester
11	2 Oct	Peterborough United	A	0-1	(0-1)	L	8460		Cawston	Worth' D	Worth' R	Elliott	Townsend	Moody	Johnson	Brace	Guthrie	Taylor	Cunn'ham	Silvester
12	5	Swindon Town	A	0-2	(0-0)	L	6690		Cawston	Worth' D	Worth' R	Coulson	Townsend	Moody	Johnson	Brace	Guthrie	Silvester	Taylor	Ford(4)
13	7	Peterborough United	H	1-2	(1-1)	L	5730	Guthrie	Webster	Worth' D	Worth' R	Dyer	Townsend	Moody	Johnson	Brace	Guthrie	Silvester	Taylor	Love
14	11	Tranmere Rovers	H	1-0	(0-0)	W	5188	Moody	Webster	Worth' D	Worth' R	Dyer	Townsend	Moody	Silvester	Brace	Guthrie	Taylor	Johnson	Lamb(3)
15	15	Halifax Town	A	1-3	(0-2)	L	1210	Silvester	Webster	Worth' D	Ford	Elliott	Townsend	Elliott	Silvester	Brace	Guthrie	Taylor	Johnson	Love(6)
16	25	Hereford United	H	0-0	(0-0)	D	5843		Webster	Dyer	Ford	Elliott	Townsend	Moody	Love	Brace	Guthrie	Silvester	Taylor	
17	29	Colchester United	A	1-1	(1-0)	D	6547	Guthrie	Webster	Dyer	Ford	Elliott	Townsend	Moody	Love	Brace	Guthrie	Cunn'ham	Taylor	Silvester
18	1 Nov	Gillingham	H	2-2	(1-1)	D	5320	Ford,Silvester	Webster	Dyer	Worth' R	Elliott	Townsend	Moody	Love	Brace	Guthrie	Ford	Cunn'ham	Silvester(4)
19	9	Preston North End	A	4-1	(3-0)	W	8295	Silvester(2),Brace,Guthrie	Webster	Dyer	Worth' R	Taylor	Townsend	Moody	Love	Brace	Guthrie	Ford	Silvester	
20	16	Wrexham	H	1-1	(0-0)	D	6041	Guthrie	Webster	Dyer	Worth' R	Taylor	Hadley	Moody	Love	Brace	Guthrie	Ford	Silvester	Worth' D(5)
21	29	Grimsby Town	H	3-0	(1-0)	W	4992	Brace,Guthrie,Silvester	Webster	Dyer	Worth' R	Taylor	Hadley	Moody	Coulson	Brace	Guthrie	Ford	Silvester	Worth' D
22	7 Dec	Brighton	A	0-2	(0-2)	L	10035		Webster	Dyer	Worth' R	Taylor	Townsend	Moody	Coulson	Brace	Guthrie	Silvester	Coulson	Worth' D(8)
23	23	Aldershot	H	1-1	(0-1)	D	5326	Elliott	Webster	Worth' D	Dyer	Elliott	Townsend	Moody	Little	Brace	Guthrie	Ford	Coulson	Ford
24	26	Crystal Palace	A	1-1	(0-0)	D	21652	Silvester	Webster	Worth' D	Taylor	Elliott	Townsend	Moody	Little	Cunn'ham	Guthrie	Ford	Silvester	Brace(8)
25	28	Port Vale	A	1-3	(0-1)	L	6327	Elliott	Webster	Worth' D	Taylor	Elliott	Townsend	Moody	Little	Cunn'ham	Guthrie	Ford	Silvester	Brace(11)
26	11 Jan	Brighton	H	1-0	(0-0)	W	5846	Little	Webster	Worth' D	Taylor	Elliott	Hadley	Moody	Little	Brace	Silvester	Love	Coulson	Ford
27	18	Grimsby Town	A	0-0	(0-0)	D	4904		Webster	Worth' D	Taylor	Elliott	Townsend	Moody	Little	Brace	Silvester	Guthrie	Cunn'ham	Hadley
28	1 Feb	Preston North End	H	1-1	(1-1)	D	9134	Brace	Webster	Worth' D	Taylor	Elliott	Hadley	Moody	Little	Brace	Guthrie	Silvester	Cunn'ham	Love(4)
29	4	Walsall	A	0-3	(0-0)	L	9894		Webster	Worth' D	Worth' R	Elliott	Hadley	Moody	Little	Brace	Guthrie	Silvester	Cunn'ham	Love(3)
30	8	Gillingham	A	1-2	(0-1)	L	7594	Silvester	Webster	Worth' D	Taylor	Elliott	Townsend	Moody	Little	Brace	Guthrie	Silvester	Cunn'ham	Coulson(11)
31	15	Huddersfield Town	H	1-0	(0-0)	W	4316	Brace	Webster	Worth' D	Taylor	Elliott	Townsend	Moody	Little	Brace	Guthrie	Silvester	Keefe	Ford
32	22	Wrexham	A	1-1	(0-0)	D	3178	Guthrie	Webster	Worth' D	Taylor	Elliott	Townsend	Dyer	Little	Brace	Guthrie	Silvester	Ford	Love(4)
33	28	Plymouth Argyle	A	0-1	(0-0)	L	16321		Webster	Worth' D	Taylor	Elliott	Ford	Dyer	Little	Brace	Guthrie	Silvester	Ford	Love(11)
34	4 Mar	Huddersfield Town	A	1-4	(0-1)	L	4538	Guthrie	Webster	Worth' D	Taylor	Brisley	Townsend	Moody	Little	Brace	Guthrie	Silvester	Cunn'ham	Keefe(2)
35	8	Blackburn Rovers	H	2-2	(2-2)	D	4711	Guthrie,Taylor	Webster	Dyer	Taylor	Brisley	MacKenzie	Moody	Little	Brace	Guthrie	Ford	Cunn'ham	
36	15	Charlton Athletic	A	1-2	(0-0)	L	9477	Hales(O.G.)	Webster	Dyer	Taylor	Brisley	MacKenzie	Moody	Little	Brace	Guthrie	Ford	Elliott	Cunn'ham
37	19	Chesterfield	A	1-1	(1-1)	D	3854	Brace	Webster	Worth' D	Taylor	Brisley	Townsend	Moody	Little	Brace	Guthrie	Ford	Elliott	Dyer
38	21	Bournemouth	H	0-0	(0-0)	D	4269		Webster	Worth' D	Taylor	Brisley	Townsend	Moody	Little	Brace	Guthrie	Ford	Cunn'ham	
39	28	Watford	H	0-0	(0-0)	D	5924		Webster	Worth' D	Taylor	Brisley	Townsend	Moody	Little	Brace	Guthrie	Ford	Keefe	
40	29	Aldershot	A	0-3	(0-1)	L	3825		Webster	Worth' D	Taylor	Brisley	Townsend	Moody	Little	Brace	Guthrie	Ford	Dyer	MacKenzie(11)
41	1 Apr	Port Vale	H	0-0	(0-0)	D	4178		Webster	Worth' D	Taylor	Brisley	Dyer	Moody	Little	Brace	Guthrie	MacKenzie	Lamb	Ford(11)
42	5	Hereford United	A	0-1	(0-1)	L	4807		Webster	Worth' D	Taylor	Dyer	Townsend	Moody	Little	Brace	Guthrie	Lamb	Cunn'ham	Elliott(6)
43	11	Swindon Town	H	2-0	(1-0)	W	4499	Brace,Moody	Webster	Worth' D	Taylor	Moody	Townsend	MacKenzie	Little	Brace	Lamb	Cunn'ham	Pountney	Elliott(11)
44	18	Tranmere Rovers	A	1-2	(0-0)	L	1744	Brace	Webster	Worth' D	Taylor	Dyer	Townsend	Moody	Little	Brace	Pountney	Lamb	Cunn'ham	Elliott
45	21	Bury	H	1-0	(1-0)	W	4294	Townsend	Webster	Worth' D	Taylor	Dyer	Townsend	Moody	Little	Brace	Guthrie	Cunn'ham	Pountney	Elliott
46	25	Colchester United	H	1-1	(1-0)	D	5924	Dominey(O.G.)	Webster	Worth' D	Taylor	Dyer	Townsend	Moody	Little	Brace	Lamb	Pountney	Cunn'ham	Ford

Abbrev.: Worth' D = Worthington D. Worth' R = Worthington R. Cunn'ham = Cunningham.

Major Cup Competitions

F.A.Cup

Rd.	Date	Opposition	Venue Score	H.T.	Res.	Att.	1	2	3	4	5	6	7	8	9	10	11	12	Goalscorers
R1	23 Nov	A.P. Leamington	(A) 2-1	(2-0)	W	3000	Webster	Dyer	Worth'n R	Taylor	Townsend	Moody	Love	Brace	Guthrie	Ford	Silvester	Worth'n D	Guthrie,Silvester
R2	14 Dec	Ilford	(A) 2-0	(1-0)	W	3486	Webster	Dyer	Taylor	Elliott	Townsend	Moody	Worth'n D	Brace	Guthrie	Coulson	Silvester	Ford	Townsend,Guthrie
R3	4 Jan	Q.P. Rangers	(H) 2-2	(0-1)	D	18100	Webster	Worth'n D	Taylor	Elliott	Townsend	Moody	Little	Brace	Guthrie	Cunn'ham	Coulson	Silvester	Guthrie,Brace
R3r	7	Q.P. Rangers	(A) 0-2	(0-0)	L	21484	Webster	Worthington D	Taylor	Taylor	Elliott	Hadley	Moody	Little	Brace	Guthrie	Love	Coulson	

League Cup

Rd.	Date	Opposition	Venue Score	H.T.	Res.	Att.	1	2	3	4	5	6	7	8	9	10	11	12	Goalscorers
R1	21 Aug	Cambridge United	(H) 2-0	(2-0)	W	5868	Webster	Dyer	Worth'n R	Elliott	Townsend	Moody	Coulson	Brace	Guthrie	Taylor	Cunn'ham	Worth'n D	Guthrie(2)
R2	11 Sep	Colchester United	(H) 0-2	(0-0)	L	7856	Webster	Worth'n D	Worth'n R	Elliott	Townsend	Moody	Johnson	Brace	Guthrie	Taylor	Silvester	Cunn'ham	

Abbrev.: Worth'n = Worthington. Cunn'ham = Cunningham.

Back Row (Left to Right) Neil Townsend, Steve Lamb, David Elliott, Malcolm Webster, Bob Worthington, Alan Moody, Chris Guthrie, Gordon Linton, Dave Worthington, Graham Byford.
Third Row (Left to Right) John Lattimer (Coach), Rodney Harrington, Roy Little, John Burney, Sean Rafter, Danny Peters, George Lay, Seamus Horgan, Martin Warwick, Paul Denny, Tony Hadley, Arthur Rowley (Manager).
Second Row (Left to Right) Frank Walton (Vice-Chairman), Willie Coulson, Stuart Brace, Andy Ford, David Cunningham, Steve Dyer, Alastair Love, Terry Johnson.
Front Row (Left to Right) Chris Hutchings, Lewis Brooks, David Keefe, Tony Wakefield, Peter Wellman, Collin Krzoska, Tony Rowell. William Rubin (Chairman)
Photographs by Southend News

13

Appearances and Goals

Name	Appearances				Goals			
	Lge.	FAC	L.C.	Total	Lge.	FAC	L.C.	Total
BRACE, Stuart	44+2	4	2	50+2	11	1		12
BRISLEY, Terry	8			8				
CAWSTON, Mervyn	10			10				
COULSON, Willie	15+1	3	1	19+1	1			1
CUNNINGHAM, Dave	26	1	1	28	3			3
DYER, Steve	29	2	1	32				
ELLIOTT, Dave	29+2	3	2	34+2	2			2
FORD, Andy	18+2	1		19+2	1			1
GUTHRIE, Chris	42	4	2	48	12	3	2	17
HADLEY, Tony	4	1		5				
JOHNSON, Terry	9+1		1	10+1	1			1
KEEFE, David	2+1			2+1				
LAMB, Steve	5+1			5+1				
LITTLE, Alan	24	2		26	1			1
LOVE, Alistair	6+5	2		8+5				
MOODY, Alan	43	4	2	49	3			3
MacKENZIE, Ian	5+1			5+1				
POUNTNEY, Ronnie	4			4				
SILVESTER, Peter	21+2	2	1	24+2	7	1		8
TAYLOR, Tony	40	4	2	46	1			1
TOWNSEND, Neil	39	3	2	44	1	1		2
WEBSTER, Malcolm	36	4	2	42				
WORTHINGTON, Bob	20	1	2	23	1			1
WORTHINGTON, Dave	27+3	3	1	31+3	1			1
Own Goal					2			2

	Ps	P	W	D	L	F	A	W	D	L	F	A	Pts.
1974/75	18	46	11	9	3	32	17	2	7	14	14	34	42

Season 1975/76 – League Division Three

No.	Date	Opposition	Venue	Score	H.T.	Res.	Att.	Goalscorers	No.	1	2	3	4	5	6	7	8	9	10	11	12
1	16 Aug	Sheffield Wednesday	(H)	2-1	(0-1)	W	6775	Parker,Moody	1	Webster	Worth'ton	Taylor	Little	Dyer	Moody	Pountney	Brace	Parker	Nicholl	Silvester	Cunn'ham(10)
2	23	Chester	(A)	1-1	(0-1)	D	4781	Silvester	2	Webster	Worth'ton	Ford	Nicholl	Dyer	Moody	Little	Pountney	Parker	Pountney	Silvester	Cunn'ham(10)
3	30	Rotherham United	(H)	1-2	(0-0)	L	4219	Brace	3	Webster	Worth'ton	Taylor	Little	Townsend	Moody	Brace	Pountney	Nicholl	Parker	Silvester	
4	6 Sep	Walsall	(A)	3-2	(2-1)	W	4380	Silvester(3)	4	Webster	Worth'ton	Taylor	Little	Townsend	Moody	Nicholl	Pountney	Parker	Cunn'ham	Silvester	Brace(8)
5	13	Port Vale	(H)	3-3	(3-0)	D	4455	Silvester(2),Parker	5	Webster	Worth'ton	Taylor	Little	Townsend	Dyer	Pountney	Cunn'ham	Parker	Silvester	Nicholl	Brace(7)
6	20	Millwall	(A)	1-2	(0-2)	L	6418	Little	6	Webster	Worth'ton	Taylor	Little	Townsend	Dyer	Coulson	Cunn'ham	Parker	Silvester	Nicholl	
7	22	Preston North End	(H)	0-2	(0-1)	L	4583		7	Webster	Worth'ton	Taylor	Little	Townsend	Moody	Pountney	Cunn'ham	Parker	Silvester	Nicholl	
8	27	Shrewsbury Town	(H)	1-3	(0-1)	L	2922	Moody(pen)	8	Webster	Worth'ton	Ford	Little	Townsend	Moody	Pountney	Dyer	Parker	Silvester	Nicholl	Brace(9)
9	4 Oct	Aldershot	(A)	1-2	(1-0)	L	3579	Silvester	9	Webster	Worth'ton	Ford	Little	Townsend	Moody	Pountney	Dyer	Cunn'ham	Silvester	Nicholl	Parker(7)
10	11	Bury	(A)	0-1	(0-0)	L	6268		10	Webster	Worth'ton	Ford	Little	Townsend	Moody	Pountney	Brace	Silvester	Nicholl	Foggo	
11	17	Mansfield Town	(H)	2-2	(1-2)	D	3248	Silvester,Foggo	11	Webster	Worth'ton	Ford	Little	Townsend	Moody	Foggo	Brace	Parker	Silvester	Nicholl	
12	20	Halifax Town	(H)	4-1	(2-1)	W	3089	Nicholl,Parker,Moody,Little	12	Rafter	Worth'ton	Ford	Little	Townsend	Moody	Brace	Foggo	Parker	Lamb	Nicholl	Keefe(10)
13	25	Crystal Palace	(A)	1-1	(0-1)	D	18438	Foggo	13	Webster	Worth'ton	Ford	Little	Townsend	Moody	Brace	Foggo	Parker	Silvester	Nicholl	Dyer(10)
14	31	Swindon Town	(H)	3-0	(2-0)	W	4256	Nicholl,Parker,Brace	14	Webster	Worth'ton	Ford	Little	Townsend	Moody	Foggo	Brace	Parker	Silvester	Nicholl	
15	8 Nov	Brighton	(A)	0-2	(0-1)	L	13500		15	Webster	Worth'ton	Ford	Little	Townsend	Moody	Foggo	Brace	Parker	Silvester	Silvester	Dyer(11)
16	29	Peterborough United	(A)	2-3	(1-1)	L	7393	Foggo,Brace	16	Webster	Worth'ton	Ford	Little	Townsend	Moody	Foggo	Brace	Parker	Nicholl	Nicholl	
17	5 Dec	Grimsby Town	(H)	5-2	(2-0)	W	3925	Silvester(3),Foggo,Ford	17	Webster	Worth'ton	Ford	Little	Townsend	Moody	Foggo	Brace	Parker	Silvester	Nicholl	Pountney(9)
18	22	Cardiff City	(A)	1-3	(0-1)	L	9342	Little	18	Webster	Worth'ton	Ford	Little	Hadley	Moody	Foggo	Brace	Parker	Silvester	Nicholl	
19	26	Colchester United	(H)	2-0	(1-0)	W	6267	Brace(2)	19	Webster	Worth'ton	Ford	Little	Hadley	Moody	Foggo	Brace	Parker	Silvester	Nicholl	
20	27	Chesterfield	(H)	2-1	(2-0)	W	4670	Foggo,Silvester	20	Webster	Worth'ton	Ford	Little	Hadley	Moody	Foggo	Brace	Parker	Silvester	Nicholl	
21	10 Jan	Rotherham United	(A)	0-2	(0-0)	L	4390		21	Rafter	Worth'ton	Ford	Little	Townsend	Moody	Foggo	Brace	Parker	Silvester	Nicholl	Dyer(5)
22	16	Millwall	(H)	0-0	(0-0)	D	7746		22	Rafter	Worth'ton	Ford	Little	Hadley	Moody	Foggo	Brace	Parker	Silvester	Nicholl	Pountney(10)
23	26	Hereford United	(H)	1-3	(0-2)	L	3722	Moody	23	Webster	Worth'ton	Ford	Little	Hadley	Moody	Foggo	Brace	Parker	Silvester	Nicholl	Glover(9)
24	6 Feb	Wrexham	(H)	2-1	(1-0)	W	4162	Brace,Silvester	24	Webster	Worth'ton	Ford	Little	Harding	Moody	Foggo	Brace	Parker	Silvester	Nicholl	
25	9	Port Vale	(A)	1-1	(1-0)	D	3494	Silvester	25	Rafter	Dyer	Ford	Little	Harding	Moody	Foggo	Brace	Parker	Silvester	Nicholl	
26	17	Brighton	(H)	4-0	(1-0)	W	4784	Silvester(4)	26	Webster	Worth'ton	Ford	Little	Hadley	Moody	Foggo	Cunn'ham	Parker	Silvester	Nicholl	
27	21	Hereford United	(A)	1-2	(1-1)	L	7264	Silvester	27	Webster	Worth'ton	Ford	Little	Hadley	Dyer	Cunn'ham	Pountney	Parker	Silvester	Nicholl	
28	24	Preston North End	(A)	1-5	(0-0)	L	5210	Parker	28	Webster	Worth'ton	Ford	Little	Hadley	Dyer	Foggo	Foggo	Parker	Silvester	Nicholl	
29	27	Crystal Palace	(H)	1-2	(1-1)	L	13500	Pountney	29	Webster	Worth'ton	Ford	Little	Hadley	Moody	Foggo	Cunn'ham	Parker	Silvester	Nicholl	
30	1 Mar	Gillingham	(A)	2-2	(2-1)	D	4722	Little,Parker	30	Webster	Worth'ton	Ford	Little	Hadley	Moody	Foggo	Pountney	Parker	Cunn'ham	Nicholl	
31	6	Swindon Town	(A)	0-0	(0-2)	D	5585		31	Webster	Dyer	Ford	Little	Hadley	Moody	Foggo	Pountney	Parker	Silvester	Nicholl	
32	8	Aldershot	(H)	0-2	(0-0)	L	3874		32	Webster	Worth'ton	Ford	Cunn'ham	Hadley	Moody	Foggo	Pountney	Parker	Silvester	Nicholl	
33	13	Bury	(H)	2-0	(0-0)	W	3844	Parker,Brace	33	Webster	Banks	Ford	Little	Hadley	Moody	Cunn'ham	Foggo	Parker	Silvester	Brace	
34	15	Mansfield Town	(A)	1-3	(0-1)	L	8043	Brace	34	Webster	Dyer	Ford	Little	Hadley	Moody	Foggo	Brace	Parker	Silvester	Nicholl	Pountney(9)
35	19	Peterborough United	(A)	0-0	(0-0)	D	4561		35	Webster	Dyer	Ford	Little	Hadley	Moody	Nicholl	Brace	Parker	Silvester	Cunn'ham	Goodwin(9)
36	23	Halifax Town	(A)	0-1	(0-1)	L	1450		36	Webster	Worth'ton	Ford	Little	Hadley	Moody	Foggo	Brace	Goodwin	Silvester	Taylor	Pountney(9)
37	27	Grimsby Town	(H)	2-2	(2-2)	D	4158	Keefe,Goodwin	37	Webster	Banks	Ford	Little	Hadley	Moody	Keefe	Brace	Parker	Goodwin	Taylor	
38	29	Cardiff City	(A)	0-2	(0-2)	L	4596		38	Webster	Banks	Ford	Little	Hadley	Moody	Foggo	Brace	Parker	Keefe	Taylor	
39	6 Apr	Shrewsbury Town	(A)	1-3	(0-2)	L	2493	Parker	39	Webster	Banks	Ford	Little	Hadley	Moody	Pountney	Dyer	Parker	Goodwin	Nicholl	Brace(11)
40	9	Walsall	(H)	2-2	(1-1)	D	3723	Parker,Nicholl	40	Webster	Worth'ton	Ford	Little	Hadley	Moody	Cunn'ham	Brace	Parker	Silvester	Taylor	
41	13	Gillingham	(A)	2-1	(0-1)	W	5776	Parker,Little	41	Webster	Worth'ton	Ford	Little	Hadley	Moody	Cunn'ham	Brace	Parker	Silvester	Cunn'ham	
42	17	Colchester United	(A)	1-2	(1-0)	L	4260	Moody(pen)	42	Webster	Worth'ton	Ford	Little	Hadley	Moody	Taylor	Brace	Parker	Silvester	Taylor	
43	19	Chesterfield	(A)	1-1	(1-1)	D	3917	Moody(pen)	43	Rafter	Worth'ton	Ford	Little	Hadley	Moody	Nicholl	Pountney	Parker	Goodwin	Taylor	
44	23	Chester	(H)	2-0	(1-0)	W	3553	Foggo,Moody(pen)	44	Rafter	Worth'ton	Ford	Little	Dyer	Moody	Nicholl	Foggo	Parker	Silvester	Taylor	
45	27	Wrexham	(A)	2-2	(0-1)	D	1965	Moody(pen),Little	45	Rafter	Worth'ton	Ford	Little	Dyer	Moody	Foggo	Nicholl	Parker	Silvester	Taylor	
46	29	Sheffield Wednesday	(A)	1-2	(0-2)	L	25802	Moody	46	Rafter	Worth'ton	Ford	Little	Hadley	Moody	Nicholl	Foggo	Parker	Silvester	Taylor	Pountney(8)

Abbrev.: Cunn'ham = Cunningham.   Worth'ton = Worthington.

Major Cup Competitions

F.A.Cup

Rd.	Date	Opposition	Venue	Score	H.T.	Res.	Att.	Goalscorers	1	2	3	4	5	6	7	8	9	10	11	12
R1	22 Nov	Swansea City	(H)	2-0	(2-0)	W	5383	Parker(2)	Webster	Worth'n	Ford	Little	Townsend	Moody	Foggo	Brace	Parker	Nicholl	Silvester	
R2	13 Dec	Dover	(H)	4-1	(3-0)	W	7696	Silvester(2),Parker,Moody	Webster	Worth'n	Ford	Little	Townsend	Moody	Foggo	Brace	Parker	Silvester	Nicholl	
R3	3 Jan	Brighton & H.A.	(H)	2-1	(1-1)	W	9878	Silvester,Brace	Rafter	Worth'n	Ford	Little	Townsend	Moody	Foggo	Brace	Parker	Silvester	Nicholl	
R4	24	Cardiff City	(H)	2-1	(1-1)	W	12863	Parker(2)	Webster	Worth'n	Ford	Little	Townsend	Moody	Foggo	Brace	Parker	Silvester	Nicholl	Hadley(5)
R5	14 Feb	Derby County	(A)	0-1	(0-1)	L	31918		Webster	Dyer	Ford	Little	Hadley	Moody	Foggo	Brace	Parker	Silvester	Nicholl	Pountney(8)

League Cup

Rd.	Date	Opposition	Venue	Score	H.T.	Res.	Att.	Goalscorers	1	2	3	4	5	6	7	8	9	10	11	12
R1L1	19 Aug	Peterborough U.	(H)	2-0	(2-0)	W	4684	Silvester,Little	Webster	Worth'n	Moody	Dyer	Ford	Nicholl	Little	Brace	Pountney	Parker	Silvester	Cunn'ham(10)
R1L2	27	Peterborough U.	(A)	0-3	(0-2)	L	4828		Webster	Worth'n	Ford	Little	Dyer	Moody	Taylor	Brace	Lamb	Nicholl	Silvester	Cunn'ham(9)

(Aggregate – Lost 2–3)

Abbrev.: Worth'n = Worthington. Cunn'ham = Cunningham.

(Back) Rafter, Little, Moody, Lamb, Ford, Silvester, Hadley, Parker, Webster.
(Middle) Nicholl, Worthington, Townsend, Brace, Taylor,
(Front) Dyer, Cunningham, Pountney.

Appearances and Goals

Name	Appearances				Goals			
	Lge.	FAC	L.C.	Total	Lge.	FAC	L.C.	Total
BANKS, Frank	5			5				
BRACE, Stuart	27+4	5	2	34+4	8	1		9
COULSON, Willie	1			1				
CUNNINGHAM, Dave	15+1		0+2	15+3				
DYER, Steve	14+3	1	2	17+3				
FOGGO, Ken	30	5		35	6			6
FORD, Andy	39	5	2	46	1			1
GLOVER, Alan	0+1			0+1				
GOODWIN, Steve	4+1			4+1	1			1
HADLEY, Tony	25	1+1		26+1	1			1
HARDING, Steve	2			2				
KEEFE, David	2+1			2+1	1			1
LAMB, Steve	1		1	2				
LITTLE, Alan	45	5	2	52	6		1	7
MOODY, Alan	42	5	2	49	9		1	10
NICHOLL, Terry	40	5	2	47	3			3
PARKER, Stuart	43+1	5	1	49+1	10	5		15
POUNTNEY, Ronnie	16+5	0+1	1	17+6	1			1
RAFTER, Sean	8	1		9				
SILVESTER, Peter	40	5	2	47	19	3	1	23
TAYLOR, Tony	16	1		17				
TOWNSEND, Neil	16	4		20				
WEBSTER, Malcolm	38	4	2	44				
WORTHINGTON, Dave	37	4	2	43				

	Ps	P	W	D	L	F	A	W	D	L	F	A	Pts.
1975/76	23	46	9	7	7	40	31	3	6	14	25	44	37

Season 1976/77 – League Division Four

No.	Date	Opponents	Venue	Score	H.T.	Res.	Att.	Goalscorers	No.	1	2	3	4	5	6	7	8	9	10	11	12
1	21 Aug	Watford	(H)	2-1	(1-1)	W	5267	Parker S,Cunn'ham	1	Freeman	Moody	Townsend	Hadley	Ford	Nicholl	Clark	Little	Cunn'ham	Parker S	Pountney	Goodwin(6)
2	25	Crewe Alexandra	(A)	1-1	(0-0)	D	2182	Parker S	2	Freeman	Moody	Townsend	Hadley	Ford	Nicholl	Clark	Little	Cunn'ham	Parker S	Pountney	Goodwin
3	28	Bournemouth	(A)	0-2	(0-1)	L	4688		3	Freeman	Moody	Townsend	Hadley	Ford	Nicholl	Clark	Little	Cunn'ham	Parker S	Pountney	Goodwin(7)
4	3 Sep	Workington	(H)	2-0	(1-0)	W	4563	Little,Denny	4	Freeman	Moody	Ford	Little	Townsend	Hadley	Nicholl	Goodwin	Denny	Pountney	Cunn'ham	Clark
5	10	Halifax Town	(H)	1-1	(1-1)	D	5163	Moody(pen)	5	Freeman	Moody	Ford	Little	Townsend	Hadley	Nicholl	Goodwin	Denny	Pountney	Cunn'ham	Clark
6	18	Hartlepool United	(A)	1-1	(1-0)	D	1612	Moody(pen)	6	Freeman	Moody	Townsend	Young	Ford	Nicholl	Little	Goodwin	Pountney	Denny	Cunn'ham	Clark(10)
7	24	Scunthorpe United	(H)	1-1	(1-1)	D	5288	Little	7	Freeman	Moody	Ford	Little	Townsend	Young	Nicholl	Goodwin	Denny	Parker S	Cunn'ham	Parker S(9)
8	2 Oct	Cambridge United	(H)	3-2	(1-0)	W	4917	Parker S(2),Goodwin	8	Freeman	Moody	Ford	Clark	Townsend	Young	Nicholl	Goodwin	Pountney	Parker S	Cunn'ham	Denny(4)
9	8	Colchester United	(A)	0-0	(0-0)	D	6690		9	Freeman	Moody	Ford	Clark	Hadley	Young	Nicholl	Goodwin	Pountney	Parker S	Cunn'ham	Denny(4)
10	16	Rochdale	(A)	0-0	(0-0)	D	2302		10	Freeman	Moody	Ford	Clark	Townsend	Young	Nicholl	Goodwin	Pountney	Denny	Cunn'ham	Dyer
11	23	Exeter City	(H)	2-0	(1-0)	W	4605	Denny,Parker S	11	Freeman	Moody	Ford	Laverick	Townsend	Young	Pountney	Goodwin	Parker S	Denny	Cunn'ham	Dyer
12	26	Barnsley	(A)	1-3	(1-0)	L	4380	Parker S	12	Freeman	Moody	Ford	Laverick	Townsend	Young	Pountney	Goodwin	Parker S	Denny	Cunn'ham	Dyer
13	29	Newport County	(H)	1-1	(0-1)	D	4821	Moody(pen)	13	Freeman	Moody	Ford	Laverick	Townsend	Young	Pountney	Goodwin	Parker S	Denny	Little	Dyer(10)
14	6 Nov	Aldershot	(A)	0-0	(0-0)	D	3845		14	Freeman	Moody	Ford	Laverick	Townsend	Young	Pountney	Goodwin	Parker S	Hadley	Little	Clark(6)
15	12	Bradford City	(H)	4-1	(2-0)	W	5417	Parker S(3),Goodwin	15	Freeman	Banks	Ford	Laverick	Townsend	Moody	Pountney	Goodwin	Parker S	Silvester	Little	Cunn'ham
16	27	Southport	(A)	0-0	(0-0)	D	1298		16	Freeman	Banks	Ford	Laverick	Moody	Young	Pountney	Goodwin	Parker S	Hadley	Little	Clark(5)
17	4 Dec	Huddersfield Town	(H)	1-1	(0-0)	D	4419	Hadley	17	Freeman	Banks	Ford	Laverick	Moody	Young	Pountney	Goodwin	Parker S	Hadley	Little	Denny
18	18	Torquay United	(A)	1-1	(0-0)	D	2151		18	Freeman	Banks	Ford	Laverick	Moody	Young	Pountney	Goodwin	Parker S	Hadley	Little	Denny
19	27	Brentford	(H)	2-1	(1-1)	W	8960	Goodwin,Little	19	Freeman	Banks	Ford	Laverick	Moody	Young	Pountney	Goodwin	Parker S	Hadley	Little	Clark
20	28	Doncaster Rovers	(A)	3-0	(2-0)	W	5605	Goodwin,Polypou,Laverick	20	Freeman	Banks	Ford	Laverick	Moody	Young	Pountney	Goodwin	Parker S	Polypou	Little	Polypou(10)
21	1 Jan	Aldershot	(H)	5-0	(2-0)	W	7150	Little(2),Laverick,Moody(pen),Parker S	21	Freeman	Banks	Ford	Laverick	Moody	Young	Pountney	Goodwin	Parker S	Polypou	Little	Hadley(7)
22	15	Crewe Alexandra	(H)	1-0	(1-0)	W	5209	Parker S	22	Freeman	Clark	Ford	Laverick	Moody	Young	Polypou	Goodwin	Parker S	Little	Cunn'ham	Hadley(11)
23	22	Watford	(A)	1-1	(0-1)	D	6934	Parker S	23	Freeman	Clark	Ford	Laverick	Moody	Young	Polypou	Goodwin	Parker S	Hadley	Little	Pountney(11)
24	28	Stockport County	(H)	0-0	(0-0)	D	6119		24	Freeman	Moody	Ford	Laverick	Hadley	Young	Polypou	Goodwin	Parker S	Morris	Little	Pountney(7)
25	2 Feb	Bournemouth	(H)	2-2	(1-0)	D	6138	Morris,Parker S	25	Freeman	Moody	Ford	Laverick	Townsend	Young	Morris	Goodwin	Parker S	Hadley	Little	Cunn'ham
26	12	Workington	(A)	3-0	(1-0)	W	1096	Laverick,Goodwin,Parker D	26	Freeman	Banks	Ford	Laverick	Moody	Young	Morris	Hadley	Parker D	Goodwin	Little	Polypou
27	19	Halifax Town	(A)	1-3	(1-1)	L	1994	Parker D	27	Freeman	Banks	Ford	Laverick	Moody	Young	Morris	Goodwin	Parker D	Hadley	Little	Cunn'ham(10)
28	21	Darlington	(A)	0-0	(0-0)	D	2743		28	Freeman	Banks	Ford	Laverick	Moody	Young	Morris	Clark	Parker D	Hadley	Little	Polypou
29	25	Hartlepool United	(H)	1-0	(1-0)	W	6383	Laverick	29	Freeman	Banks	Ford	Laverick	Moody	Young	Morris	Clark	Parker D	Goodwin	Little	Polypou(2)
30	5 Mar	Scunthorpe United	(A)	0-1	(0-1)	L	2752		30	Freeman	Banks	Ford	Laverick	Moody	Young	Morris	Clark	Parker D	Goodwin	Little	Townsend(10)
31	11	Cambridge United	(A)	0-1	(0-1)	L	9423		31	Freeman	Banks	Ford	Laverick	Moody	Young	Morris	Hadley	Parker D	Goodwin	Little	Townsend
32	15	Swansea City	(H)	1-2	(1-1)	L	3932	Hadley	32	Freeman	Banks	Ford	Laverick	Moody	Young	Morris	Goodwin	Parker D	Hadley	Little	Clark(4)
33	19	Colchester United	(H)	1-0	(0-0)	W	6637	Morris	33	Freeman	Banks	Ford	Laverick	Moody	Young	Morris	Hadley	Parker D	Clark	Little	Young
34	25	Rochdale	(H)	3-0	(0-0)	W	5430	Townsend,Hadley,Moody(pen)	34	Freeman	Banks	Ford	Laverick	Moody	Townsend	Morris	Hadley	Parker D	Clark	Goodwin	Young
35	2 Apr	Exeter City	(A)	1-3	(0-2)	L	4156	Morris	35	Freeman	Banks	Ford	Laverick	Moody	Townsend	Morris	Hadley	Parker D	Clark	Goodwin	Young
36	8	Brentford	(A)	0-1	(0-1)	L	8950		36	Freeman	Banks	Ford	Laverick	Moody	Townsend	Morris	Young	Parker D	Clark	Goodwin	Little(11)
37	9	Doncaster Rovers	(H)	2-1	(0-0)	W	4437	Parker D(2)	37	Rafter	Banks	Ford	Laverick	Moody	Young	Morris	Hadley	Parker D	Little	Young	Clark
38	12	Swansea City	(A)	0-2	(0-1)	L	8063		38	Rafter	Banks	Ford	Laverick	Moody	Young	Morris	Clark	Parker D	Little	Young	Young
39	15	Barnsley	(H)	1-1	(0-1)	D	4691	Hadley	39	Rafter	Banks	Ford	Laverick	Moody	Young	Morris	Hadley	Parker D	Hadley	Little	Young
40	18	Stockport County	(A)	0-0	(0-0)	D	2391		40	Rafter	Banks	Ford	Townsend	Moody	Young	Morris	Goodwin	Parker D	Hadley	Little	Young(10)
41	23	Bradford City	(H)	3-2	(3-1)	W	3239	Moody(2,1 pen),Parker D	41	Rafter	Banks	Moody	Young	Ford	Laverick	Little	Goodwin	Parker D	Hadley	Morris	Polypou
42	29	Southport	(H)	0-0	(0-0)	D	2371		42	Rafter	Banks	Ford	Young	Moody	Hadley	Morris	Laverick	Parker D	Goodwin	Clark	Townsend
43	2 May	Darlington	(A)	1-1	(1-1)	D	2275	Parker D	43	Rafter	Banks	Ford	Young	Moody	Hadley	Morris	Laverick	Parker D	Goodwin	Clark	Hadley
44	7	Huddersfield Town	(A)	0-3	(0-0)	L	3356		44	Rafter	Banks	Ford	Young	Moody	Townsend	Morris	Polypou	Parker D	Goodwin	Clark	Hadley(8)
45	10	Newport County	(A)	0-3	(0-2)	L	2681		45	Rafter	Banks	Ford	Young	Moody	Townsend	Morris	Polypou	Parker D	Goodwin	Clark	Polypou(2)
46	13	Torquay United	(H)	0-3	(0-2)	L			46	Rafter	Banks	Ford	Young	Moody	Townsend	Morris	Laverick	Parker D	Goodwin	Clark	

Abbrev.: Polypou = Polycarpou. Cunn'ham = Cunningham.

Major Cup Competitions

F.A.Cup

Rd.	Date	Opposition	Venue	Score	H.T.	Res.	Att.	Goalscorers	1	2	3	4	5	6	7	8	9	10	11	12
R1	20 Nov	Exeter City	(A)	1-1	(0-0)	D	4434	Pountney	Freeman	Banks	Ford	Laverick	Townsend	Moody	Pountney	Goodwin	Parker S	Hadley	Little	Cunn'ham(5)
R1r	22	Exeter City	(H)	2-1	(0-0)	W	6604	Parker S,Hadley (After Extra Time)	Freeman	Banks	Ford	Laverick	Moody	Young	Pountney	Goodwin	Parker S	Hadley	Little	Clark
R2	11 Dec	Newport County	(H)	3-0	(1-0)	W	5724	Hadley,Pountney,Parker S	Freeman	Banks	Ford	Laverick	Moody	Young	Pountney	Goodwin	Parker S	Hadley	Little	Clark
R3	8 Jan	Chester	(H)	0-4	(0-1)	L	10347		Freeman	Clark	Ford	Laverick	Moody	Young	Pountney	Goodwin	Parker S	Polypou	Little	Hadley(11)

League Cup

Rd.	Date	Opposition	Venue	Score	H.T.	Res.	Att.	Goalscorers	1	2	3	4	5	6	7	8	9	10	11	12
R1L1	14 Aug	Brighton	(H)	1-1	(0-0)	D	6254	Parker S	Freeman	Moody	Townsend	Hadley	Ford	Nicholl	Little	Cunn'ham	Pountney	Parker S	Goodwin	Clark
R1L2	17	Brighton	(A)	1-2	(1-1)	L	11907	Cunningham	Freeman	Moody	Townsend	Hadley	Ford	Nicholl	Little	Cunn'ham	Pountney	Parker S	Goodwin	Clark(11)

(Aggregate – Lost 2-3)

Abbrev.: Cunn'ham = Cunningham. Polypou = Polycarpou.

(Back) Smith (Manager), Buxton (Coach). Parker, Moody, Banks, Ford, Hadley, Lattimer (Physio), Hinchliffe (Youth Coach). (Middle) Dyer, Nicholl, Townsend, Keefe, Goodwin, Pountney. (Front) Rafter, Krzoska, Cunningham, Little, Freeman.

Appearances and Goals

Name	Appearances				Goals			
	Lge.	FAC	L.C.	Total	Lge.	FAC	L.C.	Total
BANKS, Frank	28	3		31				
CLARK, Paul	21+4	1	0+1	22+5				
CUNNINGHAM, Dave	13+1	0+1	2	15+2	1	1		2
DENNY, Paul	8+1			8+1	2			2
DYER, Steve	0+1			0+1				
FORD, Andy	46	4	2	52				
FREEMAN, Neil	36	4	2	42				
GOODWIN, Steve	40+2	4	2	46+2	5			5
HADLEY, Tony	28+3	3+1	2	33+4	4	2		6
LAVERICK, Micky	34	4		38	4			4
LITTLE, Alan	33+1	4	2	39+1	5			5
MOODY, Alan	45	4	2	51	7			7
MORRIS, Colin	23			23	3			3
NICHOLL, Terry	10		2	12				
PARKER, Derrick	21			21	6			6
PARKER, Stuart	19+1	4	2	25+1	13	2	1	16
POLYCARPOU, Andy	5+3	1		6+3	1			1
POUNTNEY, Ronnie	23+2	4	2	29+2	2			2
PRICE, Ken	1			1				
RAFTER, Sean	10			10				
SILVESTER, Peter	1			1				
TOWNSEND, Neil	27+1	1	2	30+1	1			1
YOUNG, Dave	34+1	3		37+1				1

	Ps	P	W	D	L	F	A	W	D	L	F	A	Pts.
1976/77	10	46	11	9	3	35	19	4	10	9	17	26	49

Season 1977/78 – League Division Four

No.	Date	Opposition	Venue	Score	H.T.	Res.	Att.	Goalscorers	No.	1	2	3	4	5	6	7	8	9	10	11	12
1	20 Aug	Reading	(A)	1-0	(0-0)	W	3994	Morris	1	Freeman	Moody	Banks	Laverick	Townsend	Young	Morris	Goodwin	Parker	Polypou	Foggon	Hadley(9)
2	22	Northampton Town	(H)	0-0	(0-0)	D	3499		2	Freeman	Moody	Banks	Laverick	Townsend	Young	Morris	Goodwin	Parker	Polypou	Foggon	Hadley(2)
3	26	Crewe Alexandra	(H)	1-0	(1-0)	W	4389	Goodwin	3	Freeman	Moody	Banks	Laverick	Townsend	Young	Morris	Goodwin	Parker	Hadley	Foggon	Hadley(10)
4	3 Sep	Bournemouth	(A)	3-0	(2-0)	W	3688	Morris,Parker,Moody(pen)	4	Freeman	Moody	Banks	Laverick	Townsend	Young	Morris	Goodwin	Parker	Hadley	Foggon	
5	10	Scunthorpe United	(A)	2-1	(1-1)	W	2768	Laverick,Parker	5	Freeman	Moody	Banks	Laverick	Townsend	Young	Morris	Goodwin	Parker	Hadley	Foggon	Walker(3)
6	12	Swansea City	(H)	2-1	(1-1)	W	6144	Parker(2)	6	Freeman	Moody	Banks	Laverick	Townsend	Young	Morris	Goodwin	Parker	Hadley	Foggon	
7	16	York City	(H)	0-0	(0-0)	D	7079		7	Freeman	Moody	Banks	Laverick	Townsend	Young	Morris	Goodwin	Parker	Hadley	Foggon	
8	24	Halifax Town	(A)	1-0	(1-0)	W	1573	Townsend	8	Freeman	Moody	Banks	Laverick	Townsend	Young	Morris	Goodwin	Parker	Hadley	Foggon	
9	27	Doncaster Rovers	(A)	0-2	(0-0)	L	5103		9	Freeman	Moody	Banks	Laverick	Townsend	Clark	Morris	Goodwin	Parker	Hadley	Foggon	
10	30	Torquay United	(H)	4-0	(3-0)	W	5525	Parker(4)	10	Freeman	Moody	Banks	Laverick	Townsend	Young	Morris	Goodwin	Parker	Hadley	Foggon	Polypou(8)
11	3 Oct	Stockport County	(H)	0-2	(0-2)	L	5871		11	Freeman	Moody	Banks	Laverick	Townsend	Clark	Morris	Goodwin	Parker	Hadley	Foggon	Polypou(6)
12	7	Southport	(A)	0-0	(0-0)	D	2178		12	Freeman	Moody	Banks	Laverick	Young	Clark	Morris	Clark	Parker	Hadley	Foggon	
13	14	Hartlepool United	(H)	1-1	(1-0)	D	5432	Moody(pen)	13	Freeman	Moody	Banks	Laverick	Clark	Young	Morris	Goodwin	Parker	Polypou	Foggon	Hadley(10)
14	22	Wimbledon	(A)	3-1	(1-1)	W	4448	Clark,Morris,Goodwin	14	Freeman	Young	Banks	Laverick	Moody	Clark	Morris	Goodwin	Parker	Polypou	Foggon	Hadley(10)
15	29	Brentford	(H)	0-1	(0-0)	L	7430		15	Freeman	Moody	Banks	Laverick	Townsend	Clark	Morris	Goodwin	Parker	Hadley	Foggon	
16	4 Nov	Barnsley	(A)	0-1	(0-0)	L	5356		16	Freeman	Moody	Young	Laverick	Townsend	Clark	Morris	Goodwin	Parker	Hadley	Foggon	Polypou(9)
17	12	Darlington	(A)	0-2	(0-1)	L	2337		17	Freeman	Moody	Young	Laverick	Clark	Townsend	Morris	Goodwin	Parker	Hadley	Foggon	
18	19	Watford	(H)	1-0	(1-0)	W	10990	Goodwin	18	Freeman	Moody	Banks	Laverick	Yates	Townsend	Morris	Goodwin	Parker	Hadley	Hadley	Young(10)
19	3 Dec	Rochdale	(A)	2-1	(0-1)	W	1020	Laverick,Parker	19	Freeman	Moody	Banks	Laverick	Yates	Townsend	Morris	Pountney	Parker	Fell	Hadley	
20	9	Newport County	(H)	4-2	(0-1)	W	5840	Fell(2),Hadley,Parker	20	Rafter	Moody	Banks	Laverick	Yates	Townsend	Morris	Foggon	Parker	Fell	Hadley	
21	26	Huddersfield Town	(A)	0-2	(0-1)	L	5706		21	Rafter	Moody	Banks	Laverick	Yates	Townsend	Morris	Foggon	Parker	Fell	Hadley	
22	27	Aldershot	(H)	3-1	(2-0)	W	9819	Parker,Morris,Laverick	22	Rafter	Moody	Banks	Laverick	Yates	Young	Morris	Foggon	Parker	Fell	Hadley	
23	31	Barnsley	(H)	1-1	(1-0)	D	7446	Parker	23	Rafter	Moody	Banks	Laverick	Yates	Young	Morris	Foggon	Parker	Fell	Hadley	
24	2 Jan	Grimsby Town	(H)	1-1	(1-0)	D	9973	Moody(pen)	24	Rafter	Moody	Banks	Laverick	Yates	Young	Morris	Foggon	Parker	Fell	Hadley	Pountney(11)
25	13	Reading	(H)	0-2	(0-1)	L	6215		25	Horn	Banks	Yates	Laverick	Hadley	Moody	Fell	Pountney	Parker	Abbott	Morris	
26	27	Bournemouth	(H)	5-1	(3-0)	W	4865	Morris(2),Fell,Abbott,Laverick	26	Horn	Banks	Yates	Laverick	Hadley	Moody	Morris	Pountney	Parker	Abbott	Fell	
27	1 Feb	Crewe Alexandra	(A)	1-0	(0-1)	W	1603	Parker	27	Burridge	Banks	Yates	Laverick	Hadley	Moody	Morris	Pountney	Parker	Abbott	Fell	Young(7)
28	3	Scunthorpe United	(H)	2-0	(1-0)	W	6879	Abbott(2)	28	Burridge	Banks	Yates	Laverick	Hadley	Moody	Morris	Pountney	Parker	Abbott	Fell	
29	17	Halifax Town	(A)	5-0	(3-0)	W	6128	Laverick(2),Morris,Moody,Polypou	29	Burridge	Banks	Yates	Laverick	Hadley	Moody	Morris	Pountney	Parker	Abbott	Polypou	
30	28	York City	(A)	2-1	(0-0)	W	1586	Parker,Morris	30	Burridge	Banks	Yates	Laverick	Hadley	Moody	Morris	Pountney	Parker	Abbott	Polypou	
31	4 Mar	Southport	(H)	4-2	(1-1)	W	6635	Parker(2),Polypou,Hadley	31	Burridge	Banks	Yates	Laverick	Hadley	Moody	Morris	Polypou	Parker	Abbott	Pountney	
32	7	Swansea City	(A)	0-0	(0-0)	D	11316		32	Burridge	Young	Yates	Laverick	Hadley	Moody	Morris	Pountney	Parker	Abbott	Polypou	Young(2)
33	11	Hartlepool United	(A)	0-1	(0-0)	L	2886		33	Freeman	Young	Yates	Laverick	Hadley	Moody	Morris	Pountney	Parker	Abbott	Polypou	Franklin(5)
34	17	Wimbledon	(H)	1-0	(1-0)	W	7120	Parker	34	Freeman	Banks	Yates	Laverick	Townsend	Moody	Morris	Pountney	Parker	Abbott	Polypou	
35	21	Northampton Town	(H)	0-0	(0-0)	D	2431		35	Freeman	Banks	Yates	Laverick	Townsend	Moody	Morris	Pountney	Parker	Abbott	Polypou	
36	24	Brentford	(A)	2-1	(1-1)	W	11372	Morris,Tucker(O.G.)	36	Freeman	Banks	Yates	Laverick	Townsend	Moody	Morris	Pountney	Parker	Abbott	Fell	
37	25	Aldershot	(H)	0-3	(0-1)	L	5631		37	Freeman	Banks	Yates	Laverick	Townsend	Moody	Morris	Pountney	Parker	Abbott	Goodwin	Polypou(11)
38	27	Huddersfield Town	(A)	1-3	(0-1)	L	8202	Laverick	38	Freeman	Banks	Yates	Laverick	Townsend	Moody	Morris	Pountney	Parker	Abbott	Fell	Franklin(11)
39	1 Apr	Grimsby Town	(A)	0-2	(0-0)	L	3505		39	Freeman	Banks	Yates	Laverick	Young	Moody	Franklin	Pountney	Parker	Abbott	Morris	Goodwin(10)
40	3	Doncaster Rovers	(H)	4-0	(3-0)	W	5644	Moody(2,1 pen),Morris,Yates	40	Freeman	Banks	Yates	Laverick	Young	Moody	Morris	Pountney	Parker	Abbott	Fell	Goodwin(11)
41	7	Darlington	(H)	2-0	(2-0)	W	7196	Laverick,Townsend	41	Freeman	Banks	Yates	Laverick	Townsend	Moody	Morris	Pountney	Parker	Abbott	Fell	Goodwin(11)
42	15	Watford	(A)	1-1	(0-1)	D	18947	Moody(pen)	42	Freeman	Banks	Yates	Laverick	Townsend	Moody	Morris	Pountney	Parker	Abbott	Fell	Goodwin(4)
43	18	Torquay United	(H)	1-0	(1-0)	W	2137	Moody	43	Freeman	Banks	Yates	Goodwin	Townsend	Moody	Morris	Pountney	Parker	Abbott	Fell	
44	21	Rochdale	(H)	3-1	(2-0)	W	11253	Goodwin,Morris,Parker	44	Freeman	Dudley	Banks	Laverick	Townsend	Moody	Morris	Pountney	Parker	Goodwin	Fell	
45	24	Stockport County	(A)	0-1	(0-1)	L	2394		45	Freeman	Dudley	Banks	Laverick	Townsend	Moody	Morris	Pountney	Parker	Goodwin	Fell	Dudley(3)
46	29	Newport County	(A)	2-1	(0-1)	W	2364	Townsend,Parker	46	Freeman	Banks	Dudley	Laverick	Townsend	Moody	Morris	Pountney	Parker	Goodwin	Fell	

Abbrev.: Polypou = Polycarpou.

Major Cup Competitions

F.A.Cup

Rd.	Date	Opposition	Venue Score	H.T.	Res.	Att.	1	2	3	4	5	6	7	8	9	10	11	12	Goalscorers
R1	26 Nov	Torquay United	(A) 2-1	(0-0)	W	3210	Freeman	Moody	Banks	Laverick	Young	Townsend	Morris	Pountney	Parker	Fell	Hadley		Parker,Fell
R2	17 Dec	A.P. Leamington	(A) 0-0	(0-0)	D	2540	Rafter	Banks	Moody	Laverick	Yates	Townsend	Morris	Fell	Parker	Hadley	Foggon		
R2r	19	A.P. Leamington	(H) 4-0	(2-0)	W	5879	Rafter	Moody	Banks	Laverick	Yates	Townsend	Morris	Foggon	Parker	Fell	Hadley		Moody(pen),Parker,Laverick,Morris
R3	7 Jan	Derby County	(A) 2-3	(0-2)	L	23625	Rafter	Moody	Banks	Laverick	Yates	Young	Morris	Pountney	Parker	Fell	Hadley		Parker(2)

League Cup

Rd.	Date	Opposition	Venue Score	H.T.	Res.	Att.	1	2	3	4	5	6	7	8	9	10	11	12	Goalscorers
R1L1	13 Aug	Northampton T.	(H) 2-3	(1-2)	L	4654	Rafter	Moody	Banks	Laverick	Townsend	Young	Morris	Goodwin	Parker	Polypou	Foggon		Goodwin,Foggon
R1L2	16	Northampton T.	(A) 1-2	(1-1)	L	4395	Rafter	Moody	Banks	Laverick	Townsend	Young	Morris	Goodwin	Parker	Polypou	Foggon		Morris

(Aggregate – Lost 3-5)

Abbrev.: Polypou = Polycarpou.

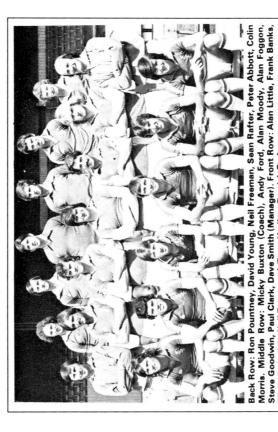

Back Row: Ron Pountney, David Young, Neil Freeman, Sean Rafter, Peter Abbott, Colin Morris. Middle Row: Micky Buxton (Coach), Andy Ford, Alan Moody, Alan Foggon, Steve Goodwin, Paul Clark, Dave Smith (Manager). Front Row: Alan Little, Frank Banks, Micky Laverick, Neil Townsend, Tony Hadley, Derrick Parker.

Appearances and Goals

Name	Appearances Lge.	FAC	L.C.	Total	Goals Lge.	FAC	L.C.	Total
ABBOTT, Peter	19			19	3			3
BANKS, Frank	42	4	2	48				
BURRIDGE, John	6			6				
CLARK, Paul	8			8	1			1
DUDLEY, Phil	2+1			2+1				
FELL, Gerry	20	4		24	3	1		4
FOGGON, Alan	22	2	2	26		1		1
FRANKLIN, Graham	1+2			1+2				
FREEMAN, Neil	33	1		34				
GOODWIN, Steve	22+4		2	24+4	4	1		5
HADLEY, Tony	28+5	4		32+5	2			2
HORN, Graham	2			2				
LAVERICK, Micky	45	4	2	51	8	1		9
MOODY, Alan	46	4	2	52	8	1		9
MORRIS, Colin	46	4	2	52	11	1	1	13
PARKER, Derrick	46	4	2	52	19	4		23
POLYCARPOU, Andy	12+4		2	14+4	2			2
POUNTNEY, Ronnie	23+1	2		25+1				
RAFTER, Sean	5	3	2	10				
TOWNSEND, Neil	29	3	2	34	3			3
WALKER, John	0+1			0+1				
YATES, Steve	27	3		30	1			1
YOUNG, Dave	22+3	2	2	26+3	1			1
Own Goal								1

	Ps	P	W	D	L	F	A	W	D	L	F	A	Pts.
1977/78	2	46	15	5	3	46	18	10	5	8	20	21	60

Season 1978/79 – League Division 3

No.	Date	Opposition	Venue	Score	H.T.	Res.	Att.	Goalscorers	1	2	3	4	5	6	7	8	9	10	11	12
1	19 Aug	Chester	(H)	0-1	(0-0)	L	4223		Cawston	Dudley	Yates	Laverick	Townsend	Moody	Fell	Goodwin	Parker	Pountney	Morris	
2	22	Bury	(A)	3-3	(1-0)	D	3243	Morris(2),Laverick	Cawston	Dudley	Yates	Laverick	Hadley	Moody	Morris	Pountney	Parker	Goodwin	Fell	
3	26	Mansfield Town	(A)	1-1	(1-0)	D	5500	Parker	Cawston	Dudley	Yates	Laverick	Hadley	Walker	Fell	Polypou	Parker	Pountney	Morris	
4	1 Sep	Plymouth Argyle	(H)	2-1	(1-1)	W	5911	Pountney,Parker	Cawston	Dudley	Yates	Laverick	Walker	Hadley	Morris	Pountney	Parker	Polypou	Fell	Hadley(2)
5	9	Sheffield Wednesday	(A)	2-3	(0-2)	L	11327	Morris(pen),Fell	Cawston	Stead	Yates	Laverick	Cusack	Walker	Morris	Pountney	Parker	Dudley	Fell	Abbott(4)
6	11	Oxford United	(H)	2-0	(1-0)	W	5260	Parker,Fell	Cawston	Dudley	Yates	Laverick	Cusack	Hadley	Morris	Pountney	Parker	Polypou	Fell	Walker(5)
7	15	Rotherham United	(H)	2-1	(0-0)	W	6515	Fell(2)	Cawston	Dudley	Yates	Laverick	Cusack	Hadley	Morris	Pountney	Parker	Polypou	Fell	
8	23	Carlisle United	(A)	0-0	(0-0)	D	4957		Cawston	Stead	Yates	Laverick	Cusack	Hadley	Pountney	Fell	Parker	Dudley	Morris	Walker(4)
9	27	Chesterfield	(A)	2-3	(2-1)	L	4153	Abbott,Parker	Cawston	Stead	Yates	Abbott	Cusack	Hadley	Morris	Pountney	Parker	Dudley	Fell	Walker(4)
10	29	Shrewsbury Town	(H)	0-1	(0-0)	L	6783		Cawston	Stead	Yates	Abbott	Cusack	Hadley	Morris	Pountney	Parker	Dudley	Fell	
11	7 Oct	Walsall	(A)	1-1	(1-1)	D	4803	Cusack	Cawston	Stead	Yates	Laverick	Cusack	Moody	Morris	Pountney	Parker	Dudley	Morris	
12	14	Blackpool	(H)	4-0	(2-0)	W	6484	Fell(2),Yates,Pountney	Cawston	Stead	Yates	Laverick	Cusack	Moody	Fell	Pountney	Hadley	Dudley	Fell	Hadley(11)
13	20	Colchester United	(A)	1-1	(1-0)	D	5647	Laverick	Cawston	Stead	Yates	Laverick	Cusack	Moody	Morris	Pountney	Hadley	Dudley	Morris	
14	23	Hull City	(H)	3-0	(0-0)	W	6629	Moody(pen),Parker,Dudley	Cawston	Stead	Yates	Laverick	Cusack	Moody	Morris	Pountney	Polypou	Dudley	Polypou	
15	27	Lincoln City	(H)	2-0	(2-0)	W	7336	Stead,Laverick	Cawston	Stead	Yates	Laverick	Cusack	Moody	Morris	Pountney	Parker	Dudley	Polypou	
16	4 Nov	Swindon Town	(A)	0-1	(0-0)	L	5647		Cawston	Stead	Yates	Laverick	Cusack	Moody	Fell	Polypou	Parker	Dudley	Pountney	Fell(3)
17	11	Plymouth Argyle	(A)	1-1	(1-1)	D	6786	Fell	Cawston	Dudley	Yates	Laverick	Cusack	Moody	Morris	Pountney	Parker	Polypou	Morris	Walker(10)
18	17	Mansfield Town	(H)	1-1	(1-1)	D	7139	Polypou	Cawston	Dudley	Stead	Laverick	Cusack	Moody	Morris	Pountney	Parker	Fell	Polypou	Walker(3)
19	2 Dec	Exeter City	(A)	0-0	(0-0)	D	2974		Cawston	Stead	Stead	Laverick	Cusack	Moody	Pountney	Polypou	Parker	Dudley	Morris	Hadley(10)
20	8	Swansea City	(H)	0-2	(0-1)	L	8969		Cawston	Stead	Yates	Laverick	Cusack	Moody	Morris	Pountney	Parker	Dudley	Polypou	Franklin(11)
21	23	Brentford	(H)	1-1	(0-0)	D	13552	Moody(pen)	Cawston	Walker	Hadley	Moody	Stead	Laverick	Dudley	Morris	Pountney	Parker	Polypou	
22	26	Gillingham	(A)	0-1	(0-0)	L	6644		Cawston	Stead	Walker	Laverick	Hadley	Moody	Morris	Pountney	Parker	Dudley	Polypou	
23	30	Peterborough United	(A)	1-0	(0-0)	W	3371	Laverick	Cawston	Stead	Yates	Laverick	Hadley	Moody	Morris	Pountney	Parker	Dudley	Fell	
24	2 Feb	Chesterfield	(H)	2-0	(2-0)	W	5499	Moody(pen),Parker	Cawston	Moody	Yates	Stead	Hadley	Cusack	Morris	Pountney	Parker	Dudley	Fell	
25	6	Rotherham United	(A)	1-2	(1-2)	L	4048	Dudley	Cawston	Stead	Yates	Cusack	Hadley	Moody	Morris	Pountney	Parker	Dudley	Fell	
26	9	Shrewsbury Town	(A)	0-2	(0-2)	L	5546		Cawston	Walker	Yates	Cusack	Hadley	Moody	Morris	Pountney	Parker	Dudley	Fell	Laverick(11)
27	13	Sheffield Wednesday	(H)	2-1	(1-0)	W	4544	Dudley,Laverick	Cawston	Stead	Yates	Cusack	Hadley	Moody	Morris	Pountney	Parker	Dudley	Laverick	
28	24	Blackpool	(A)	2-1	(2-1)	W	4566	Morris,Pountney	Cawston	Moody	Yates	Stead	Cusack	Moody	Morris	Pountney	Parker	Dudley	Laverick	
29	2 Mar	Colchester United	(H)	1-1	(0-0)	D	6957	Parker	Cawston	Moody	Yates	Stead	Hadley	Cusack	Morris	Pountney	Parker	Dudley	Laverick	
30	7	Oxford United	(A)	0-0	(0-0)	D	2913		Cawston	Moody	Yates	Stead	Hadley	Cusack	Morris	Pountney	Parker	Dudley	Laverick	Walker(2)
31	10	Lincoln City	(H)	1-1	(0-1)	D	2559	Morris(pen)	Cawston	Moody	Yates	Stead	Hadley	Cusack	Morris	Abbott	Parker	Dudley	Polypou	Laverick(8)
32	12	Carlisle United	(H)	1-1	(1-0)	D	4573	Morris	Cawston	Moody	Yates	Stead	Hadley	Cusack	Morris	Abbott	Parker	Dudley	Fell	Walker(5)
33	16	Swindon Town	(H)	5-3	(3-0)	W	4303	Polypou(2),Stead,Morris(pen),Laverick	Cawston	Moody	Yates	Stead	Hadley	Cusack	Morris	Polypou	Parker	Dudley	Laverick	Walker(5)
34	21	Chester	(A)	1-0	(0-0)	W	2108	Polypou	Cawston	Moody	Yates	Stead	Hadley	Moody	Morris	Polypou	Parker	Dudley	Laverick	
35	24	Bury	(H)	0-0	(0-0)	D	5831		Cawston	Moody	Yates	Laverick	Cusack	Cusack	Morris	Polypou	Parker	Dudley	Pountney	Pountney(3)
36	30	Tranmere Rovers	(A)	2-1	(0-0)	W	1250	Polypou,Pountney	Cawston	Moody	Yates	Stead	Hadley	Cusack	Morris	Pountney	Parker	Dudley	Laverick	Pountney(2)
37	2 Apr	Watford	(H)	1-0	(0-0)	W	11406	Pountney	Cawston	Hadley	Yates	Stead	Cusack	Moody	Morris	Polypou	Parker	Dudley	Otu'lski	
38	6	Exeter City	(H)	0-1	(0-0)	L	6733		Cawston	Dudley	Yates	Stead	Cusack	Hadley	Morris	Polypou	Parker	Pountney	Otu'lski	
39	13	Brentford	(A)	0-3	(0-1)	L	11500		Cawston	Walker	Yates	Stead	Moody	Cusack	Morris	Pountney	Parker	Dudley	Otu'lski	
40	14	Gillingham	(H)	0-1	(0-0)	L	7291		Horn	Walker	Yates	Dudley	Moody	Hadley	Fell	Pountney	Parker	Abbott	Otu'lski	
41	17	Watford	(A)	0-2	(0-1)	L	15835		Horn	Walker	Yates	Hull	Hadley	Moody	Fell	Pountney	Parker	Dudley	Abbott	
42	21	Peterborough United	(H)	0-0	(0-0)	D	3461		Horn	Stead	Yates	Dudley	Cusack	Moody	Morris	Pountney	Parker	Dudley	Otu'lski	Polypou(8)
43	24	Hull City	(A)	0-2	(0-0)	L	3960		Horn	Stead	Yates	Hadley	Cusack	Hadley	Morris	Pountney	Parker	Abbott	Otu'lski	Polypou(2)
44	28	Swansea City	(A)	2-3	(0-1)	L	15941	Parker(2)	Horn	Stead	Yates	Hadley	Moody	Cusack	Morris	Pountney	Parker	Dudley	Otu'lski	Polypou(6)
45	30	Walsall	(H)	1-0	(1-0)	W	2889	Parker	Horn	Stead	Yates	Dudley	Cusack	Walker	Morris	Pountney	Parker	Hadley	Otu'lski	Polypou(10)
46	4 May	Tranmere Rovers	(H)	0-1	(0-1)	L	3607	Parker	Horn	Stead	Yates	Dudley	Cusack	Walker	Morris	Pountney	Parker	Hadley	Otu'lski	

Abbrev.: Otu'lski = Otulakowski. Polypou = Polycarpou.

Major Cup Competitions

F.A.Cup

Rd.	Date	Opposition	Venue	Score	H.T.	Res.	Att.	1	2	3	4	5	6	7	8	9	10	11	12	Goalscorers
R1	25 Nov	Peterborough Utd.	(H)	3-2	(1-1)	W	6510	Cawston	Stead	Yates	Laverick	Cusack	Moody	Morris	Pountney	Parker	Dudley	Polycarpou		Pountney,Parker,Carmichael(O.G.)
R2	16 Dec	Watford	(A)	1-1	(0-0)	D	13377	Cawston	Stead	Walker	Laverick	Hadley	Moody	Morris	Pountney	Parker	Dudley	Polycarpou		Parker
R2r	18	Watford	(H)	1-0	(1-0)	W	15635	Cawston	Stead	Walker	Laverick	Hadley	Moody	Morris	Pountney	Parker	Dudley	Polycarpou		Polycarpou
R3	10 Jan	Liverpool	(H)	0-0	(0-0)	D	31036	Cawston	Stead	Yates	Laverick	Hadley	Moody	Morris	Pountney	Parker	Dudley	Fell		
R3r	17	Liverpool	(A)	0-3	(0-1)	L	37797	Cawston	Stead	Yates	Laverick	Hadley	Moody	Morris	Pountney	Parker	Dudley	Fell	Walker(11)	

Rumbelows Cup

Rd.	Date	Opposition	Venue	Score	H.T.	Res.	Att.	1	2	3	4	5	6	7	8	9	10	11	12	Goalscorers
R1L1	12 Aug	Wimbledon	(H)	1-0	(0-0)	W	4845	Horn	Goodwin	Yates	Laverick	Hadley	Moody	Fell	Parker	Abbott	Pountney	Morris		Donaldson(O.G.)
R1L2	15	Wimbledon	(A)	1-4	(1-3)	L	2687	Horn	Hadley	Yates	Laverick	Townsend	Moody	Morris	Pountney	Parker	Abbott	Fell	Dudley(10)	Donaldson(O.G.)

(Aggregate – Lost 2-4)

Southend United — 1979

Here is the latest Southend United senior squad picture.
Back row: Alan Moody (capt.); Steve Yates; Mervyn Cawston; David Cusack; Graham Horn; Gerry Fell; Tony Hadley; Peter Abbott.
Middle row: Dave Smith (Manager); Derrick Parker; Micky Laverick; Ron Pountney; Graham Franklin; Steve Goodwin; Colin Morris; John Lattimer (coach).
Front row: John Walker; Andy Polycarpou; Phil Dudley and Mike Stead.

Appearances and Goals

Name	Appearances				Goals			
	Lge.	FAC	L.C.	Total	Lge.	FAC	L.C.	Total
ABBOTT, Peter	7+1		2	9+1	1			1
CAWSTON, Mervyn	39	5		44				
CUSACK, Dave	37	1		38	1			1
DUDLEY, Phil	46	5	0+1	51+1	3			3
FELL, Gerry	22+1	2	2	26+1	7			7
FRANKLIN, Graham	0+1			0+1				
GOODWIN, Steve	2		1	3				
HADLEY, Tony	33+3	4	2	39+3				
HORN, Graham	7		2	9				
HULL, Jeff	1			1				
LAVERICK, Micky	29+2	5	2	36+2	6			6
MOODY, Alan	34	5	2	41	3			3
MORRIS, Colin	44	5	2	51	7			7
OTULAKOWSKI, Anton	9			9				
PARKER, Derrick	43	5	2	50	10	2		12
POLYCARPOU, Andy	21+5	3		24+5	5	1		6
POUNTNEY, Ronnie	40+2	5	2	47+2	5	1		6
STEAD, Micky	38	5		43	2			2
TOWNSEND, Neil	1		1	2				
WALKER, John	11+8	2+1	1	13+9				
YATES, Steve	42	3	2	47	1			1
Own Goal						1	2	3

	Ps	P	W	D	L	F	A	W	D	L	F	A	Pts.
1978/79	13	46	11	6	6	30	17	4	9	10	21	32	45

Season 1979/80 – League Division 3

No.	Date	Opposition	Venue	Score	H.T.	Res.	Att.	Goalscorers	1	2	3	4	5	6	7	8	9	10	11	12
1	18 Aug	Carlisle United	(H)	1-0	(1-0)	W	4140	Tuohy	Cawston	Dudley	Moody	Cusack	Yates	Stead	Otul'ski	Morris	Tuohy	Parker	Fell	Hadley(9)
2	25	Wimbledon	(A)	1-0	(0-0)	W	4173	Morris	Cawston	Dudley	Moody	Cusack	Yates	Stead	Otul'ski	Morris	Tuohy	Parker	Hadley	Fell(9)
3	1 Sep	Rotherham United	(H)	0-2	(0-0)	L	4765		Cawston	Dudley	Moody	Pountney	Yates	Stead	Hadley	Otul'ski	Tuohy	Parker	Morris	Gray(4)
4	7	Blackpool	(H)	1-2	(0-2)	L	5600	Morris(pen)	Cawston	Dudley	Moody	Cusack	Yates	Stead	Gray	Morris	Tuohy	Parker	Morris	Pountney(6)
5	15	Blackburn Rovers	(A)	1-1	(0-0)	D	6603	Cusack	Cawston	Dudley	Moody	Cusack	Yates	Stead	Otul'ski	Morris	Pountney	Tuohy	Gray	Walker
6	19	Reading	(A)	1-1	(0-1)	D	5949	Tuohy	Cawston	Dudley	Moody	Cusack	Yates	Stead	Otul'ski	Morris	Pountney	Tuohy	Gray	Walker
7	21	Plymouth Argyle	(H)	4-1	(3-1)	W	4699	Morris,Pountney,Tuohy,Gray	Cawston	Dudley	Moody	Cusack	Yates	Stead	Otul'ski	Morris	Pountney	Tuohy	Gray	Walker(3)
8	29	Brentford	(A)	0-2	(0-0)	L	6930		Cawston	Dudley	Moody	Cusack	Yates	Stead	Otul'ski	Morris	Pountney	Tuohy	Gray	Walker
9	6 Oct	Bury	(A)	1-1	(0-0)	D	2495	Pountney	Cawston	Dudley	Moody	Cusack	Walker	Stead	Otul'ski	Morris	Pountney	Parker	Gray	Hadley
10	12	Colchester United	(H)	0-1	(0-1)	L	5944		Keeley	Dudley	Moody	Cusack	Walker	Stead	Otul'ski	Morris	Hull	Parker	Gray	Nelson(9)
11	20	Swindon Town	(A)	0-1	(0-0)	L	6027		Keeley	Dudley	Moody	Cusack	Walker	Stead	Otul'ski	Nelson	Tuohy	Pountney	Morris	Hull(8)
12	24	Exeter City	(A)	2-4	(1-3)	L	3246	Gray(2)	Cawston	Dudley	Moody	Cusack	Walker	Stead	Otul'ski	Pountney	Tuohy	Gray	Gray	Hull
13	26	Chesterfield	(H)	0-0	(0-0)	D	3537		Cawston	Dudley	Moody	Hadley	Walker	Stead	Otul'ski	Morris	Pountney	Tuohy	Gray	Nelson(10)
14	29	Gillingham	(H)	0-3	(0-2)	L	4447		Cawston	Dudley	Moody	Hadley	Walker	Stead	Otul'ski	Morris	Pountney	Tuohy	Gray	Nelson(5)
15	3 Nov	Carlisle United	(A)	0-4	(0-1)	L	3744		Cawston	Dudley	Moody	Hadley	Nelson	Stead	Morris	Pountney	Tuohy	Gray	Otul'ski	Hull(9)
16	5	Exeter City	(H)	4-0	(3-0)	W	2787	Parker(2),Morris,Gray	Keeley	Dudley	Moody	Hadley	Pountney	Stead	Otul'ski	Morris	Parker	Nelson	Gray	Hull
17	9	Grimsby Town	(A)	1-0	(0-0)	W	4107	Stead	Cawston	Dudley	Moody	Hadley	Pountney	Stead	Otul'ski	Morris	Parker	Nelson	Gray	Hull
18	13	Gillingham	(A)	0-1	(0-1)	L	5286		Cawston	Dudley	Moody	Hadley	Pountney	Stead	Otul'ski	Tuohy	Parker	Nelson	Gray	Hull(10)
19	17	Sheffield Wednesday	(H)	0-2	(0-0)	L	10563		Cawston	Dudley	Moody	Walker	Pountney	Stead	Otul'ski	Hadley	Parker	Tuohy	Gray	Hull
20	1 Dec	Barnsley	(A)	2-1	(0-1)	W	11602	Franklin,Parker	Cawston	Dudley	Moody	Hadley	Hull	Stead	Otul'ski	Nelson	Pountney	Parker	Morris	Franklin(8)
21	7	Chester	(H)	4-1	(1-1)	W	3885	Parker(3),Hadley	Cawston	Dudley	Hull	Stead	Moody	Hadley	Morris	Pountney	Parker	Otul'ski	Nelson	Franklin(11)
22	21	Sheffield United	(A)	0-2	(0-1)	L	12699		Cawston	Dudley	Yates	Stead	Cusack	Hadley	Morris	Otul'ski	Parker	Tuohy	Hull	Polypou(11)
23	26	Oxford United	(H)	1-1	(0-1)	D	4213	Hadley	Cawston	Dudley	Yates	Stead	Cusack	Hadley	Morris	Pountney	Parker	Otul'ski	Gray	Polypou(2)
24	29	Wimbledon	(H)	1-3	(1-0)	L	3952	Polypou	Cawston	Dudley	Yates	Pountney	Moody	Hadley	Otul'ski	Polypou	Parker	Gray	Otul'ski	Dudley
25	12 Jan	Rotherham United	(A)	1-2	(0-1)	L	4092	Parker	Cawston	Stead	Dudley	Hadley	Cusack	Nelson	Otul'ski	Pountney	Parker	Spence	Gray18	Tuohy(10)
26	18	Blackpool	(A)	0-1	(0-1)	L	4286		Cawston	Moody	Yates	Stead	Hadley	Cusack	Gray	Parker	Spence	Spence	Pountney	Dudley
27	25	Hull City	(H)	3-0	(1-0)	W	3615	Gray,Parker,Spence	Cawston	Moody	Yates	Hadley	Cusack	Otul'ski	Gray	Pountney	Spence	Spence	Stead	Walker
28	2 Feb	Blackburn Rovers	(H)	0-1	(0-1)	L	4243		Cawston	Moody	Yates	Cusack	Hadley	Dudley	Otul'ski	Pountney	Parker	Spence	Gray	Walker
29	12	Millwall	(A)	2-1	(1-0)	W	7397	Stead(pen),Tagg((O.G.))	Cawston	Moody	Moody	Stead	Hadley	Cusack	Gray	Pountney	Spence	Mercer	Otul'ski	Polypou(4)
30	16	Brentford	(H)	3-2	(2-1)	W	3995	Gray,Spence,Kruse((O.G.))	Cawston	Dudley	Yates	Cusack	Yates	Pountney	Otul'ski	Gray	Mercer	Spence	Nelson	Polypou
31	22	Colchester United	(A)	1-2	(1-1)	L	6135	Spence	Keeley	Moody	Yates	Nelson	Dudley	Cusack	Gray	Pountney	Spence	Mercer	Otul'ski	Walker(4)
32	25	Reading	(H)	2-2	(1-0)	D	3542	Mercer(2)	Keeley	Moody	Yates	Stead	Hadley	Cusack	Gray	Pountney	Spence	Mercer	Otul'ski	Hull
33	29	Swindon Town	(A)	1-0	(1-0)	W	5282	Spence	Cawston	Moody	Yates	Stead	Hadley	Cusack	Gray	Pountney	Spence	Mercer	Otul'ski	Walker
34	8 Mar	Chesterfield	(A)	0-1	(0-0)	L	7671		Cawston	Moody	Yates	Stead	Hadley	Cusack	Gray	Pountney	Spence	Mercer	Otul'ski	Dudley
35	14	Bury	(H)	0-0	(0-0)	D	3798		Cawston	Moody	Yates	Stead	Hadley	Cusack	Gray	Pountney	Spence	Mercer	Hull	Nelson(2)
36	17	Mansfield Town	(H)	1-1	(0-0)	D	2793	Tuohy	Cawston	Dudley	Yates	Stead	Hadley	Cusack	Gray	Pountney	Spence	Tuohy	Nelson	Hull
37	22	Grimsby Town	(A)	0-1	(0-0)	L	10532		Cawston	Dudley	Yates	Stead	Hadley	Cusack	Gray	Pountney	Spence	Tuohy	Nelson	Walker(9)
38	29	Sheffield Wednesday	(H)	1-1	(1-1)	D	7455	Nelson	Cawston	Dudley	Yates	Stead	Hadley	Cusack	Otul'ski	Pountney	Spence	Tuohy	Nelson	Otul'ski(9)
39	4 Apr	Sheffield United	(H)	2-1	(0-1)	W	5959	Mercer,Pountney	Cawston	Dudley	Yates	Stead	Cusack	Cusack	Mercer	Mercer	Spence	Otul'ski	Nelson	Gray(11)
40	5	Oxford United	(A)	0-1	(0-0)	L	3548		Cawston	Dudley	Yates	Stead	Hadley	Cusack	Mercer	Pountney	Spence	Otul'ski	Otul'ski	Gray(11)
41	7	Millwall	(H)	1-0	(1-0)	W	5995	Gray	Cawston	Dudley	Yates	Stead	Hadley	Cusack	Gray	Pountney	Spence	Mercer	Otul'ski	Nelson(7)
42	12	Mansfield Town	(A)	1-3	(1-1)	L	3314	Nelson	Cawston	Dudley	Yates	Stead	Hadley	Cusack	Otul'ski	Pountney	Spence	Tuohy	Gray	Nelson(9)
43	19	Barnsley	(H)	2-1	(1-1)	W	4424	Mercer,Pountney	Cawston	Dudley	Yates	Stead	Cusack	Moody	Gray	Mercer	Spence	Pountney	Otul'ski	Hadley
44	22	Plymouth Argyle	(A)	0-0	(0-0)	D	5392		Cawston	Dudley	Yates	Stead	Moody	Cusack	Gray	Pountney	Spence	Mercer	Gray	Hadley(10)
45	26	Chester	(A)	1-2	(0-1)	L	2461	Spence	Cawston	Dudley	Yates	Stead	Moody	Cusack	Gray	Pountney	Spence	Mercer	Otul'ski	Hadley
46	3 May	Hull City	(A)	0-1	(0-0)	L	3823		Cawston	Dudley	Hadley	Moody	Cusack	Stead	Gray	Pountney	Spence	Mercer	Otul'ski	Polypou(7)

Abbrev.: Polypou = Polycarpou   Otul'ski = Otulakowski.

Major Cup Competitions

Rd.	Date	Opposition	Venue	Score	H.T.	Res.	Att.	1	2	3	4	5	6	7	8	9	10	11	12	Goalscorers
F.A. Cup																				
R1	24 Nov	Wealdstone	(A)	1-0	(0-0)	W	2400	Cawston	Dudley	Moody	Walker	Stead	Pountney	Hadley	Morris	Otul'ski	Parker	Hull	Franklin	Walker
R2	15 Dec	Harlow Town	(H)	1-1	(1-0)	D	5011	Cawston	Dudley	Hull	Stead	Moody	Hadley	Morris	Pountney	Parker	Otul'ski	Tuohy	Nelson(8)	Parker
R2r	18	Harlow Town	(A)	0-1	(0-0)	L	5000	Cawston	Dudley	Hull	Stead	Moody	Hadley	Morris	Pountney	Parker	Otul'ski	Tuohy	Nelson	
League Cup																				
R1L1	15 Aug	Brentford	(H)	2-1	(1-0)	W	3600	Cawston	Dudley	Moody	Cusack	Yates	Stead	Otul'ski	Morris	Fell	Parker	Gray	Hadley	Fell, McNicholl(O.G.)
R1L2	21	Brentford	(A)	4-1	(3-1)	W	7820	Cawston	Dudley	Moody	Cusack	Yates	Stead	Otul'ski	Morris	Tuohy	Parker	Hadley	Fell	Tuohy(2), Morris, Parker
		(Aggregate – Won 6-2)																		
R2L1	28	Bolton Wanderers	(A)	2-1	(0-0)	W	7861	Cawston	Dudley	Moody	Cusack	Yates	Stead	Hadley	Otul'ski	Tuohy	Parker	Morris	Pountney(8)	Morris(2)
R2L2	3 Sep	Bolton Wanderers	(H)	0-0	(0-0)	D	9894	Cawston	Dudley	Moody	Cusack	Yates	Stead	Hadley	Otul'ski	Tuohy	Parker	Morris	Gray	
		(Aggregate – Won 2-1)																		
R3	25	West Ham United	(A)	1-1	(1-1)	D	19658	Cawston	Dudley	Moody	Cusack	Yates	Stead	Otul'ski	Pountney	Morris	Tuohy	Gray	Hull	Pountney
R3r	1 Oct	West Ham United	(H)	0-0	(0-0)	D	22429	Cawston	Dudley	Moody	Cusack	Yates	Stead	Otul'ski	Pountney	Morris	Tuohy	Gray	Walker(5)	
R3r2	8	West Ham United	(A)	1-5	(1-2)	L	19718	Cawston	Dudley	Moody	Cusack	Walker	Stead	Otul'ski	Morris	Pountney	Hadley	Gray	Hull(7)	Gray

Abbrev.: Otul'ski = Otulakowski.

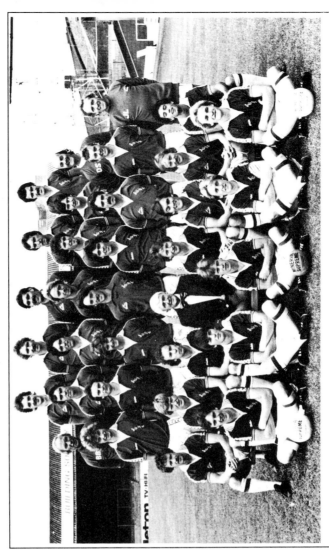

Back Row, Left to Right: Micky Tuohy, Dave Cusack, Graham Horn, Tony Hadley, Peter Abbott.
Fourth Row: Brian Beckett (Physiotherapist/Youth Coach), Alan Moody, Steve Yates, Mervyn Cawston, Gerry Fell, Derrick Parker, Dave Smith (Manager).
Third Row: Garry Nelson, Graham Locke, Jeff Hull, John Keeley, Graham Franklin, Steve Goodwin, John Walker, John Lattimer (Assistant Manager).
Second Row: Colin Morris, Mick Stead, Ron Pountney, Frank Walton (Chairman), Phil Dudley, Anton Otulakowski, Terry Gray, & Andy Polycarpou.
Front Row: Nick Edkins, Paul Foley, Alan Hull, Glen Pennyfather & John Whiskin.

Appearances and Goals

Name	Appearances Lge.	FAC	L.C.	Total	Goals Lge.	FAC	L.C.	Total
CAWSTON, Mervyn	42	3	7	52				
CUSACK, Dave	36		7	43	1			1
DUDLEY, Phil	37	3	7	47				
FELL, Gerry	1+1		1	2+1			1	1
FRANKLIN, Graham	0+2			0+2	1			1
GRAY, Terry	38+3	3	4	42+3	7		1	8
HADLEY, Tony	31+2	3	4	38+2	2			2
HULL, Jeff	6+3	3	0+1	9+4				
KEELEY, John	4			4				
MERCER, Keith	14			14	4			4
MOODY, Alan	37	3	7	47				
MORRIS, Colin	20	3	7	30	4		3	7
NELSON, Garry	16+6	0+1		16+7	2			2
OTULAKOWSKI, Anton	41+1	3	7	51+1	8	1	1	10
PARKER, Derrick	19	3	4	26		1	1	2
POLYCARPOU, Andy	1+4			1+4	1			1
POUNTNEY, Ronnie	41+1	3	3+1	47+2	4		1	5
SPENCE, Derek	22			22	5			5
STEAD, Micky	42	3	7	52	2			2
TUOHY, Micky	20+1	2	5	27+1	4		2	6
WALKER, John	7+3	1	1+1	9+4		1		1
YATES, Steve	31		6	37	2		1	3
Own Goals					2		1	3

	Ps	P	W	D	L	F	A	W	D	L	F	A	Pts.
1979/80	22	46	11	6	6	33	23	3	4	16	14	35	38

Season 1980/81 – League Division Four

No.	Date	Opposition	Venue	Score	H.T.	Res.	Att.	Goalscorers	No.	1	2	3	4	5	6	7	8	9	10	11	12
1	16 Aug	Bury	(A)	2 1	(0-0)	W	2647	Mercer,Hull	1	Cawston	Stead	Yates	Hadley	Moody	Cusack	Gray	Pountney	Spence	Mercer	Hull	Dudley
2	18	Port Vale	(H)	5 1	(3-1)	W	3948	Gray(2),Spence(2),Hadley	2	Cawston	Stead	Yates	Hadley	Moody	Cusack	Gray	Pountney	Spence	Mercer	Hull	Dudley(8)
3	22	Tranmere Rovers	(H)	2 0	(1-0)	W	4600	Mercer,Mungall(O.G.)	3	Cawston	Stead	Yates	Hadley	Moody	Cusack	Gray	Otul'ski	Spence	Mercer	Hull	Dudley
4	5 Sep	York City	(H)	3 0	(1-0)	W	5166	Spence(3)	4	Cawston	Stead	Yates	Hadley	Moody	Cusack	Gray	Pountney	Spence	Mercer	Otul'ski	Nelson
5	13	Hereford United	(A)	0 0	(0-0)	D	2464		5	Cawston	Stead	Yates	Hadley	Moody	Cusack	Gray	Pountney	Spence	Mercer	Otul'ski	Hull
6	15	Peterborough United	(H)	0 1	(1-0)	L	6063	Spence	6	Cawston	Stead	Yates	Hadley	Moody	Cusack	Gray	Pountney	Spence	Mercer	Otul'ski	Hull(11)
7	19	Doncaster Rovers	(A)	0 2	(0-1)	L	6044		7	Cawston	Stead	Yates	Hadley	Moody	Cusack	Gray	Pountney	Spence	Mercer	Otul'ski	Hull
8	23	Northampton Town	(A)	0 2	(0-1)	L	2337		8	Cawston	Stead	Yates	Hadley	Moody	Cusack	Gray	Pountney	Spence	Mercer	Otul'ski	Hull(9)
9	26	Hartlepool United	(H)	4 0	(2-0)	W	5112	Gray,Pountney,Mercer,Otul'ski	9	Cawston	Stead	Yates	Hadley	Moody	Cusack	Gray	Pountney	Spence	Mercer	Otul'ski	Nelson(6)
10	1 Oct	Peterborough United	(A)	2 5	(1-1)	L	4087	Gray,Spence	10	Cawston	Stead	Yates	Hadley	Moody	Dudley	Gray	Pountney	Spence	Mercer	Otul'ski	Nelson(2)
11	3	Mansfield Town	(H)	2 0	(1-0)	W	4440	Mercer(2)	11	Cawston	Stead	Yates	Hadley	Moody	Cusack	Gray	Pountney	Spence	Mercer	Otul'ski	Nelson
12	7	Wimbledon	(A)	1 0	(1-0)	W	1995	Spence	12	Cawston	Dudley	Yates	Hadley	Moody	Cusack	Gray	Pountney	Spence	Mercer	Otul'ski	Nelson(7)
13	11	Halifax Town	(A)	5 1	(2-0)	W	1609	Gray(2),Moody,Cusack,Spence	13	Cawston	Dudley	Yates	Hadley	Moody	Cusack	Gray	Pountney	Spence	Mercer	Otul'ski	Nelson
14	17	Scunthorpe United	(H)	2 0	(0-0)	W	5260	Hadley,Spence	14	Cawston	Dudley	Yates	Hadley	Moody	Cusack	Gray	Pountney	Spence	Mercer	Otul'ski	Nelson(10)
15	20	Wigan Athletic	(H)	1 0	(1-0)	W	5460	Hadley	15	Cawston	Dudley	Yates	Hadley	Moody	Cusack	Gray	Polycar'	Spence	Nelson	Otul'ski	Penny'er
16	25	Darlington	(A)	2 0	(1-0)	W	2083	Spence,Mercer	16	Cawston	Dudley	Yates	Hadley	Moody	Cusack	Gray	Pountney	Spence	Mercer	Otul'ski	Penny'er
17	29	Crewe Alexandra	(A)	1 1	(1-1)	D	3974	Spence	17	Cawston	Dudley	Yates	Hadley	Moody	Cusack	Gray	Pountney	Spence	Polycar'	Otul'ski	Walker
18	31	Stockport County	(H)	2 0	(1-0)	W	5842	Gray,Mercer	18	Cawston	Stead	Yates	Hadley	Dudley	Cusack	Gray	Pountney	Spence	Mercer	Otul'ski	Polycar'(11)
19	3 Nov	Wimbledon	(H)	1 0	(0-0)	W	4924	Spence	19	Cawston	Dudley	Stead	Hadley	Moody	Cusack	Gray	Pountney	Spence	Mercer	Otul'ski	Nelson(5)
20	8	Lincoln City	(A)	1 2	(0-1)	L	7128	Spence	20	Cawston	Dudley	Stead	Hadley	Walker	Nelson	Gray	Pountney	Spence	Mercer	Otul'ski	Nelson
21	10	Port Vale	(A)	0 1	(0-0)	L	2780		21	Cawston	Dudley	Stead	Hadley	Walker	Cusack	Gray	Pountney	Spence	Mercer	Otul'ski	Hull
22	15	Bury	(H)	1 0	(0-0)	W	4312	Cusack(pen)	22	Cawston	Stead	Yates	Hadley	Walker	Cusack	Gray	Pountney	Spence	Mercer	Otul'ski	Nelson(4)
23	5 Dec	Rochdale	(A)	2 0	(0-0)	W	2214	Spence,Mercer	23	Cawston	Stead	Yates	Hadley	Walker	Cusack	Gray	Pountney	Spence	Mercer	Otul'ski	Nelson
24	12	Bradford City	(H)	3 1	(1-1)	W	4761	Gray,Pountney,Thompson(O.G.)	24	Cawston	Stead	Yates	Hadley	Walker	Cusack	Gray	Pountney	Spence	Mercer	Otul'ski	Polycar'(3)
25	19	Torquay United	(A)	3 1	(1-1)	W	4206	Cusack(pen),Gray,Otul'ski	25	Cawston	Stead	Yates	Hadley	Walker	Cusack	Gray	Pountney	Spence	Mercer	Otul'ski	Nelson
26	26	Bournemouth	(A)	1 2	(0-0)	L	4381	Polycar'	26	Cawston	Stead	Yates	Hadley	Otul'ski	Cusack	Gray	Pountney	Spence	Nelson	Otul'ski	Polycar'(4)
27	27	Aldershot	(H)	3 0	(2-0)	W	6983	Gray,Pountney,Mercer	27	Cawston	Stead	Yates	Hadley	Walker	Cusack	Gray	Pountney	Spence	Mercer	Nelson	Polycar'
28	3 Jan	Wigan Athletic	(A)	1 0	(0-0)	W	5267	McAdam(O.G.)	28	Cawston	Stead	Yates	Otul'ski	Walker	Cusack	Gray	Pountney	Spence	Mercer	Nelson	Polycar'
29	9	Darlington	(H)	1 0	(0-0)	W	5070	Cusack	29	Cawston	Dudley	Yates	Otul'ski	Walker	Cusack	Gray	Pountney	Spence	Mercer	Nelson	Polycar'(7)
30	23	Northampton Town	(H)	0 0	(0-0)	D	5910		30	Cawston	Dudley	Yates	Hadley	Walker	Cusack	Gray	Pountney	Spence	Mercer	Otul'ski	Nelson(10)
31	30	Tranmere Rovers	(A)	2 2	(1-1)	D	2127	Nelson,Bramhall(O.G.)	31	Cawston	Stead	Yates	Hadley	Walker	Cusack	Gray	Pountney	Spence	Nelson	Otul'ski	Dudley
32	6 Feb	Hereford United	(H)	2 0	(1-0)	W	5285	Pountney,Spence	32	Cawston	Stead	Yates	Hadley	Walker	Cusack	Gray	Pountney	Spence	Nelson	Otul'ski	Dudley
33	14	York City	(A)	1 0	(1-0)	W	2129	Spence	33	Cawston	Stead	Yates	Hadley	Walker	Cusack	Gray	Pountney	Spence	Mercer	Otul'ski	Nelson
34	21	Hartlepool United	(A)	3 1	(2-0)	W	3751	Spence(2),Gray	34	Cawston	Stead	Yates	Hadley	Walker	Moody	Gray	Pountney	Spence	Mercer	Otul'ski	Nelson
35	27	Doncaster Rovers	(H)	0 0	(0-0)	D	6100		35	Cawston	Dudley	Penny'er	Hadley	Walker	Moody	Gray	Pountney	Spence	Mercer	Nelson	Polycar'
36	4 Mar	Bradford City	(A)	0 1	(0-1)	L	2369	Gray	36	Cawston	Stead	Yates	Hadley	Moody	Cusack	Gray	Pountney	Spence	Mercer	Otul'ski	Polycar'
37	7	Mansfield Town	(A)	1 0	(1-0)	W	4379	Gray	37	Cawston	Walker	Yates	Hadley	Moody	Cusack	Gray	Pountney	Spence	Mercer	Otul'ski	Nelson
38	13	Halifax Town	(H)	5 1	(2-0)	W	5547	Moody,Cusack(pen),Gray,Pounty,Spence	38	Cawston	Stead	Yates	Hadley	Moody	Cusack	Gray	Pountney	Spence	Mercer	Otul'ski	Nelson
39	22	Scunthorpe United	(A)	1 2	(0-0)	L	3605	Hadley	39	Cawston	Stead	Yates	Hadley	Moody	Cusack	Gray	Pountney	Spence	Mercer	Nelson	Dudley
40	27	Crewe Alexandra	(H)	3 0	(1-0)	W	6210	Gray(2),Mercer	40	Cawston	Stead	Yates	Hadley	Moody	Cusack	Gray	Pountney	Spence	Mercer	Otul'ski	Nelson
41	3 Apr	Stockport County	(A)	0 1	(0-1)	L	2278		41	Cawston	Stead	Yates	Hadley	Moody	Cusack	Gray	Pountney	Spence	Mercer	Otul'ski	Nelson(4)
42	11	Lincoln City	(H)	0 0	(0-0)	D	11955		42	Cawston	Stead	Yates	Hadley	Moody	Cusack	Gray	Pountney	Spence	Mercer	Otul'ski	Nelson(10)
43	17	Bournemouth	(H)	2 1	(1-0)	W	7372	Hadley,Spence	43	Cawston	Stead	Yates	Hadley	Moody	Cusack	Gray	Pountney	Spence	Mercer	Otul'ski	Nelson(10)
44	18	Aldershot	(A)	2 1	(2-0)	W	4433	Gray,Nelson	44	Cawston	Stead	Yates	Hadley	Moody	Cusack	Gray	Pountney	Spence	Nelson	Otul'ski	Dudley
45	25	Torquay United	(H)	3 0	(3-0)	W	1767	Hadley,Cusack(pen),Nelson	45	Cawston	Stead	Yates	Hadley	Moody	Cusack	Gray	Pountney	Spence	Nelson	Otul'ski	Dudley
46	1 May	Rochdale	(H)	1 1	(0-1)	D	10668	Hadley	46	Cawston	Stead	Yates	Hadley	Moody	Cusack	Gray	Pountney	Spence	Nelson	Otul'ski	Dudley

Abbrev.: Otul'ski = Ohulakowski   Polycar' = Polycarpou

Major Cup Competitions

Rd.	Date	Opposition	Venue Score	H.T. Res. Att.	Goalscorers
			F.A. Cup		
R1	22 Nov	Hereford United	(H) 0-1	(0-1) L 4922	
			League Cup		
R1L1	9 Aug	Oxford United	(H) 1-0	(1-0) W 3032	Pountney
R1L2	13	Oxford United	(A) 0-2	(0-1) L 2989	

(Aggregate – Lost 1-2)

Abbrev.: Pennyer = Pennyfather. Otul'ski = Otulakowski.

	1	2	3	4	5	6	7	8	9	10	11	12
	Cawston	Pennyer	Yates	Hadley	Walker	Cusack	Gray	Pountney	Spence	Mercer	Otul'ski	Nelson(8)
	Cawston	Stead	Yates	Hadley	Moody	Cusack	Gray	Pountney	Spence	Mercer	Otul'ski	Dudley
	Cawston	Stead	Yates	Hadley	Moody	Cusack	Gray	Pountney	Spence	Mercer	Otul'ski	Dudley

BACK ROW (left to right): Alan Hull, Ron Pountney, Steve Yates, Derek Spence, John Keeley, Mervyn Cawston, Keith Mercer, Micky Tuohy (now Worcester), Garry Nelson, Micky Stead, Paul Caskey, Terry Gray.
SECOND ROW: John Walker, Alan Moody, Dave Cusack, Keith Mercer, Tony Hadley, Jon Watson, Jeff Hull, Andy Polycarpou, Phil Dudley, Anton Otulakowski.
THIRD ROW: Brian Beckett (Coach), Tony Rubin (Director), Mark Rubin (Director), Frank Walton (Chairman), Dave Smith (Manager), Don Smith (Director), Fred Bonfield (Director), John Woodcock (Director), Frank Banks (Youth Coach).
FRONT ROW: Mark Whitmore, Neil Gregory, Glenn Pennyfather, John Whiskin.

Appearances and Goals

Name	Appearances				Goals			
	Lge.	FAC	L.C.	Total	Lge.	FAC	L.C.	Total
CAWSTON, Mervyn	46	1	2	49				
CUSACK, Dave	42	1	2	45	6			6
DUDLEY, Phil	15+1			15+1				
GRAY, Terry	46	1	2	49	17			17
HADLEY, Tony	44	1	2	47	7			7
HULL, Jeff	3+2			3+2	1			1
MERCER, Keith	38	1	2	41	10			10
MOODY, Alan	30		2	32	2			2
NELSON, Garry	12+10	0+1		12+11	3			3
OTULAKOWSKI, Anton	43	1	2	46	2			2
PENNYFATHER, Glenn	1	1		2				
POLYCARPOU, Andy	2+4			2+4	1			1
POUNTNEY, Ronnie	44	1	2	47	5		1	6
SPENCE, Derek	46	1	2	49	21			21
STEAD, Micky	35		2	37				
WALKER, John	17	1		18				
YATES, Steve	42	1	2	45	4			4
Own Goal					4			4

	Ps	P	W	D	L	F	A	W	D	L	F	A	Pts.
1980/81	1	46	19	4	0	47	6	11	3	9	32	25	67

Season 1981/82 – League Division Three

No.	Date	Opposition	Venue	Score	H.T.	Res.	Att.	Goalscorers	No.	1	2	3	4	5	6	7	8	9	10	11	12
1	29 Aug	Walsall	(A)	1 0	(1-0)	W	3419	Moody	1	Cawston	Stead	Yates	Hadley	Moody	Cusack	Gray	Pountney	Spence	Mercer	Otul'ski	Dudley
2	4 Sep	Newport County	(H)	0 4	(0-1)	L	4913		2	Cawston	Stead	Dudley	Hadley	Moody	Cusack	Nelson	Pountney	Spence	Mercer	Otul'ski	Pennyer
3	12	Carlisle United	(A)	2 3	(2-1)	L	3596	Cusack,Gray	3	Keeley	Stead	Yates	Nelson	Moody	Cusack	Gray	Pountney	Spence	Mercer	Nelson	Dudley
4	19	Portsmouth	(H)	2 0	(1-0)	W	4668	Gray,Spence	4	Keeley	Stead	Yates	Pountney	Moody	Cusack	Gray	Otul'ski	Spence	Mercer	Nelson	Hadley
5	21	Swindon Town	(A)	0 0	(0-0)	D	4864		5	Keeley	Stead	Yates	Pountney	Moody	Cusack	Gray	Otul'ski	Spence	Mercer	Nelson	Nelson
6	26	Huddersfield Town	(A)	2 3	(1-2)	L	7254	Pountney,Gray	6	Cawston	Hadley	Yates	Pountney	Moody	Cusack	Gray	Otul'ski	Spence	Mercer	Nelson	Dudley(11)
7	29	Fulham	(A)	1 2	(1-0)	L	4556	Otul'ski	7	Cawston	Hadley	Yates	Pountney	Moody	Cusack	Gray	Otul'ski	Spence	Mercer	Dudley	Walker(11)
8	3 Oct	Plymouth Argyle	(H)	3 0	(2-0)	W	3847	Pennyer,Mercer,Nelson	8	Cawston	Hadley	Yates	Pennyer	Moody	Cusack	Gray	Otul'ski	Spence	Mercer	Nelson	Greaves(7)
9	9	Bristol Rovers	(H)	1 0	(0-0)	W	4841	Greaves	9	Cawston	Hadley	Yates	Pennyer	Moody	Cusack	Gray	Otul'ski	Greaves	Mercer	Nelson	Greaves(9)
10	17	Chesterfield	(A)	2 1	(1-0)	W	6146	Gray,Greaves	10	Cawston	Hadley	Yates	Pennyer	Moody	Cusack	Gray	Otul'ski	Greaves	Mercer	Nelson	Stead
11	19	Brentford	(H)	1 0	(0-0)	W	5400	Yates	11	Cawston	Hadley	Yates	Pennyer	Moody	Cusack	Gray	Otul'ski	Greaves	Mercer	Nelson	Stead(9)
12	24	Oxford United	(A)	0 1	(0-1)	L	5686		12	Cawston	Hadley	Yates	Pennyer	Moody	Cusack	Gray	Otul'ski	Spence	Mercer	Nelson	Spence(2)
13	31	Preston North End	(A)	0 1	(0-0)	L	4285		13	Cawston	Hadley	Stead	Pennyer	Moody	Cusack	Gray	Stead	Greaves	Mercer	Nelson	Pountney(8)
14	2 Nov	Gillingham	(H)	3 0	(1-0)	W	6235	Mercer(2),Cusack	14	Cawston	Hadley	Stead	Pennyer	Moody	Cusack	Gray	Otul'ski	Spence	Mercer	Nelson	Greaves(2)
15	7	Lincoln City	(H)	0 2	(0-0)	L	5318		15	Keeley	Stead	Yates	Pennyer	Moody	Cusack	Gray	Pountney	Spence	Mercer	Nelson	Greaves(4)
16	14	Bristol City	(A)	2 0	(0-0)	W	6381	Pennyer,Cusack(pen)	16	Keeley	Stead	Yates	Pennyer	Moody	Cusack	Gray	Pountney	Spence	Mercer	Nelson	Greaves(7)
17	27	Reading	(H)	2 0	(0-0)	W	4847	Pountney,Mercer	17	Keeley	Stead	Yates	Pennyer	Moody	Cusack	Greaves	Pountney	Spence	Mercer	Nelson	Gray
18	5 Dec	Chester	(A)	1 1	(0-0)	D	1380	Greaves	18	Keeley	Stead	Yates	Pennyer	Moody	Cusack	Greaves	Pountney	Spence	Mercer	Nelson	Gray
19	1 Jan	Exeter City	(H)	2 1	(2-0)	W	5991	Cusack(pen),Pountney	19	Keeley	Stead	Yates	Pennyer	Moody	Cusack	Gray	Pountney	Spence	Mercer	Nelson	Greaves(11)
20	16	Doncaster Rovers	(H)	1 1	(0-0)	D	4741	Mercer	20	Keeley	Stead	Yates	Pennyer	Moody	Cusack	Gray	Pountney	Spence	Mercer	Otul'ski	Greaves(7)
21	23	Walsall	(H)	3 2	(3-0)	W	4684	Pennyer,Nelson,Greaves	21	Keeley	Stead	Yates	Pennyer	Moody	Cusack	Nelson	Pountney	Greaves	Mercer	Otul'ski	Spence(8)
22	30	Portsmouth	(A)	0 0	(0-0)	D	7371		22	Keeley	Stead	Yates	Pennyer	Moody	Cusack	Nelson	Pountney	Greaves	Mercer	Otul'ski	Hadley(8)
23	1 Feb	Millwall	(H)	2 2	(1-1)	D	5676	Mercer,Hadley	23	Keeley	Stead	Yates	Pennyer	Moody	Cusack	Nelson	Spence	Spence	Mercer	Otul'ski	Hadley(8)
24	6	Carlisle United	(H)	1 1	(1-0)	D	4911	Mercer	24	Keeley	Stead	Yates	Pennyer	Moody	Cusack	Nelson	Gray	Greaves	Mercer	Otul'ski	Hadley(7)
25	9	Swindon Town	(H)	0 0	(0-0)	D	4472		25	Keeley	Stead	Yates	Pennyer	Moody	Cusack	Nelson	Gray	Greaves	Mercer	Otul'ski	Hadley(9)
26	13	Plymouth Argyle	(A)	0 0	(0-0)	D	5058		26	Keeley	Stead	Yates	Hadley	Moody	Cusack	Nelson	Gray	Greaves	Mercer	Otul'ski	Owers
27	19	Fulham	(H)	0 0	(0-0)	D	7715		27	Keeley	Stead	Yates	Pennyer	Moody	Cusack	Gray	Nelson	Dudley	Mercer	Otul'ski	Hadley(3)
28	27	Bristol Rovers	(A)	1 2	(0-2)	L	4910	Moody	28	Keeley	Stead	Hadley	Pennyer	Moody	Cusack	Gray	Nelson	Spence	Mercer	Otul'ski	Greaves(7)
29	5 Mar	Chesterfield	(H)	0 2	(0-1)	L	5879		29	Keeley	Hadley	Stead	Pennyer	Moody	Cusack	Nelson	Phillips	Spence	Mercer	Otul'ski	Gray(7)
30	8	Brentford	(A)	1 1	(1-1)	D	3765	Phillips	30	Keeley	Hadley	Stead	Pennyer	Moody	Hadley	Pountney	Phillips	Spence	Mercer	Otul'ski	Nelson(9)
31	13	Oxford United	(A)	2 0	(1-0)	W	6252	Phillips(2)	31	Keeley	Hadley	Yates	Pennyer	Moody	Cusack	Pountney	Phillips	Spence	Mercer	Otul'ski	Gray
32	16	Gillingham	(A)	0 2	(0-1)	L	3782		32	Keeley	Hadley	Yates	Pennyer	Moody	Cusack	Pountney	Phillips	Nelson	Mercer	Otul'ski	Hadley
33	19	Preston North End	(H)	2 2	(2-0)	D	3549	Mercer(2)	33	Keeley	Hadley	Yates	Pennyer	Moody	Cusack	Pountney	Phillips	Nelson	Mercer	Otul'ski	Spence(7)
34	23	Wimbledon	(A)	0 3	(0-2)	L	2051		34	Keeley	Dudley	Yates	Pennyer	Moody	Cusack	Pountney	Phillips	Nelson	Mercer	Otul'ski	Greaves(4)
35	27	Lincoln City	(H)	1 1	(0-0)	D	5455	Yates	35	Keeley	Stead	Yates	Hadley	Moody	Cusack	Pountney	Phillips	Nelson	Mercer	Otul'ski	Dudley
36	3 Apr	Bristol City	(H)	3 0	(0-0)	W	3103	Greaves(2),Phillips	36	Cawston	Stead	Yates	Pountney	Moody	Hadley	Greaves	Phillips	Nelson	Mercer	Otul'ski	Spence(9)
37	9	Wimbledon	(H)	2 0	(2-0)	W	4779	Cusack(pen),Mercer	37	Cawston	Stead	Yates	Pountney	Moody	Cusack	Greaves	Phillips	Spence	Mercer	Otul'ski	Nelson
38	12	Millwall	(A)	1 1	(0-1)	D	3025	Phillips	38	Cawston	Stead	Yates	Pountney	Moody	Cusack	Greaves	Phillips	Spence	Mercer	Otul'ski	Nelson(7)
39	17	Chester	(H)	2 0	(1-0)	W	3427	Yates,Spence	39	Cawston	Stead	Yates	Pountney	Moody	Cusack	Nelson	Phillips	Spence	Mercer	Otul'ski	Greaves(10)
40	20	Burnley	(A)	5 3	(2-2)	W	8126	Phillips(2,1 pen),Spence(2),Nelson	40	Cawston	Stead	Yates	Pountney	Moody	Cusack	Nelson	Phillips	Spence	Pennyer	Otul'ski	Greaves
41	24	Reading	(A)	2 0	(0-0)	W	2840	Pountney,Phillips	41	Cawston	Stead	Yates	Pountney	Moody	Cusack	Nelson	Phillips	Spence	Pennyer	Otul'ski	Greaves(7)
42	1 May	Huddersfield Town	(H)	4 0	(1-0)	W	4470	Spence(2),Mercer,Phillips	42	Cawston	Stead	Yates	Pountney	Moody	Hadley	Mercer	Phillips	Spence	Pennyer	Otul'ski	Greaves
43	4	Doncaster Rovers	(A)	1 1	(0-1)	D	3374	Nelson	43	Cawston	Stead	Yates	Pennyer	Moody	Cusack	Pennyer	Phillips	Spence	Mercer	Otul'ski	Nelson(9)
44	8	Exeter City	(A)	1 1	(1-0)	D	3174	Mercer	44	Keeley	Stead	Dudley	Pountney	Dudley	Cusack	Mercer	Phillips	Spence	Pennyer	Otul'ski	Nelson
45	11	Newport County	(A)	2 3	(1-2)	L	3716	Phillips,Pennyer	45	Keeley	Stead	Dudley	Pountney	Dudley	Cusack	Mercer	Phillips	Nelson	Pennyer	Otul'ski	Nelson(9)
46	14	Burnley	(H)	1 4	(1-2)	L	4829	Mercer	46	Keeley	Stead	Dudley	Pountney	Dudley	Cusack	Mercer	Phillips	Spence	Pennyer	Nelson	Greaves(10)

Major Cup Competitions

Rd.	Date	Opposition	Venue	Score	H.T.	Res.	Att.	Goalscorers	1	2	3	4	5	6	7	8	9	10	11	12
F.A.Cup																				
R1	21 Nov	Hereford United	(A)	1-3	(0-0)	L	5310	Gray	Keeley	Stead	Yates	Penny'er	Moody	Walker	Gray	Pountney	Spence	Mercer	Nelson	Greaves(10)
League Cup																				
R1L1	2 Sep	Portsmouth	(H)	0-0	(0-0)	D	4087		Cawston	Stead	Dudley	Hadley	Moody	Cusack	Gray	Pountney	Spence	Mercer	Otul'ski	Nelson(7)
R1L2	16	Portsmouth	(A)	1-4	(1-2)	L	10019	Spence	Keeley	Stead	Yates	Nelson	Moody	Cusack	Gray	Pountney	Spence	Mercer	Otul'ski	Dudley(9)
(Aggregate – Lost 1-4)																				
Group Cup																				
Group H	15 Aug	Orient	(A)	0-2	(0-0)	L	1806		Cawston	Stead	Dudley	Hadley	Moody	Cusack	Gray	Nelson	Spence	Mercer	Otul'ski	Pountney
Group H	19	Gillingham	(H)	0-0	(0-0)	D	1974		Cawston	Stead	Dudley	Hadley	Moody	Cusack	Gray	Pountney	Spence	Mercer	Otul'ski	Nelson
Group H	24	Wimbledon	(A)	1-2	(0-1)	L	1780	Spence	Cawston	Stead	Yates	Hadley	Moody	Cusack	Gray	Nelson	Spence	Mercer	Otul'ski	Dudley
(Did not qualify for knock-out stage)																				

Abbrev.: Penny'er = Pennyfather. Otul'ski = Otulakowski.

Back Row. (left to right).
Glenn Pennyfather, John Walker, Alan Moody, Mervyn Cawston, Dave Cusack, John Keeley, Garry Nelson, Tony Hadley, Danny Greaves.
Front Row (left to right).
Brian Beckett *(First Team Coach)*, Steve Yates, Derek Spence, Phil Dudley, Ron Pountney, Micky Stead, Dave Smith *(Manager)*, Anton Otulakowski, Terry Gray, Keith Mercer, Frank Banks *(Youth Team Coach)*.

Appearances and Goals

Name	Appearances Lge.	FAC	L.C.	G.C.	Total	Goals Lge.	FAC	L.C.	G.C.	Total
CAWSTON, Mervyn	19		1	3	23					
CUSACK, Dave	43		2	3	48	5				5
DUDLEY, Phil	8+1		1+1	2	11+2					
GRAY, Terry	22+1	1	2	3	28+1	4	1			5
GREAVES, Danny	13+12	0+1			13+13	6				6
HADLEY, Tony	20+6		1	3	24+6	1				1
KEELEY, John	27	1	1		29					
MERCER, Keith	43	1	2	3	49	13				13
MOODY, Alan	44	1	2	3	50	2				2
NELSON, Garry	36+4	1	1+1	2	40+5	4				4
OTULAKOWSKI, Anton	38		2	3	43	1				1
PENNYFATHER, Glenn	34	1			35	4				4
PHILLIPS, Steve	18				18	10				10
POUNTNEY, Ronnie	33+1	1	2	1	37+1	4				4
SPENCE, Derek	32+4	1	2	3	38+4	6		1	1	8
STEAD, Micky	38+1	1	2	3	44+1					
WALKER, John	0+1	1			1+1					
YATES, Steve	38	1	1	1	41	3				3

	Ps	P	W	D	L	F	A	W	D	L	F	A	Pts.
1981/82	7	46	11	7	5	35	23	7	8	8	28	28	69

(3 points for a win)

Season 1982/83 – League Division Three

No.	Date	Opposition	Venue	Score	H.T.	Res.	Att.	Goalscorers	No.	1	2	3	4	5	6	7	8	9	10	11	12
1	28 Aug	Plymouth Argyle	(A)	0 1	(0-0)	L	3850	Phillips,Nelson	1	Cawston	Stead	Pountney	Clark	Moody	Cusack	Otu'ski	Phillips	Mercer	Pennyer	Nelson	Greaves(9)
2	4 Sep	Lincoln City	(H)	2 0	(1-0)	W	2938	Yates,Greaves	2	Cawston	Stead	Yates	Otu'ski	Moody	Hadley	Pountney	Phillips	Mercer	Pennyer	Nelson	Greaves(9)
3	6	Chesterfield	(H)	2 0	(1-0)	W	2837	Yates,Greaves	3	Cawston	Stead	Yates	Otu'ski	Hadley	Hadley	Pountney	Phillips	Greaves	Pennyer	Nelson	Walker
4	11	Brentford	(H)	2 4	(0-1)	L	5604	Mercer,Nelson	4	Cawston	Stead	Yates	Otu'ski	Moody	Cusack	Pountney	Phillips	Mercer	Pennyer	Nelson	Greaves(10)
5	18	Doncaster Rovers	(H)	3 2	(1-1)	W	2677	Phillips(2),Nelson	5	Keeley	Stead	Yates	Otu'ski	Moody	Cusack	Pountney	Phillips	Mercer	Pennyer	Nelson	Hadley
6	25	Bradford City	(A)	0 1	(0-1)	L	5150		6	Keeley	Stead	Dudley	Clark	Moody	Cusack	Pountney	Phillips	Greaves	Pennyer	Nelson	Hadley(9)
7	28	Bournemouth	(A)	2 0	(0-0)	W	4502	Phillips,Mercer	7	Keeley	Stead	Yates	Clark	Moody	Cusack	Pountney	Phillips	Mercer	Pennyer	Nelson	Otu'ski(5)
8	1 Oct	Portsmouth	(H)	4 0	(1-0)	W	4530	Otu'ski,Cusack,Pountney,Nelson	8	Keeley	Stead	Yates	Clark	Otu'ski	Cusack	Pountney	Phillips	Mercer	Pennyer	Nelson	Hadley
9	9	Wigan Athletic	(A)	0 4	(0-2)	L	4704		9	Cawston	Stead	Yates	Otu'ski	Otu'ski	Cusack	Pountney	Phillips	Mercer	Otu'ski	Nelson	Hadley
10	15	Reading	(H)	4 2	(3-2)	W	3688	Mercer(2),Otu'ski,Phillips	10	Cawston	Stead	Yates	Clark	Moody	Cusack	Pountney	Phillips	Mercer	Otu'ski	Nelson	Greaves
11	19	Huddersfield Town	(A)	1 2	(0-0)	L	4750	Yates	11	Cawston	Stead	Yates	Clark	Moody	Cusack	Pountney	Phillips	Mercer	Otu'ski	Nelson	Greaves(5)
12	23	Newport County	(H)	1 1	(1-1)	D	4338	Greaves	12	Cawston	Stead	Yates	Clark	Hadley	Cusack	Pountney	Pennyer	Greaves	Pennyer	Nelson	Dudley
13	29	Orient	(H)	1 1	(0-1)	D	5138	Otu'ski	13	Cawston	Stead	Otu'ski	Clark	Hadley	Phillips	Pountney	Pennyer	Greaves	Pennyer	Nelson	Owers(9)
14	2 Nov	Wrexham	(A)	2 3	(1-2)	L	1802	Greaves,Pennyer	14	Keeley	Stead	Yates	Clark	Otu'ski	Cusack	Pountney	Greaves	Mercer	Pennyer	Nelson	Hadley(4)
15	5	Bristol Rovers	(H)	1 0	(0-0)	W	3480	Greaves	15	Keeley	Stead	Yates	Clark	Otu'ski	Cusack	Pountney	Greaves	Mercer	Pennyer	Nelson	Phillips
16	13	Sheffield United	(A)	1 0	(0-0)	W	11032	Phillips	16	Keeley	Stead	Hadley	Clark	Otu'ski	Cusack	Pountney	Phillips	Mercer	Greaves	Nelson	Walker
17	27	Walsall	(A)	3 1	(1-0)	W	2453	Cusack,Phillips,Greaves	17	Keeley	Stead	Hadley	Clark	Otu'ski	Cusack	Pountney	Phillips	Mercer	Greaves	Nelson	Walker
18	3 Dec	Preston North End	(H)	2 3	(2-2)	L	3749	Mercer,Nelson	18	Keeley	Stead	Hadley	Hadley	Otu'ski	Cusack	Pountney	Phillips	Mercer	Greaves	Nelson	Yates(2)
19	17	Cardiff City	(H)	1 2	(0-1)	L	3476	Mercer	19	Cawston	Stead	Yates	Pennyer	Otu'ski	Cusack	Pountney	Phillips	Mercer	Pennyer	Nelson	Greaves
20	27	Gillingham	(A)	0 1	(0-0)	L	5035		20	Cawston	Stead	Yates	Pennyer	Otu'ski	Cusack	Pountney	Phillips	Mercer	Otu'ski	Nelson	Greaves(9)
21	28	Millwall	(H)	1 1	(0-1)	D	4710	Cusack	21	Cawston	Stead	Yates	Hadley	Otu'ski	Cusack	Pountney	Phillips	Mercer	Otu'ski	Nelson	Greaves
22	1 Jan	Oxford United	(A)	0 1	(0-1)	L	7021		22	Cawston	Stead	Yates	Pennyer	Hadley	Moody	Pountney	Phillips	Mercer	Otu'ski	Nelson	Clark(11)
23	3	Exeter City	(H)	1 1	(1-1)	D	3570	Phillips	23	Cawston	Stead	Yates	Clark	Otu'ski	Moody	Pountney	Phillips	Mercer	Clark	Greaves	Nelson(11)
24	14	Plymouth Argyle	(H)	3 1	(2-0)	W	3082	Yates,Phillips,Mercer	24	Cawston	Stead	Yates	Clark	Hadley	Cusack	Pountney	Phillips	Mercer	Otu'ski	Nelson	Pennyer(10)
25	22	Doncaster Rovers	(A)	0 0	(0-0)	D	3242		25	Cawston	Stead	Pennyer	Clark	Hadley	Cusack	Pountney	Phillips	Mercer	Otu'ski	Nelson	Moody
26	29	Brentford	(A)	4 2	(2-0)	W	3074	Cusack,Mercer,Otu'ski,Greaves	26	Cawston	Stead	Yates	Clark	Hadley	Cusack	Pountney	Phillips	Mercer	Otu'ski	Greaves	Moody(4)
27	5 Feb	Bradford City	(H)	1 1	(1-1)	D	2858	Phillips	27	Thomas	Stead	Yates	Moody	Hadley	Cusack	Pountney	Phillips	Mercer	Otu'ski	Greaves	Nelson(2)
28	14	Huddersfield Town	(H)	0 1	(0-0)	L	2262		28	Thomas	Stead	Yates	Clark	Hadley	Cusack	Pountney	Phillips	Mercer	Otu'ski	Greaves	Nelson(11)
29	18	Wigan Athletic	(A)	2 0	(2-0)	W	2277	Methven(O.G.),Otu'ski	29	Thomas	Stead	Yates	Clark	Hadley	Cusack	Pountney	Phillips	Mercer	Otu'ski	Nelson	Pennyer(8)
30	23	Lincoln City	(A)	1 0	(0-0)	W	4000	Phillips	30	Thomas	Stead	Yates	Clark	Hadley	Cusack	Pountney	Phillips	Mercer	Otu'ski	Nelson	Pennyer
31	26	Reading	(A)	1 1	(0-0)	D	2664	Nelson	31	Thomas	Stead	Yates	Clark	Hadley	Cusack	Pountney	Phillips	Mercer	Otu'ski	Nelson	Pennyer(11)
32	28	Wrexham	(H)	2 2	(2-0)	W	2512	Pountney(2)	32	Thomas	Stead	Yates	Clark	Hadley	Cusack	Pountney	Phillips	Mercer	Otu'ski	Nelson	Greaves(3)
33	4 Mar	Newport County	(A)	1 4	(0-2)	L	2476	Pountney	33	Cawston	Stead	Yates	Pennyer	Hadley	Cusack	Pountney	Phillips	Mercer	May	Nelson	Owers(9)
34	13	Orient	(A)	1 1	(0-0)	D	3073	Linford	34	Cawston	Stead	Pennyer	Clark	Hadley	Moody	Pountney	Phillips	Mercer	Linford	Nelson	May(9)
35	15	Chesterfield	(A)	2 0	(2-0)	W	1970	Linford,Nelson	35	Cawston	Stead	Pennyer	Owers	Hadley	Moody	Pountney	Phillips	May	Linford	Nelson	Walker
36	19	Bristol Rovers	(H)	2 2	(0-0)	D	6025	Phillips(pen),Linford	36	Cawston	Stead	Pennyer	Owers	Hadley	Moody	Pountney	Phillips	May	Linford	Nelson	Walker
37	26	Sheffield United	(H)	3 1	(1-1)	W	3769	Phillips(3,1 pen)	37	Delf	Stead	Pennyer	Owers	Yates	Moody	Pountney	Phillips	May	Linford	Nelson	Hadley
38	1 Apr	Gillingham	(H)	1 0	(0-0)	D	4234	Moody	38	Cawston	Stead	Pennyer	May	Yates	Moody	Pountney	Phillips	Linford	Owers	Nelson	Clark(5)
39	2	Millwall	(A)	1 3	(1-2)	L	3336	Nelson	39	Cawston	Stead	Pennyer	Owers	Clark	Moody	Pountney	Phillips	May	Linford	Nelson	Hadley
40	8	Preston North End	(A)	1 1	(1-0)	D	6380	Phillips	40	Cawston	Stead	Pennyer	May	Yates	Moody	Pountney	Phillips	Owers	Mercer	Nelson	Clark(9)
41	16	Bournemouth	(H)	0 0	(0-0)	D	4275		41	Cawston	Stead	Hadley	May	Moody	Clark	Pountney	Phillips	Mercer	Owers	Nelson	Pennyer(5)
42	23	Cardiff City	(A)	1 4	(0-3)	L	6141	Clark	42	Cawston	Stead	Hadley	May	Moody	Clark	Pountney	Phillips	Greaves	Owers	Nelson	Walker
43	29	Walsall	(H)	3 4	(2-2)	L	1904	Greaves	43	Cawston	Stead	Moody	May	Walker	Greaves	Pountney	Phillips	Mercer	Owers	Nelson	Pennyer
44	2 May	Exeter City	(A)	0 2	(0-1)	L	2956	Greaves,Pountney,Phillips	44	Cawston	Stead	Moody	May	Walker	Greaves	Pountney	Phillips	Mercer	Owers	Nelson	Pennyer(4)
45	7	Portsmouth	(A)	0 2	(0-1)	L	18350		45	Cawston	Pennyer	Stead	May	Moody	Clark	Pountney	Phillips	Mercer	Greaves	Nelson	Owers(10)
46	13	Oxford United	(H)	1 2	(1-1)	L	1954	May	46	Cawston	Pennyer	Stead	Clark	May	Moody	Pountney	Phillips	Mercer	Walker	Nelson	Owers(11)

Abbrev.: Otu'ski = Otu;akowski. Pennyer = Pennyfather.

Major Cup Competitions

F.A.Cup

Rd.	Date	Opposition	Venue	Score	H.T.	Res.	Att.	Goalscorers	1	2	3	4	5	6	7	8	9	10	11	12	13
R1	20 Nov	Bournemouth	(A)	2-0	(2-0)	W	4835	Cusack,Phillips	Keeley	Stead	Hadley	Clark	Otul'ski	Cusack	Pountney	Phillips	Mercer	Greaves	Nelson	Pennyfather	
R2	11 Dec	Yeovil Town	(H)	3-0	(1-0)	W	4554	Pountney(2),Phillips	Cawston	Stead	Hadley	Yates	Otul'ski	Cusack	Pountney	Phillips	Mercer	Pennyer	Nelson	Greaves	
R3	8 Jan	Sheffield Wed.	(H)	0-0	(0-0)	D	6973		Cawston	Stead	Yates	Clark	Hadley	Cusack	Pountney	Phillips	Mercer	Otul'ski	Nelson	Pennyfather	
R3r	11	Sheffield Wed.	(A)	2-2	(1-1)	D	11093	Pountney,Mercer	Cawston	Stead	Yates	Clark	Hadley	Cusack	Pountney	Phillips	Mercer	Otul'ski	Nelson	Pennyfather	
R3r2	21	Sheffield Wed.	(A)	1-2	(0-1)	L	10767	Cusack	Keeley	Pennyer	Yates	Clark	Hadley	Cusack	Pountney	Phillips	Mercer	Moody	Nelson	Moody	

League Cup

Rd.	Date	Opposition	Venue	Score	H.T.	Res.	Att.	Goalscorers	1	2	3	4	5	6	7	8	9	10	11	12	13
R1L1	1 Sep	Fulham	(H)	1-0	(1-0)	W	2671	Nelson	Cawston	Stead	Yates	Clark	Moody	Cusack	Pountney	Phillips	Mercer	Pennyer	Nelson	Greaves	
R1L2	14	Fulham	(A)	2-4	(0-1)	L	4641	Yates,Pennyfather	Keeley	Stead	Yates	Otul'ski	Moody	Cusack	Pountney	Phillips	Mercer	Pennyer	Nelson	Hadley	

(Aggregate – Lost 3-4)

Football League Trophy

Rd.	Date	Opposition	Venue	Score	H.T.	Res.	Att.	Goalscorers	1	2	3	4	5	6	7	8	9	10	11	12	13
Group A	13 Aug	Colchester Utd.	(A)	1-3	(0-0)	L	1662	Cusack	Keeley	Stead	Yates	Pountney	Clark	Cusack	Pennyer	Phillips	Mercer	Nelson	Greaves	Hadley	
Group A	16	Orient	(H)	1-1	(1-1)	D	2069	Phillips	Cawston	Dudley	Yates	Greaves	May	Cusack	Pountney	Phillips	Mercer	Pennyer	Otul'ski	Hadley	
Group A	21	Watford	(H)	1-4	(1-1)	L	2550	Pennyfather	Cawston	Dudley	Yates	Clark	May	Cusack	Pountney	Phillips	Mercer	Pennyer	Otul'ski	Hadley	

(Did not qualify for knock-out stage)

Abbrev.: Otul'ski = Otulakowski. Pennyer = Pennyfather.

Back Row (left to right).
Frankie Banks (Youth Coach), John Keeley, Dave Cusack,
Mervyn Cawston, Brian Beckett (Coach).

Middle Row (left to right).
Paul Clark, Steve Yates, Keith Mercer, Garry Nelson, Tony Hadley,
John Walker, Micky Stead.

Front Row (left to right).
Danny Greaves, Steve Phillips, Glenn Pennyfather,
Dave Smith (Manager), Ron Pountney, Phil Dudley, Anton Otulakowski.

Appearances and Goals

Name	Appearances Lge.	FAC	L.C.	Tr.	Total	Goals Lge.	FAC	L.C.	Tr.	Total
CAWSTON, Mervyn	32	3	1	2	38					
CLARK, Paul	28+3	4	1	2	35+3	1	1			1
CUSACK, Dave	28	5	2	3	38	4	2	1		7
DELF, Barrie	1				1					
DUDLEY, Phil	1			2	3					
GREAVES, Danny	17+6	1		2	20+6	8				8
HADLEY, Tony	28+2	5			33+2					
KEELEY, John	7	2		1	11					
LINFORD, John	6				6	3				3
MAY, Warren	13+1			2	15+1	1				1
MERCER, Keith	36	5	2	3	46	8		1		9
MOODY, Alan	23+1		2		25+1	1				1
NELSON, Garry	42+3	5	2	1	50+3	8		1		9
OTULAKOWSKI, Anton	30+1	5	1	2	38+1	5				5
OWERS, Adrian	10+4				10+4					
PENNYFATHER, Glenn	29+5	2	2	3	36+5	1	1		1	3
PHILLIPS, Steve	43	5	2	3	53	17	2	1		20
POUNTNEY, Ronnie	46	5	2	3	56	5		3		8
STEAD, Micky	45	4	2	1	52					
THOMAS, Martin	6				6					
WALKER, John	3				3					
YATES, Steve	32+1	4	2	3	41+1	3		1		4
Own Goal						1				1

	Ps	P	W	D	L	F	A	W	D	L	F	A	Pts.
1982/83	15	46	10	8	5	41	28	5	6	12	25	37	59

Season 1983/84 – League Division Three

No.	Date	Opposition	Venue	Score	H.T.	Res.	Att.	Goalscorers	No.	1	2	3	4	5	6	7	8	9	10	11	12
1	27 Aug	Rotherham United	(H)	2-2	(1-0)	D	3122	Shepherd,Phillips	1	Cawston	Stead	Collins	Ferguson	Yates	Clark	Pountney	Skivington	McDon'h	Shepherd	Phillips	
2	3 Sep	Bristol Rovers	(A)	1-2	(1-1)	L	4410	Ferguson	2	Cawston	Stead	Collins	Ferguson	Yates	May	Pountney	Skivington	McDon'h	Shepherd	Pennyfr	Greaves(8)
3	6	Preston North End	(A)	1-4	(0-3)	L	3967	McDon'h	3	Cawston	Stead	Collins	Ferguson	Yates	May	Pountney	Cartwright	McDon'h	Shepherd	Pennyfr	
4	10	Wimbledon	(H)	1-1	(1-1)	D	3106	Shepherd	4	Cawston	Stead	Collins	Phillips	Yates	Clark	Pountney	Kellock	McDon'h	Shepherd	Cartwright	
5	17	Bradford City	(A)	1-1	(0-0)	D	2574	Phillips	5	Cawston	Stead	Collins	Pennyfr	Yates	Clark	Ferguson	Kellock	McDon'h	Shepherd	Phillips	
6	19	Millwall	(H)	3-2	(1-1)	W	4272	Kellock,McDon'h,Phillips	6	Peyton	Stead	Collins	Pennyfr	Yates	Clark	Ferguson	Kellock	McDon'h	Shepherd	Phillips	Cartwright(9)
7	24	Walsall	(H)	0-0	(0-0)	D	3061		7	Peyton	Stead	Collins	Pennyfr	Yates	Clark	Ferguson	Kellock	McDon'h	Shepherd	Phillips	Cartwright(9)
8	30	Scunthorpe United	(A)	6-1	(2-0)	W	3335	Phillips(3),Stead,Penny'r,Shepherd	8	Peyton	Stead	Collins	Pennyfr	Yates	Clark	Ferguson	Kellock	McDon'h	Shepherd	Pountney	
9	5 Oct	Exeter City	(H)	0-3	(0-1)	L	2342		9	Peyton	Stead	Collins	Pennyfr	Yates	Clark	Ferguson	Kellock	McDon'h	Shepherd	Pountney	Skivington(11)
10	18	Burnley	(H)	0-3	(0-1)	L	5301		10	Peyton	Stead	Collins	Pennyfr	Yates	Clark	Ferguson	Kellock	McDon'h	Shepherd	Phillips	
11	21	Orient	(H)	3-0	(1-0)	W	4116	Ferguson,McDon'h,Phillips	11	Peyton	Stead	Collins	Pennyfr	Turner	Moody	Ferguson	Kellock	McDon'h	Shepherd	Phillips	Pountney(4)
12	29	Bolton Wanderers	(A)	0-2	(0-1)	L	5366		12	Peyton	Stead	Collins	Pennyfr	Turner	Moody	Ferguson	Kellock	McDon'h	Shepherd	Phillips	
13	31	Brentford	(H)	6-0	(2-0)	W	2902	Penny'r(2),Ferguson(2),Shepherd,Phillips	13	Peyton	Stead	Collins	Pennyfr	Turner	Moody	Ferguson	Pountney	McDon'h	Shepherd	Phillips	Pountney(8)
14	5 Nov	Newport County	(A)	1-1	(0-1)	D	3769	Turner	14	Peyton	Stead	Collins	Pennyfr	Turner	Moody	Ferguson	Kellock	McDon'h	Fuccillo	Phillips	
15	11	AFC Bournemouth	(H)	0-0	(0-0)	D	3277		15	Peyton	Stead	Yates	Pennyfr	Clark	Moody	Ferguson	Kellock	McDon'h	Fuccillo	Phillips	
16	26	Sheffield United	(A)	0-5	(0-1)	L	9627		16	Keeley	Stead	Collins	Pennyfr	Turner	Moody	Ferguson	Kellock	McDon'h	Fuccillo	Phillips	May(9)
17	2 Dec	Oxford United	(H)	0-1	(0-1)	L	2559		17	Keeley	Stead	Collins	Ferguson	Turner	Moody	Pountney	Kellock	McDon'h	Fuccillo	Phillips	
18	17	Wigan Athletic	(H)	1-0	(0-0)	W	1819	Shepherd	18	Cawston	Stead	Collins	Ferguson	Turner	Moody	Pountney	Kellock	McDon'h	Fuccillo	Phillips	Fuccillo(10)
19	26	Gillingham	(A)	1-5	(1-2)	L	5511	Phillips	19	Cawston	Stead	Collins	Ferguson	Turner	Moody	Pountney	Kellock	McDon'h	Fuccillo	Phillips	May(5)
20	27	Lincoln City	(H)	2-0	(0-0)	W	2824	McDon'h,Phillips	20	Cawston	Stead	Collins	Ferguson	Turner	Moody	Pountney	Kellock	McDon'h	Fuccillo	Phillips	Shepherd(10)
21	31	Plymouth Argyle	(A)	0-4	(0-1)	L	3978		21	Cawston	Stead	Collins	Ferguson	Clark	Moody	Pountney	Kellock	McDon'h	Fuccillo	Phillips	
22	2 Jan	Hull City	(H)	2-2	(2-0)	D	2737	Fuccillo,Phillips	22	Cawston	Stead	Collins	Ferguson	Clark	Moody	Pountney	Kellock	McDon'h	Fuccillo	Phillips	May(4)
23	9	Bristol Rovers	(H)	1-2	(0-1)	L	2564	Kellock	23	Cawston	Stead	Collins	Ferguson	Turner	Moody	Pountney	Kellock	McDon'h	Fuccillo	Phillips	May(10)
24	28	Wimbledon	(A)	2-3	(2-2)	L	2752	Penny'r,Phillips	24	Keeley	May	Collins	Pennyfr	Turner	Whymark	Pountney	Shepherd	Whymark	Fuccillo	Phillips	May(2)
25	30	Port Vale	(A)	1-2	(0-1)	L	3636	Phillips	25	Keeley	Stead	Collins	Pennyfr	Turner	Whymark	Pountney	Kellock	Shepherd	Fuccillo	Phillips	Ferguson(8)
26	3 Feb	Scunthorpe United	(H)	0-0	(0-0)	D	1976		26	Keeley	Stead	Collins	Pennyfr	Turner	Whymark	Pountney	Kellock	Shepherd	Fuccillo	Phillips	Shepherd(4)
27	6	Bolton Wanderers	(H)	0-1	(0-0)	L	1594		27	Keeley	Stead	Collins	Pennyfr	Turner	Moody	Pountney	Kellock	Shepherd	Whymark	Ferguson	
28	11	Walsall	(A)	0-4	(0-1)	L	8156		28	Keeley	Stead	Collins	Ferguson	Turner	Steggles	Pountney	Kellock	Whymark	Phillips	Phillips	
29	14	Brentford	(A)	0-0	(0-0)	D	3061		29	Keeley	Stead	Collins	Ferguson	Turner	Steggles	Pountney	Kellock	Whymark	Pennyfr	Phillips	
30	26	Orient	(A)	0-1	(0-1)	L	3001		30	Keeley	Stead	Collins	Pennyfr	Turner	Steggles	Pountney	Kellock	Whymark	Ferguson	Phillips	May(6)
31	2 Mar	Burnley	(H)	2-2	(1-1)	D	2567	Whymark,Phelan(O.G.)	31	Keeley	Stead	Collins	Pennyfr	Turner	Moody	Pountney	Kellock	Ferguson	Fuccillo	Phillips	May(5)
32	10	AFC Bournemouth	(A)	0-1	(0-1)	L	3615		32	Keeley	Stead	Collins	Pennyfr	Turner	Clark	Pountney	Kellock	Whymark	Fuccillo	Phillips	Shepherd(4)
33	19	Port Vale	(H)	1-2	(0-1)	L	2080	Turner	33	Keeley	Stead	Collins	Shepherd	Turner	Clark	Pountney	Kellock	Whymark	Fuccillo	Phillips	May(4)
34	23	Exeter City	(A)	3-3	(0-1)	D	1782	Ferguson,Phillips,Pountney	34	Keeley	Stead	Moody	Pennyfr	Turner	Clark	Ferguson	Kellock	Whymark	Phillips	Rogers	Pountney(2)
35	6 Apr	Preston North End	(H)	1-1	(0-0)	D	1826	Kellock(pen)	35	Keeley	Stead	Wilkins	Pennyfr	May	Clark	Pountney	Kellock	Shepherd	Phillips	Rogers	Fuccillo(6)
36	10	Rotherham United	(A)	0-0	(0-0)	D	3722		36	Pritchard	Stead	Wilkins	Pennyfr	May	Moody	Pountney	Kellock	Shepherd	Phillips	Rogers	Fuccillo(11)
37	14	Oxford United	(H)	1-2	(0-2)	L	7538	Shepherd	37	Keeley	Stead	Wilkins	Pennyfr	Clark	Moody	Pountney	Kellock	Shepherd	Phillips	Rogers	Fuccillo(6)
38	16	Bradford City	(H)	2-1	(1-1)	W	2035	Whymark,Shepherd	38	Pritchard	Stead	Collins	Phillips	Clark	Moody	Whymark	Kellock	Shepherd	Fuccillo	Rogers	
39	18	Millwall	(A)	0-4	(0-1)	L	3345		39	Pritchard	Stead	Collins	Phillips	May	Moody	Whymark	Kellock	Shepherd	Fuccillo	Rogers	
40	20	Gillingham	(H)	3-1	(2-0)	W	3218	Whymark,Shepherd,Gymer	40	Pritchard	Stead	Pennyfr	Phillips	May	Moody	Whymark	Kellock	Shepherd	Fuccillo	Rogers	Gymer(7)
41	23	Lincoln City	(A)	2-1	(1-1)	W	1834	Phillips,Kellock	41	Pritchard	Stead	Pennyfr	Phillips	May	Moody	Gymer	Kellock	Shepherd	Fuccillo	Rogers	Pountney(9)
42	28	Sheffield United	(H)	0-1	(0-0)	L	4971		42	Pritchard	Stead	Pennyfr	Phillips	May	Moody	Clark	Kellock	Shepherd	Fuccillo	Rogers	
43	30	Newport County	(H)	3-1	(2-0)	W	2108	May,Whymark,Kellock	43	Pritchard	Stead	Pennyfr	Phillips	May	Whymark	Clark	Whymark	Shepherd	Fuccillo	Rogers	
44	5 May	Hull City	(A)	1-2	(1-2)	L	6758	Phillips	44	Pritchard	Stead	Pennyfr	Phillips	May	Whymark	Clark	Kellock	Shepherd	Fuccillo	Rogers	Gymer(9)
45	7	Plymouth Argyle	(H)	1-1	(0-1)	D	3540	May	45	Pritchard	Stead	Collins	Phillips	May	Whymark	Clark	Kellock	Shepherd	Fuccillo	Rogers	Gymer(2)
46	12	Wigan Athletic	(A)	0-1	(0-1)	L	3335		46	Keeley	Pennyfr	Collins	Ferguson	May	Whymark	Clark	Kellock	Gymer	Fuccillo	Rogers	Owers(4)

Abbrev.: Pennyfr = Pennyfather. McDon'h = McDonough

Major Cup Competitions

Rd.	Date	Opposition	Venue Score	H.T.	Res.	Att.	Goalscorers	1	2	3	4	5	6	7	8	9	10	11	12	13
F.A.Cup																				
R1	19 Nov	Plymouth Argyle	(H) 0-0	(0-0)	D	3403		Keeley	Stead	Collins	Penny'er	Turner	Moody	Ferguson	Kellock	McDon'h	Shepherd	Phillips	Pountney(8)	Fuccillo
R1r	22	Plymouth Argyle	(A) 0-2	(0-0)	L	5570		Keeley	Stead	Collins	Penny'er	Turner	Moody	Ferguson	Pountney	McDon'h	Shepherd	Phillips	Clark(4)	Pennyer
Milk Cup																				
R1L1	29 Aug	Wimbledon	(H) 1-0	(0-0)	W	2577	Shepherd	Cawston	Stead	Collins	Ferguson	Yates	Clark	Pountney	Skiv'ton	McDon'h	Shepherd	Phillips	Penny'er	
R1L2	13 Sep	Wimbledon	(A) 4-6	(2-1)	L	1967	Shepherd(2),Kellock,Phillips	Cawston	Angus	Collins	Cartwright	Clark	May	Pountney	Kellock	McDon'h	Shepherd	Pennyer	Phillips(7)	Collins
						(Aggregate – Lost 5-6)														
Associate Members Cup																				
R1	20 Feb	Reading	(H) 5-0	(3-0)	W	1597	Kellock(2),Penny'er,Turner,Whymark	Keeley	Stead	Collins	Penny'er	Turner	Steggles	Pountney	Kellock	Whymark	Ferguson	Phillips	May	Fuccillo
R2	13 Mar	Colchester United	(A) 2-0	(0-0)	W	2841	Kellock,Whymark	Keeley	Stead	Collins	Shepherd	Turner	Clark	Pountney	Kellock	Whymark	Fuccillo	Phillips	May	Pennyer
QF	3 Apr	Bristol Rovers	(H) 1-2	(1-1)	L	1480	Shepherd	Keeley	Stead	Wilkins	Penny'er	May	Moody	Pountney	Kellock	Shepherd	Phillips	Ferguson	Fuccillo(6)	Collins

Abbrev.: Penny'er = Pennyfather. McDon'gh = McDonough. Skiv'ton = Skivington.

Southend United F.C. 1983/1984

Back: Roy McDonough, Brian Ferguson, Tony Currie, Gerry Peyton, Mervyn Cawston, John Keeley, Warren May, Greig Shepher, Steve Yates, Steve Collins.
Front: Glen Skivington, Adrian Owers, Steve Phillips, Ron Pountney, Paul Clark, Billy Kellock, Glenn Pennyfather, Mike Angus, Micky Stead.

Appearances and Goals

Name	Appearances					Goals				
	Lge.	FAC	M.C.	A.M.	Total	Lge.	FAC	M.C.	A.M.	Total
ANGUS, Mike	0		1		1					
CARTWRIGHT, Les	2+2		1		3+2					
CAWSTON, Mervyn	11		2		13					
CLARK, Paul	21	0+1	2	1	24+1					
COLLINS, Steve	36	2	2	2	42					
FERGUSON, Brian	28+8	2	1	2	33+8	5				5
FUCCILLO, Lil	19+4			1+1	20+5	1				1
GREAVES, Danny	0+1				0+1					
GYMER, John	2+3				2+3	1				1
KEELEY, John	16	2		3	21					
KELLOCK, Billy	40	1	1	3	45	5		1	3	9
MAY, Warren	13+8		1	1	15+8	2				2
MOODY, Alan	23	2		1	26					
McDONOUGH, Roy	22	2	2		26	4				4
OWERS, Adrian	0+1				0+1					
PENNYFATHER, Glenn	33	2	1	2	38	4			1	5
PEYTON, Gerry	10				10					
PHILLIPS, Steve	41	2	1+1	3	47+1	16		1		17
POUNTNEY, Ronnie	27+4	1+1	2	3	33+5	1				1
PRITCHARD, Phil	9				9					
ROGERS, Alan	13				13					
SHEPHERD, Greig	36+3	2	2	2	42+3	8		3	1	12
SKIVINGTON, Glen	2+1		1		3+1	1				1
STEAD, Micky	44	2	1	3	50					
STEGGLES, Kevin	3			1	4					
TURNER, Chris	22	2		2	26	2			1	3
WHYMARK, Trevor	19			2	21	4			2	6
WILKINS, Graham	3			1	4					
YATES, Steve	11		1		12					
Own Goal						1				1

	Ps	P	W	D	L	F	A	W	D	L	F	A	Pts.
1983/84	22	46	8	9	6	34	24	2	5	16	21	52	44

Season 1984/85 – League Division Four

No.	Date	Opposition	Venue	Score	H.T.	Res.	Att.	Goalscorers	1	2	3	4	5	6	7	8	9	10	11	12
1	25 Aug	Colchester United	(A)	3 3	(2-3)	D	2378	Ferguson,Phillips,Whymark	Keeley	Stead	Pennyr	Ferguson	May	Kellock	Gymer	Phillips	Whymark	Fuccillo	Rogers	Pountney(11)
2	8 Sep	Chesterfield	(A)	1 2	(0-2)	L	2692	Ellis	Keeley	Stead	Pennyr	Hadley	May	Ellis	Pountney	Ferguson	Whymark	Phillips	Rogers	Gymer(7)
3	10	Darlington	(H)	1 1	(1-1)	D	1902	Phillips(pen)	Keeley	Stead	Pennyr	Hadley	May	Fuccillo	Gymer	Kellock	Whymark	Phillips	Rogers	Ferguson(9)
4	14	Chester City	(H)	1 1	(0-1)	D	2436	Phillips	Keeley	Stead	Pennyr	Hadley	May	Ellis	Gymer	Kellock	Whymark	Phillips	Rogers	Ferguson(7)
5	17	Stockport County	(H)	1 1	(0-0)	D	1837	Phillips	Stannard	Stead	Pennyr	Hadley	Clark	Ellis	Ferguson	Kellock	Whymark	Phillips	Rogers	Gymer
6	21	Halifax Town	(A)	0 1	(0-0)	L	1120		Stannard	Stead	Pennyr	Clark	Hadley	Ellis	Fuccillo	Pountney	Whymark	Fuccillo	Rogers	Shepherd(9)
7	28	Exeter City	(H)	1 0	(0-0)	W	1952	Shepherd	Stannard	Stead	Pennyr	Clark	Hadley	Ellis	Kellock	Pountney	Whymark	Fuccillo	Shepherd	Ferguson
8	2 Oct	Crewe Alexandra	(A)	2 0	(1-0)	W	2028	Kellock,Shepherd	Stannard	Stead	Pennyr	Clark	Hadley	Ellis	Kellock	Pountney	Whymark	Fuccillo	Shepherd	Ferguson
9	6	Bury	(A)	0 2	(0-2)	L	2647		Stannard	Stead	Pennyr	Clark	Hadley	Ellis	Kellock	Pountney	May	Shepherd	Shepherd	Rogers(9)
10	13	Northampton Town	(H)	2 1	(1-0)	W	1920	Phillips,Pountney	Stannard	Stead	Pennyr	Hadley	Clark	Phillips	Kellock	Rogers	Whymark	Shepherd	Phillips	Pountney(2)
11	19	Scunthorpe United	(H)	1 1	(1-0)	D	2237	Phillips	Keeley	Ellis	Pennyr	Clark	Hadley	Phillips	Pennyr	Pountney	Whymark	Phillips	Rogers	Collins
12	24	Hartlepool United	(A)	1 1	(1-0)	D	4202	Phillips	Keeley	Ellis	Collins	Clark	May	Hadley	Kellock	Pountney	Whymark	Fuccillo	Rogers	Shepherd(11)
13	27	Aldershot	(A)	2 6	(1-2)	L	1896	May,Shepherd	Keeley	Ellis	Collins	Clark	May	Hadley	Kellock	Pountney	Whymark	Fuccillo	Rogers	Shepherd(6)
14	3 Nov	Blackpool	(H)	1 4	(1-1)	L	1904	Phillips	Keeley	Pennyr	Collins	Phillips	May	Hadley	Kellock	Pountney	Shepherd	Fuccillo	Rogers	Whymark
15	5	Port Vale	(A)	1 4	(0-1)	L	2989	Rogers	Keeley	Pennyr	Collins	Phillips	May	Hadley	Kellock	Pountney	Shepherd	Shepherd	Rogers	Whymark(8)
16	10	Peterborough United	(H)	2 1	(1-0)	W	1779	Fuccillo(2)	O'Brien	Pennyr	Collins	Phillips	Clark	Hadley	Kellock	Pountney	Shepherd	Shepherd	Rogers	Whymark
17	24	Wrexham	(A)	2 1	(1-0)	W	1129	Hadley,Kellock	Cawston	Pennyr	Collins	Phillips	Clark	Hadley	Kellock	Pountney	Shepherd	Shepherd	Rogers	Gymer
18	1 Dec	Tranmere Rovers	(H)	2 3	(1-1)	L	1845	Hadley,Kellock	Cawston	Pennyr	Collins	Phillips	Clark	Hadley	Kellock	Pountney	Shepherd	Shepherd	Rogers	Whymark(3)
19	8	Crewe Alexandra	(H)	3 1	(1-0)	W	1823	Phillips,Pennyr,Fuccillo	O'Brien	Stead	Collins	Phillips	Clark	Hadley	Pennyr	Pountney	Shepherd	Shepherd	Rogers	Gymer
20	15	Rochdale	(A)	2 2	(0-0)	D	1040	Phillips,Pennyr	O'Brien	Stead	Collins	Phillips	Clark	Hadley	Pennyr	Pountney	Gymer	Fuccillo	Rogers	Owers
21	22	Torquay United	(H)	2 2	(2-0)	D	1082	Phillips,Pennyr	O'Brien	Stead	Collins	Phillips	Clark	Hadley	Pennyr	Pountney	Whymark	Fuccillo	Rogers	Owers
22	26	Swindon Town	(H)	3 2	(1-0)	W	2942	Phillips(pen),Pennyr,Whymark	O'Brien	Stead	Collins	Phillips	Clark	Hadley	Pennyr	Pountney	Whymark	Fuccillo	Rogers	May(5)
23	29	Mansfield Town	(H)	1 3	(0-0)	L	2334	Phillips(pen)	O'Brien	Stead	Collins	Phillips	Clark	Hadley	Pennyr	Pountney	Whymark	Fuccillo	Rogers	May
24	1 Jan	Hereford United	(A)	0 3	(0-2)	L	5007		O'Brien	Stead	Collins	Phillips	Clark	Hadley	Pennyr	Pountney	Whymark	Fuccillo	Rogers	Owers
25	26	Chester City	(A)	1 5	(1-2)	L	1410	Gymer	O'Brien	Stead	Collins	Owers	Clark	Hatter	Hadley	Phillips	Gymer	Pennyr	Rogers	Fuccillo(7)
26	29	Colchester United	(H)	2 5	(0-3)	L	2190	Pennyr,Hadley	O'Brien	Stead	Collins	Seaden	Clark	Hatter	Pennyr	Owers	Engwell	Phillips	Rogers	Hadley(6)
27	1 Feb	Exeter City	(A)	1 2	(1-0)	L	2337	Phillips	O'Brien	Stead	Seaden	Phillips	May	Clark	Pennyr	Owers	Hadley	Engwell	Rogers	Gymer(10)
28	8	Halifax Town	(H)	2 1	(1-1)	W	1515	Phillips,Clark	O'Brien	Stead	Seaden	Phillips	May	Clark	Pountney	Owers	Hadley	Engwell	Rogers	Gymer
29	15	Stockport County	(H)	2 1	(1-0)	W	1039	Engwell(2)	Cawston	Stead	Seaden	Phillips	May	Clark	Pountney	Owers	Hadley	Engwell	Rogers	Gymer
30	23	Blackpool	(A)	0 4	(0-0)	L	4430		Cawston	Stead	Seaden	Hadley	May	Hatter	Owers	Pountney	Whymark	Welch	Gymer	Rogers(11)
31	2 Mar	Aldershot	(H)	1 0	(0-0)	W	1734	Gymer	Cawston	Stead	Seaden	Hadley	May	Hatter	Pennyr	Pountney	Phillips	Welch	Gymer	Rogers(10)
32	4	Hartlepool United	(H)	1 1	(0-0)	D	1552	Phillips(pen)	Cawston	Stead	Seaden	Hadley	May	Hatter	Pennyr	Pennyr	Gymer	Phillips	Rogers	Pountney
33	8	Scunthorpe United	(A)	1 2	(0-0)	L	1952	Gymer	Cawston	Stead	Williamson	Westley	May	Hatter	Pountney	Pennyr	Gymer	Phillips	Rogers	Owers(9)
34	17	Northampton Town	(A)	2 1	(1-0)	W	1702	Pennyr,Phillips	Cawston	Stead	Williamson	Westley	May	Hatter	Pennyr	Seaden	Gymer	Phillips	Rogers	Pountney
35	23	Bury	(H)	3 3	(2-1)	D	1984	Gymer,Phillips(pen),Rogers	Cawston	Stead	Williamson	Westley	May	Hatter	Pennyr	Seaden	Gymer	Phillips	Rogers	Pountney(8)
36	29	Port Vale	(H)	1 1	(0-1)	D	1816	Bromage(O.G.)	Stannard	Stead	Williamson	Westley	May	Hatter	Pennyr	Seaden	Gymer	Phillips	Rogers	Pountney(8)
37	2 Apr	Darlington	(A)	1 3	(1-1)	L	3689	Phillips	Stannard	Stead	Williamson	Westley	May	Hatter	Pennyr	Seaden	Gymer	Phillips	Rogers	Owers(8)
38	6	Swindon Town	(A)	0 2	(0-1)	L	2639		Stannard	Stead	Williamson	Westley	May	Hatter	Pennyr	Owers	Pountney	Phillips	Rogers	Gymer(9)
39	8	Hereford United	(H)	0 0	(0-0)	D	2133		Stannard	Stead	Williamson	Westley	May	Hatter	Pennyr	Owers	Gymer	Phillips	Rogers	Pountney(8)
40	13	Peterborough United	(A)	4 1	(2-0)	W	2095	Pennyr,Phillips,Gymer,Rogers	Stannard	Stead	Williamson	Westley	Clark	Hatter	Pennyr	Phillips	Gymer	Seaden	Rogers	Welch
41	19	Wrexham	(H)	0 1	(0-1)	L	1821		Stannard	Stead	Williamson	Clark	May	Hatter	Pennyr	Seaden	Gymer	Phillips	Rogers	Pountney(8)
42	23	Chesterfield	(H)	0 1	(0-0)	L	1464		Stannard	Stead	Williamson	Clark	May	Hatter	Hadley	Pountney	Welch	Phillips	Engwell	Owers(11)
43	26	Tranmere Rovers	(A)	0 2	(0-1)	L	1082		Stannard	Stead	Hadley	Phillips	May	Welch	Welch	Pountney	Welch	Clark	Westley	Engwell(5)
44	3 May	Rochdale	(H)	0 2	(0-0)	L	1540		Stannard	Stead	Pountney	Westley	May	Fuccillo	Pennyr	Clark	Whymark	Phillips	Rogers	Owers(5)
45	6	Mansfield Town	(A)	0 1	(0-0)	L	1837		Stannard	Stead	Pennyr	Westley	May	Fuccillo	Seaden	Clark	Owers	Engwell	Rogers	Phillips(9)
46	11	Torquay United	(H)	1 0	(1-0)	W	1704	Phillips(pen)	Stannard	Stead	Pennyr	Clark	Westley	Hatter	Fuccillo	Pountney	May	Phillips	Rogers	Engwell

Abbrev.: Pennyr = Pennyfather.

Major Cup Competitions

Rd.	Date	Opposition	Venue	Score	H.T.	Res.	Att.	Goalscorers	1	2	3	4	5	6	7	8	9	10	11	12	13
F.A.Cup																					
R1	17 Nov	Colchester United	(H)	2-2	(1-2)	D	2935	Phillips(pen),Clark	Cawston	Pennyer	Collins	Phillips	Clark	Hadley	Kellock	Pountney	Shepherd	Fuccillo	Rogers	Whymark	
R1r	21	Colchester United	(A)	2-3	(1-2)	L	3907	Phillips,Shepherd	Cawston	Pennyer	Collins	Phillips	Clark	Hadley	Kellock	Pountney	Shepherd	Fuccillo	Rogers	Whymark(9)	Fuccillo
Milk Cup																					
R1L1	28 Aug	Orient	(A)	1-2	(1-1)	L	2685	Pountney	Keeley	Stead	Pennyer	May	Hadley	Kellock	Ferguson	Pountney	Whymark	Phillips	Rogers	Young(3)	
R1L2	5 Sep	Orient	(H)	0-0	(0-0)	D	2340		Keeley	Stead	Pennyer	Hadley	May	Ferguson	Pountney	Kellock	Whymark	Phillips	Rogers	Ellis(8)	
		(Aggregate – Lost 1-2)																			
Freight Rover Trophy																					
R1L1	21 Feb	Millwall	(H)	0-2	(0-0)	L	1546		Cawston	Seaden	Seaden	Phillips	May	Hatter	Pountney	Owers	Hadley	Engwell	Rogers	Gymer	Fuccillo
R1L2	26	Millwall	(A)	1-3	(1-2)	L	2281	Gymer	Cawston	Stead	Seaden	Phillips	May	Hatter	Owers	Pountney	Whymark	Welch	Gymer	Rogers	Fuccillo

Abbrev.: Pennyer = Pennyfather.

BACK ROW: *(left to right).* Micky Stead, Greig Shepherd, Trevor Whymark, Micky Engwell, John Keeley, Brian Ferguson, Alan Rogers, Lil Fuccillo, Paul Clark.
FRONT ROW: *(left to right).* Ron Pountney, John Gymer, Warren May, Glenn Pennyfather, Billy Kellock (Captain), Steve Phillips, Adrian Owers, Steve Collins.

by courtesy of the Evening Echo.

Appearances and Goals

Name	Appearances					Goals				
	Lge.	FAC	M.C.	Tr.	Total	Lge.	FAC	M.C.	Tr.	Total
CAWSTON, Mervyn	9	2		2	13					
CLARK, Paul	30	2			32	1	1			2
COLLINS, Steve	15	2			17					
ELLIS, Peter	12		0+1		12+1	1				1
ENGWELL, Micky	6+1				7+1	2				2
FERGUSON, Brian	3+2		2		5+2	1				1
FUCCILLO, Lil	21+1	2			23+1	3				3
GYMER, John	16+3			1	17+3	5			1	6
HADLEY, Tony	31+1	2	2	1	36+1	3				3
HATTER, Steve	17			2	19					
KEELEY, John	9		2		11					
KELLOCK, Billy	13	2	2		17	3				3
MAY, Warren	28+1		2	2	32+1	1				1
OBRIEN, Jon	11				11					
OWERS, Adrian	9+4			2	11+4					
PENNYFATHER, Glenn	41	2	2		45	7				7
PHILLIPS, Steve	42+1	2	2	2	48+1	21	2			23
POUNTNEY, Ronnie	30+6	2	2		36+6	1		1		2
ROGERS, Alan	39+3	2	2	1	44+3	3				3
SEADEN, John	14			2	16					
SHEPHERD, Greig	11+3	2			13+3	3	1			4
STANNARD, Jim	17				17					
STEAD, Micky	38		2	2	42					
WELCH, Micky	4			1	5					
WESTLEY, Shane	12				12					
WHYMARK, Trevor	18+2	0+1	2	1	21+3	2				2
WILLIAMSON, Charlie	10				10					
YOUNG, ?	0		0+1		0+1					
Own Goal						1				1

	Ps	P	W	D	L	F	A	W	D	L	F	A	Pts.
1984/85	20	46	8	8	7	30	34	5	3	15	28	49	50

Season 1985/86 – League Division Three

No.	Date	Opposition	Venue	Score	H.T.	Res.	Att.	Goalscorers	No.	1	2	3	4	5	6	7	8	9	10	11	12
1	17 Aug	Crewe Alexandra	(A)	1-1	(0-0)	D	1431	Penny'r	1	Stannard	Stead	Lampard	O'Shea	Westley	Hatter	Penny'r	Silkman	McDon'h	Rogers	Phillips	Clark(10)
2	23	Orient	(H)	5-1	(2-0)	W	3643	Cadette(4),O'Shea	2	Stannard	Stead	Lampard	O'Shea	Westley	Hatter	Clark	Silkman	Cadette	Phillips	Rogers	McDon'h(11)
3	27	Cambridge United	(A)	2-1	(1-0)	W	2038	Cadette,O'Shea	3	Stannard	Stead	Lampard	O'Shea	Westley	Hatter	Clark	Silkman	Cadette	Phillips	Rogers	McDon'h(3)
4	30	Swindon Town	(H)	0-0	(0-0)	D	4037		4	Stannard	Stead	Lampard	O'Shea	Westley	Hatter	Clark	Silkman	Cadette	Phillips	Rogers	McDon'h(3)
5	7 Sep	Exeter City	(A)	2-0	(1-0)	W	2213	Penny'r,Clark	5	Stannard	Stead	Lampard	O'Shea	Westley	Hatter	Clark	Silkman	Cadette	Phillips	Penny'r	McDon'h(3)
6	14	Scunthorpe United	(H)	2-1	(1-1)	W	2974	Cadette,Phillips	6	Stannard	Stead	Lampard	O'Shea	Westley	Hatter	Clark	Silkman	Cadette	Phillips	Penny'r	McDon'h(3)
7	17	Halifax Town	(A)	3-2	(2-0)	W	1514	O'Shea,Cadette,Phillips	7	Stannard	Stead	Lampard	O'Shea	Westley	Hatter	Clark	Silkman	Cadette	Phillips	Penny'r	McDon'h(3)
8	20	Wrexham	(H)	3-0	(1-0)	W	4757	Westley,Silkman,Cadette	8	Stannard	Stead	Lock	O'Shea	Westley	Hatter	Clark	Silkman	Cadette	Phillips	Penny'r	McDon'h(2)
9	28	Mansfield Town	(A)	0-3	(0-0)	L	3701		9	Stannard	Stead	Lampard	O'Shea	Westley	Hatter	Clark	Silkman	Cadette	Phillips	Penny'r	McDon'h(8)
10	1 Oct	Stockport County	(H)	0-0	(0-0)	D	3672		10	Stannard	Lampard	Lock	O'Shea	Westley	Hatter	Clark	Silkman	Cadette	Phillips	Penny'r	McDon'h(10)
11	4	Tranmere Rovers	(H)	2-2	(1-0)	D	4175	Westley,Cadette	11	Stannard	Stead	Lampard	O'Shea	Westley	Hatter	Clark	Silkman	Cadette	Phillips	Penny'r	Gymer(10)
12	12	Aldershot	(A)	3-1	(1-0)	W	1816	Penny'r(2),Cadette	12	Stannard	Stead	Lampard	O'Shea	Westley	Hatter	Clark	Silkman	Cadette	McDon'h	Penny'r	Gymer(9)
13	19	Port Vale	(A)	0-4	(0-3)	L	4736		13	Stannard	Stead	Lampard	O'Shea	Westley	Hatter	Clark	Silkman	Cadette	McDon'h	Rogers	Gymer(10)
14	22	Colchester United	(H)	2-4	(0-1)	L	8120	Gymer,McDon'h	14	Stannard	Stead	Lampard	O'Shea	Westley	Hatter	Penny'r	Silkman	Cadette	McDon'h	Rogers	Gymer(11)
15	25	Preston North End	(H)	2-1	(2-1)	W	2787	Rogers,McDon'h	15	Stannard	Stead	Lampard	O'Shea	Westley	Hatter	Penny'r	Silkman	Gymer	McDon'h	Rogers	Gymer(7)
16	2 Nov	Burnley	(A)	3-1	(0-1)	W	2641	Gymer,Cadette,O'Shea	16	Stannard	Stead	Lampard	O'Shea	Westley	Hatter	Lock	Silkman	Cadette	McDon'h	Penny'r	Gymer(7)
17	6	Torquay United	(A)	2-2	(2-1)	D	1169	O'Shea,Penny'r	17	Stannard	Stead	Lampard	O'Shea	Westley	Hatter	Lock	Silkman	Cadette	McDon'h	Penny'r	
18	9	Hartlepool United	(H)	3-2	(1-2)	W	2755	Cadette(2),Gymer	18	Stannard	Stead	Lampard	O'Shea	Westley	Hatter	Penny'r	Silkman	Cadette	McDon'h	Rogers	Gymer(8)
19	29	Chester City	(H)	1-1	(0-0)	D	3523	Cadette	19	Stannard	May	Lampard	O'Shea	Westley	Hatter	Penny'r	Silkman	Cadette	McDon'h	Rogers	Gymer(4)
20	6 Dec	Northampton Town	(A)	0-4	(0-1)	L	2527		20	Stannard	May	Lampard	Seaden	Westley	Hatter	Penny'r	Silkman	Cadette	Phillips	Rogers	Gymer(10)
21	21	Orient	(A)	0-3	(0-1)	L	3545		21	Stannard	Lock	Lampard	Seaden	Clark	Hatter	Penny'r	Silkman	Cadette	McDon'h	Rogers	
22	28	Cambridge United	(H)	1-0	(0-0)	W	2528	McDon'h	22	Stannard	May	Lampard	Clark	Westley	Hatter	Penny'r	Silkman	Cadette	McDon'h	Rogers	
23	1 Jan	Peterborough United	(A)	1-1	(0-0)	D	3104	Cadette	23	Stannard	May	Lampard	Clark	Westley	Hatter	Penny'r	Silkman	Cadette	McDon'h	Rogers	Gymer(11)
24	3	Burnley	(H)	2-3	(1-0)	L	2619	Cadette(2)	24	Stannard	May	Lampard	Clark	Westley	Hatter	Penny'r	Silkman	Cadette	McDon'h	Rogers	Gymer(7)
25	12	Swindon Town	(A)	1-2	(1-1)	L	7619	Westley	25	Stannard	May	Lampard	Lock	Westley	Hatter	Clark	Stebbing	Cadette	McDon'h	Gymer	Gymer(8)
26	18	Crewe Alexandra	(H)	0-1	(0-0)	L	1814		26	Stannard	May	Lampard	Lock	Westley	Hatter	Clark	Stebbing	Cadette	McDon'h	Silkman	Neal(4)
27	24	Scunthorpe United	(A)	0-2	(0-0)	L	1463		27	Stannard	Penny'r	Lampard	O'Shea	Clark	Hatter	Seaden	Stebbing	Cadette	McDon'h	Stebbing	
28	28	Exeter City	(H)	2-0	(2-0)	W	1653	Neal,Westley	28	Stannard	Penny'r	Lampard	O'Shea	Westley	McDon'h	Clark	Stebbing	Cadette	Neal	Rogers	May(9)
29	4 Feb	Colchester United	(A)	0-2	(0-2)	L	1915		29	Stannard	Penny'r	Lock	Silkman	Westley	McDon'h	Clark	Stebbing	Cadette	Neal	Rogers	May(4)
30	3 Mar	Stockport County	(A)	1-2	(0-1)	L	2425	O'Shea	30	Stannard	May	Lampard	O'Shea	Hatter	McDon'h	Clark	Penny'r	Cadette	Neal	Rogers	
31	5	Tranmere Rovers	(H)	2-2	(1-1)	D	1006	Lampard,O'Shea	31	Stannard	May	Penny'r	O'Shea	Hatter	Lampard	Clark	McDon'h	Cadette	Neal	Rogers	
32	7	Swindon Town	(A)	1-2	(1-1)	L	1184	Neal	32	Stannard	May	Penny'r	O'Shea	Hatter	Lampard	Clark	McDon'h	Cadette	Neal	Rogers	
33	15	Aldershot	(H)	2-0	(2-0)	W	1505	Neal,McDon'h	33	Stannard	May	Penny'r	O'Shea	Hatter	Lampard	Clark	McDon'h	Cadette	Neal	Rogers	Silkman(7)
34	19	Hereford United	(A)	1-2	(0-2)	L	2002	McDon'h	34	Stannard	May	Penny'r	O'Shea	Hatter	Lampard	Clark	McDon'h	Cadette	Neal	Rogers	
35	22	Preston North End	(H)	2-3	(0-2)	L	2623	Cadette(2)	35	Stannard	May	Penny'r	Lampard	Westley	Silkman	Clark	McDon'h	Cadette	McDon'h	Rogers	Gymer(10)
36	29	Peterborough United	(A)	0-1	(0-0)	L	1687		36	Stannard	May	Penny'r	O'Shea	Hatter	Hatter	Clark	Silkman	Cadette	Neal	Rogers	Gymer(6)
37	31	Northampton Town	(H)	0-0	(0-0)	D	3527		37	Stannard	May	Penny'r	O'Shea	Hatter	Silkman	Clark	McDon'h	Cadette	Neal	Rogers	Westley(10)
38	4 Apr	Torquay United	(A)	1-2	(0-0)	L	1656	Cadette	38	Stannard	May	Penny'r	O'Shea	Westley	Hatter	Clark	McDon'h	Cadette	Pryer	Rogers	Silkman(10)
39	8	Wrexham	(A)	0-0	(0-0)	D	1055		39	Stannard	May	Penny'r	O'Shea	Westley	Hatter	Clark	McDon'h	Cadette	Silkman	Rogers	
40	12	Hartlepool United	(H)	2-1	(1-0)	W	2235	O'Shea,Hatter(pen)	40	Stannard	May	Penny'r	O'Shea	Westley	Hatter	Clark	McDon'h	Cadette	Silkman	Rogers	
41	15	Mansfield Town	(A)	3-1	(1-1)	W	1140	Cadette(2),McDon'h	41	Stannard	May	Penny'r	O'Shea	Westley	Hatter	Clark	McDon'h	Cadette	Silkman	Rogers	
42	18	Hereford United	(H)	3-4	(3-0)	L	1554	O'Shea,McDon'h,Westley	42	Stannard	May	Penny'r	O'Shea	Westley	Hatter	Clark	McDon'h	Cadette	Silkman	Rogers	
43	21	Rochdale	(A)	1-2	(0-2)	L	1060	Hatter	43	Stannard	May	Penny'r	O'Shea	Westley	Hatter	Clark	McDon'h	Cadette	Silkman	Rogers	Seaden(3)
44	26	Chester City	(A)	0-2	(0-1)	L	4453		44	Stannard	May	Penny'r	O'Shea	Westley	Hatter	Clark	Neal	Cadette	Silkman	Rogers	Engwell(2)
45	2 May	Rochdale	(H)	5-0	(3-0)	W	1153	Cadette(3),Penny'r,Engwell	45	Stannard	O'Shea	Penny'r	Seaden	Pryer	Hatter	Clark	Silkman	Cadette	Engwell	Rogers	
46	5	Port Vale	(H)	2-1	(1-0)	W	1687	Penny'r,Sproson(Own Goal)	46	Stannard	May	Penny'r	O'Shea	Seaden	Hatter	Clark	Silkman	Cadette	McDon'h	Rogers	

Abbrev.: Penny'r = Pennyfather. McDon'h = McDonough.

Major Cup Competitions

Rd.	Date	Opposition	Venue Score	H.T.	Res.	Att.	Goalscorers	1	2	3	4	5	6	7	8	9	10	11	12	13
F.A.Cup																			
R1	16 Nov	Newport County	(H) 0-1	(0-0)	L	3343		Stannard	Stead	Lampard	O'Shea	Westley	Hatter	Pennyer	Silkman	Cadette	McDon'h	Rogers	Gymer(9)	
Milk Cup																			
R1L1	20 Aug	Gillingham	(H) 1-1	(0-0)	D	2008	Clark	Stannard	Stead	Lampard	O'Shea	Westley	Hatter	Clark	Silkman	McDon'h	Phillips	Rogers	Cadette(9)	
R1L2	3 Sep	Gillingham	(A) 0-2	(0-1)	L	3106		Stannard	Stead	Lampard	O'Shea	Westley	Hatter	Clark	Silkman	Cadette	Gymer	Rogers	McDon'h(10)	
		(Aggregate – Lost 1-3)																		
Freight Rover Trophy																			
Group 14	Jan	Colchester United	(A) 1-4	(0-4)	L	1364	Clark	Stannard	May	Lampard	Lock	Westley	Hatter	Clark	Stebbing	Cadette	McDon'h	Gymer	McNeil(2)	Rogers
Group 13		Northampton T.	(H) 1-3	(0-1)	L	683	Lampard	Stannard	May	Pennyer	O'Shea	Westley	Hatter	Clark	Lampard	Cadette	Neal	McDon'h	Engwell(2)	Pryer(7)
		(Did not qualify for knock-out stage)																		

Abbrev.: Pennyer = Pennyfather. McDon'h = McDonough.

(Back) O'Shea, Hatter, O'Brien, Stannard, Oliver, Westley, McDonough. (Middle) Footman (Physio), Lock, Rogers, Gymer, Jobson (Chair.), Engwell, Seadon, Lampard, Moore (Manager), Cripps (Coach) (Front) Silkman, Phillips, Pennyfather, Cadette, Stead, May, Clark. (Foreground seated – Juniors).

Appearances and Goals

Name	Appearances					Goals				
	Lge.	FAC	M.C.	Tr.	Total	Lge.	FAC	M.C.	Tr.	Total
CADETTE, Richard	44		1+1	2	48+1	25				25
CLARK, Paul	38+1	1	2	2	42+1	1	1	1		3
ENGWELL, Micky	1+1		0+1		1+2	1				1
GYMER, John	2+11	0+1	1	1	4+12	3				3
HATTER, Steve	44	1	2	2	49	2				2
LAMPARD, Frank	33	1	2	2	38	1			1	2
LOCK, Kevin	10			1	11					
MAY, Warren	23+2			2	25+2					
McDONOUGH, Roy	32+6	1	1+1	2	36+7	7				7
McNEIL, ?	0			0+1	0+1					
NEAL, Dean	10+1			1	11+1	3				3
O'SHEA, Danny	36	1	2	1	40	9				9
PENNYFATHER, Glenn	41	1		1	43	7				7
PHILLIPS, Steve	13		1		14	2				2
PRYER, Terry	2			0+1	2+1					
ROGERS, Alan	32	1	2		35	1				1
SEADEN, John	4+1				4+1					
SILKMAN, Barry	38+2	1	2		41+2	1				1
STANNARD, Jim	46	1	2	2	51					
STEAD, Micky	17	1	2		20					
STEBBING, Gary	5			1	6					
WESTLEY, Shane	35+1	1	2	2	40+1	5				5

	Ps	P	W	D	L	F	A	W	D	L	F	A	Pts.
1985/86	9	46	13	4	6	43	27	5	6	12	26	40	64

Season 1986/87 – League Division Four

No.	Date	Opposition	Venue	Score	H.T.	Res.	Att.	Goalscorers	No.	1	2	3	4	5	6	7	8	9	10	11	12
1	23 Aug	Peterborough United	(A)	0-2	(0-1)	L	3548		1	Stannard	Roberts	Johnson	O'Shea	Westley	Hall	Clark	Pennyf'r	Cadette	McDon'h	Martin	Neal(10)
2	29	Hartlepool United	(H)	1-1	(1-0)	D	2227	Pennyf'r	2	Stannard	Roberts	Johnson	O'Shea	Martin	Hall	Clark	Pennyf'r	Cadette	Neal	Gymer	Cavener
3	5 Sep	Halifax Town	(A)	1-0	(0-0)	W	1060	Gymer	3	Stannard	Roberts	Johnson	O'Shea	Martin	Hall	Clark	Pennyf'r	Cadette	Neal	Gymer	McDon'h
4	12	Swansea City	(H)	1-2	(1-0)	L	3444	Cadette	4	Stannard	Roberts	Johnson	O'Shea	Martin	Hall	Clark	Pennyf'r	Cadette	Neal	Gymer	McDon'h(4)
5	16	Hereford United	(H)	2-0	(0-0)	W	1974	Cadette,Pennyf'r	5	Stannard	Roberts	Johnson	Martin	Westley	Hall	Clark	Pennyf'r	Cadette	Neal	Gymer	McDon'h
6	20	Lincoln City	(A)	3-1	(1-0)	W	1950	Cadette,Hall,Pennyf'r	6	Stannard	Roberts	Johnson	Martin	Westley	Hall	Clark	Pennyf'r	Cadette	Neal	Gymer	McDon'h
7	26	Rochdale	(H)	5-3	(3-2)	W	2141	Neal(2),Cadette,Hall,Gymer	7	Stannard	Roberts	Johnson	Martin	Westley	Hall	Clark	Pennyf'r	Cadette	Neal	Gymer	McDon'h
8	1 Oct	Exeter City	(A)	0-0	(0-0)	D	2736		8	Stannard	Roberts	Johnson	Martin	Westley	Hall	Clark	Pennyf'r	Cadette	Neal	Gymer	McDon'h
9	4	Orient	(A)	0-1	(0-0)	L	3634		9	Stannard	Roberts	Johnson	Martin	Westley	Hall	Clark	Pennyf'r	Cadette	Neal	Gymer	O'Shea(8)
10	10	Colchester United	(H)	1-1	(1-0)	D	4004	Cadette	10	Stannard	O'Shea	Johnson	Martin	McDon'h	Hall	Clark	Pennyf'r	Cadette	Neal	Gymer	Short(11)
11	18	Crewe Alexandra	(A)	3-1	(0-1)	W	2329	Martin,Ling,Pennyf'r	11	Stannard	O'Shea	Johnson	Martin	Rogers	Hall	Clark	Pennyf'r	Cadette	McDon'h	Ling	McDon'h(10)
12	24	Tranmere Rovers	(H)	3-1	(2-0)	W	1810	Hall(2),O'Shea	12	Stannard	O'Shea	Johnson	Martin	Rogers	Hall	Clark	Pennyf'r	Cadette	McDon'h	Ling	Neal
13	31	Torquay United	(H)	4-0	(0-0)	W	3094	Cadette(2),Ling,Martin	13	Stannard	O'Shea	Johnson	Martin	Rogers	Hall	Clark	Roberts	Cadette	McDon'h	Ling	Neal
14	4 Nov	Scunthorpe United	(H)	3-1	(1-1)	W	2789	Cadette(2),McDon'h	14	Stannard	Roberts	Johnson	Maddix	Rogers	Hall	Clark	Roberts	Cadette	McDon'h	Ling	Neal
15	8	Cardiff City	(A)	2-0	(1-0)	W	3025	McDon'h,Cadette	15	Stannard	Roberts	Johnson	Maddix	Rogers	Hall	Clark	O'Shea	Cadette	McDon'h	Ling	Pennyf'r
16	22	Preston North End	(A)	0-2	(0-0)	L	6033		16	Stannard	O'Shea	Johnson	Roberts	Westley	Hall	Clark	Pennyf'r	Cadette	McDon'h	Ling	Martin(10)
17	28	Burnley	(H)	2-1	(2-1)	W	3299	Cadette(2)	17	Stannard	O'Shea	Johnson	Roberts	Westley	Hall	Clark	Martin	Cadette	McDon'h	Ling	Gymer
18	13 Dec	Stockport County	(H)	0-0	(0-0)	D	2643		18	Stannard	O'Shea	Roberts	Martin	Westley	Hall	Clark	Pennyf'r	Cadette	McDon'h	Ling	Gymer(10)
19	20	Wolverhampton W.	(A)	2-1	(2-0)	W	4129	Ling,McDon'h	19	Stannard	O'Shea	Roberts	Martin	Johnson	Hall	Clark	Pennyf'r	Cadette	McDon'h	Ling	Westley
20	26	Northampton Town	(H)	0-4	(0-2)	L	8387		20	Stannard	O'Shea	Johnson	Martin	Roberts	Hall	Clark	Pennyf'r	Cadette	McDon'h	Ling	Westley
21	28	Cambridge United	(A)	2-1	(1-0)	W	4735	Pennyf'r,Hall(pen)	21	Stannard	O'Shea	Johnson	Roberts	Martin	Hall	Clark	Pennyf'r	Cadette	McDon'h	Ling	Neal
22	1 Jan	Aldershot	(A)	1-0	(0-1)	W	3170	Johnson	22	Stannard	O'Shea	Johnson	Martin	Roberts	Hall	Clark	Pennyf'r	Cadette	McDon'h	Ling	Rogers
23	3	Preston North End	(H)	2-2	(0-2)	L	4479	Pennyf'r	23	Stannard	O'Shea	Johnson	O'Shea	Roberts	Hall	Clark	Pennyf'r	Cadette	McDon'h	Ling	Rogers(6)
24	10	Peterborough United	(H)	2-2	(1-1)	D	2605	Neal,Gymer	24	Stannard	O'Shea	Johnson	Rogers	Westley	Hall	Clark	Pennyf'r	Cadette	Neal	Ling	Gymer(5)
25	31	Swansea City	(A)	0-1	(0-1)	L	6968		25	Stannard	Roberts	Johnson	Martin	Westley	Hall	Clark	Rogers	Cadette	McDon'h	Ling	Gymer(9)
26	3 Feb	Halifax Town	(H)	2-3	(0-0)	L	2047	Ling(2)	26	Stannard	O'Shea	Roberts	Martin	Westley	Hall	Clark	Pennyf'r	Cadette	Rogers	Ling	Gymer(7)
27	7	Hereford United	(A)	1-0	(0-0)	W	2801	Cadette	27	Stannard	Roberts	Johnson	O'Shea	Westley	Hall	Clark	Rogers	Cadette	McDon'h	Ling	Martin
28	14	Lincoln City	(H)	1-0	(1-0)	W	2451	Pennyf'r	28	Stannard	Roberts	Johnson	O'Shea	Westley	Hall	Clark	Pennyf'r	Cadette	Rogers	Ling	Martin
29	21	Rochdale	(A)	2-1	(1-0)	W	1262	Cadette(2)	29	Stannard	Roberts	Johnson	O'Shea	Westley	Hall	Clark	Pennyf'r	Cadette	Neal	Ling	Martin
30	27	Exeter City	(H)	2-1	(1-1)	W	3156	Hall,Ling	30	Stannard	Roberts	Johnson	O'Shea	Westley	Hall	Clark	Pennyf'r	Cadette	Neal	Ling	Martin(3)
31	3 Mar	Torquay United	(A)	1-2	(0-1)	L	1257	Cadette	31	Stannard	Roberts	Johnson	O'Shea	Westley	Hall	Clark	Pennyf'r	Cadette	Neal	Ling	Martin
32	6	Tranmere Rovers	(A)	3-0	(2-0)	W	3054	Cadette(2),Martin	32	Stannard	Roberts	Johnson	O'Shea	Westley	Hall	Clark	Pennyf'r	Cadette	McDon'h	Ling	Martin
33	13	Crewe Alexandra	(H)	1-2	(1-1)	L	1570	Hall	33	Stannard	Roberts	Johnson	O'Shea	Westley	Hall	Clark	Pennyf'r	Cadette	McDon'h	Ling	Martin(8)
34	17	Wrexham	(H)	0-3	(0-0)	L	2871		34	Stannard	Roberts	Johnson	O'Shea	Westley	Hall	Clark	Martin	Cadette	McDon'h	Ling	Gymer(11)
35	20	Colchester United	(A)	2-1	(0-1)	W	3357	Johnson,Cadette	35	Stannard	Roberts	Johnson	O'Shea	Westley	Hall	Clark	Pennyf'r	Cadette	McDon'h	Rogers	Martin
36	27	Orient	(H)	2-1	(1-0)	W	4160	Cadette,Rogers	36	Stannard	Roberts	Johnson	O'Shea	Westley	Hall	Clark	Pennyf'r	Cadette	McDon'h	Rogers	Martin
37	3 Apr	Cardiff City	(H)	2-0	(2-0)	W	3917	Hall,Cadette	37	Stannard	Roberts	Johnson	O'Shea	Westley	Hall	Clark	Pennyf'r	Cadette	McDon'h	Rogers	Martin
38	11	Scunthorpe United	(A)	0-3	(0-1)	L	1602		38	Stannard	Roberts	Johnson	O'Shea	Westley	Hall	Clark	Gymer	Cadette	McDon'h	Rogers	Neal(8)
39	14	Hartlepool United	(A)	0-1	(0-0)	L	1323		39	Stannard	Roberts	Johnson	O'Shea	Westley	Hall	Clark	Pennyf'r	Cadette	McDon'h	Rogers	Gymer(9)
40	18	Aldershot	(H)	2-0	(0-0)	W	3655	Hall(pen),Cadette	40	Stannard	Roberts	Johnson	O'Shea	Westley	Hall	Clark	Pennyf'r	Cadette	McDon'h	Rogers	Gymer
41	20	Northampton Town	(A)	1-2	(0-1)	L	7383	Cadette	41	Stannard	Roberts	Johnson	O'Shea	Westley	Hall	Clark	Pennyf'r	Cadette	McDon'h	Rogers	Martin(6)
42	24	Wolverhampton W.	(H)	1-0	(1-0)	W	10369	Ling	42	Stannard	Martin	Johnson	O'Shea	Westley	Hall	Clark	Pennyf'r	Cadette	McDon'h	Rogers	Gymer
43	30	Wrexham	(A)	0-4	(0-0)	L	935		43	Stannard	Martin	Johnson	O'Shea	Westley	Hall	Clark	Pennyf'r	Cadette	McDon'h	Rogers	Gymer(6)
44	2 May	Burnley	(A)	1-2	(1-1)	L	3970	O'Shea	44	Stannard	Martin	Johnson	O'Shea	Westley	Rogers	Clark	Pennyf'r	Cadette	McDon'h	Smith	Gymer(10)
45	5	Cambridge United	(H)	3-1	(2-0)	W	4370	Pennyf'r(2),McDon'h	45	Stannard	Martin	Johnson	O'Shea	Westley	Hall	Clark	Pennyf'r	Cadette	McDon'h	Rogers	Gymer(10)
46	8	Stockport County	(A)	2-0	(1-0)	W	2853	Pennyf'r,Cadette	46	Stannard	Martin	Johnson	O'Shea	Westley	Hall	Clark	Pennyf'r	Cadette	McDon'h	Rogers	Gymer(10)

Abbrev.: Pennyf'r = Pennyfather.   McDon'h = McDonough.

F.A.Cup

Rd.	Date	Opposition	Venue	Score	H.T.	Res.	Att.	Goalscorers	1	2	3	4	5	6	7	8	9	10	11	12	13
R1	15 Nov	Halesowen	(H)	4-1	(2-1)	W	4273	McDonough(2),Hall,Cadette	Stannard	O'Shea	Johnson	Roberts	Westley	Hall	Clark	Pennyer	Cadette	McDon'h	Ling	Neal	Tibbs
R2	5 Dec	Northampton T.	(H)	4-4	(1-1)	D	7412	Cadette(3),McDonough	Stannard	Martin	Johnson	Roberts	Westley	Hall	Clark	Pennyer	Cadette	McDon'h	Ling	O'Shea(3)	Gymer
R2r	10	Northampton T.	(A)	2-3	(2-1)	L	10603	Pennyfather,Cadette	Stannard	Martin	O'Shea	Roberts	Westley	Hall	Clark	Pennyfer	Cadette	McDon'h	Ling	Gymer(8)	Neal

Littlewoods Cup

Rd.	Date	Opposition	Venue	Score	H.T.	Res.	Att.	Goalscorers	1	2	3	4	5	6	7	8	9	10	11	12	13
R1L1	26 Aug	Brentford	(H)	1-0	(1-0)	W	1359	Martin(pen)	Stannard	Roberts	Johnson	O'Shea	Martin	Hall	Clark	Pennyer	Cadette	McDon'h	Gymer	Neal(10)	
R1L2	2 Sep	Brentford	(A)	3-2	(1-1)	W	2632	Hall,Neal,Cadette	Stannard	Roberts	Johnson	O'Shea	Martin	Hall	Clark	Pennyer	Cadette	Neal	Gymer	Engwell	

(Aggregate – Won 4-2)

Rd.	Date	Opposition	Venue	Score	H.T.	Res.	Att.	Goalscorers	1	2	3	4	5	6	7	8	9	10	11	12	13
R2L1	23	Manchester City	(H)	0-0	(0-0)	D	6182		Stannard	Roberts	Johnson	Martin	Westley	Hall	Clark	Pennyer	Cadette	Neal	Gymer	McDon'h	O'Shea
R2L2	8 Oct	Manchester City	(A)	1-2	(0-0)	L	9373	Pennyfather	Stannard	Roberts	Johnson	Martin	Westley	Hall	Clark	Pennyer	Cadette	Neal	Gymer	McDon'h	O'Shea

(Aggregate – Lost 1-2)

Freight Rover Trophy

Rd.	Date	Opposition	Venue	Score	H.T.	Res.	Att.	Goalscorers	1	2	3	4	5	6	7	8	9	10	11	12	13
Group	16 Dec	Cambridge Utd.	(H)	5-4	(1-3)	W	945	Pennyfer(2),Martin,Ling,McDon'gh	Stannard	Roberts	Johnson	O'Shea	Martin	Hall	Clark	Pennyer	Cadette	Neal	Ling	McDon'h(10)	Westley
Group	6 Jan	Fulham	(A)	2-1	(1-1)	W	1456	Thomas(O.G.),Cadette	Stannard	O'Shea	Johnson	Gymer	Westley	Hall	Clark	Rogers	Cadette	Neal	Ling	Pennyfer(4)	Tibbs
R2	27	Bristol City	(A)	0-1	(0-1)	L	4195		Stannard	Tibbs	Johnson	Gymer	Westley	Hall	Clark	Neal	Cadette	Rogers	Ling	Smith(6)	Wiggins(11)

Abbrev.: Pennyer = Pennyfather. McDon'h = McDonough.

Left to right, back row: D. Webb (Manager), D. Neal, D. Martin, P. Roberts, R. McDonough, P. Clark, G. Pennyfather. **Second row:** B. Silkman, D. Hall, D. O'Shea, M. Cawston, J. Stannard, S. Westley, H. Footman (Physio), K. Lock. **Front row:** R. Cadette, M. Engwell, S. Wiggins, J. Seaden, J. Gymer, K. Spires, P. Cavener.

Appearances and Goals

Name	Appearances Lge.	FAC	L.C.	Tr.	Total	Goals Lge.	FAC	L.C.	Tr.	Total
CADETTE, Richard	46	3	4	3	56	24	5	1	1	31
CLARK, Paul	46	3	4	3	56	3				3
GYMER, John	10+8	0+1	4	2	16+9	3				3
HALL, Derek	45	3	4	3	55	9	1	1		11
JOHNSON, Peter	44	2	4	3	53	2				2
LING, Martin	22	3		3	28	7			1	8
MADDIX, Danny	2				2					
MARTIN, David	28+4	2	4	1	35+4	3		1	1	5
McDONOUGH, Roy	31+2	3	1	0+1	35+3	4	3		1	8
NEAL, Dean	15+2		3+1	3	21+3	3		1		4
OSHEA, Danny	40+1	2+1	2	2	46+2	2				2
PENNYFATHER, Glenn	37	3	4	1+1	45+1	10	1	1	2	14
ROBERTS, Paul	38	3	4	1	46					
ROGERS, Andy	23+1			2	25+1	1				1
SHORT, Russell	0+1				0+1					
SMITH, Nicky	1			0+1	1+1					
STANNARD, Jim	46	3	4	3	56					
TIBBS, Jimmy	0			1	1					
WESTLEY, Shane	32	3	2	2	39					
WIGGINS, Steve	0			0+1	0+1					
Own Goal									1	1

	Ps	P	W	D	L	F	A	W	D	L	F	A	Pts.
1986/87	3	46	14	4	5	43	27	11	1	11	25	28	80

Season 1987/88 – League Division Three

No.	Date	Opposition	Venue	Score	H.T.	Res.	Att.	Goalscorers	1	2	3	4	5	6	7	8	9	10	11	12	13
1	15 Aug	Bury	(A)	2-2	(0-1)	D	1937	Robins'n(2)	Steele	Ramsey	Johnson	Rogers	Martin	Hall	Clark	Smith	Neal	McDon'h	Robins'n	Short	Clark J
2	22	Chester City	(H)	2-2	(1-1)	D	2369	Smith,Westley	Steele	Ramsey	Hall	Rogers	Westley	Martin	Clark	Smith	Young	McDon'h	Robins'n	Neal(10)	Ling
3	29	Gillingham	(A)	1-8	(0-4)	L	4145	West(O.G.)	Steele	Ramsey	Hall	Rogers	Westley	Martin	Clark	Smith	Neal	McDon'h	Robins'n	Pennyfr(8)	Ling(9)
4	1 Sep	Preston North End	(H)	1-2	(0-1)	L	2600	Robins'n	Steele	Ramsey	Hall	Rogers	Westley	Martin	Clark	Pennyfr	Neal	McDon'h	Robins'n	Smith(2)	Neal
5	5	Notts County	(A)	2-6	(2-3)	L	4166	McDon'h(pen),Rogers	Steele	Ramsey	Hall	Rogers	Westley	Martin	Clark	Pennyfr	Smith	McDon'h	Ling	Ling(5)	Neal
6	12	Brentford	(H)	2-3	(1-3)	L	2335	Pennyfr(2)	Steele	Ramsey	Hall	Rogers	Weste	Smith	Clark	Pennyfr	Robins'n	McDon'h	Ling		
7	14	Port Vale	(A)	1-4	(0-1)	L	3670	McDon'h	Steele	Ramsey	Johnson	Rogers	Westley	Hall	Clark	Pennyfr	Neal	McDon'h	Robins'n	Ling(9)	Martin
8	19	Mansfield Town	(A)	0-1	(0-1)	L	2854		Steele	Martin	Johnson	Burrows	Westley	Hall	Robins'n	Pennyfr	Nogan	McDon'h	Ling	Rogers(11)	Clark P
9	26	Brighton	(H)	2-0	(1-0)	W	3789	Westley,Pennyfr	Steele	Martin	Johnson	Burrows	Westley	Hall	Robins'n	Pennyfr	Nogan	McDon'h	Ling	Clark P(6)	Smith
10	29	Northampton Town	(H)	1-1	(1-1)	D	3407	Hall	Steele	Martin	Johnson	Burrows	Westley	Hall	Robins'n	Pennyfr	Nogan	McDon'h	Ling	Rogers	Clark P
11	3 Oct	Grimsby Town	(A)	3-0	(3-0)	W	2544	Nogan,McDon'h,Ling	Steele	Martin	Johnson	Burrows	Westley	Hall	Robins'n	Pennyfr	Nogan	McDon'h	Ling	Rogers	Clark P
12	10	Bristol City	(H)	2-3	(1-3)	L	8606	Robins'n,McDon'h	Steele	Martin	Johnson	Burrows	Westley	Hall	Robins'n	Pennyfr	Nogan	McDon'h	Ling	Rogers	Clark P
13	16	Rotherham United	(H)	1-1	(1-1)	D	2217	Robins'n	Steele	Martin	Johnson	Burrows	Westley	Hall	Robins'n	Pennyfr	Nogan	McDon'h	Ling	Clark P(6)	Rogers(9)
14	20	Fulham	(H)	0-1	(0-1)	L	3419		Steele	Martin	Johnson	Ling	Westley	Hall	Clark	Pennyfr	Neal	McDon'h	Robins'n	Rogers(9)	Ramsey(7)
15	24	Chesterfield	(A)	1-3	(0-2)	L	1726	McDon'h(pen)	Steele	Martin	Johnson	Ling	Westley	Hall	Clark	Pennyfr	Neal	McDon'h	Robins'n	Rogers(11)	Ramsey(7)
16	30	Walsall	(H)	1-1	(0-1)	D	2692	Smith	Steele	Ramsey	Johnson	Ling	Martin	Hall	Clark	Pennyfr	Robins'n	McDon'h	Rogers	Smith(6)	Westley
17	3 Nov	Sunderland	(A)	0-7	(0-3)	L	15754		Steele	Martin	Johnson	Ling	Westley	Hall	Clark	Pennyfr	Robins'n	McDon'h	Rogers	Smith(7)	Westley
18	7	Wigan Athletic	(A)	0-1	(0-1)	L	3081		Newell	O'Shea	Johnson	Ling	Martin	Hall	Clark	Pennyfr	Robins'n	McDon'h	Rogers	Smith	Short
19	21	Aldershot	(H)	0-1	(0-1)	L	2362		Newell	O'Shea	Johnson	Ling	Martin	Hall	Clark	Smith	Robins'n	Crown	Rogers	Smith(8)	McDon'h(10)
20	28	York City	(H)	3-1	(1-0)	W	2225	Smith,Crown,Ling	Newell	O'Shea	Johnson	Ling	Martin	Hall	Clark	Smith	Crown	McDon'h	Rogers		Westley
21	11 Dec	Doncaster Rovers	(H)	4-1	(1-1)	W	2268	McDon'h(2),Crown,Hall	Newell	O'Shea	Johnson	Ling	Martin	Hall	Clark	Smith	Crown	McDon'h	Rogers	Robins'n	Westley
22	19	Blackpool	(A)	1-2	(0-1)	L	3277	Crown	Newell	O'Shea	Johnson	Ling	Martin	Hall	Clark	Smith	Crown	McDon'h	Rogers	Robins'n	Westley
23	26	Brighton	(A)	0-0	(0-0)	D	11147		Newell	O'Shea	Johnson	Ling	Martin	Hall	Clark	Smith	Crown	McDon'h	Rogers	Robins'n	Westley(3)
24	28	Bristol Rovers	(H)	4-2	(2-1)	W	4094	Crown,Smith,Westley,McDon'h(pen)	Newell	O'Shea	Johnson	Ling	Martin	Hall	Clark	Smith	Crown	McDon'h	Rogers	Robins'n(11)	Ramsey
25	1 Jan	Gillingham	(H)	1-3	(0-2)	L	5254	Crown	Newell	O'Shea	Westley	Ling	Martin	Hall	Clark	Smith	Crown	McDon'h	Rogers	Robins'n(11)	Rogers
26	2	Brentford	(A)	0-1	(0-0)	L	5752		Newell	O'Shea	Johnson	Ling	Martin	Hall	Westley	Smith	Crown	McDon'h	Robins'n	Ramsey(3)	Rogers
27	9	Chester City	(A)	1-1	(1-0)	D	2065	Crown	Newell	O'Shea	Johnson	Ling	Martin	Hall	Clark	Westley	Crown	Robins'n	Smith	McDon'h(10)	Rogers
28	15	Mansfield Town	(H)	2-1	(1-1)	W	3091	Hall,Crown	Newell	O'Shea	Johnson	Ling	Westley	Hall	Clark	Smith	Crown	McDon'h	Robins'n	Rogers	Ramsey
29	22	Port Vale	(H)	3-1	(2-1)	W	3038	Crown(2),Robins'n	Steele	O'Shea	Johnson	Ling	Martin	Hall	Brush	Smith	Crown	McDon'h	Robins'n	Ramsey(6)	Rogers
30	30	Preston North End	(A)	1-1	(1-1)	D	6180	Brush	Steele	O'Shea	Johnson	Westley	Martin	Hall	Brush	Smith	Crown	Ling	Robins'n	Young(10)	Ramsey
31	5 Feb	Notts County	(H)	1-0	(1-0)	W	3904	Smith	Steele	O'Shea	Johnson	Westley	Martin	Hall	Brush	Smith	Crown	Ling	Robins'n	Young(11)	Ramsey(6)
32	13	Bristol Rovers	(A)	0-0	(0-0)	D	3092		Steele	O'Shea	Johnson	Westley	Martin	Butler	Ling	Smith	Crown	Young	Robins'n	McDon'h	Short
33	20	Bury	(H)	1-0	(1-0)	W	3003	Crown	Steele	O'Shea	Johnson	Westley	Martin	Butler	Ling	Smith	Crown	Young	Robins'n	McDon'h(10)	Hall
34	26	Grimsby Town	(H)	0-0	(0-0)	D	3409		Steele	O'Shea	Johnson	Westley	Martin	Butler	Ling	Smith	Crown	Young	Robins'n	McDon'h(10)	Hall
35	2 Mar	Northampton Town	(A)	0-4	(0-1)	L	4249		Steele	O'Shea	Johnson	Westley	Martin	Butler	Clark	Smith	Crown	McDon'h	Robins'n	Hall(8)	Young
36	5	Rotherham United	(A)	1-1	(1-0)	D	2531	Butler	Steele	O'Shea	Johnson	Westley	Martin	Butler	Clark	Hall	Crown	Young	McDon'h	Brush(7)	Ling(10)
37	11	Bristol City	(H)	2-1	(1-0)	W	3664	Crown,Westley	Steele	O'Shea	Johnson	Westley	Martin	Butler	Brush	Hall	Crown	McDon'h	Neal	Ling(9)	Smith
38	19	Walsall	(H)	1-2	(2-1)	L	4479	Brush	Steele	O'Shea	Brush	Westley	Martin	Butler	Hall	Smith	Crown	McDon'h	Neal	Ling(10)	Robins'n(8)
39	25	Chesterfield	(H)	3-2	(2-0)	W	3315	Robins'n(2),Butler	Sansome	O'Shea	Johnson	Westley	Martin	Brush	Butler	Smith	Crown	Robins'n	Neal	Smith(2)	Ling
40	1 Apr	Wigan Athletic	(A)	3-2	(3-0)	W	5003	McDon'h(pen),Ling,Crown	Sansome	O'Shea	Johnson	Westley	Martin	Brush	Butler	Hall	Crown	Robins'n	Neal	McDon'h(10)	Ling(11)
41	4	Aldershot	(A)	1-2	(0-0)	L	3436	Crown	Sansome	Hall	Johnson	Clark	Westley	Brush	Butler	Smith	Crown	McDon'h	Ling	Robins'n(8)	Short
42	9	Sunderland	(H)	1-3	(1-3)	L	8109	Crown	Sansome	Hall	Johnson	Clark	Westley	Brush	Butler	Smith	Crown	McDon'h	Ling	Robins'n(6)	Short
43	23	Fulham	(A)	1-3	(0-1)	L	5043	Johnson	Sansome	Hall	Johnson	Clark	Martin	Brush	Butler	Smith	Crown	McDon'h	Ling	Robins'n(3)	Neal
44	29	York City	(H)	3-1	(2-1)	W	3768	Ling(2),Crown	Sansome	Brush	Johnson	Martin	Westley	Clark	Butler	Smith	Crown	McDon'h	Ling	Robins'n	Hall
45	2 May	Doncaster Rovers	(A)	1-0	(1-0)	W	1306	Westley	Newell	Brush	Johnson	Martin	Westley	Clark	Butler	Smith	Crown	McDon'h	Ling	Robins'n	Hall
46	7	Blackpool	(H)	4-1	(4-0)	W	5541	Ling(2),Butler,Crown	Newell	Brush	Johnson	Martin	Westley	Clark	Butler	Smith	Crown	McDon'h	Ling	Robins'n	Hall

Abbrev.: McDon'h = McDonough. Robins'n = Robinson. Pennyfr = Pennyfather.

Major Cup Competitions

Rd.	Date	Opposition	Venue Score	H.T.	Res.	Att.	1	2	3	4	5	6	7	8	9	10	11	12	13	Goalscorers
F.A.Cup																				
R1	14 Nov	Walsall	(H) 0-0	(0-0)	D	3053	Newell	O'Shea	Johnson	Ling	Martin	Hall	Clark	Pennyf'er	Robinson	Crown	Rogers	Smith(6)	Neal	
R1r	17	Walsall	(A) 1-2	(0-0)	L	5162	Newell	O'Shea	Johnson	Ling	Martin	Hall	Clark	Pennyf'er	Robinson	Crown	Rogers	Neal(10)	Smith	Hall(pen)
Littlewoods Cup																				
R1L1	18 Aug	Brentford	(A) 1-2	(0-1)	L	2839	Steele	Ramsey	Johnson	Rogers	Martin	Hall	Clark P	Smith	Neal	McDon'h	Robinson	Short	Clark J	Neal
R1L2	25	Brentford	(A) 4-2	(2-1)	W	2111	Steele	Ramsey	Hall	Rogers	Westley	Martin	Clark P	Smith	Young	McDon'h	Robinson	Neal(10)	Pennyf'er	Westley,Robinson,Martin,Neal
			(Aggregate – Won 5-4)																	
R2L1	22 Sep	Derby County	(H) 1-0	(1-0)	W	4605	Steele	Martin	Johnson	Burrows	Westley	Hall	Robinson	Pennyf'er	Nogan	McDon'h	Ling	Smith	Clark P	McDonough(pen)
R2L2	7 Oct	Derby County	(A) 0-0	(0-0)	D	12118	Steele	Martin	Johnson	Burrows	Westley	Hall	Robinson	Pennyf'er	Nogan	McDon'h	Ling	Rogers	ClarkP	
			(Aggregate – Won 1-0)																	
R3	27	Ipswich Town	(A) 0-1	(0-1)	L	13444	Steele	Ramsey	Johnson	Ling	Martin	Hall	Clark P	Pennyf'er	Robinson	McDon'h	Rogers	Westley(9)	Smith	
Sherpa Van Trophy																				
Group	13 Oct	Fulham	(H) 1-0	(1-0)	W	1442	Steele	Martin	Johnson	Rogers	Burrows	Hall	Clark	Pennyf'er	Nogan	McDon'h	Robinson	Westley(9)		Nogan
Group	25 Nov	Brighton & H.A.	(A) 2-3	(1-3)	L	3565	Steele	Ramsey	Edinburgh	Ling	Westley	Hall	Short	Smith	Crown	McDon'h	Robinson	Martin(2)		Westley,Hall
R2	20 Jan	Brighton & H.A.	(A) 2-4	(2-2)	L	6654	Steele	O'Shea	Johnson	Ling	McDon'h	Hall	Clark	Smith	Crown	Robinson	Rogers	Ramsey(3)	Short(7)	Ling,McDonough(pen)

Abbrev.: Pennyf'er = Pennyfather. McDon'gh = McDonough.

(Back) Smith, O'Shea, Steele, Neal, Short, Robinson.
(Middle) Footman, McDonough, Young, Newell, Westley, Martin, Lock
(Front) Johnson, Rogers. Ling, Bate (Manager), Clark, Pennyfather, Hall.

Appearances and Goals

Name	Appearances Lge.	FAC	L.C.	Tr.	Total	Goals Lge.	FAC	L.C.	Tr.	Total
BRUSH, Paul	13+1				13+1	1				1
BURROWS, Adrian	6	2		1	9					
BUTLER, Peter	15				15	3				3
CLARK, Paul	28+2	2	3	2	35+2					
CROWN, David	28	2		2	32	17				17
EDINBURGH, Justin	0			1	1					
HALL, Derek	39+1	2	5	3	49+1	3	1	1		5
JOHNSON, Peter	39	4	2	2	47	1				1
LING, Martin	35+7	2	3	2	42+7	7			1	8
MARTIN, David	41	2	5	1+1	49+1	1		1		2
McDONOUGH, Roy	37+5	0+1	5	3	45+5	9		1	1	11
NEAL, Dean	10+2	1+1		1	11+4	2				2
NEWELL, Paul	13	2			15					
NOGAN, Lee	6		2	1	9	1			1	2
O'SHEA, Danny	22	2		1	25					
PENNYFATHER, Glenn	16+1	2	3	1	22+1	3				3
RAMSEY, Chris	8+5		3	1+1	12+6					
ROBINSON, Martin	31+6	2	5	3	41+6	8		1		9
ROGERS, Andy	17+4	2	3	2	24+4	1				1
SANSOME, Paul	6				6					
SHORT, Russell	0			1+1	1+1					
SMITH, Nicky	29+5	0+1	2	2	33+6	5				5
STEELE, Eric	27		5	3	35					
WESTLEY, Shane	35+1		3+1	1	39+2	5		1	1	7
YOUNG, Richard	5+2		1		6+2					
Own Goal										1

Ps P W D L F A Pts.
1987/88 17 46 10 6 7 12 23 50 55

Season 1988/89 – League Division Three

No.	Date	Opposition	Venue	Score	H.T.	Res.	Att.	Goalscorers	1	2	3	4	5	6	7	8	9	10	11	12	13
1	27 Aug	Bolton Wanderers	(H)	2 0	(1-0)	W	4075	O'Shea,Crown	Sansome	O'Shea	Johnson	Martin	Westley	Brush	Butler	Hall	Crown	McDon'h	Ling	Young(10)	Clark
2	3 Sep	Fulham	(A)	0 1	(0-0)	L	4754		Sansome	O'Shea	Johnson	Martin	Westley	Brush	Butler	Hall	Crown	McDon'h	Ling	Smith	Matthews
3	9	Swansea City	(H)	0 2	(0-1)	L	4357		Sansome	O'Shea	Johnson	Martin	Westley	Brush	Butler	Hall	Crown	McDon'h	Ling	Matthews(6)	Smith(8)
4	17	Aldershot	(A)	2 4	(0-2)	L	2170	Crown,Ling	Sansome	O'Shea	Johnson	Martin	Westley	Brush	Butler	Hall	Crown	McDon'h	Ling	Matthews(9)	Smith
5	21	Reading	(H)	0 0	(0-0)	D	4062		Sansome	O'Shea	Johnson	Martin	Westley	Brush	Butler	Hall	Crown	McDon'h	Ling	Matthews(10)	Smith
6	21	Cardiff City	(A)	0 0	(0-0)	D	3199		Sansome	Edin'gh	Johnson	Martin	Brush	O'Shea	Butler	Hall	Crown	McDon'h	Ling	Matthews(10)	Smith(11)
7	23	Preston North End	(H)	2 3	(2-0)	L	5348	Crown,Hall	Sansome	Edin'gh	Johnson	Martin	Brush	O'Shea	Butler	Hall	Crown	McDon'h	Ling	Matthews	Smith
8	1 Oct	Mansfield Town	(A)	1 1	(1-0)	D	2436	Ling	Sansome	Edin'gh	Johnson	Martin	Brush	Smith	Butler	Hall	Crown	McDon'h	Ling	Matthews	O'Shea
9	4	Brentford	(H)	0 4	(0-0)	L	5016		Sansome	Edin'gh	Johnson	Martin	Brush	Smith	Butler	Hall	Crown	McDon'h	Ling	Matthews(6)	O'Shea(2)
10	15	Gillingham	(H)	2 1	(1-0)	W	3200	Ling,Crown(pen)	Sansome	O'Shea	Johnson	Butler	Westley	Brush	Clark	Hall	Crown	McDon'h	Ling	Martin	Smith
11	22	Chesterfield	(H)	3 1	(3-0)	W	2662	Crown(2,1 pen),McDon'h	Sansome	O'Shea	Johnson	Butler	Westley	Brush	Clark	Hall	Crown	McDon'h	Ling	Martin	Smith
12	25	Bury	(A)	1 3	(0-0)	L	2419	Crown(pen)	Sansome	O'Shea	Johnson	Butler	Westley	Brush	Clark	Hall	Crown	McDon'h	Ling	Robinson(10)	Martin(7)
13	28	Wigan Athletic	(H)	1 2	(0-1)	L	3120	Robinson	Sansome	O'Shea	Johnson	Smith	Westley	Brush	Clark	Hall	Crown	McDon'h	Ling	Robinson(8)	Martin
14	5 Nov	Wolverhampton W.	(A)	0 3	(0-2)	L	10432		Sansome	Edin'gh	Johnson	Martin	Westley	Brush	Clark	Matthews	Crown	Robinson	Ling	McDon'h(8)	Hall(6)
15	8	Bristol Rovers	(H)	2 2	(1-1)	D	2453	Crown(2)	Sansome	Edin'gh	Johnson	Martin	Westley	Hall	Clark	Robinson	Crown	McDon'h	Ling	Smith(7)	Jones(10)
16	12	Notts County	(A)	1 1	(0-1)	D	5037	Crown(pen)	Sansome	Edin'gh	Johnson	Martin	Westley	Hall	Clark	Robinson	Crown	Bennett	Ling	Smith	Ramsey
17	26	Chester City	(A)	4 2	(1-1)	W	2050	Ling,Crown,Robinson,Bennett	Sansome	Edin'gh	Johnson	Martin	Westley	O'Shea	Smith	Robinson	Crown	Bennett	Ling	Hall	Schneider
18	2 Dec	Port Vale	(H)	1 1	(1-1)	D	3245	Robinson	Sansome	Edin'gh	Johnson	Martin	Westley	O'Shea	Smith	Robinson	Crown	Bennett	Ling	Hall	McDon'h
19	10	Wigan Athletic	(A)	0 3	(0-1)	L	2027		Sansome	Edin'gh	Johnson	Edwards	Brush	O'Shea	Smith	Robinson	Crown	Bennett	Ling	McDon'h(8)	Hall
20	17	Sheffield United	(A)	3 1	(0-0)	W	9556	Robinson,Pike(O.G.),McDon'h	Sansome	O'Shea	Johnson	Butler	McDon'h	Brush	Smith	Robinson	Crown	Bennett	Ling	Hall(8)	Edwards
21	26	Northampton Town	(H)	2 1	(2-1)	W	5034	Martin,McDon'h	Sansome	O'Shea	Johnson	Martin	Westley	Brush	Butler	Hall	McDon'h	Bennett	Ling	Edin'gh(4)	Young(9)
22	31	Bristol City	(H)	1 2	(0-1)	L	4012	Bennett	Sansome	Martin	Johnson	Butler	Westley	Brush	Hall	Edin'gh	Crown	Bennett	Ling	McDon'h(8)	Short
23	2 Jan	Huddersfield Town	(A)	2 3	(0-1)	L	6403	Crown,McDon'h	Sansome	Martin	Johnson	Butler	Westley	Brush	Hall	McDon'h	Crown	Bennett	Ling	Edin'gh	Short
24	13	Fulham	(H)	0 0	(0-0)	D	4844		Newell	Roberts	Johnson	Martin	Westley	Butler	Clark	Hall	Crown	Bennett	Ling	McDon'h	Brush
25	21	Swansea City	(A)	0 2	(0-1)	L	3388		Sansome	Roberts	Johnson	Martin	Westley	Butler	Clark	Hall	Crown	McDon'h	Ling	Robinson(9)	Brush
26	28	Aldershot	(H)	1 1	(0-0)	D	3014	Crown	Sansome	Roberts	Johnson	Martin	Westley	Butler	Clark	Hall	Crown	McDon'h	Ling	McDon'h(10)	Brush
27	3 Feb	Preston North End	(H)	2 1	(2-0)	W	2948	Crown,Hall	Sansome	Roberts	Johnson	Martin	Westley	Robinson	Clark	Hall	Crown	Bennett	Ling	McDon'h(10)	Brush
28	11	Mansfield Town	(A)	0 4	(0-2)	L	2414		Sansome	Roberts	Johnson	Martin	McDon'h	Brush	Hall	Robinson	Crown	Bennett	Ling	Smith(8)	Tilson(10)
29	25	Gillingham	(A)	1 1	(0-1)	D	3574	Crown	Sansome	Roberts	Edin'gh	Martin	Prior	O'Shea	Hall	Tilson	Crown	McDon'h	Ling	Smith(8)	Bennett
30	28	Bury	(A)	1 1	(0-1)	D	2479	Crown	Sansome	Roberts	Edin'gh	Martin	Prior	O'Shea	Hall	Tilson	Crown	McDon'h	Ling	Butler(7)	Johnson
31	4 Mar	Chesterfield	(H)	1 2	(1-0)	L	3261	Butler	Sansome	Roberts	Johnson	Martin	Westley	Butler	Clark	Tilson	Crown	McDon'h	Ling	Smith	Brush
32	10	Wolverhampton W.	(H)	3 1	(2-0)	W	5924	Crown(2,1 pen),Tilson	Sansome	Roberts	Johnson	Butler	Westley	Tilson	Clark	Hall	Crown	McDon'h	Bennett	Martin	Robinson
33	18	Bolton Wanderers	(A)	0 0	(0-0)	D	3505		Sansome	Roberts	Johnson	Butler	Westley	Tilson	Clark	Hall	Crown	Ling	Bennett	Martin	Robinson
34	25	Huddersfield Town	(H)	2 4	(0-2)	L	3582	Crown(2)	Sansome	Roberts	Johnson	Butler	Westley	Tilson	Clark	Hall	Crown	McDon'h	Bennett	Martin(6)	Ling(11)
35	27	Northampton Town	(A)	2 2	(0-0)	D	3707	Crown,Robinson	Sansome	Roberts	Johnson	Butler	Westley	Tilson	Clark	Hall	Crown	McDon'h	Ling	Robinson(6)	Martin(7)
36	31	Sheffield United	(H)	2 1	(1-1)	W	4584	McDon'h,Thompson(O.G.)	Sansome	Roberts	Johnson	Bennett	Westley	Prior	Martin	Hall	Crown	McDon'h	Ling	Tilson	Robinson
37	4 Apr	Blackpool	(H)	2 1	(1-1)	W	2795	Hall,McDon'h	Sansome	Roberts	Johnson	Butler	Westley	Prior	Martin	Hall	Crown	McDon'h	Ling	Tilson(4)	Robinson
38	8	Bristol City	(A)	2 0	(1-0)	W	6213	Ling(2)	Sansome	Roberts	Johnson	Butler	Prior	Brush	Martin	Hall	Crown	McDon'h	Ling	Tilson	Robinson
39	14	Reading	(H)	2 1	(1-0)	W	4623	Crown(2)	Sansome	Roberts	Johnson	Butler	Prior	Brush	Martin	Hall	Crown	McDon'h	Ling	Tilson	Robinson
40	18	Brentford	(H)	1 1	(0-0)	D	4119	Tilson	Sansome	Roberts	Johnson	Butler	Prior	Brush	Martin	Hall	Crown	McDon'h	Ling	Tilson(8)	Robinson(9)
41	22	Cardiff City	(H)	0 2	(0-1)	L	3268		Sansome	Roberts	Johnson	Butler	Prior	Brush	Martin	Hall	Tilson	McDon'h	Ling	Bennett(11)	Robinson(8)
42	28	Notts County	(H)	1 1	(1-0)	D	3931	Crown	Sansome	Roberts	Johnson	Butler	Prior	Brush	Martin	Hall	Crown	McDon'h	Ling	Tilson(11)	Robinson(8)
43	1 May	Bristol Rovers	(A)	1 1	(1-0)	D	6250	Robinson	Sansome	Roberts	Johnson	Butler	Prior	Brush	Martin	Hall	Crown	McDon'h	Robinson	Tilson(11)	Bennett
44	6	Port Vale	(A)	0 2	(0-2)	L	6250		Sansome	Roberts	Johnson	Butler	Prior	Brush	Martin	Hall	Crown	McDon'h	Robinson	Tilson(10)	Ling(4)
45	9	Blackpool	(A)	2 3	(0-3)	L	3999	Butler,Crown	Newell	Roberts	Johnson	Butler	Prior	Westley	Ling	Tilson	Crown	McDon'h	Robinson	Smith	Edin'gh
46	13	Chester City	(H)	1 0	(0-0)	W	4089	Prior	Sansome	Roberts	Johnson	Butler	Prior	Brush	Clark	Tilson	Crown	McDon'h	Ling	Bennett	Robinson

Abbrev.: Edin'gh = Edinburgh. McDon'h = McDonough.

Major Cup Competitions

F.A.Cup

Rd.	Date	Opposition	Venue	Score	H.T.	Res.	Att.	Goalscorers	1	2	3	4	5	6	7	8	9	10	11	12	13
R1	19 Nov	Bristol City	(A)	1-3	(0-2)	L	7026	Ling	Sansome	Edinb'gh	Johnson	Martin	Westley	Hall	Clark	Robinson	Crown	Bennett	Ling	Smith(4)	Ramsey(7)

Littlewoods Cup

Rd.	Date	Opposition	Venue	Score	H.T.	Res.	Att.	Goalscorers	1	2	3	4	5	6	7	8	9	10	11	12	13
R1L1	30 Aug	Brighton & H.A.	(H)	2-0	(1-0)	W	3072	Gatting(O.G.),Crown	Sansome	O'Shea	Johnson	Martin	Westley	Brush	Butler	Hall	Crown	McDon'h	Ling	Clark	Young
R1L2	7 Sep	Brighton & H.A.	(A)	1-0	(0-0)	W	4614	Ling	Sansome	O'Shea	Johnson	Martin	Westley	Brush	Butler	Hall	Crown	McDon'h	Ling	Matthews	Smith

(Aggregate – Won 3-0)

Rd.	Date	Opposition	Venue	Score	H.T.	Res.	Att.	Goalscorers	1	2	3	4	5	6	7	8	9	10	11	12	13
R2L1	28 Sep	Derby County	(A)	0-1	(0-1)	L	9703		Sansome	Edinb'gh	Johnson	Martin	Brush	O'Shea	Butler	Hall	Crown	McDon'h	Ling	Matthews	Smith
R2L2	11 Oct	Derby County	(H)	1-2	(1-2)	L	4422	Ling	Sansome	Edinb'gh	Johnson	O'Shea	Westley	Brush	Butler	Hall	Crown	Martin	Ling	McDon'h(8)	Clark(2)

(Aggregate – Lost 1-3)

Sherpa Van Trophy

Rd.	Date	Opposition	Venue	Score	H.T.	Res.	Att.	Goalscorers	1	2	3	4	5	6	7	8	9	10	11	12	13
Group	22 Nov	Lincoln City	(H)	2-1	(1-1)	W	1176	Crown(2)	Sansome	Edinb'gh	Johnson	Schneider	Westley	O'Shea	Smith	Robinson	Crown	Bennett	Ling	Hall	Short
Group	20 Dec	Colchester Utd.	(A)	1-2	(1-1)	L	993	Young	Sansome	O'Shea	Johnson	Butler	McDon'h	Brush	Smith	Hall	Young	Matthews	Ling	Edin'gh(6)	Jones(10)
R1	17 Jan	Northampton T.	(A)	1-2	(0-0)	L	2539	Crown	Newell	Roberts	Johnson	Butler	Westley	Hall	Clark	Robinson	Crown	McDon'h	Ling	Brush	Edinb'gh

(After Extra Time - 90 mins.)

Abbrev.: McDon'h = McDonough. Edinb'gh = Edinburgh.

SOUTHEND UNITED

Back Row (Left to Right): Martin Robinson, Danny Schneider, Danny O'Shea, Paul Brush, David Crown, Russell Short, Peter Johnson, Kevin Lock (Youth Team Coach)
Middle Row: Buster Footman (Treatment/Injury Officer), Justin Edinburgh, Ray McDonough, Paul Sansome, Shane Westley, Paul Newell, Richard Young.
Front Row: Nicky Thurston, Peter Butler, Derek Hall, Paul Clark (Player/Manager), Frank Banks (Asst. Manager), David Martin, Nicky Smith, Martin Ling, David Mathews.

Appearances and Goals

Name	Appearances Lge.	FAC	L.C.	Tr.	Total	Goals Lge.	FAC	L.C.	Tr.	Total
BENNETT, Gary	16+1	1		1	18+1	2				2
BRUSH, Paul	28		4	1	33					
BUTLER, Peter	34+1		4	2	40+1	2				2
CLARK, Paul	16	1	0+1	1	18+1					
CROWN, David	44	1	4	2	51	25	1	3		29
EDINBURGH, Justin	14+1	1	2	1+1	18+2					
EDWARDS, Andy	1				1					
HALL, Derek	38+2	1	4	2	45+2	3				3
JOHNSON, Peter	43		4	3	51					
JONES, Matt	0+1			0+1	0+2					
LING, Martin	42+2	1	4	3	50+2	6	1	2		9
MARTIN, David	34+3	1	4		39+3	1				1
MATTHEWS, David	1+5			1	2+5					
McDONOUGH, Roy	36+4		3+1	2	41+5	5				5
NEWELL, Paul	2			1	3					
O'SHEA, Danny	19+1		4	2	25+1	1				1
PRIOR, Spencer	14				14	1				1
RAMSEY, Chris	0	0+1			0+1					
ROBERTS, Paul	23			1	24					
ROBINSON, Martin	12+7	1	2	2	15+7	6				6
SANSOME, Paul	44	1	4	2	51					
SCHNEIDER, Danny	0			1	1					
SMITH, Nicky	7+4	0+1		2	9+5					
TILSON, Steve	10+6				10+6	2				2
WESTLEY, Shane	28	1	3	2	34					
YOUNG, Richard	0+2			1	1+2				1	1
Own Goal										1

	Ps	P	W	D	L	F	A	W	D	L	F	A	Pts.
1988/89	21	46	10	9	4	33	26	3	6	14	23	49	54

Season 1989/90 – League Division Four

No.	Date	Opposition	Venue	Score	H.T.	Res.	Att.	Goalscorers	No.	1	2	3	4	5	6	7	8	9	10	11	12	13
1	19 Aug	York City	(H)	2-0	(1-0)	W	2725	Walsh,Crown	1	Sansome	Dixon	Roberts	Martin	Prior	Brush	Cook	Butler	Crown	Walsh	Bennett	McDon'h(10)	Ling
2	26	Wrexham	(A)	3-3	(1-1)	D	2011	Prior,Crown,Bennett	2	Sansome	Dixon	Roberts	Martin	Prior	Brush	Cook	Butler	Crown	Walsh	Bennett	Smith N	Ling
3	1 Sep	Hartlepool United	(H)	3-0	(3-0)	W	2793	Ling(2),Walsh	3	Sansome	Dixon	Roberts	Martin	Prior	Ling	Cook	Butler	Crown	Walsh	Bennett	Smith N	McDon'h
4	9	Aldershot	(A)	5-0	(2-0)	W	2255	Crown(2),Bennett,Brown(O.G.),Smith(O.G.)	4	Sansome	Dixon	Roberts	Martin	Prior	Ling	Cook	Butler	Crown	Walsh	Bennett	Brush	McDon'h
5	15	Torquay United	(H)	1-0	(1-0)	W	7070	Bennett	5	Sansome	Dixon	Roberts	Martin	Prior	Ling	Cook	Butler	Crown	Walsh	Bennett	Brush	McDon'h
6	23	Doncaster Rovers	(A)	1-0	(1-0)	W	2386	Crown(pen)	6	Sansome	Dixon	Martin	Roberts	Prior	Ling	Cook	Butler	Crown	Walsh	Bennett	Brush(6)	McDon'h(10)
7	26	Gillingham	(A)	0-5	(0-1)	L	3842		7	Sansome	Dixon	Roberts	Martin	Prior	Tilson	Cook	Butler	Crown	McDon'h	Bennett	Brush(6)	McDon'h(10)
8	30	Lincoln City	(H)	2-0	(1-0)	W	4833	Butler,McDon'gh	8	Sansome	Dixon	Roberts	Martin	Prior	Brush	Cook	Butler	Crown	McDon'h	Bennett	Walsh	Edinbh
9	7 Oct	Scarborough	(H)	1-0	(0-0)	W	3432	Crown	9	Sansome	Roberts	Edinb'gh	Martin	Prior	Brush	Cook	Butler	Crown	McDon'h	Bennett	Tilson(7)	Walsh
10	14	Hereford United	(A)	3-0	(2-0)	W	2975	Crown(2),McDon'gh	10	Sansome	Roberts	Edinb'gh	Tilson	Prior	Brush	Cook	Butler	Crown	McDon'h	Bennett	Daley(9)	Jones(11)
11	16	Stockport County	(H)	0-1	(0-0)	L	6591		11	Sansome	Roberts	Edinb'gh	Tilson	Prior	Brush	Cook	Butler	Crown	McDon'h	Jones	Smith N(11)	Daley
12	21	Maidstone United	(A)	0-1	(0-1)	L	4016		12	Sansome	Roberts	Edinb'gh	Tilson	Prior	Brush	Cook	Butler	Crown	Walsh	Bennett	Daley(7)	Jones(10)
13	28	Chesterfield	(A)	1-1	(0-1)	D	3096	Crown	13	Sansome	Roberts	Edinb'gh	Martin	Prior	Brush	Cook	Butler	Crown	McDon'h	Bennett	Walsh	Tilson
14	31	Burnley	(H)	3-2	(2-2)	W	3765	McDon'gh,Crown(pen),Bennett	14	Sansome	Roberts	Edinb'gh	Martin	Prior	Brush	Cook	Butler	Crown	McDon'h	Bennett	Walsh	Tilson
15	4 Nov	Peterborough United	(H)	0-0	(0-0)	D	4895		15	Sansome	Roberts	Edinb'gh	Martin	Prior	Brush	Cook	Butler	Crown	McDon'h	Ling	Tilson(5)	Walsh
16	11	Halifax Town	(A)	2-1	(1-0)	W	1908	Ling,Martin	16	Sansome	Roberts	Edinb'gh	Martin	Tilson	Brush	Clark	Butler	Crown	McDon'h	Ling	Clark(5)	O'Connell
17	24	Cambridge United	(H)	0-0	(0-0)	D	4068		17	Sansome	Roberts	Edinb'gh	Martin	Tilson	Brush	Clark	Butler	Crown	McDon'h	Ling	Clark	Walsh
18	2 Dec	Scunthorpe United	(A)	1-1	(1-0)	D	3714	Ling	18	Sansome	Roberts	Edinb'gh	Martin	Cook	Brush	Clark	Butler	Crown	McDon'h	Ling	Tilson	Walsh
19	19	Grimsby Town	(A)	0-2	(0-0)	L	4001	Ling	19	Sansome	Roberts	Edinb'gh	Martin	Cook	Brush	Clark	Butler	Crown	McDon'h	Ling	Tilson(5)	Walsh
20	26	Colchester United	(H)	0-2	(0-0)	L	5563		20	Sansome	Roberts	Edinb'gh	Martin	Edwards	Brush	Cook	Smith N	Walsh	McDon'h	Ling	Bennett(9)	Smith N(8)
21	30	Exeter City	(H)	1-2	(1-1)	L	3761	McDon'gh	21	Sansome	Roberts	Edinb'gh	Bennett	Edwards	Clark	Cook	Butler	Walsh	McDon'h	Ling	Daley	Clark
22	1 Jan	Rochdale	(A)	1-0	(1-0)	W	1521	Ling	22	Sansome	Roberts	Edinb'gh	Bennett	Edwards	Clark	Cook	Butler	Crown	McDon'h	Ling	Daley	Walsh
23	6	Carlisle United	(A)	0-3	(0-1)	L	6196		23	Sansome	Roberts	Edinb'gh	Bennett	Edwards	Clark	Cook	Butler	Crown	McDon'h	Ling	Martin(2)	Walsh(9)
24	12	Wrexham	(H)	2-1	(1-0)	W	3005	Crown,Cook	24	Sansome	Dixon	Roberts	Martin	Edwards	Brush	Cook	Butler	Crown	McDon'h	Bennett	Ling	O'Connell
25	20	York City	(A)	1-2	(0-0)	L	2397	Crown(pen)	25	Sansome	Dixon	Roberts	Martin	Butters	Brush	Cook	Butler	Crown	McDon'h	Bennett	Ling(7)	Clark
26	27	Aldershot	(H)	5-0	(3-0)	W	2821	Crown(3),Ling(2)	26	Sansome	Dixon	Roberts	Martin	Butters	Brush	Tilson	Butler	Crown	McDon'h	Ling	Clark	Bennett
27	2 Feb	Doncaster Rovers	(H)	2-0	(1-0)	W	3174	McDon'gh,Ling	27	Sansome	Dixon	Roberts	Martin	Clark	Brush	Tilson	Butler	Crown	McDon'h	Ling	Bennett(7)	O'Connell
28	6	Torquay United	(A)	0-3	(0-1)	L	2007		28	Sansome	Dixon	Roberts	Martin	Butters	Clark	Tilson	Butler	Crown	McDon'h	Ling	Bennett(7)	Brush
29	13	Hartlepool United	(A)	1-1	(1-0)	D	3628	Ling	29	Sansome	Dixon	Roberts	Cook	Butters	Clark	Cook	Butler	Crown	McDon'h	Ling	Bennett(11)	Brush
30	17	Scunthorpe United	(H)	0-0	(0-0)	D	3154		30	Sansome	Dixon	Roberts	Martin	Butters	Clark	Cook	Butler	Crown	McDon'h	Ling	Bennett(3)	Bennett(11)
31	25	Cambridge United	(A)	1-2	(0-1)	L	4573	Crown	31	Sansome	Dixon	Brush	Martin	Butters	Clark	Smith N	Butler	Crown	McDon'h	Jones	O'Connell(11)	Tilson
32	3 Mar	Carlisle United	(H)	2-0	(2-0)	W	3465	Butters(2)	32	Sansome	Dixon	Brush	Martin	Butters	Clark	Smith N	Butler	Crown	Benjamin	Tilson	O'Connell(4)	McDon'h
33	7	Lincoln City	(A)	0-2	(0-1)	L	4860		33	Sansome	Dixon	Brush	Martin	Butters	Clark	Smith N	Butler	McDon'h	Benjamin	Tilson	O'Connell(11)	Walsh
34	9	Gillingham	(H)	2-0	(1-0)	W	4514	Benjamin,Butters	34	Sansome	Dixon	Brush	Martin	Butters	Clark	Smith N	Butler	Crown	Benjamin	Bennett	McDon'gh	Cook
35	17	Scarborough	(A)	1-1	(0-0)	D	2179	Smith N	35	Sansome	Dixon	Brush	Martin	Butters	Clark	Smith N	Smith P	Crown	Benjamin	Bennett	O'Connell(11)	McDon'h(12)
36	20	Hereford United	(H)	2-0	(2-0)	W	2669	Benjamin,Martin	36	Sansome	Dixon	Brush	Martin	Butters	Clark	Cook	Butler	Crown	Benjamin	Smith N	Smith P(7)	McDon'h
37	23	Stockport County	(A)	2-0	(2-0)	W	3917	Butler,Benjamin	37	Sansome	Dixon	Brush	Martin	McDon'h	Clark	Ling	Butler	Crown	Benjamin	Smith N	McDon'gh(9)	Smith P
38	31	Maidstone United	(H)	0-3	(0-1)	L	3550		38	Sansome	Dixon	Brush	Martin	McDon'h	Clark	Ling	Butler	Crown	Benjamin	Smith N	Ansah(7)	McDon'h
39	7 Apr	Chesterfield	(H)	0-2	(0-1)	L	2892		39	Sansome	Dixon	Edinb'gh	Martin	Butters	Clark	Ling	Butler	Ansah	Benjamin	Smith N	McDon'gh(9)	SmithP(3)
40	10	Burnley	(A)	0-0	(0-0)	D	3967		40	Sansome	Austin	Edinb'gh	Martin	Butters	McDon'h	Cooper	Smith P	Ansah	Benjamin	Smith N	Butler(7)	Ling
41	14	Rochdale	(H)	3-2	(1-0)	W	2464	Ansah,Martin,Brown(O.G.)	41	Sansome	Austin	Edinb'gh	Martin	Butters	Clark	Ansah	Smith P	Crown	Benjamin	Cooper	McDon'gh	Cooper
42	16	Colchester United	(A)	2-0	(1-0)	W	5283	Benjamin,Daley	42	Sansome	Austin	Edinb'gh	McDon'h	Clark	Clark	Ansah	Smith P	Crown	Benjamin	Cooper	Daley(8)	Edwards
43	20	Grimsby Town	(H)	0-2	(0-1)	L	4945		43	Sansome	Austin	Edinb'gh	McDon'h	Clark	Clark	Ansah	Smith P	Crown	Benjamin	Cooper	Tilson(7)	Roberts(8)
44	25	Exeter City	(A)	1-2	(0-1)	L	8271	Crown	44	Sansome	Austin	Edinb'gh	Butler	Butler	Clark	Ling	Smith P	Crown	Benjamin	Cooper	Edwards(4)	Tilson(11)
45	27	Halifax Town	(H)	2-0	(1-0)	W	3656	Ling,Smith P	45	Sansome	Austin	Edinb'gh	Edwards	Butler	Clark	Ling	Smith P	Crown	Benjamin	Ansah	Daley(8)	Tilson
46	5 May	Peterborough United	(A)	2-1	(2-0)	W	7958	Crown(2)	46	Sansome	Austin	Edinb'gh	Martin	Edwards	Clark	Ling	Smith P	Crown	Benjamin	Butler	Daley(8)	Tilson

Abbrev.: Edinb'gh = Edinburgh. McDon'h = McDonough.

Major Cup Competitions

Rd.	Date	Opposition	Venue Score	H.T.	Res.	Att.	Goalscorers	1	2	3	4	5	6	7	8	9	10	11	12	13
F.A.Cup																				
R1	18 Nov	Aylesbury U.	(A) 0-1	(0-0)	L	4043		Sansome	Roberts	Edinb'gh	Martin	Tilson	Brush	Cook	Butler	Crown	McDon'h	Ling	Walsh(11)	Clark
Rumbelows Cup																				
R1L1	22 Aug	Colchester United	(A) 4-3	(1-2)	W	3537	Crown(2),Bennett,Martin	Sansome	Dixon	Roberts	Martin	Prior	Brush	Cook	Butler	Crown	Walsh	Bennett	Smith N(7)	Ling
R1L2	29	Colchester United	(H) 2-1	(1-0)	W	3763	Crown(pen),Bennett	Sansome	Dixon	Roberts	Martin	Prior	Brush	Cook	Butler	Crown	Walsh	Bennett	Smith N(6)	Ling
							(Aggregate – Won 6-4)													
R2L1	20 Sep	Tottenham H.	(A) 0-1	(0-0)	L	15734		Sansome	Dixon	Roberts	Martin	Prior	Ling	Cook	Butler	Crown	Walsh	Bennett	Brush	McDon'h
R2L2	4 Oct	Tottenham H.	(H) 3-2*	(2-1)	W	10418	Bennett(2),Martin	Sansome	Dixon	Roberts	Martin	Prior	Brush	Cook	Butler	Crown	McDon'h	Bennett	Edin'gh(2)	Walsh(7)
							* (After Extra Time – 90 mins. 3-2)													
							(Aggregate 3-3 – Lost on (A) Goals)													
Leyland Daf Cup																				
Group	7 Nov	Gillingham	(H) 1-0	(0-0)	W	1650	Tilson	Sansome		Edinb'gh	Martin	Tilson	Brush	Cook	Butler	Crown	McDon'h	O'Conn'l	Walsh(10)	Ling(11)
Group	12 Dec	Cambridge Utd.	(A) 3-3	(2-1)	D	1304	Walsh,Edinburgh,Ling	Sansome	Roberts	Edinb'gh	Martin	Cook	Brush	Clark	Butler	Walsh	McDon'h	Ling	Smith N(5)	Tilson(10)
R1	17 Jan	Northampton T.	(H) 2-1	(2-0)	W	1346	Cook,Crown	Sansome	Dixon	Roberts	Martin	Butters	Brush	Cook	Butler	Crown	McDon'h	Bennett	Ling	Clark
R2	30	Walsall	(A) 1-4	(0-2)	L	2255	Butter	Sansome	Dixon	Roberts	Martin	Butters	Brush	Tilson	Butler	Crown	McDon'h	Ling	Clark(6)	Bennett(10)

Abbrev.: McDon'h = McDonough. Edin'gh = Edinburgh. O'Conn'l = O'Connell.

SOUTHEND UNITED

Back row (left to right): S. Tilson, M. Lawrence, G. Bennett, M. Walsh, D. Crown, M. Jones, J. Edinburgh

Middle row: P. Clark, D. Martin, R. McDonough, P. Sansome, P. Newell, S. Prior, J. O'Connell, K. Lock

Front row: N. Smith, P. Butler, P. Roberts, D. Webb (Manager), P. Brush (Capt), M. Ling, J. Cook

Appearances and Goals

Name	Appearances Lge.	FAC	R.C.	L.D.	Total	Goals Lge.	FAC	R.C.	L.D.	Total
ANSAH, Andy	6+1				6+1	1				1
AUSTIN, Dean	7				7					
BENJAMIN, Ian	15				15	4				4
BENNETT, Gary	20+5		4	1+1	25+6	4		4		8
BRUSH, Paul	28+3	1	3	4	36+3	3				3
BUTLER, Peter	40+1	1	4	4	49+1					
BUTTERS, Guy	16			2	18				1	1
CLARK, Paul	24+1			1+1	25+2	2				2
COOK, Jason	29	1	4	3	37				1	1
COOPER, Mark	4				4					
CROWN, David	41	1	4	3	49	19		3	1	23
DALEY, Peter	0+5				0+5	1				1
DIXON, Andy	24		4	2	30					
EDINBURGH, Justin	22	1	0+1	2	25+1				1	1
EDWARDS, Andy	7+1				7+1					
JONES, Matt	2+2				2+2					
LING, Martin	24+1	1	1	2+1	28+2	10			1	11
MARTIN, David	38+1	1	4	4	47+1	3		2		5
McDONOUGH, Roy	27+6	1	1	4	33+6	5				5
O'CONNELL, Iain	0+4			1	1+4	1				1
PRIOR, Spencer	15		4		19					
ROBERTS, Paul	30+1	1	4	4	39+1	1				1
SANSOME, Paul	46	1	4	4	55					
SMITH, Nicky	12+2		0+2	0+1	12+5	1				1
SMITH, Paul	8+2				8+2	1				1
TILSON, Steve	11+5	1		2+1	14+6				1	1
WALSH, Mario	10+1	0+1	3+1	1+1	14+4	2			1	3
Own Goal						3				3

	Ps	P	W	D	L	F	A	W	D	L	F	A	Pts.
1989/90	3	46	15	3	5	35	14	7	6	10	26	34	75

Season 1990/91 – League Division Three

No.	Date	Opposition	Venue	Score	H.T.	Res.	Att.	Goalscorers	1	2	3	4	5	6	7	8	9	10	11	12	13
1	25 Aug	Huddersfield Town	(A)	2-1	(1-1)	W	5219	Angell,Edwards	Sansome	Edwards	Hyslop	Martin	Cornwell	Tilson	Clark	Butler	Ansah	Benjamin	Angell		
2	1 Sep	Crewe Alexandra	(H)	3-2	(1-1)	W	2994	Benjamin,Martin(pen),Angell	Sansome	Edwards	Powell	Martin	Cornwell	Tilson	Clark	Butler	Ansah	Benjamin	Angell		
3	9	Cambridge United	(A)	4-1	(1-0)	W	4790	Angell(2),Benjamin,Butler	Sansome	Austin	Powell	Martin	Cornwell	Tilson	Clark	Butler	Ansah	Benjamin	Angell		
4	14	Preston North End	(H)	3-2	(0-1)	W	4614	Martin,Benjamin,Cornwell	Sansome	Austin	Powell	Martin	Cornwell	Tilson	Clark	Butler	Ansah	Benjamin	Angell		
5	18	Shrewsbury Town	(H)	2-1	(2-1)	W	5100	Tilson,Ansah	Sansome	Austin	Powell	Martin	Cornwell	Tilson	Clark	Butler	Ansah	Benjamin	Angell		
6	22	Stoke City	(A)	0-4	(0-2)	L	11901		Sansome	Austin	Powell	Martin	Cornwell	Tilson	Clark	Butler	Ansah	Benjamin	Angell	Cook(11)	
7	29	Mansfield Town	(A)	1-0	(0-0)	W	2120	Benjamin	Sansome	Austin	Powell	Martin	Prior	Tilson	Clark	Butler	Ansah	Benjamin	Angell	Locke(9)	
8	2 Oct	Swansea City	(H)	4-1	(1-0)	W	3635	Martin(2,1 pen),Tilson(2)	Sansome	Austin	Powell	Martin	Prior	Tilson	Clark	Butler	Ansah	Benjamin	Angell	Locke(9)	
9	5	Bournemouth	(H)	2-1	(1-1)	W	5255	Martin,Angell	Sansome	Austin	Powell	Martin	Prior	Tilson	Clark	Butler	Ansah	Benjamin	Angell	Locke(9)	Cawley(7)
10	13	Birmingham City	(A)	1-1	(0-0)	D	9333	Ansah	Sansome	Austin	Powell	Martin	Prior	Tilson	Cawley	Butler	Ansah	Benjamin	Angell	Locke(11)	Cornwell(6)
11	20	Wigan Athletic	(A)	1-4	(0-2)	L	2691	Cawley	Sansome	Austin	Powell	Martin	Prior	Tilson	Cawley	Butler	Ansah	Benjamin	Angell	Ling(9)	Cornwell(4)
12	23	Exeter City	(H)	2-1	(1-1)	W	4280	Powell,Benjamin	Sansome	Austin	Powell	Martin	Prior	Tilson	Cawley	Butler	Ansah	Benjamin	Angell	Cornwell(4)	
13	27	Bury	(H)	2-1	(1-1)	W	4001	Angell,Tilson	Sansome	Austin	Powell	Cornwell	Prior	Tilson	Cawley	Butler	Ansah	Benjamin	Angell		
14	4 Nov	Brentford	(A)	1-0	(1-0)	W	8021	Benjamin	Sansome	Austin	Powell	Cornwell	Prior	Tilson	Cawley	Butler	Ansah	Benjamin	Angell	Locke(11)	
15	10	Fulham	(H)	1-1	(1-0)	D	5808	Cornwell	Sansome	Austin	Powell	Cornwell	Prior	Tilson	Cawley	Butler	Ansah	Benjamin	Angell	Locke(11)	
16	24	Reading	(A)	4-2	(1-0)	W	3927	Martin(2),Tilson,Angell	Sansome	Austin	Powell	Martin	Prior	Tilson	Clark	Butler	Locke	Benjamin	Angell		
17	1 Dec	Rotherham United	(A)	1-0	(0-0)	W	3465	Benjamin	Sansome	Austin	Powell	Martin	Prior	Tilson	Clark	Butler	Smith	Benjamin	Angell		
18	15	Grimsby Town	(H)	2-0	(2-0)	W	8126	Tilson,Martin	Sansome	Austin	Powell	Martin	Prior	Tilson	Clark	Butler	Locke	Benjamin	Angell		
19	22	Chester City	(H)	0-1	(0-0)	L	1523		Sansome	Austin	Powell	Martin	Prior	Tilson	Clark	Butler	Locke	Benjamin	Angell		
20	26	Bolton Wanderers	(H)	1-1	(0-0)	D	7539	Tilson	Sansome	Austin	Powell	Martin	Prior	Tilson	Clark	Butler	Locke	Benjamin	Angell		
21	28	Bradford City	(H)	1-1	(1-0)	D	6767	Tilson	Sansome	Austin	Powell	Martin	Prior	Tilson	Clark	Butler	Locke	Benjamin	Angell	Ansah(9)	
22	1 Jan	Tranmere Rovers	(A)	1-3	(1-2)	L	7214	Angell	Sansome	Austin	Powell	Smith	Prior	Tilson	Clark	Butler	Ansah	Benjamin	Angell	Ling(4)	
23	12	Crewe Alexandra	(A)	2-0	(1-0)	W	3595	Angell(2)	Sansome	Austin	Powell	Martin	Scully	Tilson	Clark	Butler	Ansah	Benjamin	Angell		
24	19	Huddersfield Town	(H)	0-1	(0-1)	L	5509		Sansome	Austin	Powell	Martin	Scully	Tilson	Clark	Butler	Ansah	Benjamin	Angell		Cornwell(8)
25	26	Preston North End	(A)	1-2	(0-1)	L	4351	Ansah	Sansome	Austin	Powell	Martin	Scully	Tilson	Clark	Butler	Locke	Benjamin	Angell	Locke(11)	
26	2 Feb	Shrewsbury Town	(H)	1-0	(1-0)	W	4377	Angell	Sansome	Austin	Powell	Ling	Scully	Tilson	Clark	Butler	Ansah	Benjamin	Angell	Ansah(9)	
27	5	Stoke City	(H)	1-0	(1-0)	W	5164	Angell	Sansome	Austin	Powell	Martin	Scully	Tilson	Clark	Butler	Ansah	Benjamin	Angell		
28	19	Reading	(H)	1-2	(1-0)	L	4588	Benjamin	Sansome	Austin	Powell	Martin	Scully	Tilson	Clark	Cornwell	Ansah	Benjamin	Angell	Locke(8)	
29	23	Fulham	(A)	3-0	(2-0)	W	5113	Benjamin,Martin,Ansah	Sansome	Austin	Powell	Martin	Scully	Tilson	Clark	Butler	Ansah	Benjamin	Angell		
30	1 Mar	Rotherham United	(H)	2-1	(2-0)	W	5622	Benjamin(2)	Sansome	Austin	Powell	Martin	Scully	Tilson	Clark	Locke	Ansah	Benjamin	Locke	Angell(6)	
31	9	Grimsby Town	(A)	0-1	(0-1)	L	9689		Sansome	Austin	Powell	Martin	Scully	Tilson	Clark	Butler	Ansah	Benjamin	Angell	Locke(11)	
32	12	Swansea City	(H)	4-1	(1-1)	W	2712	Locke(2),Benjamin,Ansah	Sansome	Austin	Powell	Martin	Scully	Tilson	Clark	Butler	Ansah	Benjamin	Angell		
33	15	Mansfield Town	(H)	2-1	(0-1)	W	5400	Martin,Butler	Sansome	Austin	Powell	Martin	Prior	Tilson	Clark	Butler	Ansah	Benjamin	Locke		
34	18	Birmingham City	(H)	2-1	(0-1)	W	6328	Martin,Angell	Sansome	Austin	Powell	Martin	Prior	Tilson	Clark	Butler	Ansah	Benjamin	Locke	Angell(9)	
35	23	Bournemouth	(A)	1-3	(1-1)	L	7421	Angell	Sansome	Austin	Powell	Martin	Prior	Tilson	Clark	Butler	Moran	Benjamin	Angell	Cornwell(7)	Hyslop(9)
36	30	Bolton Wanderers	(A)	0-1	(0-0)	L	10666		Sansome	Austin	Powell	Cornwell	Scully	Tilson	Clark	Butler	Ansah	Benjamin	Angell		
37	2 Apr	Chester City	(H)	1-1	(0-0)	D	6190	Ansah	Sansome	Austin	Powell	Martin	Scully	Tilson	Clark	Butler	Ansah	Benjamin	Locke		
38	6	Bradford City	(H)	1-2	(0-1)	L	5846	Angell	Sansome	Austin	Powell	Martin	Scully	Hyslop	Clark	Cornwell	Locke	Benjamin	Angell	Ansah(9)	
39	9	Leyton Orient	(A)	1-0	(1-0)	W	6306	Ansah	Sansome	Austin	Powell	Martin	Scully	Hyslop	Clark	Cornwell	Ansah	Benjamin	Angell		
40	12	Tranmere Rovers	(H)	1-0	(1-0)	W	8622	Ansah	Sansome	Austin	Powell	Martin	Scully	Hyslop	Clark	Cornwell	Ansah	Benjamin	Locke		
41	19	Wigan Athletic	(H)	0-2	(0-1)	L	7550		Sansome	Austin	Powell	Martin	Scully	Hyslop	Clark	Butler	Ansah	Benjamin	Locke	Angell(11)	
42	27	Exeter City	(A)	2-1	(1-1)	W	4941	Ansah,Locke	Sansome	Austin	Powell	Martin	Scully	Hyslop	Clark	Butler	Ansah	Benjamin	Locke	Angell(11)	
43	30	Cambridge United	(H)	0-0	(0-0)	D	10664		Sansome	Austin	Powell	Martin	Scully	Hyslop	Clark	Butler	Ansah	Benjamin	Angell		
44	4 May	Bury	(A)	1-0	(0-0)	W	4254	Benjamin	Sansome	Austin	Hyslop	Martin	Scully	Locke	Clark	Butler	Ansah	Benjamin	Angell	Powell(6)	
45	7	Leyton Orient	(H)	1-1	(0-0)	D	8760	Locke	Sansome	Austin	Hyslop	Martin	Scully	Powell	Clark	Butler	Ansah	Benjamin	Angell	Locke(11)	Cornwell(11)
46	11	Brentford	(H)	0-1	(0-0)	L	9666		Sansome	Austin	Hyslop	Martin	Scully	Tilson	Clark	Butler	Ansah	Benjamin	Locke	Angell(6)	Powell(3)

Major Cup Competitions

F.A. Cup

Rd.	Date	Opposition	Venue Score	H.T. Res.	Att.	Goalscorers	1	2	3	4	5	6	7	8	9	10	11	12	13
R1	17 Nov	Leyton Orient	(A) 2-3	(0-0) L	6095	Angell(2)	Sansome	Austin	Powell	Cornwell	Prior	Tilson	Cawley	Butler	Ansah	Benjamin	Angell	Martin(4)	Locke(7)

Rumbelows Cup

Rd.	Date	Opposition	Venue Score	H.T. Res.	Att.	Goalscorers	1	2	3	4	5	6	7	8	9	10	11	12	13
R1L1	28 Aug	Aldershot	(H) 2-1	(0-1) W	2254	Butler,Martin	Sansome	Edwards	Hyslop	Martin	Cornwell	Tilson	Clark	Butler	Ansah	Benjamin	Angell	Cook	McDonough
R1L2	4 Sep	Aldershot	(A) 2-2	(2-0) D	2400	Austin,Angell	Sansome	Austin	Powell	Martin	Cornwell	Tilson	Clark	Butler	Ansah	Benjamin	Angell	Cook	McDonough

(Aggregate – Won 4-3)

Rd.	Date	Opposition	Venue Score	H.T. Res.	Att.	Goalscorers	1	2	3	4	5	6	7	8	9	10	11	12	13
R2L1	25	Crystal Palace	(A) 0-8	(0-2) L	9653		Sansome	Austin	Powell	Martin	Cornwell	Tilson	Clark	Butler	Ansah	Benjamin	Angell	Cook(5)	McDonough
R2L2	9 Oct	Crystal Palace	(H) 1-2	(0-1) L	5199	Angell	Sansome	Cornwell	Powell	Martin	Prior	Tilson	Cawley	Butler	Locke	Benjamin	Angell	Ansah(10)	Smith

(Aggregate – Lost 1-10)

Leyland Daf Cup

Rd.	Date	Opposition	Venue Score	H.T. Res.	Att.	Goalscorers	1	2	3	4	5	6	7	8	9	10	11	12	13
Group	6 Nov	Aldershot	(H) 10-1	(5-0) W	1281	Angell(4),Tilson(3),Prior,Ben'n,Ansah	Sansome	Austin	Powell	Cornwell	Prior	Tilson	Cawley	Butler	Ansah	Benjamin	Angell	Edwards	Locke
Group	7 Dec	Reading	(A) 4-1	(1-1) W	1472	Benjamin(2),Butler,Angell	Sansome	Austin	Powell	Martin	Prior	Tilson	Cawley	Butler	Ansah	Benjamin	Angell	Hyslop	Smith
R1	8 Jan	Maidstone United	(H) 2-0	(1-0) W	1849	Cooper(O.G.),Angell	Sansome	Austin	Powell	Ling	Prior	Tilson	Clark	Butler	Locke	Benjamin	Angell	Edwards	Hyslop
R2	26 Feb	Torquay United	(H) 7-0	(0-0) W	2273	Ansah(3),Martin(2),Edwards,Angell	Sansome	Austin	Powell	Martin	Edwards	Tilson	Clark	Butler	Ansah	Benjamin	Locke	Angell(10)	Cornwell
R3	5 Mar	Brentford	(H) 0-3	(0-2) L	3937		Sansome	Austin	Powell	Martin	Edwards	Tilson	Clark	Butler	Locke	Benjamin	Angell	Ansah(9)	Cornwell

Appearances and Goals

Name	Appearances Lge.	FAC	R.C.	L.D.	Total	Goals Lge.	FAC	R.C.	L.D.	Total
ANGELL, Brett	37+5	1	4	4+1	46+6	15	2	2	7	26
ANSAH, Andy	37+3	1	3+1	3+1	44+5	9			4	13
AUSTIN, Dean	44	1	2	5	52			1		1
BENJAMIN, Ian	46	1	4	5	56	13			3	16
BUTLER, Peter	42	1	4	5	52	2		1	1	4
CAWLEY, Peter	6+1	1	1	1	9+1	1				1
CLARK, Paul	40		3	4	47					
COOK, Jason	0+1		0+1		0+2					
CORNWELL, John	13+6	1	4	1	19+6	2				2
EDWARDS, Andy	2		1	2	5	1			1	2
HYSLOP, Christian	10+1		1		11+1					
LING, Martin	1+2			1	2+2					
LOCKE, Adam	18+10	0+1	1	3	22+11	4				4
MARTIN, David	40	0+1	4	3	47+1	11		1	2	14
MORAN, Paul	1				1					
POWELL, Chris	43+2	1	3	5	52+2	1				1
PRIOR, Spencer	19	1	1	3	24				1	1
SANSOME, Paul	46	1	4	5	56					
SCULLY, Pat	21				21					
SMITH, Paul	2				2					
TILSON, Steve	38	1	4	5	48	8			3	11
Own Goal									1	1

	Ps	P	W	D	L	F	A	W	D	L	F	A	Pts.
1990/91	2	46	13	6	4	34	23	13	1	9	33	28	85

Season 1991/92 – League Division Two

No.	Date	Opposition	Venue	Score	H.T.	Res.	Att.	Goalscorers	No.	1	2	3	4	5	6	7	8	9	10	11	12	13
1	17 Aug	Bristol City	(H)	1-1	(1-0)	D	6720	Benjamin	1	Sansome	Austin	Powell	Martin	Edwards	Prior	Ansah	Sussex	O'Call'n	Benjamin	Angell	Tilson(9)	Locke
2	24	Derby County	(A)	2-1	(2-0)	W	12284	Sussex,Angell	2	Sansome	Austin	Powell	Martin	Edwards	Prior	Ansah	Sussex	Tilson	Benjamin	Angell	Cornwell	Locke
3	31	Leicester City	(H)	1-2	(0-0)	L	6944	Martin	3	Sansome	Austin	Powell	Martin	Scully	Prior	Ansah	Locke	Tilson	Benjamin	Angell	Edwards(5)	Sussex
4	3 Sep	Cambridge United	(A)	1-0	(0-0)	W	6413	Benjamin	4	Sansome	Austin	Powell	Martin	Scully	Prior	Ansah	Cornwell	Tilson	Benjamin	Angell	Sussex	Locke
5	7	Ipswich Town	(A)	0-1	(0-0)	L	12732		5	Sansome	Austin	Powell	Martin	Scully	Prior	Ansah	Cornwell	Tilson	Benjamin	Angell	O'Call'n(4)	Sussex(9)
6	14	Bristol Rovers	(H)	2-0	(0-0)	W	4670	Ansah,Angell	6	Sansome	Austin	Powell	Sussex	Scully	Prior	Ansah	Cornwell	Tilson	Benjamin	Angell	Edwards	Hall
7	17	Plymouth Argyle	(H)	2-1	(1-0)	W	4585	Angell,Benjamin	7	Sansome	Austin	Powell	Sussex	Scully	Prior	Ansah	Cornwell	Tilson	Benjamin	Angell	Edwards	Hall
8	21	Port Vale	(A)	0-0	(0-0)	D	5988		8	Sansome	Austin	Powell	Sussex	Scully	Prior	Ansah	Cornwell	Tilson	Benjamin	Angell	Hall(7)	Edwards
9	28	Wolverhampton W.	(H)	0-2	(0-0)	L	8368		9	Sansome	Austin	Powell	Sussex	Scully	Prior	Hall	Cornwell	Tilson	Benjamin	Angell	Locke(7)	Cagigao
10	4 Oct	Tranmere Rovers	(A)	1-1	(1-0)	D	7358	Angell	10	Sansome	Austin	Powell	Sussex	Scully	Prior	Locke	Cornwell	Tilson	Benjamin	Angell	O'Call'n	Hall
11	12	Millwall	(A)	2-3	(1-2)	L	7266	Sussex,Tilson	11	Sansome	Austin	Powell	Jones	Scully	Prior	Ansah	Cornwell	Tilson	Benjamin	Sussex	Angell(11)	Locke
12	19	Watford	(A)	2-1	(1-0)	W	6862	Sussex,Dublin(O.G.)	12	Sansome	Austin	Powell	Jones	Scully	Prior	Ansah	Cornwell	Tilson	Benjamin	Sussex	Locke(11)	Hall
13	26	Charlton Athletic	(H)	1-1	(1-0)	D	7320	Austin(pen)	13	Sansome	Austin	Powell	Jones	Scully	Prior	Ansah	Cornwell	Tilson	Benjamin	Sussex	Hall(11)	Edwards
14	30	Oxford United	(A)	2-3	(1-3)	L	4873	Angell,Tilson	14	Sansome	Austin	Powell	Jones	Scully	Prior	Ansah	Cornwell	Tilson	Benjamin	Angell	Edwards	Locke
15	2 Nov	Middlesbrough	(A)	1-1	(1-0)	D	9664	Angell	15	Sansome	Austin	Powell	Jones	Scully	Prior	Ansah	Cornwell	Tilson	Benjamin	Angell	Locke(7)	Edwards
16	5	Blackburn Rovers	(H)	3-0	(1-0)	W	4860	Angell(2),Benjamin	16	Sansome	Austin	Powell	Jones	Scully	Edwards	Ansah	Cornwell	Tilson	Benjamin	Angell	O'Call'n	Locke
17	9	Swindon Town	(H)	3-2	(1-0)	W	7709	Angell(2),Tilson	17	Sansome	Austin	Powell	Jones	Scully	Prior	Ansah	Cornwell	Tilson	Benjamin	Angell	O'Call'n(10)	Locke
18	20	Newcastle United	(A)	2-3	(1-3)	L	14740	Angell,Tilson	18	Sansome	Austin	Powell	Jones	Scully	Prior	Ansah	Cornwell	Tilson	Benjamin	Angell	O'Call'n	Edwards
19	23	Barnsley	(H)	2-1	(0-0)	W	5060	Angell,Tilson	19	Sansome	Austin	Hyslop	Jones	Scully	Prior	Ansah	Cornwell	Tilson	Benjamin	Angell	O'Call'n	Butter
20	30	Sunderland	(H)	2-1	(1-1)	W	13575	Angell,Scully	20	Sansome	Austin	Powell	Jones	Scully	Prior	Ansah	Cornwell	Tilson	Benjamin	Angell	O'Call'n	Butter
21	7 Dec	Brighton & H.A.	(H)	2-1	(1-0)	W	6303	Ansah,Tilson	21	Sansome	Austin	Powell	Jones	Scully	Prior	Ansah	Cornwell	Tilson	Benjamin	Angell	O'Call'n	Butter
22	14	Portsmouth	(A)	1-1	(1-1)	D	9006	Scully	22	Sansome	Austin	Powell	Jones	Scully	Prior	Ansah	Cornwell	Tilson	Benjamin	Angell	Locke	Butter
23	22	Cambridge United	(H)	1-1	(1-1)	D	9353	Benjamin	23	Sansome	Austin	Powell	Jones	Scully	Prior	Ansah	Cornwell	Tilson	Benjamin	Angell	Locke	Butter(10)
24	26	Oxford United	(A)	1-0	(0-0)	W	5601	Angell	24	Sansome	Austin	Powell	Jones	Scully	Prior	Ansah	Cornwell	Tilson	Benjamin	Angell	Locke(9)	Locke
25	28	Leicester City	(A)	0-2	(0-0)	L	15635		25	Sansome	Austin	Powell	Jones	Scully	Prior	Ansah	Cornwell	Tilson	Benjamin	Angell	Butter(4)	Locke
26	1 Jan	Newcastle United	(H)	4-0	(2-0)	W	9458	Angell(2),Jones,Ansah	26	Sansome	Austin	Powell	Jones	Scully	Prior	Ansah	Cornwell	Tilson	Benjamin	Angell	Butter(4)	Edwards
27	11	Derby County	(H)	1-0	(1-0)	W	8295	Ansah	27	Sansome	Austin	Powell	Jones	Scully	Prior	Ansah	Cornwell	Tilson	Benjamin	Angell	Locke	Jones(7)
28	18	Bristol City	(A)	2-2	(2-0)	W	9883	Angell,Ansah	28	Sansome	Austin	Powell	Butter	Scully	Prior	Ansah	Cornwell	Tilson	Benjamin	Angell	Edwards(6)	O'Call'n(9)
29	1 Feb	Watford	(H)	1-0	(0-0)	W	7581	Benjamin	29	Sansome	Austin	Powell	Butter	Scully	Edwards	Ansah	Cornwell	Tilson	Benjamin	Jones	Sussex(10)	O'Call'n(9)
30	8	Charlton Athletic	(A)	0-2	(0-1)	L	9724		30	Sansome	Austin	Powell	Butter	Scully	Edwards	Ansah	Cornwell	Tilson	Benjamin	Jones	Locke(11)	Hyslop
31	15	Barnsley	(A)	0-1	(0-0)	L	5328		31	Sansome	Austin	Powell	Butter	Scully	Edwards	Ansah	Cornwell	Tilson	Benjamin	Sussex	O'Call'n	Edwards
32	18	Grimsby Town	(A)	2-3	(0-1)	L	5337	Austin,Ansah	32	Sansome	Austin	Powell	Jones	Scully	Edwards	Ansah	Cornwell	Tilson	Benjamin	Angell	Butter(7)	Butter
33	22	Sunderland	(A)	2-0	(2-0)	W	7473	Angell,Jones	33	Sansome	Austin	Powell	Jones	Scully	Prior	Ansah	Cornwell	Tilson	Benjamin	Angell	Edwards	Butter
34	29	Brighton & H.A.	(A)	2-3	(1-1)	L	8271	Benjamin,Angell	34	Sansome	Austin	Powell	Jones	Scully	Prior	Ansah	Cornwell	Tilson	Benjamin	Angell	Edwards	Butter
35	10 Mar	Blackburn Rovers	(A)	2-2	(2-1)	D	14404	Ansah,Angell	35	Sansome	Austin	Powell	Jones	Scully	Prior	Ansah	Cornwell	Tilson	Benjamin	Angell	Sussex	Sussex
36	14	Middlesbrough	(H)	0-1	(0-0)	L	7272		36	Sansome	Austin	Powell	Jones	Scully	Prior	Locke	Cornwell	Tilson	Benjamin	Angell	Butter(7)	Locke
37	17	Portsmouth	(H)	2-3	(2-2)	L	6832	Tilson,Jones	37	Sansome	Austin	Hyslop	Jones	Scully	Prior	Locke	Cornwell	Tilson	Benjamin	Angell	Sussex	O'Call'n
38	21	Swindon Town	(A)	1-3	(1-1)	L	8628	Ansah	38	Sansome	Austin	Powell	Jones	Scully	Prior	Ansah	Cornwell	Tilson	Benjamin	Angell	Sussex	O'Call'n
39	28	Grimsby Town	(H)	3-1	(2-1)	W	4591	Angell,Scully,Ansah	39	Royce	Austin	Powell	Jones	Scully	Prior	Ansah	Cornwell	Tilson	Benjamin	Angell	Sussex	Edwards
40	1 Apr	Bristol Rovers	(A)	1-4	(1-0)	L	5375	Jones	40	Sansome	Austin	Powell	Jones	Scully	Prior	Ansah	Cornwell	Tilson	Benjamin	Angell	O'Call'n(10)	Locke
41	4	Ipswich Town	(H)	1-2	(1-0)	L	10003	Prior	41	Sansome	Austin	Powell	Jones	Scully	Prior	Ansah	Cornwell	Tilson	Benjamin	Angell	O'Call'n	Locke
42	11	Plymouth Argyle	(A)	2-0	(1-0)	W	7060	Marker(O.G.),Benjamin	42	Sansome	Austin	Powell	Jones	Scully	Prior	Ansah	Cornwell	Tilson	Benjamin	Angell	O'Call'n	Sussex(11)
43	15	Port Vale	(H)	0-0	(0-0)	D	4462		43	Sansome	Austin	Powell	Jones	Scully	Prior	Ansah	Cornwell	O'Call'n	Benjamin	Angell	Tilson(7)	Sussex
44	20	Wolverhampton W.	(A)	1-3	(1-1)	L	10953	Benjamin	44	Sansome	Austin	Powell	Jones	Scully	Prior	Locke	Cornwell	Tilson	Benjamin	Angell	O'Call'n	Sussex(11)
45	25	Tranmere Rovers	(H)	1-1	(1-0)	D	4761	Jones	45	Sansome	Austin	Powell	Jones	Scully	Prior	Ansah	Cornwell	Tilson	Benjamin	Angell	O'Call'n(9)	Sussex
46	2 May	Millwall	(A)	0-2	(0-0)	L	7574		46	Sansome	Edwards	Powell	Jones	Scully	Prior	Ansah	Cornwell	Tilson	Sussex	Angell		Locke

Abbrev.: O'Call'n = O'Callaghan

Major Cup Competitions

Rd.	Date	Opposition	Venue	Score	H.T.	Res.	Att.	Goalscorers	1	2	3	4	5	6	7	8	9	10	11	12	13
F.A.Cup																					
R3	4 Jan	Everton	(A)	0-1	(0-1)	L	22605		Sansome	Austin	Powell	Jones	Scully	Prior	Ansah	Cornwell	Tilson	Benjamin	Angell	Locke	Butler
Rumbelows Cup																					
R1L1	20 Aug	Watford	(A)	0-2	(0-2)	L	6231		Sansome	Austin	Powell	Martin	Edwards	Prior	Ansah	Sussex	O'Call'n	Benjamin	Angell	Tilson(9)	Locke
R1L2	28	Watford	(H)	1-1	(1-1)	D	3802	Angell	Sansome	Austin	Powell	Martin	Scully	Prior	Locke	Sussex	Tilson	Benjamin	Angell	Ansah(10)	Edwards
Zenith Data Systems Cup																					
R1	2 Oct	Watford	(A)	1-0	(1-0)	W	1700	Sussex	Sansome	Austin	Powell	Sussex	Scully	Prior	Locke	Cornwell	Tilson	Benjamin	Angell	O'Callaghan	Hall
R2	22	Crystal Palace	(A)	2-4	(1-0)	L	7185	Jones,Angell	Sansome	Austin	Powell	Jones	Scully	Prior	Ansah	Cornwell	Tilson	Benjamin	Angell	Locke	Hall

(A.E.T. 90 min. – 2-2)

Abbrev.: O'Call'n = O'Callaghan.

Back row – Dean Austin, Ian Benjamin, Brett Angell, Andy Sussex, Spencer Prior, Pat Scully, Andy Edwards, Paul Smith
Middle row: David Webb (manager), Kevin Lock (team coach), Steve Tilson, John Cornwell, David Martin, Paul Sansome, Tony Parks, Christian Hyslop, Steve Heffer, Danny Greaves (youth coach), Alan Raw (physio).
Front row: Adam Locke, Spencer Barham, Mark Hall, Andy Arsah, Jason Cook, Chris Powell, Peter Butler and Kevin O'Callaghan.

Appearances and Goals

Name	\	Appe	arance	s \	\	\	Goals	\	\	\
	Lge.	FAC	R.C.	Z.D.	Total	Lge.	FAC	R.C.	Z.D.	Total
ANGELL, Brett	42+1	1	2	1	46+1	21	1	1		23
ANSAH, Andy	40	1+1		1	43+1	9				9
AUSTIN, Dean	45	1	2	2	50	2				2
BENJAMIN, Ian	45	1	2	2	50	9				9
BUTLER, Peter	4+5				4+5					
CAGIGAO, Francisco	0			1	1					
CORNWELL, John	43	1		2	46					
EDWARDS, Andy	7+2		1		8+2					
HALL, Marcus	1+2				1+2					
HYSLOP, Christian	2				2					
JONES, Keith	33+1	1		1	35+1	5			1	6
LOCKE, Adam	5+5		1	1	7+5					
MARTIN, David	5		2		7			1		1
O'CALLAGHAN, Kevin	2+6		1		3+6					
POWELL, Chris	44	1	2	2	49					
PRIOR, Spencer	42	1	2	2	47	1				1
ROYCE, Simon	1				1					
SANSOME, Paul	45	1	2	2	50					
SCULLY, Pat	44	1	1	2	48	3				3
SUSSEX, Andy	12+3		2	1	15+3	3	1			4
TILSON, Steve	44+2	1	1+1	2	48+3	3	1			4
Own Goal						2				2

	Ps	P	W	D	L	F	A	W	D	L	F	A	Pts.
1991/92	12	46	11	5	7	37	26	6	6	11	26	37	62

ADVANCED SUBSCRIBERS

Southend United Football Club
Karen Goody
Jim Goody – Well Done Dave
Otto Burnham
Traci–Leigh Scarlett
Victoria Scarlett
Mike Smith & little Chloe
Tony, Christmas '92 Love Vicky
To Martin Love the Chris's!
Ian & Karen Hoskins
David Brabbing
Whitey In The West Bank
Stephen Swift of Brentwood
Lee Garrett
Dean Garrett
Martin George Hinton
Julie & Michael Pearce
Supporter Since 1932 David Jennings
Good Luck from Stephen Cubitt
Mr. Don Cannon
M.A. & C.M. Eighteen
To Gary Happy 21st Birthday
To Darren Happy 18th Birthday
Thanks Ted Hankey – Dave & Jim
To Lee, Happy Christmas, Dad
Barry Venus
Stalky
Bob Sills Christmas 1992
Best Wishes Mike, Mum & Dad
B.E. Fance
T.M. Taylor
Love Steph & Manny February 1993
John Treleven
K.P. Wood
David Keats, Thornton Heath
G.D. Painter
Harry Kay
David Earnshaw, Belper, Derbyshire
Raymond Shaw
Steve Emms
P.R. Rowe
J. Motson
Phil. Hollow
Graham Spackman
Duncan Watt
Mark Tyler
Barry Watson
Derek Hyde
Terje Ovrebo – Norway
L.A. Zammit
British Non League Programme Club
Derek Wheatcroft
W.D. Phillips
For Russell
J. Ringrose
David Downs & Marion Peer

Willy Østby – Norway
Fred Lee – Plymouth Argyle
Jonathan Hall
Rob Jex
David Jowett
Mr. R. Betts
Andrew Anderson
Stephen Kieran Byrne
Douglas Lamming
Martin Simons
Alan Davies
Dave Smith
Chris Hooker, Ajax, Ontario, Canada
Philip H. Whithead
B.H. Standish
Lars–Olof Wendler – Sweden
Arthur Atkins – Toronto, Canada
Michael McConkey – Luton
Geoffrey Wright
David Lumb
Brian Tabner
Donald Noble, Dunkeld, Perthshire
Bob Lilliman
Gareth M. Davies
Jonny Stokkeland – Norway
To Frank love from Tina
Christer Svensson
Peter Baxter
M.D. Edroff
Bryan Horsnell
Ian Atkins
John, Julie & Simon Armstrong
Clifford Vincent, with love Lesley
Cyril Bailey, Supporter 1922–1992
Russell Baker
Frankie Banks, Southend Community Officer
Through Thick & Thin, BM4
Steve Batchelor
David Baxter, Supporter since 1966
Nigel Bedford, A Loyal Supporter
Dave Bell, Up The Blues
Chris Bent
46 Years of Fondest Memories
D.R. Bidgood
Geoff, Jenny, Toby & Greg.
Mum Branscombe
The West Bank Bridge Family
Charlie, Alan & Peter Bushell
Barry, Forever Blues, love Penny
Marion & Chris Cave.
Loving Memories of Martin Clark
David Clenshaw, life long supporter
Peter Coster, Die Hard Extravagent
Norman L. Cockerill
Gavin Cotgrove
Roger Cousins, with love Hazel

Phil Cox
Timothy Charles Davis, Que Sera.
Carol-Ann Manser
Mike Davies - Rayleigh
Part of Life, Mike Davies
Thanks for years of enjoyment
Southend United Supporters Billericay Branch
Kevin & Laura Eaton
Up the Blues, Peter Ebbs
Phil Esdaile
James Leadbetter
Happy Christmas Ken, from Mum.
Mick Happy 40th, love Gill.
Charlie Finch
E.B. Findlay
I.C. Findlay
David Fitzgerald
To Ken Foakes, from Kevin.
Mark Robert Folwell
Peter Frier
In Memory of E.A. Glasscock
J.R. Goodwin, Go On You Shrimps
Kevin Pethick Gordon Ladies Coach
Peter Green, Arcadian Gardens, Hadleigh
C.E. Gunning
Derek Hall, Leigh on Sea
Happy Christmas Eddie love Susannah xx
Wayne Harris
Mike Harvey Supporter since 1960
Bob & David Hill
Darren Hines
The Hood Family, Forever Blue
Harry Hoverd
Paul Holland, Always There Supporting
David Homan-Smith
Kevin Hoverd
Chris Hussey, Essex
David A. Jones
Mick Joiner, Happy 50th Birthday
Mark, Happy 18th Birthday
Stephen, Happy 18th Birthday
Kevin Jones - Forever Blue
Paul Kelsey, Dedicated Loyal Supporter
To Daddy, from Sammy & Buttsie
Cleveland Key
To Dave, An Old Supporter
Andrew J. Leeder, Hadleigh, Suffolk
Tony Leeder, Isle of Wight
Irwin Lewis
Tom Lister
Bonkers Bob Mid Van Mob
Paul Mason - Loyal Since 1955
Merry Christmas Tony
David & Stephen, Lifelong Supporters
Bill Messer, A Lifetime Supporter
Colin & Graham Moody
John Morgan, Loyal Supporter
William Leonard Nunn
Neil Oakley, Supporter Since 1972
Eric Osborne

Simon, Asa, & Elliot Osborne
Arthur Byford, A Lifelong Supporter
Ted & Hazel Parsons
Dave, Much love Katy.
Ian Perryman - Bristol Exile
Chris & Gina Perryman
Colin Pollard
Robin A. Port
Laurie Potkins, Life Time Supporter
David Potkins
Ray Rippon, Linda & Peter Holohan
Good Luck Blues, Ron Rayner
Peter William Reeve
Mid Van Boys Turtle Hawklord
Dave Russell
Derrick Sawyer
Michael Shaw
Duncan Sheekey
Barry & Peter Smart, Benfleet
Garry N. Smith BA (Hons.) MA.
Martin Smith, Great Wakering, Essex.
With All My Love, Sandra.
Ken St. John - February 1993
Stuart Stoner
Paul & Barbara Strutt
Long Live The Blues!
With Love - Craig.
Glenn Taylor
Thompson's East Stand Blue Army
Nicholas Frederick, Kim Lesley Timms
Sean Tyrell, Wakefield, West Yorks.
Wag & Sam
Mark Wallis
John Wallis
A. and J.A. Waterman
Oliver Graham St. John Ware-Lane
Paul & Mark Wellington
Norman Meddle Jnr. & Snr.
Dave Wellington
Tom White
Stephen, Love Mum & Dad
Russell, All My Love Julia
Stephen Wilson
David Wilson
Scott & Gary
In Memory of 'Bob' West
David Woodyard
Two-nil from the Nans
John, Southend's No.1 Fan.
Alan Watkins 1955-1992
Gary Lockett, Happy 30th Birthday
To Chris, Love Pat/Stuart
Joe, Justin & Sebastian Sims
Basil, Kitty, Peter & Simon Butler
Best Wishes from Mum & Dad
Steven John Norrington
Happy Birthday, Mum & Dad
In memory of Stan Gee
Robert Hinton - Baby Blues
Arran Matthews

Groundsmen Joe Augur (left) and Sid Broomfield try to clear the pitch of snow

When the match is postponed, or during the summer, what better than to settle down in the armchair (or the deckchair) and have a good read!

YORE PUBLICATIONS
Specialists in Football Books generally with an historic theme

Our current titles include:
The Official and detailed histories of *Cardiff City* (320 pages) and *Peterborough United* (240 pages).
'The Ironsides', a complete 'Who's Who' of Newport County players.
'Through The Turnstiles', a fascinating well illustrated book on the history of football, angled towards attendances; includes the average attendance of **every** Football League club from **every** season – since 1888!
'Rejected F.C.' – The detailed and well illustrated histories of all the ex-Football League clubs (from Aberdare to Workington). (Also a 90 minute home video with the same title)
'History of the Lancashire Football Association 1878 - 1928' – a reprint of this rare book from a bygone age.
'More Defunct F.C.' and *'Gone But Not Forgotten'* – histories of famous (and not so famous) defunct non-League Clubs and grounds.

For further details of these and other titles, please send a S.A.E. (free newsletters are issued three times per year) to: